"It is a hopeless endeavour to attract people to a theatre unless they can be first brought to believe that they will never get in."

Charles Dickens (1812-1870), *Nicholas Nickleby*

"Every proper quality and convenience of a good theatre has been sacrificed or neglected to show the spectator a vast triumphal piece of architecture."

Colley Cibber (1671-1757), actor-manager, on Vanbrugh's 1705 Haymarket Theatre

"The modern theatre building is a hyper-sophisticated and very expensive architectural, mechanical, and electronic monument, all designed to conjure up a rainbow. But a rainbow that shifts, that fades, and reappears in unexpected places. Sometimes it appears ridiculous to hope that so heavy and inert a piece of real estate can catch a rainbow as it moves over the landscape of society's dreams."

Michael Elliott (1931-1984), director, founder of the Royal Exchange Theatre, Manchester

"I beg the government not to be too grandiose in the matter of architecture; and not to be led astray by the enthusiasm of architects, who are always prone to exaggerate the importance of their own art. After all, aren't we all? I beg them to consider the quality of the productions, rather than any exaggerated grandeur of the producing medium."

Mr E.P. Smith, MP for Ashford, in debate on the National Theatre Bill, 21st January 1949

"Theatre will never die because, as a culture and as a species, the value of story is immense and that live connection between the storyteller and the audience is a really vivid, vital thing."

Rufus Norris, National Theatre artistic director 2015-2025

"The theatre is too complex and delicate a machine, depending on the harmonious cooperation of too many talents, ever to reach perfection for more than a passing moment."

Harley Granville-Barker (1877-1946), pioneering theatre director

"I do know that the answer to our theatre building in the future does not lie with architecture. It must emerge from our fumbling and inarticulate endeavours to pin down the relationship between the platform and that seat - whatever that is."

Sean Kenny (1932-1973), designer, member National Theatre Building Committee 1962-63, speaking on 2nd July 1964

"I was proud of my position as the director of the National, and always will be. And I'm certain that the work we did there was a great credit to the British theatre as a whole. I am convinced that, pound for pound, for a while we were the best troupe of players in the world. Although I maintain we must forever be looking forward, it is still very important to hold on to our theatrical roots and listen."

Sir Laurence Olivier (1907-1989)

> "One of the weaknesses of the theatrical profession in this country is that producers and designers and theatre architects are apt to be extraordinarily ignorant of what was going on in the theatre just before their own time."
>
> Norman Marshall
> Joint Chairman, NT Building Committee
> *TABS*, April 1962

> "One day, no doubt, the complete annals of the National Theatre will be written, based on the archives of the theatre itself, and prolonged from age to age. While memories are still fresh, it is possible to recall the steps whereby the National Theatre idea was first imposed on a more or less unwilling public; and then, as an eyewitness, to tell the story of the outstanding events which led to the actual foundation of the theatre."
>
> Geoffrey Whitworth CBE
> *The Making of a National Theatre*
> Faber & Faber Ltd, 1951

Laurence Olivier and Denys Lasdun at the first public showing of the model of the new National Theatre, December 1967

A Sense of Theatre
The Untold Story of Britain's National Theatre

Richard Pilbrow
with Fred Pilbrow, Rob Halliday

**Foreword by
Sir Richard Eyre**

A Sense of Theatre
The Untold Story of Britain's National Theatre
by Richard Pilbrow

Editors: Rob Halliday & Fred Pilbrow
Research Assistant: Acatia Finbow
Graphic Design: Flora Cox, Pilbrow & Partners

With thanks to Paule Constable and John Runia

Produced by: P2+H Ltd,
in association with The Society for Theatre Research.

Published in the UK in 2024
by Unicorn, an imprint of Unicorn Publishing Group
Charleston Studio, Meadow Business Centre,
Lewes BN8 5RW, UK
www.unicornpublishing.org

Copyright © Richard Pilbrow 2023.

Richard Pilbrow has asserted his right under the Copyright, Designs and Patents Act 1988 to be identified as the author of this work.

All rights reserved. No part of the contents of this book may be reproduced, stored in or introduced into a retrieval system, or transmitted, in any form or by any means (electronic, mechanical, photocopying, recording or otherwise) without the prior written permission of the copyright holder and the publisher of this book.

Cover Photographs:
Front, upper: The National Theatre in 2016, photographer Philip Vile.
Front, lower: *War Horse*, photographer Brinkhoff/Mögenburg.
Rear: The Olivier Theatre drum revolve under construction, photographer Philip Sayer.
Rear inset: Richard Pilbrow on Waterloo Bridge overlooking the National Theatre, 1974. *Evening Standard*/Hulton Archive via Getty Images.

Other illustrations are credited at the end of the book.

Every effort has been made to trace the copyright holders and to obtain their permission for the use of copyright material. The publisher apologises for any errors or omissions and would be grateful if notified of any corrections that should be incorporated in future reprints or editions of this book.

Email: info@asenseoftheatre.com
Web: www.asenseoftheatre.com

Printed in Türkiye by FineTone Ltd.

Hardback ISBN: 978-1-916846-03-6
10 9 8 7 6 5 4 3 2 1

Contents

Foreword by Sir Richard Eyre ix

Introduction xiii

The Theatres xix

Part One: The Quest 1
1.1 The Quest for a National Theatre 3
1.2 British Playhouse Design 19
1.3 A Company of Players under Laurence Olivier 51

Part Two: The Minutes 67
2.1 Beginnings: Finding An Architect 69
2.2 Design Begins 105
2.3 Blood Dripping From Concrete Walls 147
2.4 Full Scenic Capability 195
2.5 Getting To The Poetic 215

Part Three: Construction and Chaos – Realisation 229
3.1 Peter Hall Takes Charge and Writes a Diary 231
3.2 Her Majesty: "Is The Theatre Ready, Mr. Pilbrow?" 253

Part Four: Concrete Versus Theatre 259
4.1 Peter Hall - The Show Goes On 261
4.2 Richard Eyre 289
4.3 Trevor Nunn 313
4.4 Nicholas Hytner 329
4.5 Rufus Norris 355

Part Five: Five Decades of Theatre Design and Architecture 373
5.1 Our Theatres Examined in a Changing World 375
5.2 The Shape of Theatre 387
5.3 Genoa: A Design Revolution 397
5.4 Designing Theatres 405
5.5 Theatres for People 427

Part Six: Five Decades of a Working Theatre 433
6.1 Fifty Years of Performance Design 435
6.2 Technical Evolution 443
6.3 Acoustics 451
6.4 Theatre Makers and Architecture 457
6.5 Theatre In Challenging Times 473

Part Seven: Finale 479
7.1 A Personal Conclusion 480

Appendices 485
Author's Notes and Thanks 486
Epilogue 488
The National Theatre Building 490
Bibliography 498
Credits and Archives 499
Endnotes 509
Index 515

Supporters

This book would not have been possible without the generous and gratefully received support and encouragement of these wonderful individuals and organisations – some of whom have a connection with the National Theatre going back to its creation. We thank them all.

Neil Austin
Dear Richard, you are deeply missed. Your energy, enthusiasm and joy for life was inspirational. The schoolboy that devoured your book can't believe his luck that he got to know you and call you a friend.

Psyche Chui
It was my privilege to have known Richard for over three decades in a number of capacities, as a guest artist at the Hong Kong Academy for Performing Arts, and joining him at lighting seminars around the world. Together with his wife Molly, we also struck up a friendship over the years and I can truly say I have lost a wonderful friend and close acquaintance. I will miss Richard as many will, and am delighted to be a small part of this, your final book.

Robert Bell
Millions of people around the world have sat in their seats, not fully appreciating all the work that Richard and TP put into planning spaces where cast and audience ignite in what we call theatre. Well done!

Mike Simpson
I read Richard's book *Stage Lighting* in 1970 and was inspired by the creativity possible with lighting. This influenced both my career and my life. It's my pleasure to support this book.

David Hersey
I first met Richard in early 1968 when I came to London from New York on a mission to discover what the English Theatre was all about. He was kind enough to offer me a job even though I had been extremely off hand about a play I had seen without realising he had lit it. He even loaned me the down payment on my first boat which I lived on for seven years just upstream from the National. I will forever be in his debt. I was extremely proud to be part of the commando team charged with the task of wresting the New National from the grip of the contractors and lighting the opening productions in the Lyttelton and the Olivier.

Clifton Taylor
Richard was a friend and mentor. Ever grateful for all he invented, discovered, and shared. His first books inspired me at the beginning of my career, and his humour and abiding friendship sustained us in the Wednesday Group for the pandemic years and beyond.

Bryan Raven
Here's to the memory of Richard Pilbrow and of John Simpson, two great men who touched my life and career, and the lives and careers of so many, over the decades we were fortunate enough to have them with us.

John Harris
Beckenham to Broadway and all the places in between. It always surprises us how much vibrant activity there is everywhere in our lighting world. With unending respect and thanks.

Pat MacKay
There is no doubt about it. Richard was the most charming man in the world. So admired. So loved. So inclusive. So sharing. It was my joy and privilege to be his co-author, his friend, his colleague. He invariably supported – with enthusiasm – my next 'bright' idea. It was a particular joy that we had this second layer of connection. My husband, Ralph Pine, was the US publisher of Richard's first book: *Stage Lighting*. That grew into the second book, *Stage Lighting: the art, the craft, the life*. Ralph encouraged Richard to add more interviews for another edition. Being Pilbrow, he had other projects to finish first. The lighting profession and the theatre consulting business are what they are today because of Richard. And may we carry on remembering him and his grace, humility, humour, intelligence... and fun. Thank you, Richard!

Benny Ball
Not so long ago Richard did a video chat; he recalled the tale of friends advising him not to write his book *Stage Lighting* "because then everyone will be able to do it!" Well, you can give a person the best canvas, brushes and paints, it doesn't mean they become a Rembrandt. Richard was a Rembrandt; he attracted many Rembrandts, inspired and nurtured all of us TeePee'ers. My enduring thanks and love. 'The Letraset Kid.'

Anne Minors
Richard Pilbrow's experience of shaping the National Theatre for performance led to his founding a new profession, theatre consultancy, creating the institutional pillars of the technical theatre industry and inspiring generations of lighting designers. His lifelong quest to Make Theatre Better is the lens through which this book is focussed and a fitting tribute to his restless creativity.

Andrew Bridge
Richard was the beacon that literally made our paths brighter, he was the most enthusiastic artist in our profession. Richard was a brave pioneer that forged the creative position of Lighting Designer, against many obstacles he pushed the technical and lighting design process to become a new essential department in all theatre projects. Creating beautiful Theatre and Theatres in all forms was his passion. Ever supportive of new talent and excited about new technologies and passionate about painting with light, moving the darkness around to create emotions. His colour sense and the clarity of his work came from always keeping his eyes open and observing the beauty of light. Richard was a theatre wizard.

Ken Billington
Richard's history of the National Theatre must be known by historians and theatre lovers. I am happy my very small contribution will help to get this story out there for the future theatre makers.

Steve Terry
Richard will forever be a part of theatre history, with a lasting imprint on buildings, design, and lighting designers. I am grateful to have had the joy of knowing him, learning from him, and laughing with him.

Charcoalblue
We have so much to thank Richard for, not least inspiring and teaching us so much - we'll miss him greatly. With love to Molly, Fred, Abigail, Daisy and families, from all your friends at Charcoalblue; particularly Andy, Gavin, Jon and Katy x

The Directors of Triple E
The National has been a key player in the lives, professionally and personally, of all three Directors. David Edelstein was at the NT for four years from the opening in 1976. Brenda and Lucy have also worked there over the years. The experience of being involved at Richard's NT has proved invaluable.

Asociación de Autores de Iluminación
Back in the eighties it was not possible to study lighting design in Spain (... sadly still difficult today). And then we discovered Richard Pilbrow's book *Stage Lighting*. For many of us it became a guide to start our professional career in lighting design. We called it 'the bible.' AAI is proud to collaborate in making possible the publishing of this book. Thanks Richard for sharing your knowledge and inspiring us. Your legacy will remain forever.

Michael Ferguson
Thank you for your generosity of time and spirit. You are missed...

John A. Williams
I was introduced to Richard at an ALD meeting in the early 1980s. At that time there weren't many of us – Richard was member #1, I'm #23 – so meetings were intimate affairs. We struck up a friendship that brought us together in various parts of the world. I invited him to the Hong Kong Academy for Performing Arts where he led captivating masterclasses, always happy to share his expertise, knowledge and experiences. On his last visit he was conferred Academy Fellow. We didn't know then that would be the final time we would meet. Will miss you dear friend.

Theatreplan
Dick Brett, to whom Richard has dedicated this book, created the innovative engineering for the NT as Richard's close partner. Later, Dick formed his own theatre consultancy, now known as Theatreplan, where his engineering designs revolutionised the re-build of the stage of Barcelona's fire ravaged Gran Teatre del Liceu and his career highlight was the technical design and realisation of the stage systems for the Operaen, Copenhagen in 2004. His memory lives on in theatres and concert halls around the world.

Association for Lighting Production and Design
Richard, our founder, our guiding light, forever in the heart of our Association.

Others who supported us through Kickstarter
Rachel Bowen; Richard Bunting; Dawn Chiang; Martin Chisnall; BT Clark; Emma Jayne Davis; Paul & Ros Deegan; Tony Gill; Polestar Productions; Natalie Gyles; Byron Harrison; Simon Hicks; Peter Hunter; Andrew Kimpton; Jules Lauve III; Rachel McCutcheon; John McGarrigle; Keith Mitchell; Dan Murfin; Gareth Owen & Carmen Bierens; Shaun Perry; Chris Patton; Gordon & Sondra Pearlman; Simon Prior; Lori Rubinstein & John McGraw; Jay Scott; Andy Torble; Andrew Voller; Simon Wilkinson.

Association of British Theatre Technicians

The Association of British Theatre Technicians was founded in 1961 by a far-seeing and passionate group of technicians of which Richard Pilbrow was one. It is a charity and membership organisation setting and upholding standards in technical excellence, safety and compliance for theatre and live performance: a resource to support all technical, production and building design practitioners involved in live performance. The ABTT regularly presents technical training, industry visits, the annual ABTT Theatre Show and the quadrennial International Theatre Engineering and Architecture Conference.

Richard received the ABTT's Technician of the Year Award. Subsequently he was appointed a Fellow of the Association in recognition of the signal service he gave to the technical aspects of the art of the theatre.

In 2016 the ABTT presented a symposium at the National Theatre in celebration of the 40th anniversary of the opening of the building. Richard created the event and the transactions were published as *The National Theatre: A Place for Plays*.

The ABTT is now hugely proud to help bring into being this fantastic work of reference, produced by Richard with his characteristic energy and dedication.

Richard was a truly legendary icon of our industry and a founder of the concept of modern stage lighting. He blazed a trail of innovation, invention, and proactivity in the world of light and lighting which brought recognition and understanding of the discipline as well as of the power and importance of light in storytelling. He was passionate about everything he did, be it lighting a show, designing a new performance space, or writing a book. His legacy and influence will be inspirational to generations of future lighting professionals all over the world.

The Robe Family is honoured and humbled to be involved in *A Sense of Theatre*, and the story it tells of a groundbreaking theatrical phenomenon that continues to produce some of the finest, most relevant and significant performance works for all audiences.

For decades Autograph Sound have been privileged to work with the National Theatre, at their London homes and on many of their touring productions - in a coincidental synchronicity, both organisations celebrated their 50th anniversaries in 2023. Autograph are honoured to support this unique historical record of our National Theatre.

Richard Pilbrow was a brilliant lighting practitioner and author whose books provide an important lighting education to those across our industry, both experienced professionals and students alike. Continuing education was important to our founder, Fred Foster and has been a core foundation of ETC's corporate culture since the beginning. We're proud to help enable the publication of this seminal work by an industry giant.

The Steeldeck platform was created back in the day when we were the theatre scenery makers P.L. Parsons. The National Theatre was our best customer; we supplied a number of the shows included in these pages, as well as, of course, many Decks! We are very proud indeed to have worked with the National and all of its wonderful people, and of course with Richard, who will be missed immeasurably. May his final book be a source of inspiration for theatre creators for many decades. And may our friend and mentor rest in perpetual light.

Richard's inexhaustible curiosity and people-first approach to design are evidenced in every project he touched, every new initiative launched, and every individual he championed. The National is an indelible example of that spirit. We're moved to celebrate his legacy in this wonderful story and to cherish his influence on our community now and into the future.

    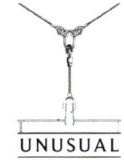 

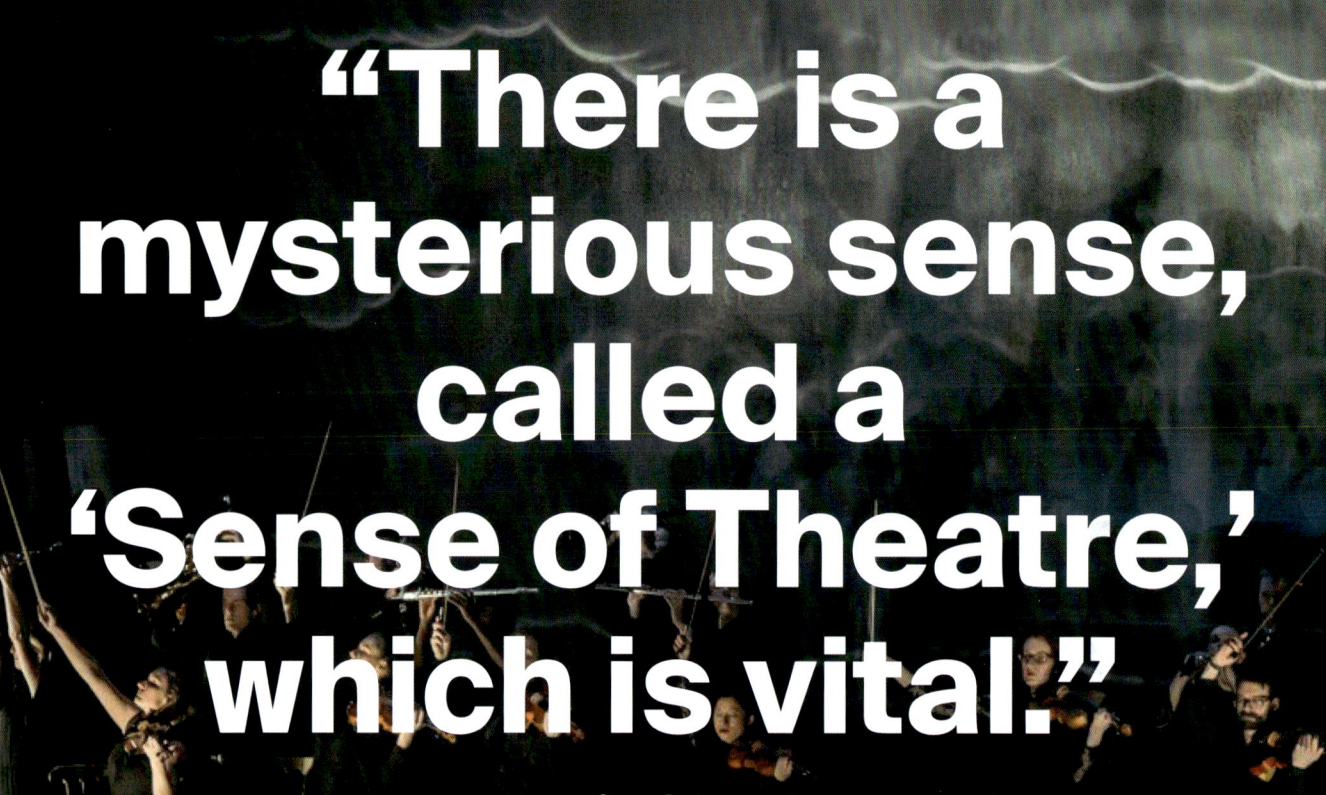

"There is a mysterious sense, called a 'Sense of Theatre,' which is vital."

George Devine

Amadeus, Olivier Theatre, 2017: Lucian Msamati as Salieri

Foreword

Sir Richard Eyre

I've lived in a house in West London for the last thirty-four years but I doubt if I've spent as much time in it as I have in the National Theatre on the South Bank. I've worked there, on and off, since 1982, and I've been as happy there as anywhere on earth. Perhaps I've had too much time to consider its faults as well as its virtues but that's one of the reasons why I welcome a book which seeks to explain how this idiosyncratic and sometimes exasperating building came to be designed and built. The story is told by one of the participants in its making, Richard Pilbrow. It could not be better told: he's a very diligent researcher, a very able writer, a very accomplished artist - the godfather of modern stage lighting – and the most influential theatre design consultant in the world.

The National Theatre on the South Bank was conceived with three auditoria (well, two; the Cottesloe – now Dorfman – was an afterthought) under one roof, each playing a rotating repertoire of three plays. This principle is at the heart of its activities and its source of artistic adventure. To have three theatres in one building is, to say the least, a noble project. It was the triumph of Laurence Olivier's will, his wilfulness, and his ambition. He was once asked what his policy was for the National Theatre. "To make the audience applaud," he said. When the National Theatre was built, a "dream made concrete" (a metaphor made literal), he was asked what he thought of it. He smiled wryly: "It's an experiment."

It's an experiment which has been a wild success. The building, designed by Denys Lasdun, is stern, elegant, forceful and ascetic. In its intentions and its realisation, it's a classical building, which won't go out of fashion. It represents a social and political utopia – an imagined age in which public funding for the arts would be virtually unchallenged and an age in which the 'art' theatre and the commercial theatre would walk hand in hand – this, after all, is a building so certain of its purpose, its commercial chastity and the respect of its audience, that it was built without any sign of any sort advertising its purpose on its exterior.

The building attracted a storm of hostility when it first opened. The torrent of criticism was directed partly towards the building and partly towards the whole enterprise: inflated, grandiose, hubristic, it was said. But it's proved itself, if numbers are anything to go by, to be a genuine expression of popular desire. And, like all successful buildings, it's been colonised by the many hundreds of thousands of people who have visited it, worked in it and shared some sort of communal experience. Like worn paving stones in a cathedral, it's become humanised by use. It's acquired a heart.

To paraphrase Gertrude Stein: A theatre is a theatre is a theatre, which is to say that any theatrical space needs to recognise the capacities of the human voice and the scale of the human body. A theatre needs to create a relationship between the performer and the audience in a space which enfolds them both; it should make you feel as if your presence has made a difference. No one in an audience should feel that they're getting an unreasonably privileged or deprived view of the actor. They need to hear, to see, to feel in contact with what's happening onstage and, if an auditorium dwarfs the human body, there's something wrong with it.

The model for successful theatres is readily accessible to us – from Epidaurus with its one equitable tier of seating, to the Globe Theatre where the audience was wrapped around the stage, to the theatres designed by Frank Matcham in the late 19th century, whose horseshoe-shaped auditoriums clasp the stage in a friendly embrace. In the 20th century, with the birth of modernism, the friendly embrace became suspect. These theatre spaces, went the modernist battle cry, were "old-fashioned," theatre was an "irrelevant" art form, the art was "redundant," its humanism "out-dated." How can a work of art become "redundant"? How can the representation of the human figure become "irrelevant"? How can portraying the lives of human beings be seen as "outdated humanism"? By that measure, theatre will always seem outdated because it can never dissolve its reliance on the scale of the human figure, the sound of the human voice, and the disposition of humankind to tell each other stories.

The history of the creation of the National Theatre, like that of most public buildings, is one of utopianism, pragmatism, wilful ego and confusion. Out of its foggy origins, the architect, Denys Lasdun, built something which has more than endured, it has become loved. The front of house is superb; It has a sense of grandeur and occasion combined with a demotic accessibility. Worn and warmed by time and use, the public spaces have become indisputably one of the most welcoming places in London.

However, two of the National Theatre's three auditoriums – the Olivier and the Lyttelton – are not easy spaces, at least if they are measured against the criteria that theatre practitioners and audiences would understand. If you sit in the centre of the centre block of the Olivier Theatre you think: this is thrilling, I'm at the centre of this marvellous space, there's a real sense of event. But, if you sit at the back of the circle you feel remote and detached: disenfranchised. The volume of the auditorium is much larger than it needs to be to accommodate 1160 people. It feels larger than the Theatre Royal Drury Lane, which seats over 1000 more people. A disproportionate volume of space has to be energised by actors' voices in order to make themselves audible – to be exact nine times the ideal volume.

To compound this difficulty there are large areas of wall and balcony made of an acoustically unfriendly material: concrete. It's very hard for even the most technically accomplished actors to make themselves heard without amplification. I once told Albert Finney that Peter Brook had said that a theatre should be like a violin, its tone coming from its period and age. "Yes," said Albert. "And who'd build a violin out of fucking concrete?"

The first production I did in the Olivier was a musical, *Guys and Dolls*. The designer John Gunter was at that time Principal of the Theatre Design course at the Central School. For several years he had set his students the task of designing for the Olivier space and they had been confounded. "What do you do?" he said to me. "How do you make this space work? The architecture intrudes on the space of the artist. If you leave it bare, the concrete jaws either side of the stage and those concrete boxes, like gun emplacements, intrude ostentatiously on the actors' territory. It's an unfocused space. You have to create a form of false proscenium." And he did: a porous proscenium built of neon signs. We were absolved of the audibility problem: it was a musical, voices were amplified.

The problems of the Lyttelton Theatre are no less testing: the concrete-clad auditorium is wholly unsympathetic to the human voice, the circle has no relationship to the stalls, and the human scale is diminished by the continental width of the proscenium. Actors suffer from 'the nodding dog syndrome,' their heads bending side to side and from floor to ceiling to embrace the whole audience.

The only wholly successful space in the NT, loved by actors, directors, writers and audiences is the Cottesloe/Dorfman. In the planning of the original it had been ignored by the artistic committee: it was a hole that was referred to somewhat patronisingly, as a 'studio'. The auditorium was designed as a flexible space by Iain Mackintosh and Richard Pilbrow. You can more or less do what you like in it: it's the artists' territory.

I first met Denys Lasdun in 1982 when I directed *Guys and Dolls*. He congratulated me on "the use of the space." He was still raw about the gross and gratuitous abuse he had received when the building opened. Which is perhaps why he was so thin-skinned when, as Director of the NT, I spoke to him some ten years later about making changes to his building in a much-needed renovation project.

I told him how much I admired the public spaces, the sense of adventure, the classicism of the building. I tried to suggest that there might be ways of making the Olivier and Lyttelton Theatres more genial for the practitioners and for the audiences. He announced – in a public lecture – that he had no intention of changing an atom of "the room" (i.e. the Olivier), a space, he averred, that embraced audience and actors in a unifying hug. In the same lecture he quoted Arthur Clough, "Pure form nakedly displayed/And all things absolutely made," and I wanted to protest: If concrete is the medium of our century and its pure form is nakedly displayed, why was the concrete shuttered and is therefore impregnated with the pattern of a million pine planks? Surely a brutalist version of flock wallpaper?

I never asked him why the catering refuse bins had been placed at the first corner that a theatre-goer would encounter if coming from the east; nor did I ask why the building was angled at a right-angle to Waterloo Bridge rather than aligned with the river, allowing a view of St. Paul's as well as Somerset House. Nor did I ask why the stages, which should be at the epicentre of any theatre building, were so elusive when you were backstage.

But I did ask him why he designed a road that bisected the space between the theatre and the river. It was placed there, Lasdun told me, to give a sense of the city, like the road that divided the Regency terraces and hotels from the Brighton esplanade. I also asked him, cautiously, if it was possible to remove one of the walkway terraces which entirely blocked the view of the river from the Lyttelton circle level. To remove it, he said, would be like removing a pediment of St. Paul's.

In our many conversations he veered from the mandarin to the combative, vague, lyrical, often patronising and occasionally incomprehensible. In short, he was intimidating. Nevertheless, I was still surprised to discover that he had described me to his friends and to the press as a "barbarian who had insulted, vandalised, and mutilated his building." Was it "mutilation" to take away the road that separated the theatre from the river and create a large pedestrian area that linked the building to the South Bank walk? Was it "vandalism" to move the cramped temporary bookshop from the foyer to the existing porte-cochère? And was it not "insulting" to those who directed, designed, performed and wrote plays for the Olivier and Lyttelton

Theatres to be prohibited by Lasdun and by English Heritage from changing any features of those auditoriums?

The problems with the NT's auditoriums are very far from unique but, in spite of their problems, you can't say that the National Theatre doesn't work. You can't say it's not a successful theatre. It's worked because of the will of very gifted people who have, year after year, said, "We're going to make the best of it, we can't change this, so we'll find ways of making this space work." It's a truism that the art of theatre can survive pretty much whatever architects might throw at it, and it's also a truism that all directors, writers and actors feel warmly about theatres in which they've had a success.

Only Richard Pilbrow could have had the patience, the application and the wisdom to write this book. That I find it utterly absorbing is predictable; after all, it deals with matters that haunted my waking and sleeping hours for years. But its appeal is much wider than that: It addresses a problem that applies to almost all bespoke theatres, galleries, museums, cinemas and concert halls. How does a committee of professionals, expert in their own fields, sanction spaces so ill-suited to the art form that they are designed to serve?

Sir Richard Eyre
Director of the National Theatre 1988-1997

Guys and Dolls, Olivier Theatre, 1982. Bob Hoskins as Nathan Detroit, Julia McKenzie as Adelaide, Ian Charleson as Sky Masterson, directed by Richard Eyre.

Introduction

Richard Pilbrow

Theatre is a magical art that has captivated humans since the dawn of time. Theatre is about telling stories, about actors creating magic by telling stories. Theatre is one of the most ancient and revered methods of communication between people.

Modern theatre can be accompanied by music, dance, scenery, costumes, make-up, props, lights, sound and video to support telling stories. Theatre can be performed in a village clearing, upon a simple wooden platform, or in a special building: a theatre.

A theatre may be complex or very simple. It may provide a place where the audience encircles the stage; gathers around it, or sits to one side. The stage may be simple boards, or a machine of great complexity. The communication between actor and audience, telling the story, is all.

We theatre makers, we actors, we who work backstage to tell stories, generally accept the place where theatre is made. But a theatre's architecture – the architecture of the place where we tell our stories – influences every aspect of story telling.

This book is about theatre buildings. How the place in which we make theatre has evolved over time is a fascinating story.

This book is about the National Theatre, about one of the most successful theatre companies in the world. This book is about the Denys Lasdun building and, equally importantly, about the life within, the people who bring those stories, and the theatre, to life.

The National Theatre
The National Theatre is the most significant theatre building of the 20th century. It was born at the end of a time when

"Cannot we concentrate on making a place where the actors feel marvellous?"

Sir Laurence Olivier

construction of new London theatres had dried up and the building of new regional repertory theatres had hardly begun, leaving the stakeholders with few reference points from which to begin. The theatres of the West End didn't seem relevant in the mid-20th century and, in any case, everyone involved harboured ambitions of creating a world-class building: the "exemplary theatre" envisaged by Granville-Barker, an early advocate of a national theatre in 1903.

Thus, the birth of the National is a kind of Big Bang in the history of theatre architecture, an explosion of ideas that took place almost in a historical vacuum. The National's founding artistic director, Sir Laurence Olivier and his colleagues weren't just designing a building; they were asking profound questions about what makes a theatre.

The creation story of the National contains all of the issues and conflicts that are associated with the design of any new theatre. The fact that the National was born with some defects only makes it more interesting. The purpose of this book is to illuminate the conflicts and challenges behind the National's creation, to show how it has evolved over time, and to chart how subsequent generations of artists have engaged with the building's flaws and successes to create great art.

The Architecture of Performance
Architecture and theatre: two aspects of human endeavour that are amazingly disparate. The one devoted to housing the human spirit in built form, a form almost always intended to last for decades, or even centuries. The other, the most ephemeral of all the arts, only realised in real time in the real presence of performer and spectator, here today – and then gone forever. A concrete house for a fleeting emotion. A cage for a butterfly?

No wonder misunderstandings can arise.

Creating The National Theatre
The National Theatre was a dream, a dream that began in 1848. The British establishment took 101 years to come to its support with the passing of the National Theatre Act in 1949. Thirteen years were to pass before Sir Laurence Olivier was appointed to bring the National Theatre – company and building – to reality. Four previous designs that had been prepared by architects remained on the drawing boards. Advisory committees had repeatedly debated the needs of the theatre. Their views, although sometimes quite prescient, were forgotten, relegated to the archives.

Sir Laurence had just taken the reins of Britain's first purpose-built thrust stage theatre, which opened in Chichester in 1962. Now he had a new company to create... and a new building to conceive. To assist him he assembled some of the most distinguished theatre people of the time, to form the National Theatre Building Committee.

At their second meeting, they passed a resolution: *"The panel is convinced that the long history of failure in modern theatre architecture in England is due to a basically wrong relationship between the architect and the theatre people."*

Nine months later, in 1963, the architect, Denys Lasdun, was appointed. His distinctive attribute was his innocence about theatre. The chairman of the National Theatre Board, Lord Cottesloe, reported, "He said he knew nothing about designing theatres and would have to sit down and learn what was needed from our committee." He came to the interview alone. He stated he was a blank slate, willing and anxious to work with the committee to deliver more than they might ever dream of. Sir Laurence recalled, "Very theatrical. Just him and nobody else. During the interview he said, 'Surely the most important aspect of what we're talking about is the spiritual one.' Oh my dear! We all fell for that one."

With perhaps a foretaste of what was to come, Lasdun himself also said, "If you want me as your architect, you will have to work hard with me. When you have nothing more to tell me, only then will I want to be left alone to design the building." Lord Cottesloe again: "I took the view that once you appointed an architect, you have to give him his head."

Your Author and the National Theatre
In the summer of 1962, Sir Laurence had invited me to Chichester to "sort out the bloody awful lighting." Unfortunately, he asked me two days before opening night. There was nothing that could be done in time. He said, "Well, you're no bloody use, are you?" I withdrew in considerable confusion. The following April, he phoned me: "Dickie, dear boy. It's April, we open in June. Does that give you enough fucking time?"

Soon afterwards, after an elegant lunch at The Dorchester with Sir Laurence and theatre director and building committee member John Dexter, I became Sir Laurence's lighting director for the brand-new National Theatre Company at The Old Vic, which had become its temporary home. We opened with Peter O'Toole as *Hamlet*, a shaky start to what soon became a glorious period of British theatre history. The lighting design team I had built at Theatre Projects, the company I had created to allow me to subsidise my career as a lighting designer by renting equipment to shows, by then included a remarkable group of other designers. With the wonderful Old Vic crew, led by Lennie Tucker, we lit almost every production for that first amazing decade.

As planning for the new theatre began, I became involved in various technical subcommittees with NT colleagues: technical director Coeks Gordon, production stage manager Neville Thompson, general manager George Rowbottom, and Sir Laurence's loyal long-time stage manager, Diana Boddington. We worked alongside architect Denys Lasdun's team, formulating the backstage brief for the building.

From its earliest days Theatre Projects had found itself assisting architects seeking to understand what backstage theatre meant. Few new theatres had been built in the UK since the 1930s, but public funding in the 1960s led to a new regional theatre boom. I had become quite an 'expert,' working on ambitious productions in the West End and on Broadway, but I knew little or nothing of architecture. As a small team, we soon discovered that however little we knew, we still had much to offer the architect who knew less about theatre than we knew about architecture.

In April 1966, during the 24th meeting of the National Theatre Committee, I was nominated to join the National Theatre Building Committee after the passing of director and English Stage Company founder George Devine:

OLIVIER: I think we should record our very deep sorrow at the death of George Devine who was of inestimable help to the Committee.

DEXTER: I think we should bring in Richard Pilbrow. We are sadly lacking on the technical side.

I joined this distinguished group. The secretary, Kenneth Rae, gave me a file of the preceding minutes, which made fascinating reading. I sat (usually somewhat tongue-tied in such august company) and listened to their deliberations. There was clearly little consensus about theatre architecture and what constituted good theatre design.

During subsequent meetings, I found myself seated beside Lasdun. One day, while we were leaving, he took me aside and asked my advice. He'd been confused by what he was hearing. "Richard, at the last meeting, didn't so-and-so say something that contradicted his view today?" Well, I had to admit that I believed he had.

Some months later, Sir Laurence called me into his office in Aquinas Street. "Richard, Lasdun wants the theatre to appoint a permanent representative… a theatre consultant to represent our position. I think you at Theatre Projects have been doing this type of work. Could you take it on?"

A great adventure had begun.

The Untold Stories
Your author was a witness to this forging of our National Theatre. It is a remarkable tale in human terms. A committee of brilliant men and women, an architect of exceptional brilliance. The result, a building of extraordinary distinction, one of the most famous concrete structures in Britain – though one that divides opinion: King Charles, then Prince of Wales, reportedly likened it to a nuclear

power station, but it is now protected by Grade II* listing. Of the three theatres, one, the smallest, a courtyard, is imitated around the world; the two larger, alleged exemplars of proscenium and open-stage forms, remain controversial, their epic concrete form too often offering an unsympathetic rigidity. It has been inhabited by a company of international renown, home to their countless successful theatrical productions under outstandingly able artistic directors. It has been both loved and criticised by actors, actresses, directors and designers.

Extraordinary talent, ambition, misunderstanding, ego, folly and delight: a truly human fusion of elements created our National Theatre. This book is a unique examination of the design of this great building, combined with analysis of how the stages within have performed. It reveals how talented theatremakers have risen above any possible limitations set in concrete to create great art.

I have sought to elucidate the mystery of the relationship between building and art, between theatre and architecture. I've tried to do this through historical overview, hitherto unpublished history - particularly the minutes of the National Theatre Building Committee, which met from January 1963 to January 1969 to prepare the brief for the proposed new National Theatre. These have not previously been published in full. Between the notes of each meeting I have added commentary, drawing on my personal papers, recollections and other documents.

I have also included the voices of many other artists, including their (often contradictory) impressions of the meeting between these two disparate worlds of theatre and architecture - at the National Theatre, and elsewhere.

This meeting is not always successful. Achieving success - creating magical performance spaces - needs, as we shall see, humility, listening and true collaboration from everyone involved.

Richard Pilbrow

Richard Brett, with the original model of the Olivier Theatre drum revolve

For my friend Richard (Dick) Brett, and the people of the National Theatre.

The Olivier Theatre

> "On the Olivier stage, one man could play Beckett or a hundred men could fight the Wars of the Roses…"
>
> Peter Hall, Director, 1972

> "It is a really, really hard space. You can't be passive in there - and I think that's what I love about it."
>
> Paule Constable, Lighting Designer, 2023

First performance
16th September 1976
Royal Gala opening performance 25th October 1976

Seating capacity
1160

Design
Open stage notionally inspired by the outdoor theatre at Epidaurus in Greece.

Named for Lord Olivier, the National's founding artistic director, who would only perform there once, on the night the Queen came to open the National Theatre.

Thanks to its concrete construction, the robust defence of its architect and, later, the building's grade II* listed status, the Olivier of now is immediately recognisable as the Olivier that opened in 1976. But that isn't to say nothing has changed. Surface finishes have been modified to try to tame the complex acoustics, the concrete of some surfaces now concealed. And experiments have been made with the relationship of stage to audience, Peter Hall lifting it up, Richard Eyre trying an in-the-round version, Trevor Nunn and designer John Napier moving it up further and dramatically forward, Nichoas Hytner pulling it back to Peter Hall's line, most recently it receding back to the original 1976 front edge.

Technically, the theatre incorporates a complex 'drum revolve' as part of its stage, able to create complex scene changes by rotating and lowering scenery to the basement below, and what was at the time a ground-breaking power flying system for lifting scenery.

For audiences arriving in 1976, it felt like a revelation – so different from those traditional theatres of the West End, so spacious, vast, open, epic (and also comfortable, and air-conditioned!) Of course all of those things are what make it challenging to mount shows in, and from the back of the circle the stage can feel a long way away. Nonetheless, generations of young theatregoers have grown up watching shows all the way back there, in the standing spaces that have always been the very cheapest way of seeing shows at the National.

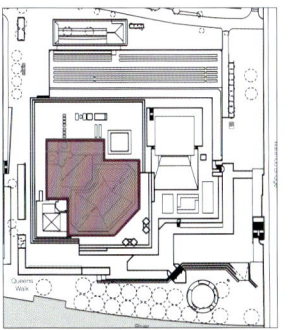

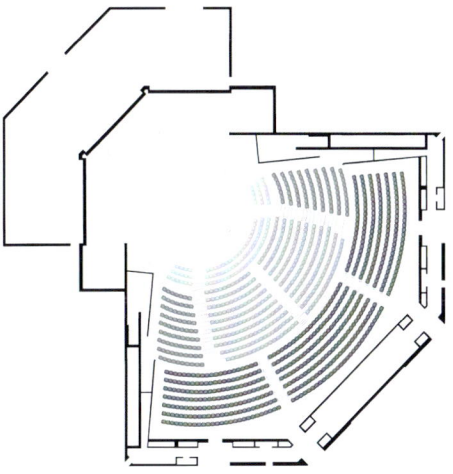

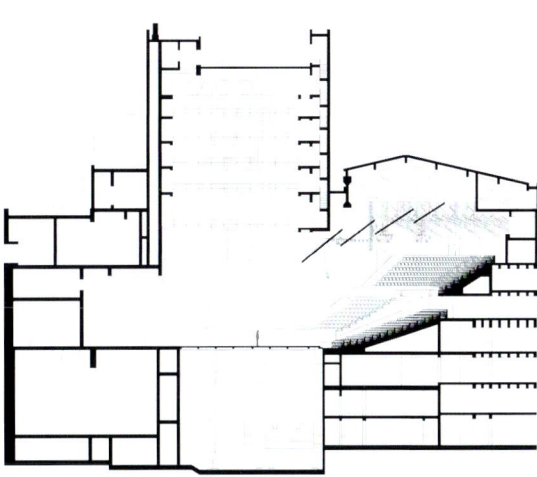

The Lyttelton Theatre

> "You need a rectangle and the audience frankly just facing. That is the essence of the Lyttelton Theatre."
>
> Denys Lasdun, 1966

> "Because this is such an entirely new kind of auditorium, with a different focus and a different rhythm, I find it enormously stimulating."
>
> Peter Hall, Director, 1974

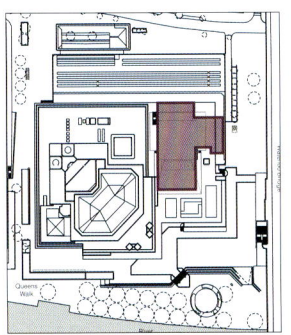

First performance
8th March 1976

Seating capacity
897

Design
Two level auditorium facing a proscenium-arch stage with adjustable proscenium zone.

Named for Oliver Lyttelton, Lord Chandos, whose drive to win the establishment's support of the National continued that of his parents, Alfred and Edith Lyttelton, who were involved in the campaign for a national theatre from its very earliest days.

The first of the National's three theatres to open back in 1976, the Lyttelton had a form familiar to theatregoers – two levels of seating facing a proscenium stage – yet felt radically different to those traditional theatres, with its very formal structure, its beautifully lit textured concrete instead of plaster and ornamentation and the spacious foyers that led in to it. For theatre makers, the big, well equipped stage wth rear and side stages to support changeovers between shows in rep provided boundless opportunity.

That familiar form is perhaps why there appears to have been almost no discussion about the theatre in the planning committee meetings, compared to the countless discussions and versions of the Olivier Theatre. Yet for all the familiarity of the proscenium, it turned out to be a challenging space to energise, the auditorium's design giving a sense of two smaller audiences – one upstairs, the other downstairs – rather than one unified whole.

It has perhaps always been hampered by the decision to give it fewer seats than the Olivier: a theatre is sometimes chosen for a show based on perceived demand for tickets rather than which style of space might best suit the show as those involved in creating the National perhaps intended.

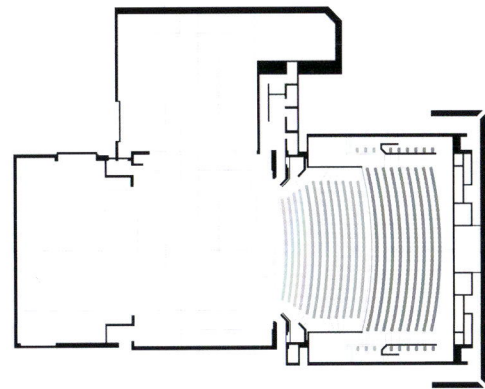

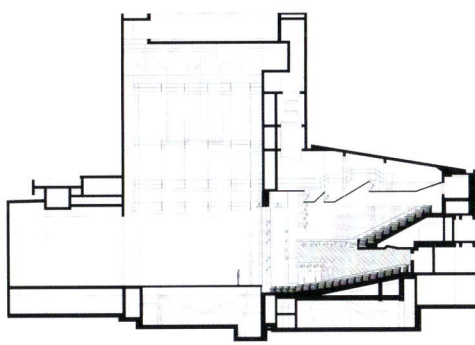

The Cottesloe Theatre, later renamed the Dorfman Theatre

> "The truth is that the South Bank Board cannot avoid having the Studio. Denys Lasdun has built it as the cornerstone of the building."
>
> Peter Hall, Director, 1972

> "I love the Cottesloe, and I thank you all for that!"
>
> William Dudley, Designer, 2015

First performance
4th March 1977

Seating capacity
Variable – around 400

Design:
Adaptable courtyard theatre with audience on three sides.

Named originally for Lord Cottesloe, Arts Council chair from 1960-1965, and from 1962 chair of the South Bank Theatre and Opera House board. In 2014, renamed for Lloyd Dorfman, founder of the Travelex company, in recognition of his support of the National's low-cost ticket schemes.

The Cottesloe was the only part of the National not designed by Denys Lasdun. A space had been set aside for a studio theatre, but budget cuts meant it was to be left empty. As a condition of taking over the company, Peter Hall insisted the studio be reinstated. With Lasdun busy on the rest of the building, coming up with a design was handed to your author's company, Theatre Projects, with Iain Mackintosh creating a design he initially called the 'Cottesloe Cockpit' over a weekend.

The courtyard form he created has been replicated many times in many places in the years since, not always as well when designers fail to understand the key ingredients of its success – particularly tightly packing the audience vertically.

Built quickly and on a tight budget, equipped with hand-me-downs from the Old Vic rather than the glamorous new equipment of the rest of the building, and disconnected from the other two theatres, with its own entrance through its own lobby around the side of the building, the Cottesloe was the last part of the building to open, but quickly acquired a loyal audience and the love of those making shows in it.

The theatre is enormously flexible, able to be reconfigured into different formats, with seating on a steep or shallow rake facing a stage, or with seating on either side of a stage, or, as in a number of acclaimed productions, with no seating at all, the audience promenading with the actors.

The seperate lobby space was reworked and expanded in the 2015-2016 NT Future scheme, but attempts to find a route through or around or even over the building to connect it to the main lobby spaces failed, so a trip to the Dorfman still means a walk around the building, under the dramatic buttresses of the building's eastern edge.

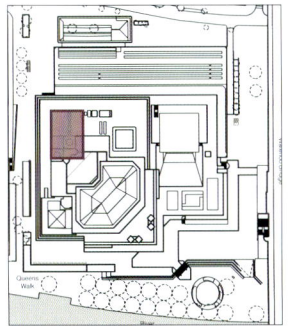

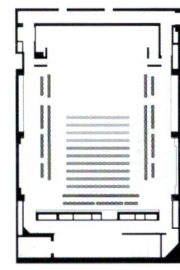

Cottesloe Theatre at the time of opening, 1977

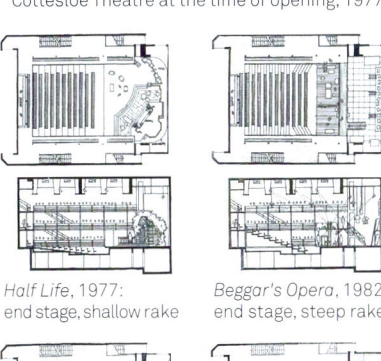

Half Life, 1977: end stage, shallow rake

Beggar's Opera, 1982: end stage, steep rake

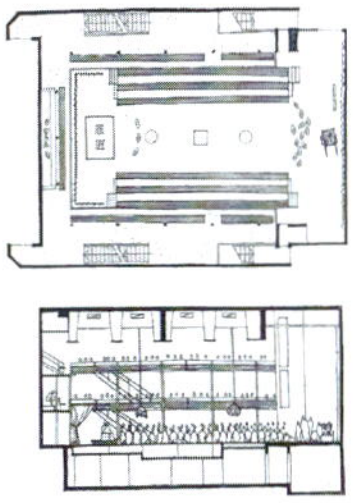

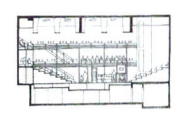

Fuente Ovejuna, 1992: long traverse

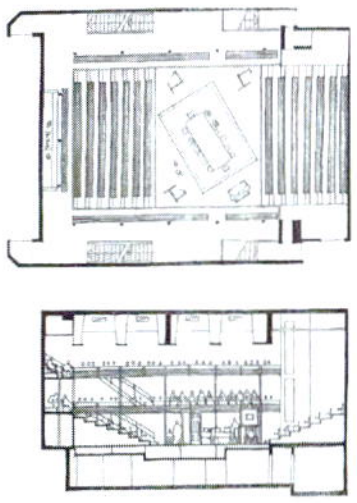

Voysey Inheritance, 1989: short traverse

The Fourth Theatre

> "The building offers thoroughfares in exactly the same way a city offers them. There are streets, squares, gardens, cul-de-sacs, where I hope life will cross the building."
>
> Denys Lasdun, 1976

Opening date
8th March 1976

Design
The architect intended the National's public spaces as a fourth theatre, with the public as the performers.

The design – spacious, open, comfortable, welcoming – was radical compared to the cramped foyers of the West End theatres across the river. Just as radical was that they were open all day, not just immediately prior to a show. The National invited you to hang out and relax. This was revolutionary.

As many people have moved from working in an office to working from wherever, the National during the day has become a thriving work and social hub, the foyers full of people and laptops taking advantage of the strong WiFi, good coffee and comfortable surroundings – so much so they now almost have to be shoo-ed away come show time. Amongst them, as has been the case since the building opened, are others just looking for a comfortable place to spend some time – parents with young kids, pensioners playing Scrabble, tourists just stopping for a coffee. And, often, NT staff having meetings, sometimes preferring Lasdun's fourth theatre to the backstage office spaces!

There have been changes over time: facilities rearranged, a new lift installed to provide better access to the Lyttelton circle, one window to the west moved dramatically outwards in the 1997 updates, another to the east in the 2015-2016 upates, to a line that reflects Lasdun's original line of the western window. The old window lines are visible in the columns and in the ceiling if you look up. Most controversially, at the time, the porte-cochère was filled in to create a bookshop; this was revised in the 2015 scheme to create new lobby and box-office space. The removal of the road that used to encircle the building allowed the creation of a new outdoor space, known as Theatre Square, between the building and the river.

The National's foyers when new in 1976

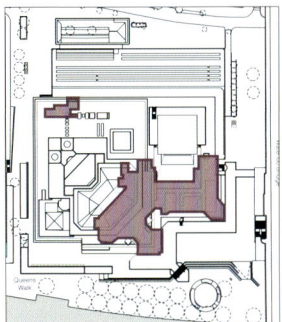

The foyers today: a thriving work and social hub

The foyers between 1997 and 2016

xxvii

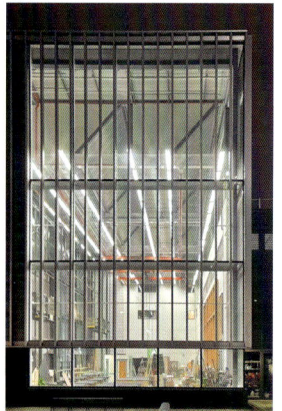

Far left: drum road; top right: stage door; mid left: Max Rayne Centre; mid right: drum corridor; bottom right: dock door

Behind The Scenes

Design

The National Theatre building had always been conceived as a complete machine for making theatre – not just the auditoria for presenting shows, but the rehearsal rooms for creating them, and on-site workshops for building them. This, too, was a revolution compared to so many other theatres, and a source of delight to theatre practitioners – particularly actors and directors who for so long had been used to rehearsing in whatever cramped, cold, draughty halls could be found. Once their show moves on to the stage, those performers move to the National's dressing rooms, built around a hidden courtyard at the heart of the theatre so giving plenty of daylight and the opportuntiy for all those appearing on the National's stages on a given night to see each other and – as new shows open – celebrate each other.

For those designing shows, the National's spacious workshops allowed their designs to be built and painted on site, necessitating the creation of an enormous paint frame big enough to deal with the hugely wide backcloths that the Olivier's stage would require. All of this was housed in the rear portion of the building, which from the exterior is quite distinct in its finish from the rest of the building, using exposed brick rather than raw concrete.

Though parts of this work have always been accessible to the public through the Backstage tours that the National has long run, the 2015 NT Future project opened it up further, providing new windows in the building's facade that allow passers by a glimpse of the work required to get a show onto the stage, and allow visitors inside a new walkway above the workshops to get an even closer look.

National Theatre rehearsal room one at the time of opening

> "The particular rehearsal room in the new theatre that we are using is quiet, has good daylight, height, and is properly warmed. After twenty-one years of rehearsing in cupboards, leaky halls, and bars smelling of last night's drink and tobacco, at last I am in a place with good conditions. I count this one of the greatest merits of our South Bank building. The work can be created in a proper place."
>
> Peter Hall, Director, 1975

Dressing room courtyard

> "The dressing rooms, all around the courtyard, you see everybody getting ready. I love that. Love it."
>
> Judi Dench, Actor, 2018

Cover of *Drama* illustrating the prize-winning design submission by William Lyon Somerville of Toronto to the National Theatre architectural competition of 1924.

Part One

The Quest: Setting the Scene

The story of the 101-year quest for the National Theatre that culminated in the establishment of Laurence Olivier's National Theatre Company at the Old Vic. The story is set alongside that of the evolution of British theatre architecture since the 16th century.

"We British were a little behind the curve."

Your author

The Old Vic Theatre in around 2006

1.1 The Quest for a National Theatre

The National Theatre was a dream that began in 1848. Encouraged by such luminaries as Sir Henry Irving, Charles Dickens and Bernard Shaw, and proselytised by the outstanding Edwardian dramatist/director Harley Granville-Barker, the British establishment took over one hundred years to come to its support with the passing of the National Theatre Act in 1949.

Four attempts to erect a National Theatre building produced much deliberation, some of it quite prescient, but no results, in concrete or even lathe and plaster. Thirteen years were to pass before Sir Laurence Olivier was appointed to finally bring the National Theatre to reality.

Beginnings

In his epic volume *The National Theatre Story*, Daniel Rosenthal points out that the story really began in 1564 with the birth of William Shakespeare, who did indeed inspire generations of theatre lovers around the globe. I will not attempt to repeat the history in Daniel's encyclopaedic book, but will simply touch on some of the more dramatic highlights.

These highlights were epic indeed. For years, conflict raged between Britain's theatrical excellence personified by Shakespeare, the world's most beloved playwright, and the British cultural heritage of prudery and government indifference. On countless occasions, financial disaster threatened; even during the National's construction serious argument often raged about cancelling the half-finished concrete monolith.

Without any help from the Bard of Avon, France had possessed a national theatre since 1680, while other European countries, such as Austria, Sweden and Denmark, had boasted national theatres for more than 200 years. We British were a little behind the curve.

The first record of a British initiative came in 1848, when a London publisher, Effingham Wilson, prompted by the 1847 purchase of Shakespeare's birthplace in Stratford, issued a pamphlet: *A House for Shakespeare: A Proposition for the Consideration of the Nation*. Wilson felt that serious drama was being overwhelmed by frippery and lightweight fare. His paper suggested some principles: affordable tickets, education in addition to entertainment and the need to strive for the highest quality. These ideas were supported by notable Victorians: Charles Dickens and actor/manager Charles Kemble. Despite the fact that other major cultural institutions were being supported – the National Gallery, the British Museum and others – to many Victorians, theatre remained hardly respectable. Large segments of society shared my very own Methodist grandfather's belief that theatre was still a place of moral turpitude.

In 1880, after seeing the Comédie Française in London, English critic Matthew Arnold called for a 'Comédie Anglaise' with a clarion summons: "The theatre is irresistible: Organise the theatre." This created only modest interest, as stars such as Sir Henry Irving were already presenting their own versions of Shakespeare, in the West End and on tour. Nevertheless, Sir Henry was a supporter and, with his own company, seemed to come close to a Victorian 'National' ideal. Sadly, commercial pressures led to his company's financial collapse by the 1890s. This renewed calls for a very different type of theatre, an endowed, 'exemplary' non-commercial institution.

Harley Granville-Barker[1]

In 1903, the critic William Archer met with Edwin Sachs, author of the extraordinary multi-volume classic on theatre architecture *Modern Opera Houses and Theatres* (and who had been responsible for the electrification of the stage machinery at the Theatre Royal Drury Lane) to discuss "tentative plans." Then, after exchanging "fistfuls, then stacks of paper" and along with a 27-year-old friend, actor-director-author Harley Granville-Barker, the two men produced: *Scheme & Estimates for a National Theatre* for private publication, "on no account to be communicated to, criticised, or mentioned, in the Public Press."[2] This was a detailed proposal for staff, size of company (sixty-five), budget and repertoire of a national theatre. The estimated total capital cost was £300,000.

Harley Granville-Barker is today remembered as a brilliant playwright, yet he was also one of the most important men of early 20th century theatre. "He would spend the next 24 years working on the stage as an actor, director, manager and playwright, then 30 years more as a critic and theorist. He would establish Shaw as the first dramatist of his age. He would effectively invent the position of director in England, establish the principle of playing in repertoire, and create, with his partner J.E. Vedrenne, two of the most

 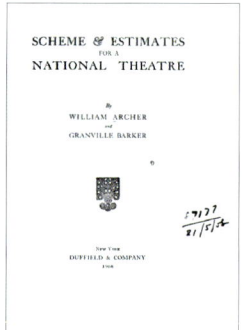

Harley Granville-Barker   *Scheme & Estimates*

important theatre managements. He would show the way for the establishment of a national theatre, and struggle for it all his life."[3]

The practical plan they wrote was privately printed in 1904 and referred to as the Blue Book. It was formally published with a revised title, *A National Theatre: Schemes and Estimates,* by Duckworth and Company in 1907. The authors assumed a company of actors consisting of forty-two men and twenty-four women, and one house with 1500 seats. They were deliberately cautious in the sample repertoire, omitting the provocative names of Ibsen and Shaw, emphasising Shakespeare and drama within the late Victorian tradition. "It is not an 'Advanced' Theatre that we are designing… experiment would not be its primary function."[4] Perhaps feeling slighted, Shaw criticised their "musty" list of plays and suggested they deserved to be ignored if they lacked the courage to propose a bolder repertoire. The 1907 revision included a bold change: "I advocate the inclusion of every author we excluded four years ago – Ibsen, Hauptmann, D'Annunzio, Shaw and the rest."[5]

The radical notions in the Blue Book were the proposal for a training school as part of a national theatre, and the insistence on a new and specially designed building to house all of the functions related to it. The collaborators specified "A theatre building wholly different from any now existing in London. We believe that such an enterprise would be almost impossibly handicapped in any building not specially designed for this particular purpose." They concluded, "There never was and never will be an ideal theatre. The theatre is too complex and delicate a machine, depending on the harmonious cooperation of too many talents, ever to reach perfection for more than a passing moment. The very greatest theatres at their greatest periods have been criticised, not, as a rule, without reason."[6]

Archer and Granville-Barker also wrote, "The National Theatre must be its own advertisement – must impose itself on public notice, not by posters and column advertisements in the newspapers, but by the very fact of its ample, dignified and liberal presence."[7] Sixty years later, in designing the National that was finally built, Denys Lasdun was to keep a copy of these words by his desk as a source of inspiration.

Granville-Barker, in partnership with the more experienced J.E. Vedrenne, began to put theory into practice. From October 1904 to June 1907, they organised seasons of repertory at the Royal Court Theatre, presenting 946 performances of thirty-two plays, with twenty-eight premieres. This was a trailblazing event, revolutionising the British theatre of the time and doing much to introduce George Bernard Shaw and the principles of repertory. While artistically a breakthrough, the season failed financially, the losses worsened by subsequent seasons at the St. James, Little, Kingsway and Savoy Theatres.

But then came a complication. A wealthy 84-year old brewer, Richard Badger, wrote to *The Times* in 1903 about his dream of a statue of Shakespeare, "worthy of his fame," in Portland Place (near the site of the present headquarters of the British Broadcasting Corporation). This idea attracted a public meeting in 1905, leading to the formation of a general committee that attracted hundreds of distinguished and aristocratic supporters, including the Archbishop of Canterbury, Edward Elgar, Thomas Hardy and even Henry Irving. The committee liked the idea of a statue, rejecting the competing controversial, and much more expensive, alternative of building a proper theatre.

Winston Churchill, at the time secretary of state for the colonies, speaking in 1906 at a banquet in honour of actress Ellen Terry, said, "Think with what excitement and interest people witness the construction of a dreadnought – what a pity it is that some measure of that interest cannot be turned in the direction of

"Surely a subsidised theatre is the only fitting memorial."

Ellen Terry, English Actress

launching, say, a National Theatre."[8] Archer and Granville-Barker who were in the audience that night, thanked Churchill for his support, and sent him a copy of their paper.

There ensued something of a civil war between 'monument' and 'theatre.' In May 1908, Lord Lytton (Victor Bulwer-Lytton, the 2nd Earl of Lytton) summoned a meeting at the Lyceum Theatre to appoint another committee, this one to draft a scheme to build the Shakespeare Memorial National Theatre. The committee was to be an ideal blend of the establishment and the "rebels, of practical businessmen and academics,"[9] including Shaw, Pinero, Archer and Granville-Barker, with Herbert Beerbohm Tree, Johnson Forbes-Robertson, Edith Lyttelton and Professor Israel Gollancz (honorary secretary). The vice-chairman was Viscount Esher, then aged just 27.

Opposition from the theatrical old guard of the West End was considerable, and a spirited public discourse ensued. William Archer: "It is absurd to raise an inert and lifeless statue to Shakespeare while he lacks the living monument of a National Theatre."[10] Ellen Terry added, "Surely a subsidised theatre is the only fitting memorial."[11] Eventually, the two groups merged to begin a fund under a new committee: the Shakespeare Memorial National Theatre Committee (SMNTC).

Important figures of the establishment were key campaigners; they were led by Alfred Lyttelton, a late Victorian noble and sports figure, with his wife Edith, a friend of George Bernard Shaw. It was their son, Oliver Lyttelton, Lord Chandos, who was to push the establishment in support of the theatre in the 1950s and '60s – leading to the naming of the Lyttelton Theatre in his family's memory. The first significant donation, of £70,000, came from the wealthy businessman Carl Meyer, solicited by Edith Lyttelton with the aid of the young actress Lillah McCarthy (Mrs. Harley Granville-Barker). Meyer was soon made a baronet!

In 1909, the new committee published an illustrated prospectus setting out its aims. It included that the building should be "at once conspicuous and dignified… one of the great buildings of the Metropolis." It included the admonishment that "it would be a fatal mistake to make the auditorium too large, yet the space between seats ought to be so liberal that ladies can, if they wish, pass out into fresher air during the intervals."[12]

The prospectus listed the following aims:
1. To keep the plays of Shakespeare in its repertory.
2. To revive whatever else is vital in English classical theatre.
3. To prevent recent plays of great merit from falling into oblivion.
4. To produce new plays and to further the development of modern drama.
5. To produce translations or representative works of foreign drama, ancient and modern.
6. To stimulate the art of acting through the various opportunities it will offer to members of the company.[13]

On 24th November 1910 at the Haymarket Theatre, Bernard Shaw's one-act play *The Dark Lady of the Sonnets* ingeniously sought establishment support. (Granville-Barker himself played Shakespeare.) In an imagined midnight tryst between Shakespeare and the Virgin Queen:

SHAKESPEAR: The boon I crave is that you do endow a great playhouse, or, if I may make bold to coin a scholarly name for it, a National Theatre, for the better instruction and gracing of your Majesty's subjects.

ELIZABETH: Why, sir, are there not theatres enough on the Bankside and in Blackfriars?

SHAKESPEAR: Madam: these are the adventures of needy and desperate men that must, to save themselves from perishing of want, give the sillier sort of people what they best like; and what they best like, God knows, is not their own betterment and instruction, as we well see by the example of the churches, which must needs compel men to frequent them, though they be open to all without charge. Only when there is a matter of a murder, or a plot, or a pretty youth in petticoats, or some naughty tale of wantonness will your subjects pay the great cost of good players and their finery, with a little profit to boot.

ELIZABETH: Master Shakespear: I will speak of this matter to the Lord Treasurer.

SHAKESPEAR: Then am I undone, madam; for there was never yet a Lord Treasurer that could find a penny for anything over and above the necessary expenses of your own government, save for war or a salary for his own nephew.[14]

But establishment circles were moving – albeit painfully slowly. In 1913, there was a first debate on a private member's bill in Parliament on the proposed theatre, with an estimated cost of £500,000. A one-acre site in Keppel Street, behind the British Museum in Bloomsbury, was acquired for £50,000.

Emma Cons, Lilian Baylis, and the Old Vic
The Old Vic, later to be the birthplace of the National Theatre, was built in 1818 and named the Royal Coburg. Initially successful, the area and theatre then declined until, in 1831, the great actor Edmund Kean, playing in *Richard III,* met an audience he described in a tempestuous curtain call speech as a set of ignorant, unmitigated brutes! In 1871, the theatre was rebuilt by architect Jethro T. Robinson (father-in-law of theatre architect Frank Matcham) into a house with twin lyre-shaped balconies, intended for melodrama, pantomime… and copious drinking!

Such was the state of debauchery that met Emma Cons when she visited in 1880. She was a remarkably determined social reformer who, supported by powerful backers, took over the theatre and renamed it the Royal Victoria Coffee Palace and Music Hall. Alcohol not permitted! The programme under Miss Cons included polite concerts, readings from Shakespeare and lectures. The latter became so important that they evolved into the full-time Morley College.

In 1912, Lilian Baylis, the niece of Emma Cons, took over the theatre and, while opera was her first love, she expanded operatic recitals and began a policy of 'Shakespeare for Her People.' Baylis was a deeply religious character of powerful conviction; one night, "Miss Baylis had a vision. She had been trying to sleep, when a strong manly voice out of the dark enquired: 'why have you allowed my beautiful words to be so murdered?' She replied that it was not she but others who had done it. The voice then said: 'you must run the plays yourself as you do the operas.'"[15] Thus she created a theatre company devoted to low-cost productions of Shakespeare to accompany her opera and, later, ballet companies. (These later developed into The Royal Opera and The Royal Ballet. Miss Baylis was a high achiever!)

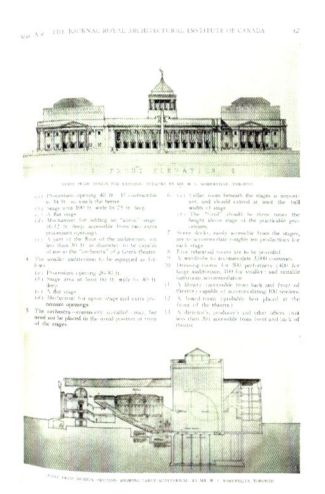

By 1923, celebrating the 300th anniversary of the publication of Shakespeare's First Folio, the Old Vic had produced every one of his plays – an extraordinary achievement.

World War I
The advent of war brought considerations of a national theatre to a halt. In 1916, the Bloomsbury site was lent to the YMCA to erect a 'Shakespeare Hut' for the entertainment of the troops. The Old Vic continued bravely presenting low-cost Shakespeare throughout the war, despite the Zeppelin air raids.

And war brought other stirrings on behalf of the drama.

While serving with the army in France, a young director, Basil Dean, had found time to organise, with the approval of the military, concert parties and stage entertainments behind the lines. At almost the same time, Lena Ashwell, one of the leading actresses of pre-war days, conceived the notion of starting musical and dramatic entertainment in YMCA huts at Le Havre and elsewhere.

During the war, Granville-Barker travelled to New York to present a season of plays. There he met and fell in love with Helen Huntington, a wealthy American poet and writer. This led to the breakup of his marriage and his retirement from active production to concentrate on writing plays and scholarly works advocating community theatre, with his brilliantly influential *Prefaces to Shakespeare*.[16]

It might be noticed that efforts on behalf of a national theatre dream so far came mainly from the aristocracy, the professional classes, and only some of the theatrical profession. When advocating for the national theatre, people spoke of the memory of Shakespeare, the forging of bonds of empire and the progress of the dramatic arts. But little was done to encourage the support of the wider public.

But war had spurred a wider interest in the theatre. Basil Dean went on to become England's premier director through the 1920s and '30s. And other stirrings were also afoot.

Geoffrey Whitworth and Theatre for the People
Amateur theatre in Britain had been a widespread and popular pastime since the turn of the century, much encouraged by enthusiasm for the works of Gilbert and Sullivan.

In 1918, a young publisher, Geoffrey Whitworth, delivered a lecture on *The History of the Stage* to a chapter of the YMCA at a munitions factory in Crayford, Kent. He remembered, "After the lecture, I was informed of a surprise item. The Crayford Reading Circle was about to present a one-act play by Stanley Houghton. Would I not stay and hear it? The first thing that happened was that the hall, which previously had

Lilian Baylis

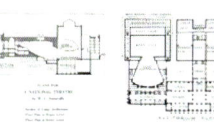

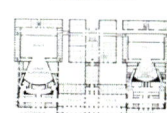

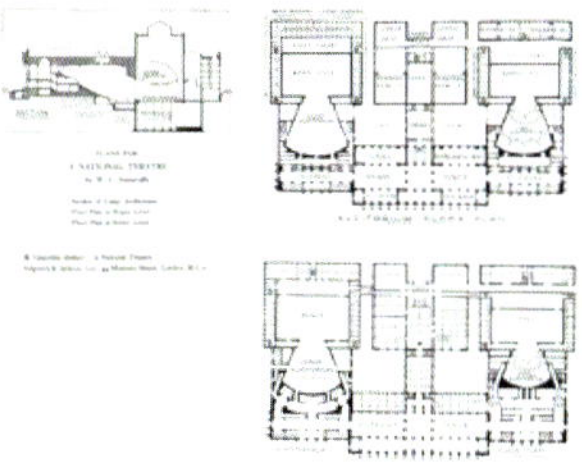

National Theatre Proposal 1924

National Theatre Proposal 1924

been half empty, began to fill. The women laid aside their knitting-needles, and the men their newspapers. This was no lecture. This was real and this was earnest. This was a Play.

"Yet here were no actors in the proper sense of the word. They just sat, on a semi-circle of chairs. They were not dressed for their parts. They had not even memorised them. With books in their hands and with a minimum of action, they did not do much more than read the words of the play. And yet, through the emotional sincerity of their interpretations, the characters came to life and, as I watched, I felt that I was coming close to the fundamental quality of dramatic art in a way that I had never understood it before." [17]

Whitworth's conversion was to the realisation that theatre was not only for the elite but might be vitally important to the emotional life of a broader population. His new enthusiasm led him to found the amateur British Drama League. "In a flash I saw that a national theatre, for all its costly elaboration, was no more or no less than community theatre writ large." [18] In 1924, frustrated by the lack of progress of the national theatre, the League sponsored an architectural competition for its design in association with *Country Life* magazine.

Granville-Barker devised the brief for a building, now with two theatres. "With but one stage to work on, useful actors would be left idle." The large stage was to be 100 feet wide, 75 feet deep, with a 10-12 foot forestage and the potential to create a "Greek orchestra," [19] an extension in the auditorium some 30 feet in diameter. The smaller stage was to be 60 feet wide, 40 deep.

On 27th June 1924, a winner was declared: William Lyon Somerville, from Toronto. Unsurprisingly, nothing came of this ambitious scheme, but Granville-Barker was so pleased with the results that he incorporated Somerville's drawings as a foldout endpaper to his new book, *The Exemplary Theatre*, originally published in 1922 and revised in 1930.

The proposals for the architecture of the theatre were a departure from the past as well. Where the Blue Book had assumed a single, conventional auditorium, the new edition insisted on two unconventional ones. Two houses would allow more performances and permit the retention of a larger company, but Granville-Barker was mainly interested in greater dramatic flexibility. The two theatres would provide not only "the picture stage, but a platform with footlights abolished and suitable entrances for Elizabethan plays." [20] For Greek drama, the second house must be able to convert "part of the stalls into an arena for a Greek chorus." [21] He also asked for a removable proscenium that could be lifted into the flies and for provisions for performing in daylight – a wonderfully radical notion. To encourage a sense of community in the audience, the seats should be arranged in a horseshoe shape so that spectators never quite lose their consciousness of each other: "The relations of the spectators among themselves are part of their united good relations to the play, and people should feel free to turn around to strangers and speak without restraint." [22]

What an amazingly farsighted suggestion... and what a tragedy that none of us who later were to be on the building committee of today's National remembered (or even knew anything about) these words of special wisdom.

British Theatre in the 1930s

In 1930, Geoffrey Whitworth became honorary secretary of the Shakespeare Memorial National Theatre Committee, which continued to meet. Various efforts to raise funds were held, including a Shakespeare matinee, directed by Ivor Novello, and a coronation ball for George VI. During the '30s, many other sites were considered, in Leicester Square and Bloomsbury. Theatres under consideration included the Lyceum; the New (now the Noël Coward) and Wyndham's Theatre (as a single block); the Theatre Royal Drury Lane, Her Majesty's and others.

Interestingly enough, in 1930 Granville-Barker wrote, "The site facing the river, between County Hall and the Surrey approach to the new Charing Cross Bridge, is about all that one could wish for. A national theatre could hardly be better placed." A prescient suggestion.

National Theatre Building #1

In 1937, a new 16,000-square-foot site in Cromwell Gardens, opposite the Victoria and Albert Museum, was acquired. A new building committee, consisting of Ashley Dukes, Sidney

Bernstein, William Bridges-Adams, Lewis Casson, Nicholas Hannen and Whitworth were to supervise Sir Edwin Lutyens (1869-1944), president of the Royal Academy, who was chosen as architect. He was experienced in war memorials (The Cenotaph, Whitehall), but not in theatre design, so he was to collaborate with Cecil Masey (1880-1960), pupil of the noted theatre architect Bertie Crewe. Masey was the designer of many commercial cinemas in the Granada chain and of the Phoenix Theatre in Charing Cross Road.

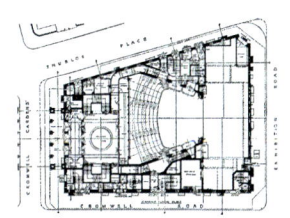

Granville-Barker, now living in Paris, declined the invitation to be the director: "A ridiculous address... excellent for a pillar-box, but no use for a factory of drama." [23] However Lutyens and Masey completed their first design, squeezed onto this cramped triangular site. Lutyens boasted his plans included the "largest revolving stage in London... although it can be used for 'intimate' plays." [24]

Also in 1937, Lilian Baylis died. The already emerging director Tyrone Guthrie took over management of the Old Vic, along with the Sadler's Wells Opera and Ballet.

On 22nd April 1938, Shaw and Whitworth attended a pre-construction celebration together with, according to ancient custom, a symbolic twig and a clump of Kensington earth. Madrigals were sung. Shaw famously remarked, "Do the British people want a national theatre? Of course they do not. They never want anything. They got the British Museum, the National Gallery and Westminster Abbey, but they never wanted them. But once these things stood as mysterious phenomena that had come to them they were quite proud of them and felt the place would be incomplete without them." [25]

World War II, ENSA and CEMA

In March 1939, Lutyens watched as work on the Cromwell Gardens site actually began, but the outbreak of war once again brought the National to a halt. The site was returned to the government and was utilised as one of many fire-fighting water reservoirs, anticipating the Blitz.

The impact of World War II brought other profound changes to the arts in Britain. Under Basil Dean's direction, the Entertainments National Service Association (ENSA) was installed at the Theatre Royal, Drury Lane and proceeded to send out theatrical tours to all fronts of the widening world war, entertaining – it is estimated – over three million people. In 1940, the Council for the Encouragement of Music and Arts (CEMA) was formed, introducing the revolutionary concept of state support for the arts to Britain; CEMA would evolve into the Arts Council in 1946. Supported by CEMA, the Old Vic and Sadler's Wells Opera and Ballet, under the leadership of Tyrone Guthrie, began touring deprived industrial areas of Britain.

In a remote Welsh mining village, a well-meaning cleric welcomed "Dame Sybil Thorndike, a member of the oldest profession in the world." [26] Art, however confusing, was coming to the British people – surprisingly, paid for by the public purse, albeit very modestly!

National Theatre Building #2

The widespread destruction of the Blitz began serious consideration of how a postwar London might be rebuilt. In June 1942, Lord Latham, leader of the London County Council (LCC), met with members of the Shakespeare Memorial National Theatre and discussed a possible new site on the South Bank of the River Thames, adjacent to County Hall. In 1943, Lutyens, although suffering from cancer, designed a new building, to include a second stage on this larger rectangular site, completing this work just before his death at the age of 74.

After Lutyens' death, his former assistant, Sir Hubert Worthington (1886-1963) developed a revised scheme. Worthington reported to the SMNT executive committee: "The position will be midway between Waterloo and Charing Cross Bridges." He also noted, "Mr. Masey had, with great ingenuity, produced a new plan for the theatre so that it would occupy no more than one acre and, at the same time, maintain the accommodation as previously specified." [27] However, planning permission was later refused and the SMNT and Worthington parted company.

The new site, closer to the Old Vic than hitherto, prompted discussion about likely future competition with the Vic, the governors of which agreed to merge with the SMNT. This was announced at an all-parties press conference in January 1946. Representing the Conservative Party was Oliver Lyttelton (son of Alfred and Edith, later Lord Chandos), fresh from his place in history as minister of production (Albert Speer's opposite number) in Churchill's war cabinet.

National Theatre Building #3, Part I
At the first meeting of the Joint Council of the Shakespeare Memorial and Old Vic on 13th February 1946, an agreement was signed. Whitworth explained the past history of architects Lutyens, Worthington and Masey. It was agreed that Masey's plans for the interior should continue to be a point of departure, but might be subject to criticism in the light of modern developments: technical developments on the Continent, the latest acoustic developments and whether Masey's plans were designed "to include the latest lighting devices." [28]

At the second meeting on 3rd May 1946, Masey was reappointed technical architect, and the search for a new architect for "elevations of the theatre" was begun.

Austerity Britain and a New Welfare State
Of course, other, more momentous, events were occurring in Britain. Most significantly, on 26th July 1945, a Labour government under Clement Attlee replaced Winston Churchill's wartime administration. This led to massive social changes: the welfare state, National Insurance and the National Health Service, nationalisation of major elements of the economy, decolonisation of the empire... and, for the first time in history, a start to significant funding for the arts.

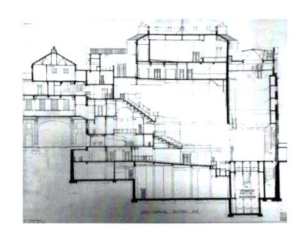

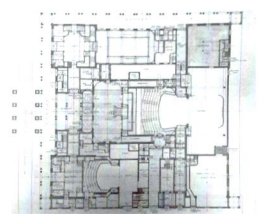

National Theatre #2 section

National Theatre #2 plan

"Do the British people want a national theatre? Of course they do not."
George Bernard Shaw

Melodrama Back at the Vic
Back at the Vic, a bizarre story began to unfold: triumph, jealousy, bureaucratic arrogance, backstabbing and betrayal. A triumphant moment in British theatre history pivoted into a farcical disaster. I'm going to enlist the help of the late critic Irving Wardle to help tell this bizarre backstage drama:

"In 1944, at the request of the Old Vic Governors, Olivier and Ralph Richardson were released from the Fleet Air Arm to operate the company jointly with Guthrie and John Burrell. There followed one of the most brilliant and lucrative chapters in the Vic's history, beginning with the 1944-5 seasons at the New Theatre of Richardson's *Peer Gynt, Cyrano De Bergerac,* and Olivier's *Richard III* and *Oedipus*. Armed with the bargaining power of these successes, the directors proposed that the Vic's mandate should be expanded to include a new centre run by the former heads of the prestigious, pre-war London Theatre Studio,

French director Michel Saint-Denis, George Devine and Glen Byam Shaw. Not realising what was involved, the Governors gave this scheme their blessing." [29] Guthrie, weary from his extraordinary efforts keeping the organisation going on a shoestring through the war years and somewhat sceptical about these ambitious plans, resigned.

"The Old Vic Theatre Centre would consist of a school of theatre, a children's theatre company (The Young Vic) and an experimental thrust stage – the last, known as EXP, being the most important to Saint-Denis. It was intended as a spearhead in his crusade against the picture-frame stage. With the French architect Pierre Sonrel, he prepared a design for a new forestage for the Old Vic."

Wardle continues, "Lord Lytton, the Chairman of the Governors, was an irregular attender at Board meetings. The plan had to be explained again and again for those who had not yet quite grasped the details. Devine commented: 'Why should we sell this idea to these people? If they are stupid enough not to see the value of the plan, then let them go to hell.'" [30]

At the Vic, divergent views emerged. The governors (among whom, following the quaint British custom, the theatrical profession had no representative) wanted to see their efforts crowned with the founding of a great national institution. Saint-Denis' group – known to the rest of the organisation as the 'Three Boys' – wanted to carry through their new action plan. While money was flowing in from the Olivier-Richardson seasons, the two sides achieved some sort of common ground. Wardle continues, "Olivier recalls a meeting when Ralph Richardson said to him, 'You know, old fellow, this will be the end of us. These boys are not going to stand for two actors bossing the place around any more. Under Lord Lytton, the sweet old friendly governors were eating out of our hands. Then Esher came on the scene. We shall be out, old cocky.'" [31]

Lord Esher, the new chairman, allegedly dreaded the prospect of Britain's National Theatre falling into the hands of a Frenchman and confessed he "could never understand a word Saint-Denis said." [32]

Ralph Richardson as Peer Gynt

Laurence Olivier as Richard III

But Esher was the man who talked Chancellor Stafford Cripps' Treasury into authorising the National Theatre's £1 million building grant. Esher seemed determined to get the National Theatre built and launched, no matter what happened to the Old Vic. Olivier, Richardson and Burrell as directors had immensely advanced the fortunes of the Old Vic, and now Olivier's company was performing the same service on tour to an enthusiastic Australian public. Setting these contributions aside, Esher wrote to Olivier informing him that the five-year contracts of the three directors would not be renewed when they expired in 1949. Olivier, then playing in *Richard III*, cabled to London, "I feel like a pioneer disowned by his countrymen in the midst of a distant campaign." The role that Tyrone Guthrie played in influencing this decision is unclear. "Lord Esher's view was that "Continuity of direction was essential, and directors who failed to supply it – no matter how great as artists – were expendable." The Board, accordingly, envisaged a system where the man mainly responsible for making the whole thing work would be an administrator. Llewellyn Rees, the ambitious, somewhat Machiavellian, drama director of the Arts Council, was picked to take over as this administrator, while the director of the Bristol Old Vic, Hugh Hunt, was promoted to be artistic director of the London company." [33]

Devine wrote an embittered letter to Esher, restating the circumstances that had infected the organisation with "an atmosphere of petty squabbling and jockeying for position… which has turned the Vic into a miserable place." He concluded, "We feel strongly enough to bring ourselves to offer, with the greatest regret and difficulty, that we should resign if these matters cannot be resolved."[34] On 7th May, without further consultation, Esher replied, accepting the resignations and, two days later, they were announced to the press. "The governors of the Old Vic", said actor and director, Glen Byam Shaw, "had quite a good record for getting rid of directors. Tyrone Guthrie, Richardson, Olivier, Saint-Denis, Devine and myself. All sacked."[35]

Retraction would have cost the governors what shreds of credibility they still retained. Meanwhile, time was fast ticking away to 13th July, when the King was due to lay the foundation stone of the National Theatre on the South Bank. By then, perhaps, the Old Vic would have injured itself beyond repair.

The only chance was to find a leader with authority from outside, to halt the collapse. Hunt and his general manager, Stephen Arlen, appealed to Tyrone Guthrie to return to the rescue. He agreed, not as co-equal with Hunt, but as a general manager with sweeping powers. Glad to have found their strongman all parties agreed, including the Three Boys, even though they had not been consulted. Guthrie, after all, was an old comrade.

Guthrie then invited his three old friends to dinner in Soho for a scene, here recalled by Byam Shaw. "He started off by saying, 'I think I'd better tell you that I've advised the Governors to close the school.' Michel said, 'but why?' He said, 'because I don't believe in training for actors.' Michel said, 'but are you mad? Do you remember that you gave me £1,000 of your own money to help start the London Theatre Studio? Why have you changed?' Tony said, 'I don't know, but I have changed and that's it.' Michel said, 'and what about the Young Vic?' Guthrie said, 'I've told them that in my opinion it's not worth the money being spent on it.' Michel said, 'but have you ever seen a performance of the Young Vic?' Tony went red and said, 'no, I haven't.' And that was the end of the party. It was, to us, inexplicable.

"One can only assume there was a feeling of resentment towards Michel because of his nationality and his possible influence on the English theatre." To actor Marius Goring, who was equally stunned by this move, Guthrie gave another explanation: "Pity. Two sports masters in love with the head. Very unhealthy. Got to be stopped."[36]

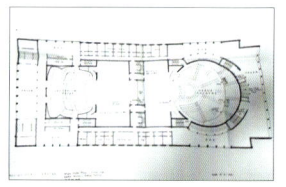

National Theatre #3

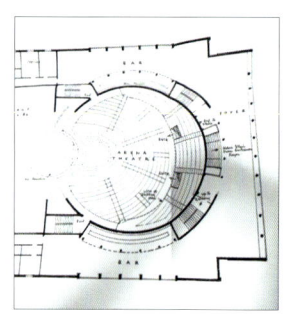

The O'Rorke thrust stage theatre

Brian O'Rorke

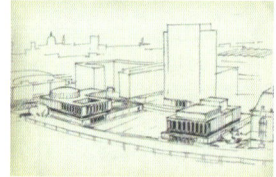

National Theatre #3. The O'Rorke concept

The National Theatre Act
Despite all this seemingly bizarre infighting, Lord Esher was most effectively marshalling the Treasury and the political establishment. That the political mood had shifted, there was little doubt. In 1942 at the inaugural meeting of the Provincial Theatre Council, one of the greatest of Labour leaders, Ernest Bevin, Minister of Labour, had said, "I have no doubt that the theatre, like all other institutions, will undergo great changes before the end of this titanic struggle, I hope it will. In the British people there exist great divergencies of character which are endangered by the current tendency toward uniformity, and I look forward to the living theatre, not only coming into its own as a means of livelihood, but to its becoming one of our great national institutions to convey to the peoples of the world the real character of the British people."[37]

In August 1946, just as hope seemed to be rising, Granville-Barker, age 68, died in Paris. A 1956 biography included this: "That there was greatness in Granville-Barker is suggested by the fact that he has become a legend so soon after his death. He is the myth of 20th century English Theatre."[38] Three years before his death, Granville-Barker had written, "By the new Waterloo Bridge might not be bad.

But you must have ample space… enough room in the factory for all its essential machinery, unless the manufacture [of plays] is to be extravagantly costly; and, above all, you must have your two auditoria and be prepared to argue for three. They are a sheer economic necessity… as William Archer and I ought to have foreseen in 1903. For why? You must aim at a triple elasticity; as to the sort of play you do; as to the sort of audience you will attract, and (in consequence) as to the number of performances you give. You must go for quality, first and last." [39]

On 23rd March 1948, even under a returned Tory government, Chancellor of the Exchequer Sir Stafford Cripps made the following statement in the House of Commons: "I propose to introduce legislation during the present Parliament to the effect that, if the LCC provides a suitable site for the purpose of a National Theatre, the Treasury may make a contribution not exceeding £1 million towards the cost of building the theatre, to be used by the Government of the day as soon as it becomes possible to start on the scheme." [40]

The National Theatre bill received its affirmation, first in the Commons, then the House of Lords, in February 1949. The way was clear… All that was required was the money.

National Theatre #3, Part II
In October 1946, a new architect had been appointed: Brian O'Rorke, a New Zealander celebrated for his work on luxury liner interiors. His building was to balance the Royal Festival Hall, then in construction as the permanent element of the 1951 Festival of Britain. The board insisted that O'Rorke continue to partner with Cecil Masey, explaining that he was "as good a technical theatre expert as could be found," because "no architect of eminence would want to be bothered with curtain drops and sightlines." [41]

This forced marriage was, however, to be short-lived. O'Rorke reported to Secretary of the Joint Council Kenneth Rae, "[Masey and I] had lunch together. As a result of these meetings, I am afraid that I still find myself in a difficult position. I think that architecturally I must say at once that we obviously have very different views. There is a difference of 20 years in our ages and with the changes in architectural trends that have taken place since the 1920s, this gap does not tend to make collaboration easier." [42]

In a letter to Kenneth Rae on 13th November 1948, Cecil Masey wrote, "Theatre building with all its problems and intricacies is widely different from any other form of building, and having been on this all my life, I can with assurance say that the technical specialist side of the work is very considerable, more so perhaps when there are two architects working together." [43]

However, Masey's services were dispensed with in February 1950, "with regret." By the spring of 1951, O'Rorke's scheme was approved. To be built in Portland stone, it was estimated at £1.2 million, twenty percent more than had been anticipated.

In 1950, the presiding building committee, including Sir Bronson Albery (chairman), Norman Marshall, Laurence Olivier, Hugh Hunt, actor Sir Lewis Casson, producer Donald Albery and pioneer theatre consultant Richard Southern, stated in their minutes that perfect sightlines were "not possible, except in a fan-shaped theatre, to which the committee has always been strongly opposed, involving as it did, the sacrifice of that intimacy which the committee felt was so desirable." [44] Sadly, this canny recommendation was lost in the archives when the later, and final, NT Building Committee under Sir Laurence, took over in 1963. Even he, seemingly, would forget the strictures against the "fan-shaped" theatre when presented with the charismatic Denys Lasdun's fan-shaped "Scheme A".

The committee's other deliberations included stage arrangements that proposed a 60-foot revolve, discussion of a cyclorama – "acoustic experts preferred a solid cyclorama, but a Schwabe-Hasait rolling one on spools might be better" – and, later, an elaboration on the revolve "on a drum principle with a lower floor so traps could be installed." [45]

Over the years of talk that followed, there was extended discussion over the form of the auditorium. At a meeting in 1954, Tyrone Guthrie spoke. "The present plans were merely a duplication of the Old Vic stage. In his opinion this 'semi-proscenium' stage would soon be very dated. He begged that serious consideration be given to the erection of a theatre something along the lines of that constructed in Stratford Ontario." [46] Sir Lewis Casson and Michael

Benthall were of the opinion that the public whose money would be spent… were not yet ready for an arena theatre. Dr. Guthrie wished it put on the record that he was in no way criticising Mr. O'Rorke's fulfilment of the mandate, which he thought had been carried out to perfection, but remained of the opinion that he would prefer to see, particularly for Shakespeare, an arena stage rather than this "compromise." [47]

However, planning permission for O'Rorke's building was refused because of its "massive bulk." The site moved again to alongside County Hall, and O'Rorke began a new design. An emergency meeting of the joint council declared that Her Majesty must be immediately informed of the move. She replied: "Her Majesty… is in truth delighted by the new suggestion… The original site never commended itself very much to Queen Elizabeth, and the new one appears to be a distinct improvement." [48]

Meanwhile, O'Rorke had just completed a redesign for the Shakespeare Memorial Theatre interior in Stratford-upon-Avon, and felt "the experience gained… will be invaluable [for the NT]." He saw the NT as an "isolated building" with "foyers… on the river front in a light glazed structure… something between a yacht club and a Victorian conservatory." [49]

Geoffrey Whitworth died at his home in Oxford in 1951, aged 68. "Who is this man named Whitworth?" Bernard Shaw had asked in 1934. "He is not a great actor… If he has written any plays, I have not seen them. And yet, wherever I go I hear the name: Geoffrey Whitworth. He is one of the most important people in the theatre today." [50]

At the 17th meeting of the joint council in March 1951, an inscription for the NT foundation stone, written by Geoffrey Whitworth, originally read: "'TO THE LIVING MEMORY OF WILLIAM SHAKESPEARE ON A SITE PROVIDED BY THE LONDON COUNTY COUNCIL IN CONFORMITY WITH THE NATIONAL THEATRE ACT MCMXLIX AND IN THE YEAR OF THE FESTIVAL OF BRITAIN THIS FOUNDATION STONE FOR THE NATIONAL THEATRE WAS LAID ON XIII JULY MCMLI BY HIS MAJESTY KING GEORGE VI." In the minutes approving that wording, the name of the King, who was then ill, was superseded in ink by the name of "HER MAJESTY THE QUEEN." [51]

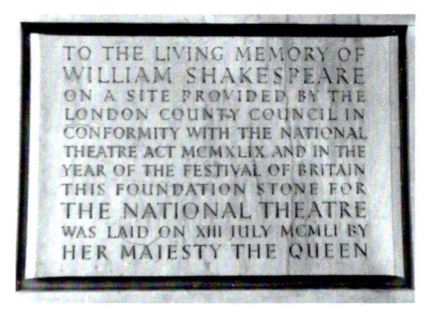

1951, your author's Box Brownie shot

On 13th July 1951, as part of the Festival of Britain, Queen Elizabeth, soon to be widowed and become the Queen Mother, laid the foundation stone of the National Theatre on the South Bank site, accompanied by her daughter, the soon-to-be queen, with a dedication from the Archbishop of Canterbury. As an 18-year old schoolboy, I took its photograph on my Box Brownie camera just after the ceremony!

Four days later, the Old Vic controversy disturbed the political arena. One of the more rebellious theatre students, Frank Dunlop[52], set the wheels turning to raise the matter in Parliament.[53] Saint-Denis was touched by the loyalty shown by his students.[54] "In the House of Commons on 17th July, Labour MP Wedgwood Benn opened up, by asking the Chancellor of the Exchequer to make future grants to the Arts Council conditional on their providing funds to maintain the [Old Vic] school. Philip Noel-Baker followed with a question, 'In view of the fact that the Governors of the Old Vic have received very large sums of public money, and since, instead of making the theatre into a national theatre – as we had all hoped they would – they have lost money, lost the best directors and producers, lost the best artists, closed the Young Vic and now have closed the school, can the Government do nothing to secure a better system of administration for this great national institution?' (Cheers)." [55]

In January 1956, a letter from building committee member Sidney Bernstein to Sir Bronson Albery: "There is the incontrovertible fact that there is a great deal of experimental production… which incorporates film into live production. I ask you to consider again that the theatre may find new and vigorous forms of expression through these new tools at its disposal." He also suggested that theatres be equipped with television cameras so that productions may be broadcast to a much larger audience.

Construction was scheduled to begin in April 1956. But in September 1957, Prime Minister Harold Macmillan, struggling with soaring costs across a collapsing economy, announced drastic deflationary measures. Esher told Kenneth Rae: "That puts the lid on our plan. We must wait for better times – if any." [56]

In 1958, critics Kenneth Tynan and Richard Findlater were pictured on the front cover of the magazine *Encore*, holding a mock memorial service for the shifting foundation stone, as a symbolic tomb of the National Theatre.

The Joint Council of the National Theatre and the Old Vic, now led by Oliver Lyttelton (since 1954 titled Lord Chandos) with Lord Esher, who had dismissed Olivier in 1949, now invited Olivier to join them. Olivier described Esher's approach, "We don't believe you'll be much use, but what we need is a glamour-puss, and you're it." [57] *Daily Telegraph* critic John Barber characterised: "Britain's starriest actor… rooting for Britain's stuffiest notion… the National Theatre… a vast mausoleum, half cinema and half public baths." [58] But Olivier realised that Chandos and Esher, with long-serving secretary Kenneth Rae upholders of the National flame, viewed him as the NT's director-in-waiting. Olivier asked them directly if this was so. "Yes, are you surprised?" "Do you realise what a cunt I am? Well. You'll find out now." [59] He was more than ready.

Peter Hall
And then came Peter Hall. Born in 1930, the son of a stationmaster, he read English at St. Catharine's College Cambridge, and developed a passion for directing theatre. After earning £7 per week script reading for director John Fernald at the tiny Arts Theatre in London, he'd taken over as director, shooting to fame at the age of 24 with the first London production of *Waiting For Godot*.

The Shakespeare Memorial Theatre director, Glen Byam Shaw, saw Hall as a potential successor. He became the unanimous choice of the Shakespeare Council, led by the brewer Edward

Peter Hall

Tynan and Findlater: pall bearers for the National's moving foundation stone

Fordham Flower, and was thrilled to accept directorship of "the most important theatre in the country" [60] one week before his 28th birthday.

In 1959, Hall was rehearsing Olivier in the title role of *Coriolanus*. They talked:
Olivier: "I'm going to have a go at making the National… will you join me as Number Two?"

Hall: "I'm very flattered, Larry, I'd love to… but I'm going to make my own company, as Number One." [61]

In 1960, Hall announced the creation of a permanent ensemble for Stratford-upon-Avon, and a West End base at the 1200-seat Aldwych Theatre (rented by owner Prince Littler at the exorbitant rent of twenty-five percent of the gross box-office). [62] He persuaded Flower to back him with all the Royal Shakespeare Theatre resources. "You're absolutely mad," [63] Flower said, but he supported this massive expansion… to create a second National, perhaps, before the first had even emerged.

Evening News critic Felix Barker wrote, "the most ambitious theatrical venture in British history… I don't suppose wild horses would drag from [Hall] the admission that at the back of his mind is the idea of becoming the first director of our NT. But if he succeeds… he will be ready for the theatre's biggest job." [64]

Might It Happen At Last?
In 1960 the recently appointed chairman of the Arts Council, Lord Cottesloe (John Fremantle), produced a report on the viability of the National project for the SMNT and Old Vic joint

council. The joint council was supportive; it met with Selwyn Lloyd, Chancellor of the Exchequer, in December 1960.

In 1961, the executive committee of the joint council invited Hall and Flower to join them, thus now potentially combining the Old Vic, the National dream, and Stratford. The issue of who was to be Number One remained unresolved: talks about leadership always ground to a halt. Correspondence between Hall and Olivier veered between the hilarious and vituperative. Olivier to Hall: "…Your letter carries to me a slightly hysterical [tone]… which… makes me feel you are not in a good state – or… are pulling wool over my eyes which I don't like much better (!) (Never shit a shitter)." [65]

Even the press joined in: the sixth issue of the satirical magazine *Private Eye* imagines Peter Hall as the National's director, talking of "plans to build a new theatre on the South Bank, which will probably be called Peter Hall. Along the lines of the Albert Hall? Yes, only obviously rather larger." [66]

Then, catastrophe: The Chancellor of the Exchequer announced there would be no National Theatre. Instead, a subsidy of £400,000 would be spread across regional theatres to save them from the onslaught of commercial television. It appeared that the emergent RSC had won this round.

But the news brought outrage. Lord Chandos protested that it was an insult to the Queen Mother, who had laid the itinerant foundation stone. Sir Isaac Hayward, leader of the London County Council, observed that the LCC had given the site that was now effectively sterilised. Lord Cottesloe, from the House of Lords, complained that the South Bank development would now be "unbalanced." Politics, too, intervened. Labour retained control of the LCC; the actors' union Equity, and then the entire Trades Union Congress came out in support of the National.

A volte-face. The LCC Labour leader, Isaac Hayward, led the decision to force the release of funds. He persuasively offered Government the product of a penny rate (a penny in the pound of property ratable value), which meant £1,300,000 plus the South Bank site, if the Government would reverse its position. It quickly did so, adding the unlikely complication that the new National should be accompanied by a new opera house, to be home to the Sadler's Wells company. This must have seemed a very bright idea at the time: to achieve two theatres for the price of one!

Stratford was cast aside and withdrew from the joint council in February 1962.

What finally broke the long-running stalemate? Perhaps the National story had finally become irresistible. Behind the scenes, the drive and determination of Oliver Lyttelton, coupled with that of Jennie Lee, then Labour Minister for the Arts, and Lord Cottesloe, Arts Council chairman, was followed by Lord Goodman: the initiative of the LCC, under Isaac Hayward, prevailed. Labour councillor Hugh Jenkins, a later Arts Minister, finally moved a resolution that the theatre should be built without delay.

At the 32nd meeting of the joint council, Lord Chandos reported that recent high-level conversations indicated that the climate of opinion in favour of the NT had undoubtedly become more propitious. For the Arts Council, both parliamentary parties, British Actor's Equity and the LCC, the NT was no longer a controversial subject. Sir William Emrys Williams, on behalf of the Arts Council, stated that the council was now unreservedly behind the NT project. Steps might be taken toward the establishment of a company as soon as building operations began. He warned, however, that the draft plans of the NT needed considerable revision.[67] In April 1960, at an NT Building Committee meeting, Hugh Willatt, for the Arts Council, said that the NT plans should be reviewed. They had been drawn up ten years earlier and, since then, much theatre building had taken place on the Continent and fashions in theatrical production had changed. The relationship between stage and auditorium might well need reconsidering and a greater degree of flexibility introduced. The architect should be given a new brief.

A month later brought a memorandum from Tyrone Guthrie. "I have already expressed my view that the erection of a proscenium theatre of 'traditional' (i.e. 19th century) style, is not a wise plan." Guthrie proposed sticking out for two theatres. "Since no sensible advocate of the open stage, however fervent, would recommend it for Congreve, Sheridan or Wilde; whereas no one who has seen a respectable production on a well-designed open stage could possibly recommend anything else for Shakespeare, Greek tragedy or *Peer Gynt*. The other option is for a flexible stage such as Lincoln Centre." He advocated the former position, even though it could lead to the whole National Theatre project being shelved again by Government.[68]

But shelved it was not. In 1962, the South Bank National Theatre and Opera House Board, intended to build the building, and the National Theatre Board, to create the company, were established. On 9th August 1962, Sir Laurence's appointment as director of the National Theatre was announced.

A Theatre is to be Built in Chichester
Sir Laurence was very busy that summer of 1962.

A Chichester businessman and amateur drama enthusiast, Leslie Evershed-Martin, had watched a BBC television programme about how a theatre was to be built in Stratford, Ontario, under the direction of Tyrone Guthrie. It was to be a thrust stage theatre, an 'open' promontory stage, three-quarters surrounded by audience, which had been Guthrie's dream since the 1930s. When leading the Old Vic company in *Hamlet* on location in Elsinore Castle, rain had stopped the open-air performance and the company had improvised in a hotel ballroom with a stage surrounded by loose seating. It had been a triumph. The open stage also promised to be cheap. There was no expensive stage house to build and Guthrie himself advocated economy, minimal scenery and simple lighting.

Evershed-Martin had a brainwave: he could build one of these thrust stages in Chichester for the modest sum of money that he could raise privately, without any Government support. He approached Guthrie about running his enterprise, but he declined, suggesting Evershed-Martin aim high: Sir Laurence Olivier. Olivier saw his chance. Leadership of such a venture in a new experimental theatre space was a risk, but a worthy one. A roll of the dice. Triumph would confirm him as the only conceivable candidate to be the first director of the National Theatre, powerful enough to at last bring this dream to reality and change British theatre forever.

Chichester Festival Theatre, 1962

Chichester Festival Theatre auditorium, 1962

This is where your author enters the scene. Just before opening, Olivier telephoned me to come and "sort out the bloody awful lighting." When I walked into the unfinished auditorium with Sir Laurence rehearsing among builders' chaos, the lighting was pretty poor. I knew what had to be done, but not that Sir had left his request rather late. Opening was only a day away. Rehanging half the installation was impossible. Sir Laurence said to his new lighting 'expert,' "Well, you're no bloody good then, are you?"

The first two productions, selected and directed by Sir Laurence, were not too good either. *The Chances*, by John Fletcher, and *The Broken Heart*, by John Ford, were disappointing. The reviews were poor and the critic for the *Observer* newspaper, Kenneth Tynan, wrote a fiercely critical letter to Sir Laurence. After being initially furious ("How shall we slaughter the little bastard!"), with prompting from his wife, Joan Plowright, Sir Laurence surprised everybody by inviting Tynan to join him as literary manager of the National. ("God, anything to get you off that *Observer*.")

Happily, the third production of the season was *Uncle Vanya*, with a stellar cast – Michael Redgrave, Sybil Thorndike, Lewis Casson and Joan Plowright, among others – in a performance of the play that will surely never be bettered. The world flocked to Chichester. The gamble had worked. Triumph carried Sir Laurence back to the Old Vic to fulfill his long-held dream – to lay the very foundations of the National Theatre of Great Britain.

Destiny had met its man.

Strollers performing *Macbeth* in a barn, 1788

1.2 British Playhouse Design

The design of the playhouse evolved over centuries from the Elizabethan courtyard to the Victorian/Edwardian spaces of London's West End and New York's Broadway – a lineage broken by Richard Wagner at Bayreuth with the world's first frontal, fan-shaped auditorium. The subsequent proliferation of the necessarily frontally oriented cinema created further confusion: What was a real theatre? A place for looking and listening or a place also of participation? Theatre-in-the-round, thrust stage, or proscenium…

Epitomised by the conflicts over Elisabeth Scott's 1932 Stratford Theatre, which was praised by architects and vilified by theatre artists, all that was remembered by the 1960s was that the recent history of theatre architecture in Britain was fraught with confusion and disappointment…

The very first meeting of the National Theatre Building Committee took place on 3rd January 1963 – some ten months before the NT's first performance at the Old Vic in October of that year, and so before anyone had really had a chance to explore what the National Theatre company would be. At that meeting, Sir Laurence reported:

"I had originally agreed to become a Trustee of the National Theatre in order to insist on proper artistic representation where the building of the Theatre was concerned.

"It was the function of this panel to decide upon the form of the stage and auditorium to be recommended to the National Theatre Board which had been asked to present their conclusions to the South Bank Board no later than February 12th." [69]

This gave the new committee just six weeks to create the brief for the long-awaited National Theatre. A challenging task indeed! Since Granville-Barker's 1903 initiative, successive building committees had at least twice before prepared such a brief for previous architects. However, none of these previous deliberations were even discussed by the new building committee. The focus in the '60s was all about looking forward, not backward. The future was about to to be invented!

British theatre in the '60s was in quite a ferment. Growth of subsidy, led by post-war Labour governments, had driven several major concurrent events: new regional repertory theatres were being commissioned; Peter Hall, building upon Anthony Quayle's successes at the Stratford Memorial Theatre, had created the Royal Shakespeare Company, with homes in Stratford-upon-Avon and London; George Devine's English Stage Company 'broke through' with John Osborne's play *Look Back In Anger;* Joan Littlewood was breaking all the rules at Stratford East with her wondrous artisan designer John Bury… and the long-awaited National Theatre seemed finally ready to emerge.

The 1960s were also a period of complete confusion about theatre architecture. The great theatre architects of Victorian/Edwardian England were gone and, at the time, quite unappreciated. Few new theatres had been built since the 1930s and one of those few was notorious… the theatre built in 1932 for Shakespeare at Stratford-upon-Avon.

This was the result of an architectural competition, won by Elisabeth Scott. Its story is significant indeed.

Stratford-upon-Avon
The original, rather quaint looking, Stratford-upon-Avon Shakespeare Theatre was designed by William Frederick Unsworth (1851-1912) and Edward Dodgshun (1854-1927); it opened in 1879. It was a bizarre mix of styles: Gothic revival and Elizabethan half-timbering. Inside was an inadequate stage yet a charming horseshoe-shaped auditorium. Director and designer William Bridges-Adams (1889-1965), who ran the festival from 1919, said of the latter that it had "a warm and friendly atmosphere where the horseshoe tiers take the stage, as it were, in their embrace; the play's magnetism runs around the house in an unbroken circuit." [70] This was a telling observation… sadly forgotten in 1963.

The theatre burned down in March 1926, though its burnt-out shell remained. George Bernard Shaw wrote to Stratford's chairman, Archibald Flower, "Congratulations. It will be a tremendous advantage to have a real theatre." [71]

Stratford immediately embarked on a competition to pick a new architect. To satisfy the architectural profession, this had to be headed by a panel of assessors appointed by the Royal Institute of British Architects (RIBA). Its president wrote the competition brief and led the panel, advised by Bridges-Adams. He, in consultation with Harley Granville-Barker, drew up detailed specifications for the stage and auditorium: a two-tiered, 1000-seat, horseshoe-shaped house, with boxes, a removable forestage and spacious wings. Bridges-Adams added "The need is for absolute flexibility, a box of tricks out of which the child-like mind of the producer may create whatever shape it pleases. It should be able to offer Mr. Poel [actor, director and pioneer of simplified staging of Shakespeare] an Elizabethan stage after his heart's desire. It should be no less adequate to the requirements of Professor Reinhardt [Max Reinhardt, leading director of the German theatre]." [72] This call for absolute flexibility – a familiar one even today – may have been a regrettable, yet frequently repeated, mistake. The appearance of the theatre exterior was not specified, simply that it should harmonise with the spirit of a theatre and the town of Stratford.

Seventy-two architects entered the competition. Six were shortlisted and, to general amazement, a young woman won: only three years graduated from college at the Architectural Association, Elisabeth Whitworth Scott (1898-1972) was the first woman in British history to win a major architectural competition. Her design was a functional, modernistic one, sitting next to the remains of the old building. She became an overnight celebrity. Conservative Stratford was shocked: There were to be no Elizabethan timbers for their river frontage, rather a cool and modern exterior – more Scandinavian than English, a style that was yet to have an impact in Britain.

Scott said, "I belong to the modernist school of architects. I believe the function of the building to be the most important

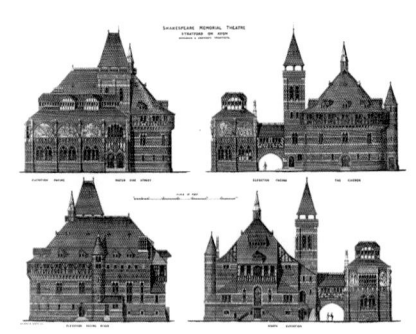

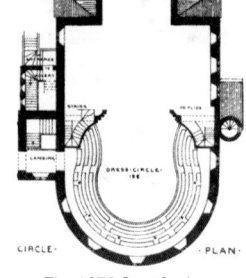

The 1879 Stratford-upon-Avon Theatre – elevation

The 1879 Stratford-upon-Avon Theatre – plan

thing. In terms of theatre... this means the acoustics and sightlines must come first."[73]

In January 1928, she went on a tour to Germany seeking their technical expertise – the Künstlertheater, Munich,[74] by Max Littmann (1908) and Oskar Kaufmann's Stadttheater (1909) in Bremerhaven – and to Paris for Auguste and Gustave Perret's Théâtre des Champs Elysées (1913). At home, she had advice from the artist Norman Wilkinson (1878-1971), designer/director Sir Barry Jackson (1879-1961), founder of the Birmingham Repertory Theatre with Russian director/designer Theodore Komisarjevsky (1882-1954). Acoustic advice was given by the then current expert, Hope Bagenal (1888-1979). A year was spent refining the design of the building – intended to be one of Britain's most modern theatres.

I remember my first visit to Stratford, when I was a teenager in the 1950s. I was deeply impressed by this quite noble modern building fronting onto the River Avon. The lobbies and front of house were gracious, but the auditorium did seem cold and the stage remote. And backstage...

Bridges-Adams had been forced to fit his backstage dreams to the selected design – an all-too-frequent outcome of architectural competitions.[75] The resultant proscenium was too small and the forestage was disconnected from the elaborate stage behind. The gap between stage and the front row was too wide and the balcony sightlines bad. The concept, written in the brief, of surrounding horseshoe balconies had been ignored and blank side walls – like a cinema – substituted. (Very 1930s!) Onstage, the wings were too narrow for the mechanised sliding stages. Dressing rooms were poor and there was no green room.

Twenty years later, Bridges-Adams commented sadly, "What we eventually got, when the architects, pressure groups, quacks and empirics had finished, was a theatre, of all the theatres in England, in which it is hardest to make an audience laugh or cry."[76]

The architectural press loved it: "perfect sightlines...

The Shakespeare Memorial Theatre Stratford-upon-Avon, 1932

The original Stratford balcony: "A monstrosity" – Anthony Quayle

Architect Elisabeth Scott

acoustics like a giant horn… modernist 'intelligent' use of materials." All the woods used in the interior were mentioned by Shakespeare!

Performers were less impressed. Actor-manager, Balliol Holloway observed, "You can just about see the boiled shirts in the front row: it is like acting to Calais from the cliffs of Dover." Later, he added: "The acreage of blank walls between the proscenium arch and the ends of the circle completely destroy all contact between actor and audience. It is doubly hard on the actor that the audience does not realise this and is aware only of the actor's comparative ineffectiveness." [77] These words should be noted and remembered.

Stratford Herald theatre critic Ruth Ellis discussed the negative reaction of the traditional theatre goers, whom she described as dreaming of winking gilded cupids. Instead they found the building "to be on its guard lest it should rouse any emotion at all." [78]

Controversy persisted, but Elisabeth Scott, in the *Daily Telegraph* of 30th September 1943, said, somewhat plaintively, that in her view it was the limited approach of the producers/directors rather than the fault of the theatre itself that caused so much dissent and adverse criticism.[79] An architect's hurt reaction that would be echoed by Denys Lasdun thirty-five years later.

Various changes were made through the 1930s and '40s, partly to increase seat count and partly to try and improve the actor-audience relationship. Sadly, by the time Anthony Quayle became director in 1950, he could still say: "The building was of a hideousness that nobody who had not sat in it could possibly appreciate. It was built like a cinema, a long shoe-box of a place. The dress circle was set so far back that you were almost sitting outside the theatre. It was a monstrosity."[80] Quayle's changes, including re-raking the stalls, adding two rows to the circle to bring it forward, adding side boxes and changing the decor, were carried out (somewhat ironically) by Brian O'Rorke, who had recently replaced Lutyens as potential architect of the National Theatre.

Change continued. In 1960, upon his appointment as director, Peter Hall brought in stage designer/architect Sean Kenny to remove the proscenium and open up the stage. But the proscenium arch could not be removed without endangering

The Shakespeare Memorial Theatre Stratford-upon-Avon, 1974

The Swan Theatre Stratford-upon-Avon, 1986

the structural stability of the entire fly tower and so the scheme was dropped. Hall, with his designer Henry Bardon, then created a hexagonally shaped raked stage and forestage. Later, stage designer Christopher Morley continued the effort to create a horse-shoe-style auditorium by adding side balcony seats. In 1968, under Trevor Nunn and designer John Napier, another redecoration and reseating occurred, then again in 1976 when two rows of seats were temporarily added on towers onstage surrounding the acting area.

The Swan
Years later, it was, apparently, a visit by the Royal Shakespeare Company to Christ's Hospital School Theatre in Horsham, with which I'd been involved in the design of after the National Theatre, that sparked Trevor Nunn's interest in building a new theatre within the long-ago burnt-out shell of the old 1897 theatre. The Swan, designed by architect Michael Reardon based upon the Christ's Hospital model, opened in 1986 and proved to be instantly loved for the intimacy of its thrust stage, surrounded by warm-hued, timbered galleries.

The 'New' Royal Shakespeare Theatre
A little detour in time, if I may, just to complete this piece of theatre design history…

In 2010, the RSC finally replaced their theatre, and a strange circular stroke of fate seemed to play a part in it. We at Theatre Projects in the US had a few years before been commissioned to design a new theatre for Shakespeare on a pier in Chicago. Our client Barbara Gaines, the amazingly dynamic artistic director of the Chicago Shakespeare Theater, knew exactly what she wanted: a theatre just like the Swan in Stratford, albeit with perhaps a hundred more seats. As great admirers of the Swan, we set to work, carefully assessing where a small number of seats might be added while preserving the intimacy of the original. The result, with 550 seats, was an enormous success. Sir Peter Hall described it as "one of the best, if not the best, Shakespeare spaces in the world."[81]

Soon after opening, Adrian Noble, artistic director of the RSC, visited Chicago. We saw a production together. Afterward, he

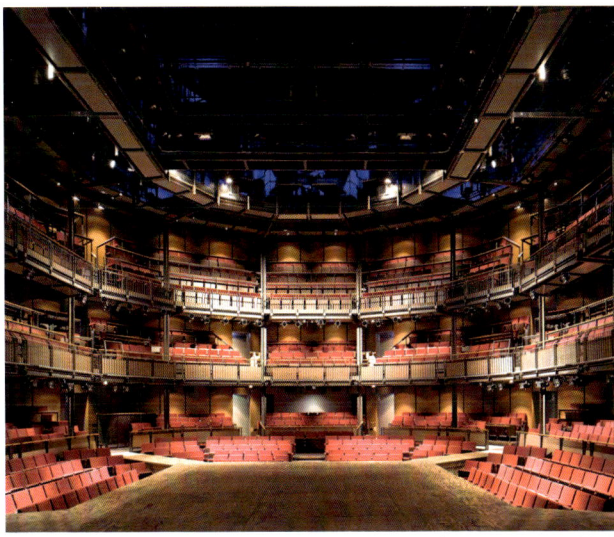

Royal Shakespeare Theatre Stratford-upon-Avon, 2010

said, "Richard, this is what I want in Stratford. Exactly what I want… only with 1100 seats."[82]

"Adrian," I replied, "with respect, theatre design doesn't quite work like that."

Stratford proceeded to explore its options. The possibility of demolishing the Scott theatre completely was debated. Various consultants were hired to give advice, including TP's Iain Mackintosh. An exceptionally stylish Dutch architect, Erick van Egeraat, was engaged. There was an extended debate as to whether the new theatre should be only a thrust stage, or whether it should be capable of modification to some form of proscenium, or end stage, for non-Shakespearean productions during the winter season. Egeraat's plan included the total demolition of the old theatre. This was deemed to be overambitious and his proposals were dropped.

Artistic directors and direction changed. Michael Boyd took over from 2003 and decided upon a thrust stage within a

1.2 British Playhouse Design

completely new, courtyard-style auditorium, but preserving the original 1932 Scott stage and the building's facade. In 2006, as a trial, a full-size mock-up, a courtyard containing a narrow thrust stage with 1000 seats, was designed by Ian Ritchie Architects working with theatre consultants Charcoalblue, scenic designer Tom Piper and the RSC's Flip Tanner, and built on the site formerly occupied by RSC's The Other Space studio theatre. This seemed full of promise.

Finally, architects Bennetts Associates, again with Charcoalblue, designed a new theatre set within a partial redevelopment of the public areas of the Scott building, which opened in 2010 at a cost of £112.8 million. The juxtaposition of the differing periods of the building's Victorian architecture, Scott's 1930's modernism and the new spaces provided a promising patina. At its core lies a one-room narrow thrust stage surrounded by three levels of courtyard-style balconies. The deep thrust stage shapes the surrounding balconies, but it is claimed that the depth of the thrust is adjustable. The auditorium certainly brings actors and audiences closer, with the distance of the furthest seat from the stage being reduced from 27 metres (89 feet) to 15 metres (49 feet). The technical facilities were hugely expanded, with an expensively excavated deep traproom and an elaborate flying capability covering the entire thrust. But, compared to its courtyard prototype, something seems missing. Almost identical in dimension, the new space seems larger, the higher seats more vertiginous and the sightlines even more extreme.

It is worth noting that they were at least able and allowed to make these dramatic changes, in contrast to the National where, as we shall see, changes to the auditoria were always hard because of their concrete construction and are now not permitted because of the building's listed status. And also worth noting that as Andy Hayles, one of the ex-TP founders of Charcoalblue notes, there was a lesson learnt from the National: concrete is only used in the building's outer shell so the auditorium could be removed should there be a desire for something different in the future. Nevertheless, the result is that the RSC now has two courtyard theatres, large and small. The Swan remains a jewel, but the larger space, albeit offering a very different experience to the playgoer than the Scott cinema-style space, seems locked in something of a straight jacket: a very deep, narrow, tongue of a thrust, with massive technical infrastructure, but one surrounded by too many seats with extreme viewing angles. Perhaps big theatres cannot be designed by simply blowing up a small, seemingly ideal, model like a balloon.

The narrow thrust, strongly influenced by the Guthrie model seen in Stratford Ontario, Minneapolis and Sheffield's Crucible, is promoted as being Shakespearean, yet the evidence of the Rose and the Globe suggests otherwise. These classic precedents present a lozenge-shaped stage, wider than its depth, not a deep tongue.

Perhaps theatre practitioners are not the most aware of what makes theatre architectural space actually work. Maybe they're too busy 'putting on a show' to stop and think about what is all around them.

Misunderstanding between architecture and theatre seems perpetual.

To understand the depth of this misunderstanding, we need to go back a bit in history… way back, long before 1848, back to the 16th century.

The history of the English playhouse has been the subject of much scholarship and many books. This chapter cannot begin to compete with such expertise. But to put the National's design process into context, I'll touch upon the highlights of development, as changing demands of audiences and entrepreneurs, philistine destruction and, most often, fire led to a process of constant renewal.

The reader might note that the needs of actors were not often seen as a high priority – and this would continue during planning of the National, where only one, Sir Laurence, was part of the planning committee. But by way of some spiritual compensation, this chapter will take advice from Sir Laurence and remember some of our greatest actors amongst this story of the development of the playhouse.

'The Theatre' to 'The Globe'

The origins of British theatre seem lost in the mists of time. But, while that mist may obscure our view, we can be sure that even in the darkest ages, theatre was alive and kicking. We know that in early mediaeval times, religious mystery plays were performed, initially in churches and then out and around the town. Similarly every form of performance must have taken place on makeshift platforms in the village square, or the great hall of the manor house. Our forbears, strolling players, who may have been little more than wandering vagabonds, will have sought popular acclaim in sundry and diverse places.

The chronicler Raphael Holinshed wrote of Edward II: "He furnished his court with companies of jesters, ruffians, flattering parasites, musicians and other vile and nasty ribalds, that the king might spend both days and nights in jesting, playing, banqueting and in such other filthy and dishonourable exercises." [83]

Theatre has always been controversial and, all too often, stood in the cross-hairs of puritanical outrage. Seeking protection and patronage, groups of players sought the respectability of attachment to a noble household. Many groups travelled constantly – English players were popular in Germany and elsewhere in Europe during the 16th century.

But the centre of British life increasingly focused on London. Between 1520 and 1600, its population quadrupled from about 50,000 to 200,000, as Britain transformed from a feudal to a capitalist society.

There is some evidence that Puritan outrage actually contributed to the first custom-designed theatres being built. In the City of London initially, players were forced to make use of public inn-yards. They were tolerated and had to content themselves with hastily built, inadequate stages. For their income they had to rely on hat collections, an unreliable means of collecting money.

Itinerant players. c.1540. Bibliotheque Municipale, Cambrai

Richard Flecknoe, in his *A Short Discourse on the English Stage* (1664), calls these reconstructed inns "theatres." At first, he says, the players acted "without any certain theatres or set companions, till about the beginning of Queen Elizabeth's reign they began here to assemble into companies and set up theatres, first in the city (as in the inn-yards of the Cross Keys and Bull in Grace and Bishop's Gate Street), till that fanatic spirit [i.e., Puritanism], banished them thence into the suburbs" [86] – that is, into Shoreditch and the Bankside, where, outside the jurisdiction of the puritanical city fathers, they erect their first regular playhouses.

1566-7

1572

The Act for the Punishment of Vagabonds makes the freelance actor's life more precarious than ever.

1575

The Bel Savage Inn is readied for performance; possibly also the Bell, the Bull and the Cross Keys.

1576

James Burbage, by trade a joiner but also an actor and leader of a band of players licensed by the Master of the Revels, borrows a sizeable sum of money and builds a permanent home for his company, naming it **The Theatre**. Built outside the confines of the City of London in Finsbury Fields, little is known about this structure. Burbage's indebtedness leads to constant legal problems, but he retains the right to remove the physical structure of the theatre. Twenty-two years later, on the night of 28th December 1598, his son Cuthbert Burbage (brother of Richard, the famous actor), a friend William Smith, Peter Street, "cheefe carpenter," and twelve others described as "laborers such as wrought for wages," gather at The Theatre and begin to tear down the building. We learn that the widow of James Burbage "was there, and did see the doing thereof, and liked well of it;" and we may suspect that, at some time during the day, Shakespeare and the other actors are present, at least as interested spectators.[84] The timbers are taken down and used in building the first **Globe Theatre** o 1599 on the South Bank of the River Thames.

Where did these very first concepts for custom-built theatre space come from? Seemingly, inspired by the conditions to which those early players were well accustomed: a 'fit-up' theatre within the great hall of a palace, manor house or barn, or within the open-air courtyard of an inn.

The only picture that exists of the interior of an Elizabethan theatre is that of **The Swan**, built between 1594 and 1596. This is a copy of a sketch by a Dutch tourist, de Witt, sent with a description to a friend. He said that the theatre seated 3000 persons, was built on "a concrete of flint stones" and "supported by wooden pillars painted in such an imitation of marble that it might deceive even the most prying." Other descriptions of the early theatres – **The Theatre** itself, **The Curtain**, and **The Rose** – agree there were three galleries encircling a central yard for standing spectators, a rectangular thrust stage[85], tiring house behind (dressing rooms and backstage) with a room above. There was also 'my lord's room' for the use of the players' patron. The theatres resemble the often-adjacent bear-baiting yards and, indeed some stages may have been removable to allow these other 'multi-purpose' activities to take place.

The author's timeline commentary is highlighted in purple text.

Standing Audiences

A standing audience fills me with wonder. London's more modern **Globe** (1997) clearly demonstrates the energy generated by a standing crowd. A seated audience can all too often be sleepy and withdrawn; the standees become the most active of all participants, at worst shifting from discomfort but, at best, reacting to every move on stage; backing away from the action, forward to observe, rocking with laughter, sharing with neighbours a dramatic moment, constantly in movement like a field of corn in the wind. Remember the passion and excitement of standing spectators in a football stadium compared to seated fans. The orgiastic thrills of mosh-pit or standing crowd at a rock-and-roll concert only parallels the excitement of London's annual classical Promenade Concerts. And, to jump forward in theatrical time, the promenade productions in the Cottesloe Theatre, such as *The Mysteries*, will long remain highlights of the National's success. One can well imagine that the Elizabethan audience was a roisterous, excitable crowd: we know that food, drink and other sundry favours must have been part of the excitement.

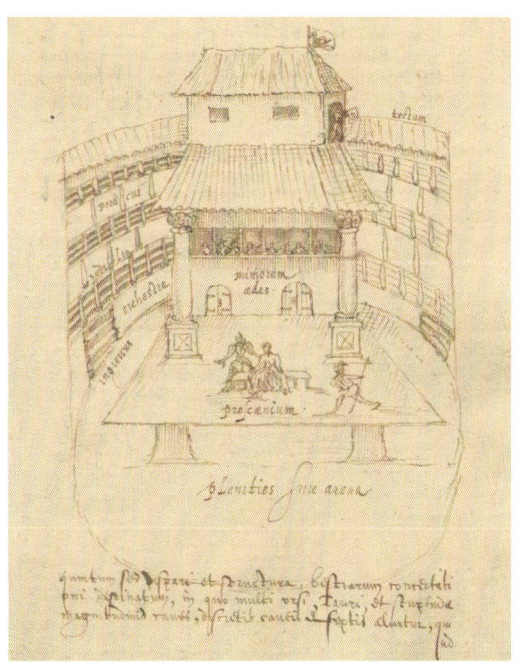

The Swan Theatre, 1594

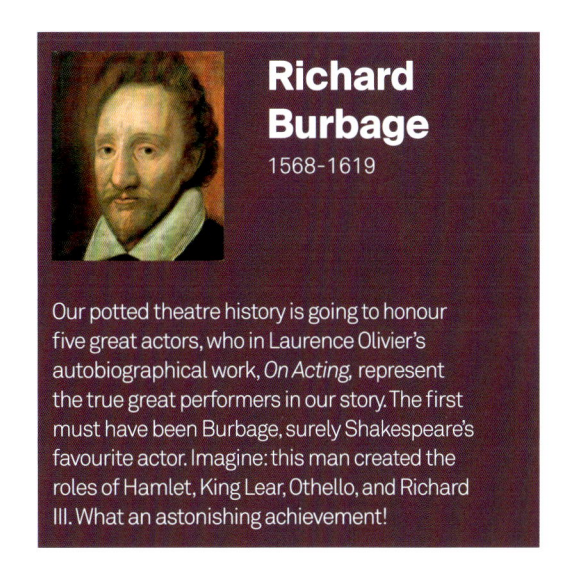

Richard Burbage
1568-1619

Our potted theatre history is going to honour five great actors, who in Laurence Olivier's autobiographical work, *On Acting*, represent the true great performers in our story. The first must have been Burbage, surely Shakespeare's favourite actor. Imagine: this man created the roles of Hamlet, King Lear, Othello, and Richard III. What an astonishing achievement!

Indoor Theatre and the Masque

The lesser-known, contemporaneous theatres of London are those built indoors. The first, **St. Paul's**, is built in 1575, followed by **Blackfriars,** also built by James Burbage, in 1576. These are constructed within existing structures. Admission is more expensive: 6 pennies to 2 shillings and 6 pennies, compared to 1 penny for standing at the Globe. Each seats only around 500; they are lit by daylight from high windows, and also by candlelight. Initially they are occupied by companies of boy actors until 1609, when Burbage obtains permission for the King's Men to perform at the Blackfriars as well as at the **Globe.**

1575-1576

Inigo Jones (1573-1625), the architect and stage designer, famed for his introduction of perspective scenery to England, is active during Shakespeare's lifetime; indeed, playwright Ben Jonson is his frequent collaborator. The indoor theatres have galleries on three sides, and audiences in the pit are now seated. Before the theatre closures caused by the Puritan Revolution, 1642-1660, indoor theatres flourish, and Jones produces a number of designs for theatres that crossed the bridge between the open non-scenic Elizabethan platform and the Renaissance scenic stage. It is likely that *The Tempest* is first played indoors and within a scenic environment, probably in 1611.

The Courtyard Theatre

The Elizabethan courtyard theatres bear remarkable affinity to the French tennis court theatres of Molière, the Spanish Corrales of Lope de Vega and Calderón, even the almost contemporary theatres across China and Japan. All clustered their audiences tightly around a central space shared by performers and audience. And in all these 'primitive' theatres, the art of the playwright reached a level of accomplishment that has never been surpassed. Something is very right about these courtyard theatre spaces.

1578

The playhouses of London are immensely popular. In one of his sermons preached at Paul's Cross, the Protestant clergyman John Stockwood says, "Will not a filthy play, with the blast of a trumpet, sooner call thither a thousand, than the tolling of a bell bring to the sermon a hundred… They pleased to have call it a theatre, that is even after the manner of the heathenish theatre at Rome, a show-place of all beastly and filthy matters." [87]

1587

The **Rose** is built by Philip Henslowe. The first playhouse to be built on the South Bank of the Thames and the first to stage the plays of Shakespeare.

The discovery of the foundations of the **Rose Theatre** in 1989 caused much excitement. Here, at last, was hard evidence of the shape of these revered theatres. Of extraordinary interest was the clear evidence of both the original theatre and Henslowe's reconstruction in 1592. The original was a twelve-sided regular polygon with space for groundlings standing on three sides of the stage. The later house provides evidence of typical theatrical pragmatism. The stage and stage end of the building are pushed back about 8 feet (2.44 metres) to increase the standing/ seating capacity (it is estimated by about twenty-five percent) and the tiring house backstage was expanded, perhaps to allow more room for backstage storage (so often short changed in a new theatre). The result was a rather lop-sided building. This lasted for eight years before being replaced, by Henslowe in 1600, with the square-shaped **Fortune** which continued in use until the Puritan's closure of the theatres in 1642.

The **Rose** today looks very small. It reputedly held about 2000 people, yet from the stage edge to the front of the middle tier was only about 30 feet (9.1 metres). Audiences were packed in a space that today would only hold about a quarter as many. Yet in this tiny theatre, the mighty *Tamburlaine the Great* by Marlowe was first played.

Henslowe expands **The Rose**. Robert Greene describes Shakespeare as "the upstart crow."

The plague closes London theatres for two years.

1592

The **Swan Theatre** opens.

1595

The second **Blackfriars Theatre** is taken over by Richard Burbage.

1596

The first **Globe Theatre** opens.

1599

Queen Elizabeth dies. James I takes the throne.

1603

Henslowe builds the **Fortune Theatre.**

1609

The Globe, Bankside, London, 1997 historically accurate re-creation of the original Globe

The Rose Theatre, 1587

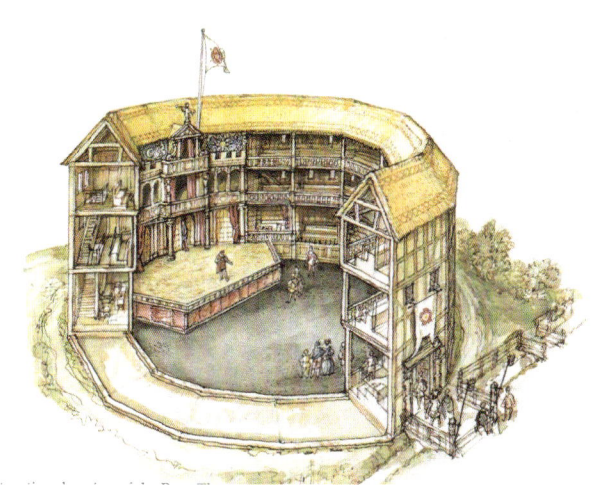

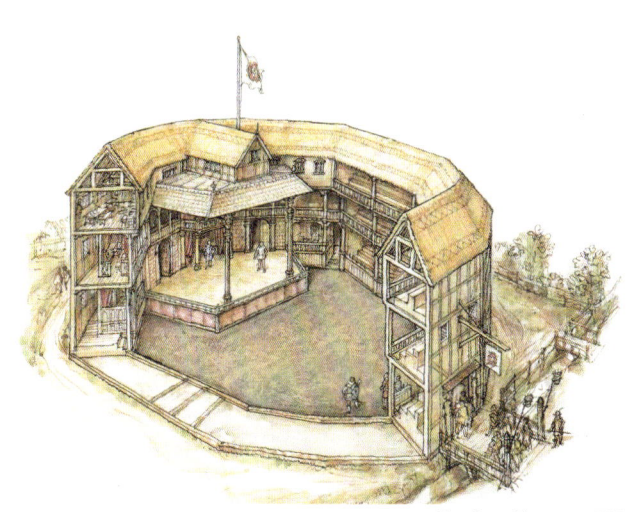

The Rose Theatre, 1592

1.2 British Playhouse Design

29

Shakespeare Retires

For a summary of the Elizabethan theatre we should go to a contemporary witness, Thomas Middleton in his *The Roaring Girl* that took to the stage of **The Fortune** in 1611:

"Within one square a thousand heads are laid, So close that of heads the room seems made; As many faces there, filled with blithe looks, Show like the promising titles of new books Writ merrily, the readers being their own eyes, Which seem to move and give plaudities, The very floor, as t'were, waves to and fro, And, like a floating island, seems to move, Upon a sea bound in with shores above." [88]

The Elizabethan theatre certainly kindles passion and enthusiasm. The outdoor theatres are all built during a short period (1566 to 1614). Within their walls, some of the greatest dramatic literature of all time is produced. What other age has seen Shakespeare, Marlowe, Jonson, Chapman, Dekker, Heywood, Middleton, Webster, Tourneur, Massinger and Beaumont & Fletcher filling the theatres with an audience representing an entire cross-section of society?

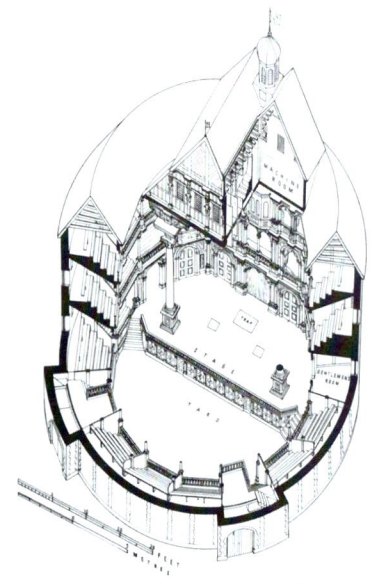

1611

The second Globe: conjectural 20th century drawing by Richard Leacroft

1614

The Globe burns down. The second **Globe** opens.

1616

The Death of Shakespeare

Worcester College Oxford holds two pairs of drawings long thought to be by Inigo Jones, for the conversion of two different cockpits into playhouses. In 1973 one set was identified[89] as the **Cockpit in Drury Lane**, acquired by actor-manager Christopher Beeston in 1616; it burns the next year in a riot, then is rebuilt as, appropriately, the **Phoenix**. Sam Wanamaker,[90] instigator of the re-imagined Globe in London of 1997 was persuaded to build a second, indoor theatre based on these plans. By the time the money was raised, Wanamaker had died. Other scholars suggested these drawings were actually by Jones' erstwhile assistant John Webb, drawn some decades after Shakespeare's death. The 2014 Wanamaker Theatre uses a modified version of these drawings intended to make the resulting Wanamaker Playhouse more Jacobean. It does successfully suggest how candle-lit playhouses evolved between Shakespeare's time and the Restoration of the monarchy in 1660.[91]

The second set of drawings show Henry VIII's **Cockpit-in-Court** in Whitehall (1529), definitely adapted into a theatre by Jones in 1629-1630. The Shakespeare North Playhouse (2022) in Prescot near Liverpool was inspired by these drawings.[92]

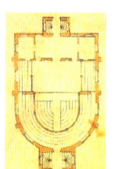

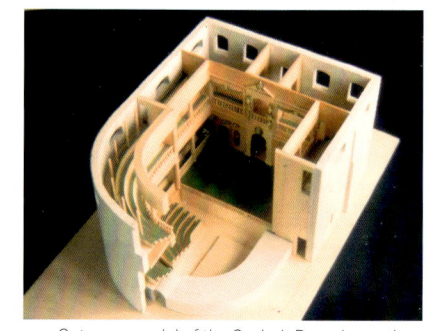

Cutaway model of the Cockpit Drury Lane, then believed to be by Inigo Jones. Model made in 1974 by John Ronayne, later used as the basis for the proposed indoor playhouse at the Globe in London.

A Sense of Theatre

The Puritan Revolution
In England on 2nd September the Puritan revolution bans theatre and all are closed: "Public stage-plays shall cease and be forborne." Under Cromwell, actors might be arrested as "rogues" if they are caught "in the act." The theatre is forced to go underground.

1642

Evolution of Theatre Architecture
Conventional wisdom used to suggest that theatre totally changed after the accession of Charles II and the theatres' reopening, but this is not so. Italian-style perspective scenery is introduced during Shakespeare's life in the court theatre masques, and the intimacy of the Elizabethan indoor theatres continues for many decades after the Restoration, indeed through until the late 19th century, in the smaller theatres of both England and America.

Lincoln's Inn Fields is
created by Davenant from Lisle's Tennis Court. Davenant employs John Webb, as his designer. Actors played on the forestage, while increasingly spectacle occurs on the stage behind them. Davenant, with Webb, thus provides the more attractive spectacular competition, apparently influencing Killigrew to upgrade his facilities to create the first **Theatre Royal Drury Lane**.

1661

Theatre Royal Drury Lane, attributed to Christopher Wren, 1663

The first **Theatre Royal Drury Lane** (Bridge Street) built by Killigrew, is attributed to Christopher Wren. It extends the scenic capability of theatre.[94]

1663

1656

Advent of Spectacle
The Siege of Rhodes is designed by John Webb, who is Inigo Jones' pupil, son-in-law and assistant. It presents the first recorded use in England of Italian-style perspective scenery for the first English opera.[93] The Italian Renaissance introduces spectacle to the stage. Encouraged by Inigo Jones, the indoor theatres and courtly masques, too, see perspective scenery and effects grow in popularity. For the next 400 years, the battle between stage spectacle and the performer rages.

During the close of theatres, short sketches - 'drolls' - are performed instead. This frontpiece, from a 1662 book possibly showing Salisbury Court, suggests how indoor performance spaces were developing during this era, with a gallery and lighting by candelabra and footlights.

1660

The Restoration
When Charles II is restored to the throne, he establishes the post of Master of the Revels, responsible for licensing all public entertainment, and provides two Royal Patents, one to poet laureate Sir William Davenant (1606-1668) of The Duke's Company at **Lisle's Tennis Court**, and one to dramatist and manager, Thomas Killigrew of the King's Men first at **Gibbon's Tennis Court.** These theatres are not radically different in form or capacity; they continue in the tradition of the indoor theatres of the past, seating perhaps 400 or 500, with a stage width of between 16 and 33 feet, a deep forestage with doors to either side and surrounding balconies. Some part of the audience sits at the sides or around the stage, further reducing the stage area.

1665

The Great Plague. Theatres closed. The following year the Great Fire destroys four-fifths of London.

1.2 British Playhouse Design

In 1671 **Sir Christopher Wren,** architect of St. Paul's Cathedral and master planner of the new city, builds the **Duke's Theatre, Dorset Garden,** for Davenant, and later, in 1674, the first **Theatre Royal Covent Garden** for Killigrew (on the site of the current Royal Opera House, but differently oriented). These theatres continue to combine continental innovations with some of the features of the Elizabethan stage. The latter building is a three-tiered wooden structure, with a fan-shaped auditorium, 112 feet (34 metres) long and 59 feet (18 metres) wide; it could hold an audience of about 700. Set well back from the broader streets, the theatre is accessed by narrow passages between surrounding buildings.

1671

Perhaps the more exciting event comes with the introduction of actresses to the English stage, the most famous being Nell Gwynn (1650-1687). An undoubtedly jolly, outspoken figure, she begins her career as an orange seller, becomes an actress at age 14, then graduates to become mistress to the King. Samuel Pepys describes her as "pretty, witty Nell." The King himself frequently attends productions, as does Pepys, whose private diaries provide much of what we know of London theatre-going in the 1660s. The day after the **Theatre Royal Drury Lane** opens, Pepys attends a performance of John Fletcher's *The Humorous Lieutenant*. He has this to say in his diary:

"The house is made with extraordinary good contrivance and yet hath some faults, as the narrowness of the passages in and out of the Pit and the distance from the stage to the boxes, which I am confident cannot hear." [95]

In 1668 John Dryden (1631-1700) is contracted to write three plays a year for the King's Company.

The weakness of Restoration theatre is that, by concentrating on its aristocratic audience, it excludes most of the populace and is therefore far from representative of English society. The theatre struggles to survive and, after the 1670s, audiences dwindle. In 1682 the King's Company and the Duke's Company merge to form the United Company, under the leadership of the Duke's Company people. For thirteen years, London supports only one theatre. In 1672, Drury Lane burns.

1674

Drury Lane #2 is built..

1676

Fabrizio Carini Motta was an Italian man of the theatre, in charge of the theatres of the Gonzagos. He writes: *Trattato Sopra la Struttura de' Teatri e Scene* in 1676. It is the first book on theatre architecture of the modern age. "A theatre is so called because it has an auditorium and stage on which to perform." He describes good entrance and exits, quiet, good wardrobes and dressing rooms, good sightlines, a spacious stage and a division of the auditorium into three parts: the floor for the nobility, the tiers for the lesser nobility and the gallery for the commoners. He postulates single, or triple, tiers, all in a bell-shaped plan. He describes as essential, the forestage, with a width between 4'9" and 9'6", in which the players and speakers who walk on the stage, that is to say, those who do not have to depend on machines, perform. Motto directs that the upstage edge of the forestage should be narrower than the downstage (audience) side and, thus, those who perform here, are heard beautifully. This differentiation between 'main stage' for machines, and 'forestage' for actors is to last 100 years.

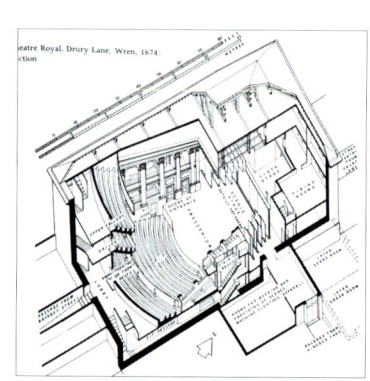

Theatre Royal Drury Lane #2, 1674

32 A Sense of Theatre

1682

Christopher Rich
The two theatre companies combine to play in the **Theatre Royal Drury Lane** and Rich renovates the space for larger audiences.

Rich is a lawyer and, by all accounts, an unpleasant, litigious creature who buys a controlling share in the patent of Drury Lane and proceeds to fight with the leading actors of the day, led by the brightest star, Thomas Betterton. This forces Betterton to quit and start his own company at **Lincoln's Inn Fields**, opening with Congreve's *Love for Love*. Of Rich, Cibber writes, "He was as sly a tyrant as ever was set at the head of a theatre; for he gave the actors more liberty and fewer days' pay than any of his predecessors; he would laugh with them over a bottle and bite them in their bargains… He kept them poor that they might not rebel and sometimes merry that they might not think of it. All their articles of agreement had a clause in them that he was sure to creep out at." [96]

It's refreshing to learn that 'sharp' producers are not a solely 21st century invention.

1705

Queen's Theatre, Haymarket
by architect Sir John Vanbrugh, begins the trend toward building ever larger theatres. Cibber writes of it: "The best play… could not be under greater disadvantage." The theatre becomes established for opera and musical theatre and twenty-five operas of Handel are premiered there between 1711 and 1739. The theatre's name changes with the sex of the monarch, becoming **The King's Theatre** in 1714.

Colley Cibber (1671-1757)
Colley Cibber, who at last secures control of Drury Lane, is an entrepreneur, actor, playwright, theatre manager and a colourful show-off who rises, to the surprise of many of his contemporaries, to be poet laureate. He famously writes *An Apology for the Life of Mr. Colley Cibber, Written by Himself* in two volumes, which remains a detailed telling of his life and the backstage gossip of his age, from the Restoration to his retirement in 1733. Two extracts will suffice to illuminate the theatre scene in his contemporary England. The first about the habits of some audience members who enjoyed showing themselves upon the stage:

"Aesop: How do you spend your evening sir?

Fine Gent: I dress in the evening and go generally behind the scenes of both playhouses; not, you may imagine, to be diverted by the play; but to intrigue and show myself. I stand upon the stage, talk loud and stare about, which confounds the actors and disturbs the audience; upon which the galleries, who hate the appearance of one of us, begin to hiss and cry, Off! Off! While I, undaunted, stamp my foot so – loll with my shoulder thus – take snuff with my right hand and smile scornfully – thus. This exasperates the savages and they attack us with volleys of sucked oranges and half-eaten pippens.

Aesop: And you retire?

Fine Gent: Without doubt. If I am sober, for orange will stain silk and an apple disfigure a feature."

Cibber adds, "This is proof that Garrick saw and felt the evil [of onstage audiences] in his younger days; and he at last mustered courage by one bold stroke to put the hatchet to the tree and thereby annihilate the grievance."

Cibber again: "The platform of the old stage, projected about four foot forwarder, in a semi-circle the usual station of the actors was advanced at least ten foot nearer to the audience, than they now could be. When the actors were in possession of that forwarder space, the voice was then more in the centre of the house; all objects were thus drawn nearer to the sense; every painted scene was stronger, every grand scene and dance more extended; nor was the minutest motion of a feature ever lost, as they frequently must be in the obscurity of too great a distance." [97]

Of the **King's Theatre** (1703), Cibber writes in 1740, "Every proper quality and convenience of a good theatre has been sacrificed or neglected to show the spectator a vast triumphal piece of architecture. And the best play, for reasons I am going to offer, could not be under greater disadvantage… This extraordinary and superfluous space occasioned such an undulation from the voice of every actor that generally what they said sounded like the gabbling of so many people in the lofty aisles of a cathedral."

By the time Cibber writes his criticism, Vanbrugh's theatre has undergone various alterations, but even Handel has vacated the theatre, seeking the more focused environment of Covent Garden.

The Beggar's Opera
Opening in Lincoln's Inn Fields on 29th January 1728, John Gay's ballad opera produced by John Rich is the first musical megahit. Between 1728 and 1731 William Hogarth created a sketch and five oil paintings of the event. In 1993 Iain Mackintosh pointed out that while the final paintings, now at the Yale Center for British Art and the Tate in London, portray some audience on stage within a grand Newgate prison and upstage a crowd of prisoners, while in earlier versions things are more modest. The same actors are crowded by the audience and the small orchestra is placed upstage, Lincoln's Inn Fields having no orchestra pit. It had a tiny stage space, with the actors performing, effectively, in-the-round.[38]

Thomas Davies, writing of Garrick, reports a playbill as stating "for the better accommodation of the ladies the stage will be formed into an Amphitheatre." The onstage audience reduces the stage area into something more suitable for a cockfight. Packing the audience into any available space is particularly popular with the actors, for whom a benefit performance is a valuable source of income.

The Licensing Act (also known as the 'Gagging Act') is introduced by prime minister Robert Walpole to reduce criticism of the Government, as with the savage satire of *The Beggar's Opera*, and enhance its power. It gives the Lord Chamberlain exclusive authority to license spoken drama in theatres, and restricts the activities of strolling players across the country. Only with the Theatres Act of 1968 is this stage censorship abolished.

The Half-Price Riots, Theatre Royal Covent Garden, 1763

At Covent Garden, managers end the customary sale of half-price tickets. Furious audiences riot, closing the theatre and causing considerable damage.

1728

1737

1763

1732

Theatre Royal Covent Garden reopens with William Congreve's *The Way of the World*.

David Garrick, at the time England's leading actor, controls the **Theatre Royal Drury Lane** from 1747 to 1776. He tolerates the onstage audience until late in his career, and only in 1775 commissions Robert Adam to renovate his theatre. Even then, he keeps many of the much-loved traditional features: a deep forestage with proscenium doors to the side, and the stage only 28 feet (8.5 metres) wide.

The theatre under Garrick reaches unprecedented levels of popularity. "In the days of David Garrick, the theatre engrossed the minds of men to such a degree that it may now be said that there now existed in England a fourth estate; King, Lords, Commons and Drury Lane Theatre," [39] wrote Arthur Murphy, one of Garrick's early biographers.

In 1714, there is one legitimate theatre in Britain; in 1777, there are 150-200, by 1814, over 300. Almost all are of similar scale and might have been accommodated within the dimensions of a tennis court.

David Garrick
1717-1779

The second actor in Sir Laurence's pantheon of greats is David Garrick. He was an actor, playwright, manager and producer, who had an enormous influence on every aspect of theatre: acting, set design, lighting, costumes and even audience behaviour during his long career. After initial rejection he came to the public's attention with his Richard III, in which the naturalism of his performance was the talk of London. From 1747, during his 29-year management of Drury Lane, it became one of Europe's leading theatres. Dr. Johnson wrote an ode for his inaugural production: "The drama's laws the drama's patrons give, For we that live to please must please to live." Words that summarise Garrick's approach, balancing art, integrity and the fickle tastes of the public. True then, of course, and equally true today, if you find yourself running the National Theatre. In 1769, Garrick staged the first Shakespeare Jubilee in Stratford-upon-Avon, doing much to confirm Shakespeare's predominance in the public imagination. Garrick was granted a lavish funeral in Westminster Abbey.

A Sense of Theatre

Theatre Royal Bristol opens. Built to designs by James Saunders, David Garrick's carpenter at Drury Lane. Outside London, theatres continued to be sized on a modest scale until late in the 19th century.

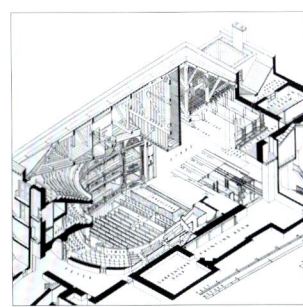

Theatre Royal Bristol, 1764-66

1766

Sir Robert Talbot in the *The Oxford Magazine*: "As it was in Athens, the playhouse in London is for all classes of the nation." [101]

1771

1767

Count Francesco Algarotti (1712-1764) writes *An Essay on the Opera,* 1767, which he dedicates to Prime Minister William Pitt.

"Let us consider that the measure of the length of the parterre or pit and size of a theatre is the performer's reach of voice and none other. For it would be as ridiculous in any person to have a theatre built so large that people could not hear in it as in an engineer to make the works of a fortress in such a manner as it could not be defended.

"The architect's principle care should be to leave no article unremedied that might in any way impede the view; and at the same time let no gaping chasm appear by any space remaining unoccupied and lost to every serviceable purpose. Let him also contrive that the audience may appear to form part of the spectacle to each other, ranged as books are in a library." [100]

Algarotti adds, "The actor, instead of being so brought forward, ought to be thrown back a certain distance from the spectator's eye and stand within the scenery of the stage in order to make a part of a pleasing illusion for which all dramatic exhibitions are calculated."

This versus Cibber, who in 1740 remembered, "When the actors were in possession of the forwarder space to advance upon, the voice was then more in the centre of the house, so that the most distant ear had scarce the least doubt in difficulty of hearing… All objects were thus drawn nearer to the sense… Every rich or fine coloured habit had a more lively lustre; nor was the minutest motion of a feature… ever lost as they must be in the obscurity of too great a distance."

Pierre Patti (1723-1814) in his *Essai sur l'architecture théâtrale* writes on theatre architecture and publishes comparative plans of the theatres he describes.

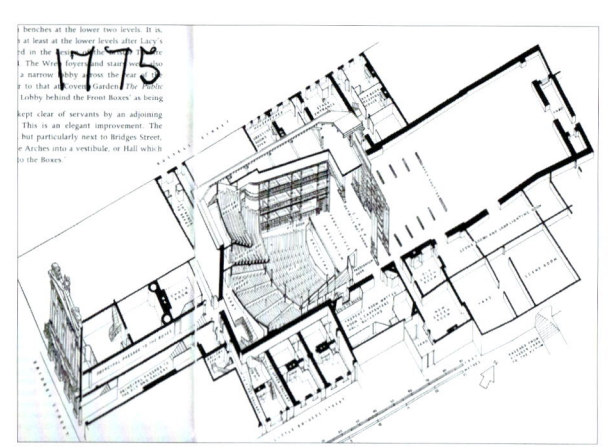

Theatre Royal Drury Lane renovation, 1775

1775
Theatre Royal Drury Lane renovation by Robert Adam. For his penultimate season Garrick hires Adam to renovate the auditorium, thus enhancing the value of his large shareholding! This theatre lasts until 1792.

1785
The Argand lamp introduces more intense and constant light compared to the flickering candle.

1788
Theatre Royal Richmond opens, built by actor-manager Samuel Butler. The Theatrical Representations Act is passed, allowing local magistrates to license performances for up to 60 days. In France, M. Clément Contant publishes another collection of comparative theatres: *Parallèle des Principaux Théâtres Modernes de l'Europe*.

1771
Garrick engages Philippe-Jacques de Loutherbourg from the Paris Opera as his designer. Many innovations in atmospheric scene design, lighting and effects follow. Visible lights on the stage are concealed, side lighting with reflectors increases brightness on the stage.

Oliver Goldsmith's (1728-1774) *She Stoops to Conquer* is produced at Covent Garden in 1773.

1774
Gabriel Pierre Martin Dumont publishes in Paris his *Parallele De Plans des plus Belles Salles de Spectacles d'Italie et de France Avec des détails de Machines Théatrales*, a series of engravings of theatre architecture including plans, sections and elevations with details of stage machinery construction that prompt a renewed interest in the principles of theatre architecture and construction.

1777
An engraving of a performance of *The School for Scandal* at Drury Lane in 1777 shows the actors on stage and the audience in boxes around them. From that, we get an idea of the actual scale of the theatre.

Another engraving from around 1775 has a view from the stage in which the theatre appears far larger – perhaps to exaggerate its value. This second engraving is, however, immediately suspect as the actors in the foreground appear to be only four feel tall!

The School for Scandal at Drury Lane, 1777

Engraving with miniature people onstage!

A Sense of Theatre

George Saunders, (1762-1839) *A Treatise on Theatres*. "The great advance of the floor of some stages into the body of the theatre is too absurd ever to be again considered." [102]

The Growth of Theatres Accelerates

1790

Theatre Royal Covent Garden stage and auditorium enlarged, rebuilt by Henry Holland.

1792

Theatre Royal Drury Lane #3, 1794

1791

King's Theatre Haymarket is rebuilt even larger by architect Michael Novosolieski.

1794

Theatre Royal Drury Lane rebuilt with the first iron safety curtain and water drencher by architect Henry Holland.

The stage is the largest in Europe. Iron columns support five tiers of audience.

1797

At **Drury Lane**, actors succeed in having proscenium arch doors reintroduced.

1800

Theatre Royal Bristol is remodelled.

1.2 British Playhouse Design

What the extraordinary increase in scale does to acting styles is illustrated by the accounts of two theatregoers who compared old Drury Lane, where Garrick held sway from 1747 to 1776, to the new, greatly enlarged Drury Lane created by Holland in 1794. Reflected playwright Richard Cumberland in his *Memoirs* published in 1806: "Since the stages of Drury Lane and Covent Garden had been so enlarged in their dimensions as to be henceforward theatres for spectators rather than playhouses for hearers, it is hardly to be wondered at if managers and directors encourage those representations, to which their structure is best adapted. The splendour of the scene, the ingenuity

1806

of the machinist and the rich display of dresses, aided by the captivating charms of music, now in a great degree supersede the labours of the poet. There can be nothing very gratifying in watching the movement of an actor's lips when we cannot hear the words that proceed from them, but when the animating march strikes up and the stage lays open its recesses to the depth of a hundred feet for the procession to advance, even the most distant spectator enjoys his shilling's worth of show… On the stage of Old Drury in the days of Garrick, the moving brow and penetrating eye of that matchless actor came home to the spectator. As the passions shifted and were by turns reflected from the mirror of his expressive countenance, nothing was lost; upon the scale of modern Drury many of the finest touches of his act would of necessity fall short." [103]

A few years earlier John Byng, later Viscount Torrington, recorded in his diary a visit to the newly opened mega-Drury Lane of 1794: "14 May 1794. I adjourned to Drury Lane Playhouse where I enjoyed the highly wrought exhibition of Mrs. Siddons's performance as Katherine in *Henry VIII* although lost and sent to waste in this wide wide theatre where close observation cannot be maintained – nor quick applause received! Restore me, ye overruling powers of the dramas, to the warm close observant seats of Old Drury where I may comfortably criticise and enjoy the flights of fancy. These now are past. Garrick, thou did'st retire at the proper time for were't thou restored to the stage, in vain would now thy byplay, thy whisper, thy aside, even thine eye assist thee." [104]

1809

Theatre Royal Covent Garden is entirely rebuilt by Robert Smirke. Theatre Royal Drury Lane is destroyed by fire; Benjamin Dean Wyatt builds a new version which opens in 1812.

Wyatt wrote in his *Observations on the Design of the Theatre Royal Drury Lane,* "Nothing being so incongruous as the indiscriminate use of such [proscenium] doors."

A veteran actor, Dowton replied, "Don't tell me of frames and pictures. If I can't be heard by the audience in the frame, I'll walk out of it." Wyatt continues on Drury Lane: "I was aware of the very popular notion that our theatres ought to be very small; but it appeared to me that if that very popular notion should be suffered to proceed too far it would in every way deprive the proprietors of that revenue which is indispensable to defray the heavy expenses of such a concern." [105]

Thus the 'needs' of the proprietors, rather than that of the actors or the drama, drives a massive increase in the size of our theatres.

Theatre Royal Drury Lane 1794-1809, designed by Henry Holland, as modified with proscenium arch doors in 1797

Edmund Kean
1787-1833

The third great actor lauded by Sir Laurence was Edmund Kean. Noted for his short stature, firebrand temperament but utter dedication, his portrayals of Shakespeare's villains were legendary. After a long apprenticeship, troubled by an excess of alchohol, his breakthrough came in 1814 at Drury Lane, where his Shylock caused a sensation. His performances as Richard III, Iago, Macbeth, Othello, and Hamlet were legendary. In his maturity, his excesses made him increasingly unpopular on tours in England and in the United States. In 1833, while playing Othello to his son Charles' Iago, he collapsed. He died a few days later.

Olivier wrote, "He presented a raw freshness that knocked the audiences sideways. I think he opened their minds to the truth and thrilled them out of their boxes."

The **Adelphi Theatre** by architect Samuel Beazley introduces cantilevered construction allowing balconies to overhang each other without pillars and bringing more audience closer to the stage. **Theatre Royal Covent Garden** again remodelled. **Old Vic Theatre** designed by Rudolph Cabanel is built. **Bury St Edmunds** remodelled.

1819

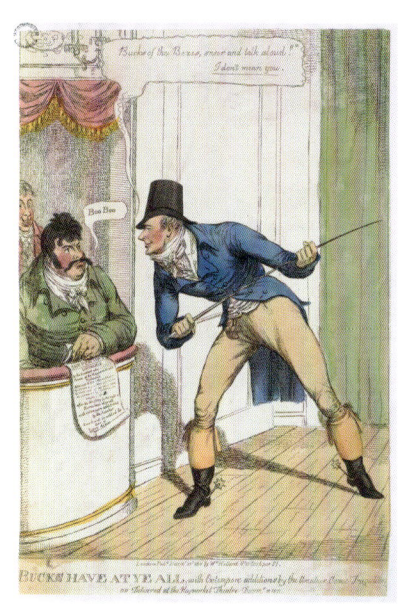

The intimate contact of boxes

1813

As the theatres of the metropolis mushroomed in size, acting styles had to grow in scale, developing a whole new 'Romantic' style exemplified by the tragic hero John Philip Kemble and his sister, Sarah Siddons. As the victories of Trafalgar and Waterloo inspire a nation, romantic spectacle takes over our stages.

With the end of the Napoleonic wars, however, peace, agricultural and social challenges and the rise of Methodism also lead to a lessening interest in theatregoing.

1817

Gaslight is installed in the **Lyceum Theatre** then **Drury Lane.** The enhanced ability to control light levels on stage and in the auditorium lead to the lowering of light in the latter, increasing the sense of spectacle on the stage. But does this new ability to remotely control lighting allowing a darkened auditorium make theatregoing seem a more perilous pastime?

1825

Stephenson's Rocket
The first commercial railways enter service. Through the 19th century, the explosion of railway travel both expands the world of touring theatre across Britain and brings larger audiences into urban centres.

1837

Queen Victoria's Coronation
Actor William Macready introduces the powerful beam of limelight to the stage.

1.2 British Playhouse Design

1843

The Theatre Regulations Act is passed, restricting the Lord Chamberlain's powers to ban plays where it is "fitting for the preservation of good manners or public peace." Additional power to local authorities to license theatres gives rise to the spread of pub theatres and music halls.

1856

Covent Garden is destroyed by fire and rebuilt by Edward Middleton Barry, opening in 1858. This auditorium with the adjacent Floral Hall and extensive stage additions forms the current **Royal Opera House**.

1862

C.J. Phipps (1835-1897) wins a competition for the rebuilding of the **Theatre Royal Bath** after a fire. He goes on to become a leading theatre architect, responsible for the **Queen's Theatre** (1867), the **Gaiety** (1868) and the **Vaudeville** (1871).

1865

The Builder magazine condemned current theatre design: "Those venerable archaic theatres must be confessed to have been most bunglingly contrived, or rather not contrived at all, to produce anything like scenic illusion or stage effect. Visitors are piled up to the very ceiling and consequently have to look down on the heads of the performer." [106]

1870

Thomas Verity, theatre architect (1837-1891) wins the competition to build the **Criterion Theatre**. He is also involved with the **Royalty**, the **Scala** and the **Comedy Theatres**.

1871

The Old Vic (original architect Rudolph Cabanel) is rebuilt by **J.T. Robinson** (1829-1878), father-in-law to Frank Matcham. He is also responsible for the **Theatre Royal Margate**.

Audience Density

It is an indisputable fact that audience members in the 16th and 17th centuries were physically smaller than people are today. Standards of comfort, and regulations related to audience safety, were a great deal laxer in times past.

The **Old Vic Theatre** when built in 1818 was meant to hold 4000, whereas *The Stage* reported that in 1912 it seated 2000, and the same sized auditorium today seats only 878.

Humans are getting larger!

Fire and Safety

As theatres grow larger, so does the need for regulation to mitigate the frequent disaster of fire. The fire curtain is introduced, followed by water deluges and sprinklers and greater control over the regulations of access and egress.

Darkness and Morals

Ever-larger theatres, brighter stages, more extravagant styles of acting, melodrama and a darkened auditorium all enhance for some Victorian playgoers a sense of looming danger. Theatre seems again to become the "the house of Satan," so feared by their puritanical forbears.[107] The upper classes begin to confine themselves to the more socially acceptable opera; the professional classes still patronise the Theatres Royal, while the broader public drift away to the newly popular music halls and lesser theatres.

Another Type of Restoration

But from the 1860s, theatre begins to recover. The railways bring ever-larger audiences to urban centres. New theatres, designed for the age of gas and accommodating the innovations of the last decades, begin to appear. Steel cantilevers bring balconies closer to the stage. Larger audiences enjoy more equitable sightlines, while the side boxes are relegated to places where it might be better to be seen, rather than places from which to see.

Stages reveal ever more wondrous illusions and the modern proscenium stage is born, rapidly being accepted as *the* theatre for the ages.

The opening of the **Paris Opera** by Charles Garnier, who creates surely the world's ultimate classic horseshoe-shaped house. A magnificent stage is over-matched by stupendously glorious lobbies, staircases and auditorium.

1875

Garnier Opera Paris, 1875

Festspielhaus Bayreuth, 1876

1876
Revolution

Festspielhaus Bayreuth
Richard Wagner

By a strange irony, at almost the same time as Garnier's masterwork opens in Paris, Richard Wagner leads a major change in the design of the theatre auditorium with his new opera house in Bayreuth, which opens only one year later in 1876. Fed by his revolutionary political instincts and determined to create an ideal venue for his new form of *Gesamtkunstwerk* (total work of art, combining poetry, music and visual effect in unified balance), he first strives to conceal the orchestra pit from the audience in a "mystic gulf" between stage and audience. Side box seats could break the illusion, allowing the audience to see down into the pit, so he abolishs them. Despising the social snobbery he sees as a fundamental of the horseshoe auditorium, he introduces the first 'continental' (without dividing aisles) fan-shaped auditorium, seating 1345 people. Everyone sits on a single level facing the stage, with boxes located only at the rear. The stage is seen by all through a series of frames that distance the stage beyond his mystic gulf. Designed for the long reverberation time needed for his richly orchestrated work, this presents a totally new form for the opera house.

Perhaps surprisingly, it has been little imitated in opera house design (only at the Prinzregententheater in Munich) – maybe because of its specificity to Wagner's own work – but the model was to influence a hundred years of theatre design for drama.

While Wagner succeeds in creating a new form of auditorium, onstage he continues to employ all the techniques of contemporary stagecraft… or, rather, as much as his limited resources would allow. Wagner's poetic visions are realised only with the flapping backcloths, wings and borders of tradition.

1.2 British Playhouse Design

Frank Matcham (1854-1920) is England's most prolific theatre architect. He begins with the practice of Jethro T. Robinson, who becomes his father-in-law. His innovative use of the cantilever brings balconies closer to the stage and optimises sightlines and seating capacity. His firm, Matcham and Co., is estimated to have completed over 170 theatres.

Walter Emden (1847-1913), theatre architect, is responsible, with C.J. Phipps, for the **Garrick**, the **Duke of York's**, and the **Tivoli**.

Bertie Crewe (1860-1937), theatre architect, is responsible for the **Royal Court Theatre** as assistant to Walter Emden. He is also responsible for such theatres as the **Theatre Royal Lincoln**, the fifth **Sadler's Wells**, the **Shaftesbury Theatre** and the **Lyceum**.

William Poel creates the Elizabethan Stage Society and begins the attempt to rediscover the simplicity of the platform stage of Shakespeare's time.

The Old Bedford, painting by Walter Sickert

1879

1888

1894

1887

Electricity is first installed in the **Savoy Theatre** and spreads rapidly. Ellen Terry is appalled: "When I saw the effect on the faces, I entreated Henry to have the gas restored and he did. The thick softness of gas with the lovely specks and motes in it, so like natural light, gave illusion to many a scene." [108] It takes several decades for electric stage lighting to attain a similar warmth.

Catastophic fire breaks out in the **Theatre Royal Exeter** with around 150 fatalities.

In London, the creation of Shaftesbury Avenue and Charing Cross Road open the way for twelve new theatres to be built.

1891

The Royal English Opera House (now the **Palace Theatre**) was designed by Richard D'Oyly Carte with G.H. Holloway providing the drawings and J.G. Buckle as consultant. The architect was T.E. Collcutt. The English Opera House's stage was equipped with then revolutionary counterweight flying and stage equipment patented by Walter Pfeffer Dando. However the theatre was not a success and was soon adapted to a variety house by Walter Emden.

1897

Theatre Royal Nottingham C.J. Phipps' theatre of 1865 is remodelled by Frank Matcham. **Her Majesty's Theatre**, the last theatre to be designed by C.J. Phipps, opens in the Haymarket. Actor manager Herbert Beerbohm Tree is famed for his spectacular production of Shakespeare's *Midsummer Night's Dream* there, featuring real rabbits. It is the first London theatre to have a flat stage rather than the traditional rake that had been commonplace since the advent of perspective scenery in the 17th century.

Backstage in Victorian times

Edwin Sachs FRSE FRGS (1870–1919), stage engineer, writes and illustrates one of the most astonishingly comprehensive surveys of theatre construction. Sachs who dies at the age of 49, is an expert on fire and safety, and is the engineer in charge of re-equipping the **Royal Opera House** and **Drury Lane**.

1898

W.G.R. Sprague (1863-1933) designs outstanding pairs of theatres: **Wyndham's** and the **New** (now **Noël Coward**), the **Aldwych** and **Novello,** and the **Gielgud** and **Queen's** (now the **Sondheim**) **Theatres**.

1899

Royal Court season for Granville-Barker and Vedrenne launches Granville-Barker as the leading young new-wave director and establishes George Bernard Shaw as a major dramatist.

1904

1905

Edward Gordon Craig (1872-1976) departs for Germany. Craig is the illegitimate son of Ellen Terry and architect Edward William Godwin. He apprentices as an actor under Irving and later turns to design.

Craig is a visionary who rejects the standards of Irving's romantic theatre and seeks a new stagecraft of imagination, beauty and power... pure theatre. He leaves Britain and soon becomes a prophet of the new theatre. He wrote:

"The art of the theatre is neither the acting nor the play, it is not scene or dance, but it consists of all the elements of which these things are composed: action, which is the very spirit of acting; words, which are the body of the play; line and colour, which are the very heart of the scene; rhythm, which is the very essence of the dance."[109]

Somewhat tragically, Craig's designs and writing are contradicted by his actual achievements. His designs were inspiring, but are seldom practical. In 1912, Stanislavski invites Craig to design *Hamlet* for the **Moscow Art Theatre**. Despite evocative designs, on a real stage Craig's moving screens tended to jam or collapse. Craig certainly inspired many (including your author), but his dreams were indeed a dream. Half a century had to pass before such techniques became remotely practical.

The other philosopher of modern stagecraft is **Adolphe Appia** (1862-1928), a Swiss designer/director, who sees Wagner's creaky scenery at Bayreuth as absurd. He envisages a world of the stage that is not of illusion, but of atmosphere that envelopes the singers, seamlessly evoking the music and poetry imagined by Wagner. "A man in the atmosphere of a forest... Siegfried bathed in moving shadows instead of strips of cloth jiggled by strings."[110]

Henry Irving
1838-1905

Ellen Terry
1847-1928

Fourth in the pantheon of Olivier's "greats," but this time accompanied by his long-term leading lady, Ellen Terry. Irving was the foremost stage actor of the Victorian era. He took complete responsibility (supervision of sets, lighting, direction, casting, as well as playing the leading roles) for season after season at the Lyceum Theatre, establishing himself and his company as representative of English classical theatre. In 1895, he became the first actor to be awarded a knighthood, indicating full acceptance into the higher circles of British society. Olivier: "He became the master and champion of his profession."

Craig – A Self Portrait

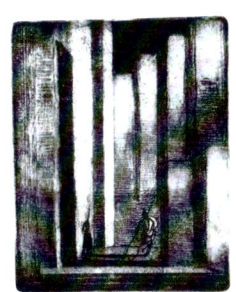

Scene by Edward Gordon Craig

1.2 British Playhouse Design

Hellerau. Scenery and lighting by Appia

1912

Reaction: The Open Stage

A movement against the proscenium and toward the open stage starts to form, a reaction against the Victorian proscenium theatre that sought to place the performer in a separate room behind a proscenium picture frame. The battle continues against the degraded cinema-style, frontally seated auditorium of the early 20th century.

In 1910, the **Festspielhaus Hellerau** by Heinrich Tessenow is a large double cube space with raked seating and a raised stage. The ceiling and walls are translucent and backlit – with scenery and lighting by Appia.

In Paris in 1913, Jacques Copeau creates the **Théâtre du Vieux-Colombier** (interior by architect Francis Jourdain according to drawings by Louis Jouvet). It is a plain rectangular space with an open stage and without a proscenium. In 1919, he constructs a permanent 'Elizabethan-style architectural' setting with steps on either side of the back wall leading to an upper stage with inner stage below. This is found to be too restrictive and the theatre closes in 1924. Attempts to provide fixed architectural settings seem doomed to failure.

The immensely prolific Austrian-born director Max Reinhardt (1873-1943) is Germany's leading director and entrepreneur of the early 20th century. While he is noted for his productions of vast spectacle such as those staged in the 3500-seat **Grosses Schauspielhaus** in Berlin, he also pioneers work on very modest open stages, as in the **Redoutensaal** in Vienna.

1914

The Art Theatre

Reacting against the crowded popular theatres of the day, the 'art theatre' movement at the turn of the 20th century also wants a frontal viewpoint, concentrating upon a realistic stage picture. In *The Theatre of Today* by Hiram Kelly Moderwell, published in 1914, the author writes with passion about the newly emerged "ideal art of theatre." He dismisses with "utter contempt" the ordinary "horseshoe" theatres that "make the stage partly or wholly invisible," with "wretched acoustics" contributing to an evening of "torture." He hails the new Wagnerian designers, in particular Professor Littman of Munich, for his new style of theatre (the **Prinzregententheater**, and **Münchener Künstler-Theater** in Munich), in which "there shall be no bad seats; there shall not even be any worse seats." His "amphitheatre playhouse has all its rows nearly parallel to the proscenium and its floor rising at such an angle that every spectator can look clean over the head of his neighbour in front. A new democratic playhouse." [111]

The **Goodman Theatre** in Chicago (1927) is a deliberate copy of the vaunted **Münchener Künstler-Theater**. So too is the original **Birmingham Repertory Theatre**, on which the young British director Basil Dean gives technical advice to its founder Barry Jackson. But, by the middle of the 20th century, enthusiasm for the frontal auditorium begins to wane. In hindsight, in such a house there were all too many bad seats – almost all those more than half way back – and the lack of encircling audience made the theatre seem more an antiseptic lecture hall than a theatrical space. (In 2000, after a fifteen-year struggle, the highly successful Goodman Theatre Company opened two new theatres in Chicago, one an 800-seat two level proscenium theatre with side boxes, the other, a flexible courtyard theatre.)

Künstler Theatre Munich, 1908

1926

Reaction: The Art Theatre
Terence Gray (1895-1986) is a pioneer. Without previous experience, he takes over the **Theatre Royal, Barnwell, Cambridge**, renaming it the **Festival Theatre** (built in 1808 by William Wilkins) and converts this Georgian horseshoe-shaped theatre into an experimental theatre space. He removes the entire proscenium, creating an open-end platform stage with a permanent cyclorama and a small revolve. With his cousin, Ninette de Valois, founder of the Royal Ballet, he creates revolutionary productions of a largely European repertoire. His young stage director is the fledgling Norman Marshall, later to become a leader of the avant-garde in London, and then Olivier's co-chair on the National Theatre Building Committee. There he admitted that the Cambridge experiment ran out of steam because of a lack of plays suitable for such radical treatment. The company lasts until 1931.

Festival Theatre, Cambridge

1927

Erwin Piscator (1893-1966) is a German theatre director, pioneer with Bertolt Brecht of 'epic' theatre and an early enthusiast for the use of projection and three-dimensional constructed settings. He commissions architect Walter Gropius to design the **Total Theatre**, a vast space with a revolve that transfigures part of the auditorium, surrounded by a vast domed surface for projection. It is unbuilt, but its influence upon aspirant directors (and perhaps on the Las Vegas Sphere) remains. Dear architect reader: beware of unbuilt dreams.

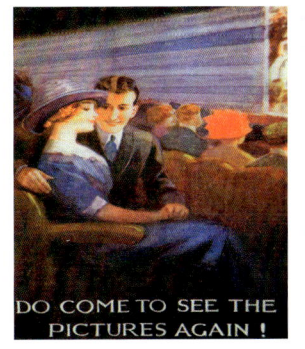

Total Theatre, Walter Gropius, 1927

1936

Reaction: The Thrust Stage
The thrust stage brings the performer out amongst the audience that surrounds him or her on three sides. The modern thrust rediscovery begins almost by accident. In 1936, the Old Vic Theatre Company is to present Laurence Olivier's *Hamlet* 'on location' outdoors in the Kronborg Castle at Elsinore in Denmark. At the last minute, the rain begins to pour and the performance is moved inside to a ballroom, with seats hastily improvised around the stage. It is a great success. It brings director Tyrone Guthrie "the conviction that, for Shakespeare, the proscenium stage was unsatisfactory... the performance related the audience to the play in a different, and I thought more lyrical, satisfying and effective way than can ever be achieved in a theatre of what is still regarded as orthodox design."

The Cinema Phenomenon
Then the movies are invented. At first, a flickering sideshow, then the nickelodeon, the new phenomenon sweeps all before it. Turn-of-the-century vaudeville houses and theatres are taken over for, at first, a mix of film and live performance. The first purpose-built movie palaces are akin to theatres, but quickly become more specialised. The side boxes are overtaken by sumptuous decorations and the stages shrink to mere platforms for the ubiquitous screens. Cinema sweeps the world, rapidly becoming the most popular form of entertainment. The lavish, almost baroque interiors created a fairy-tale world that must have been particularly effective when one remembers that the first films were small, silent, flickering and in black and white.

1.2 British Playhouse Design

1948

In 1948, Guthrie converts the **Assembly Hall, Edinburgh** into a thrust stage. He and his designer, Tanya Moiseiwitsch, went on to develop the purpose-built thrust stage theatre, first at **Stratford Ontario** (a tent enclosure in 1953 then a permanent building in 1957), then **Minneapolis** (1963), and finally the **Sheffield Crucible**[112] in England (1013 seats, 1971). His formula is to create a stage that is quite narrow and deep (about 18 feet, 5.48 metres, wide by 24 feet, 7.3 metres, deep), surrounded by three steps and a moat.[113] Actors could thus stand in the moat slightly lower than the stage, and be partially out of sight to the front row audience. Audience seating begins at the level of the stage beyond the moat. Access to the stage is from the rear or from vomitoria at 45° to the front of the stage. The centre of the stage becomes a crossroads for actors entering from stage or vomitorium. Behind the stage is a rear stage which, in Guthrie's original, consists of a permanent setting with entrances and inner and upper-stages in the Elizabethan style. By the time of the **Crucible**, this permanent structure has evolved into a series of movable towers that divided the thrust from a rear stage. In Guthrie's original aesthetic, the stage is a bare platform for the plays, expressed using costume and properties, but no illusionistic scenery. There is little provision for theatrical lighting other than bare illumination, but this soon proves to be unsatisfactory, and modern lighting, and considerable quantities of scenery, are now found on every thrust stage.

Each of Guthrie's theatres features a stage surrounded on three sides by audience in a Greek-style amphitheatre layout, rather than vertically stacked as in the Elizabethan model. **Stratford** has a narrow balcony around the rear, as does **Minneapolis**, although in the latter the architect introduced an asymmetric section that links the circle to the audience's right down to orchestra level, a feature that Guthrie himself told me he disliked. Fresh from his dispute over the **Minneapolis** architecture, in Sheffield he returned to basics, with the audience on one level. But he was working from the fundamental theatre design premise of the 1950s: that theatres should not be stacked vertically. Multiple levels in an auditorium denoted class (and in some countries, racial) segregation. Only with Frank Dunlop's **Young Vic**, and the rediscovery of the courtyard, in the late 1970s, has a return to multiple balconies become acceptable.

Reaction: The Arena Stage

The Russian director Nikolay Okhlopkov is remembered for his experimental staging in Moscow of the early 1930s. Employing a simple rectangular space with a balcony at one end, he tried traverse, thrust, surround, and arena staging.

It was in the United States that in-the-round staging came to fruition. In 1932, the University of Washington School of Drama experiments with a surrounding audience, in 1936 adapting the existing space into the 140-seat **Penthouse Theatre**. It was replaced in 1940 with a new theatre seating 185. The stage and theatre are elliptical, with three rows of seating. In Dallas, Texas, Margo Johns creates her arena stage **Theatre 47** in 1947, which she was subsequently to rename every year until her death in 1955. The **Playhouse Theatre** in Houston, Texas opens in 1950, seating 306 around a circular revolving stage 6½ inches (0.17 metres) high. In contrast to the **Penthouse,** it was painted black to minimise stray light in the audience. Also in Houston, Nina Vance built her original **Alley Theatre** (1949) using a rectangular plan.

Stephen Joseph and Scarborough

The pioneer of arena staging in Britain was Stephen Joseph (see Part 5.4). After years of valiant struggle, he finally establishes his theatre in Scarborough, originally in the public library, then in a former school.

Despite Joseph's premature death, the theatre flourishes under the leadership of Alan Ayckbourn until his retirement in 2008, though he continues to write and direct for the company.

In 1996 the company moves again, creating two theatres inside the town's former Odeon cinema and in doing so bringing the building back to life.

The current Stephen Joseph Theatre, Scarborough, 1996

Crucible Theatre, Sheffield, 1971

1958

English Repertory Theatre

The English repertory theatre movement begins in the early 1900s in Liverpool, Manchester, and Birmingham. It brings drama to cities across the country, often under quite impoverished conditions, and often presenting a different show every week. World War II and the development of what becomes the Arts Council brings a new impetus to the movement.

In his recent book *Modern Playhouses*, Alistair Fair describes the spate of theatre building in Britain that began after World War II.[114]

The first is in Coventry in 1958. The **Belgrade Theatre** (Donald Gibson of the Coventry City Architect's Department) seats 910 people. As a pioneering effort, its stage and backstage are criticised, but the three-level auditorium with wraparound boxes is accepted, albeit then viewed by some as being rather old fashioned.

Your author's career in stage management begins in 1955, and I founded Theatre Projects two years later. It is in 1959 that we stumble upon our first consulting client. A wealthy businessman walks into our tiny office and asks if we design theatres. "Of course," I reply. He takes me to his home in Barmouth, North Wales that weekend and thus begins our first project: the conversion of an old Methodist chapel into a 180-seat theatre, the **Dragon Theatre**. Thus begins my life as a theatre consultant. My first major project is a new home for the **Birmingham Repertory Theatre**, with architect Graham Winteringham. The concept is already decided; it is to be a 900-seat version of the old 1913, 460-seat Rep originally guided by Sir Barry Jackson, with a young Basil Dean as technical advisor. This had been directly inspired by Munich's **Künstler Theatre**, symbolic of the new Wagner-inspired, frontal, single-tier auditorium, extolled in print by Moderwell a year later. My role is to design the stage and all its equipment. Did I understand then that with double the seat count, the new theatre might be problematic? No, I did not.

Other regional theatres follow, all with more modest seat counts, all following the rules: single-level, socially equal, frontal auditoria, no old-fashioned side boxes, proscenium stages and the latest in 1960s technology. We consult on theatres in Leatherhead, Derby, Swindon, Warwick, and elsewhere.

Then a big change. Colin George, director of the existing proscenium Sheffield Playhouse, approaches me to join the team for his new Sheffield **Crucible**. This is to be a real thrust stage, highly controversial at the time, as the argument rages between supporters of the proscenium versus new-fangled 'open stage'. Colin directly approaches Tyrone Guthrie to advise him, and Tanya Moiseiwitsch is engaged as designer. Sir Laurence (for whom I am lighting *Three Sisters*) gives me a glowing reference… and we are off! Tanya immediately guides us toward the essential proportions of the 'Guthrie' stage that had been so misunderstood at **Chichester** (1962), which was too wide, flat and lacking in focus. With architects Renton Howard Wood, led by partner Nick Thompson, we achieve at Sheffield what Guthrie himself considered, before his death, to be his best thrust-stage theatre.

The Old Birmingham Rep, 1953

The New Birmingham Rep

Thorndike Theatre, Leatherhead. 1969

Forum Theatre, Billingham, 1967

1.2 British Playhouse Design 47

1958 cont...

The Ubiquitous Fan – Izenour and the Engineered Rational Theatres

The overwhelming competition from cinema and radio, later joined by television, buries much theatre and vaudeville activity. Perhaps cinema's most pernicious influence is upon the design of the theatres that are built between the 1930s and the 1970s. Wagner's frontal theatre, the new 'art theatre' form, and the movie palace combine to support the design of fan-shaped auditoria with blank side walls, so-called 'perfect' sightlines and at most, a single balcony. The 'rational' theatres advocated by American theatre engineer George Izenour offered 'engineered' sightlines, but resulted in spaces that now seem quite alien to human communication.

'Equality,' with all seats on one or, at most, two levels, all sharing an equal view of the stage, seems to actually be very unequal – unless you are seated near the front.

German Reconstruction – 'Improved' Sightlines Versus The Golden Horseshoe

After World War II, the Germans embark – astonishingly – on an orgy of theatre building. Unlike perhaps any other nation on earth, rebuilding their theatres becomes their highest priority. Most are to be theatres for opera and ballet with a smaller drama house attached, all built by the state on a scale unimaginable in Britain.

Some seek to develop a modern equivalent to the classic horseshoe opera by lining the side walls with ski-slope blocks of side seating, facing toward a flexible proscenium zone and massively mechanised stages. A later generation in cities such as Munich and Dresden find something missing with these 'modern' manifestations of theatre form, and return to the classic encircling horseshoe of tradition.

The Mermaid Solution

In contrast, in London the **Mermaid Theatre** (architect Elidir Davies) opens in 1959. This causes a sensation, for it is a simple one-level, 500-seat open-end stage, built within a renovated, brick-walled warehouse that had been bombed during the war. It seems to be everything that the new future needed: no old-fashioned picture frame proscenium; no stupid, old-fashioned balconies and boxes; social equality with everybody on one level of seating. The modern theatre person's dream. Nobody seems to notice that it is even better if you have a seat closer to the stage. But a rough brick enclosure seems to bring some special quality of experience, an informality long lost to the traditional theatre. Thus begins the move toward the 'found space,' out of which comes the multiple excitements of fringe theatre that are to change the theatre world out of all recognition.

Unknown auditorium with engineered sightlines

Ski-slope boxes at Cologne's Oper der Stadt

1960

Theatre Design

So this is the climate of theatre design by the 1960s, when work starts on what will finally become the National Theatre. Guthrie and his thrust stage revival, which seeks to break out of the proscenium picture frame and bring the performers into the audience, is striving to recapture the excitement of 'classic' intimate theatre. This also creates a new interest in arena, in-the-round and the open stage.

An important moment at the very beginning of the NT's design is when Sir Laurence leads a group of company actors to several West End theatres. One by one, the actors and 'Sir' perform a Shakespeare soliloquy onstage, while we run out with tape measures. Finally, Sir Laurence decides that he cannot act to anyone who is seated more than 65 feet (19.8 metres) away. This dimension drives the quantity of seats and ultimate shape of the two main theatres, the **Olivier** and **Lyttelton**. We establish the distance to the farthest seat, but – sadly for posterity – we actually miss the most important point: distance to the farthest seat does not determine a good theatre. It is how many people can be brought as close to the actor as possible that is the root of intimacy. This is the legacy that theatrical tradition left us but which, through lack of understanding, we abandoned.

The Mermaid Theatre, London, 1959

48   A Sense of Theatre

> "Blazing away out there are the spirits of Burbage, Garrick, Kean, and Irving, lighting the theatrical sky forever. Smiling, grinning, laughing, and saying, 'follow that!!!' "
>
> Laurence Olivier

Sir Laurence Olivier
(1907-1989)

Follow that, Sir Laurence surely did. He become one of the most acclaimed actors of his generation, arguably of the 20th century, his work commanding the stage like those greats before him, but also the new mediums of film and, later, television. Like those others he so admired, he was never content with merely appearing in the show: he also became one of the greatest actor-director-managers.

He began performing at school: an early appearance as Brutus impressed an audience that included Ellen Terry. After attending the Central School he found work for companies including the Birmingham Rep, and quickly became the leading man in the debuts of new plays including *Journey's End*, and Noël Coward's *Private Lives*.

The movies came calling in 1931; he did not make an immediate breakthrough but would return to enormous acclaim in films such as *Wuthering Heights* and then Alfred Hitchcock's *Rebecca*. Later he would also direct movies, including the World War II *Henry V*. As the war ended, he found himself part of a triumvirate running the Old Vic for three seasons, including a tour of Australia and New Zealand.

Sir Laurence had a knack for knowing when to reinvent himself, taking the lead in John Osborne's play *The Entertainer* for the Royal Court in 1957 then appearing in Stanley Kubrick's film *Spartacus*. In 1961 he took the directorship of the new Chichester Festival Theatre, positioning himself perfectly for the arrival of the National. After his time at the National his health declined, but he continued to appear on film and in television productions such as *Brideshead Revisited*.

Sir Laurence and his contemporaries Ralph Richardson and John Gielgud perhaps represented the last of a particular era of theatre performance style, originally playing to audiences not used to the camera's close-up. As directors they were the last generation who had directly overseen every aspect of their productions, including lighting - but Sir Laurence happily embraced what a new wave of specialists, such as myself, could bring to their productions.

Photographs of Sir Laurence, in his prime and as his younger self, watch over the National's backstage scenic roadway

> "My sister shelters a large wooden packing case that was my first stage when I was almost six. I used to draw curtains in front of it. My father always brought gold flake cigarettes in fifties, in circular tins, and I would put candles in each so that I'd have my own footlights.
>
> "There it was, lit by candles in cigarette tins: the first Olivier Theatre."
>
> Laurence Olivier

The Old Vic, 1963

1.3 A Company of Players

Laurence Olivier
NT Director 1963-1973

Sir Laurence – on watch

Only Sir Laurence Olivier could create such a company of actors in such a theatrically eclectic environment.

In 1963 Lilian Baylis' dream, the Old Vic, is transformed into the new NT: *Hamlet, Uncle Vanya, Othello, The Royal Hunt of the Sun, Love for Love, Rosencrantz and Guildenstern are Dead,* and *The Front Page* exemplify an exceptionally creative period. The Young Vic is created by Frank Dunlop.

Contemporary backstage scenes captured by photographer Chris Arthur illustrate this chapter.

Laurence Olivier
"Larry had a real, almost an idealistic young man's dream about a national theatre, peopled by the best actors in the world doing the best plays in the world. Nobody can talk about those days at the Vic without a catch in the throat and a furtive tear. Are we being elegiac – too adulatory? Perhaps, but those were heady times."
Director Peter Wood [115]

"1963 was a momentous year in myriad ways. There was a sense of an old order crumbling: the pathetic charade of the Profumo scandal, with its lies, evasions and hints of orgies in high-class places, made the British establishment into a laughing stock. But it was also a period of creative excitement: of, as Philip Larkin famously noted, the Beatles' first LP; of Joan Littlewood's *Oh, What A Lovely War!*, which saw the 1914-18 conflict from the perspective of the common soldier; of a new view of the Cold War reflected in Le Carré's *The Spy Who Came in from the Cold*."
Michael Billington, *The Guardian* [116]

Introducing Chris Arthur
I first met Chris in 1957 when he was a student at Wimbledon School of Art, then again when he was a member of the wonderful Old Vic lighting department as the National began. It was soon evident that Chris was also a brilliant photographer, with an uncanny ability to capture informal backstage portraits that uniquely illustrate the extraordinary period in theatre history: the ten-year reign of Sir Laurence that laid the foundation for our National Theatre.

Chris' talent soon found him a career as a professional photographer, with an extraordinary range of work from theatre productions to portraiture to architecture. His work has been selected for a number of exhibitions; notably the 2013 show *Chris Arthur: Scenes from National Life* that was seen by over 40,000 people.

Views of the Old Vic auditorium

Lighting *Back to Methuselah* with portable stalls lighting desk

A Sense of Theatre

Not Enough Room at The Old Vic

There was no room at The Old Vic to house the offices of the new National Theatre Company. Instead on an old bomb site in Aquinas Street, about a ten-minute walk away – complete with rubble, nettles, brambles and feral cats – a row of building contractors' wooden weatherboarded prefabricated huts was occupied. In these 'elegant' surroundings were a rehearsal room and rows of far-from-soundproof offices. Sir Laurence's office was adjacent to the main entrance, from where he could keep a beady eye out for who was doing what to whom! The huts were like a Royal Navy barracks where Olivier acted like the captain of the ship. He loved the thunder of feet on the companionway. Kenneth Tynan remembered, "One has the sense of participating in the theatrical equivalent of the Battle of Britain."[117]

Sir Laurence picked carefully and seemingly sought out people who would not roll over to his every whim. Directors John Dexter and William Gaskill joined him from the Royal Court. The casting was strong, with stars such as Peter O'Toole (to play Hamlet) and Michael Redgrave alongside the as yet not-so-well-known Robert Stephens, Derek Jacobi, John Stride, Frank Finlay, Ronald Pickup, Geraldine McEwan and Michael Gambon. This was a tightly knit ensemble, taking inspiration from their leader even if they didn't always immediately recognise him. "Many are the junior members of the company who, while grabbing a rapid lunch in the canteen, were disconcerted and delighted to find a rather undistinguished-looking and bespectacled middle-aged man settle beside them and to realise that God had come down to earth."[118]

At the Old Vic, modifications were made for the arrival of the National Theatre under the eye of designer Sean Kenny. Sean and I together with my business partner, sound designer David Collison, had worked together on the Lionel Bart musical *Blitz!* Now we set about renovating the Vic. The forestage was extended far into the front stalls, with a brown double proscenium looming overhead. A new khaki-coloured festoon house curtain, affectionately nicknamed after a pair of Women's Army pantaloons, filled the opening and was intended to be lifted by an electric motor. This mechanism was somewhat temperamental and Sir Laurence was not adverse to assisting the crew, manually winching it out to allow the play to proceed. New lighting and sound controls, by David and me, were installed in the front-of-house. In later years, Sir Laurence was reported to have regretted the extent of the forestage. "Much further and we'd have been playing in The Cut! [the street outside]."

Aquinas Street

Rehearsal room at Aquinas Street

The fly floor at the Old Vic

1.3 A Company of Players

Key Moments

After a lifetime fighting for the NT, Lord Esher dies two weeks before the opening of the first production, Hamlet.

1963
22nd October
The National's first production opens at the Old Vic – *Hamlet*, directed by Laurence Olivier, stars Peter O'Toole. *The Recruiting Officer*, directed by William Gaskill, follows. The shows all play in repertoire.

1964
The first premiere of a new play, Peter Shaffer's *The Royal Hunt of the Sun,* directed by John Dexter, with Robert Stephens and Colin Blakely.

Continuing in a tradition from Burbage, Kean, Garrick, Irving, and his contemporaries, Gielgud, Scofield and Orson Wells, Olivier creates Othello as a black man through make-up and a bravuro performance.

"It was like watching Shakespeare by lightning bolts." Peter Shaffer *Telegraph Weekend Magazine*, 1988.

1965
September
Tour to Moscow's Kremlevsky Teatr with *Othello, Love for Love* and *Hobson's Choice.*

1966
Peter Shaffer's *Black Comedy* and Strindberg's *Miss Julie. A Flea In Her Ear,* directed by Jacques Charon.

1967
Tom Stoppard's *Rosencrantz and Guildenstern are Dead* premieres at the Old Vic, and transfers to the Alvin Theatre, New York.

1967
The NT board, led by Lord Chandos, cancels a production of Rolf Hochhuth's *Soldiers,* a play about World War II and Churchill's role in the bombing of Dresden, that had been promoted by Ken Tynan. This exacerbates tensions between Sir Laurence and Chandos.

1968
Peter Brook's controversial *Oedipus,* with Sir John Gielgud.

1969
Peter Nichols' *The National Health*, directed by Michael Blakemore.

1970
The success of the NT generates a financial surplus that is used to fund Frank Dunlop's plan for building the Young Vic Theatre. Sir Laurence is made a life peer, the first such honour given to an actor.

1971
The National overreaches itself. Seasons at the Cambridge and New Theatres in the West End generate losses; only *Long Day's Journey Into Night,* with Olivier as James Tyrone, reverses the decline.

Sir Max Rayne (later Lord Rayne) succeeds Lord Chandos as chairman of the NT board.

Othello by William Shakespeare with Laurence Olivier. Kremlevsky Teatr, Moscow, 1965.

1972
Four productions at the Old Vic support a recovery: *The School for Scandal*, *The Front Page*, *Jumpers* and *Equus,* directed by Jonathan Miller, Michael Blakemore, Peter Wood and John Dexter respectively.

1973
Trevor Griffiths' *The Party* features Sir Laurence's last performance on stage. Peter Hall, former director of the RSC, succeeds him as director of the NT.

Hamlet

By William Shakespeare
The Old Vic
22nd October 1963

Director: Laurence Olivier
Production design: Sean Kenny
Costumes: Desmond Heeley
Lighting: Richard Pilbrow
Sound: David Collison
Production photographer: Angus McBean

"The National Theatre that opened to a star-studded audience last week is the Old Vic with a new coat of paint; and its first production, Hamlet, what else? It is played up and down a marvellous set by Sean Kenny, an ominous wedge of rock curled around the circumference of the revolving stage. Add to this a sumptuous range of costumes by Desmond Heeley, and the subtle and sympathetic lighting by Richard Pilbrow, and you have a production as visually satisfying as you could ask."
B.A. Young
The Financial Times, 23rd October 1963

"After a wait of 100 years this will do for a start."
Bernard Levin
Daily Mail, 23rd October 1963

Uncle Vanya

By Anton Chekhov
Chichester Festival Theatre and The Old Vic
The Old Vic: 19th November 1963

Director: Laurence Olivier
Production design: Sean Kenny
Costumes: Beatrice Dawson
Lighting: John B. Read / Leonard Tucker
Production photographer: Angus McBean

"The most purely moving presentation of this tough and exquisite play I ever saw. Michael Redgrave's self-wasted landowner has haunted me through the years – surrounded as he was by great (not merely good) actors in an exterior set of a dacha by Sean Kenny, which a mere change of lighting turned into a convincing Russian interior."
Peter Shaffer
Telegraph Weekend Magazine, 1988

"The supreme achievement of the contemporary English stage."
Harold Hobson
The Sunday Times

The Recruiting Officer

By George Farquhar
The Old Vic
10th December 1963

Director: William Gaskill
Production design: Rene Allio
Lighting: Richard Pilbrow
Production photographer: Lewis Morley

"Gaskill has directed [this] mixture of near farce and biting comment with a touch that keeps the play spinning along, the wit shines, the broad humour is full of vitality… Fine shaping and weaving of motivation, character, fun and seriousness that make [the play] a classic work."
R.B. Marriott
The Stage

"Every scene on this stage acquired an air of sharpened reality, like life on a winter's day with frost and sun."
Bamber Gascoigne

The Royal Hunt of the Sun

By Peter Shaffer
Chichester Festival Theatre and The Old Vic
Chichester: 7th July 1964

Director: John Dexter
Production design: Michael Annals
Lighting: Brian Freeland
Production photographer: Angus McBean

"Only a subsidised theatre could have properly presented my play concerning the conquest of Peru, thereby assuaging in me a huge longing to help rekindle the fire of epic theatre in England. I believe John Dexter agreed to direct it mainly because of the instruction in the script 'the soldiers now climb the Andes'. In the process he provided audiences with the most tremendous essay in Total Theatre. I recall the sighs of disappointment coming from a sophisticated English audience when the corpse of Robert Stephens's golden Inca remained unmoving. In that moment a beam of electric light actually touched the nerve of Theatre."
Peter Shaffer
Telegraph Weekend Magazine, 1988

"A virtuoso production in a dazzlingly bold design of a darkly questioning play, cast in epic form, performed by a company at a peak of physical fitness."
Simon Callow
The National: the Theatre and its Work

Love for Love

By William Congreve
Kremlevsky Teatr, Moscow and The Old Vic
Kremlevsky Teatr: 20th October 1965

Director: Peter Wood
Production design: Lila de Nobili
Lighting: Richard Pilbrow.
Production photographer: Zoë Dominic

"I believe Peter Wood to be the best director of Restoration comedy we have. The set was by Lila de Nobili and was laid boldly out-of-doors, defying the confinement of boudoirs and cabinets. I recall best Lynn Redgrave's bouncy Prue, Miles Malleson's incomparably doddering old Foresight, and Colin Blakely's stalwart sailor Ben."
Peter Shaffer
Telegraph Weekend Magazine, 1988

Rosencrantz and Guildenstern are Dead

By Tom Stoppard
The Old Vic and Alvin Theatre, New York
The Old Vic: 11th November 1967

Director: Derek Goldby
Production design: Desmond Heeley
Lighting: Richard Pilbrow
Production photographer: Anthony Crickmay

"This is the NT's biggest gamble to date… and, praised be to audacity, it wins at 66 to 1. We have a stunning new playwright."
Peter Lewis
Daily Mail

"The most important event in the British professional theatre of the last nine years."
Harold Hobson
The Sunday Times

"A most remarkable and thrilling play."
Clive Barnes
New York Times

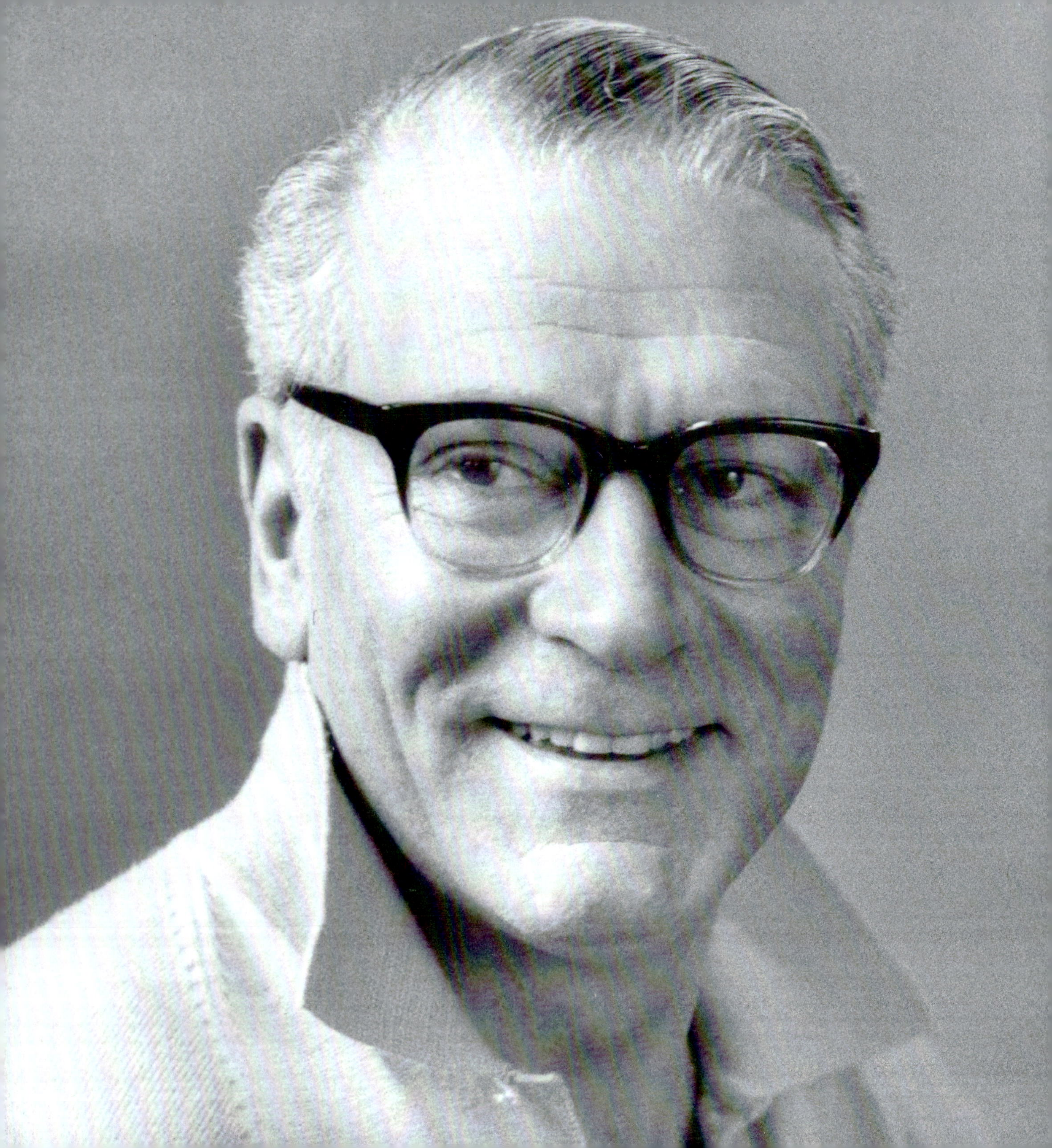

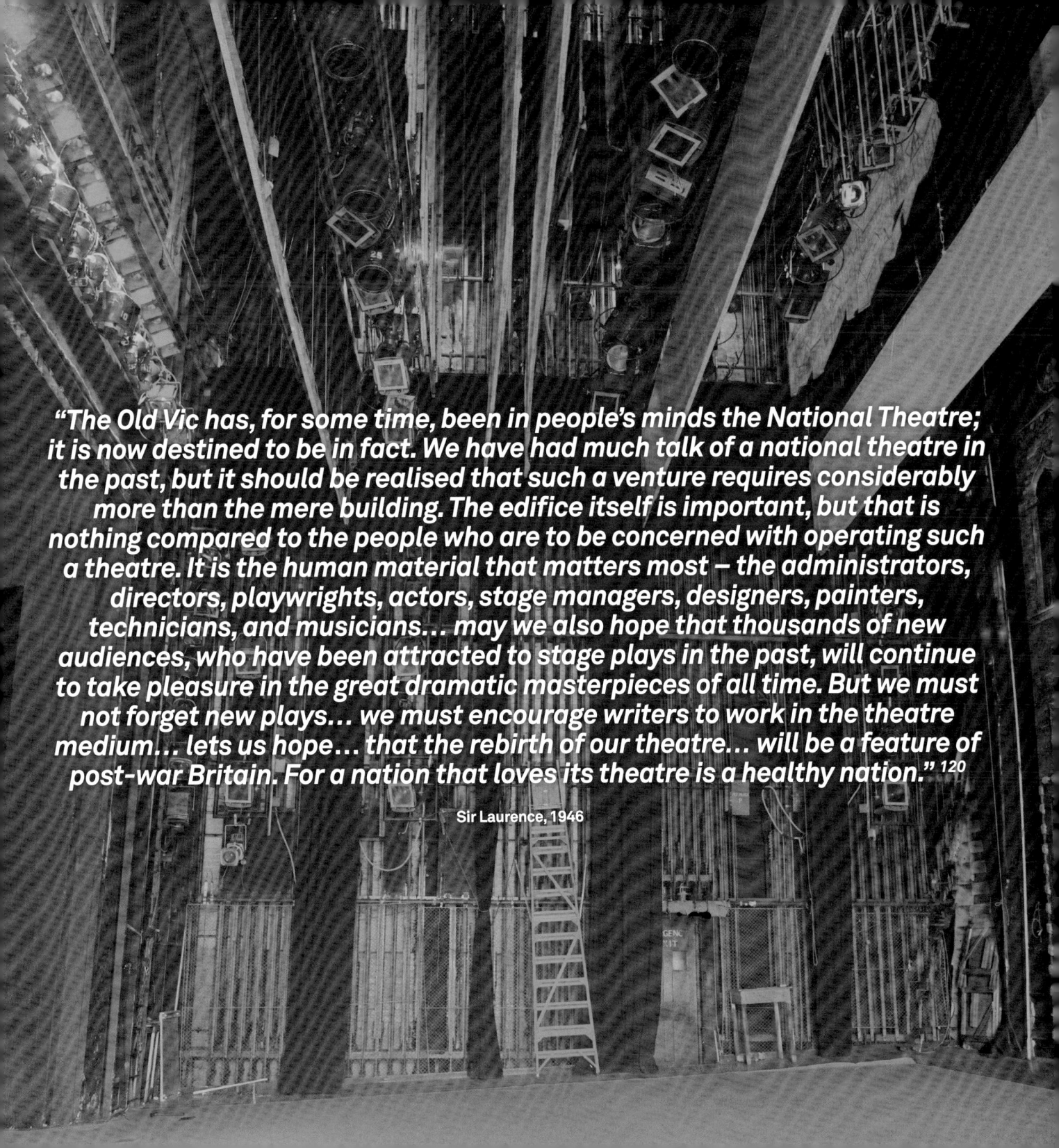

"The Old Vic has, for some time, been in people's minds the National Theatre; it is now destined to be in fact. We have had much talk of a national theatre in the past, but it should be realised that such a venture requires considerably more than the mere building. The edifice itself is important, but that is nothing compared to the people who are to be concerned with operating such a theatre. It is the human material that matters most – the administrators, directors, playwrights, actors, stage managers, designers, painters, technicians, and musicians… may we also hope that thousands of new audiences, who have been attracted to stage plays in the past, will continue to take pleasure in the great dramatic masterpieces of all time. But we must not forget new plays… we must encourage writers to work in the theatre medium… lets us hope… that the rebirth of our theatre… will be a feature of post-war Britain. For a nation that loves its theatre is a healthy nation." [120]

Sir Laurence, 1946

Rupert Rhymes – House Manager

Tom Gillon – Property Master

Pat Leighton – Box Office (right, back to camera)

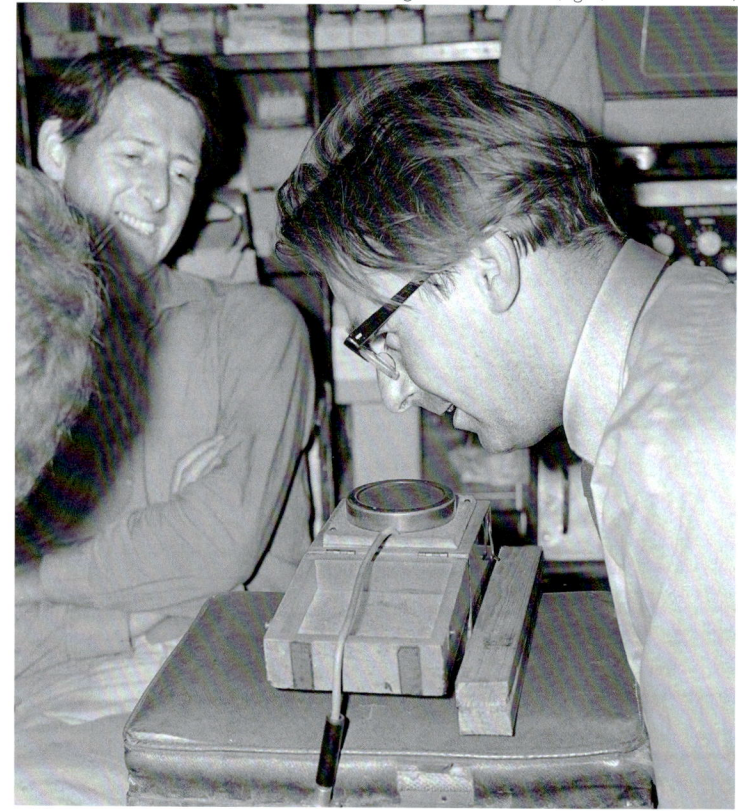

The young Michael Gambon – Actor

Ronald Cox and Leonard Tucker – Lighting

A Sense of Theatre

Lynn Holm and Jennifer Carveth – Wigs

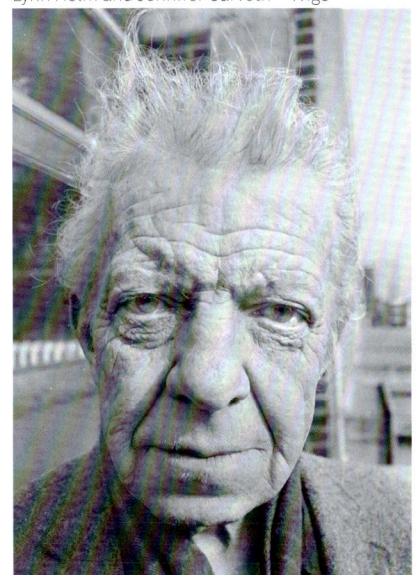

Roger Ramsdell – Painter

Harry Henderson – Housekeeper

Fred Taylor – Master Carpenter

Diana Boddington – Stage Manager

Ernie Davis – Stage Door Keeper

1.3 A Company of Players

Backstage: Olivier Remembered

How to convey the absolute magic of those golden days? I remember only a blur of frenzied, exhilarating activity – one of the most exciting episodes in my entire life. Moving shows from Chichester to the Old Vic was a thrilling lighting experience. Three-dimensional light demanded by the thrust stage proved equally relevant to the proscenium; 3D light for the living actor in a way that was unprecedented in the early 1960s. And acclaim and recognition for what we were achieving.

Sir Laurence was our leader. We would do anything for this man.

"In the beginning it was great fun. We were at the Old Vic and had offices and a canteen in huts in Waterloo. We thought the new building would be open in about three years. In the end it took thirteen." [121]
William Gaskill (associate director of the National Theatre, 1963-1965)

"The ones he liked best were the old actor laddie jokes, like the actor playing Richard III to whom someone in the gallery shouted, 'You're drunk!' 'You think I'm drunk?' the villainous king wandered unsteadily down to the footlights to enquire. 'Well, wait till you've seen the Duke of Buckingham!' It was stories like that which made him laugh most, and he would laugh until the tears came to his eyes and his voice rose to a high tenor note of delight." [122]
John Mortimer (translated *A Flea In Her Ear* for the National at The Old Vic, 1966; National Theatre board 1967-1989)

"I'm not sure if Larry had such a thing as an 'aesthetic.' What attracted him were bloody good plays, wonderful, theatrical situations – something to keep the audience awake at night. He belonged to an earlier age when the actor's art was to celebrate, and he looked at plays with the attitude of the vanished West End." [123]
Peter Wood (directed Olivier at the Old Vic in *The Master Builder* and *Love for Love*)

"He had an amazing ability to know everyone who worked for him – he knew all the birthdays of the stage staff. He was the governor, and everyone respected and loved him." [124]
Anthony Hopkins (member of the acting company at the Old Vic, 1965-72)

"He was the most specific technician of any director I ever met. He knew how to build a crew around him in whom he had faith. I had a love for him almost as deep as for my family. What more could one want? He basked in my spotlight and I basked in his." [125]
Leonard Tucker (National Theatre lighting manager, 1963-85)

"He was the sort of bloke that if another war started, you would willingly say: 'That's it. I'll go anywhere with him.' You'd be safe with him. He was a gentleman and an ordinary chap." [126]
Harry Henderson (housekeeper for the National Theatre at the Old Vic, 1963-76)

"He was always very interested in the returns – particularly if he was appearing in that night's show. He would go onstage for his first scene, have a squint around the auditorium and, a few minutes later, the internal phone would go, and it would be Sir Laurence asking for the night's figures. The thing was, sometimes he would find it difficult to come out of character during the show – so in *Long Days' Journey*, say, he'd ring with his American accent, and the next night I'd have Shylock on the end of the line, asking why there were six empty seats in Row O." [127]
Tom Pate (theatre manager for the National Theatre, 1969-79)

"He had an extraordinary ability to retain information and was concerned about every department–every area of the National. Everything had to be discussed in minute detail, especially the actors' salaries, the allocation of dressing rooms and, of course, casting. He even took an interest in the colour of the leaflets. He insisted on red and green for the Christmas season. Purple, of course, was his favourite colour." [128]
Michael Hallifax (executive company manager for the National Theatre from 1966-74; later company administrator)

"In his office at the National Theatre, he had a picture of Henry Irving, who in the 19th century rescued the theatre and returned it to its proper status as one of the great arts. Larry had worked for Lilian Baylis when Tyrone Guthrie was director of the company at the Old Vic. Guthrie firmly believed that theatre could be about things other than money and success – it could be part of what one might call The Good Fight. That tradition informed and fed Olivier throughout his career." [129]

Michael Blakemore (directed Olivier in *Long Day's Journey into Night*; associate director of the National Theatre, 1971-1976)

"He wasn't a cosy actor. He fought for the 'language' in my play. He told me, 'You've got to remember this is the first time the word cunt has ever been uttered on the stage of the National Theatre.' I said, 'You're not serious?' He said, 'Well, at least as part of the play.' " [130]

Trevor Griffiths (author of *The Party*)

"He epitomised English theatre more than any other performer and seemed to represent England rather like Winston Churchill did. He rose to his finest hour at our finest hour. He was a father to the company in every sense of the word – positive and negative. Working in those sheds in Aquinas Street was like being in a small airfield or naval station of which he was Commanding Officer.

"No one ever addressed him as Lord Olivier. His secretary and many of his staff called him Sir Laurence. He never bridled at being called Larry. Most people referred to him as Sir. He was surprisingly anonymous in public life. Then he underwent this werewolf change when he went on stage and something fierce, distinctive and alarming appeared." [131]

Jonathan Miller (associate director of the National Theatre, 1973-1975)

[Recalling Franco Zeffirelli on Olivier's performance in *Othello*]:
"I was told that this was the last flourish of the romantic tradition of acting. It's nothing of the sort. It's an anthology of everything that has been discovered about acting in the last three centuries. It's grand and majestic, but it's also modern and realistic. I would call it a lesson for us all." [132]

Kenneth Tynan (literary manager of the National Theatre from 1963-1969; literary consultant 1969-1973)

Making up

Geraldine McEwan, Robert Long, Jacques Charon, Laurence Olivier

1.3 A Company of Players

The Young Vic: "To the Old Vic, A Son." [133]

Frank Dunlop was administrative director of the NT from 1967 to 1971. He was born in Leeds, England, and studied with Michel Saint-Denis at the Old Vic Theatre School in London.

With designer Richard Negri, Frank founded and directed his own theatre company, The Piccolo Theatre, in Manchester in 1954. He became resident director at the Bristol Old Vic in 1955 and ran the Nottingham Playhouse from 1961 to 1964.

In 1967, he joined the National Theatre as associate director and was administrative director from 1968 to 1971. In 1969, while at the National and under its auspices, he created the Young Vic, aiming to attract a new, younger audience. The Young Vic Theatre became an independent body in 1974. Frank went on to run the Edinburgh Festival from 1984 to 1991. He was appointed CBE in 1977 and received the Chevalier of the Order of Arts and Letters, presented to him by the French Government in 1987.[134]

"While in college I had a tutor, Professor Terence Spencer, later to be chair of the Shakespeare Institute, who excited my interest in the Elizabethan theatre. Together we drew out the dimensions of the Elizabethan Fortune Playhouse. When I began on the Young Vic, the Fortune influenced my decision to add a gallery to the thrust stage. Thus I suppose I became the true originator of the modern galleried 'courtyard' theatre.

"For the Young Vic, I was working with designers Carl Toms and Patrick Robertson. Patrick introduced me to Bill Howell, who became the architect. It was a tremendously collaborative relationship. Patrick, Bill and I agreed entirely about the primacy of the human actor and the human voice.

"McAlpine's [the construction company that would build the National] bid for the Young Vic was very high, so Bill introduced a church builder from Birmingham, who won the contract. The building was on budget and constructed in nine months. I remember ringing you to get some lighting before the opening of *Scapino*. The acoustics proved to be superb.

"I loved the original Young Vic's red-coloured balconies. The

Director Michael Bogdanov rehearsing the *Action Man Trilogy* (*Hamlet, Richard III and The Tempest*) at the Young Vic in 1978.

renovation has lost much of that popular feel in the more muted decoration. I am disappointed by the renovation. It was ridiculous to add another balcony level for technology and not for audience (as I had originally hoped for). The theatre now has too much volume and the acoustics have suffered.

"When I ran the Nottingham Playhouse, through its opening, I had Peter Ustinov and Tyrone Guthrie as associates. We discussed the Old Vic School and the Young Vic, the closure of which I thought was disastrous. We discussed Guthrie's role in that debacle. I thought Guthrie regretted his part in the closures. I thought that Llewellyn Rees was a self-opinionated fraud, who was to blame for the collapse of the school and Young Vic Company.

"I feel strongly influenced by the Old Vic School, and loved the Young Vic Company that led me to the later naming of the Young Vic Theatre. The aim of the theatre was to appeal to a younger audience.

"I was close to Lord Chandos, who supported me at the NT. I know of a letter from Chandos to [fellow board member] Kenneth Clark saying Frank was one of the few people who can deal with Olivier."

Lasdun and the Young Vic

The design and construction of the Young Vic seems something of a miracle – achieved in months instead of the years it took to design and then build the National Theatre on the South Bank. Frank drove the entire process – and incurred the displeasure of Denys Lasdun, by then appointed the National's architect, along the way.

21st May 1968, Dunlop writes to Lasdun:
"You may have read in the Press that we are thinking of building a temporary Young People's Theatre on a bomb-site near the Old Vic. I have assumed that it is to be built very fast and your firm would have quite enough on their hands. I hope this is not treading on your toes. I met Mr. Bill Howell last week and he is very interested. I know he is a great friend and admirer of yours and I'm asking the Board to approve his appointment. Do let me know if you have any suggestions." [135]

23rd May 1968, Lasdun's notes on telephone call with Dunlop: "Regarded his letter as impertinent and discourteous. It is not up to him to assess the capacity of DL&P, nor should he have approached another architect without reference to this office. The Youth Theatre, which will be up for at least four years, is to be used as a test for the main theatre. He expects DL&P to discuss the shape of the stage, etc., with the other architect and this can only sow confusion to an already intolerable situation, since it will involve not only ourselves but consultants, etc. DL told Dunlop that he would be getting in touch with the Board directly and would not reply to his letter." [136]

23rd May 1968, Dunlop to Lasdun: "Thank you for your phone call. My letter was intended as a polite one. I do realise that it might have been better if you could have been informed earlier. However, the plans came to a head quickly and there was a great deal of urgency. The building has to be up by next Christmas. As this temporary building has no official link whatsoever with the South Bank scheme, I do not consider our action has been as despicable as you seem to think.

"I hope this disagreement does not affect our abilities to work together in the future. Certainly I won't let it affect me."

> "I was always dreaming of marching my little troupe up the road but that wasn't for me. I was hoping to feel a glow of satisfaction but I was so tired out, I was just glad to let it go." [139]
> Laurence Olivier

Olivier – A Farewell Fanfare
"The blazing success of [Olivier's] tenure was like a glorious and sustained fanfare for the more measured and solid achievements that were to follow."
Simon Callow [137]

"Treachery of the Highest Order"
"A combination of Olivier's poor health and a grumbling dissatisfaction with a string of failures at the New Theatre led to a search for a new director. And, at this point, the story gets somewhat murky. What seems to have happened is that the NT's chairman, Max Rayne, and that Richelieu of the London arts scene, Lord Goodman, sounded out Peter Hall as a successor to Olivier. Hall, sworn to secrecy, behaved perfectly honourably and said he would take over only with Olivier's consent. But, in the end, Olivier was confronted with a fait accompli and felt he had been stitched up. It's a situation that rankles to this day, as is clear from a first-rate, two-part BBC Arena documentary in which Joan Plowright (Lady Olivier) talks darkly of 'treachery of the highest order.'"
Michael Billington
The Guardian [138]

National Theatre: architects and discarded models (front: Malcolm Minjoodt and Philip Wood – modelmaker; mid: Peter Softley, Theo de Rouw; rear: Denys Lasdun)

Part Two

The Minutes: Design

The minutes of the National Theatre Building Committee, a body created by Sir Laurence to create the brief for the building and guide the architect. An architect is chosen because he promised to come entirely fresh to the theatre as a building form. The minutes are accompanied with contemporaneous notes of backstage discussions with the participants.

London's South Bank at the time of the Festival of Britain in the early 1950s, showing the Dome of Discovery on one of the sites later proposed for the National Theatre, the Skylon, the Royal Festival Hall and, just behind the glowing white Waterloo Bridge, the final site of the National Theatre

2.1 Beginnings

**Finding An Architect
Meetings #1-14**

How it could have been: 1943 County of London plan for the South Bank

Astonishingly, the newly formed National Theatre Building Committee is given just six weeks to write the brief for the long-awaited new theatres. Four previous National Theatre schemes are cast aside, unexamined. Almost immediately confusion reigns: what is a theatre? Are there to be one or two auditoria? Thrust, proscenium, or multiform? How might an architect be chosen? How might the architectural mistakes of the past be avoided?

The Two Boards
In 1962 two boards were formed. The first – the South Bank Theatre and Opera House Board – to build our new National Theatre and originally, as the title suggests, a new opera house alongside it. The other – the National Theatre Board – to operate the new company, initially at the Old Vic and, eventually, in the new building.

The terms of reference are dated 13th August 1962. They include: "Submit for the approval of the Government and the London County Council plans for the erection on the South Bank of an amphitheatre auditorium for the National Theatre and an opera house to replace Sadler's Wells for the opera company [that later became the English National Opera]... for a capital sum not to exceed £2.3m in all. To be responsible for building [the same] and to advise how, when built, it should be used." [1]

On 10th October 1962, after the first Chichester season, Sir Laurence attended his first board meeting as director designate. His salary had been agreed at £5000 per year, which the board described as "very public-spirited, terms far less generous than those he could command elsewhere." [2]

Forgetting the Past
This was to be a new beginning. The four previous attempts at a National Theatre were cast aside. Innumerable committee meetings over fifty years were forgotten. The most obvious casualty in this new pursuit of excellence was the previous architect, Brian O'Rorke, who had battled through the 1950s, attending endless boring meetings and sticking to his post beyond the call of duty. Olivier felt O'Rorke was "a fine architect and a really nice man," but his theatre "lacked, well, some spirituality, shall we say?" [3]

Hindsight suggests that some good things were thrown out with the old. In 1950, an earlier committee planning the O'Rorke theatre stated in its minutes that perfect sightlines were "not possible, except in a fan-shaped theatre, to which the committee has always been strongly opposed, involving as it did the sacrifice of that intimacy, which the committee felt was so desirable." [4] This truly important comment was quite lost in the very fervent 1960s pursuit of the new.

A New Future
Sir Laurence was determined upon a clean slate. To start from scratch in the creation of a new exemplary theatre for the future. This was his driving mission. But how to begin? Always maddeningly uncertain about his own opinions, he sought an advisory committee, representing a cross section of leading thinkers in the theatrical profession, including his rivals from the Royal Shakespeare Company. A 'Theatre Panel,' subject to his approval and that of Norman Marshall (his co-chair), was to be invited "to advise the board on the draft specifications and technical requirements for the National Theatre." [5]

Members of the NT building committee were approved in South Bank Board Minute #42 and included a preponderance of directors: Sir Laurence Olivier and Norman Marshall (joint chairmen) with Michael Benthall, Peter Brook, George Devine, Michael Elliott, Peter Hall and Michel Saint-Denis with designers Roger Furse, Sean Kenny and Tanya Moiseiwitsch. Notably, Sir Laurence was the only actor to be part of the deliberations about these new spaces for actors to work in.

Chichester and the Building Committee
The first meeting of the National Theatre Building Committee took place in January 1963. This followed the previous summer's first Chichester season, on the new thrust stage, with a new company led by Sir Laurence.

During that season, somewhat to his annoyance, his appointment to head the National Theatre had been leaked to the press. Olivier remembered, "An enemy hath done this." [6] (He meant Peter Hall!) He thought it bound to provoke snide criticism for his new Chichester venture.

And, indeed, things began badly. The first two productions chosen and directed by Sir Laurence, the Jacobean plays *The Chances* by the Duke of Buckingham, and *The Broken Heart*, by John Ford, were something of an embarrassment. (The lighting that I had failed to fix had been one of the lesser problems.)

> "The next two years were spent unravelling what did they [the building committee] really mean. There is a document which I hold, which, I suppose when I'm dead and gone, I shall release to the public, of what they all said over two years; fascinating, some of it contradictory, some of it maddening, and some of it so to the point that you had to reread what they said several times until you had got the point. That is the kind of human relationship out of which architecture can spring for me."

Denys Lasdun, recorded interview, 1996

But the third production, also directed by Sir Laurence, saved the day. An incandescently wondrous *Uncle Vanya*, it was perhaps the best production of Chekhov ever staged in Britain. Starring Michael Redgrave and Sir Laurence, with Joan Plowright, Dame Sybil Thorndike and her husband Lewis Casson, it shattered preconceived notions of what type of play might work on a thrust stage.

The South Bank Board was to be responsible for the design and construction of the new National Theatre. Since Olivier was the only actor on the board, he felt his contribution to be particularly significant. Years later, he told Sarah Miles, "No one listened to what I wanted; my way was the only way it could work." [7]

But Olivier was also "deliciously and probably maddeningly vague" [8] over what actually might work. He never seemed quite certain as to the ideal solution. In 1969, a new theatre was being opened in Sheffield (the Crucible Theatre, designed with the guidance of Tyrone Guthrie and Tanya Moiseiwitsch – and your author as theatre consultant). Bernard Miles, founder of the Mermaid Theatre in the City of London, was asked to sponsor that enterprise. He refused,

A Sense of Theatre

indignantly. He protested to Sir Laurence that it was "worse than Chichester. They have even got 40 or 50 seats at the back. All that is required is a glass stage (through which) to look up the girls' skirts!" He sent a copy of the brochure to Olivier. "Here's another FUCKER! Worst of the lot to date. Acting is largely a frontal job, as you well know." Olivier was not sure how well he knew or, indeed, what he knew. It all depended what one meant by "largely." When Miles denounced the enterprise in the newspapers and cited Olivier as being on his side, Olivier took him to task: "Do learn to manage the opening of your pretty mouth with more discretion, dear boy. That was a really shitty note you wrote." Miles replied, "After all, I'm only doing it for you and your doubtless gifted progeny, who will one day be faced with the problems of this stupid, bookish theory."9

Olivier was determined to obtain the best advice that he could. He sought Peter Brook's involvement in his own charmingly idiosyncratic way. On 2nd August 1962, he wrote to Peter: "My dear Peterkin, I am as certain as I can be that your best advice is going to be needed in the planning of the National Theatre and it is with regard to this that I am writing to you now privately, to ask if you would be so very good as to come to Chichester again and see the rest of the stuff. The thing is, it's an experiment and it's a testing ground and it really should be scrutinised carefully and thoughtfully and I would love it to be so scrutinised by you. Please try and come, if you can bear it. Always, with love to you and Natasha, Laurence Olivier." 10

But, at the beginning (and perhaps reflecting his own uncertainty), Olivier had come to the view that one main theatre was what was needed. He sought a new form of theatre, one that might be 'adaptable,' that could somehow combine the refreshing virtues of the open stage at Chichester and the familiarity of the proscenium of the Old Vic.

So, the National Theatre building committee's deliberations began.

I am quoting the record of these meetings almost in full, with only very minor edits for space. Minutes were taken of all the meetings by Yolande Bird, assistant to the secretary, Kenneth Rae. Many meetings reportedly took several hours, and Michael Elliott always told me that he was left with

"Architecture has to begin from some set of ideas. An architect needs to provide for himself the area of certainty within which he can work." 11

Denys Lasdun

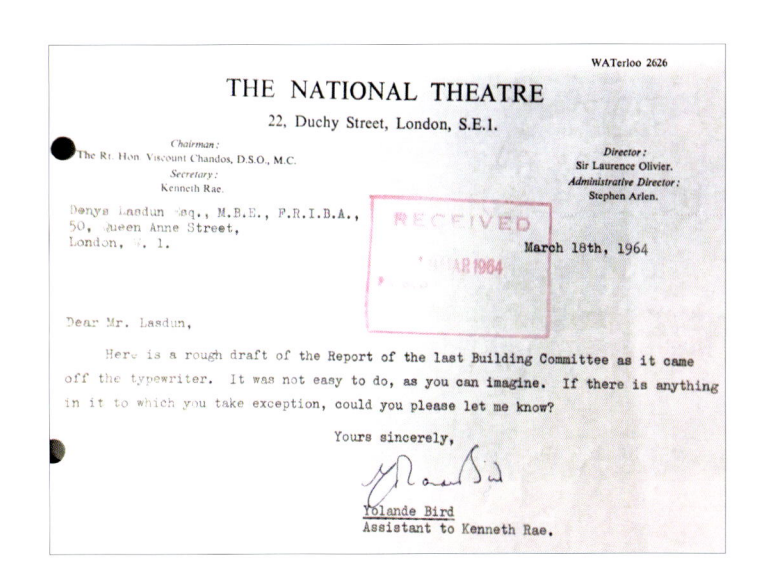

a hangover. These minutes remain the only evidence of their deliberations. In 2015, Yolande herself told me that she distributed the minutes after each meeting for comment, but seldom received back any suggestions or alterations. At the end of each meeting I have added some commentary of my own and extracts from other relevant correspondence, or contemporaneous meeting notes by others, in particular, where relevant, by the architect.

2.1 Beginnings. Finding An Architect: Meetings #1-14

The National Theatre Building Committee

In 1962 Olivier assembled an expert group to advise on the choice of architect, agree the theatrical brief and make real the inspiration for the National Theatre.

Sir Laurence Olivier
(1907-1989) Co-chair

Actor-manager extraordinaire, producer and director. First director of the National Theatre, 1962-1973.
Sir Laurence was a godlike figure to me and to many at the National. While he was clearly the world's greatest actor, he was also a father figure to those in his company. We would do anything for him. As a director, he was decisive and had a great deal of technical theatre knowledge. He was proud of his ability to light his own productions and was both amused and frustrated at how lighting technology was changing, opening the way for lighting designers (like me) to supersede him. His foreword to my 1970 book *Stage Lighting* included some insightful reminiscences and concluded, "The difference is about the same as that of flying before and during the War 'by the seat of your pants' and the technological expertise required for handling the jumbo jets of today." In hindsight, his technical knowledge and vast experience makes it all the more surprising that he appeared so curiously indecisive about his views for the new National Theatre and its architecture.

Norman Marshall
(1901-1980) Co-chair

Director, writer. Worked with innovator Terence Grey in the 1930s. First chairman of the Association of British Theatre Technicians (ABTT).
As a founder of the Association of British Theatre Technicians, I met Norman when he accepted our invitation to become the organisation's first chairman in 1961. At the time, in my ignorance, I hardly knew who he was. I soon learned that he was a man of great common sense and experience. Only later did I understand some part of the role he played in the avant-garde of British theatre in the '30s and his role on previous NT building committees back into the 1940s. Norman was a gentleman, quietly spoken, wise and always reasonable.

Sir Peter Hall
(1930-2017)

Founder and director of the Royal Shakespeare Company (1960-68) and second director of the National Theatre (1973-1988).
Peter was the most ambitious man I ever met. I lit John Mortimer's play *The Wrong Side of The Park* for the very young Peter in 1960. Later shows for his RSC included Vanessa Redgrave's debut in *As You Like It*. I was angered by the way Sir Laurence was shifted aside from the NT's leadership and rather resented Peter for breaking up Sir's 'family.' But Peter did endorse my plans for the NT stages, although he grew angry (with much justification) at the interminable delays. I became the focus of that anger in the horrors surrounding 1976. It was only in the 1990s that he asked me to light *Four Baboons Adoring the Sun,* by John Guare, at the Vivian Beaumont Theater in New York. Working with him again proved a pleasure and any old bitterness vanished as we collaborated on several other productions in the US. Peter always was brilliant with his actors, but, technically, he always seemed surprisingly naive. He seemed to find it impossible to imagine how the stage would actually appear until every single detail was exactly in place.

Peter Brook
(1925-2022)

Director, Royal Shakespeare Company (1962-1970), and of Théâtre des Bouffes du Nord, Paris. Author and guru of theatre space.
Peter was clearly a genius of our theatre world. His productions have inspired and his innate sense of theatre, displayed through his writings and his work, will continue to illuminate the future. Where was his head in 1963? His instincts were usually correct and his search for a new architecture of theatre should have worked more positively alongside Lasdun's brilliance.

George Devine
(1910-1965)

Actor, pioneer lighting designer, director. Founder of the English Stage Company at the Royal Court Theatre. Keenly interested in architecture and a source of inspiration to Denys Lasdun before his premature death in 1965.
I lit *Platanov,* designed by Richard Negri and directed by George, at the Royal Court in 1960. I had no idea then that, before World War II, he had been Britain's leading lighting designer. He was gruff, but amiable, and the experience was good. Of course, I only joined the building committee after his demise, so I can only tell from others of his interest in architecture and his influence on Lasdun.

Michel Saint-Denis
(1897-1971)

Actor, director and educator. Nephew of Jacques Copeau and French theatre pioneer with the Compagnie des Quinze. Founded the London Theatre Studio in 1936 with George Devine and Glen Byam Shaw, all of whom went on in 1946 to create the short-lived Old Vic Centre, which included the Young Vic Company and Old Vic Theatre School. Artistic adviser to the Vivian Beaumont Theater at Lincoln Center in New York.
My close friend, the designer Richard Negri, had studied at the Old Vic Theatre School under George Devine and Michel Saint-Denis. He had the greatest respect for Saint-Denis' grasp of essentials that proved a modest, but important, influence upon the committee.

John Dexter
(1925-1990)

Assistant director of the Royal Court in the 1950s. Associate director, National Theatre (1963-1966), Director of production Metropolitan Opera (1974-1981).
I met John at the Central School of Speech and Drama where, for a short period, he ran the stage management training course, long before he became a celebrated director. Why, at one time, I even briefly shared an apartment with him... an interesting experience! As a director, John could be cruel, caustic, aggressive, but was always brilliant. I lit many shows for John, including the West End musical *Half A Sixpence* and others for the NT at the Old Vic and Chichester Festival Theatre.

The National Theatre Building Committee

William Gaskill
(1930-2016)

Associate director of the National Theatre. Artistic director of Royal Court Theatre (1965-1972). Founder, with director Max Stafford-Clarke, of the Joint Stock Theatre Group (1974).

I lit numerous productions for Bill, including *Richard III* at the RSC and the West End, and *Baal* (both designed by Jocelyn Herbert), where we explored the Brechtian use of white light long before it became so fashionable. For the NT at the Old Vic, our most memorable collaboration was *The Recruiting Officer*.

Michael Elliott
(1931-1984)

Director of 59 Theatre Company and the Old Vic Theatre Company for the latter's final season before the National took over the building. Founder of the Royal Exchange Theatre, Manchester (1962-1963).

Michael, Richard Negri, and I were a close-knit team from the 59 Theatre Company to the RSC, West End, Old Vic and, twenty years later, the Royal Exchange, Manchester. Richard was a small dormouse-like man of profound insights and real genius, while Michael was tall, gaunt, inspiring, and our leader. He was the most brilliant man I ever met and I worshipped him. Michael was the father of Marianne Elliott, the director of many successes for the NT including *War Horse* and *The Curious Incident of the Dog in the Night-Time*.

Michael Benthall
(1919-1974)

Director of the Old Vic Theatre Company (1953-1962). Succeeded in reviving the waning reputation, in the early 50s, of the Old Vic.

I only met Benthall briefly when I lit *Richard II* at the Old Vic with Richard Negri and director Val May. During his reign, I guess, was when I introduced three-dimensional lighting to that venerable theatre.

Michael began a five year programme at the Old Vic in 1953 that included all thirty-six plays in the first folio of Shakespeare, a feat accomplished only once before by the Old Vic, between 1914 and 1923.

Broadway saw some of his earlier work with Shaw's *The Millionairess* and *As You Like It*, both with Katharine Hepburn, and *Antony and Cleopatra* and *Caesar and Cleopatra*, with Sir Laurence Olivier and Vivien Leigh.

Roger Furse
(1903-1972)

Designer for stage and film, friend of Laurence Olivier.

Olivier's *Henry V* was a film emblazoned on my memory. I lit a show for Roger in the West End very early in my career. I was startled by my first viewing of his set – he had left no room for any lighting at all! Did I dare tell such an iconic figure that something had to be changed?

Roger began working as a stage designer in 1934. He joined the navy at the outbreak of World War II. In 1943 he was granted a temporary release to design the *Henry V* film.

He won two Oscars in 1949, for his art direction and costume design of Olivier's *Hamlet* (1948). He also worked with Olivier on his films *Richard III* (1955) and *The Prince and the Showgirl* (1957).

Sean Kenny
(1932-1973)

Designer who sprung to prominence with Lionel Bart's *Oliver!* and *Blitz!* Trained as an architect under Frank Lloyd Wright. Responsible for remodelling the Old Vic for the NT in 1969.

I met Sean on *Blitz!*, the Lionel Bart musical about the Nazi bombing of London. It was an amazing spectacle, perhaps more spectacular than any ever staged since. Sean was a wild Irishman with the gift of the blarney above all else… but what an imagination!

As a theatre designer, Sean was responsible for the concept designs of the New London Theatre, Drury Lane, London (now the Gillian Lynne Theatre) and the Sussex University Gardner Arts Centre.

Tanya Moiseiwitsch
(1914-2003)

Designer, collaborator with Tyrone Guthrie on development of thrust stages at Stratford, Ontario; Minneapolis, Minnesota; and Sheffield, UK.

I had the honour of lighting several plays for Tanya and she taught me how to handle "bright white light" for Tyrone Guthrie. She became a good friend and we collaborated on realising the Crucible Theatre in Sheffield.

Richard Pilbrow

From meeting #24.

Lighting designer, producer, theatre design consultant. Founder of Theatre Projects. Lighting design supervisor to the National Theatre 1963-1969.

I began my career as an Assistant Stage Manager at Her Majesty's Theatre in London, a theatre that I was to return to many times over as a producer in the West End. I began Theatre Projects in 1957 in the basement of Her Majesty's Theatre as a lighting design and rental company to launch my career as a designer. This led me to become Sir Laurence's lighting designer when the National began at the Old Vic.

Jocelyn Herbert
(1917-2003)
From meeting #24.

Designer of many productions at the Royal Court, National Theatre and RSC. A strong proponent of a bleak and spare aesthetic in stage design.

I lit several early productions for Jocelyn, a delightful, insightful and brilliant designer.

They included *Baal*, an early play by Bertolt Brecht, which opened at the Phoenix Theatre in February 1963. It was staged fluently with elegant fragments of reality and evocative projections abstracted from nature.

Jocelyn was married to George Devine; she, I and Tyrone Guthrie were invited to join the committee after his death. Guthrie declined.

2.1 Beginnings. Finding An Architect: Meetings #1-14

In Attendance

Kenneth Tynan

Stephen Arlen

Kenneth Tynan (1927-1980)
Critic, literary advisor to the National Theatre (1962-1973).
Ken was quite a character. I got to know him quite well, being later involved in lighting his revue *Oh! Calcutta!* in London and Paris (the latter with lighting designer Jules Fisher), and then co-producing his subsequent sex show *Carte Blanche*. He combined brilliance as a writer, critic and dramaturg with an apparent love of controversy.

George Rowbottom
General manager, National Theatre.
Close friend and colleague.

Anthony Easterbrook
General manager, National Theatre.
Another friend and colleague.

Stephen Arlen (1913-1972)
Administrator, National Theatre & Sadler's Wells Opera.

Kenneth Rae (1927-1980)
Long-serving secretary to the South Bank Theatre Board.
Kenneth Rae served the National Theatre from his demobilisation after World War II. He was the ideal government servant, urbane, patient and wise to all the variables of human nature.

Yolande Bird (1925-2021)
Equally long-serving assistant secretary to the National Theatre Board and loyal right hand to Kenneth Rae.
An amazing person who knew everything, everybody and every skeleton in every cupboard. I met her while a student at drama school when she introduced me to the noted German theatre consultant and guru Walther Unruh, who expedited for me a tour of recently completed German theatres.

The South Bank Theatre & Opera House Board
Established in July 1962

Lord Cottesloe

Lord Chandos

Lord Cottesloe (1927-2018)
Chairman
Lord Cottesloe (John Fremantle), a member of the London County Council, vice-chairman of the Port of London Authority and chairman of the Arts Council of Great Britain (1960-1965).

Lord Chandos (1893-1972)
Chairman of the National Theatre Board
His family's history of support for the National, almost since its inception, was legendary.

Sir Laurence Olivier (1907-1989)
Joint Chairman of NT Building Committee

Prince Littler (1901-1973)
A powerful theatre owner and entrepreneur.

Norman Marshall (1901-1980)
Joint Chairman of NT Building Committee

David McKenna (1911-2003)
Chairman of Sadler's Wells Trust

Norman Tucker (1910-1978)
Administrator of Sadler's Wells

Sir Isaac Hayward (1884-1976)
Labour Leader, London County Council

Sir Percy Rugg (1906-1986)
Conservative Leader, London County Council

Sir William Hart
London County Council Clerk

Sir Leslie Rowan
Representative of HM Treasury

Richard Lynex
Secretary to the South Bank Theatre Board

The Architects

Sir Denys Lasdun
Peter Softley 
Harry Pugh 

Sir Denys Lasdun
(1914-2001)
Architect, Denys Lasdun & Partners (DL&P)

Peter Softley
Architect (DL&P)

Harry Pugh
Architect (DL&P)

Malcolm Minjoodt
Architect (DL&P)

Philip Wood & Robert Kirkman
Modelmakers (DL&P)

Structural Engineers
Flint & Neill

Quantity Surveyor
Davis, Belfield & Everest

Acoustic Consultants
Henry R. Humphries and Sound Research Laboratories

Stage Engineering, Lighting and Sound
Theatre Projects Consultants Limited

Main Contractor
Sir Robert McAlpine

The Theatre Projects Consultants Team

Richard Pilbrow
Richard Brett 
David Collison 

Iain Mackintosh
Bob Anderson 
John Pilcher 

Richard Pilbrow
Founder and Chairman

Richard Brett
Managing Director, Chief Engineer

David Collison
Sound Design

Iain Mackintosh
Cottesloe Design

Bob Anderson
Electrical Engineer

John Pilcher
Sound and Communications

Peter Turner
Site Engineer

2.1 Beginnings. Finding An Architect: Meetings #1-14

77

Meeting 1

1st Meeting of The National Theatre Building Panel

8 Hamilton Place, W1
Thursday 3rd January 1963, 11:40 am

Present:
Sir Laurence Olivier, Mr. Norman Marshall (Chairmen); Mr. Roger Furse, Miss Tanya Moiseiwitsch, Mr. Michael Benthall, Mr. Michael Elliott, Mr. Peter Hall, Mr. George Devine, Mr. Sean Kenny. Mr. Stephen Arlen and Mr. Kenneth Rae were in attendance.
Apologies:
Apologies for absence were received from Mr. Michel Saint-Denis and Mr. Peter Brook.

Sir Laurence welcomed those present.

He explained that he had originally agreed to become a Trustee of the National Theatre in order to insist on proper artistic representation where the building of the Theatre was concerned.

It was the function of this Panel to decide upon the form of the stage and auditorium to be recommended to the National Theatre Board which had been asked to present their conclusions to the South Bank Board no later than February 12th.[12] The South Bank Board would be represented by two of its members on the Board of Assessors which would decide which architects should be invited to take part in a limited competition.

DEVINE: After this panel of experts has made its recommendation does it then hand over to another body?

MARSHALL: The Panel is to provide a brief for an architectural closed competition open only to six people. The R.I.B.A.[13] representation on the Board of Assessors will be very strong.

OLIVIER: We are to study the practical aesthetics of the question.

RAE: The same Panel will probably be invited to advise the South Bank Board at a later date.

MARSHALL: The S.B.B.[14] will also need assistance from technical experts on such matters as box office, acoustics, etc., over which it should be unnecessary to trouble this Panel.

DEVINE: Will we have a say in how the theatre will eventually work and look as a whole?

OLIVIER: If we keep together, the S.B.B. Panel may become redundant. At the moment we are an appendage of the National Theatre Board.

To start off the discussion I would like you to put forward your thoughts on what a National Theatre building should be, and I will begin with a short record of my experience gained at Chichester.

DEVINE: Do we assume there will be two stages; and if so, when.

MARSHALL: Have we any guarantee that there will be a second theatre? This affects the entire problem.

RAE: Two theatres, eventually are an integral part of the National Theatre plan.

MARSHALL: Are we to design an all purpose theatre for ten years or so?

DEVINE: We must make clear our assumptions when we submit our findings.

HALL: The Old Vic is not suited to be the proscenium theatre of the National Theatre. The only way to get a second theatre is to be absolutely uncompromising about the first.

MARSHALL: Should we put it on record that the Old Vic Theatre is not suited to become the second theatre of the National Theatre.

OLIVIER: I think we ought to consider departing from the idea of two theatres. The only reason would be in order to have one large and one small. We do not want large theatres. Two are unnecessary. Let us have one flexible theatre and use any extra space on the site for rehearsal rooms, and a small experimental theatre. With two theatres we will get confusion. Let us have one perfect theatre, its capacity not exceeding eleven hundred.

After that the craft of acting becomes split between the people who can act broadly and those who can't. With the people who can it is embarrassing in the front row, and all right in the back.

We must find a perfect compromise whereby the acting will be equally good for every one in the house. What I have found at Chichester is this. All our lives the critics have been saying that plays should be produced on the form of stage for which they were written. I think the playwrights wrote for what they had got and they were glad to get behind the proscenium arch.

I found *Uncle Vanya* the easiest play to produce at Chichester. With Beaumont and Fletcher and Ford I found myself longing for the proscenium. Anything that required frontal presentation needs a proscenium. I therefore put it to you that the generally accepted opinions as to the best purpose for the arena stage are not so. The plays best suited to it are the least expected. What came out of Chichester was the fact that it was a different experience for the audience. As every lounge in the country has a proscenium arch in television hadn't we better offer something different? Now what are your opinions?

MOISEIWITSCH: I had four questions in mind. You have answered them all. Will the backbone of the National Theatre Repertory be Shakespeare?

OLIVIER: No. Shakespeare will be about ten per cent. We have lots of Shakespeare at Stratford and elsewhere.

MOISEIWITSCH: Stratford Ontario is too big.

OLIVIER: Chichester is too big.

DEVINE: Is this due to the rake?

OLIVIER: Economics governed the size of Chichester.

MOISEIWITSCH: I think a capacity of eleven hundred is all right if the audience is squashed together and not spread out; otherwise people feel lonely. Minneapolis will be around fifteen hundred.

FURSE: The Chichester stage is too big.

BENTHALL: There is the case for one perfect theatre, but the bigger it is the more difficult is it to make it adaptable.

OLIVIER: Is this true?

HALL: Adaptable theatres cannot hold more than six hundred people. Is an auditorium seating a thousand to eleven hundred big enough for the National Theatre in social terms? That would be the effect on prices. There should be plenty of five shilling seats. Otherwise the whole thing becomes a middle class enterprise. One way to get young people into the theatre is to make it cheap.

DEVINE: I agree.

ARLEN: For the new Sadler's Wells we started with the idea of about two thousand seats. Because of acoustics it was cut down to sixteen hundred. The Arts Council are still urging us to cut down the number, so we say all right, but you must give us a higher subsidy.

OLIVIER: I see Peter Hall's point about the social implications of a small house, but I am more determined to build a theatre where we can present plays properly. If we distort them no one gets a fair deal.

MARSHALL: It is agreed all over Europe that you cannot go beyond eleven hundred.

OLIVIER: The design of Chichester is fairly cunning, but the theatre is too big.

ELLIOTT: An amphitheatre is no smaller to play in. Though the audience are nearer the actor, he still has to cope with the same

The Old Vic 1962

> "Let us have one perfect theatre, its capacity not exceeding eleven hundred."
> — Laurence Olivier

> "As every lounge in the country has a proscenium arch in television, hadn't we better offer something different?"
> — Laurence Olivier

Chichester, 1962

> "If an open stage is to be built we shouldn't disregard modern resources, such as lighting."
>
> Michael Elliott

cubic capacity of space. Before we decide that we should incorporate all functions in one building, we must decide whether we can do this. I am not aware of any theatre where this has been achieved. Any adaptable theatre is bound to be a compromise.

OLIVIER and KENNY: That's what they say, it hasn't been tried.

ELLIOTT: You can have a wholly adaptable theatre but it is a question of altering the focal point in the building. To do this you need to change the seats around in the auditorium as well. Very expensive.

MARSHALL: It is possible, viz L.A.M.D.A.[15], but that will be un-intimate. It takes the audience too far back and there will be three hundred and sixty people at the most.

ELLIOTT: If we designed two ideal auditoriums it would be difficult to adapt the one into the other.

MARSHALL: Why are you (Olivier) against two theatres?

OLIVIER: There is not enough room on the site.

HALL: I agree that we should have one ideal theatre. It is dire aesthetically to limit ourselves to producing one type of play in the proscenium and another in the arena.

DEVINE: What we have got to do is to make a statement of the experience of our time.

HALL: I agree.

KENNY: The problem over adaptable theatres hasn't yet been solved, but we can try. Leave the space left open on the site with a question mark.

HALL: I don't believe it is as simple as 'do you have a proscenium' or 'do you have a Chichester, or Stratford Ontario'. When you make a verbal statement on the stage you've got to command the whole house, and the problem of Chichester and Stratford Ontario is that you must have perpetual movement.

OLIVIER: I made mistakes there.

DEVINE and HALL: Even if you hadn't, the problem remains.

OLIVIER: In *Uncle Vanya* there was only ten per cent more movement that I would have put in the proscenium arch.

HALL: An open stage non-proscenium theatre hasn't yet been attempted. If you have the picture-frame, you automatically have a picture.

DEVINE: I agree.

BENTHALL: You often get your greatest sense of intimacy in a large theatre with a good shape.

ELLIOTT: If an open stage is to be built we shouldn't disregard modern resources, such as lighting, etc., There is no incompatibility between modern theatrical resources and the open stage. We could still have scenery.

HALL: We can have a fly-tower over the open stage.

OLIVIER: The great problem is lighting. This is so for any arena theatre.

HALL: I feel that no member of the audience should be distracted by seeing other members of the audience beyond the actors.

KENNY: If the rake is steep enough you won't.

ELLIOTT: Let us have a theatre where the actor at the focal point can be seen by all in the audience without moving.

OLIVIER: I'll have a model of Chichester here for the next meeting.

DEVINE: We should have a tape-recording of what we say. How else are we going to convey all this to the R.I.B.A? We can never say the same things twice. Minutes are not enough.

BENTHALL: The National Theatre architect has to be chosen as the result of a competition?

MARSHALL: Yes. We seek the best architect in the land.

ELLIOTT: It is assumed by the R.I.B.A that the designing of theatres is routine. It is not, it is an art.

DEVINE: I'm just back from Brazil where architecture is the current thing. In every case the hospitals are superb but the theatres are hopeless.

OLIVIER: You should see the one at Coventry.

RAE: What Devine says is important. All the architects to the S.B.B, will be preoccupied primarily with the elevation and the relationship between one building and another on the South Bank. They will want "a pretty South Bank".

DEVINE: It must look nice, and it must all be joined up. The whole thing must be a statement.

HALL: Given time we could give a precise specification that would satisfy us all, but is this going to be enough? We want as architect a collaborator who will say 'if you want that sort of thing, why not have it like this'. Collaboration with the architect is essential.

OLIVIER: I think we must stick to saying what the inside of the theatre must be like, otherwise we won't get anywhere.

DEVINE: But this attitude is why we don't get good theatres. I think the theatre is the whole building.

FURSE: We have the advantage of being able to present the essential kernel. We can only talk about the inside.

ARLEN: The danger is not so much the architect, but the S.B.B., the Arts Council, the Drama Panel of the Arts Council and any other advisory panel that may come between the architect and this panel. The problem is the relationship of the architect to this panel.

ELLIOTT: We must have authority.

DEVINE: We must say 'this is what we want and if you don't like it you are on your own!'

HALL: We must be firm about it, otherwise, when all the committees have finished messing the theatre about it will be a square blank.

DEVINE: The question of the competition is very difficult. The people produced as great architects won't necessarily have a conception of a theatre as we want it.

MARSHALL: There is no reason why a young architect shouldn't come into it somewhere.

BENTHALL: Shouldn't we get hold of the original brief on which the National Theatre Building Committee spent so long time years ago?

RAE: The "Basic Requirements"[16], which are before you, are the result of their work. They take into account the fact that there are to be two theatres. If we now propose that there should be only one they should be revised.

ARLEN: They can be; they were merely provisional.

DEVINE: Next time when we meet let us have pieces of paper with our individual ideas set down, and a model of Chichester.

MARSHALL: I want to say something about Chichester. Already we have become hidebound about what an open stage should be. The concept is currently dominated by Guthrie. Let us forget Chichester, and start all over again.

OLIVIER: From Chichester you will get certain technical details. That's all.

MARSHALL: Don't let us try to make an improved Chichester.

BENTHALL: There is a section over here that feels there should not be a theatre in the round but a semi-circle.

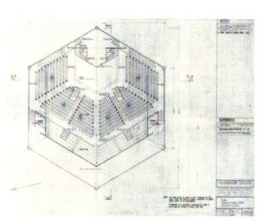

Chichester Festival Theatre, 1963: plan

> "I'm just back from Brazil where architecture is the current thing. In every case the hospitals are superb but the theatres are hopeless."
>
> George Devine

> "The problem is the relationship of the architect to this panel."
> Stephen Arlen

Théâtre National de Chaillot, Paris, 1963

Théâtre National de Chaillot, Paris, 2009, after re-design

> "We must have authority."
> Michael Elliott

MARSHALL: We seem to have reached certain conclusions:

The actor must be able to command the audience. The audience must be able to see the actor without there having to be too much movement.
There should be a fly-tower.

We must avoid too much austerity.

DEVINE: Everywhere we see a more baroque, more colourful type of theatre coming in. The dry type of intellectual theatre is not going to be it, though we should have somewhere where we can do that sort of theatre.

HALL: To me the most interesting thing is the Vilar Theatre in Paris. The Chaillot is a horrible place but a new public in France doesn't think so. Vilar Theatre is spreading throughout France; To return to capacity, we must think about the people who will have to run the National Theatre after us. How will they make it pay? A theatre of a thousand will have too many seats at a pound and twenty-five shillings, making the National Theatre too established and middle-class. It is no part of our brief to comment on subsidies but if we are asked to put forward our ideas on an ideal theatre we must make this point.

ELLIOTT: What Larry said about the perfect performance is vital.

FURSE: We have not got to think of subsidy considerations.

HALL: The pressure on people running the National Theatre to make the audience pay will be great if it is too small.

ARLEN: If you go to the Empire Theatre, Liverpool, which seats between two and three thousand and you have a packed house the generation of excitement is terrific and such as you will never get with a six hundred seater.

HALL: I agree.

ELLIOTT: I would qualify that.

DEVINE: I couldn't ask for anything better than our experience of playing "Luther" in the Opera House, Manchester.

ELLIOTT: I am amazed. In my experience playing there was terrible.

KENNY: A capacity of twelve hundred would be the maximum for adaptability.

ARLEN: You should bear in mind that the current restrictions regarding fireproofing, etc., can be got around. When the L.C.C. built the Festival Hall they got themselves waivers. There is a movement inside the L.C.C. at the moment towards a realisation that the old regulations no longer apply today.

HALL: The old regulations apply to 1870!

ARLEN: They are beginning to realise that regulations applicable to a timber grid need not apply to steel.

MARSHALL: The Association of British Theatre Technicians has had a most valuable meeting with the L.C.C. on all this.

MOISEIWITSCH: I was horrified to hear that people in the theatre don't like to see the rest of the audience.

HALL: What we meant was that when we look at the actors we don't want to be too aware of the audience beyond.

OLIVIER: If they had maintained the rake at Chichester it would have made a great difference on this point.

ARLEN: Summing up my experience of Chichester, I would say that I got excitement from the stage, but no corporate excitement from the audience.

KENNY: I think it will take four meetings of this panel before we can get anything down on paper.

MOISEIWITSCH: I am afraid that this is the last meeting that I can attend.

A Sense of Theatre

An Uncertainty Principle

On this somewhat regretful note from Tanya Moiseiwitsch (who was heavily involved in her work with Guthrie at Stratford, Ontario), the first meeting closed. It sets the tone for many. Sir Laurence was leader, but behind the scenes he was anxious not to dictate, but to reach consensus. The world-famous leader of men as *Henry V* ("Once more unto the breach, dear friends") was not the "Sir" of our offstage world. If you met him in his cramped office in the huts at Aquinas Street, you might presume he was your bespectacled bank manager. In the pub, he could easily disappear into the guise of your ragged local street-corner tramp.

In seeking to persuade, he could be wondrously flirtatious. Bill Gaskill reported, "Larry was not easily put off. His technique… was to treat me like a woman. I don't think he actually sent me flowers but I was regularly lunched at the Dorchester. 'The wooing of Billy Gaskill,' he called it. Of course, I succumbed."[17] So, too, did I, after an equally persuasive lunch at The Dorchester in April 1963.

Sir Laurence was uncertain as to where his opinion lay about theatre forms. Chichester had surprised him. He was amazed and delighted by the success of *Uncle Vanya*, which he never thought could work so well on a thrust stage. He knew of the ongoing debate of open versus proscenium stages and he was grappling with establishing his own viewpoint. His desire for an adaptable space was his hope to cover both bases with one space.

Points of significance from this first meeting:

1. The initial instruction that the brief should be submitted to the South Bank Theatre Board (SBTB) within six weeks was absurdly impractical.
2. Sir Laurence was, at the outset, for a single multiform theatre. This very '60s view had been adopted in New York for the Vivian Beaumont at the Lincoln Center, against the advice of Jo Mielziner, the theatre designer. It was a view that Denys Lasdun later dismissed.
3. The committee was quite aware of the challenge of designing a new theatre and was sceptical of an architect's willingness to listen and collaborate. This was based upon an almost historic degree of mistrust between the theatre and architecture.
4. But, as a preview of what was to come, almost all the views expressed were surely divergent, contradictory and often confusing. This would be challenging to an architect to whom theatre was a new and mysterious world.

Festival Theatre, Stratford, Ontario

Vivian Beaumont Theater, New York

Meeting 2

2nd Meeting of The National Theatre Building Panel

8 Hamilton Place, W1
Wednesday 9th January 1963, 11:00 am

Present:
Sir Laurence Olivier, Mr. Norman Marshall (Chairmen), Mr. Roger Furse, Mr. Michael Benthall, Mr. Michael Elliott, Mr. Peter Hall, Mr. George Devine, Mr. Sean Kenny, Mr. Peter Brook. Mr. Stephen Arlen and Mr. Kenneth Rae were in attendance.
Apologies:
Apologies for absence were received from Mr. Saint-Denis.

OLIVIER: What came out of our last meeting was that February 12th was too tight a deadline by which to give the South Bank Board any decision. As a Panel we want to be taken seriously and to see the job right through.

DEVINE: We were worried about the choice of the six architects.

BROOK: Why six architects?

MARSHALL: The R.I.B.A. have inescapable rules.

BROOK: Does that mean that no other architect can take part in the competition?

MARSHALL: Yes.

The Panel agreed that this was a bad thing.

DEVINE: They are looking at it from the point of view of the outside of the building.

OLIVIER: The choice of the architects is finally up to the S.B.B.

Discussion on the various Panels of the S.B.B.

OLIVIER: I managed to persuade Chandos to persuade Cottesloe to delay calling the S.B.B. Panel for the National Theatre. At the moment we are an informal Panel.

MARSHALL: We are officially appointed to advise the National Theatre Board. The original building committee for the National Theatre had over fifty-six meetings.

BENTHALL: Most distinguished architects haven't time to go in for competitions.

Discussion on the architects for Stratford and Coventry having been chosen by competition.

MARSHALL: The L.C.C argue that such an important project as the N.T, should be done under the auspices of the R.I.B.A.

BROOK: What happens if we find the designs are no good? Can we bring in someone else?

OLIVIER: If the designs are unacceptable to the S.B.B. and this Panel we can say so.

BROOK: Do we then have to go back to the R.I.B.A. or will we have fulfilled the gesture to them?

MARSHALL: This question should be asked of the S.B.B.

BROOK: Anyone chosen by the R.I.B.A. could come up with a bad design.

MARSHALL: Could one of the six architects be a foreigner?

RAE: It would be regarded as a national disgrace were the theatre not built by a British architect.

OLIVIER: There will tremendous pressure for a British architect.

MARSHALL: Are the six to be chosen in collaboration between this Panel and the R.I.B.A?

OLIVIER: The S.B.B. will finally approve the choice of the six architects and the design.

ARLEN: Representatives of the S.B.B. were asked to put forward names of architects.

DEVINE: Last time we also talked about whether we were to consider the whole building.

OLIVIER: We're not supposed to concern

ourselves with the exterior.

DEVINE: I mean the general character of the whole place.

RAE: There is a N.T. Board meeting on Monday 14th January, and only one a month, so let this Panel make recommendations to it:
- That the deadline of 12th February is too tight.
- That this panel would like to be assured that it will be taken on by the S.B.B to advise as their Panel..

OLIVIER: If the second point is made the first is not too vital.

BENTHALL: But this is the responsibility of the S.B.B. and not the N.T. Board.

OLIVIER: As Norman Marshall, Lord Chandos and myself are on the S.B.B. we can help over this.

Details are given of the membership of the N.T. Board and the S.B.B.

ARLEN: Remember that the N.T., Sadlers Wells and Norman Marshall have collectively a very strong representation on the S.B.B. (Five votes).

DEVINE: Where is the Treasury?

OLIVIER: They attend as Assessors.

BROOK: Have all the old N.T. plans been ditched?

RAE: The S.B.B. would not consider themselves bound by any previous commitment.

OLIVIER: O'Rorke[18] may be one of the candidates.

DEVINE: Is it advisable that we say something about the choice of architects? We are important and busy people, therefore our voice should be heard.

DEVINE: Why isn't the competition open?

MARSHALL: Because of the delay and expense involved.

BROOK: I can't see how serious designing can be done by competitions. Unless someone is chosen on the grounds of intelligence, imagination and merit and works in proper collaboration with us, I don't see how we can get anywhere.

RAE: This Panel is entitled to make its views known on the entire conception of the theatre.

BENTHALL: We should be firm and say that we don't intend to give advice unless we can see it carried through

The panel agreed that this was essential.

RAE: I think that you will be asked to act as Panel for the S.B.B. Cottesloe has it in mind but I am all for putting the idea in the form of a recommendation to the N.T. Board. We must produce a series of resolutions to submit to the N. T. Board on Monday 14th.

MARSHALL: It is really up to the S.B.B.

RAE: It is up to Olivier and Chandos to get the proposal through the S.B.B. I don't anticipate any difficulty.

BENTHALL: Do our proposals have to go through tho Arts Council Drama Panel?

MARSHALL: Yes.

ARLEN: Judging by the experience of Sadler's Wells in submitting its Basic Requirements you need not worry about the Arts Council Drama Panel.

DEVINE: It would not do for it to come out that our proposals had been rejected.

BENTHALL: Let us rough out some resolutions for the N.T. Board for consideration at this Friday's meeting (11th Jan.) of this Panel.

OLIVIER: Last time we explored different ideas and conceptions and talked about the arena stage, etc., I suggested that we should have an adaptable theatre. In my experience at Chichester I found the classical plays were more difficult to do in an arena than the "thoughtful" ones.

BROOK: I think that was everyone's experience of Chichester. In watching *The Chances* I found the

Nottingham Playhouse, opened 1963, architect Peter Moro, shown in 2018 (top) and 2010 (bottom)

> "Unless [an architect] has thought about theatre as such he is no use."
>
> Peter Brook

spectacle came out, but I had little idea of the plot. On the other hand when I saw *Women Beware Women* at the Arts it came over in close-up. I am convinced there is no issue of principle involved in all this. It is all a matter of precision of design.

OLIVIER: If the [Chichester] rake had been maintained, etc., it would have made all the difference.

BROOK: The open stage and the closed stage is a journalistic simplification. One could evolve something that is neither one or the other that would be a proper evolution.

DEVINE: What you are saying is that in the brief we should put forward certain principles rather than lay down the type of stage.

BROOK: Yes; that is where the architect should be carefully briefed. I couldn't say at this point whether we should have an open or a closed stage. What must be taken into account are:
- The relationship of the actor to the stage.
- Scenic problems.
- We cannot make clearcut recommendations which is what the R.I.B.A. want. The Stratford architect was told to make something suitable for modern drama and Greek tragedy; the result was disastrous. 'Adaptable' is an umbrella word that will make the architects think they must design in limbo.
- Discussion on the mistakes made in the Royalty Theatre and new Nottingham Theatre

HALL: To design the theatre properly one should work with the architect as with a stage designer.

ELLIOTT: An open competition might reveal potential talent.

BROOK: If the R.I.B.A. know their stuff they should be able to bring forward men with a potential for designing theatres.

DEVINE: The architect chosen should be someone who is prepared to work with the people who are going to work in the building.

BROOK: The architect's brief should be regarded as something evolutionary and not recommendationary. We should bear in mind that architecture in this country is appalling and the R.I.B.A. reflects this.

OLIVIER: The trouble is that the architect is going to be chosen as a result of a design to which he is already committed.

MARSHALL: Whatever happens we are outvoted on the Assessors' Panel which chooses the competing architects.

ELLIOTT: If we take a strong line they cannot afford to put up a National Theatre against our recommendations. If they insist on a design which we have rejected they will find themselves in a stupid position.

RAE and MARSHALL: The S.B.B. has the right to reject a design.

DEVINE: If we put our recommendations down on paper and they pick their six architects, what will the six initially produce?

KENNY: Sketch designs in six months.

BROOK: It could be six months wasted.

DEVINE: We would know if they were any good if we could see the candidates first.

BROOK: Can we not talk to the architects immediately and make an immediate choice. Why give them six months to waste if within a month we can assess by interview whether those people are likely to be right for the job. In the remaining five months those people could work with us.

DEVINE: If we don't do this we shall make our recommendations, six months later the sketches will arrive and we shall choose whoever seems the best man. But he will already be committed to his design and he is not going to start again.

KENNY: Brook's suggested method of working is difficult but not impossible.

MARSHALL: Can an architect produce a practical scheme in a month?

BROOK: He is not going to produce a scheme. What we want is not a competition but an audition. We want a smell of his talents. He will still be uncommitted to a scheme.

KENNY: I think we should have about 12 architects from whom to select.

MARSHALL: What should they submit?

KENNY: They must have some kind of brief.

MARSHALL: What are they to bring on paper? Rough sketches?

KENNY: I would bring my ideas on theatre and also about twelve sketches of different kinds of theatres showing their inherent difficulties.

OLIVIER: Would this Panel see them singly or collectively?

DEVINE: The candidates should come with their ideas, and talk.

BROOK: We don't want their submissions to be a reflection of their design for the National Theatre, but their thoughts on the problem of designing a theatre. Unless a man has thought about theatre as such he is no use.

ELLIOTT: What matters most is to find people who have the right attitude of mind. There is a danger that candidates will use the National Theatre for egocentric purposes. The right man must have curiosity, humility, and adaptability.

DEVINE: We also want the man who will not be put off by us disagreeing among ourselves, but will be stimulated thereby.

HALL: If the only final authorities are the R.I.B.A. and the architect, we are lost. Responsibility has got to be vested in us.

BROOK: An architect today is bound to think in showy terms and he will start, say, with a hexagon. Once he stands on some geometric principle and makes it the beginning rather than the end we have disaster.

DEVINE: He should start from the stage and auditorium and go outwards.

BROOK and DEVINE: Your R.I.B.A. man will start with a pre-determined geometric shape.

ELLIOTT: If this project goes wrong it will be a disaster not only for the National Theatre, but for the theatre as a whole. If this Panel has responsibility without authority we shall be blamed for any mistakes.

HALL: I put it as a resolution that unless we can collaborate with the architect we are wasting our time.

OLIVIER: Should there be more than six architects?

It was agreed there should be twelve.

OLIVIER: And we see them all?

BROOK: Yes. Each interview will be creative for everyone including ourselves.

RAE: There will be practical difficulties.

DEVINE: Yes; but if we go the old way it will be a dead loss.

BROOK: Better to spend more time profitably than waste a lot to no good purpose.

HALL: I don't see why we need twelve sessions; we could have say four meetings with all twelve candidates. If we don't it will be unfair on number one.

FURSE: We can see them all at once.

BROOK: What we are saying is let's have a competition, but we will make the rules, sketches, conversations etc, We could then make a short list.

DEVINE: At the end of the period we could produce a list of our people and then the R.I.B.A. could say what they want from them.

ARLEN: What we have to do first is unpick the S.B.B.'s views. We could prepare a paper, but I think it is better to send a representative of this Panel to address the S.B.B.

DEVINE: Are we getting to a hard position over all this?

> "We should bear in mind that architecture in this country is appalling and the R.I.B.A. reflects this."
> Peter Brook

> "If we say that we don't know whether we want an adaptable theatre, etc., and that we would like to meet the architects and tell them that the theatre is a great mystery, it may not look so good."
>
> Laurence Olivier

HALL: Yes. We say to the S.B.B. 'Unless you see your way to meeting us on all this we are more of a danger to you than a help.'

KENNY: We are the people who will use the theatre, so we should have a big say.

RAE: Could we detail the resolutions?

MARSHALL: This is a departure from what Arlen proposes.

ARLEN: No. The resolutions should be taken to the S.B.B by the representative of this Panel for him to amplify.

BROOK: I propose Devine as spokesman.

RAE: I second.

ARLEN: We tell the N.T. Board that the way things are going at the moment are not right for the National Theatre. The Chairman of the N.T. Board asks the Chairman of the S.B.B. for permission for our spokesman to address the S.B.B.

DEVINE: I will draft something for our Friday meeting.

MARSHALL: There is a problem in the suggestion that the same architect should design the Opera House as well as the N.T. It means that Sadlers Wells is affected.

ARLEN: The Sadler's Wells problem is not so difficult as it is a working organisation. Sadler's Wells has specified that the architect, should start in the middle and work outward.

BROOK: Aren't Sadler's Wells' needs more conventional?

ARLEN: A bit, but Sadler's Wells has asked for a new form of presentation to be studied.

BENTHALL: We should lobby members of the S.B.B. before its meeting, if possible.

KENNY: Would it be a help if Sadler's Wells' Panel sat in on the auditions of this Panel?

ARLEN: I am already thinking along those lines.

DEVINE: Sadlers Wells could set up a similar attitude.

MARSHALL: Would it not be better if our Scheme goes through that we should have two architects, one for the National Theatre and one for the Opera House?

BROOK: Is there time for any one man to absorb all the problems relating to opera and drama.

OLIVIER: Let's minute it that we consider it impossible for one man to do both.

KENNY: Should Bennett[19] and the R.I.B.A. sit in on our auditions?

DEVINE: Yes.

BENTHALL (to Olivier): Are you in agreement with us on all this, or are we making things too difficult for you?

OLIVIER: We were supposed to provide the Boards with specifications.

BROOK: But the National Theatre cannot suddenly be stopped; their dates and preconceptions must yield to us.

ARLEN: In terms of time there is one vital date – when the L.C.C. goes out of existence.

DEVINE: What will happen then?

ARLEN: The Council for Greater London will take over, and we don't know what their attitude will be. We know the L.C.C. is anxious to complete Morrison's[20] South Bank, and there is a hope that they will pay for it. The problem is easier if we know by 1965 what the financial cost will be.

BROOK: The building won't start until nearly 1965 anyway.

OLIVIER: If we go to the Board and say what we want they may tell us that we were asked to provide ideas. If we say that we don't know whether we want an adaptable theatre, etc., and that we would like to meet the architects and tell them that the theatre is a great mystery, it may not look so good.

BROOK: 'Don't know' is not a fair reflection on this morning's work. We have precise ideas on theatre, but we won't give them off pat.

HALL: No good our giving precise recommendations; the building will only work as a result of collaboration directed towards making an organic theatre.

DEVINE: The answers to the Board's questions are 'it all depends.'

HALL: That is right, because we know what it all depends on.

BENTHALL: After we've auditioned the candidates, can we choose three?

BROOK: An optimistic figure.

OLIVIER: Let us think up recommendations of our own and get them included in those submitted by the R.I.B.A.

MARSHALL: We must remember that we won't got rid of the R.I.B.A. completely.

ELLIOTT: Is there any point of contact between this Panel and the R.I.B.A. outside the S.B.B.?

DEVINE: Shouldn't Larry meet Mathews on an informal basis? [E.D. Jefferiss Mathews, architect and RIBA hon. treasurer]

RAE: Cottesloe is a vital factor.

ELLIOTT: In theory the R.I.B.A. should have as much say in the choice of architect for the National Theatre as anyone.

HALL: Don't agree!

BROOK: Who has been in touch with the R.I.B.A.?

ARLEN: Cottesloe.

BROOK: Is he the best person to be our intermediary outside ourselves?

RAE: I should say Cottesloe has already intimated that we should not think along the lines of an adaptable theatre as it is too expensive.

DEVINE: An adaptable theatre could cost half as much if done the right way.

HALL: Current thinking on adaptable theatres is hidebound by the German approach.

BENTHALL: I would also like to propose that Peter Brook should go with George Devine to address the S.B.B.

BROOK: I am going to New York, otherwise I would be delighted to do so.

BENTHALL: Perhaps it would help Devine if Peter Brook drafted the resolutions with him.

MARSHALL: What is very important is the feeling of the Panel against the suggestion of one architect for both theatres.

RAE: Dangerous to talk to the R.I.B.A. behind Cottesloe's back.

BENTHALL and DEVINE: Ask Cottesloe to set up the lunch.

OLIVIER: What about Chandos?

RAE: We must get Chandos behind us because what we propose to do is a reversal of the whole procedure agreed by the S.B.B.

OLIVIER: I understand Mr. Benthall's concern about George being left alone to confront the S.B.B.

It was agreed that Peter Hall should go with George Devine to address the S.B.B.

BROOK: It will be a good thing to have representatives of two major theatrical organisations [Royal Shakespeare Company and Royal Court Theatre] to plead our case with the S.B.B.

It was agreed that the Secretary should ask Chandos to facilitate the above. It was agreed that the bringing together of the R.I.B.A. and the Panel should be delayed until after Monday's meeting of the N.T. Board.

BROOK: We have to put it on record that the reasoning behind the proposals that we would put to the S.B.B. is our conviction that it is the only way to get a proper National Theatre. We know that we are making things more difficult initially.

> "What matters most is to find people who have the right attitude of mind. The right man must have curiosity, humility and adaptability."
>
> Michael Elliott

The National Theatre Building Panel

11th January 1963

THE NATIONAL THEATRE BUILDING PANEL
11 January 1963

The National Theatre Building Panel submits the following recommendations:

1. The Panel is convinced that the long history of failure in modern theatre architecture in England is due to a basically wrong relationship between the architect and the theatre people who are to function in the building.

2. The Panel considers that the method of procedure at present proposed will not produce the best results for the National Theatre. This procedure anticipates that the Panel will produce certain aesthetic and technical requirements to be handed over to the competitive architects as their brief, for which six months later the sketch plans will be submitted.

3. The Panel fundamentally disagrees with this method as being wrong and a waste of time, because it believes that all basic issues of principle (type of stage, style of auditorium, etc.) involved are matters of precision of design. No successful theatre has ever been built on a series of theoretical specifications.

4. In other words, the Panel considers that from the moment of conception to the completion of the design there should be a real collaboration between the Panel and the architect.

5. The Panel realises that what it proposes will make greatly increased demands on the time of its very busy members. However, it is convinced that the choice is between more time well spent or less time wasted, and consequently feels bound to make those its conditions of continued service. The method of procedure is, naturally, open to discussion but the Panel proposes the following:

(a) The competitive architects should be nearer twelve in number than six. Their selection should be based on a potential for designing theatres, rather than any other sort of building, and amongst architects who will welcome a deep and detailed collaboration with theatre people from the start.

(b) To begin with the Panel would hold a few sessions of discussion with the competitors, whether in groups or separately; during which ideas would be discussed, sketches, etc. produced, and the total experience of the Panel exposed to the architects, thus creating a fluid rather than a rigid series of requirements. The architects in turn would not be judged by any rigid proposals or solutions. The aim of the sessions would be to discover which amongst maybe equally talented architects shows the most specific feeling for theatre. The Panel would propose that representatives of the R.I.B.A. be present at those sessions.

(c) After this, the Panel should be in a position to recommend a short list to the South Bank board for final selection. This process might take, at the most, two to three months, but, in any case, the architect finally chosen would be able to start work considerably sooner than under the original scheme.

(d) The architect finally chosen would then continue to work in collaboration with the Panel through the various phases toward the final design, expert consultants being called in as necessary.

The Panel considers that the National Theatre should comprise one stage in one building, and that the idea of a second stage be dropped. It recommends however that the provision of a small studio theatre on the site be considered alongside the main auditorium.

An Impossible Brief

This was a quite remarkable meeting that faced the impossibility of preparing a comprehensive written specification for the architect, and that the eventual process must be one of close collaboration.

The conviction grew that the building committee had to take a more aggressive role in the architectural selection process. Merely advising the South Bank Theatre Board and a selection committee led by RIBA was not going to be sufficient. The theatre itself should take the lead on the selection. The committee members felt they were uniquely qualified to provide such expertise.

The South Bank Board minutes later included the following extract:

"George Devine and Michael Elliott presented to the Council the ideas of the Theatre Panel. Discussion followed, after which the following principle points were made:

'The National Theatre Board and the South Bank Theatre Board need to work in close harmony; and there must be full collaboration between architects invited to submit initial sketch schemes and the technical panels advising the Council, and subsequently between those panels and the architect or architects ultimately appointed for the project. The importance for this was stressed because in theatre architecture there seems to be little or no tradition of collaboration between architects and the theatrical profession.'" [21]

The South Bank Board accepted the recommendation. The architectural Panel of Assessors was demoted to become a Panel of Advisors only. Architects would not be required to submit schemes, but would first express interest, after which a short list would be prepared by the assessors for interviews by the theatre and opera house representatives, leading to a final interview round.

There follows a gap in the existing minutes. There are no records of Meeting 3, 4, 5 and 6. Strangely, there doesn't appear to be an obvious gap in the committee's deliberations.

View of the Old Vic stage from the fly floor

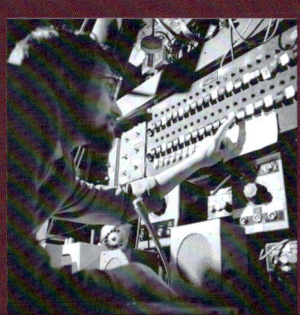

Old Vic – two views of the prompt corner

Meeting 7

7th Meeting of The National Theatre Building Committee

6 Rossetti Studios
Tuesday 19th February 1963, 10:45 am

Present:
Sir Laurence Olivier, Mr. Norman Marshall (Chairmen), Mr. Peter Hall, Mr. George Devine, Mr. Michel St Denis, Mr. Roger Furse, Mr. Michael Elliott, Mr. Sean Kenny and Mr. Stephen Arlen were in attendance.
Apologies:
Apologies for absence were received from Mr. Michael Benthall and Mr. Peter Brook.

The Chairmen made a Report on informal discussions held by the Panel of Assessors with both the National Theatre Building Committee and the equivalent Sadler's Wells body. The outcome was most satisfactory.

The Panel of Assessors had volunteered to step down and to become a Panel of Advisers. The idea of a limited competition, governed by RIBA rules, to choose the architect or architects, had been abandoned in favour of a process of selection. The selection procedure had been discussed and it was suggested that architect candidates should be divided into two categories:

1. <u>Those with established reputations.</u>
   A list would be drawn up with the help of the Panel of Advisers of those wishing to be considered. It was not anticipated that they would exceed twenty in number. The National Theatre Building Committee would interview them individually and would reduce them to a short list not exceeding six. Unknown talent and non-architects. An open "competition" or survey would be held that would provide:
   a) unknown qualified architects and firms.
   b) non-architects e.g. theatre designers with an opportunity of showing their talent and appreciation of Theatre.

Up to 400 people might be expected to enter for this competition. Entries would not be confined to sketch plans but could include models, essays, or anything that would demonstrate the candidate's ideas. Non-architects would have to associate themselves with a qualified architect or firm before they could compete. The Panel of Advisers would help make public the terms of the open "competition" and would also organise the exhibits.

Out of this larger body of competitors a further, say, six candidates would be chosen.

The final list of, say, twelve candidates would then be interviewed and a choice of architect made.

The Committee agreed that the above suggestions, which it was understood would be presented in outline to the South Bank Board the following day, were acceptable.

The procedure governing the interviewing of the established architects, which should take place as soon as possible, was then discussed. It was decided that at least five members of the Building Committee should hold themselves available to do the interviewing, possibly over a period of three consecutive days – a Saturday, Sunday and Monday. In fairness to the candidates and to facilitate selection, the five members should be the same throughout the interviewing period which should be fixed for at least a month or six weeks from the present date.

During the meeting the following points were made in connection with the survey
1. A preference was expressed for models as evidence of competitors' talent.
2. As many young architects might wish to submit what was called a "Research and Development Survey", these should be presented in a form comprehensible to laymen.
3. A problem could arise in that the Building Committee might want to make a synthesis of ideas expressed by a number of competitors.
4. With a view to avoiding the danger of exhausting the original impulse of a promising competitor the briefing should not be too specific.

Two Comparative Theatre Types

It is of some passing historical interest that the meeting with the Panel of Assessors resulted in this seemingly extraordinarily 'democratic' outcome. Not only was it agreed to widen the field to other potential architects, but they also added the consideration of "unknown, or even non-qualified architects." Surely an amazing concession from the RIBA.

There is, however, no record of any such widening of the competitive field ever being pursued further, except in discussion about the possible future role of Sean Kenny at the next meeting.

Musiktheater Gelsenkirchen, Germany

Chichester Festival Theatre at the time of opening, 1962

Meeting 8

8th Meeting of The National Theatre Building Committee

8 Hamilton Place, W1
Tuesday 7th May 1963, 10:40 am

Present:
Sir Laurence Olivier, Mr. Norman Marshall (Chairmen), Mr. Roger Furse, Mr. Michael Elliott. Mr. Stephen Arlen and Mr. Kenneth Rae were in attendance.

Apologies:
Apologies for absence were received from Mr. Peter Brook, Mr. Michel Saint-Denis, Mr. Peter Hall, Mr. Michael Benthall, Mr. George Devine and Miss Tanya Moiseiwitsch.

Resignation of Mr. Kenny
Sir Laurence said that Mr. Kenny wished to resign from the Committee in order to become a candidate-architect for the National Theatre. All the members of the committee had been consulted on this and had agreed that, although Mr. Kenny's advice would be much missed, he must be released.

Sir Laurence pointed out that Mr. Kenny's resignation would leave a gap on the committee. He suggested that Mr. Dexter and Mr. Gaskill, the National Theatre Associate Directors, should be invited to serve on it.

Selection of Architect
Sir Laurence read the draft announcement on the method of selecting the architect which had been agreed by the Panel of Advisers and which was to be made public the next day.

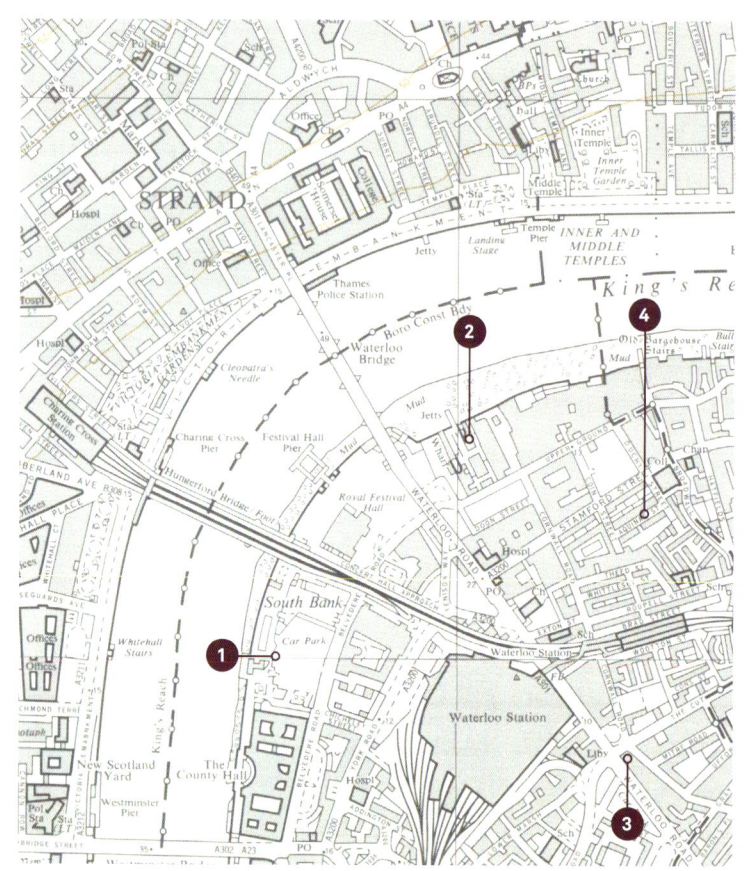

London's South Bank, mid 1960s. 1: Proposed site of the National Theatre-Opera House, 2: Eventual site for the National Theatre, 3: The Old Vic, 4: Aquinas Street

A Sense of Theatre

Sean Kenny and Architecture

16th April 1963. Peter Brook to Olivier: Peter suggested that Sean Kenny should be appointed as "Theatre Designer," like the famous American scene designer Jo Mielziner had been for the Vivian Beaumont Theater. Then the architect would be bound to accept his recommendations. This idea seems never to have been followed up.

Fifteen months later Sean Kenny wrote to Sir Laurence:

"Once again the theatre is back in the old formula of having to explain carefully to an outside designer of building what it wants. One is always hopeful that Mr. Designer will be sympathetic and understanding, and that he won't go off and design another monument to himself or architecture. Up to now we have always failed with the inside although we have many interesting outsides. Unless an architect totally immerses himself in theatre... there will be nothing of the inside.

"Ordinary interest is not enough even for us theatre people who work with it every day – maybe it is better to have a man build a great tent around our activities. Speaking as simply as I can and without going into a blind rage, I do know that the answer to our theatre building in the future does not lie with architecture. It must emerge from our fumbling and inarticulate endeavours to pin down the relationship between the platform and that seat – whatever that is.

"I should not rejoin the committee... I'm off to play in someone else's backyard." [22]

This backyard was to be, in fact, Las Vegas, the Dunes Hotel, where Sean designed a girlie spectacular on a series of elevating, pivoting, circular platforms, with sound design by my friend and Theatre Projects colleague David Collison: an early Theatre Projects adventure into the Americas.

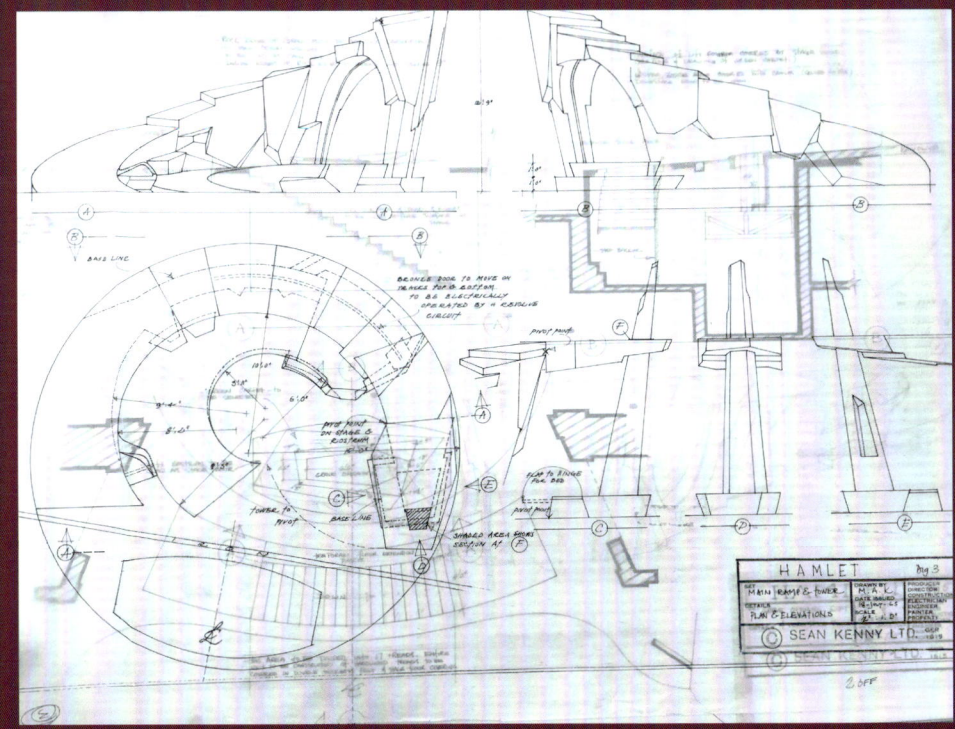

Sean Kenny's design for *Hamlet*, the opening production of the National Theatre at the Old Vic

Meeting 9

9th Meeting of The National Theatre Building Committee

22 Duchy Street, SE1
Monday 16th July 1963, 11:30 am

Present:
Sir Laurence Olivier, Mr. Norman Marshall (Chairmen), Mr. George Devine, Mr. Roger Furse, Mr. John Dexter, Mr. Peter Brook, Mr. Michael Elliott, Mr. Michael Benthall and Mr William Gaskill. Mr. H. Bennett [head of the L.C.C.'s architects department 1956-1971] was in attendance.
Apologies:
Apologies for absence were received from Mr. Michel Saint-Denis, Mr. Peter Hall and Miss Tanya Moiseiwitsch.

Mr. Bennett explained the background of the South Bank development, which had been planned as a comprehensive scheme some ten years before. If the sites for the National Theatre and Opera House were not large enough they could, subject to the consent of the L.C.C., be expanded slightly at either end, towards Hungerford Bridge in the case of the former and towards County Hall in the case of the latter. It was also possible to approach Shell to find out if they would modify their attitude on their right to an unrestricted view of the river.

Mr. Bennett said that the document received from the Building Committee in reply to the comments of the Arts Council and its Drama Panel on the National Theatre Basic Requirements indicated that it had moved away from some of the assumptions contained in the early suggestions for Basic Requirements. It was most important that the Committee should, if possible, clarify its attitude on the type and size of the two theatres envisaged.

Mr. Elliott agreed and suggested that it was up to the National Theatre organisation, which was to use the theatres, to decide on their functions.

Sir Laurence Olivier said that it was the responsibility of the Building Committee to give a decision as representatives of the theatrical profession.

During the subsequent discussion on the most suitable size and form for the two theatres, Mr. Bennett showed plans of German theatres, including Bochum, Gelsenkirchen and Frankfurt. He reassured the Committee on the problem of the fire curtain and suggested that a proscenium could be treated as flexible both horizontally and vertically.

Sir Laurence Olivier said that he was in favour of one perfect adaptable theatre, with another smaller experimental theatre.

Mr. Elliott expressed economic and technical reservations on the building of a theatre satisfactorily adaptable to both the proscenium and open stage.

The following resolutions were finally agreed:

1. One theatre should be adaptable to open stage and proscenium stage, seating 1,000 in its amphitheatre form.

2. One theatre, of three to four hundred seats, should be completely adaptable to any shape.

3. The two theatres should be planned together so that account could be taken of common services and accessibility.

Mr. Devine raised the question of procedure in selecting the architect for the National Theatre. It was agreed to delay discussion of this until the meeting on July 18th with the Panel of Advisers.

Panel of Advisors

The Panel of Advisors consisted of three distinguished architects: Sir Robert Matthew, the London County Council (LCC) Chief Architect 1946-1953; Hubert Bennett, then present LCC Chief Architect; and Sir William Holford, an important planner. They were joined by the painter John Piper and Norman Marshall, co-chair with Sir Laurence of the building committee.

Meeting 10

10th Meeting of The National Theatre Building Committee

22 Duchy Street, SE1
Thursday 25th July 1963, 10:45 pm

Present:
Sir Laurence Olivier, Mr. Norman Marshall (Chairmen), Mr. George Devine and Mr. Roger Furse. Mr. Stephen Arlen was in attendance.
Apologies:
Apologies for absence were received from Mr. Peter Hall, Mr. Peter Brook, Mr. Michel Saint-Denis, Mr. John Dexter, Mr. William Gaskill, Mr. Michael Benthall, Mr. Michael Elliott and Miss Tanya Moiseiwitsch.

Confidential lists of short-listed architects, and of those persons under consideration in an advisory capacity and of those candidates whose submissions were rejected by the Panel of Advisers as a result of the survey, were examined and discussed by the Committee. It was agreed that the deletion of some names be recommended and Mr. Marshall undertook to report this to the Panel of Advisers.

It was agreed that members of the Building Committee should be given an opportunity to examine the submissions of those rejected as a result of the survey. Arrangements for this would be finalised with the Secretary of the South Bank Board and a letter detailing them should be sent to members of the Building Committee.

It was further agreed that the next meeting of the Building Committee should be called after members had examined the survey rejects.

Listing the Architects

The building committee had clearly won its way over the selection process. The selection would be based not upon submitted schemes but upon a process of interview by a broader group of theatre and architectural advisors, followed by selection. This unusual competition was advertised in the architectural press and drew letters of complaint from some architects, who suspected that the results might be preordained.

A wide range of architects was considered. The list on 24th May 1963 included Hugh Casson; Peter Moro (then the leading theatre architect in the UK, with the Nottingham Playhouse to his credit); Ahrends, Burton and Koralek; Stirling and Gowan; and Denys Lasdun. George Devine, who had always had a keen interest in architecture, put forward Ernö Goldfinger; Powell and Moya (responsible for the Chichester Festival Theatre and also endorsed by Sir Laurence); Howell Killick Partridge and Amis; Elidir Davies (Mermaid Theatre). Theo Crosby led a team of Chalk, Crompton and Herron of Archigram. Also included were Cedric Price, and Eldred Evans and Dennis Gailey.[23]

Extensive discussion led to seven firms being invited to submit themselves: Casson, Richard Llewelyn-Davies, Gibberd, Martin, Powell and Moya, Spence, and Lasdun. Powell and Moya, Spence, and Martin declined on grounds of being already overcommitted.

Through the summer of 1963, this list was refined. The final list for interview consisted of: Ahrends, Burton and Koralek; Architects Co-Partnership; Philip Dowson of Arup Associates; Bridgwater Shepheard & Epstein; Burnet, Tait & Lorne, with the German theatre architect Walter Ruhnau; Peter Carter; Casson and Conder; James Cubitt with American architect Philip Johnson; Elidir Davies; Evans and Gailey; Frederick Gibberd; Ernö Goldfinger; Howell Killick Partridge and Amis; Denys Lasdun; Richard Llewelyn-Davies; Peter Moro; Brian O'Rorke; Richard Sheppard, Robson & Partners; Stirling and Gowan; and Yorke, Rosenberg Mardell.[24]

Meeting 11

11th Meeting of The National Theatre Building Committee

22 Duchy Street, SE1
Tuesday 21st August 1963, 5:15 pm

Present:
Sir Laurence Olivier, Mr. Norman Marshall (Chairmen), Mr. John Dexter, Mr. William Gaskill, Mr. Roger Furse and Mr. George Devine. Mr. Stephen Arlen and Mr. Kenneth Rae were in attendance.
Apologies:
Apologies were received from Mr. Michael Benthall, Mr. Peter Brook, Mr. Michel Saint-Denis, Mr. Michael Elliott, Mr. Peter Hall and Miss Tanya Moiseiwitsch.

The Letter received by the Secretary from the Secretary of the South Bank Board inviting the Committee to send three representatives, including Mr. Norman Marshall to the interviews due to take place, with architect candidates on the 17th, 24th and 25th of October, 1963, was discussed.

It was considered essential that Sir Laurence should attend all three interview sessions.

It was further agreed to ask Lord Cottesloe if at least five members of the National Theatre Building Committee could be present at the interviews.

The Secretary drew attention to the request stated in the letter for a revised version of the basic requirements for the National Theatre as submitted to the South Bank Board in December 1962. It was agreed that a technical sub-committee composed of Heads of Departments, should be convened to deal with this matter.

It was agreed to ask the Secretary of the South Bank Board for the questions likely to be asked by the architects at the interviews.

Meeting 12

12th Meeting of The National Theatre Building Committee

22 Duchy Street, SE1
Wednesday 18th September 1963, 5:30 pm

Present:
Mr. Norman Marshall (in the Chair), Mr. William Gaskill, Mr. Michael Elliott and Mr. Michael Benthall. Mr. Stephen Arlen and the Secretary were in attendance.
Apologies:
Apologies for absence were received from Sir Laurence Olivier, Mr. Peter Brook, Mr. George Devine, Mr. Michel Saint-Denis, Miss Tanya Moiseiwitsch, Mr. Peter Hall, Mr. John Dexter and Mr. Roger Furse.

It was unanimously agreed to send five members of the committee to the architectural selection interviews, as there was no-one who could not make a special contribution. It was agreed that the five representatives should be Sir Laurence Olivier, Mr. Peter Brook, Mr. George Devine, Mr. Michael Elliott and Mr. William Gaskill.

The Secretary thought it was essential that the Committee should meet before the October interviews. Mr. Elliott considered that all five members should have a detailed, unanimously agreed viewpoint about the major points of the design of the theatre. He offered to draw up a detailed questionnaire as a basis for discussion at future meetings. Mr. Marshall agreed to ask Mr. Hubert Bennett for a list of questions prepared by Sir Robert Matthew to which the architect candidates would require answers.

Mr. Marshall thought that the first question to be asked by potential architects would be the amount of money available for the building. It was agreed that the £1,000,000 voted would prove insufficient but that this was a problem beyond the competence of the Building Committee. It was their function to see that the ideal theatre was designed. The Secretary however undertook to raise the matter of finance with the Chairman of the National Theatre Board in case it should prove politic for the matter to be raised by him at the South Bank Board.

National Theatre Board Minute 80/63
Building Committee – South Bank Board

The Secretary reported that negotiations with Lord Cottesloe and the Panel of Advisors had resulted in dates being fixed for the interviewing of architect candidates which would enable the Director to attend, The interviews would be held on October 24th, 25th and 26th and it had been agreed that five members of the National Theatre Building Committee should attend along with three representatives from the Sadler's Wells Committee. On November 22nd short-listed architects would be interviewed by the South Bank Board. Mr. Moore [Board member Henry Moore] asked at 'what point the National Theatre Board would be consulted on the choice of an architect,' the Chairman said that the matter would be reported back to the National Theatre Board after the South Bank Board meeting on November 22nd.

QUESTIONS CONCERNING THE DESIGN OF THE NATIONAL THEATRE
It has been suggested, following the inspection of the architects' submitted evidence, that the basic requirements for the design of the National Theatre must be specified and agreed upon by the Building Committee, particularly as at the interviews the Building Committee will be on trial at least as much as the individual architect, and must be able to give clear answers to certain questions.

The following is an attempt to suggest a basis for the Committee's discussions preceding the interviews. These discussions will presumably also form a starting point for the eventual briefing of the chosen architect.

A. THE MAIN STAGE
1. What is this theatre to be used for?
2. What seating capacity should the theatre have?
3. To what degree should the stage be adaptable?
4. Does an adaptable stage demand an adaptable auditorium?
5. Should it be possible to mount conventional proscenium arch productions when desired or can all drama at all times at a National Theatre be produced on an open stage?
6. Should the theatre be able to receive the major foreign classical companies?
7. Should there be a fly tower? Should it have any unusual characteristics?
8. What should be the relative sizes of auditorium?
9. Are full electrical and mechanical facilities to be provided? (i.e, revolve, lifts, Sliding stages, etc.)
10. Will unprecedented technical flexibility for repertory change-over be a primary feature of the design?
11. Will the large number of productions available for repertory at any one time vitally affect the size and nature of the servicing areas? (i.e. scenery and costume workshops and stores, etc.)
12. Can the need for flexibility be allowed to limit drastically every individual production at a National Theatre? If not, must methods not previously used in this country be found to avoid these limitations?

B. THE SMALL STAGE
1. What is this theatre to be used for?
2. What seating capacity?
3. What degree of adaptability?
4. What basic forms must this theatre be able to assume?
5. In each form can there be any major sacrifice of facilities for that form?
6. Should intimacy be one of its main design requirements?
7. Will the same degree of repertory be required as on the main stage?

C. REHEARSAL STAGES
1. Should there be a rehearsal stage for each theatre the same size as their respective acting areas and provided with minimal flying, mechanical and electrical facilities to allow for dress rehearsals?
2. Should it be possible for an entire production to be mounted on a traveling stage that can pass from set-up in the workshops, to dress rehearsal in the rehearsal stages, to performance on the public stages with the minimum of dismantling and time?
3. Should there be a major concern with public activities other than the evening performances, and facilities provided accordingly? (i.e. Children's performances in the morning, restaurants, film performances connected with international theatre, lectures and conferences on international drama, play library, exhibitions of stage design, recording and television facilities, etc.)

Lasdun Emerges

On 19th June 1963 the second Chichester season began with a revival of the sensational *Uncle Vanya*. I was now the lighting designer and had the great experience of working with Sir Laurence and designer Sean Kenny on his wondrously simple set of a clapboard back wall to the thrust stage. Changing only the lighting could make the wall represent an interior or exterior. More successes followed, including *Saint Joan* with an incandescent performance from Joan Plowright. The whole season was a magical experience for me as lighting designer, and a personal introduction to being part of Sir Laurence's 'family.' Wow!

Meanwhile at the National, from the time that Lasdun's name came to the attention of the selection panel it was annotated with the comment "v. good." His growing reputation as an architect of special ability had been enhanced by the Royal College of Physicians, which was under construction in Regent's Park, and his project for the University of East Anglia.

Lasdun had always taken particular pains to ensure his reputation was nurtured with care. He worked hard to create a legend around his name. He knew the pivotal importance of projects being well-photographed and he would be extremely painstaking about picture selection. He also took great care over the words that accompanied those images. He felt inadequate as a writer and sought assistance from friends, staff, and even his own son, James.[25] He would seek to encapsulate his intentions with a catchphrase; such as the "Fourth Theatre," which he later used to describe the lobbies of the National.

Once the National project was won, its design was conducted, even within his own office, in great secrecy. His staff recall that the National designs were developed in rooms that were off-limits and the windows of the basement model room were screened by brown paper.[26] Everything seemed concerned with maintaining his personal control.

Lasdun's extreme sensitivity in regard to his image and publicity goes some way to explaining much that was to occur in the months and years to come. A Lasdun memo on an architectural press visit to the National in 1975 gives an insight: "Visited site in pouring rain and no lights on in the Lyttelton. They seemed to understand relationship of building to the city. DL volunteered that Denys Lasdun & Partners (DL&P) would stand one shot if it were a really good one. […] DL&P must certainly find out exactly who they are using for all aspects of the writing and DL&P should edit anything from Theatre Projects."[27]

Meeting 13 & 14

13th & 14th Meetings of The National Theatre Building Committee

22 Duchy Street, SE1

Thursday 26th September 1963, 6:00 pm
Present:
Sir Laurence Olivier, Mr. Norman Marshall (Chairmen), Mr. Michel Saint-Denis, Mr. William Gaskill, Mr. Michael Elliott and Mr. George Devine, Mr. Stephen Arlen and Mr. Kenneth Rae.
Apologies:
Mr. Michael Benthall, Mr. Peter Brook, Mr. Roger Furse, Mr. Peter Hall, Mr. John Dexter and Miss Tanya Moiseiwitsch.

Monday 30th September 1963, 6:00 pm
Present:
Sir Laurence Olivier (in the Chair), Mr. William Gaskill, Mr. Michael Elliott and Mr. George Devine, Mr. Stephen Arlen and Mr. Kenneth Rae.
Apologies:
Mr. Michael Benthall, Mr. Peter Brook, Mr. Roger Furse, Mr. Peter Hall, Mr. John Dexter and Miss Tanya Moiseiwitsch, Mr. Michel Saint-Denis, Mr. Norman Marshall.

Referring to the Record of the Meeting on the 18th September, the Secretary drew the attention of the meeting to the paper prepared by Mr. Elliott, which had been circulated. A copy of the paper had been recorded in the Record Book.

Very full discussion took place during the two meetings, and the following overall conclusions were reached.

<u>Main auditorium and Acting Area.</u>
A single theatre would be required with an adaptable stage/acting area. Adaptability of the stage area would in all probability make it necessary for the auditorium to be adaptable to ensure maximum comfort and visibility for the audience. It was considered that the proscenium aspect of the adaptable stage should go as far as the solution reached at Gelsenkirchen, and in the amphitheatre form as far as Chichester. The whole potential acting area should be covered with a flytower, the grid of which should be designed for the special requirements of repertory working. The minimum stage area, i.e. the area in the rear of the amphitheatre stage should be calculated as follows:-
- Width – three times the overall width of the amphitheatre stage
- Depth – twice the overall width of the amphitheatre stage.

The size and nature of the servicing areas with access to the stage should be suitable to store the large number of productions in the repertory at any one time. The most complete electrical and mechanical devices should be provided on the acting area. The seating capacity to be determined from a prime instruction to the architect that, from a focal and dominating point on the acting area, all members of the audience must be able to see facial expression. It was thought that this figure would be about 1,000 in amphitheatre form.

These conclusions clarified a great number of the points in the memorandum.

Further points made were:
Nothing in the design would inhibit the main purpose – that of the presentation of drama.
1. That, within the conclusions listed above, the theatre should be able to invite foreign classical companies.
2. That the technical flexibility of the equipment should permit rapid repertory change-overs, and even the provision of a rehearsal stage from which scenery could be set up and transferred complete to the main stage.
3. That the relationship between workshops, rehearsal stage and main stage should allow scenery when completed and painted to be set up in the workshops and transferred complete to the rehearsal stage and main stage. It was considered that this scheme would be both practical and economic.
4. The foyers of the theatre should be constructed as to allow adequate room for exhibitions, etc.

<u>The Small Theatre</u>
The size of the small theatre should permit seating of up to a maximum of 400. The theatre should be entirely flexible, and admit of infinite variations in both seating and staging arrangements. The architect should study and improve upon all experimental areas which have been recently constructed. The entire area should be covered by flying facilities and the whole floor space should be in sectional lifts.

The Selection of the Architect

The interviews took place on 17th and 24th-25th October 1963 in the Council Room at 4 St. James Square, London. The panel included, for the theatre, Sir Laurence, George Devine, Peter Brook, Michael Elliott and Bill Gaskill.

Hamlet, with Peter O'Toole, under Sir Laurence's direction – the first production of the National Theatre at the Old Vic – opened on 22nd October! Completion of the renovation work at the Vic, with new forestage, lighting and sound installations had, of course, been late. Rehearsals survived alongside builders working, but the new curtain did go up on time – just! This was one extraordinarily busy time!

Each architect had submitted evidence of his qualifications.[28] There were three broad categories of architect. First, those with theatre experience: Peter Moro had recently completed the well-received Nottingham Playhouse. He had also been on the design team of the Royal Festival Hall in 1951. Peter and I had become friends through the ABTT and were then working together on the new flexible Gulbenkian Theatre for the University of Hull; I was part of Peter's team at his National interview. Elidir Davies was another architect with extensive theatre experience, most particularly with the then-popular open-end-stage Mermaid Theatre. Burnet, Tait & Lorne applied with Walter Ruhnau, the noted German theatre architect (responsible for the highly regarded recent theatre in Gelsenkirchen) as consultant.

Hugh Casson (with whom I had worked as a lighting designer, when he designed the scenery for the Michael Codron musical *The Golden Touch*) spoke of the need to be "imaginative and liberating without resort to the tiresomely self-assertive or bizarre."[29] Goldfinger included an *Architectural Design* issue illustrating his work. Stirling and Gowan stressed their lack of experience and preconceptions about theatre architecture. The Ahrends team spoke of architectural abstractions; Yorke Rosenberg Mardell spoke of modernity that may have alienated the theatre representatives. Bridgwater suggested, "Others might appear to be more qualified, but none would approach [the project] with keener interest."[30] Architects Co-Partnership expressed an interest in the theatre form debate and expressed reservations about adaptability.

James Cubitt presented with the American architect Philip Johnson, then designing the New York State Theater in the Lincoln Center. They made a statement derived from Johnson's experience in New York with George Balanchine, who had completely changed Johnson's original design concept. "Not only do we believe that the theatre should be enjoyed for its festive aspects, as well as for the drama, but that this can be most reasonably obtained by revitalising the baroque auditorium (as distinct from that conceived by Wagner and Semper) with its tiers of balconies embracing the proscenium opening."[31] This statement, in 1963, was amazing, yet went completely unrecognised. In the '60s, balconies and boxes were almost universally condemned as being socially divisive and the proscenium was seen only as an illusionistic barrier. It was to be nearly twenty years before the truth of the statement (and a return to three-dimensional theatre) was to be recognised.

Richard Sheppard's team spoke of the importance of backstage function driving the planning of the building. Bill Howell wrote, "We have never built a theatre, but considering the record of those who have, we do not think this is necessarily a fatal drawback."[32] It must be regretted that this was not taken more seriously. Bill went on to design Frank Dunlop's Young Vic, which became a landmark achievement – the first modern courtyard theatre. This led to my partnering with him to design Christ's Hospital School, Horsham – which, in turn, later inspired the Royal Shakespeare's Swan Theatre at Stratford.

The record of the interviews[33] suggest there was extended discussion of theatre matters. Stirling suggested stacking the opera house and theatre vertically to overcome the limited site area. Rosenberg proposed emulating the sparkling character of the West End. Bridgwater talked of the riverside site and a floating pier restaurant. Peter Moro told the panel that he was sceptical about the adaptable auditorium – he later felt his rejection was due to this pessimism. Others sparked little interest.

On 26th October eight names ended up on the short list. Architects Co-Partnership (annotated second); Yorke Rosenberg Mardell; Ahrends, Burton and Koralek (also annotated second); Howell Killick Partridge and Amis; Stirling and Cowan; Richard Llewelyn-Davies and John Weeks; and Richard Sheppard, Robson and Partners. Annotated first: Denys Lasdun.

The summary sheet opens beneath the heading "Very Confidential", with the words "Unanimously Lasdun." [34]

Richard Lynex, secretary to the South Bank Theatre Board, reported "three days of grueling interviews." He described the interviewing panel thusly: "It would be hardly an exaggeration to say that no two of them think the same about anything." [35]

But the final selection meeting ended twenty minutes early. Denys Lasdun was appointed.

Stories abound about how Lasdun succeeded in so impressing the selection panel. Peter Moro always contrasted his honesty with Lasdun's ability to impress. Moro said, "I'm very bad at interviews. I'm far too honest. I've lost any amount of jobs by saying, 'Don't attempt this; I've tried it and it can't be done.'" [36] He told the committee that an adaptable theatre was impossible and the design process would take six years. Lasdun, without any knowledge of theatre design, readily agreed to try to solve the adaptable theatre challenge and in response to the question on timing he said, "Not a minute longer than necessary." [37]

Lasdun did describe his process. He explained the need for close artistic collaboration with the users for six to twelve months, "during which the architect must absorb your wants but also your dreams," [38] but he noted that the relationship changes after twelve months; then it was his business to produce the designs and that would be done without their interference.

Undoubtedly, Lasdun, in his twenty minutes of allotted interview time, impressed the panel. His charm and confidence were overwhelming. Secretary Richard Lynex, in a letter to the chairman of the boards of both the opera and theatre, wrote, "Lasdun was outstandingly the best of those interviewed. It was an incredible result, and I can only regard it as a direct intervention of providence." [39]

In 1982, Olivier recalled, "Lasdun made an immediate impression by coming in unaccompanied and sitting entirely alone at the other side of the table. He seemed to carry a quiet conviction. He said things like 'I imagine the supremely vital element in such a building to be the spiritual content of it.'

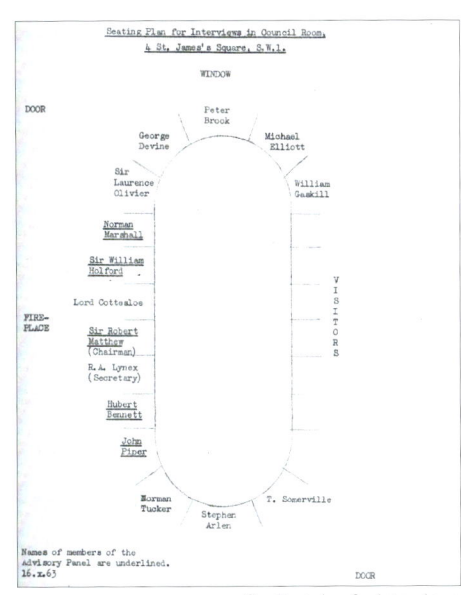

Seating plan for interviews

Of course, we all fell like a hod of bricks for that one. When we asked if he could agree that our [building] committee might be of some small assistance in an advisory capacity, he declared that he would welcome any comments of any kind that we might care to make and that the relationship should surely be regarded as a partnership. He was the one for us alright." [40]

Lasdun's interview didn't overrun its twenty minutes. He admitted that he had no experience in theatre design.

On Friday 22nd November 1963 Lasdun's appointment was announced to a press conference. Lasdun had a handwritten note to explain his design principles to the press: "SCALE SPACE MOVEMENT ANATOMY... COHERENCE / UNITY NOT UNIFORMITY + AUTONOMY." [41]

We had been warned... and the dye was cast.

But there was to be almost no publicity about the appointment: that evening, the BBC announced that President Kennedy had been shot in Dallas, Texas.

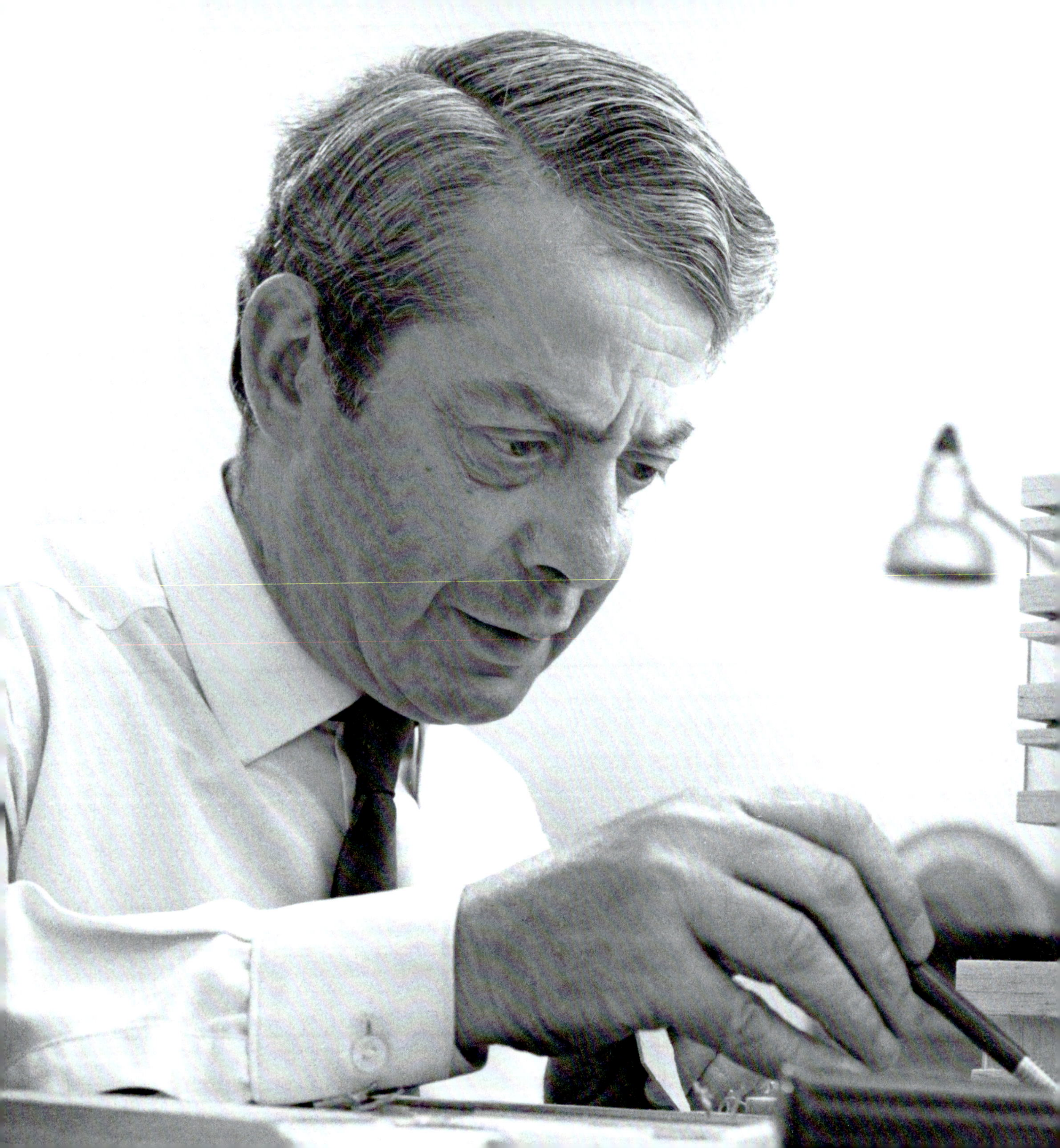

2.2 Design Begins

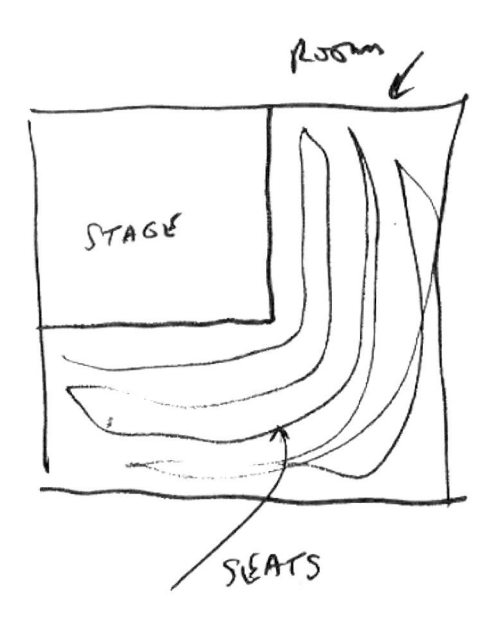

Meetings #16-21

In the same week Lasdun was interviewed, the National Theatre Company was born at the Old Vic, opening on 22nd October 1963 with Sir Laurence's production of *Hamlet* starring, briefly, Peter O'Toole, fresh from his triumph in the film *Lawrence Of Arabia*. His Hamlet was less impressive.

The production was designed by Sean Kenny, who had re-designed the forestage of the Old Vic, removing the Victoriana of the proscenium and pushing the stage yet further into the auditorium. David Collison and I had installed innovative new sound and lighting systems.

Olivier was creating a new company, one that proved to be of extraordinary import, with a cast of players who were stars in the making. In those early years they included, from the Royal Court, his two assistant directors, John Dexter and William Gaskill, with actors Robert Stephens, Frank Finlay, Colin Blakely and Joan Plowright. Others in the company included veterans Michael Redgrave and Edith Evans; West End stars Maggie Smith, Geraldine McEwan, and Max Adrian; with newcomers Albert Finney, Ian McKellen, Derek Jacobi, Edward Petherbridge, Anthony Hopkins, Ronald Pickup, Michael York and Michael Gambon.

Hamlet was followed by *Saint Joan* and *Uncle Vanya*, transferred from Chichester, and then a new and brilliant production of *The Recruiting Officer*, directed by Bill Gaskill and designed by René Allio, which I also lit. The climax of the season on 23rd April 1964 was undoubtedly Sir Laurence's extraordinary performance in *Othello*, directed by Dexter and designed by Jocelyn Herbert.

In one year, Olivier had created a new theatrical enterprise, directed two productions, played in two more and made British theatre history. He had led on every detail, down to the typography of programmes and the uniforms for the ushers. Now he had to turn to designing a new theatre… with his brand-new architect.

That architect was later to describe the two-year process which he was now embarked upon as "two year's fairly good hell with the greatest intelligences the British theatre can offer." [42]

An architect entirely new to theatre is appointed, a National Theatre company finally arrives. Despite Lasdun having explained the need for six to twelve months of discussion, in just four months, Scheme B emerges – a theatre with stage and audience in one square room. At the request of the South Bank board, a proscenium arch theatre is added to the plan.

Then: to Lasdun's fury, the plans are leaked to a national newspaper…

Meeting 16

Note: There is a record of Meeting 15 being scheduled for October 1963; there is no record of that meeting ever having taken place.

16th Meeting of The National Theatre Building Committee

22 Duchy Street, SE1
Thursday 9th January 1964, 5:30 pm

Present:
Sir Laurence Olivier, Mr. Norman Marshall (Chairmen). Mr. Michel Saint-Denis, Mr. Michael Benthall, Mr. Michael Elliott, Mr. John Dexter and Mr. William Gaskill. Mr. Stephen Arlen and Mr. Kenneth Rae were in attendance. Mr. Denys Lasdun and Mr. Peter Softley were present by invitation.

Apologies:
Apologies for absence were received from Mr. Peter Brook, Mr. George Devine, Mr. Peter Hall and Miss Tanya Moiseiwitsch.

OLIVIER: The National Theatre Board is the customer. The South Bank Board is the party responsible to the Treasury for the building of the theatres, the paying of the bills and all the legal side.

LASDUN: Let us discuss the nature and anatomy of the theatre.

OLIVIER: We get back to the problem of what is a theatre. I suppose to us the most deeply essential aspect of a new theatre exists in the conditions for the work in it. When we visited the Berliner Ensemble, we found that the heart was in the canteen. We have a good company at the moment with a strong sense of unity, and this sense of unity has to be catered for whenever and wherever possible.

BENTHALL: The actor/audience relationship is very important.

ELLIOTT: Would Mr. Lasdun welcome a series of controversial discussions?

GASKILL: Would he welcome a series of personal statements?

LASDUN: It seems to us that we must work from the centre outwards, and that everything else must spring from that.

ST. DENIS: Is there any point in saying what we want the public to feel like outside, as well as inside the auditorium?

LASDUN: The whole building is the theatre, but I want to concentrate on a point and work outwards.

GASKILL: Most of us feel that the impulse for a new form of theatre springs from an attempt to present the play – or whatever happens – to the audience in a more open and humble way than has sometimes been the case in the past. The movement towards the open stage looks backward and at the same time looks forward to a new concept of society. Though the old theatres have charm, they are hierarchical. We should have a theatre that expresses unity and in which all have a fair chance to see and hear. The desire to create a greater emotional relationship between the actor and the audience has led people back to the open stage.

ELLIOTT: While agreeing with William Gaskill that there is a social connection, I think there is greater significance in the parallel in development between church architecture and theatre architecture. You get a change of impact when the actor passes across the curtain line. He becomes dimensional and one gets a greater sense of his personality on the fore-stage. The open stage has not only a social but a ritualistic significance.

LASDUN: I agree. The church is now also going "in the round".

OLIVIER: It was not entirely a sociological instinct that made the actors go back from the public. Comedy and comic acting is a main consideration in placing the audience in one direction. Comedy is very difficult in theatre in the round. In the seventeenth century, growing use of the aside made it imperative to put the audience in one direction. The soliloquies of *Richard III* are asides and not meditations. The Italian theatre led the way due to its use of mime. Personally, I don't think the actors took much notice of the people sitting on the side of the stage in Elizabethan days. The inn-yard was a useful form and the theatre could always be converted to a bear-pit if it fell on evil days, but I think the actors wanted their backs against the wall more and more.

BENTHALL: Historically speaking, the Greek

shape gave the most contact between the actor and the audience. Socially the audience were all on one slant, concentrating on one spot.

MARSHALL: The lines of sight at Delphi are marvellous even from the side seats. The Greek theatre came round the chorus, not round the actor.

ST. DENIS: The feeling that the public gets when it comes into the theatre plays an important part in what it feels later on. The public of today wants to receive a different impact from what it did thirty or forty years ago. The artifice of opera, which you have inside the box, is ready to be replaced by another convention. An impact of reality that is often anti-theatre. Every member of the audience should be in a position to hear and see from wherever he is sitting. That is why the problem of numbers is so important. Everywhere there is a conflict between the number of people that one wants for economic and social reasons and the impulse for a diminution of numbers called for by impact. What do we want the public to feel in a National Theatre before they come into the auditorium?

MARSHALL: A Canadian told me that Minneapolis was unpopular because there was no feeling of warmth, gaiety or entertainment. It could be a lecture hall or library. It imparts an intellectual feeling to the audience. The auditorium doesn't welcome them.

ST. DENIS: The first time I went to the Mermaid I got a completely new feeling in the main hall.

ARLEN: Taking account of what you have said, what is the optimum number of people to generate the right feeling?

ST. DENIS: Every time you get above 1,100 or 1,200 you get beyond sixty feet from the curtain line to the furthest seat, and feeling becomes lost and dissipated. In the new, adaptable Lincoln Centre Theatre, you have 1,170 seats and a distance of sixty foot from the curtain line to the back seat.

RAE: Do they get a capacity of 1,170 all the time, or does it vary in its different forms?

ST. DENIS: The capacity does not fall below 1,100.

BENTHALL: The emotional problem of getting in touch with the actor is not just a physical thing.

ELLIOTT: To put an audience on one plane should create a greater sense of unity, but in doing so the volume of space created can be so big that you get a feeling of bareness which is difficult to overcome in the open stage. Circles can, in fact, bring people closer together.

OLIVIER: In our present theatres people can look at the stage from two directions – up from the stalls or down from the circles. In early days the audience looked up to the actors on a platform in the market place. In many proscenium theatres most people look up, e.g. the Old Vic. What do you, as an audience, want to do: look up or look down?

ARLEN and RAE: Look down on the actor.

ELLIOTT: We should provide the audience with an alternative.

OLIVIER: The best seat for me is the fifth row in the Birmingham Repertory theatre.

LASDUN: I don't know yet where I prefer to sit.

ST. DENIS: The lines of sight are very important for the shape of the auditorium. At Chichester and in the round more movement is dictated. The shape of the auditorium influences the shape of a production and has acoustical consequences.

OLIVIER: I like movement. When I did "Vanya" at Chichester, I thought I added 15% to what I would have done in a picture frame. Now I find that I have cut out very few moves in transferring it to the proscenium of the Old Vic.

MARSHALL: Do we want anything as definite as a picture frame at any time? In the new German theatres you get the feeling that the stage and auditorium are in one room. The Old Vic now seems to me very good.

DEXTER: It is very difficult when you get to *Hobson's Choice*.

ST. DENIS: Even now the Old Vic remains a picture frame.

ARLEN: With *Hobson* you run into sight-line trouble.

> "It seems to us that we must work from the centre outwards, and that everything else must spring from that."
> — Denys Lasdun

> "Circles can, in fact, bring people closer together."
> — Michael Elliott

2.2 Design Begins: Meetings #16-21   107

> "What I am dreaming about is a space stage that would give a feeling of audience and actors being in the same room."
> Michel Saint-Denis

> "How can we get the atmosphere of an old theatre in a new one? Plaster and wood is better for voice."
> Laurence Olivier

MARSHALL: The audience/actor relationship at the Old Vic in the case of "The Recruiting Officer" is excellent.

GASKILL: Yes, but the Old Vic stage is now an approximation to the restoration stage.

ELLIOTT: The world of the actors is not the world of the audience in the proscenium stage. Out of that magical world something is presented to the audience. With the open stage there is no such separate world. There is a wide gulf fixed here philosophically and ascetically.

GASKILL: Isn't it easier to do naturalistic plays in a picture frame?

ELLIOTT: That is not the point. The actor has different functions in the two different forms of stage.

ARLEN: The effect of the open stage on me is that I want to go back. I am embarrassed when I am too close to it. This doesn't mean that I don't like the open stage.

OLIVIER: I don't know how to suggest a claustrophobic room on an open stage or at the Old Vic.

BENTHALL: The magic of spectacle has been diminished by the film and TV screen. That is why we are trying to get back to human relationships in the theatre. The actual acting, between me and you, is conveyed better on the open stage, though I am very worried about comedy and "Richard III".

ARLEN: I got more impact in Chichester than in any other theatre, but I would have been embarrassed if too close.

DEXTER: Have you sat in the first two rows?

ARLEN: No.

ST. DENIS: At Delphi there is a gap between the actors and the audience and a stone wall and a step.

ARLEN: One always feels there is enough distance between actor and audience in the proscenium theatre.

MARSHALL: At Stratford, Ontario, they are moving the audience back and up a bit.

OLIVIER: As far as actors are concerned, acting at Chichester is horrible.

DEXTER: Some actors prefer it.

ST. DENIS: The actors at the T.N.P (Théâtre National Populaire), hated arena acting at first, but have come to like it.

MARSHALL: Can't we get the freedom of movement of the open stage without putting so many people at the sides?

ELLIOTT: Can't we get it without jettisoning all we have learnt about scenery and lighting in the last three centuries?

ST. DENIS: What I am dreaming about is a space stage that would give a feeling of audience and actors being in the same room.

DEXTER: The National Theatre must be able to accommodate a very wide repertory of plays.

MARSHALL: At Minneapolis, *The Three Sisters* and the Moliere play worked but *Death of a Salesman* failed.

OLIVIER: I am not worried about human relationships on an open stage but about comedy and the aside plays.

BENTHALL: The full three sides or semi-circle may not be the answer.

DEXTER: Coming back to a play like *Hobson*, you need certain real elements.

GASKILL: As soon as you start thinking that you won't go all the way, you start to think that a glorified proscenium theatre is the best.

ST. DENIS: It is the size of the auditorium, not the size of the stage, that governs intimacy.

OLIVIER: We are all agreed that whatever

we do the audience must be engaged in as equal an intensity as possible. Every member of it must see every wink, hear every whisper of the actor.

DEXTER: The first three rows of the Gallery are very good at the Old Vic.

ARLEN: You get a good ring on the voices in the first three rows of the Gallery.

OLIVIER: How can we get the atmosphere of an old theatre in a new one? Plaster and wood is better for voice. Acoustically, the theatre at Antwerp, which has plaster and wood, is the best for me.

ST. DENIS: Mr. Lasdun should see the Aldwych Company in the Histories at the Aldwych and at Stratford, *Othello* at the Vic, at Chichester and on tour.

LASDUN: "Engaged intensity" is the central thing. We cannot duplicate the furnishings of an old theatre except by pastiche. We have looked at the Lincoln Theatre and Loeb. They are adaptable but they lack the operative intensity.

ST. DENIS: Why?

LASDUN: In the mechanics of conversion some of the seats virtually turn their backs on the acting area. We are going to try for adaptability, But we must find out what suffers in the process.

ST. DENIS: The National Theatre should not be adaptable in terms of Lincoln or Loeb. As soon as you play about with seats, it doesn't work.

LASDUN: We will see what happens. I believe adaptability is not a mechanical thing – it's to do with you and the theatre. An idea will come when we get our attitudes clear, but we will go through the motions of adaptability and see what it costs us in terms of engaged intensity. We have got Chichester and good, bad or indifferent, it is a laboratory to work in.

Lines of Confusion

The first meeting with the architect and the lines of confusion are already drawn. Denys Lasdun, quite rightly, begins by seeking to focus on the core essential: "the nature of theatre." But Olivier responds with a confusing opinion: "The conditions for the work… the heart was in the canteen."

Benthall brings it back into focus: "The actor/audience relationship."

Gaskill: "The old theatres have charm, [but] they are hierarchical."

Elliott: "The open stage has not only a social, but a ritualistic significance."

St. Denis (a good question): "What do we want the public to feel?"

Elliott: "Circles can, in fact, bring people closer together."

Discussion of the proscenium versus the open stage. Amidst the confusion, some specially significant statements were made:

St. Denis: "What I am dreaming about is a space stage that would give a feeling of audience and actors being in the same room." This phrase became central to the future conversations. But also: "It is the size of the auditorium, not the size of the stage, that governs intimacy." So, so true.

Olivier: "How can we get the atmosphere of an old theatre in a new one? Plaster and wood is better for voice."

Lasdun avoiding a response to this fundamental, instinctive plea for a 'theatrical' atmosphere, replies, "Engaged intensity is the central thing. We cannot duplicate the furnishings of an old theatre except by pastiche."

An architect's response… which, in fact, is only partially correct. "Engaged intensity is indeed the thing"… but it is that single attribute that Lasdun eventually failed to achieve. And Olivier's plea for plaster and wood was immediately rejected as old fashioned. Nobody on the committee was aware that the materials used in a theatre's construction might adversely affect the acoustics.

An Architect's Education Begins

Parallel to the monthly meetings of the building committee with the architect, Lasdun began his education into the weird world of theatre. Throughout the next months, he visited theatres and had meetings with individuals on the committee, which he noted with internal DL&P memoranda.

His first meeting was with the always flamboyant and always controversial Kenneth Tynan, on 28th January 1964. At their first meeting, Lasdun asked Tynan, "What is it that you could not do in an amphitheatre?"[43]

Ken's answer was characteristically provocative: "Practically everything! The preoccupation with the amphitheatre springs from an economic consideration and Guthrie is misleading because he is a director who likes to arrange crowds and does not care if people can hear the spoken word. The theatre of tomorrow might well want to make use of film, back-projection, etc. You could not do this in amphitheatre form. Very few plays could be performed in amphitheatre form, but the majority [would be] far better off with a proscenium."

Ken was very enamored with the Brecht's Berliner Ensemble. "The Theater am Schiffbauerdamm provides as good an experience of theatre as might be experienced anywhere."

An interesting comment. This famous theatre, a centre of German drama from Max Reinhardt to Bertolt Brecht, is a spectacular, baroquely decorated, 1892 auditorium which had housed a theatre company that for decades had been at the cutting edge of the European theatrical avant-garde. An ultimate demonstration perhaps of 'a sense of theatre' in architecture. But, sadly, this comment passed unnoticed.

Stratford, Ontario

Theater am Schiffbauerdamm, Berlin

Meeting 17

17th Meeting of The National Theatre Building Committee

22 Duchy Street, SE1
Wednesday 5th February 1964, 5:00 pm

Present:
Mr. Stephen Arlen (in the Chair), Mr. Michel Saint-Denis, Mr. William Gaskill, Mr. Michael Benthall, Mr. Michael Elliott, Mr. John Dexter and Mr. George Devine. Mr. Kenneth Rae was in attendance. Mr. Denys Lasdun and Mr. Peter Softley were present by invitation.

Apologies:
Apologies for absence were received from Sir Laurence Olivier, Mr. Norman Marshall, Mr. Peter Brook, Mr. Peter Hall and Miss Tanya Moiseiwitsch.

Mr. Lasdun said that since the last meeting of the Committee he and his colleagues had been considering the nature of their brief. The last document submitted by the National Theatre Board to the South Bank Board had suggested an amphitheatre that could be adapted to a proscenium, though he had been assured that this was in no way a final decision. In the last few weeks he had examined such data and photographs on the Lincoln Center and Gelsenkirchen as were available, and had also visited Chichester. Mr. Lasdun then circulated a document showing in juxtaposition rough ground plans for the theatres at the Lincoln Center, Gelsenkirchen, Chichester and Minneapolis. He described the mechanical device in the fore-stage area at the Lincoln Center which could either bring up a thrust stage for the amphitheatre or seating for the proscenium action and made the following observations on its so-called adaptability for both forms of presentation:

1. It involved two points of focus. The seating, which was fixed, was focused mainly on the thrust stage.
2. The thrust stage was a quarter the size of the Chichester stage.
3. If everyone in the audience was to see more than half the stage during a proscenium production, the width of the opening could not be less than 60'. If this 60' opening were masked in, the outer zones of seating would be put out of commission.
4. Even when adapted for amphitheatre presentation, the feeling generated had not the same feeling of one-room intimacy as at Chichester. This was probably due to the difference in proportion where the auditorium/stage was concerned as compared to Chichester.

The Committee agreed unanimously that the above were not admissible premises and went on to discuss the most desirable width of opening for a proscenium production. It was agreed that, bearing in mind the sort of plays which would be done in a proscenium, the width should not be more than 40'.

Mr. Arlen asked whether it was possible to design an adaptable theatre on the following premises:
- a proscenium opening of an absolute maximum of 40', it being noted that the width at the Old Vic was 29'.
- a seating capacity of not more than 1,200.
- an amphitheatre stage that was smaller than Chichester but larger than that at the Lincoln Center.

Mr. Lasdun said that he had not as yet found any solution that would accommodate these premises. The discussion proceeded as follows:

GASKILL: Is it not possible if you move the seats in the auditorium?

LASDUN: It is not just the seating but the walls as well which would have to be moved.

ELLIOTT: Hear, hear.

LASDUN: The Lincoln solution leaves you looking at a thrust stage that is no longer there.

DEVINE: Can you design anything that has two focal points?

LASDUN: I think we might do it another way, if you are prepared to forego the facilities

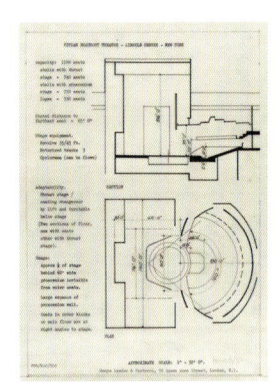

DL&P sketch: Vivian Beaumont Theater, New York

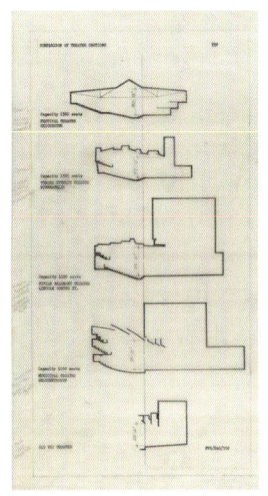

DL&P sketch, comparative sections, from top: Chichester, Guthrie Minneapolis, Beaumont NY, Gelsenkirchen Old Vic.

of flying. For instance, you could have a fan-shaped auditorium converging on a two-sided stage. The ceiling area would be continuous and unbroken over both auditorium and stage. The scenery could be changed by means of wagons brought in through doors in the walls of the stage area.

DEVINE: Why can't you have a hole for the flies?

LASDUN: You then get a frame. Cannot you conceive of getting scenic effects through ways other than flying?

ELLIOTT: There is no known alternative that is as satisfactory as flying.

LASDUN: The only immediate objection to this idea seemed to me to be that visiting companies geared to flying facilities couldn't operate in such a theatre.

ELLIOTT: There is more to it than that. Various kinds of scenic effects require a means of letting in objects, some of them quite large.

LASDUN: If you accept that, you are in the principle of Gelsenkirchen. You are out of the amphitheatre world altogether. It doesn't work.

DEXTER: What emerges from this is the fate of the experimental theatre. Should we make the second theatre less and not more experimental?

ARLEN: You are then back to the original brief as outlined in the proposals to the Treasury: that there should be a new amphitheatre built on the South Bank as the first phase, and that the Old Vic should serve as the proscenium theatre for some years until a new one was built. But in the early debates of this Committee it became clear that a clean division between an amphitheatre and a proscenium was not what the Committee wanted. They were hoping for a new form that would express a unity of what everybody wanted.

ELLIOTT: Lasdun is saying that we have produced a brief without examining its possibility.

GASKILL: Olivier feels that the idea of dividing plays into open stage and proscenium categories is bad – particularly as the result of his experience in producing "VANYA".

DEVINE: No-one has yet defined for Lasdun what the flies mean to us. It is an area that is free of actors and things that are already on the stage.

LASDUN: Softley has called the flies 'a filing system'.

DEVINE: There is something dramatic about an object that comes down and goes up, viz the curtain. It has an emotional effect.

ARLEN: Taking the history of the Old Vic in recent years, is it not true to say that producers have come forward rather than use the flies?

DEVINE: If you had to make a choice would you rather have flies or an audience/actor relationship?

GASKILL: I would choose the audience/actor relationship.

BENTHALL: Can we get two theatres for the price of one or can the National Theatre afford two?

ELLIOTT: To me the only solution seems to be three theatres – proscenium, open stage and studio/experimental. It seems that we must have two main theatres.

DEVINE: Do we want to have a theatre that is a statement of our time but with no flies, or a compromise, i.e. two different stages.

ARLEN: Mr. Lasdun is making the observation that our brief contains two things that are inadmissible.

LASDUN: After three and a half weeks of study – yes.

ARLEN: What re-briefing do you require?

DEVINE: Supposing we had all said "yes" to the premise of a 60' proscenium opening?

A Sense of Theatre

LASDUN: I would have been very unhappy.

DEVINE: Would you have given us flies?

LASDUN: Only with some reluctance. If you really care about the unity of audience and actor, this means a room. If you destroy the room with a void I have misgivings.

GASKILL: What we all feel is that we have been committed to an old type of theatre. We see the possibility of a new one but are frightened definitely to commit ourselves. It could be that the particular feeling that we have about the theatre at the moment will only last for thirty years.

LASDUN: If you are trying to make a theatre of today, you must change something to do it.

DEVINE: The trouble is that we are acting as a Committee on behalf of the whole profession and cannot entirely follow our individual inclinations.

LASDUN: I have not yet fully examined the possibilities of the site. I don't know whether there is room for two theatres on the South Bank, but there is the Old Vic.

ARLEN: If you have a one-room theatre and an experimental theatre on the South Bank would you be happy to keep the Old Vic as a proscenium theatre?

GASKILL: Only if we could have proper flying and wing space.

LASDUN: My visit to the Old Vic showed me the necessity for space to work in. Gelsenkirchen is designed for a proscenium in depth. As such it does its job much better than Lincoln can ever do as an adaptable theatre.

DEVINE: Can we design something with two points of focus?

Mr. Lasdun said that his experience so far seemed to show that the sculptural quality of a production depended largely upon one's proximity to it. Mr. Elliott felt that a great many other factors were involved.

BENTHALL: If we can have the Vic adapted for proscenium theatre and a new one and an experimental theatre on the South Bank site, why not?

LASDUN: If we opt for three theatres the problem becomes financial.

DEVINE: Can we all think over the implications of not having flies?

GASKILL: Disregarding our opinions, does Mr. Lasdun himself see a theatre that would be a statement for this time.

LASDUN: No, I don't. Excellence is my only criterion, but my instincts are against adaptability as a solution.

Mr. Lasdun's idea was then discussed further. Mr. Elliott felt the apertures in the stage walls made obligatory by the necessity to bring on scenery would in any case diminish the feeling of being in one room. He believed Mr. Lasdun's solution could be either the worst or the best of both worlds.

LASDUN: I can't say that I reject the principle of adaptability after three and a half weeks, but my instincts are against it.

DEVINE: Has Mr. Lasdun got enough out of us today for the meeting to be considered satisfactory?

LASDUN: No. Until there is some consensus as to the nature of the brief, we won't get anywhere.

DEVINE: What would you like us to have said?

LASDUN: I would have got much enjoyment by your having said: "To hell with the flies"!

It was agreed that Mr. Lasdun's idea should be examined further and that he should elaborate it before submitting copies of a sketch to the members of the Committee for their consideration.

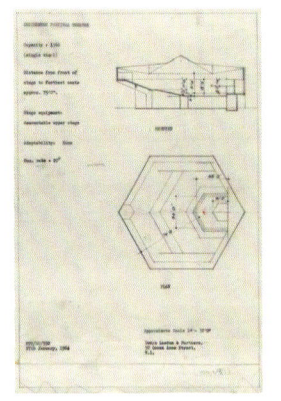

DL&P sketch: Chichester

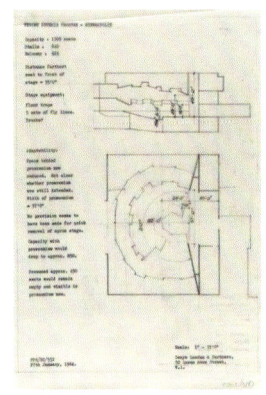

DL&P sketch: Guthrie Theater, Minneapolis

2.2 Design Begins: Meetings #16–21

The Room

At this second meeting of 5th February, the concept of 'the room' has already emerged. By the next meeting this idea had evolved into a wide, fan-shaped auditorium, with an open-end stage, which Lasdun entitled Scheme A.

It is sad and disquieting that such a wide fan, which Lasdun described as being quite unique, was, of course, not original at all. It bore a troubling similarity to a type of theatre that the American theatre consultant George Izenour was propagating throughout the United States, as the perfect 'engineered' theatre of the future. Neither Lasdun, in his theatrical naiveté, nor the committee, noticed how commonplace the idea actually was. There's a further irony here. In 1950, the previous building committee, working with Brian O'Rorke, had spoken out against such an auditorium, resolving against "a fan-shaped theatre, to which the committee has always been strongly opposed, involving as it did, the sacrifice of that intimacy which the committee felt was so desirable." By the '60s, such verities had been forgotten.

Arlen and Elliott agreed with Lasdun that the lack of clarity of the brief was an ongoing problem. Lasdun seemed overly focused on 'the flies' as a major problem, perhaps anything that created a gap in his 'room.'

Lasdun: "My instincts are against adaptability as a solution. Until there is some consensus as to the nature of the brief, we won't get anywhere."

On 11th February, Lasdun met with Michael Elliott, who had been the director of the Old Vic for its last season before the NT took over the building. Michael began surveying the history of theatre development and then added some personal views, which Lasdun noted:

"In the Greek theatre, the seating occupied more than a semicircle in plan; it embraced the orchestra. The chorus was the link between the audience and the principal actors. Medieval theatre and Elizabethan theatre… the plays were acted in the midst of the audience. The break came as a result of the masque, which required the audience be placed on one side.

"The actor is a medium through which an impulse is given to the audience so that what happens onstage becomes real. Something must happen in the audience. It is easier to achieve this on an open stage. An amphitheatre with some scenic facilities would be valid.

"When an open stage is placed against a wall, there is the desire to make the wall respond in the creation of a place. Nothing yet suggested seems to take the place of flying. Since a new form of theatre has not yet arrived, it would seem most sensible to build an improved Gelsenkirchen.

"If you asked 100 directors what kind of theatre they would like, at least half would opt for a proscenium. Mr. Elliott said that if he had to make a decision now, he would choose a proscenium."[44]

Two weeks later, George Devine met with Lasdun. In later years, Lasdun was to describe this lengthy meeting as one that had deeply influenced him.

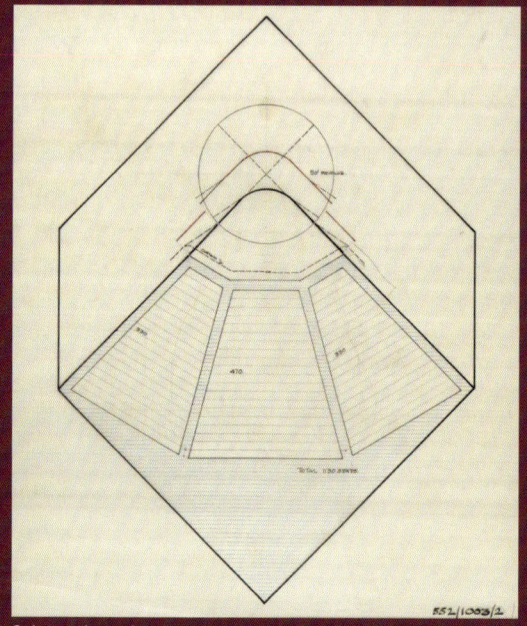

Scheme A version 1

25th Feb 1964: Memo DL&P.: Record of Conversation [45]
Present: George Devine, Denys Lasdun, Peter Softley [Denys Lasdun's principal lieutenant], Malcolm Minjoodt [design assistant on the open stage].

LASDUN: One of the things I detected… is that when you explained the triangulation of action… My reaction was that you instinctively felt that the profile of the apron that we've got is sloppy from that point of view. It is not sufficiently dynamic for triangulation to be built up. It is a little weak…

DEVINE: The height of the stage is another point which I think is a personal one. This business of just feeling that the actors are not part of you.

MINJOODT: We have to avoid the people in the front getting a crick in the neck, so it is a matter of inches.

SOFTLEY: Would you expect the stage to have a rake on it?

DEVINE: No. With revolves and things, they work so much better, and it is much easier. It makes moving scenes difficult.

LASDUN: The other point – going back to the committee – we talked about limiting the proscenium to forty feet, and maybe this requires review. If you reduce it geometrically, we are going to drop numbers within a range of 65' [to the furthest seat], which we think is important to keep.

DEVINE: 65 feet is a much more important figure, than whether it's 40 feet, 45 feet, or 50 feet, because it's not a proscenium in that sense. It hasn't got the proscenium feeling. It's a one-room feeling.

LASDUN (to SOFTLEY): What do you think in terms of adjustment? There's nothing to stop the adjustment of the profile of the apron, is there?

SOFTLEY: This one happens to fall naturally into place, because you can only increase the number of seats in one row by a whole seat. The LCC expect smooth gangways, so we've increased by one. If you increase by two you get an enormous splay. Without wasting any space, one could spread the seats out as you go back, and so change the angle.

LASDUN: It rather fights against uniting the acting area within the auditorium.

SOFTLEY: The apron and the auditorium are the same thing.

DEVINE: They must be because that's your room.

LASDUN: And you still think it's sloppy?

DEVINE: Yes.

LASDUN: You've seen the attitude to proscenium. You've seen attitude to the floor. Assuming we make all the adjustments we've been talking about, or could do, would you think we are on the right lines?

DEVINE: I would. But I would ask you to give me a plan, because you've had my immediate reaction, but I would like to think about it.

LASDUN: I'm not asking you to make a decision.

DEVINE: I think that something can be got out of a plan and letting me think about it. Of course, my immediate reaction is to be excited, there's no question about that.

LASDUN: You've got to look at it a bit from our point of view. We come into the theatre world as strangers, we can see – because we've been brought up with it – pretty well what the proscenium can offer. It's not changed much in 200 years. We can see the Minneapolises, Chichesters of this world, and we can listen to the dilemma that the theatre is in at the moment, and then when we come up with something

George Devine

> "We've been brought up with what the proscenium can offer. It's not changed much in 200 years."
>
> Denys Lasdun

> "I think it would be good for you to provide, within this rather austere background, the maximum of tricks."
>
> George Devine

like this, it doesn't appear to have any parentage anywhere – or very little.

DEVINE: I would say to myself, let's take the National Theatre repertoire… let's take six plays and see could they be done. I'd like to think about that because that's what my responsibility is. I've an immediate reaction. With the qualifications I've made, I think it's very interesting. You seem to have made a compromise between the two requirements without having an adaptable theatre.

LASDUN: That's what the objective was… we are at a midway point, unless you tease it over one side or the other, and one or the other starts collapsing.

SOFTLEY: We could strengthen the appearance of it without altering it much.

LASDUN: For the moment, we divided that audience into three equal sections, but it's quite possible to distort them with two, different from the middle one, to have an effect on the apron. It's static. There's a year's work of 'finesse' ahead of us, but we can't get to that situation until we can get confidence in the line of attack. But at the moment we are examining form.

DEVINE: I think we ought to show this to the committee.

MINJOODT: Can we just clarify the apron. Is it weakest from the audience or from the actor's point of view? One dictates the seating. Both? Do you think it is equally bad?

DEVINE: It's not all that bad, but it is a little bad.

LASDUN: Are you sure that it's the angle that's weak and not the fact that it's equilateral. What about changing the angle to give it more thrust?

DEVINE: I think the provision of three little [figures] 6' high on pins would be worth having. What is the height at the moment?

MINJOODT: Approximately 26'. You have to picture that the ceiling goes right through. It's just an unseen division.

SOFTLEY: We were wondering whether these [surfaces] were movable as well.

DEVINE: Once you start that, you are in the brothel department; everybody wants a different frame.

MINJOODT: It's extremely dangerous to say that you could fly those ceiling baffles, because you could take them away and leave a big hole.

DEVINE: We haven't talked about an iron curtain at all.

SOFTLEY: This could be accommodated if necessary.

DEVINE: If you ask for everything to be made with fireproof material it is a frightful bind… There's no question that people are going to want house tabs… you could just accept that the scene is changed in front of the audience.

SOFTLEY: They did very well with *King Lear* at the Aldwych. They even removed the corpse in full view.

MINJOODT: That worried me, how they were going to do it.

DEVINE: This is where you might find Larry with a certain idea how you should behave toward the audience. That you shouldn't let them in on the secret. I think the essence of theatre is not contained in that at all. Strong conventional theatres, like the Chinese or Japanese or the Elizabethan or Greek theatres, they never minded about this.

LASDUN: But you see it's this sort of intellectual assessment which dictates whether the form of theatre is going to change or not.

DEVINE: It will not change unless there is a strong architectural form.

LASDUN: You have to accept a sort of space, and it's

got to have it's own characteristics. Now if you doll it up to look like something else, then you are going to go around in circles. So I'm not terribly pro-curtain.

DEVINE: In certain styles of great theatres, there is something that comes down and makes a punctuation mark at the end.

LASDUN: We can fly right out to here if you want to… then we could have a revolve.

MINJOODT: This is rather up to the producer isn't it? What are the other possibilities?

SOFTLEY: Trucks.

MINJOODT: Do you like trucks or hate them?

DEVINE: I don't particularly hate them.

MINJOODT: It might be useful, too, if the revolve could be raised or lowered within reason.

DEVINE: I think it would be good for you to provide, within this rather austere background, the maximum of tricks.

LASDUN: If we go forward on this, as far as the action area is concerned it can have any trick that anybody wants.

DEVINE: You will still find people like Michael Elliott talking about repertory. How long does it take you to change from show A to show B? It might be valuable to have these sections of grid dragged further on, so you could have one set of scenery on a grid here, waiting, and a second here, then this lot could go on, and this lot could go off.

LASDUN: These are going to be matters of finance… what sort of equipment they want. When we get to that stage we shall be home and dry, because this is purely what can be done technically. It still doesn't alter the basic design.

DEVINE: It's an architectural theatre, not an Italian theatre. You don't pretend. It's an anti-realistic theatre. Must be. I'm only warning you because some people may say it. That's why I think the composition of the committee is so important. I don't think that necessarily Larry will be in that direction. All you need to say is that you're asking me for an 18th century theatre. There are certain things, like the ceiling, that are fundamentals. If you chip that away, you're getting something else. I think it's very important that this principle is the right one, I think that Larry has probably studied the question. It's always the directors who have designed the theatres. Directors are not architects.

LASDUN: I think this has been most helpful; it hasn't dampened enthusiasm for the line of attack that we are on.

DEVINE: I can assure you that if I felt like dampening it, I would have done. I will write a letter to Larry, which I will ask to be read out at the meeting – so he can't get out of it really – telling him how I feel.

One of my problems at the [Royal] Court is that the stage is so small. One could make a very interesting diagram of this formation.

LASDUN: It's never been done?

DEVINE: Never been done. I think the angularity of it is important; everything can be triangulated.

LASDUN: From our point of view, what is attractive about the angularity and geometry is that it generates every room in the whole theatre.

DEVINE: When we taught kids about 18th century theatre, they used to learn it through the dance, and all the movements were always in the round. People [today] don't want this kind of elaboration, which is why the director is such an important dramatist, although he's not particularly popular. It's an angular attitude to a situation. That's all very highfalutin' stuff, but good stuff.

> "From our point of view, what is attractive about the angularity and geometry is that it generates every room in the whole theatre."
>
> Denys Lasdun

2.2 Design Begins: Meetings #16–21

Lasdun and Devine

Interesting how Devine describes this as "highfalutin' stuff." Some of this transcript, particularly the last paragraph, is indeed hard to understand. It's also hard to understand what in the conversation Lasdun found so particularly interesting. Was it Devine's apparent enthusiasm for triangulation? The angularity of Scheme A certainly appealed to Lasdun and, even as the straight lines and angles of Scheme A became softened by the curves of the eventual Scheme E, the angularity was maintained through the Olivier Theatre ceiling, and underpinned Lasdun's entire geometry of the building.

Note too Lasdun's remark: "The proscenium [has] not changed much in 200 years." Sadly this, too, indicates his naiveté about theatre. The proscenium theatre had changed enormously during the previous two centuries, from the Georgian courtyard playhouse, in which the actors actually performed on the forestage within the audience chamber, up to the extraordinary sophistication of the Edwardian Matcham theatre, by which time the actor was secured behind the proscenium arch. Denys' failure to understand this change undoubtedly later led to the Lyttelton, and his theory of a 'theatre of confrontation.' Three days later Devine did write to Sir Laurence:

28th February 1964
George Devine to Olivier & NTBC [46]
"I consider Lasdun's project to be a remarkable achievement and in principle I whole-heartedly support it. There are of course many points of finesse to be worked on, but as a point of departure it has my enthusiastic support.

"It seems to me that he has provided a solution which, whilst avoiding the basic incongruity of what has been called an adaptable theatre (i.e. switching from proscenium to open stage and vice-versa) it provides an actor audience relationship of great flexibility. It must be obvious that to do this certain sacrifices will have to be made, because we will not have a pure Italian stage, but I have always been convinced that if an exciting, flexible and different architectural form were to be provided, this would create its own style, a style which would incorporate the major possibilities of open and closed stages without attempting to reproduce them. This project seems to me to potentially produce the answer."

Devine's enthusiasm for this early, very simplistic, fan-shaped concept of Lasdun's is curious. However, it must be placed in the context of Devine's other current enthusiasm at the time... only too typical of the period. He was actually planning to gut the multi-level, horseshoe-shaped Royal Court Theatre into a single-level, rectangular, 'Mermaid-style' frontal, open-end, stage space. Thankfully (for posterity) he was unable to fund the redevelopment and the project was aborted.

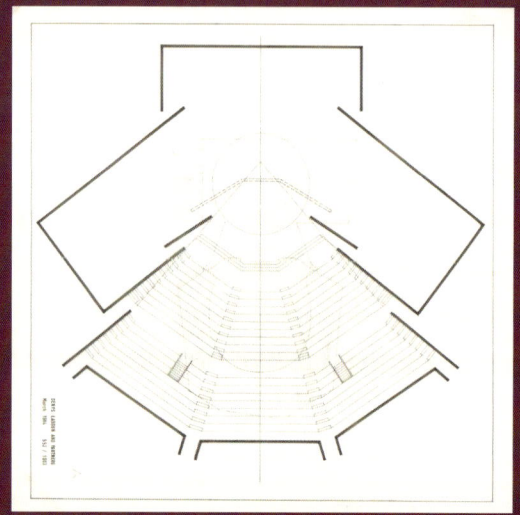

Scheme A version 2, dated March 1964; note faint outline of the Old Vic stage and auditorium

> **"I have always been convinced that if an exciting, flexible and different architectural form were to be provided, this would create its own style."**
> George Devine

Meeting 18

18th Meeting of The National Theatre Building Committee

22 Duchy Street, SE1
Wednesday 4th March 1964, 5:00 pm.

Present:
Sir Laurence Olivier (in the Chair), Mr. John Dexter, Mr. Peter Brook and Mr. William Gaskill. Mr. Stephen Arlen and Mr. Kenneth Rae were in attendance. Mr. Denys Lasdun and Mr. Peter Softley were present by invitation.

Apologies:
Apologies for absence were received from Mr. Norman Marshall, Mr. Michael Benthall, Mr. George Devine, Mr. Michael Elliott, Mr. Peter Hall, Miss Tanya Moiseiwitsch and Mr. Michel Saint-Denis.

Mr. Lasdun summarised the position to date. He recapitulated the terms of the brief and said that he and his colleagues had examined the premise of adaptability in particular. The formula achieved at the Lincoln Center had, by general consent of the Building Committee, been ruled out.

His suggestion that the flies should be eliminated had not met with enthusiasm, so he and his colleagues had given further thought to the problem, bearing in mind the following points in as much as they were a positive and consistent expression of the members of the Committee:

1. The auditorium and acting areas should together give a feeling of one room.
2. The auditorium should be non-hierarchical.
3. The audience should be engaged in equal intensity.
4. No member of the audience should be more than 60' to 65' from the stage.
5. An actor should be able to confront the audience.
6. The performance should have a dimensional quality.
7. An attempt should be made to capture in one form the essence of what could be done at Chichester and at the Old Vic without moving any seats or resorting to complicated mechanical aids.

Mr. Lasdun then produced a diagram-model [Scheme 'A'] which he said was an attempt to embrace all these criteria including flying facilities. Mr. Brook said that he would have applauded the idea of getting rid of the flies.

Commenting on the diagram Mr. Lasdun said that there was no proscenium. The ceiling was devised as a series of gradated planes, one of which was where the proscenium would normally be. It proceeded from flatness to depth, from the back of the auditorium to the back of the acting area and it was possible to fly scenery and to light within the voids. No seat was further from the acting area than 65'. The auditorium was fan-shaped. There were no walls as such, but gradated screens, and it was possible to light from the apertures. There was an apron, a 40' revolve, and a numerical capacity of some 1,100. Mr. Lasdun then invited comments and discussion which proceeded as follows:

ARLEN: My immediate reaction is to get alarmed in terms of dissipation at the sides of the auditorium, where I get the feeling of an enormous amphitheatre.

OLIVIER: Could we not reduce the Gothic severity by having the auditorium more circular?

LASDUN: No. The angular relationship is deliberate. I would want compelling reasons why it should be circular. There is a relationship between the gradations of planes that you wouldn't get with a circle, but if you feel strongly we must soften it.

OLIVIER: I just rather like it circular.

LASDUN: It could be written as a circle.

BROOK: This is what I dreaded in the sense that the moment you produce the model the outside form immediately strikes one. The principle of the auditorium is so conventional that it looks like what would come out if you fed the requirements into a computer. I believe it is possible to make something that fulfils the requirements and yet is ahead of the times.

Mr. Brook then spoke highly of the new Berlin Philharmonic Hall.

LASDUN: An architect is neither a magician nor a computer. At this stage he is a sponge and

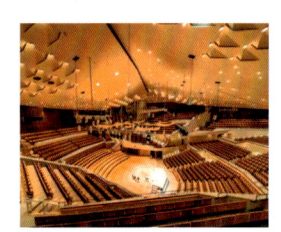

Berliner Philharmonie

"An architect is neither a magician nor a computer."

Denys Lasdun

he can only be as good as what you give him to absorb.

BROOK: If your brief makes it impossible for you to transcend certain things, you are forced to come to conclusions that are not as exciting and radical as one would have hoped. In the Berlin Phiharmonic Hall the architect has imposed a new conception on the idea of listening to music. There is a radical breakthrough.

LASDUN: Would it be fair to say that the radical issue in our case is how you deal with scenery?

BROOK: Not entirely. I would beg you to continue to query certain things:

Non-hierarchical seating
The current conception of scenery and how to change it.

LASDUN: With regard to your first point I must stress that the model is only a diagram.

GASKILL: Is Brook not asking us to alter our brief rather than making a criticism of Lasdun?

LASDUN: Here you have a diagram. You can alter it but every alteration must have a sanction from you.

BROOK: The logic of the brief is this diagram.

LASDUN: We are discussing the brief and not architectonic values. I asked the Committee what it wanted to do in the theatre. This question has never been answered, though I have been given interesting personal vignettes, some of them cancelling out, some not. The architect is going to work with you and not produce an idea that is going to solve what is essentially your problem. Are you prepared to get rid of the flies? The clue, the anchor and the blockage is the flies.

BROOK: You maintain the flies are the only snag?

LASDUN: Yes Everything else is related. So long as the Italian formula is at work you are inhibited. So long as you hold to it I can't see the next move.

BROOK: If your work brings you to this conclusion then we must explore the problem as the core of the matter.

LASDUN: We should not be concerned whether this diagram is exciting or poetic. We cannot get to the poetic till we have bled dry the functional. We can not get to the functional till we have an agreed brief.

BROOK: If this is the core of the argument why duck the issue?

OLIVIER: As I see it a theatre in the round imposes two great inhibitions upon the director and the actor: it makes two things excruciatingly difficult - the aside and comedy.

GASKILL: We have got to say that the National Theatre must satisfy a number of directors including foreign ones. I wouldn't think that our urge to change is so great that we will feel differently in five years' time.

BROOK: The theatre that satisfies so many requirements is not going to be as good as the one which stimulates. I can't believe that the all-purpose anthology aim is as good as the one that stimulates.

LASDUN: You couldn't reproduce the Italian theatre in this diagram.

GASKILL: Even this diagram would worry the Comedie Francaise.

LASDUN: The object of the exercise is to get something out of attack and defence. Brook has made one false assumption: this diagram is not a conventional theatre. There is no theatre as yet where you can get scenery in depth in one room.

OLIVIER: Can Brook help me over my two worries (comedy and the aside)?

BROOK: I watched LEAR from an on-stage box in Budapest. I was with someone who had not seen the production before. We had a different but none the less rewarding view.

GASKILL: But you had a front row seat!

BROOK: I was seeing the production

against the axis.

GASKILL: But you directed the play! You were in a privileged position.

BROOK: The Italian theatre sets up a social hierarchy which we cannot accept today. On the other hand, when the seats in it are offered for free some people choose one place and some another. I question the theory that in abolishing social hierarchy you have to give everyone an equal view.

LASDUN: You can shatter the auditorium in this diagram: you can raise some portions of it and depress others but we can't get onto this aspect till we have a clearer picture from the centre outwards.

BROOK: I am on Lasdun's side on the question of flies. I beg you all to re-examine your premises.

LASDUN: (to Brook) In your experience would you agree that the flies are the key?

BROOK: I think they might well be.

GASKILL: Did Lasdun get the impression that as a group we could ever arrive at an unanimity for or against the flies?

LASDUN: One of the dilemmas that we have to face is to what extent the National Theatre main auditorium should eliminate all connection with the past.

OLIVIER: What do we do about comedy?

GASKILL: A clown in a circus gets a laugh from the whole house if what he does is sufficiently crude and physical. All subtlety is lost. If this theatre is to be directed by Olivier one has to think to a certain extent in classic forms. This would not necessarily involve a compromise.

BROOK: It would.

OLIVIER: Supposing Brook were running the National Theatre. Has he a particular form of theatre in mind?

BROOK: I am not proposing a theatre-in-the-round. Did Lasdun see the Theatre of Cruelty at LAMDA?

LASDUN: I did.

BROOK: What to me was interesting was turning things inside out. We would not have used it in the way we did if the architecture hadn't been there in the first place.

GASKILL: The point of LAMDA is that it is a tiny theatre.

LASDUN: A capacity of 350 people. We are dealing with 1,100.

GASKILL: I have worked at Strawberry Hill in a completely flexible theatre - a huge room. I have also worked in something rather like this diagram. I tend to believe that the experimental theatre should not be 100% adaptable.

BROOK: The absence of flies and the concrete steps imposed something at LAMDA which had contemporary possibilities. I would have been happy to say that this was a characteristic of the theatre and to use it for five years.

GASKILL: Would you be happy to do a wide repertory in it? I personally wouldn't. There comes a point where it stereotypes itself more than anything else.

LASDUN: From what Brook is saying, all he seems to want is a bombed site in Bethnal Green. It's dead easy. And we could do it on the South Bank site but is this a National Theatre? I am a layman, one of your audience. When I saw VANYA at the Vic, I got a feeling of a relationship, and I wasn't conscious of proscenium arches, boxes or galleries. If I could produce the quality of that relationship for 1,100 people I would be happy.

GASKILL: What we are discussing here is the difference between an actor's and a director's theatre.

BROOK: I don't agree.

GASKILL: The Greek theatre was a director's theatre and the value of the individual actor was comparatively slight. Provided he was well-trained, virtually anyone could have played the parts.

BROOK: I preferred Olivier's performance as Titus at the Stoll. He dominated the whole theatre.

GASKILL: What was Olivier's reaction as an actor?

Scheme A version 1

> **"We cannot get to the poetic till we have bled dry the functional."**
>
> Denys Lasdun

> "From what Brook is saying, all he seems to want is a bombed site in Bethnal Green. It's dead easy. And we could do it on the South Bank site but is this a National Theatre?"
>
> Denys Lasdun

OLIVIER: I don't think that what Brook says is true. The art or craft of acting has to deal with something that has changed because of other media – films and television.

BROOK: Yet in America Beatrice Lillie was highly successful in the Shubert Theatre.

OLIVIER: The Beatrice Lillie example is of one actor only.

BROOK: I question the premise that intimate acting demands intimacy of space.

DEXTER and GASKILL: When you (Brook) go to the theatre do you always buy seats in the gallery?

GASKILL: Olivier is a great actor: he has learnt to condition the muscles of his face so that his expression can be seen at a distance.

OLIVIER: I don't think operatic acting is right.

BROOK: What would be the consequences for Lasdun if we were prepared to dispense with the flies?

LASDUN: I don't know, I would have to think. As I have said before, the flies destroy the feeling of one-roomness.

OLIVIER: What is wrong with a room that has a loft?

ARLEN: Lasdun has said that continuity of ceiling is what is specific about a room. Why can't you cut a hole in it, let things through and then fill the hole in again?

LASDUN: We set out to avoid a hole in the wall and the sense of another room, i.e. proscenium and flies.

BROOK: In this diagram if you can only fly in the voids, you are creating bad flying.

OLIVIER: The audience is not conscious of the ceiling once the action of the play has begun.

GASKILL: Olivier has a good point there. When I sit eight rows back at the Mermaid Theatre I feel out of contact with the stage. The feeling of being close to the stage is not necessarily a matter of the stage projecting.

BROOK: I come back to the question of asymmetry. It seems to me that the excitement felt by a crowd of people coming into a theatre today is somehow related to a principle of irregularity. Even the stage itself should perhaps be a combination of the formal and informal. Is it worth investigating this at the price of the perfect view for everyone?

OLIVIER: Anything that is a theatre has to choose between being an exciting place and something that is good to see and hear in.

LASDUN: What has the Mermaid got that this diagram hasn't?

BROOK: I can only answer in shocking terms. The Mermaid has bare walls related to its budget.

LASDUN: You're not reading marble into here, are you? This is a superficial point. You are talking about the superficialities of a cheap building, not the essence.

BROOK: I am asking you to look at the fact that there is something very interesting that can be achieved in a circus tent or at LAMDA. A curious life that one wants to recapture.

GASKILL: At LAMDA Brook used part of the building as the stage. At the Mermaid the architect used walls that were already there. He wants architecture to be part of the theatre. He likes the sense of the auditorium being used. The logical conclusion is that he does not want the stage built as a separate area.

OLIVIER: I think what Brook is talking about is an emotional thing. Lasdun said something about the life of a building depending upon what goes on there. Chichester was an extraordinary experience. Everyone was against it. It was something about the building. This sounds silly but we felt it keenly. We rehearsed there from when it was a mess of concrete to half an hour before the curtain went up. Once the seats had been filled with people, it was different. The use of it has become something. I worry about the National Theatre being a place where acting and plays are seen to best advantage. I don't care whether people think it is nice or nasty as long as it's alright when the play begins.

GASKILL: The Berliner Ensemble theatre is all right because the Berliner Ensemble is in it.

LASDUN: What I don't go along with yet is the way to get topographical compulsion. I understand the point about roughness and eccentricity. What is wrong with this diagram?

OLIVIER: Cannot we concentrate on making a place where the actors feel marvellous? As an actor, I think I could manage that place (the diagram). The auditorium is still a bit hierarchical. The public would book from the middle.

LASDUN: They would do this if it was circular.

ARLEN: They wouldn't do it so much if it was circular. I wouldn't like to sit at the side because of the feeling of the walls.

GASKILL: I agree.

ARLEN: There is less distinction between seats within a circle. We know from the Old Vic that the customers don't like the side seats.

LASDUN: Forget the side walls for a while. You are dead right, but it is a problem that is architecturally malleable.

OLIVIER: We said we should not inhibit the Master's voice with illustrative intentions. That was the origin of going back to theatre-in-the-round. We could say that it is all right to do Shakespeare that way for ever and other drama that is poetic, but there is a lot we do that isn't poetic.

The meeting returned to the question of the flies.

GASKILL: Brook used thunder-sheets in LEAR which were flown.

BROOK: I could have used louvres in the wall.

GASKILL: It wouldn't have had the same effect.

LASDUN: We could achieve our objective with flies in this diagram if the objective is right.

BROOK: Whatever you do, you must do properly. I am not proposing a theatre without flies, but it is no good having bad flies. This arrangement is the worst of all possible worlds. If it is to be a theatre with something called scenery this conditions all manner of things. You could have a principle other than flies.

Mr. Brook spoke of a theatre in which he had worked with Sean Kenny in Paris, in which the technical means of scene-changing contributed to the physical nature of the place.

GASKILL: Why is Brook not giving the lead? Why is he expecting Lasdun to? You can't expect the architect to solve your problems.

OLIVIER: Brook has often been most successful by designing productions himself within the disciplines imposed by the building.

GASKILL: You can't have a building in which there are no disciplines at all.

LASDUN: I do not believe that you can make a place by variable elements. I believe in spatial impact but it is a fixed affair. It has proportion and clarity. It has something before you start your game of theatre. You must say what is wrong with this test case (the diagram).

BROOK: The curious nature of a theatre building depends on something which you can't get out of specifications. This diagram has got bad flies and doesn't give me anything. I want some exciting new possibility.

GASKILL: Lasdun expects you to bring up the exciting new possibility.

BROOK: You can't reconcile the exciting auditorium with perfect sight-lines.

LASDUN: I don't agree with you.

GASKILL: Should we put it to the vote whether all the audience should get a good view or not?

BROOK: They could still have differences of view.

GASKILL: What is the next stage?

LASDUN: I don't want there to be any impression that we are proposing to build this diagram.

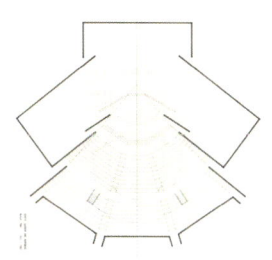

Scheme A version 2

> "Cannot we concentrate on making a place where the actors feel marvellous?"
> — Laurence Olivier

> "I would require a written directive if some seats are to be bad."
> — Denys Lasdun

Scheme A version 1

> "To find a single room with dynamic possibilities needs an arrogance from the architect."
>
> Peter Brook

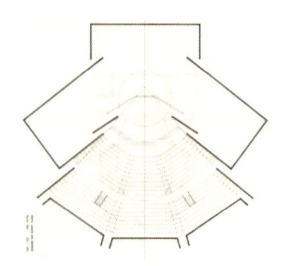

Scheme A version 2

We are going through an evolutionary process, but Brook's attitude is destructive. I would require a written directive if some seats are to be bad. I can understand your feeling about the flies not being good but the Committee cannot abdicate its responsibility.

We must have constructive criticism. We will leave you the diagram and the drawing. Produce on it. Shove it around.

BROOK: I had better be silent in future if what I say is of no help.

LASDUN: Why must you be so abstract? I don't want to impose an architectural idea. I work with people. Be positive. Talk about the flies, confrontation, apertures etc. We won't get anywhere with abstractions.

BROOK: In my mind everything that I have been trying to say is specific. What I am looking for is a building in which the stage is conceived and designed like the auditorium. I believe that there must be an imaginative solution.

GASKILL: Everybody should see the diagram and make specific observations.

OLIVIER: Why does Brook want something asymmetric?

BROOK: I want something lively.

LASDUN: I understand that.

OLIVIER: But if you have an asymmetrical auditorium all you do as director, surely, is to shift your centre?

BROOK: Not necessarily.

OLIVIER: If you want a centre, you'll make it in the bulge or whatever you have, whatever asymmetry you have you will emphasise a centre elsewhere.

BROOK: That is the problem.

LASDUN: This diagram has no ancestry. The ground that is being broken has nothing to do with shape but with human relationships.

BROOK: Lasdun is saying that work over the next six months will make this diagram different. What I am driving at is, that if an architect, having absorbed all the problems of theatre, applies his thinking to the nature of the playing area there are solutions in terms of mass and machinery that are more telling than a stage that can be filled in as you wish. There is such a thing as a designed stage. If an architect wanted to treat the stage radically, it is possible to find things such as a wall that moves, an area that is built up, etc. To find a single room with dynamic possibilities needs an arrogance from the architect.

LASDUN: A theatre man must pose this point. You will get nothing till you give a lead. We don't want an architect's whim to design the National Theatre. At abstract level I am with Brook 100%, but I can't operate on it.

BROOK: In the case of Stratford, Ontario, the whole notion of the building sprang from the conception of the stage. In the Japanese theatre stage design conditions everything.

LASDUN: We put down a synthesis of stated opinions. We have got immense problems quite apart from what we have discussed tonight. We can't get onto them until I know we are roughly on the right lines and the National Theatre will be held up until then.

OLIVIER: I distrust Brook's notion that the stage by itself can have a dynamic unrelated to the auditorium.

BROOK: A man in France designed three stages. They were impractical etc. but from that conception sprang the whole building. I can't give you a design but if I were asked to do it I would. In my view more attention should be focused on the stage: whether a stage should be open or not, contain certain features or not.

OLIVIER: Brook is talking about a set.

BROOK: A stage exists for the 20th century with a dynamic of its own.

LASDUN: For the National Theatre you need a fixed dynamic space.

It was agreed that members of the Building Committee, not present at the meeting, should be asked to submit their comments on the diagram before the next meeting.

A Sense of Theatre

Scheme A

This is the meeting that introduces Lasdun's Scheme A, a wide-fan, directional auditorium, without a proscenium, but with ceiling and walls sloping toward the stage, and with slots for lighting and flying. Again, confusion continues between issues of general principle and issues of flying and seating.

Olivier complains of the "Gothic severity," while Peter Brook attacks it as "so conventional that it looks like what would come out if you fed the requirements into a computer."

The confusion of multiple levels of misunderstanding pervades the discussion. Lasdun defends the "angular relationship." Olivier replies, "I just rather like it circular." Lasdun instantly reverses himself: "It could be written as a circle."

The argument between Brook and Lasdun quickly became somewhat personal, with Lasdun's comment: "All [Brook] seems to want is a bombed site in Bethnal Green. It's dead easy. And we could do it on the South Bank site, but is this a National Theatre?"

Lasdun's ignorance of theatre is compounded by the committee's confusion, contradictory opinions, and lack of leadership. One might sense that this was a conversation between blind men describing an elephant. One feels the trunk, the other the tail. What is in the middle? The sadness of this dispute is that it actually conceals how Brook and Lasdun were both each seeking something more from the other; both sought an architectural solution that created new theatrical possibilities. Lasdun: "What I don't go along with yet is the way to get topographical compulsion. I understand the point about roughness and eccentricity. What is wrong with this diagram?" Sir Laurence's reply: "Cannot we concentrate on making a place where the actors feel marvellous?"

A pivotal moment: Lasdun stating he'd require a written instruction before he'd add "bad" seats. Brook was clearly of the view that any good theatre must have some "different-viewpoint" seats. Yet nobody was able to help Lasdun toward understanding this fundamental truism: To achieve a lively theatre, some seats must have different view sightlines. Brook: "A stage exists for the 20th century with a dynamic of its own." "Actors feeling marvellous" and a new architectural stage with "a 20th century dynamic." How might that be achieved? Both Lasdun and Brook actually agreed that it was for the architect to bring that special insight to convert concept into spacial reality.

After this meeting, Kenneth Tynan, Rae, and Olivier were concerned at Brook's attacks on Lasdun. Indeed on 20th March, Devine met with Lasdun at the Queen's Theatre to privately convey Olivier's concern with his own committee. Lasdun responded: "This was water off a duck's back and part of the design process..." Indeed he hinted that some of the points Brook had made might be good sense.[47]

Lasdun's own notes on the meeting include: "The following three hours were occupied largely by an exposition by Peter Brook of his attitude to the National Theatre... he thought it was too early to settle on a solution and wanted more exploration in the hope of finding a more radical and exciting conception."[48]

Two Versions

The DL&P Archives contain two versions of proposals entitled Scheme A. There is no record in the minutes of these options, though in meeting 19 there is mention of a "rough diagram" made in meeeting 17. What I have called Version 1 does seem to have been first despite its label including a /2: the three blocks of seating are described in the 25th Feb meeting with Devine. My Version 2 (dated March 1964) appears to be a second thought with the addition of some further backstage provision. The careful observer might also notice that the Version 2 sketch shows a very faint outline of The Old Vic stage and auditorium with the outline of the front of the dress circle indicated. That Scheme A appears massively larger was apparently not noticed. 'Topographical compulsion' might perhaps not be obtained in an auditorium over three times the width of The Vic.

The Critical Dimension

While these seemingly theoretical discussions between committee and architect continued, Sir Laurence and a small band of his selected actors were conducting practical experiments in several West End theatres. How far away from the actor might the furthest spectator be satisfactorily seated? These tests resulted in a maximum distance of 65 feet., which was adopted throughout all subsequent discussions.

Scheme B Emerges

Peter Brook

Scheme B model

John Bury

Peter Hall

25th March 1964: DL&P with Peter Brook[49]

"PB was shown the first model of Scheme B. He felt that the concept was generally excellent. He wondered whether the *'proportion of people at the limits of the auditorium were not too great.*

"'Shape of the right angle stage front was slightly disturbing. New York has many small theatres of every type, those with right angle stages, seemed somewhat intolerable.

"'Not difficult to create intimacy on this stage. Jean Vilar with his T.N.P. at the Chaillot, had a hideous building, with an enormous stage, but it had proved successful for Chekhov.'

"Best seats would be in the centre of the diagonal. Acting area was excellent, but he had doubts about the seating. A theatre must have a major axis: an ideal seat: 'where you would put your friends'.

"He thought Olivier might say 'I don't want to act in a corner.'

"Worst feature of Scheme A was the dominance of the side walls. This had been overcome in Scheme B."

Brook's summary of theatre development was:

"The Elizabethan theatre emphasised social division. There were three levels on the stage and in the auditorium. In the 18th and 19th centuries, the stage became a closed, unreal world of the imagination. In the first half of the 20th century there was a desire for absolute democracy, characterised by bare stages and non-hierarchal sweeps of banked seats. Society was now changing, not toward greater uniformity, but toward a multitude of non-conformists living side by side. This was reflected in the theatre by a greater degree of variety in the auditorium and stage. It was an open world, but not a desert, with many possibilities, and certain contradictions, not cancelling each other out."

21st April 1964: DL&P notes on meeting with George Devine[50]

Mr. Devine is shown the second model of Scheme B. He makes the following comments:

"If it were mine, I'd buy it! In a classical play the commanding position would be behind the line joining the extreme seats in the front row. An actor on this stage would feel as if he had the audience in his hands, but more onus would be placed upon the actor.

"Designers would be delighted with this stage. You cannot expect all types of play to be equally good on any particular stage. Wonderful visual concentration could be achieved with a properly composed scene. This is a progressive theatre. The National Theatre should not be a museum.

"It must be possible to create a mysterious 'off stage' for the Ibsen Strindberg type of realistic play.

"An intimate scene would be destroyed if it were necessary for the actor to raise their voices unduly to make themselves heard."

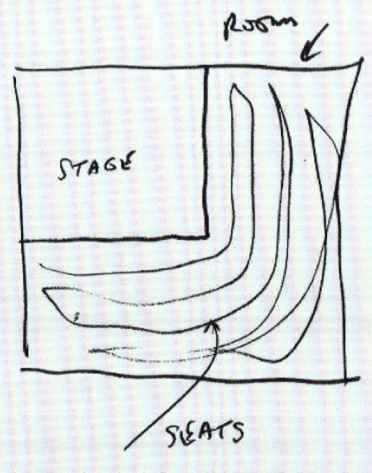

Lasdun's first sketch - "The Room"

27th April 1964: Discussion with Designer John Bury[51]

The designer John Bury visited Lasdun to view Scheme B. He made the point that based upon his experience with Joan Littlewood at Stratford East, he preferred an auditorium decorated in a pale colour to allow sufficient reflection for the actors to see their audience. This idea maybe later led Lasdun to have light concrete walls at the sides of both large theatres.

29th April 1964: DL&P Notes on meeting with Peter Hall[52]

"Mr. Hall thought the one room conception was excellent. There was something in the forward corner of the stage that worried him. The commanding position was too far back, a fatal defect. He believed actors demanded proximity to the nearest seat.

"The stage would be satisfactory for naturalistic drama. Plays in which the text was paramount would be difficult, if you had to rush around rationing your face, you could not give the words their true value.

"He thought that the audience would have an excellent view of all the objects on the stage, which would be seen as sculpture, but they would not have such a good view of the actor, whose face needed to be seen.

"The problem of creating a satisfactory open stage theatre was an enormous one. He had been searching for a solution for the past two years. And still had not found one."

30th April 1964: DL&P Notes on Second meeting with Peter Hall[53]

"An optimum size for an acting area was 25 feet square. If this area was placed at the forward edge of the stage, 50% of the area was unusable for Shakespeare, and became a no-man's-land. He would move the acting area back and put in additional seats in the remaining triangle.

"He felt the blandness of the right angle was not right for 'now'. He would want an actor to play about 10 feet back on the diagonal. The weakness was that this would be uncomfortable for the audience at the extremes of the auditorium."

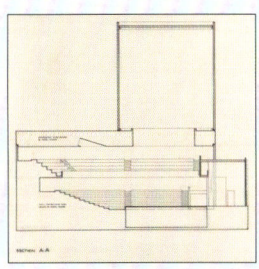

Scheme B section

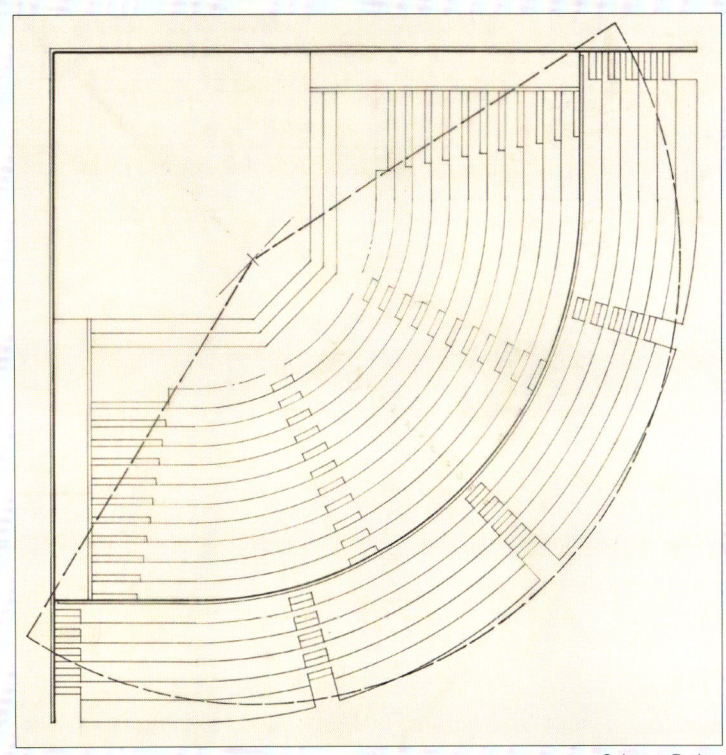

Scheme B plan

Meeting 19

19th Meeting of The National Theatre Building Committee

22 Duchy Street, SE1
Wednesday 6th May 1964, 5:00 pm

Present:
Sir Laurence Olivier, Mr. Norman Marshall (Chairmen), Mr. George Devine, Mr. Michael Benthall, Mr. William Gaskill, Mr. Michael Elliott and Mr. Peter Brook. Mr. Stephen Arlen, Mr. George Rowbottom and Mr. Kenneth Rae were in attendance. Mr. Denys Lasdun, Mr. Peter Softley and Mr. Minjoodt were present by invitation.
Apologies:
Apologies for absence were received from Mr. John Dexter, Mr. Peter Hall, Miss Tanya Moiseiwitsch and Mr. Michel Saint-Denis.

Mr. Lasdun outlined the process of thinking which had led to the evolution of Scheme B, which he was about to submit to the Committee.

A model known as Scheme A had developed from a rough diagram which he drew at the meeting of the Committee on February 5th, 1964. This had been based on the principles of a non-hierarchical auditorium and a one-room relationship between auditorium and acting area. The general feeling of the Committee had been that it was too severe: the side walls seemed oppressive. Mr. Lasdun then produced a ground plan of a further development, Scheme B, with the following main features:
1. A seating capacity of about 1,150.
2. A distance of 65' from the stage to the farthest seats.
3. No walls in the usual sense.
4. Perfect visibility from all seats.
5. A balanced relationship between auditorium and acting area.

Mr. Lasdun placed overlays of the stage/auditorium of the Old Vic and of Chichester on the Scheme B plan. The upper tier in Scheme B was in the same position relative to the stage as the Dress Circle at the Old Vic which was usually considered to be the best part of the house. There were several times the number of seats in the Scheme B upper tier as in the centre of the Old Vic dress circle. He emphasised that compared with Chichester the point of confrontation on the stage was 16' nearer the audience, the audience rake was much steeper and the seats on each side of the stage were moved back through 45°.

The design of a theatre was, of course, an art and it was necessary to go beyond functional criteria to achieve a satisfactory solution.

Mr. Lasdun said that no single theatre could do everything but a satisfactory actor/audience relationship was a fundamental requirement in all theatres.

He suggested that, unless there was an 80% feeling of confidence at the meeting that the principles on which the model was based were right, it was useless to discuss it in detail, enlarge the scale or develop the scheme further. He felt that the meeting should, at this stage, assess the model from the viewpoint of actor and audience only and under the following headings:-
1. Confrontation - an actor feeling that he is face-to-face with an audience.
2. Command - a compelling place where an actor could feel he could command an audience even with his back.
3. "Ripple" - the actor's ability to generate a ripple of feeling passing through the whole audience possibly depending on his relationship with the members of the audience in the front seats.
4. Focus - the concerted effect of all seating directing the attention of the audience to the acting area.

Finally Mr. Lasdun quoted a remark made by Michel St.Denis at an earlier meeting of the Building Committee. "What I am dreaming about is a space stage that would give a feeling of audience and actor being in the same room."

During the subsequent discussion, Mr. Lasdun made the following points:-
1. Most members of the Building Committee who had seen the model prior to the meeting had expressed misgivings concerning some

aspect of the relationship between the forward corner of the stage and the centre bank of seating. He was aware of these misgivings but felt that it was wrong to make alterations to meet these early reactions before allowing time for mature consideration.
2. Three stage designers had seen the model. They regarded the stage as a working proposition which presented a new challenge.
3. There would not be a fire curtain.
4. It would be possible to drop things onto the stage from above over more or less the whole of the acting area.

Sir Laurence said that the fact that the aisles in the Scheme B auditorium were screened from the actor's view had been claimed as an asset. He had thought about this a lot and had come to the conclusion that this was not so and that there was some advantage in the actor being able to look up the aisles. Mr. Lasdun said that subsequent development of the scheme would take this into account.

There was considerable discussion on whether the National Theatre would also need a proscenium theatre of average capacity, either in the same complex on the South Bank, should there be enough room on the site, or elsewhere. This point was not resolved.

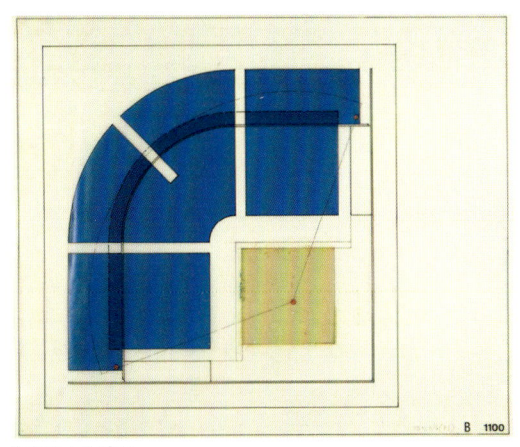

Scheme B plan

Scheme B

It is worthy of note that on 23rd April, two weeks earlier, Olivier's triumphant (albeit physically exhausting) *Othello* opened.

Scheme B arrives, prepared at DL&P, within 20 days of the previous meeting. Note too, that this was only the fourth meeting between Lasdun and the building committee.

Despite the generally favourable reaction, certain issues disturbed the committee and led to extended discussion into the future.

First was the square stage shape with a right angle at the front. Brook "found the shape of the stage slightly disturbing, and thought this was due to the right-angled point." [54]

The second concern was the balcony around the stage that might severely restrict scenery. Lasdun, told by Brook that his role was to produce a radical space, felt this "spacial quality" more important than flexibility. The theatre people generally disagreed. The reader needs to remember that the thrust stage at Chichester was backed by a permanent concrete balcony, which had been a constant irritant to every designer until it was finally removed in the renovation of 2015.

The third problem was the placement of the 'point of command.' This seemed to be too far upstage. Olivier: "The commanding position was, in his opinion, too far back. He believed that actors demand proximity to the nearest seat. This is where the ripple starts which infects the audience." [55]

Despite these reservations, the building committee passed a resolution: "The committee, having studied it individually and collectively, unanimously approved and recommended the adoption of the principles of a scheme known as Scheme B." [56]

Lasdun felt this resolution was sufficient for him to use it as the basis for the main theatre design, while he and his team proceeded with development of the overall building design, exploring the arrangement of workshops, dressing rooms, rehearsal rooms, and front of house. While Lasdun knew the design of Scheme B was unfinished, he clearly was strongly drawn to the concept and continued to push for its acceptance…

A Proscenium.... And A Pause

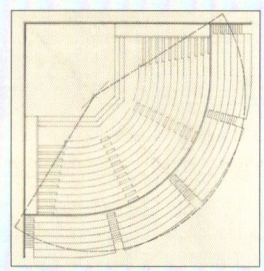

Scheme B plan

> "He thought a solution was lurking within 10ft. or so. He was willing to go that far, but no further."
>
> Denys Lasdun

11th May 1964: National Theatre Board Meeting. A Proscenium Theatre[57]
With the building committee's recommendation, the NT Board approved Scheme B. However the chairman, Lord Chandos, added his hope that the NT might also include a proscenium theatre.

12th May 1964: DL&P Meeting with Michel Saint-Denis and Ken Tynan[58]
"Mr. Saint-Denis thought the scheme was very logical and said that it could be French. Although his French nature responded to its logic, there was something in it, possibly the front edge of the stage or the angle of the balcony over the stage or the centre bank of seating, against which he instinctively rebelled. He thought that it was very satisfactory to the mind, but so satisfactory that there was a frigidity about it.

"Tynan found the lower half of the model more fluid and he suggested that the angular balcony over the stage should be removed. So many dramatists, Shaw, Chekhov, Ibsen, who gave detailed instructions about the setting and he wondered how these could be followed on this stage. He suggested that *Look Back in Anger* would be difficult to do here.

"Mr. Saint-Denis thought the theatre was anti-illusion by nature. Mr. Tynan said he would call it anti-experimental.

"Mr. Saint-Denis was absolutely against building a proscenium theatre. He said we need this theatre and a studio. But it was important that naturalism could be handled. He was not yet completely sure, but he thought it could.

"Mr. Lasdun said that Peter Hall had been against the Mermaid-type of compromise and said that he was convinced that an open stage solution was lurking somewhere, although he had not found it in two years. Mr. Lasdun said he thought a solution was lurking within 10 ft. or so. He was willing to go that far, but no further.

"Mr. Saint-Denis said he agreed with that attitude. Mr. Lasdun asked about vomitories for actors. Mr. Saint-Denis said he thought they were useful and on this theme he said he did not want to take away the impact of the point of the stage, but he thought a vomitory there might animate it and allow further subtle adjustments that could alleviate the rigidity of the design."

Time Out...
Denys Lasdun then requested a pause in the building committee meetings throughout the summer, while his team worked on on the overall building, explaining that he found the meetings time-consuming. The next meeting was not to be until six months later, on 7th October 1964.

Meeting 20

20th Meeting of The National Theatre Building Committee

22 Duchy Street, SE1
Wednesday 7th October 1964, 5:00 pm

Present:
Sir Laurence Olivier, Mr. Norman Marshall (Chairmen), Mr. George Devine, Mr. William Gaskill and Mr. Michael Benthall. Mr. Stephen Arlen, Mr. George Rowbottom, Mr. Kenneth Tynan and Mr. Kenneth Rae were in attendance. Mr. Denys Lasdun and Mr. Peter Softley were present by invitation.

Apologies:
Apologies for absence were received from Mr. Peter Brook, Mr. John Dexter, Mr. Michael Elliott, Mr. Peter Hall, Miss Tanya Moiseiwitsch and Mr. Michel Saint-Denis.

LASDUN: In May last, we presented Scheme B to the National Theatre Board and the South Bank Board and it was adopted in principle by them with the rider that we should examine the possibility of including on the site a proscenium theatre seating 700 people. In the last few months we have examined the implications of this and, with many reservations, we can tell you that a proscenium theatre is possible if you want it. The original brief was for an adaptable theatre and an experimental theatre and there was also a document detailing basic requirements, with regard to services, etc. We have recently had to interpolate that document in the light of there being Scheme B and a proscenium theatre. You have now to decide whether that programme of accommodation is relevant to such a project.

GASKILL: I didn't realise that we had scrapped the idea of an experimental theatre.

LASDUN: That is for you to say. My brief from the South Bank Board is specific. What I have just said above is Part 1 of what you have to decide. Part 2 is what we have never yet discussed – everything else to do with the theatre. Paint-shops, paint-frames, etc. will have to be reviewed. My office has done a great deal of work on this, which will soon be ready to be scrutinised by this Committee. You have got to decide that it is the sort of thing you want before we report to the South Bank Board that the proscenium theatre is a possibility. In about three weeks, we should have cock-shy plans showing the location of the lavatories, dressing-rooms etc. They may be where you don't want them and it is up to you to say so.

DEVINE: Was the Committee consulted about the change of principle (the incorporation of a proscenium theatre)?

OLIVIER: No. We were trying to get away with one theatre and an experimental theatre that would be more or less a room – something the size of LAMDA and involving only a small section of the public. We chose to forget about the proscenium theatre. The Board said they would still like to know whether it was possible to have a proscenium as well as Scheme B. We thought Scheme B would embrace the proscenium to a certain extent.

LASDUN: We do not envisage building the two theatres at the same time but the site implications are terrific as between Scheme B and an experimental area and Scheme B and a proscenium theatre. Your job is to discuss the implications of the latter where the supporting accommodation is concerned.

MARSHALL: The feeling of the South Bank Board was that they were happy about Scheme B subject to the "full exploration of the possibility of including a proscenium theatre" seating 700.

GASKILL: This Committee recommended the principle of Scheme B. We have never accepted it as our theatre. It was agreed as a starting-point.

MARSHALL: I thought we said various people should plan productions on the model. Lasdun said it had its own limitations and could not do all a proscenium theatre could do.

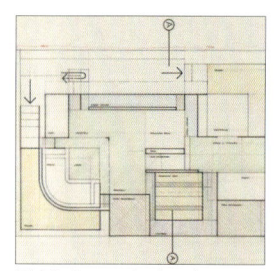

DL&P site study sketch

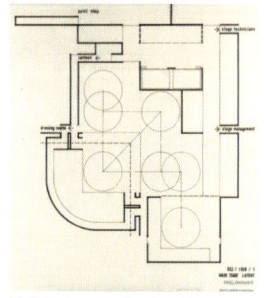

DL&P site study sketch

> "To make headway you've got to take it (Scheme B) as an act of faith."
>
> Denys Lasdun

LASDUN: To make headway you've got to take it [Scheme B] as an act of faith. We couldn't make an adaptable theatre. Scheme B in principle was the evolution of what we thought the National Theatre main auditorium should be. If you change it fundamentally we go back to square 1. We now have the possible addition of a proscenium theatre but we don't have to argue about what a proscenium theatre is.

TYNAN: Don't we? We don't necessarily have to have a picture frame.

GASKILL: By proscenium theatre we mean a directional theatre.

LASDUN: Yes. You mean, basically, Scheme A; but at the National Theatre Board meeting the word "antiquarian" was used by Sir Kenneth Clark. We must get certain priorities right. The decision about the exact nature of the proscenium theatre can remain to be settled in the future.

GASKILL: It has to have flying space and wing space.

LASDUN: You must examine now what is possible in principle on 1.9 acres.

GASKILL: What is the position on the Old Vic as a theatre?

RAE: Fluid.

BENTHALL: Hugh Beaumont [Managing Director of the commercial producer H.M Tennant] says that you must have a theatre with a curtain if you are to put the Comedie Francaise in it.

DEVINE: Surely it is a great advance to have the Boards agreeing to Scheme B?

OLIVIER: If the Board heard that we had to reduce the facilities they would give up the idea of a proscenium theatre being incorporated on the site.

MARSHALL: I don't agree. They might go back on Scheme B.

DEVINE: (re: Old Vic) There used to be a thing about widening the Waterloo Road.

BENTHALL: This has been postponed.

RAE: They might widen it on the other side of the road (to the Old Vic).

LASDUN: Our findings are that it is possible to include a proscenium theatre subject to certain reservations.

RAE: The Comedie Francaise found it very difficult to run successfully theatres that were geographically separated.

GASKILL: I think the reason for the recent division was to give Barrault a theatre.

DEVINE: Would the incorporation of a proscenium theatre jeopardise Scheme B?

LASDUN: What we have done at the moment will not inhibit Scheme B but it might inhibit the proscenium theatre.

GASKILL: It would be foolish not to have a proper proscenium theatre.

MARSHALL: If the Comedie Francaise were to come over here under the auspices of the National Theatre, it need not go to the National Theatre building itself, it could always go to another theatre.

RAE: The Basic Requirements document was drawn up many years ago by a different Committee and before the new Old Vic workshops were built. Is the revision of the necessary ancillary accommodation to be done before or after we see your plans or after?

LASDUN: I think you should start now. It would quicken things up when you see our plans, as you will do in three weeks' time.

DEVINE: Can we have them before a meeting?

LASDUN: You will have a week before the next meeting to study them.

OLIVIER: Is there any thing you would

want in a National Theatre that you would have to sacrifice if you had a second, proscenium, theatre? For example, a library or a museum.

RAE: People enquiring whether there will be a library or museum have been firmly told there would be no room on the site for anything like that.

MARSHALL: We can't consider a library or a museum. They take up too much space.

DEVINE: Wasn't Lasdun thinking about the supporting accommodation all the time that we thought we were going to have Scheme B and a small experimental theatre?

LASDUN: No. We didn't think about it at all to start with.

GASKILL: Is there a restaurant planned?

LASDUN: We must have a directive on this.

OLIVIER: We have five plays in rehearsal at the moment, and for two or three days now we have been rehearsing THE MASTER BUILDER in this Board room. We must have ample rehearsal space.

TYNAN: With two theatres you would have two stages to rehearse on.

GASKILL: Stages are not available for routine rehearsals.

LASDUN: Incorporated in the present plans are four rehearsal rooms. The problem is the supporting accommodation. To sum up:

Do you want a proscenium theatre or not?

If you have one, what will the supporting accommodation be?

For the moment we have made provision for a single-tier proscenium theatre with a 30' opening and a numerical capacity of the order of Nottingham.

OLIVIER: I'm not interested in a proscenium theatre. Do we all feel strongly enough to throw it out?

DEVINE: A bit late to say that now. We must go through the tedium of the hoop.

GASKILL & TYNAN: I'm for a proscenium theatre as well as Scheme B.

MARSHALL: I'm for it because I think a National Theatre should have two theatres. Everywhere I have been on the Continent, the necessity for this has been underlined.

TYNAN: I'm in favour, partly because of Marshall's argument, also because I think that certain intimate plays - THE CARETAKER - need a smaller theatre; also because there are certain staging and atmospheric effects that you can get only on a straight-edged stage. Many people have confirmed this when comparing the productions of OTHELLO at Chichester and at the Old Vic.

GASKILL: I must admit I was greatly relieved to get back to the Old Vic with THE DUTCH COURTESAN. Setting aside all romantic considerations, I believe that any kind of intellectual or didactic theatre is better in a proscenium. A theatre like Chichester works for the highly-introvert or spectacular type of play. If someone can see an entirely new vision of theatre, the best of luck to them, but I am not sure that I could make the same impact where some plays are concerned.

LASDUN: You won't be able to make the same impact (with Scheme B). It will be a different one.

MARSHALL: I think it would be exciting to have a building that would contain both theatres.

GASKILL: To create a link with tradition, we need the two. I am now convinced that the actors of Shakespeare's day played directionally. If there were spectators on the side they had a tough time.

LASDUN: I would not like to take the

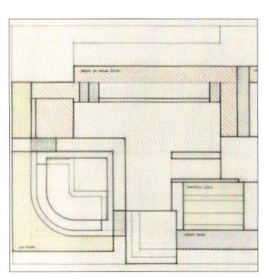

DL&P site study sketch

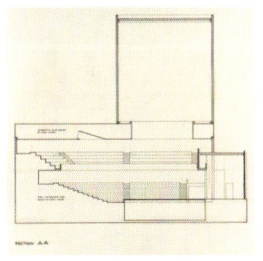

Scheme B section

> "The Festival Theatre, Cambridge, was a marvellous theatre to work in, but certain plays could not be done to advantage there. I feel strongly that two theatres would be the best solution."
>
> Norman Marshall

responsibility for Scheme B without, say, six producers playing about with the model, and we should also, at some time, need a mock-up in a field somewhere.

Devine, Gaskill and Benthall then agreed to experiment with productions on the plans of Scheme B.

BENTHALL: On second thoughts, I am not a very good person to choose because I shall shortly be unavailable. I must say however that I do not really think it is the answer to the problem. If you are a director, you make use of what you've got at your disposal.

If you have to do THE CARETAKER in the Opera House, New York, you mask it in etc. and make the best of it.

DEVINE: When I had my private session with Lasdun I did PLAY [by Samuel Beckett].

OLIVIER: (to Benthall) Would you undertake to do a play written between 1600 and 1700?

BENTHALL: I think any of us could make a play work but that's not the answer.

LASDUN: You have to think what you would gain and what you would lose. I have always said that Scheme B had limitations: it cannot do everything.

TYNAN: Would the gap left by Scheme B be filled by a proscenium theatre?

DEVINE: I'd rather take all the productions I'd done and not a particular period in drama and see what would happen. If someone would give me the plans I'd do it.

OLIVIER: (to Gaskill) Have you got time?

GASKILL: I will have in a week.

DEVINE: Let's make Dexter do CHIPS WITH EVERYTHING on it (Scheme B)

OLIVIER: I still think we'd better have three different types of plays:
  i. one modern one - not earlier than Chekhov.
  ii. one Elizabethan.
  iii. and one in between.

GASKILL: I'll do RECRUITING OFFICER and DUTCH COURTESAN.

OLIVIER: (to Devine) Will you do THE SEAGULL or something modern?

DEVINE: EXIT THE KING?

OLIVIER: If John Dexter has not the time to do some productions on Scheme B, we'll ask Michael Elliot if he can help.

RAE: Why not have both?

OLIVIER: I think we should also involve Motley, John Bury and Jocelyn Herbert as designers.

MARSHALL: The Festival Theatre, Cambridge, was a marvelous theatre to work in, but certain plays could not be done to advantage there. I feel strongly that two theatres would be the best solution.

GASKILL: The proscenium theatre is still a very good theatre.

OLIVIER: I was convinced that the proscenium theatre had certain advantages until I did UNCLE VANYA at Chichester. Wasn't UNCLE VANYA better at Chichester than at the Old Vic?

GASKILL: I wouldn't go to the stake on that.

OLIVIER: Scheme B is not Chichester anyway but you could do LOOK BACK IN ANGER at Chichester.

GASKILL: Great plays would be marvellous anywhere but if you do the less good, and we will have to do them, I think you run into trouble without the possibility of a proscenium theatre.

MARSHALL: Have we any more information about fire regulations?

LASDUN: They're under review by the L.C.C. Undoubtedly certain restrictions will continue to be imposed on materials.

RAE: Have we any further news about the South Bank parking problems?

LASDUN: It all depends on what you decide here.

OLIVIER: Please send me six sets of plans for three producers and three designers.

RAE: The next meeting is due to be held on November 4th.

OLIVIER: I'm on tour then but I could come back for a meeting at this time on Friday the 6th. We'll try to get a report for you by then from three directors.

LASDUN: I'm sensing a feeling of ambivalence about Scheme B which could put us back to square 1. There are immense decisions about the South Bank that will be held up until we get a decision on whether or not there is to be a proscenium theatre.

GASKILL: Then we must establish whether or not we want a proscenium theatre.

LASDUN: I have always said Scheme B can never be an Italian theatre.

GASKILL: If we come back in one month and say we can do any play on Scheme B do we then go back to the Boards and say we don't want a proscenium theatre?

DEVINE: Am I right in saying that in three weeks' time we get a piece of paper saying what the services are, plus plans showing Scheme B in detail?

OLIVIER: The dressing rooms are the same for the two theatres?

LASDUN: Yes. The moment you have a proscenium theatre (as well as Scheme B) you have to put the dressing-rooms, paint-frame etc. in a certain place. You may have reservations about the accommodation or you may be satisfied with it. If you say you must have six rehearsal rooms that may kill the proscenium theatre.

OLIVIER: Can one theatre go on top of the other?

LASDUN: No.

MARSHALL: Has it been minuted that the second theatre will be built later?

RAE: No.

MARSHALL: The South Bank Board realises very clearly that it would cost less to build two theatres simultaneously than defer one to a later date.

GASKILL: Can Lasdun envisage building a theatre with a gap for another at a later date?

LASDUN: We've cracked that nut. The second theatre will be at a different level. We build a roof to start with.

OLIVIER: Myself apart, is the feeling of the Committee for a second theatre?

DEVINE: I'll do my work (on Scheme B) before I decide.

BENTHALL: I'd be against it if it prejudices Scheme B.

OLIVIER: I don't feel the necessity for a second theatre.

ARLEN: Speaking as a manager, I must say that we could do with two theatres. I think there is a grave problem here: to satisfy the demand of the public for seats. It is a terribly serious one that we haven't yet faced up to. Inevitably you'll have at any one time one or two productions that the public are screaming to see. The problem would be eased by two theatres.

GASKILL: Performances of OTHELLO are limited by Olivier's physical endurance!

OLIVIER: I hate the idea that certain sections of the public might develop a preference for one theatre or the other and I am worried in case they should opt for a proscenium theatre. I love Scheme B. I want to force producers to produce in it, and the public to accept it. I don't want to divide interest between two theatres.

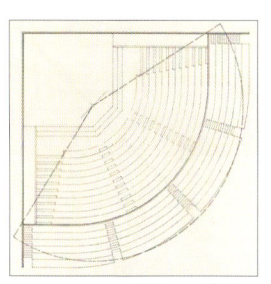

Scheme B plan

> "I think it's necessary for the National Theatre to have a theatre which won't look bad if it's half full."
>
> William Gaskill

> "The most revolutionary thing in this country could be a perfectly designed proscenium theatre."
>
> Kenneth Tynan

GASKILL: I think it's necessary for the National Theatre to have a theatre which won't look bad if it's half full.

MARSHALL: If there is only one theatre there will be a public outcry for it to contain another 300 seats.

LASDUN: There is a great merit in deferring a decision to a later date. Let us have a proscenium theatre on paper.

OLIVIER: I don't want a second National Theatre. What happens if you've got UNCLE VANYA and OTHELLO in the smaller theatre?

GASKILL: You could transfer productions to the larger theatre.

ARLEN: What would you say if you had room on the site for two Scheme B's?

OLIVIER: If we open both theatres at the same time I think we will be making the biggest mistake of our lives. We ought to go on with Scheme B till the effect of another theatre would be merely useful. We'd be cutting our throats if we tried a simultaneous opening.

GASKILL: I don't think so. A year between the openings would suffice.

LASDUN: I suggest that we suspend this conversation till you've seen the plans. We will have to reserve certain architectural positions so the whole thing doesn't look a mess, but you'd be totally aware of the proscenium theatre except for the fly-tower. The space could be a proscenium theatre or a LAMDA theatre. You could leave the whole thing as an open question for five years, provided someone pays for the roof to go over the area.

TYNAN: The most revolutionary thing in this country could be a perfectly designed proscenium theatre.

It was decided that the next meeting of the Committee should be on Friday, November 6th at 5.00 p.m.

Scheme B model, showing the permanent structure wrapping around the rear of the stage

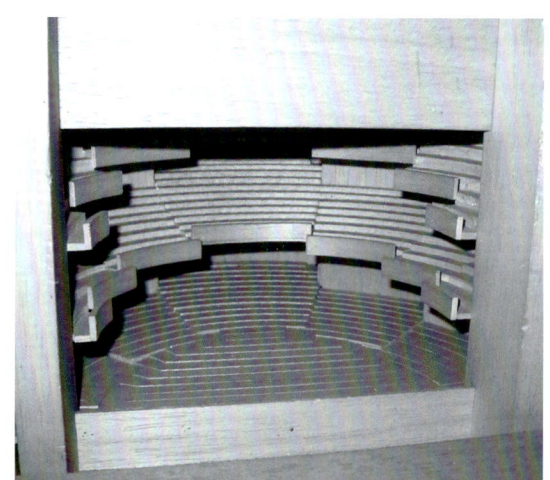

A forgotten evolutionary point? A model possibly showing the auditorium design Lasdun was simultaneously working on for the Opera House part of the NT-Opera scheme. Two versions of this model, the other a wider proscenium, can just be glimpsed, often overlooked, in the centre of the famous 'discarded model' photographs (p66, p146). This one is now in the RIBA Collections.

Meeting 21

21st Meeting of The National Theatre Building Committee

22 Duchy Street, SE1
Friday 6th November 1964, 5:00 pm

Present:
Sir Laurence Olivier (Chairman), Mr. William Gaskill, Mr. Michael Elliott, Mr. George Devine, Mr. Peter Brook, Mr. Michel Saint-Denis and Mr. Peter Hall. Mr. Stephen Arlen, Mr. George Rowbottom, Mr. Kenneth Tynan and Mr. Kenneth Rae were in attendance. Mr. Denys Lasdun, Mr. Peter Softley and Mr. Minjoodt (DL&P) were present by invitation.

Apologies:
Apologies were received from Mr. Norman Marshall, Mr. Michael Benthall, Mr. Roger Furse, Miss Tanya Moiseiwitsch and Mr. John Dexter.

SOFTLEY: We have brought this small "stack-up" model of the theatre complex which has been based on the original "basic requirements" submitted. It is designed to study the relationships of the various groups of accommodation, taking account of a proscenium theatre seating about 700 on the site. It is not a complete answer because we have not yet fully studied the traffic problem. The L.C.C. have taken the latter into consideration – for example it is possible that there will be an underpass in Belvedere Road. The model is a diagram in abstract that bears in mind the space available, which may be reduced if there is to be an underpass.

Mr. Minjoodt then explained the model pointing out the salient features. Provision had been made for five rehearsal rooms. During discussion and in answer to questions by Sir Laurence and Mr. Arlen on "levels," Mr. Lasdun stressed that the model was an abstract exercise that was concerned only with inter-relationships of the various parts of the theatre complex. It had not yet been determined where and at what level the streets would be. Mr. Softley said that various questions called for consideration:

1. PAINTSHOP. This was the largest element in the scheme.

   What was the requirement for a paint frame in relation to Scheme B and a proscenium theatre? Conventional cloths would not be used for Scheme B. Would the committee consider painting cloths on the floor as on the continent?

2. DRESSING ROOMS. Would it be more flexible to have one centralised dressing room area for the two theatres or two sets of dressing rooms, one for each theatre?

   Mr. Gaskill and Mr. Elliott suggested, and it was agreed, that such technical questions should be considered in detail by a smaller sub-committee.

   Sir Laurence said that before leaving these questions he would like to say that he considered a communal dressing room area between the two theatres would be preferable and that it would be desirable to have facilities for painting cloths on the floor should there be sufficient room.

3. REHEARSAL ROOMS. In connection with these, Sir Laurence and Mr. Gaskill pointed out that they should be at least as large as the acting area of the stage.

4. SCHEME B. Mr. Softley's observation that the opening at the back of the stage leading into the assembly area was limited to a height of 20ft. led to a discussion on scene-changing and flying facilities.

DEVINE: But the room is 35ft. high.

LASDUN: Yes.

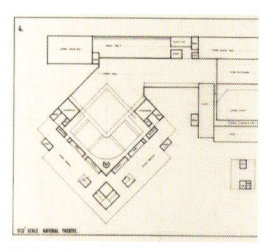

DL&P site sketch

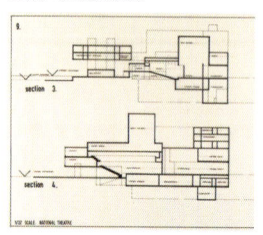

DL&P initial sections

ELLIOTT: What have you intended where flying facilities are concerned?

MINJOODT: There is provision over the whole of the stage area.

TYNAN: Could the gallery be a bit higher?

MINJOODT: In that case the volume goes up and you run into trouble with acoustics.

GASKILL: How high is the "ceiling" of the Old Vic stage?

ARLEN: A little less than 40ft.

ST. DENIS: The gallery imposes a certain convention of playing in one room.

OLIVIER: Yes. But you can be in a room and look out of a window. We want to be able to come into a room from an immense outer world.

ST. DENIS: But what are the means of doing that?

LASDUN: You could go up 30ft but you would then hide the gallery.

ST. DENIS: The question is: Is it good to constrict or not?

HALL: If we start saying the gallery is not there we destroy the feeling of one room.

LASDUN: The room is a room because of that gallery. Above and below the room you have a great deal of space. Take the gallery away and we start again.

MINJOODT: You can punch holes in the gallery but not take it away.

OLIVIER: Is there an L-shaped flytower behind the gallery?

MINJOODT: That is possible with certain reservations.

DEVINE: I have laid this stage out in my garden and it is quite big. Anything that took place that far away would be in the nature of spectacle mob scenes.

MINJOODT: If you have something as high as 60ft you start to influence the facilities behind that area.

GASKILL: Is the stage too big, I wonder?

LASDUN: We are dealing with a spatial conception. The stage is what you choose to make it.

ELLIOTT: When you have worked the theatre for a year every actor will know just where the stage is.

HALL: To what extent does a chimney or a funnel for flying dissipate the feeling of a room?

LASDUN: When we presented Scheme B it was described how the soffit of the ceiling would be continuous and there would be a hole within it.

OLIVIER: I think we are asking you to convert the room into a barn with a loft.

HALL: What everybody is going to want to do is to put something in front of the gallery. The limitations of flying space will confine the stage area.

BROOK: When I was last at a meeting the general feeling was that Scheme B was lovely but the problem remained that we were looking into a corner. Has that problem been resolved?

LASDUN: I was not a party to that feeling. We haven't looked into it yet.

BROOK: Everything was related to the point of the stage.

LASDUN: We took notes of comments on that corner. What we are now arguing about is the other corner, and I am resisting changing the conception of one room.

GASKILL: What should the next stage be? If we

have any doubts about Scheme B, surely now is the time to voice them.

LASDUN: You were given plans on which to work out productions. What has happened?

DEVINE: Did we say the proscenium theatre was desirable?

OLIVIER: Though I was personally opposed to one, the feeling of the meeting was that there should be a proscenium theatre.

For the benefit of those not present at recent meetings Olivier outlined the position regarding the attitude of the South Bank Board and the National Theatre Board to the inclusion of a proscenium theatre.

Further discussion threw up the following points and observations:

BROOK: I get the impression that there is a danger now that we are taking Scheme B too much for granted and are afraid to open up certain questions.

LASDUN: Don't deceive yourselves. There is a lurking feeling in this room that you are hankering back to a proscenium theatre. We have always told you that Scheme B has its limitations.

GASKILL: My doubts have grown in the last six months.

ELLIOTT: I do not think there is any point in my working productions out on Scheme B ground plan. The idea that this would be of use is based on the assumption that all directors work better on an open stage. I cannot find an answer in relation to a given play. An answer exists only in relation to a given director and a given production. You can only divide the plays objectively – if you can do so at all – by taking them according to the period in which they were written.

LASDUN: You are going to have to cope with a theatre that you don't know. It must be an act of faith.

DEVINE: I agree with Elliott that every approach must be subjective but given we can't say that we have no idea what we would do with any given production on Scheme B.

LASDUN: You will be forced to direct according to the dictates of the space that you are given. You cannot do plays conventionally on Scheme B.

HALL: I don't like Scheme B. I don't accept that we should be forced to choose between the concept of a proscenium and an open stage. Is the proscenium theatre to be an insurance against the deficiencies of Scheme B?

OLIVIER: Probably. I preferred UNCLE VANYA at Chichester to UNCLE VANYA at the Old Vic. The relationships between people were more lively. I think Scheme B is a smashing theatre and I would like to embrace it and say "That is the National Theatre." Considerations of comedy could dictate a picture frame, however.

ST. DENIS: Cannot we have a studio theatre that would embrace the proscenium theatre?

OLIVIER: We might use one of the rehearsal rooms as such.

LASDUN: The fly in the ointment is that we must have a proscenium theatre for 700 people.

OLIVIER: Let's say we want one for 450 people only because of limitations of space and that it must be of an experimental nature.

Sir Laurence then left the meeting.

ST. DENIS: If the intention is to house visiting foreign companies a capacity of 700 would not be big enough for the Comedie Francaise, etc.

TYNAN: The Berliner Ensemble theatre seats only 750 people. We are enough in danger of not allowing enough people to see the work of the National Theatre.

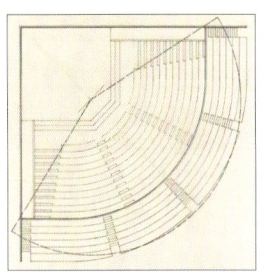

Scheme B plan

> **"You are going to have to cope with a theatre that you don't know. It must be an act of faith."**
>
> Denys Lasdun

> "Ideally the National Theatre needs three stages. Something like Scheme B, a proscenium theatre and an experimental theatre."
>
> Michael Elliott

HALL: Will the productions be interchangeable?

DEVINE: One has to admit that there are certain plays for which a smaller theatre is desirable.

ELLIOTT: Ideally the National Theatre needs three stages. Something like Scheme B, a proscenium theatre and an experimental theatre.

BROOK: It seems to me that there is a major clash of ideas here.

1. From every theatrical point of view it would be better if the second theatre were limited to 350 seats.

   VERSUS
2. Tynan's idea that 750 people should have the opportunity of seeing the productions at the second theatre.

LASDUN: 400 seats is the limit for adaptability.

DEVINE: That doesn't answer Tynan's argument.

TYNAN: I would like to see the first perfectly equipped proscenium theatre for 750 people in this country.

GASKILL: Then you've got to have wing space and flying space.

HALL: Then you can't confuse it with an experimental theatre.

LASDUN: Nottingham has already been criticised for inadequate wing space. Tynan wants a jewel of a proscenium but there isn't room.

GASKILL: If you can't have a properly equipped proscenium there is no point in having it at all. Ideally we need a total stage width of 90ft and a depth of 60ft though we could settle for a width of 60ft.

MINJOODT: You have got 30ft of wing space each side of the stage allowed for in this model.

GASKILL: That's all right then. We don't need more dressing room space. The same company acts in both theatres. Having a proscenium theatre doesn't mean that you have to double your dressing room accommodation. It is a matter of planning the repertory. What depth is there?

MINJOODT: There is 30ft behind the stage.

BROOK: We all think it is a great pity for the experimental theatre to be lost. Cannot Lasdun be asked to study if one of the rehearsal rooms can be made into an experimental theatre? It can be used for many other purposes including rehearsals.

RAE: While Lasdun is doing that, the technical committee will study the facilities as far as this theatre complex is concerned.

LASDUN: I am under instructions from the South Bank Board. I can do nothing without their mandate.

DEVINE: Then we will recommend a resolution to the National Theatre Board which they can submit to the South Bank Board.

TYNAN: When the Kammerspiele built their experimental theatre they called it a large adaptable rehearsal room. There was no need to refer it to any Board or equivalent authority.

LASDUN: Every additional enquiry has enormous implications concerning parking, etc. I need documents and I cannot act without them.

DEVINE: The experimental theatre might have to be open only to a supporters' club.

RAE: Could we now draft a resolution satisfactory to everybody here?

TYNAN: Let us keep out words like "experimental theatre".

The following resolution was recommended for submission to the National Theatre Board and the South Bank Board:

THAT the architect should be asked to consider the possibility of adapting one of the rehearsal rooms for use as a studio theatre where performances could be given before small audiences.

BROOK: Where do we go with Scheme B? I have a terrible feeling that a certain impatience to get going may freeze Scheme B.

DEVINE: We must get it into a form that we all understand – something as simple as a half inch model.

BROOK: I think we need a full size mock-up as well.

GASKILL: The problem is the point of command on the stage in relation to people watching it.

HALL: I support that.

It was agreed that a half-inch model and a full size mock-up of Scheme B were essential.

GASKILL: Where could we build a mock-up?

ARLEN: Probably in a film studio. We could find out whether the South Bank Board would finance a mock-up.

HALL: We also need more ground plans of Scheme B. I have never had one.

GASKILL: Could we have ground plans on a half-inch scale?

Mr. Lasdun agreed to provide ground plans of Scheme B on a half-inch scale for the purpose of a half-inch model.

ARLEN: (to Lasdun) Can you tell us what the thinking was behind your brief regarding the proscenium theatre? If the South Bank Board were thinking that visiting foreign companies might be housed there, it must be made clear that in the present circumstances of subsidy that consideration is out. It would be economically impossible to bring companies like the Comédie Française, Moscow Arts Theatre, etc. to a theatre seating only 750.

GASKILL: But those circumstances of subsidy might change.

ST. DENIS: What is the National Theatre to be? A creative force in itself or a building that will take all the companies of the world?

DEVINE: Could we say that we are building for posterity and there might be people who don't like Scheme B?

GASKILL: Should we now ask whether we want the proscenium theatre?

LASDUN: I think it would be easy to get out of the proscenium theatre where the South Bank Board is concerned.

RAE: Not where the National Theatre Board is concerned.

BROOK: If a large company has two outlets instead of one it seems to me admirable.

ELLIOTT: We need to accept that Scheme B and the proscenium are two different instruments. One is not inherently better and the other inferior.

BROOK: If we have a proscenium theatre we must guard against the danger that less attention will be devoted to Scheme B. We must concentrate on Scheme B. We know what we want from the proscenium theatre.

ST. DENIS: But there are many kinds of proscenium theatre. It shouldn't be a conventional one.

LASDUN: But that is just what Sir Kenneth Clark wants. He used the word "antiquarian".

HALL: I don't like Scheme B but I would be worried if the inclusion of a proscenium theatre would make the National Theatre a middle-of-the-road theatre.

GASKILL: What difference will the inclusion of a proscenium theatre make to the cost of the National Theatre?

LASDUN: It will cost what it will cost.

> "But there are many kinds of proscenium theatre. It shouldn't be a conventional one."
>
> Michel Saint-Denis

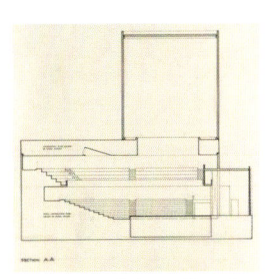

Scheme B section

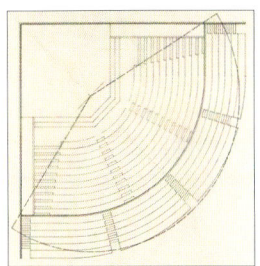

Scheme B plan

Doubts and Success... And Costs...

This was only the second meeting to discuss Scheme B, and after a four-month gap. To and fro went the inconclusive discussions, with the growing concern that Scheme B, without any further development, was being forced upon the committee. Gaskill: "My doubts have grown in the last six months." Peter Hall: "I don't like Scheme B." What should be the size and role of the proscenium theatre? Could a studio be included by double use of a rehearsal room?

A minor, historically significant comment by Norman Marshall: he had been "brought up on an open stage, the Festival Theatre Cambridge. This theatre died because some plays could not be done on its stage, and they ran out of suitable pieces."[59]

Meanwhile, the National company continued to yet greater success. Sir Laurence's extraordinary *Othello* was joined by the first sensationally successful new play, Peter Shaffer's *Royal Hunt of the Sun*, directed by John Dexter and designed by Michael Annals. Sir Laurence directed Arthur Miller's *The Crucible*, while *Much Ado About Nothing*, directed by Franco Zeffirelli, further confirmed the astonishing eclecticism of the company.

16th December 1964: South Bank Board. It was made clear that the existing commitments totalled £2.3 million (£1 million by the Government and £1.3 million by the LCC) and that any increase and/or its division between the two parties would still have to be considered. It was agreed that at the earliest possible practicable opportunity ministers should be informed fully that the project would certainly cost far more than was at present earmarked. The council agreed that the general requirement for more finance should then be presented to ministers by the chairman, supported by Lord Chandos, Sir Isaac Hayward, and Sir William Hart, together with Mr. W.B. Fiske, the Leader of the Greater London Council, the body which replaced the LCC after the elections of April 1964.

... And Sabotage

Then on 21st February 1965 a bizarre development. *The Sunday Times* published an article by Peter Sullivan: *The National*

The Sunday Times, 21st February 1965

Theatre Plan – and how it evolved.[60] It included extensive leaks of information about the NT design. The article wrote of the changes in auditorium design in Britain since 1945 and introduced the proposed new concept represented by Scheme B. However it added, "it is Peter Hall [in the RSC's Barbican Theatre], however, that returns to the actor and his demands." Worse, it adds the comparative costs of various theatres, with the National quoted at £2 million and the Barbican, with surprising precision, at £1,307,500.

It not only implied that the RSC plan might be superior, but that it would be cheaper!

Kenneth Rae reported, "They were sailing dangerously close to being without an architect as a result of damaging and irresponsible statements in *The Sunday Times*."[61] Kenneth reported that Lasdun was convinced that Peter Hall had been responsible for the leak. He and Olivier were at pains to persuade Lasdun that Hall was not responsible.

Lasdun did indeed go ballistic. He accused Peter Hall of being behind the leak and reported that Olivier agreed with his suspicion. "DL considers that Peter Hall should be removed from the committee and has said so, and has alternatively suggested that we will cease to be architects for the project."[62]

Lasdun said he considered the NTBC a bad security risk, was not prepared for further discussion with its members and under no circumstances would they be shown the nature of the masterplan.

Lasdun then outlined all the requests and amendments that had come from the building committee since November 1964. He said that every single request had been met and Olivier would have to say that DL&P had both given them everything they had asked for and that everything they had asked for was the minimum reasonable requirement of the NT.

Lasdun warned that if there was any ambivalence on this issue, it would put paid to the scheme. (His private notes suggested Olivier was not quite as safe as he had previously thought in his confidence in Scheme B.) He underlined that whatever damages had been done to the NT, the effect on the morale of the architects working at high pressure could only have been worse. This he stressed because Olivier gave great attention to the morale of his own company. Lord Chandos fully agreed with Lasdun's attitude (Lasdun had advised them that he had taken legal opinion on the matter) and the best thing to do was to bury the story. He would see that no further mention of the NT took place in *The Sunday Times* or elsewhere.

But Lasdun demanded the return of all the plans that he had released to the committee. No more drawings were issued to them until 1966 – a year later.

It's hard in retrospect to understand the extent of Lasdun's outrage… other than his habitual extreme sensitivity about any publicity falling outside his control.

Lasdun had had only six meetings with the building committee. The third had produced Scheme A and the fourth Scheme B. Then, at his request, there had been four months without further committee contact while he developed a total building that incorporated Scheme B without any further development. This, despite the two further subsequent meetings of the committee that had expressed concern over lack of progress with Scheme B. Now a breach had occurred.

On 21st February 1965, the South Bank Board recorded: "The Chairman reminded the Council that the article on 'The National Theatre Plan – and how it evolved', which appeared in *The Sunday Times* of 21st February 1965, meant that there had been a leakage of confidential information, which had naturally much disturbed the architect. It was not known where the leakage had originated. The Chairman wished to give a warning about the importance of keeping the South Bank Board's confidential information as such, until the board releases it.

"Lord Chandos said that quite rightly Mr. Lasdun had taken grave exception to this disclosure and that, after he (Lord Chandos) had spoken to the editor and seen the writer of the article, *The Sunday Times* had agreed to say no more at that time, in return for Lord Chandos's promise of a press interview with himself when the South Bank Board is ready to make a public announcement. The Chairman said that at that time the South Bank Board might decide to hold a press conference."[63]

Unfortunately, there followed a fourteen-month gap to the next meeting with the committee over the design of the theatres. Meanwhile, Lasdun was preoccupied by other problems surrounding the project: its site and, most importantly, its cost.

Costs and Site

On 21st April 1965, Lasdun reported to the South Bank Board that since the earlier idea of an adaptable theatre had been abandoned as impractical, it became clear that something extra would be needed and that one of the main rehearsal rooms might be adapted as an experimental studio or workshop theatre where performances might be given before a small invited audience of 150 to 200 persons. The recommendation was accepted by the Board.

But costs remained a grave concern. When Lasdun first unveiled the site model, he said, "The standards for his proposals, in work and equipment, had been dictated by the essential needs proscribed by those acquainted with theatres and opera houses who had been advising him; if economies in expenditure were to be made, the point of no return would be quickly reached, and his firm's considered advice to the council would be not to build at all rather than accept a lower standard."[64]

Even so, the future of the opera house remained uncertain, and DL&P was advised to concentrate on the theatres.

In May 1965 Lasdun produced a splendid model of his scheme for a National Theatre and Opera House to be built alongside County Hall in front of the massive tower of the Shell Building. He described it as "deeply concerned with the creation of a cityscape on a metropolitan riverside site which can be enjoyed day and night... by everyone whether they are going to the theatre or not... A series of terraces... cascade into a central valley which, in turn, gently steps down to the riverside. The night scene will take on the quality of fairyland."[65]

Olivier's first sight of the model prompted this letter to Lasdun: "Sleep I could not, for excitement and heart-bubbling joy at what you had shown us... Oh my God, if the government don't... promulgate and extol the enterprise now, I think I shall... go and eat bananas in Pitcairn Island. Please let me now congratulate and thank you from my heart for the genius which combines such ravishing imagination with such shrewd, wise, cunning and disciplined order."[66]

The new cost however was a big shock: £2.3 million had been expected – now it was estimated at £9.5 million, not including £5 million of site costs!

From the Treasury to the GLC on 25th May 1965: "The cost of the project had not taken the Treasury by surprise for it had been evident for some time that the Theatre Board were thinking in grandiose terms." The two funding bodies seem to be figuring out, at this point, who would be responsible for cancelling the project – the Government or the GLC.[67]

Lasdun site model of the National Theatre - Opera House scheme: opera house (left) and theatres (right), 1965

A Sense of Theatre

The National Theatre, Alone

DL Memo, 15th June 1965. Meeting with Arts Minister to Harold Wilson's government, Jennie Lee[68]
"Miss Jennie Lee was sympathetic to the proposals, but, nevertheless, with a Government majority of two, it was impossible to contemplate the expenditure of £9.5 million at present. Nor could Lord Cottesloe persuade her that the architects should, in the meantime, continue with the work."

Panic ensued and efforts were made to find economies. As a member of the technical sub-committee, I was very involved with my NT colleagues in seeking economies. The entire area of the building was shrunk (literally changing the scale of the existing drawings of theatre and opera house), saving £250,000, but making some backstage spaces – like dressing rooms – exceptionally compact (they have been particularly 'cosy' ever after!). The proscenium theatre might be left as a shell (another £650,000), and the restaurant and opera studio omitted (£540,000). Replanning reduced the ground works by £500,000. Altogether a possible saving of £2.5 million.[69] But this was hardly enough.

In June 1965, Olivier wrote to Lord Cottesloe: "May we hope therefore, that every effort is made to see that Denys Lasdun's inspired 'Fairyland' does not become a 'Never-Neverland'."[70]

23rd June 1965: House of Lords. Lunch. Lord Cottesloe, Chancellor of the Exchequer, Selwyn Lloyd, Secretary of State for Education and Science Anthony Crosland, Lasdun, etc.
A cordial lunch, but Her Majesty's Government was very nervous. The pound was weak and this could not have come at a worse time. Crosland said that the cost of the NT had "escalated." Lasdun strongly countered this: "That is not so." The original figure of £2.3 million had never been an estimate, it was simply a theoretical figure that had been used in the press, but one that was unconnected to any estimate for any actual building.[71]

Black Times Indeed
On 10th December 1965, Secretary to the South Bank Board Richard Lynex, wrote to warn Lasdun of the possibility that the entire project might be abandoned by the end of 1965.

But, in February 1966, the Treasury announced to the South Bank Board that it would contribute half the cost of the theatre but nothing toward the opera house. The Greater London Council, formed by elections of April 1964 and fully established in April 1965, at first offered to take over the opera house cost, but then Jennie Lee countered by saying there would be no increase of annual grant to Sadler's Wells to cover any extra costs.[72] This led to the cancellation of the opera house.

That was only part of the remaining problem. The new cap of £7.5 million for the theatres alone was regarded by Government as an absolute limit. Indeed, Lasdun, even then still negotiating his contract with the SBB, was initially asked to guarantee that cap, which he, quite understandably, refused to do.

As an aside: in Australia, the problem of funding the Sydney Opera House, running a few years ahead of the National, was solved by creating a lottery specifically for this purpose. It would be three decades before the British government discovered this approach to arts funding.

In March 1966, it was reported that the National would be situated between County Hall and Hungerford Bridge and include three theatres (an 1100-seat open stage, 750-seat proscenium, and 200-seat experimental space). It would be built in three-and-a-half years and open in 1972.

During all these momentous developments, the building committee remained in ignorance of these financial crises. It remains a mystery why Sir Laurence, who must have been aware of these dramas, never shared this information with his committee. Since numerous meetings had been cancelled since the dramatic stop-work caused by *The Sunday Times* leak, most of the committee members felt isolated and worried that their principle concern, Scheme B, was being pushed through despite their expressed reservations. Sir Laurence was, at the time, going through grave personal problems. His wife Joan Plowright had a miscarriage in 1965 and he went into a period of extreme and crippling stage fright that was to haunt him for almost five years.

What on earth was going on?

Abandoned models of abandoned ideas for the National Theatre and Opera House, at the DL&P Office

2.3 Blood Dripping From Concrete Walls

Meetings #24-30

The models, conjecturally: 1: Scheme Av2; 2: Part of Scheme B; 3: Proscenium theatre; 4: Opera House wide opening; 5: Proscenium theatre; 6: Opera House square opening; 7: 180° scheme seen nowhere else, curtailed version in plan on p.173; 8: Early Olivier model; 9: Scheme B; 10: partial Scheme Av2; 11: alternate Scheme B; 12: NT-OP exteriors; 13: perhaps workshop block; 14: Proscenium theatre variations

The Opera House is abandoned, but the National gets the go-ahead. The committee meet after a fourteen month hiatus, deeply suspicious that Lasdun is pushing them into Scheme B despite most members' growing reservations. In the face of continuing criticism, Lasdun prepares three more schemes, the last the forerunner of today's Olivier. At Sir Laurence's request, Richard Pilbrow prepares a concept for the stage and fly tower that infuriates Lasdun. He finds it "impossible to accept"... but eventually does so.

As the state of Britain's finances continues to worsen, so budgetary pressures increase on the National.

Missing Months

Great news: the National Theatre gets a go-ahead from Government and GLC.[73] Yet, for the building committee, fourteen months had elapsed. The dramatic interruption of *The Sunday Times*' 21st February 1965 "breach of security" had deeply offended Lasdun, and he had demanded the withdrawal of all the drawings of Scheme B from the committee and NT staff. For the committee, no progress on the theatre design had been made, and their initial enthusiasm had turned to doubt.

Nevertheless, on 9th March 1966, the architect was instructed to proceed with Stage Two (detailed design) and report back in twelve months' time with a more accurate estimate of costs.

Meanwhile, Olivier's company at Chichester, which he continued to run alongside the National, was flying high. The fourth year was another success. It began with a new John Arden play, in a wildly invented Scottish language, starring Albert Finney: *Armstrong's Last Goodnight*, then a revival of *Trelawney of the "Wells"*, finally, a special double bill: a production by Michael Elliott (with Richard Negri designing and myself lighting) of *Miss Julie*, starring Maggie Smith and Albert Finney, together with a hilarious new comedy by Peter Shaffer, *Black Comedy*, brilliantly directed by John Dexter. My lighting had become even more assured with the three-dimensional needs of the thrust stage... and it was a truly glorious English summer.

Going International

Meanwhile, an adventure: the National toured three productions to Moscow. The international situation in 1965 was dramatic, Russia was an iron-fisted police state, and for an English company to be invited to visit was a major event. We played right within the Kremlin, in the Kremlevsky Teatr, built as Stalin's private cinema.

The load-in and fit up were nightmares. The Russian crew, described to us as the cream of Moscow theatre… were not. The opening of Olivier's *Othello* was a lighting nightmare, but who cared? It was a public triumph. Olivier, in the performance of a lifetime, overwhelmed the audience, who stood and cheered and cheered. This magnificent image of blackness stalked to downstage centre. "Tovarischi!" he began. The audience went crazy and it seemed the applause would go on forever.

Next to open was my personal all-time favourite production, Peter Wood's *Love for Love*, designed by Lila de Nobili. I'm not sure the Russian audience really understood restoration comedy, but the visuals of the show were magical.

Then to Berlin, the Freie Volksbühne, to repeat our success. Here a practical lesson was learnt. Lila's main setting for *Love For Love* was a huge, three-dimensional exterior of a Georgian house and garden. It took a crew of twenty-five four hours to build it each time at the Vic. In Berlin, with its mechanised side stage wagons, the setup took maybe two minutes. We noted this for our future theatre.

Then home. For me, in 1966, lighting two productions at the Vic: *Juno and the Paycock*, directed by Olivier, then an epic production of Ostrovsky's *The Storm* with John Dexter, director, and the genius Czech scenographer, Josef Svoboda.

Then back to planning the new building. The building committee was in a dark and suspicious mood.

While Sir Laurence and Norman Marshall, as members of the SBB, must have been aware of the overall picture, building committee members seemed unaware of the traumas, of cost cutting and site changes, with which Lasdun had been struggling. They only knew that Scheme B, to which Lasdun seemed so committed, fell far short of their hopes.

Poster for the National's 1965 visit to Moscow

Meeting 24

24th Meeting of The National Theatre Building Committee

10a Aquinas Street, London, SE1
Friday 1st April 1966, 5:00 pm

Present:
Sir Laurence Olivier, Mr. Norman Marshall (Chairmen), Mr. Michael Benthall, Mr. John Dexter, Mr. Michael Elliott, Mr. William Gaskill, Mr. Peter Brook and Mr. Peter Hall, Mr. George Rowbottom, Mr. Kenneth Tynan and Mr. Kenneth Rae were in attendance.

OLIVIER: I thought it best to have a meeting between ourselves without the inhibiting influence of Lasdun. You know things are now going ahead. Before we begin, I think we should record our very deep sorrow at the death of George Devine who was of inestimable help to the Committee.

ALL: Hear, hear.

RAE: Within the last three weeks, the Treasury and the G.L.C. have each agreed to give £3-4 million towards the building of the National Theatre, embracing an open-stage auditorium seating about 1,150 and a proscenium theatre seating about 750.

MARSHALL: Lasdun has sent a message that any delay will cost £35,000 a month.

OLIVIER: Read the Minute of 6th May 1964 recommending the principles of Scheme B which would be classed as an open-stage auditorium. This had subsequently been recommended by the National Theatre Board to the South Bank Board and approved by the latter.

What has gone forward and now passed by the Treasury and handed back to the South Bank Board to build is a larger open-stage and a smaller proscenium. Opinions have been going up and down and left and right since Scheme B was first shown. Doubts were brought to a head after the Building Committee's examination of the model in Lasdun's office and his high-handed attitude when challenged on the point. Subsequently we challenged Lasdun on this and he said that nothing was final until the 1/2" model was built and the full-scale "mock-up" tried out.

RAE: The building of the 1/2" model is now underway.

OLIVIER: I'll go round the table and ask everyone what they now think.

BENTHALL: How did we get the second theatre? I thought it was ruled out.

RAE: No, the proscenium theatre has been incorporated.

BENTHALL: I suppose the question is "what do we think of the Point?".

OLIVIER: What do you think of any of it?

BENTHALL: I think an open theatre is fine but I don't approve of the Point.

MARSHALL: Do you approve of the Corner?

DEXTER: I am committed to an open-stage but not to that one (Scheme B) and it's not just the question of the Point. The two side walls are difficult to cope with. I have tried out theoretical productions and you are always backing onto the two walls. Then there is the factor of the 16' Gallery and the construction seems locked round that back Corner.

ELLIOTT: I accepted the principle of Scheme B as an open-stage theatre not subtending at so wide an angle as Chichester. When we accepted this principle a stage with an audience on two sides – we didn't discuss it in enough detail. As a result of political circumstances, Scheme B hardened

> "Are we confident that when there is a 'mock-up' there will be something to mock?"
>
> Peter Hall

into something not properly discussed. I am not satisfied with Scheme B.

GASKILL: I am not personally enthusiastic about Scheme B. We are no nearer the stage any of us want. In its initial concept, Scheme B was more striking.

TYNAN: I think Scheme B is too big. The 70' diagonal is too much. I have become more interested in decor in the last year or two. With Scheme B, everything will be shoved into the back corner, with its back against this permanent wall. My minority opinion is to cut down Scheme B to equal size with the proscenium theatre. I'm for a drastic curtailment of Scheme B.

OLIVIER: Our Committee has been seriously weakened by the death of George Devine. Can we make any serious suggestions about people whom we might like to join the Committee? I personally think it would be bad if we didn't ask Tyrone Guthrie.

MARSHALL: Guthrie is a fanatic for the thrust stage. This doesn't rule him out but it should be remembered. His case is that it provides a more economic use of space, generates a higher voltage, discourages the use of scenery and discourages illusion.

GASKILL: I think the Committee is too large at the moment. We must face the practical considerations of getting the theatre designed and built towards the vision of two or three directors. I can't see us building one for six directors.

ELLIOTT: I agree about inviting Guthrie. With his experience he would know all about the practical implications of the open-stage.

DEXTER: I think we should bring in Richard Pilbrow. We are sadly lacking on the technical side.

MARSHALL: If Pilbrow is going to put in as a contractor, he would have to resign.

Mr. Peter Brook and Mr. Peter Hall then joined the meeting. Sir Laurence outlined what had transpired so far and put forward the suggestion that Richard Pilbrow, Tyrone Guthrie and Jocelyn Herbert should be invited to join the Committee.

TYNAN: Is it possible to ask someone right outside, like Svoboda[74], what he thinks of Scheme B?

OLIVIER: With his views on design, he would hate it so there is no point.

It was agreed to ask Richard Pilbrow, Tyrone Guthrie and Jocelyn Herbert to join the Committee.

HALL: Scheme B got set too early, We all said an open-stage would be fine but I expressed great concern about the Point.

BROOK: The resolution to build Scheme B was conditional upon the result of the "mock-up" and that we would have ample opportunity in the future to work productions out on the "mock-up". We can't take Scheme B without that proviso.

HALL: Are we confident that when there is a 'mock-up' there will be something to mock?

TYNAN: Lasdun says that if you remove the other Corner you remove Scheme B.

DEXTER: The Technical Sub-Committee is being rushed for decisions on the basis of Scheme B.

OLIVIER: The Balcony round the stage is what creates his room.

ELLIOTT: Lasdun has produced a theatre on the specious idea that it must be one room. We wanted an open proscenium or a Chichester closed down ... with the audience not so far round and with scenic facilities.

OLIVIER: We are all worried by the Point. We really want a quarter circle.

HALL: It is not tenable to say a room must be right-angled.

BROOK: An architect always believes a solution must be a pure one, where every good theatre contains antagonistic principles. (Looking at the model) This should be slightly more impure... not geometric. We could get the model right if we pulled it about a bit,

ELLIOTT: Lasdun has always seen it rigidly. He has made it geometric.

ALL: We always said it must be the feeling of one room.

GASKILL: Will Lasdun not argue that the point of the stage works against the curve of the auditorium?

HALL: The only way to approach Lasdun is by talking about specific staging problems.

ELLIOTT: Scheme B has no focal point. It is a deliberate dispelling of such.

OLIVIER: How do we put this all to Lasdun?

RAE: Wait for the model.

DEXTER: Why build a "mock-up" of that (Scheme B) and waste time and money?

HALL: We have solved the Barbican by being impure.

TYNAN: Surely there is nothing against building two identical theatres if they are good theatres?

BROOK: We want to do something that will stir Lasdun creatively. We must make what we all think and feel clear to him. We may be able to make him think dramatically.

ELLIOTT: The pressure on him to be rigid is enormous.

HALL: I am bothered if the brief of the Committee is to make the theatre as comprehensible as possible for future ages. If Scheme B is accepted, at some point someone will say it is too particular a solution and this will throw the weight onto the conventional theatre. In the last four years we have tended to retrace our steps anyway.

ELLIOTT: I would like a theatre subtending at 90° and having full scenic possibilities.

HALL: You've just described the Barbican. If Scheme B were a 400 seater with a stage 20' x 20' it would work.

TYNAN: Would it help if the two theatres were of an equal size - 900 each?

BROOK: For me, the situation has changed enormously since we first met. In the early days, the National Theatre had no particular identity. I was pressing then for a stage that would force an overall approach to production. What bothers me is that the National Theatre has now acquired collectively an approach to the plays you want to do, and therefore at this moment the root question should be looked at again. Does a Chichester theatre solve enough of your wishes and problems?

OLIVIER: All our work finds a benefit in being responsive to a discipline of some kind. The Old Vic stage is awful but you get clever about it. The same thing applies to Chichester. Look what a surprise it was to find TRELAWNY OF THE "WELLS" working so well on it.

DEXTER: The open-stage offers a different experience.

BROOK: Are you basically with Chichester or against it?

OLIVIER: Chichester is too big. If the cant of the seating had been raised up it would have been ten times more dynamic. The sound will never be any good, the theatre is too squashed down. Once the curtain is up, an audience is watching a show. They don't know if it's still a room or not.

TYNAN: If the audience is conscious of the Balcony in Scheme B, they will hate it. If they can't see it, why have it?

BROOK: What sort of stage do you want for your repertory?

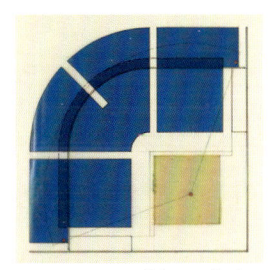

Scheme B plan

> "We want to do something that will stir Lasdun creatively. We must make what we all think and feel clear to him. We may be able to make him think dramatically."
>
> Peter Brook

> "No geometric solution can take precedence over dramatic necessity. The point of a theatre is not how geometric the building is. Attack Lasdun – we've been the victims of a sort of confidence trick."
>
> Peter Brook

GASKILL: It is difficult to start from the unknown. Why not start from what you know and what you have learned? I like working at Chichester and at the Vic. I don't like the Royal Court stage so much. It's all related to one's experience.

BROOK: Do you want an improved Chichester or an improved Old Vic?

DEXTER: An improved Chichester.

TYNAN: We need a theatre of both illusion and non-illusion. All sorts of plays are being written for both.

OLIVIER: We've discovered so many surprises about staging. In our youth we were dogged by the learned critics who had definite ideas on how we should do Shakespeare. Experience has led us to question this.

HALL: What seems to emerge is that the right organic growth for the National Theatre lies through an improved Chichester.

DEXTER: What happens if we say it's off (Scheme B)?

ELLIOTT: It's better to design a new building than spend £7-5 million on a white elephant.

MARSHALL: What about the idea of looking at both theatres as of equal size auditoriums?

BROOK: That won't solve it. It would only be viable if you bring Scheme B down to 400 capacity. Beyond that figure, it won't work. The point of command is too far away. A changed Scheme B based on Michael Elliott's solution will have a focal point: a quarter circle, with an open back.

OLIVIER: What do we do?

BROOK: Attack the core of the problem and put it back on Lasdun's plate. I thought he would produce lots of schemes. He must be presented with the situation as a horrendous crisis. He may be landing us with a white elephant. He must go into two months of crisis and use that pressure to face the problem. Something must come out of it.

TYNAN: If Lasdun hesitates and doesn't produce something new, his reputation is at stake. If we are united, we can conquer him.

HALL: Shall we try to make up some sort of resolution? That we find after mature consideration that Scheme B is not workable. The theatre has no point of command. We say to Lasdun "You have come up with a marvellous scheme, but it doesn't work". No person must be more than 70' from the point of command and everybody's eye must go through the point of command. The capacity is determined by the point of command.

OLIVIER: Also we don't want to be limited by the point of a room.

ELLIOTT: We say that the concept of a room has been interpreted too literally. Everything that happens behind and above the actors should be dictated only by scenic possibility.

BROOK: No geometric solution can take precedence over dramatic necessity. The point of a theatre is not how geometric the building is. Attack Lasdun – we've been the victims of a sort of confidence trick.

HALL: We were promised developments of Scheme B.

ELLIOTT: We want to pick up where we left off and consider Scheme B.

HALL: If the proscenium theatre is going to be the general purpose theatre, I feel the other auditorium should be informed by the aesthetic of you of the National Theatre.

BROOK: Going back for a minute to how we deal with Lasdun. All of us went on in our own way trying to explain what we felt about the mystique of the theatre. If all of us agree that we feel that the living actor-audience relationship is not caught in Scheme B, we must say to him "you haven't produced the feel of a living performance." The yardstick was not whether we should have a proscenium or a non-proscenium theatre but whether it was possible for an actor to get onstage and make Richard III a living and vital exchange for all. If we can prove that the actor is too far away on Scheme B, we can say Lasdun hasn't implemented his brief.

There followed more discussion on the best way of dealing with the architect, and it was finally decided that a set of resolutions or conclusions should be drafted; that Lord Chandos's advice should be sought and his help enlisted; that Lasdun should then be invited to meet the whole Building Committee.

Discussion then followed on the best way of working with the architect in the future.

HALL: I think the best thing is to have a small group working closely with Lasdun.

BROOK: I agree. We all much appreciated the fact that Sir Laurence invited us onto the National Theatre Building Committee, but it is up to us now to give you of the National Theatre your freedom back again. We wouldn't mind if we were left out of the discussions for a while and were then invited back to comment as things developed.

ELLIOTT: The Building Committee should, perhaps, continue to work as a full committee on a monthly basis but a smaller sub-committee should probably have weekly meetings with Lasdun.

HALL: We will do all we can to help. It is up to you of the National Theatre if you want us to come in on the sub-committee or not. I, personally, couldn't be of any help in initiating a new concept but I am prepared to help someone else's concept along.

It was agreed that Richard Pilbrow should be invited on to the Building Committee, but that no other invitations should be extended at this stage.

> **"If all of us agree that we feel that the living actor-audience relationship is not caught in Scheme B, we must say to him 'you haven't produced the feel of a living performance.'"**
>
> Peter Brook

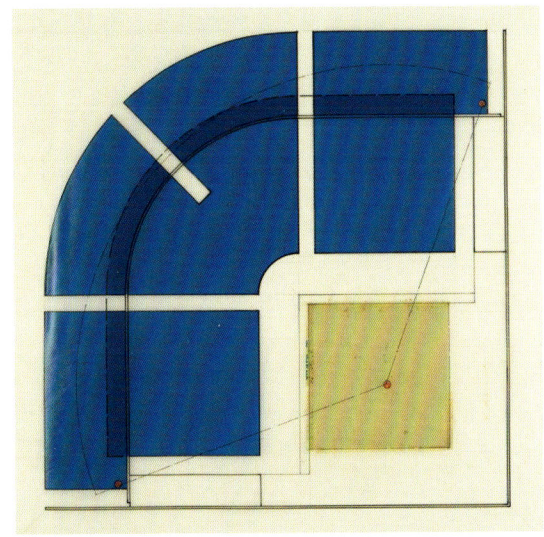

Scheme B plan

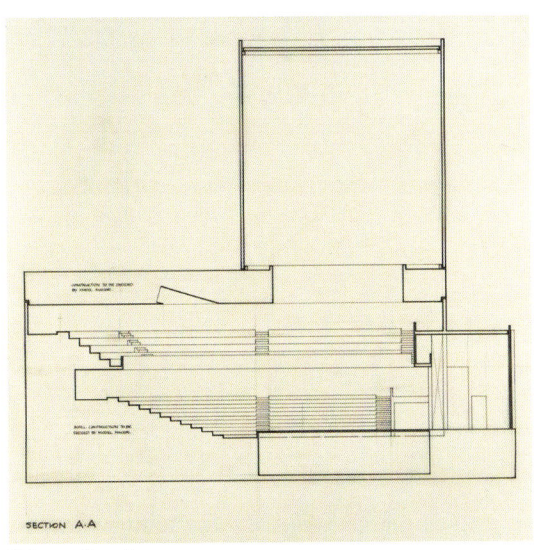

Scheme B section

2.3 Blood Dripping From Concrete Walls: Meetings #24-30

The Conclusions

1st April 1966
The Conclusions extract: Item #3.
"The Committee also agrees, that the concept of a one-room-auditorium stage is, in Scheme B as at present developed, interpreted too literally. There must be an atmosphere of one room, but the pattern of all stage facilities both behind and above the actor must be dictated only by scenic possibilities. The Committee is also aware that the above qualifications with regard to the present Scheme B may affect the pure geometry of the scheme as it stands at the moment. It would submit, however, that the most exciting theatre generally results, architecturally speaking, from an impure geometry of design."

26th April 1966
Sir Laurence met with Denys Lasdun, who recorded:
"This meeting [with Olivier] appeared to be a gentle icebreaking preparation for the fact the Scheme B now appears to have been unanimously rejected by the Building Committee, who are speaking with one voice." [75]

4th May 1966
Ken Tynan to Sir Laurence: "Scheme B gives the illusion of one room." He has a problem with the corner. "If it can be seen, the audience will tire of it, if it is never to be seen, why have it. It will always be covered in drapes." [76]

5th May 1966
A meeting between Lasdun and Gaskill, Olivier, Marshall, Benthall, and Tynan was less pleasant.[77] Lasdun felt himself attacked. He reported: "Tynan considered DL&P entrenched in their views on Scheme B." He withdrew this when he, Lasdun, said he would reconsider both the point of command and the upstage corner. Lasdun's note confirmed his distress, adding, "DL thinks that the matter must be brought to a close now fairly soon since the whole reputation of the office is now in jeopardy. We should be blamed for producing plans that don't work and wasting government money."

TECHNICAL SUB-COMMITTEE WEDNESDAY 6 APRIL 1966 (extracts)

Present:
Mr. George Rowbottom (Chair), Mr. John Dexter, Mr. Coeks Gordon, Mr. Richard Pilbrow, Mr. Neville Thompson. Also present Mr. Peter Softley, Mr. Malcolm Minjoodt.

<u>Workshops and Paint Frame.</u>
An extensive discussion in favor of the scenery shops being on one rather than three levels.

<u>Rehearsal Rooms.</u>
Agreed one rehearsal room for each theatre with direct access and height for full scenery. Other rehearsal spaces of limited height for properties only.

<u>Dressing Rooms and Wardrobe.</u>
PS said dressing rooms were presently without daylight. The committee felt that Equity would strongly object to this.

TECHNICAL SUB-COMMITTEE THURSDAY 21 APRIL 1966 (extracts)
Present: Mr. George Rowbottom (Chair), Mr. John Dexter, Mr. Coeks Gordon, Mr. Richard Pilbrow, Mr. Neville Thompson.

Paint frame size, cloth lift and scenery lift dimensions, dressing rooms with windows, office accommodation, discussed. Setting out area in workshops of 50' square required. Pilbrow and Rowbottom to meet Softley on 29 April.

Meeting 25

25th Meeting of The National Theatre Building Committee

10a Aquinas Street, London, SE1
Wednesday 11th May 1966, 5:00 pm

Present:
Sir Laurence Olivier, Mr. N. Marshall (Chairmen), Mr. J. Dexter, Miss Jocelyn Herbert, Mr. R. Pilbrow, Mr. P. Brook and Mr. M. Benthall. Mr. G. Rowbottom and Mr. K. Rae were in attendance. Mr. D. Lasdun, Mr. P. Softley and Mr. Malcolm Minjoodt were present by invitation.

Apologies:
Apologies for absence were received from Mr. Michael Elliott, Mr. William Gaskill and Mr. Peter Hall.

Before the Architects joined the meeting Sir Laurence summarised the position to date for Miss Herbert and Mr. Brook. He explained that he had personally visited Mr. Lasdun and had left with him a copy of The Conclusions reached by the Committee at its meeting on 1st April. A few members of the Committee who had been available, Mr. W. Gaskill, Sir Laurence, Mr. Norman Marshall, Mr. Michael Benthall and Mr. Kenneth Tynan, had an informal meeting with Mr. Lasdun on May 5th and he and Mr. Marshall had had a further talk with Mr. Lasdun on the 7th.

LASDUN: The situation in May 1965 was that there should be a proscenium theatre seating 750 with all that a proscenium theatre implies. We were also to provide as a main auditorium what was classified as an "open stage" seating about 1,100 people. We saw the second one as complementary to the first. This decision was not unanimously approved in the early days because it was not agreed that we should have two auditoriums. You chose an architect who knew nothing about the theatre, presumably to work out what an open stage is supposed to be.

In May 1965, both collectively and individually, there was a feeling that we were along the right lines with Scheme B and upon that assumption all the designs and developments of the subsequent eighteen months were based. Now one year later, I think there has been a change in feeling and we must nail down what the changes are, if we can. They devolve around three basic issues: 1) The point of command in an open stage theatre, 2) Its capacity, 3) The desire to have a background. This is not the same thinking that went into Scheme B and one of the main difficulties between us is language. Scheme B was hard-edged, anti-illusion and with a failure at the point of command. The first thing we did when we got your recent Conclusions was to see if we could define the point of command.

The cold facts are in a document which is not on this table but is inherent. On May 5th there was a paper which we did not take away defining the point of command and I obtained the consent by telephone this morning, this paper, it would seem to us, would reduce the capacity to about 950 people.

OLIVIER: The paper has not been shown to the Committee as a whole.

LASDUN: The initiative was ours. We asked you to define the point of command.

OLIVIER: We didn't give it to you because we didn't feel it was good enough and it represented the views of only three or four of us.

LASDUN: It is important because I feel one of the things the Committee is unhappy about is the point of command; it's fundamental. We, the architects, were already on a not dissimilar tack. We were already at work on a relaxation of Scheme B. I sensed that there was a feeling that we were entrenched and inflexible and unwilling to listen to criticism.

I want to show you a model, showing you how our minds were working. There are two differences between what you are going to see in the model and your thinking in the Conclusions. The first is that we have not accepted that those seated in the front seats of the auditorium should have their knees on the stage. You said you were unhappy about the proximity of the front seats at the Old Vic. Is that fair?

2.3 Blood Dripping From Concrete Walls: Meetings #24–30

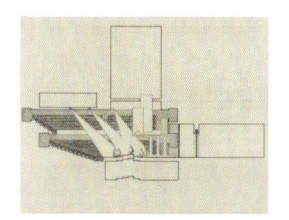

Scheme C section

> "You chose an architect who knew nothing about the theatre, presumably to work out what an open stage is supposed to be."
>
> Denys Lasdun

OLIVIER: This proximity may well be responsible for some of the complaints of inaudibility. An inhibition may subconsciously take place in the actor because of his nearness to the front seats. The complaints are mostly from the Gallery which is extraordinary and it may be that the intense proximity of the actors to the front row subconsciously reduces their pitch.

LASDUN: The second point of difference is this. In your specification of the point of command all seats focus on the point of command and every seat on its axis is facing that point, in the model you will see we reject this. We focus the seats roughly 9' beyond the point of command, otherwise the actor cannot approach gracefully to the point of command. I would also like to say that we have brainwashed ourselves out of Scheme B. It is now for you to, question, for you to tell us whether this new model is moving towards what you want.

This is not a final design – only a guess of what might happen,

BENTHALL: Do you visualise a curtain?

LASDUN: No. There will come a moment if we are not careful when we will tell you that you will be better off with a proscenium. When you ask if you can have a curtain you are already signaling what you see in that model.

BROOK: What is the difference between this and Scheme A?

LASDUN: Very little. We didn't give you full flying facilities in Scheme A.

OLIVIER: This has less feeling of classification of the audience. Why doesn't the line of the front stalls seating follow the line of the stage?

LASDUN: Because we haven't yet discussed scenery.

ROWBOTTOM: Why not put the fly tower further back?

LASDUN: Another 5' back and we will be having two rooms. You'll be back to the proscenium and the theatre of illusion. Why do you want to extend the area of the tower?

ROWBOTTOM: You are thinking in terms of performance, I am thinking in terms of making two other productions ready for performance.

BROOK: The possibility of hanging more things is absolutely vital to the repertory system.

OLIVIER: What about the flying system that they have on the continent which has changeable grids?

BENTHALL: You can't have changeable grids in an open stage theatre

PILBROW: It could be that a bigger space than that allowed in the model is desirable.

LASDUN: The issue is it shouldn't be.

OLIVIER: If this theatre seats 1,010 can we increase the capacity of the proscenium theatre by some 90 seats?

LASDUN: For every seat to be within 70' of the stage, the capacity of the proscenium theatre will be in the order of 750. We wouldn't be able to increase capacity even if we had no problem with regard to the site. Are you right to hold to the idea that another row of seats in a theatre like that indicated in the new model would be disastrous?

OLIVIER: You mean the furthest seat would be some 74' away?

LASDUN: If these empirical figures were true, you wouldn't need an architect, only a computer. Figures are only a rough guide. The simple phenomenon is that you can get more people into an open stage theatre. That is the one where you can best increase capacity.

OLIVIER: I think we feel that audience interest is lost when the expression on the face of the actor is lost.

LASDUN: There is the point about the angle of vision also. We know what the range is, but don't entrench yourself in mathematics. For a moment, a member of the audience may have to move his head a little. I repeat you can increase capacity more easily in this model than in a proscenium theatre.

MARSHALL: A painter will say that he can't see the faces on stage properly beyond the 7th row of the stalls. The Association of British Theatre Technicians have never been able to reach a consensus of opinion on this point. It is the design of the theatre that really counts.

LASDUN: It is the room, not statistics. To come back to capacity, we could increase that of the proscenium theatre by 10 or 15 seats, no more.

OLIVIER: Not 50?

LASDUN: No. You have to take into consideration fire regulations, gangways etc.,

We were most unhappy about the last paragraph of your Conclusions, and its reference to geometry.

BENTHALL: This was born out of your square.

BROOK: The situation is more serious and more potentially tragic than that. Let us remember that this Committee has been unanimous on one issue only. A deep feeling that a theatre can't be built on specifications. We now come to the point where you are saying this to us. There is a danger that because of the inevitable delays that have occurred and the current time pressure, that we might come to a wrong agreement simply because one can agree on specification. You spoke of the difficulties of language between us and this is shown up tragically in that my entire feeling and experience of theatre backs the paragraph in the Conclusions to which you take exception. If you feel that it is nonsense it underlines our difficulties. Let me quote a metaphor that we used when we all discussed what we felt about Scheme B after one and a half years. It may give you a glimmer about what we felt and now feel about Scheme B. An actor can say at the end of a first week of rehearsals "how is my performance?" and the producer replies "marvellous." Three weeks later the producer is saying that "it is no good." We are all used to that in the theatre. We felt Scheme A was a conventional theatre. Scheme B we felt was not the result of a computer; it was creative. Real people were being moved about in relation to one another. The plan evoked enthusiasm and opposition.

We felt the next stage should be that of putting something up in a rough form – for your sake as well as ours. It should be like a playwright seeing a play in rehearsal. A process was beginning to blossom, and we hoped Scheme B would lead to many schemes. For historical reasons this process was interrupted but nothing ever stands still; everyone's experience develops, and then we all came together in April and saw a Scheme that hadn't moved. We attacked it by being specific and tried to talk in terms of 70' and angles. Scheme B was only an embryo and now we find ourselves back in an unhappy discussion of a form of Scheme A, where everyone's requirements are fulfilled, and a fairly conventional, safe committee-style theatre is suggested.

LASDUN: Your speech is a repetition of your reaction to Scheme A.

BROOK: This new model is a repetition of Scheme A.

LASDUN: Your reaction to Scheme B was based on its potential. What is tragic is that you haven't tried to make Scheme B work. We produced diagrams and put in hand the building of a 1/2" scale model. Don't blame us, we are deeply hurt at the Conclusions.

RAE: The diagrams and the model were withdrawn at your request.

LASDUN: Yes. But what it adds up to is that you should be working on the model. This is an intellectual issue not a procedural one. We could start on that embryo (Scheme B) but that would not be in conformity with the Conclusions.

BROOK: We are agreed that when we all last met we were at the beginning of a concept that caused both enthusiasm and concern. We

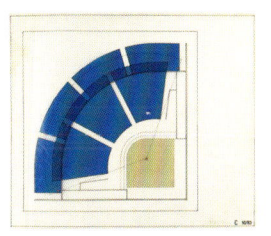

Scheme C plan

> "Your speech is a repetition of your reaction to Scheme A."
> Denys Lasdun

> "This new model is a repetition of Scheme A."
> Peter Brook

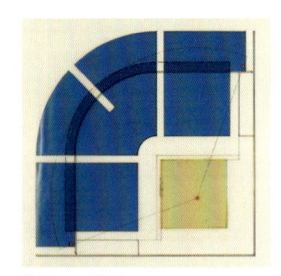

Scheme B plan

> "The embryo Scheme B was an anti-illusion room with more scenic possibilities than any other open stage theatre in the world, and with it went the inhibiting factors of that statement."
>
> Denys Lasdun

all said this is not the last word. We left Scheme B a year and a half ago at a certain point. Either we pretend nothing has happened and go ahead with the model etc, or we try to be more constructive. We put our worries to you. No-one has said we should come to you with a new brief, destroying all that had gone before and produce a computerised result. What we are saying is that the Conclusions defined the areas where people were worried about Scheme B.

LASDUN: Let me bring it to earth. In the Conclusions there appears the phrase "an atmosphere of one room". I was very clear on the 5th when we met, about the objections to Scheme B as it stood. There was tremendous uneasiness on the point of the stage and the background.

The embryo Scheme B was an anti-illusion room with more scenic possibilities than any other open-stage theatre in the world, and with it went the inhibiting factors of that statement. May 5th showed anxieties about the point of command, the background, and the ambivalence of going full-blooded into a room as against harping back to the proscenium.

BROOK: This is where you are resisting us. You are implying that any feeling of incomplete involvement with Scheme B will stop a development towards a Scheme C. You have gone backwards in offering us a more conventional article. We were caught by the imaginativeness of Scheme B but everyone had reservations about it in performance though we liked the approach and the vision.

LASDUN: Without giving any names I would like to quote a statement that was made on May 5th. It was to the effect that maybe the truth of the National Theatre was that it was conventional and its role that of a museum.

OLIVIER: Ignore that statement. It was an individual expression of opinion.

LASDUN: There is a feeling that the most tragic situation would be not to get the theatre right if one could get it right. For me there is no such thing as an ideal theatre. Time does play a very important factor in all this and with this size committee I fear we won't get agreement, close in on the model and work on it.

MARSHALL: It would take us months to do this.

BROOK: I repeat what I have said before. In eighteen months, the National Theatre Company has developed and it now has a clear knowledge of what it needs for its own work. I propose that we have a small committee working in close co-operation with the Architect and it could, of course, come back to us all periodically. The Committee should work forward empirically with models and mock-ups.

BENTHALL: If that is a motion, I second it.

MARSHALL: It should be a case of a management building a theatre.

OLIVIER: I don't agree at all.

BENTHALL: There is no other solution.

BROOK: The committee can come back to us as often as it likes but must find a practical way of working.

OLIVIER: It would be O.K. if the entire committee could meet every fourteen days, but I fear that there are philosophical differences at stake. When we first called you together as a committee it was to avoid the possibility of building a theatre without inviting all the current experts. As things are going, it is possible that there is a great philosophical difference that should be threshed out. Your solution is to vote three people on to a Committee.

MARSHALL: No, Let us have a small body of people working intimately together. Already something has emerged in the days since May 5th.

BROOK: I want to make it clear that I don't want to resign from the Committee to give myself the freedom to denounce the theatre when it is built. The National Theatre now exists as a major company and I am prepared to support wholeheartedly any decision taken by the National Theatre people. I am prepared to help and to suggest. I don't see any other working method.

OLIVIER: For some time now we have been bewailing the fact that we have had no designer working with us on the Committee. Now we have Jocelyn Herbert, but you Peter Brook, are also a designer. You hated Scheme A as class-conscious and dull. I always felt something circular would be better and out of that came Scheme B - a vivid statement of fact. The fact that none of us have been able to visualise, more than two or three productions on it has now brought us to a compromise but perhaps you have a better philosophical idea than an amphitheatre? As a statement Scheme B worked.

BENTHALL: In its initial concept Scheme B excited us. Now that we have got a proscenium theatre as well, can we not afford to have the other auditorium as a committed, uncompromising space?

OLIVIER: I don't see why we should be condemned to one form of rigidity just because we've got another (the proscenium). If you have a theatre that is committed to follow the laws of anti-illusion you may have one that is more rigid and soon becomes more old fashioned than a proscenium.

HERBERT: What was exciting about Scheme B was its powerful, stimulating conception. Is it not possible to discuss with models how to develop Scheme B rather than develop a compromise?

LASDUN: We are at one on this. This (new model) was a gesture to show you we are not taking up an entrenched position, but we can never be philosophically behind the new model. It is an extraordinary phenomenon to me and there must be a blockage of communication here, that what you see as rigidity in a non-illusory way, I see as extreme flexibility. Can anyone else see this?

DEXTER: Yes, I can. I do think the time has come to boil the Committee down and work practically on Scheme B. I have objections to it regarding the side walls, the corner etc. How immoveable is the point of Scheme B? The point area is dead. How do you get an actor there?

LASDUN: We deny this. Supposing there was a vomitory there (facing the point)

DEXTER: It still wouldn't help.

LASDUN: We can work with you, we can do it on a half-inch model. You may be right about the point? We don't know.

BROOK: The Committee as a whole has never rejected Scheme B. We were suddenly frozen in our tracks. The provisos at our last meeting together were that we shouldn't be rushed, and that work should go forward from the stage it had previously reached.

LASDUN: I think it is true to say that two points have emerged. Olivier has a love/hate relationship for the point of the stage; other people have a hate relationship with the other corner.

DEXTER: We need the model to work on for four weeks to block out a production. My personal plan is to try to put on Scheme B a production I already have in my mind, and am going to do in the next year.

LASDUN: In our other work we sometimes work with scientists, sometimes with people in the humanities. The scientists, and it perhaps portrays our dilemma, come roughly under two philosophical headings. The Baconians, who observe and measure facts and draw conclusions, and those who follow Poppa. These last take an imaginative hunch and verify later. We are in the second category and that is what Scheme B is about. If we assemble a few people - an actor, a director, a designer, audience - we could verify Scheme B and modify it a bit if that is what you want to do.

BROOK: I feel that any possible approach must go from the stage of the hunch to verifying the practicalities, but we also need some supplementary hunches. Scheme B hunch is 90% satisfactory. When you see it in relation to our hunches, there will be a development.

LASDUN: No architect, not even working with you, will invent a new theatre.

BROOK: Scheme B is an invention.

> "I don't see why we should be condemned to one form of rigidity just because we've got another (the proscenium)."
>
> — Laurence Olivier

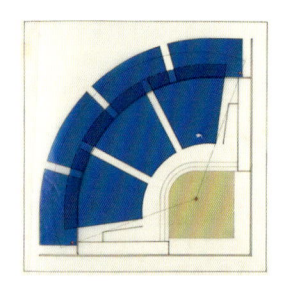

Scheme C plan

> "Scheme B says to me something the new model can never say. It is sharp, non-compromising, anti-illusion theatre. Blood dripping from concrete walls."
>
> Denys Lasdun

LASDUN: It isn't.

BROOK: When you have seen the result of your hunch in relation to the work John Dexter is proposing, your resolution of the stumbling blocks will take place without going back on the leap forward of Scheme B. Let us go back to the idea of a smaller Committee.

BENTHALL: We must not lose courage as the new model might suggest.

MINJOODT: As designers, we can visualise certain things, but not the point of command from the viewpoint of the actor. Does the director tell the actor where to go?

BROOK: The question doesn't arise. It is a process of evolution and collaboration.

OLIVIER: Everybody who is anybody working on a play thinks of the whole.

LASDUN: Will you work on the model and we will then tell you whether the alterations you want are possible within architectural terms? Scheme B says to me something the new model can never say. It is sharp, non-compromising, anti-illusion theatre. Blood dripping from concrete walls.

HERBERT: All theatre, even the most avant-garde, is based on illusion of some kind. When you say anti-illusory...

LASDUN: That is just shorthand.

OLIVIER: You always offer the audience some belief.

HERBERT: Scheme B puts much more onus on the actor.

OLIVIER: If you are having a theatre that is not a proscenium type, you have to agree to having an audience round you to some extent. The new model is a basis for observation. The spectator basis is reasonable. As a designer what sort of stage would you, Brook, put into a room like that?

BROOK: I can only say that this (new model) makes a logical and unchanging relationship and a boring one.

MINJOODT: Either you fit the stage to the audience by computer or you put your audience into a space.

BROOK: Do we take Scheme B and the new model as the only two possibilities, or do we reject both, and say we want to look for a third?

LASDUN: How do you search for a third?

BENTHALL: In Scheme B you are sitting in a room and communication is total; the new model is more conventional; you have a bit of mystery etc.

BROOK: Are we trying to choose between developing Scheme B or the new one, or are we trying to choose a completely different solution?

OLIVIER: What would you do?

BROOK: I keep trying to put the onus back on the National Theatre. I am convinced that Scheme B is embryonically a very exciting theatre, but I am not convinced that it is in keeping with what you are trying to stage.

OLIVIER: We have two theatres.

BENTHALL: What it boils down to is that ten people can't make a Committee of this kind work.

BROOK: Out of Scheme B could come a most exciting theatre that might not accommodate the plays you want to do. Out of the new model would come the conventional. The third possibility is that the National Theatre people now lock themselves up with models and the architects and search for another solution.

OLIVIER: The object in choosing this Committee was not that anyone should be on the fringe. Suppose I ask you (Brook) and Jocelyn and John to be in on this, does your association with another theatre prevent it?

BROOK: Yes, it does make it difficult.

LASDUN: It was very distressing for us to be told that the Royal Shakespeare had solved its own particular problem and would build in eighteen months. Would it be possible for us to see your plans?

BROOK: You can.

LASDUN: It will be most interesting and the interchange of ideas should be helpful.

BROOK: We of the Royal Shakespeare have never withheld anything; no-one has ever asked to see the plans before.

OLIVIER: I can explain why we feel we are not getting the whole benefit of Brook's brains. It is because the bit that we are getting exists somewhat in the abstract. It is divorced from the practicalities. How you would do it is what we want from you.

BROOK: What would prevent me from sitting on a smaller sub-committee is this. The National Theatre knows what it wants to do and how to do it. Similarly, we at the Royal Shakespeare know what plays we are going to do in the next five years, the way we want to do them and the actors who are going to be in them. The work of the National Theatre is not dissimilar to that of the Royal Shakespeare.

OLIVIER: You don't know what you'll be doing in fifty years time. The National Theatre and Royal Shakespeare repertories are really very close to each other.

BROOK: Look at the summer season at the Aldwych!

OLIVIER: We will both be doing the same work in fifty years. The fact is that what you are building is a theatre that will be O.K. for the *Marat/Sade* and Shakespeare's *Henry IV*.

BROOK: We are building a theatre not for posterity but for what Hall and I want to do.

OLIVIER: Pretend you (Brook) are now the Director of the National Theatre. What would you do?

LASDUN: Hall said there was a fatal defect in Scheme B. Since the Royal Shakespeare is building in eighteen months time please could it show us that defect?

OLIVIER: I'll show it to you. On Scheme B every line and every laugh has to be got over twice.

BENTHALL: You can't have a point of command in a theatre with the audience on three sides.

LASDUN: That is the problem, and I hate that last sentence in the Conclusions because it says that the architects have imposed their geometry on the art of the theatre.

DEXTER: I'm stuck on the long exits and entrances where Scheme B is concerned. I can't see any dramatic way to make someone's entrance.

OLIVIER: We are all meeting again on the 20th at 6 p.m, except for Michael Benthall.

LASDUN: We must face the fact that we are at a standstill, and this has serious implications in terms of building the National Theatre. We can't begin the work on the operation side until we have taken a major decision.

BENTHALL: If we saw a model of the proscenium theatre on the table as well, would it be a help?

OLIVIER: I don't believe the proscenium theatre is relevant. I don't believe one should be committed to having a certain type of play in one theatre and another in the other.

BROOK: Maybe you need two theatres.

OLIVIER: There are certain plays for which you can say "this must have a box set"; for them you are building your proscenium.

DEXTER: With the new model you are too near the proscenium theatre.

OLIVIER: I would rather say, and it's a dangerous statement, that one should be a theatre for comedy and one for non comedy.

DEXTER: No. *Black Comedy* worked at Chichester.

LASDUN: Whatever you achieved at Chichester, you can achieve better on Scheme B. We are further forward in what we call "command!"

BROOK: What we think may be good about the theatre in The Barbican is that the stage has been designed by the Architect and the resident Scene Designer working together

> **"We must face the fact that we are at a standstill, and this has serious implications in terms of building the National Theatre."**
>
> Denys Lasdun

from the start. When I do a production I nearly always start by pulling the model of the set about and in this way problems start to get analysed. I would approach this by pulling the model about. Gradually by touch, sense and feeling something that seems to be right in equilibrium might evolve. What we have in The Barbican is a mixture defying definition, but it seems to us to be a good set of living relationships. The difference between the model of The Barbican and this one here is that the one at The Barbican has evolved like a scene design, whereas in the case of this one we have up to now worked only through an exchange of theoretical ideas. Does this give you (Lasdun) any idea of what we mean by purity as against impurity?

LASDUN: Does this manipulation involve the audience?

BROOK: It would be possible to move the seats around, change angles. Why couldn't something evolve from Scheme B that would be quite as exciting and original as the initial impetus? It is agreed that we don't take the Conclusions as literal but as spirits of unease. Suppose we agreed to take them as points from which we can develop the practicalities.

LASDUN: I don't believe it, but am willing to try it.

DEXTER: When you talk of working with us do you mean that you are prepared to sit through a whole production?

LASDUN: Yes, if it will help.

OLIVIER: Let us give ourselves, the money at stake, and posterity, nine more days (meeting on 20th).

LASDUN: Is there anything you would like us to do meanwhile?

OLIVIER: Please think again.

HERBERT: Could Scheme B be made in sections so that we can move it all around and do what Peter Brook says?

Lasdun and Herbert

18th May 1966. Lasdun: Notes on Meeting with Jocelyn Herbert at Queen Anne Street [78]
"Her objection to Scheme B concerned three aspects.
a. Distance of point of command from furthest seats.
b. Limitations imposed by ring behind stage.
c. Difficulty of using the triangle at the point of the stage.

The architects maintained that arbitrary rules based on experience in other types of theatre did not necessarily apply in Scheme B.

The point of command was certainly in the centre of the stage at a distance of 85' from farthest seat, but taking into account the shape and rake of auditorium, the architects felt command was possible.

The ring behind the stage must impose some limitations, but the architects felt they were outweighed by advantages. Acting area purposely kept well forward so that the ring could be subdued by lighting or hanging scenic objects in front.

Flattening the arc of seating would push the acting area nearer the ring. Architects did not expect the point of the stage to be used much. The steep rake made it possible to act in the centre of the stage.

The architects recognised that these points could only be tested by working on the model. We would expect to tackle each of these problems in turn and action taken on one or other might compel further reconsideration."

We must note the references above to 'the architects.' These notes were prepared by DL&P. To me, fifty years later, they sadly reveal that after eighteen months labouring on the National project, Denys and his team were still far from a real understanding of the essential dynamics of theatre design. Ignorance of tradition coupled with – it has to be said – a certain arrogance about an architect's sense of possessing a uniquely insightful perspective.

Jocelyn Herbert

Meeting 26

26th Meeting of The National Theatre Building Committee

10a Aquinas Street, London, SE1
Wednesday 20th May 1966, 6:00 pm

Present:
Sir Laurence Olivier, Mr. Michael Elliott, Mr. J. Dexter, Miss Jocelyn Herbert, Mr. William Gaskill, Mr. Peter Hall, Mr. R. Pilbrow, Mr. G. Rowbottom and Mr. K. Rae were in attendance. Mr. D. Lasdun, Mr. P. Softley and Mr. Malcolm Minjoodt were present by invitation.
Apologies:
Apologies for absence were received from Mr. Norman Marshall, Mr. Michael Benthall and Mr. Michel Saint-Denis.

The Chairman proposed that the following members should be invited to serve as a sub-committee to work in close cooperation with the Architect.

Miss Jocelyn Herbert
Mr. Peter Hall
Mr. John Dexter
Mr George Rowbottom

Sir Laurence Olivier (Chairman)

The sub-committee should meet at frequent intervals, and would report progress to and invite comment from full meetings of the Building Committee once a month. The Committee approved, and those invited agreed to serve.

It was agreed that work on the development of the non-proscenium theatre auditorium should take account of the requirement for scenic facilities, it being understood that these would be of a dimensional rather than a perspective nature. Particular attention must be given to the resolution of the problem of the actor's command over his audience on an open stage, and to the size and shape of the stage itself.

It was agreed that the theatrical potential of Scheme B should be put to a practical test by producers undertaking to block-out various productions on it as follows:

Laurence Olivier – *King Lear, Three Sisters*

Michael Elliott – *The Master Builder*

William Gaskill – *The Recruiting Officer*

John Dexter – *Dandy Dick, A Bond Honoured, Chips With Everything*

Peter Hall – *The Homecoming, Macbeth.*

Work would proceed as soon as the 1/2" model was completed, which would be by May 31st. After the five producers had viewed the model, ground plans indicating the "area of concentration" or "focal zone", would be given to the producers to work on.

The first meeting of the sub-committee would be on Wednesday 8th June at 6.00 p.m.

The dimensions of the stage of the present Scheme B were given as a 45' square with a diagonal of approximately 64'.

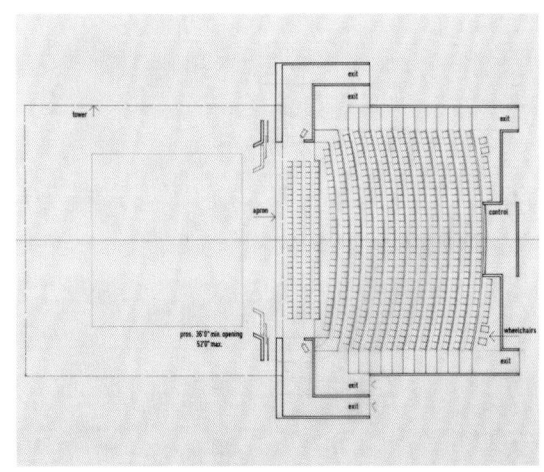

Proscenium theatre preliminary stalls plan

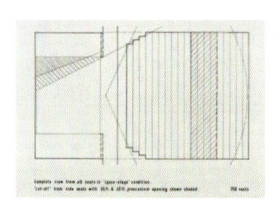

Examination of proscenium seating sightline options in plan

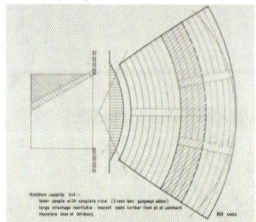

Examination of proscenium seating sightline options in plan

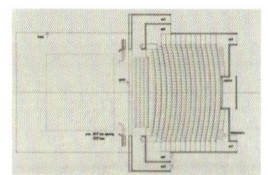

Proscenium theatre preliminary stalls plan

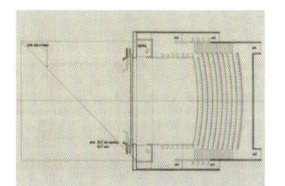

Proscenium theatre preliminary circle plan

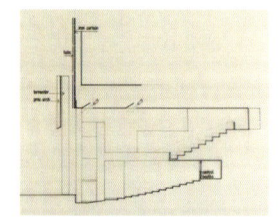

Proscenium theatre preliminary section

Meanwhile – The Proscenium Theatre
3rd June 1966. Sub-committee Meeting.
Peter Softley presented the first version of the proscenium theatre. He said, 'it had evolved without consultation with the building committee.'[79]

Lasdun had formed the opinion that a proscenium theatre was simply one in which an audience faced a stage. The design was driven by his conviction that a proscenium theatre was a "theatre of confrontation" – the opposite to the open stage with its principle of the audience surrounding the stage. The simplicity of the design was initially greeted with enthusiasm.

Lasdun later said, "I remember George Devine saying, 'every play, every playwright, has his own special need – there is a space to fit every play.' There are discursive plays where it is important that we talk to each other, actor and audience, and confront each other. Now, the characteristic of confrontation is very straightforward – you need a rectangle and the audience frankly just facing. That is the essence of the Lyttelton Theatre." [80]

Softley's summary reads:
"*The architects had therefore to make their own assessment of the criteria on which the design should be based and these were as follows:*
1. *The proscenium theatre should provide the best possible conditions for those productions which could take place only within a proscenium and, having done this, should have maximum flexibility.*
2. *A large apron (forestage) was assumed to be unnecessary.*
3. *The standard width of the proscenium was assumed to be 40' and the height 24'.*
4. *By opening up to a maximum of 52' the proscenium would be virtually eliminated, and the stage could be used as a space stage.*
5. *As the picture frame with its simulated perspective is seen at its best from the centre of the auditorium, the object had been to get as many of the audience as possible into a central position.*
6. *All seats in the model are within 70' of the point of command.*
7. *The audience are seated on two tiers rather than one in order to give as many people as possible a central view.*
8. *The overhang of the upper tier had been kept as low as possible.*
9. *The seating was arranged in straight rows in order to bring the audience as close as possible.*[81]

Minor changes were suggested to Softley. The adjustability of the proscenium was initially curtailed, the seating was curved and the blankness of the side walls was slightly modified by bringing the balcony sides forward to create an effect like a box… albeit unpeopled by audience.

The concept was accepted. The South Bank Board later insisted upon an increase of seat count to 850.

Back to the Upper Theatre
Concern continued about the progress on the 'upper theatre.' Despite his not having attended recent building committee meetings, on 6th June Michel Saint-Denis wrote to Sir Laurence: "*It seems that the main theatre plan has not altered since the last time I saw it, ages ago now; this I find difficult to understand. It seems we have been kept away, as if, after our exchange of ideas, our absence was necessary for our considerations to have effect and take shape. To me there was a very good project to begin with and we had expressed our view with enough clarity for a few alternate schemes to have evolved from them. Are we being kept away as if to avoid our input?*" [82]

The Subcommittee
The ongoing crisis of confidence in Scheme B led to the creation of a subcommittee to work more closely with the architects.

Brook had said: "Out of Scheme B could come a most

exciting theatre that might not accommodate the plays you want to do. Out of the new model would come the conventional. The third possibility is that the National Theatre people now lock themselves up with models and the architects and search for another solution."

Essentially, this is what now occurred. The smaller group of Olivier, John Dexter, Jocelyn Herbert, Peter Hall, George Rowbottom (general manager), with myself in attendance, met on 31st May, 3rd, 8th, 15th June, 11th, 29th July, trying to finesse details of seating, vomitories and stage dimensions, as well as issues related to office, wardrobe and dressing room accommodations.

Sir Laurence was anxious for Peter Brook to be involved in the vitally important subcommittee. On 15th June he wrote:

"My dearest Peter, I implore you to forgive this being in type. I was hoping today to find the time to write to you in longhand… but things are boiling up to a high point of centigrade, and I can see I'm not going to manage this. Forgive this please. I am dreadfully distressed to hear that you have been offended by my not including you in the invitations to the Building Sub-Committee. Please will you allow me to explain myself. I may have taken too seriously something you said at one of our Committee meetings, and my impression of what your feelings were may have been wrong. In my anxiety over the rights and wrongs of this, I have gone back now to the roots of my impression and I find these in the Minutes of a meeting on 11th May: (Peter Hall was not at this meeting by the way). Do you mind if I quote to you?

"'OLIVIER: The object in choosing this Committee (the big one) was not that anyone should be on the fringe. Suppose I ask you (Brook) and Jocelyn and John to be in on this, does your association with another theatre prevent it? BROOK: Yes it does make it difficult."[83]

Meanwhile, during the subcommittee's deliberations, John Dexter had tried two productions and had developed his own conclusions. He found that the action was best pushed downstage and emphasised that sufficient lighting positions would be needed.[84]

John and Jocelyn continued to be in favour of the balcony or 'ring' surrounding the stage, although they suggested that it might be raised to allow the passage of scenery from backstage. George Rowbottom and I remained profoundly sceptical about such a structural element placed in what we saw as the middle of the stage.

22nd June 1966, Subcommittee Meeting re Scheme B. JH & JD. DL. FPS. MJM.

The meeting was an informal discussion between Jocelyn Herbert and John Dexter with the architects, examining the 1/2" model.
1. Looking at the stage with the centre section of seating removed.

JD felt main characteristic was the thrust and he wanted to bring the action forward toward the audience. Softley felt that the natural zone of command lay in the centre of the stage at the intersection of the centre line of the two blocks of side seats. To bring the action forward the side seats would need to recurved.

JD felt the desire to oppose the pitch of the audience with a raked stage. This would complicate scene changes, although part of the floor might be raised on lifts.

A corrugated paper background was added and the enclosure helped to define the stage.

JD was worried that the audience would be too conscious of the fly tower. Some 3D masking might be needed. DL suggested that visible lights might solve the problem, [he thought] the lights in Chichester effectively masked the roof above.

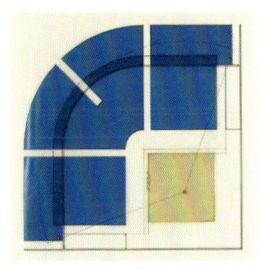

Scheme B plan

> "Forgive this please. I am dreadfully distressed to hear that you have been offended by my not including you in the invitations to the Building Sub-Committee."
>
> Laurence Olivier

2.3 Blood Dripping From Concrete Walls: Meetings #24-30

> "He would like the audience to be more powerfully concentrated on the stage."
>
> Denys Lasdun notes of Peter Brook comments

2. Looking at the seating with the stage removed.

Central quadrant of seating was unsatisfactory. DL suggested adding voms and moving the gangways. JD pointed out the position opposite gangways was useful to the director.

JD suggested that the point of command should be moved forward. DL felt it was near the end seats of the front row. JD and JH agreed this was all right for the single actor, but would not work for a conversation piece with a number of actors.

3. Looking at the stage with the centre seating removed.

JD & JH agreed that the definition of the stage edge was helpful in overcoming their preconceptions about the square. A circular raked stage seemed to work very well on top of the square stage.

JD made the point that many plays with only 1 or 2 actors would require the whole stage, but a crowded scene would require a smaller space… easier to make a smaller space look crowded.

JD said that if he wanted to create a room he would place it close to the audience. He felt LO would cling to the back wall.[85]

The Paymasters
It's fascinating that, even at this advanced stage, 'behind the scenes' in the bureaucracy of the South Bank Board, the Treasury and the Arts Council, tensions continued.

24th June 1966, Arts Council to Mr Lynex: "The Arts Council continues to feel disturbed by the relatively low seating capacity announced for the two auditoria of the National Theatre."[86] In August, the Department of Education and Science to Lord Cottesloe: "potentially exceeding the budget for the project and it is suggested that a single, large, proscenium theatre be the sole focus of the building project."[87] From the Arts Council, Lord Goodman seemed to be pressing Lord Chandos to drop the 'experimental' open stage over worries of expense. He even suggested the purchase of an existing large theatre, Theatre Royal, Drury Lane, rather than building a new one!

Pressure from all sides, from both the building committee and the paymasters, led Lord Cottesloe to write to the minister, Miss Lee, on 3rd July 1966. "It would be a real disaster if we lost the architect who is, by common consent, much the best man for this particular job."[88]

14th July 1966: Brook Meets with DL&P to Review the 1/2" Scale Model of Scheme B
"He thought the vomitories were very ugly and disruptive. He was not one of those who believed there was a fixed point of command… the point of command in a boxing ring is wherever the fighters happen to be (provided the fight is interesting enough). It was obvious that Scheme B would only take bold and simple scenery… those who wanted 'cosy' naturalistic settings were doomed to disappointment… so long as this was understood, it was potentially an exciting and interesting stage. He was concerned with the balance between the size of the stage and the auditorium. Softley explained that it was not intended that the whole of the visible stage should normally be used – the action could only be drawn well into the room by leaving space behind the action. PB was doubtful whether one could limit the use of the stage in any way. He did not think it was desirable to isolate the stage in space… this was something that had been tried by [Norman] Bel Geddes and others and was rather an old fashioned idea. He would like the audience to be more powerfully concentrated on the stage. He suggested that the fact that people were uneasy about Scheme B should indicate there was something wrong. When the thing was right everything would fall into place in an inevitable way."[89]

1st August 1966: Notes Brook to Olivier on Scheme B[90]

"As the new model is only a larger version of what we already know, it proves once again how important the 'mock-up' will be – so all new impressions are offered very tentatively.

The interest of this stage is that it offers us a square. This is only interesting if every bit of it is equally useful. It is like a boxing ring and the focus is wherever the fight takes place. As such, it is utterly opposed to the notion of a point of command. The point of command is always on the move. This reflects a very contemporary view of the world where points of command are continually defined and redefined. I'm all for a stage that offers this.

It dictates a rigorous style of production, acting and scenery. Conventional scenery can never be used. Yet many productions may call for the use of conventional scenery, in painted styles, etc. This need could truly give the proscenium theatre it own separate definition. With the present Scheme B, the two will never be interchangeable, so a major policy decision is involved.

We all share a sense of unease. What is this? In some way we are not comfortable with Scheme B. We sense that were we sitting in that auditorium we would not completely relax and feel at one with the stage. One man says the stage is too vast; another that it is too oppressive. This is naturally confusing to the architect, but only means that the audience-stage relation is not quite right. May I here sound a warning? All criticism recently has centred on the stage, its size, the shape of the tip, the placing of the main acting area. I suggest it would be worthwhile accepting the stage area and reconsidering the whole arrangement of seats and auditorium? If the shifting point of command is to be commanding, then the audience should hug and embrace the square. The angle and layout become crucial. If the audience can feel that it is enveloping the acting area, it will be in one room. If it sits back, watching detachedly, then, whatever the label, it will be in two rooms."

8th August 1966: Olivier to Brook

"Dearest Peter,
This is just a word to thank you so infinitely much for your most illuminating notes on Scheme B, which are so very helpful in providing an abundance of food for thought. It was enormously helpful to be permitted to see the model of The Barbican and the kind generosity which prompted this was vastly appreciated by all of us. I do hope to see you again very soon. Always with love, Laurence Olivier"[91]

9th August 1966: Lasdun's Notes on a Meeting at Aquinas Street[92]

Present: Laurence Olivier, Norman Marshall, Denys Lasdun.

Anxieties were: Size of the stage, lack of auditorium embrace, upper level corner 'shelf,' and the failure of the left and right sections of seating to converge on the stage.

Sir Laurence said he had his own difficulties with the committee. Was terrified that if we built the wrong theatre, there would be a court of enquiry and a public scandal if the thing was wrong. That, in no circumstances, would he relax his desire to keep the Stratford group on the committee, because he does not want to take personal responsibility and does not want the Stratford group to say, 'Well, we told you so.'

DL said that the mock-up must go forward. This was the only way to settle anxieties.

Olivier then handed DL an official building committee resolution which said they had grave reservations about Scheme B.

Lasdun noted that Olivier will be at the next Council meeting, though 'God knows what he will say then'.

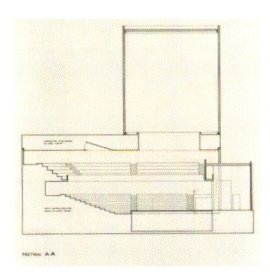

Scheme B section

> "If the audience can feel that it is enveloping the acting area, it will be in one room. If it sits back, watching detachedly, then, whatever the label, it will be in two rooms."
>
> Peter Brook

> "The chairman gave a summary of what he understood to be grave reservations: doubts about the size of the stage, the configuration of the seating, the no-man's-land behind the acting area and the rear corner."

Lasdun questioned how things had changed after three month's progress, now there was this volte-face for yet another time. Olivier just gabbled on about the difficulties of his committee.

Lasdun was blamed for lack of enthusiasm for Scheme C. (Brook's speech). He was blamed for his reaction when Brook said it was too geometric. Generally Lasdun expressed the view that it is just a question of panic, when they are faced with a decision.

10th August 1966. Southbank Board Meeting. The Upper Theatre Impasse. "Grave Reservations."

The chairman read conclusions from the NTBC of 8th August and gave a summary of what he understood to be grave reservations: doubts about the size of the stage, the configuration of the seating, the no-man's-land behind the acting area, and the rear corner.

Olivier confirmed this summary and said there was a dichotomy about the NTBC's feelings about the scheme. There was a tendency, having both a proscenium theatre and an open theatre, to assume that they should be extreme versions of each form. He accepted that the proscenium theatre could not be compromised (experiments with fore-stages of the Old Vic and the Aldwych having largely failed). But he believed it might be necessary to compromise on the open stage to extend its range. No one was sure what future generations might want – we could only work from our own experience.

Marshall agreed that it was a matter of policy whether the full limitations of an open stage should be acceptable for the main auditorium.

SBB members felt that the extreme side seats in the balcony were too withdrawn and were disturbed by the fact that they were not inclined toward what one member called the area of maximum interest. Olivier said he would like these seats to be linked in some way to the lower tier. The NTBC generally felt the scheme was "lacking in warmth."

The mock-up was needed. The proscenium theatre model was shown: "Few members took much interest in it."

Lasdun's letter of 3rd August 1966 was submitted regarding the budget of £7.5 million and noted that this was unrealistic. The GLC representatives warned over costs: "Steps should be taken now to effect reductions." [93]

The First Questionnaire

Two days after this crisis meeting in August, when Olivier had shared the building committee's grave reservations about Scheme B to the South Bank Board, he wrote to all the committee members asking them to set down their opinions in writing. Here is the copy that your author received:

```
The National Theatre 12th August, 1966.
URGENT AND CONFIDENTIAL

Dear Richard,

It is so very difficult to achieve a full
committee meeting and consequently to keep
in touch with opinions which are influenced
by sporadic meetings, re-influenced by the
catching up process and possibly subject in
all the interim times by second thoughts and
changes of mind.

When our committee first met in Hamilton
Place on January 3rd, 1963, hopes were
high and gay, practical considerations
such as scale, forms, shapes, volumes and
measurements were turned aside as being
workaday banalities spoiling the limitless
skies serenely and confidently dedicated
to celestial inspiration. Soon after this
Lasdun was chosen to be our architect and
since then something has happened: Scheme B;
and, since our wordless reception of Scheme
C, in essential conception, again Scheme B.

In some apt and clear remarks concerning
this Peter Brook asks What is it about Scheme
B that gives us a feeling of unease? I think
```

we must all face now that time is of the essence and will no longer indulge any more reluctance to specific definition.

Certain basic principles have gone forward, having been minuted and passed up to the top councils and been accepted by them and in statutory fashion have joined the original briefs.

In order to save wasted exploration in areas that can no longer be considered, may I remind you of the following points of original briefing or carried motion:
1. The Amphitheatre is to be the larger of the two theatres and the Proscenium the smaller.
2. They must together cater for about 2,000 capacity. The Amphitheatre holding about 1,150 and the Proscenium about 850. Minor variations of these totals can be tolerated providing the sum total is achieved.
3. The Larger Theatre to be an "Open Stage" Theatre with scenic possibilities.
4. The general layout of the amphitheatre, namely one quarter of a square for the acting area and the rest for the auditorium, has been agreed.

Lasdun has to some extent relieved the much vexed question of the downstage point of the stage by simply removing the stage or clear outline of it altogether and leaving an acting space the shape of which is to be indicated only by the configuration of the front row of the audience.

This has at present been broken by three vomitoria, one in the centre and one at each wing of the acting area.

There are three main features which confront us, and which carry with them implications of vital and basic principle,
1. The upstage corner imposed by the architecturally logical completion of the upper gallery.
2. The size of the stage.
3. The audience/actor relationship now dictated by the configuration of the front seating.

One great question which arises from these points at issue is this:-

In light of the adjacent presence of a conventional illusory Theatre, how extreme should be the doctrinal difference between the two theatres? Or how far should the amphitheatre go in the non-illusory direction?

We find it impossible to serve the committee's interests any longer without some kind of consensus, and we beg that you put down your considered answers to the questions overleaf at your earliest convenience.

We would greatly appreciate your kind cooperation at this time, and please, as speedy a reply as possible.

A full Committee meeting will be called following hard upon the reception of these answers.
1. Do you think there should be a permanent architectural feature (e.g. the upstage hanging corner), or should it be possible to dispense with this?
2. Bearing in mind that the first of the following alternatives will incline towards more illusory possibilities, and the second towards more purely abstract disciplines, should the acting area be placed -
   (a) within accessible distance from the upstage corner (in which case the point of command will be obvious)? or
   (b) placed well away from the "corner" and towards the body of the house (in which case the point of command will be variable)?

   (N.B. The configuration of the front row of audience would presumably skirt whichever of these is decided upon).
3. In consideration of audience/actor relationship the frontal configuration the acting area is emphatic, so please specify what shape you would favour for this perimeter
   (a) The right angle according to the original Scheme B "sketch"?
   (b) any other angular conception?
   (c) a quarter-circle?

(d) a third-circle (120°)?
(e) a more elliptical thrust still?
(f) any other shape (please sketch if required)
4. How wide should the acting area be at its widest point?

The only detailed response to the questionnaire is my own, which I quote in full. Following that, I list Kenneth Rae's summary for Sir Laurence of the other member's comments.

ANSWERS TO QUESTIONNAIRE by RICHARD PILBROW REGARDING SCHEME B 29th August, 1966
1. I emphatically do not believe there should be a permanent architectural feature (e.g. the upstage hanging corner) and believe it is ESSENTIAL to dispense with this absolutely. Any structure that a director or designer wishes to place at the back centre of his acting area should be considered as theatrical scenery and NOTHING more permanent. Should the architect wish to provide for POSSIBLE use an architectural surround to the stage, he may have that option (if it is not taking funds needed elsewhere) but in that case it must be capable of easy removal.
2. I believe that the "point of command" will not be made more obvious by the position of the acting area in relation to the square room. The point of command is the point upon which the whole auditorium focusses. (The "Freie Volksbuhne" in Berlin seemed particularly successful in that the almost "seashell" shaped auditorium that raked not only front to back but side to side seemed to force the audience's attention toward stage centre.) Scheme B does not at this time focus anywhere, there is no architectural compulsion in directing the audience's attention to the stage.
3. The acting area must be within accessible distance from the corner (since I do not believe such a corner should exist). But this does not mean that the whole should be pushed toward this corner. The quality of "open stage" decided upon (i.e. a stage subtending an audience of 90°) should I believe be preserved. But around this open stage must be SPACE. Space can always be screened in but once shut in in concrete can never be opened out.
4. The acting area, indeed and more importantly, the whole volume of the "room" is too vast. (I suspect it can be reduced but if necessary seats may have to be cut out.) Scheme B is not a room but a large hangar. Peter Hall may be correct in asserting that the Scheme B form would only work on a small scale (300-400 seats I believe he mentioned), but certainly everything must be done to squash the audience volume down. Then the acting area will assume viable proportions and still be 1/4 of the "room".

The front of the stage itself can, and should, be variable, just as the floor areas in *Armstrong* or *Hobson's Choice* etc. were shaped scenically. The front row of the audience however must embrace and focus on the stage. A right angle and a quarter circle feel too dead, too geometric! An elliptical or parabolic envelopment is to be preferred: that can still stop before the end seats face directly their opposite numbers.

5. The width of the acting area (being that part of the stage upon which the auditorium is focussed and that part that appears fully within the 'room') should not be much greater, I suspect, than 50 feet.

OTHER COMMENTS
I do take issue with your "great question" (page 2 of your letter) "In the light of the adjacent presence of a conventional illusory theatre"

Why is a proscenium theatre an illusory theatre? Since when?

The proscenium theatre can be as illusory or non illusory as director, designer and actors choose. The Berliner Ensemble use a proscenium theatre as a non illusory instrument. A theatre-in-the-round can be completely illusory when the stage is lit, the auditorium dark and actors and audience can together live a dramatic story. (Albeit with perhaps less scenery than usual).

Any stage is only illusory as far as the theatre people working on it wish it to be illusory.

There has been a recent (and maybe only temporary) theatrical movement away from illusory theatre. Brecht led this movement in a proscenium theatre.

If a piano can be used to play any music ranging from Beethoven concerto to jazz, WHY should any theatre be even considered that will not prove to be a fine instrument in which any type of theatre can be played?

FURTHERMORE:
Our friends from the Royal Shakespeare have with increasing frequency stressed that the National Theatre Building MUST grow out of the young roots that the company have laid down in the last few years. Their own theatre in The Barbican reflects completely their own work. The strength of the success of the National is superb acting, theatricality and an eclecticism of theatrical style in repertory that is a revelation to the English theatre-going public and most of its successful productions are illusory in style. Surely we cannot even consider a theatre that will limit this eclectism. We should have an open stage form, but let it not be an open stage shut in a concrete box; let it be:

"What I'm dreaming about is a space stage that will give the feeling of audience and actor in one room"
St.Denis. Meeting 9.1.64

"But you can be in a room and look out of a window. We want to be able to come into our room from the immense outer world."
Sir Laurence. 6.11.64

I consider that the theory that the "open" stage has to be the opposite of the "proscenium" stage extremely dangerous. It illustrates the dangers of theoretical discussion losing touch with reality. They are both STAGES for THEATRES.

The modern proscenium stage is emphatically not a stage divided from its audience (sitting in a straight rows) by an architectural picture frame. This is a poorly designed proscenium theatre of the 1930s.

If the present sketch plans of the proscenium theatre represent a contrast to the open stage, I remain deeply concerned for the success of either.

Lasdun once said:-
 "Engaged intensity is the central thing."
 (9.1.64)

As a lighting designer, occasional producer and theatre consultant I attempt to stand in for the audience. My deepest concern for both theatres in the complex is an emotional concern. I find them both geometric, rigid, inhuman and un-theatrical.

As a so-called practical, "technical" person, I have much sympathy with Lasdun in the face of all the "advice" he has received:
 "Why must you (Brook) be so abstract. I don't want to impose an architectural idea. Be positive. We won't get anywhere with abstractions."
 Lasdun 4.3.64

But the greatest problem does STILL seem to be one of abstractions. The National Theatre Company has performed a miracle in English Theatre. It needs a <u>theatrical</u> home. These are not theatrical stages. Yet.

It is terribly difficult to judge a theatre without a production, or at least a setting lit upon the stage and an audience in the seats. What would a model of the Duke of York's Theatre or the Royal Opera House look like with dirty brick walls bare around the stage?

Theoretical discussion and a live performance are poles apart:
 "The audience is not conscious of the ceiling once the action of the play has begun."
 Sir Laurence 4.3.66

 "I don't accept that we should be forced to choose between the concept of the proscenium and an open stage."
 Hall. 6.11.64

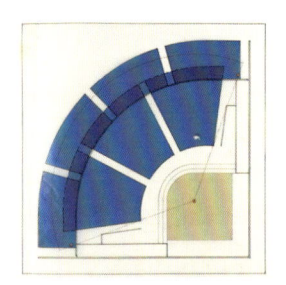

Scheme C

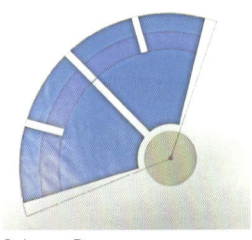

Scheme D

The Committee's Responses [94]
Kenneth Rae summarised for Sir Laurence, the other members' responses to the questionnaire.

1. Do you think there should be a permanent architectural feature (e.g. the upstage hanging corner?
   NO: George Rowbottom, Jocelyn Herbert, John Dexter, Kenneth Tynan, Norman Marshall, William Gaskill, Peter Hall.

2. Should the acting area be placed within accessible distance from the upstage corner?
   YES: Peter Hall, Kenneth Tynan, George Rowbottom.
   NO: Norman Marshall, William Gaskill, Jocelyn Herbert.

3. What shape of stage would you favour?
   Right Angle: William Gaskell.
   Quarter Circle: Peter Hall, Kenneth Tynan.
   120°: George Rowbottom, Norman Marshall, William Gaskill.

4. How wide should the acting area be at its widest?
   35 feet: Peter Hall, William Gaskill.
   40 feet: Norman Marshall.
   45 feet: Ken Tynan, Jocelyn Herbert.
   50 feet: George Rowbottom.

Committee Further Reactions
On 18th August Peter Hall wrote to Sir Laurence: "My basic worry is the idea of theatre in a quarter of a square. This will lead to bad sightlines and volume too large… bad for acoustics." [95]

Meanwhile, correspondence between Olivier and Lord Cottesloe recorded by Olivier's biographer: "Olivier… was beginning to be a bit frustrated at the intractability of the architect. He wanted to see more plans and hoped that Cottesloe's board would not be swept off its feet by what he now recognised as Lasdun's superb salesmanship and accept his designs as they stood. Cottesloe supported Olivier, but remarked that how Olivier could get into Lasdun's head that the wishes of the end user were dominant, as in all buildings, was quite beyond him." [96]

During August, DL&P prepared two new variants: Schemes D and E. They were similar, but the seating of Scheme D was single level, while E added a balcony and – a remarkable innovation from Lasdun – both sides of the stalls were raised some five feet to create a bowl-like impression, partially linking the stalls to the circle. These were viewed at the architect's office on 16th September. Sir Laurence seemed to prefer Scheme D as it seemed to minimise "class distinction." [97]

19th August 1966: Lasdun Notes on NTBC Meeting [98]
The following revised specifications were agreed: seating within a right-angle; front row 20' radius extended through 120°-180°; preferred single tier, two vomitoria, stage height plus 2', stage in sections so profile can be altered, fly tower from front seats to background wall to escape light spill, three or four lighting bridges, two to three lighting positions on side walls.

Questioned by Softley, concentric seating would produce "zone of command rather than a point of command."

Scheme B upper tier was too detached. Softley said two tiers might eliminate cross gangways.

These guidelines might reduce seat count. The proscenium theatre might be enlarged. Discussion of the Berlin Freie Volksbühne, seating over 1100, which was thought to be very good.

Peter Hall said the conventional proscenium was not needed. He'd prefer this theatre and one more 'in-the-round'. Marshall suggested that could be provided by the studio theatre. Jocelyn Herbert suggested that this auditorium would suffice for the proscenium and that a smaller Scheme B might be better.

Hall said The Barbican had a 40' wide pros, but it was set back out of sight. They were experimenting with seating groups suspended off the side walls. Yolande Bird said that it was her initiative that Softley and Minjoodt were invited to the meeting to hear the unanimous decision on the recommendations above.

Five days later, on 21st September, another meeting. Olivier, Dexter, Herbert and myself. We all preferred Scheme E. Dexter: "exciting with no suggestion of a proscenium." Jocelyn: "intimate, with a bowl-like feeling." [99]

'The Project'
DL&P recorded the following: "LO said that he and Richard Pilbrow had been doing some home-work on the backstage arrangements which would be necessary, and if DL would not consider it an impertinence, he would like to show him the drawing that RP had prepared. The drawing was produced with a large printed title 'PROJECT' (DL said that the title was an impertinence verging on the unprofessional)." [100]

The background to this development was that Michael Elliott had discussed the questionnaire and my responses, with which he was in complete agreement. But the committee appeared divided on the issue of scenery. John Dexter and Jocelyn Herbert were for a purist 'Guthrie' approach of limiting scenic capability. Michael and I were against the shape of the actor/audience relationship dictating – forever – the style of presentation. As Michael had said, why does the form of the auditorium force us to give up centuries of stagecraft – scenery and lighting? We decided to talk to Sir Laurence directly.

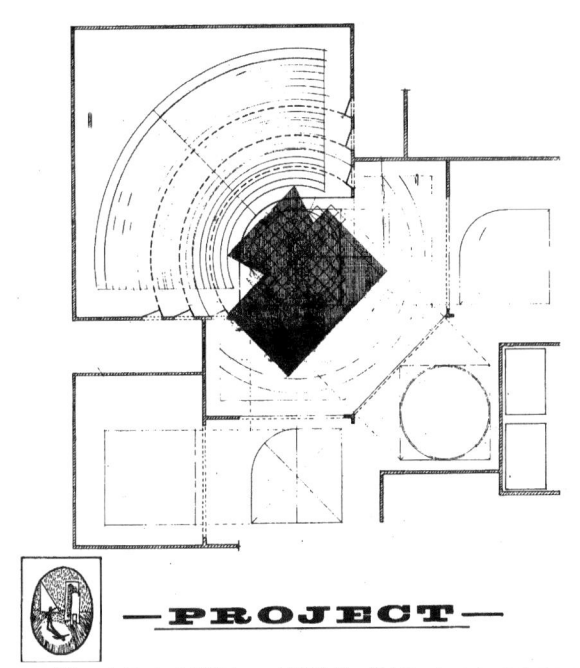

Pilbrow's Project, 29th August 1966. The Old Vic stage in dark grey overlaid on a sketch of the proposed Upper Theatre

We met Sir Laurence in his flat at Roebuck House, near Victoria, after a performance, at 11pm. We discussed the limitations of the stage and our view that the surrounding concrete balcony seemed to contradict Sir Laurence's hope that the new stage should not shackle the rich traditions of stagecraft but unleash a new potential. What were we to do about the balcony? Michael argued passionately against it. Sir Laurence himself seemed uncertain. He wanted a stage that was "within the audience room" but he "wanted to enter from space beyond that room." For example, he could imagine himself in *King Lear*, entering through the storm from the furthest distance and then coming into the heart of the audience. I suggested that if a production wanted a balcony it could always be specified by the scene designer and built for the production. Why inhibit the theatre for all time with a mass of concrete at centre stage? Look at the problems the concrete balcony had caused us in Chichester.

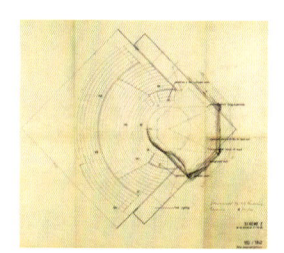

Scheme E plan

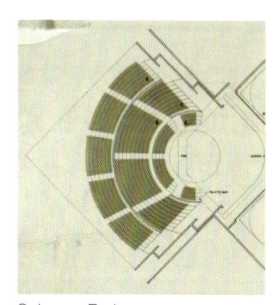

Scheme E plan

Sir Laurence asked me to go away and sketch a suggestion for a new stage shape. I did this the next day. My colleague, Tony Corbett, drew it up and I sent it to Sir Laurence for his reaction. I was shattered when he passed it enthusiastically to Lasdun, who was not amused at all. I was commanded to appear at his office forthwith. "I am the architect, how dare you!? Why, your 'ears' on my fly tower will change the silhouette of the building and the skyline of London for all time!" He was right. They did. They still do, and, presumably, will – for many ages.[101]

Architectural historian Barnabas Calder confirms the architect's anger: "Lasdun – and one of Lasdun's architectural contemporaries (who preferred to remain anonymous) – found it impossible to accept." [102]

However, my sketch did provide a moment of breakthrough. From a square stage surrounded by a concrete balcony, it provided a 'space stage' that surrounded the thrust. Essentially, it created what Michel Saint-Denis had dreamt of: "What I am dreaming about is a space stage that would give a feeling of audience and actors being in the same room." It provided Sir Laurence with what he sought, "a thrust stage with full scenic possibilities" – a stage within the audience room – but a room that could be opened out to an outer space.

There was not universal acceptance. Dexter and Herbert – both inclined toward the 'purity' preached by Guthrie for a non-illusory stage – thought my stage too large. Jocelyn felt "that the existence of so much space would dissipate concentration in the room." Olivier responded, in his peculiarly exposed position, "the best he could do was to say to John and Jocelyn: 'If you want to close it in, you can and at the same time give himself the option of opening it up'. " [103] But, in fact, they were both right. My initial plan showed a very large stage overlaid with the plan of the Old Vic and forestage. It did create the eccentric fly tower shape, but, as redrawn by DL&P, the stage depth was modified in a perfectly sensible manner. My 'ears' on the fly tower that allowed the end of any full masking surround to the stage to be hidden, remained.

Lasdun went on to comment that he strongly opposed this attitude [that maximum flexibility should be sought], saying that one should not try to make it possible to do things which are contrary to the nature of this particular auditorium. He was sure that most designers would welcome being given some limitations within which to work and quoted Margaret Harris of Motley[104] in support of this contention.

A decision had to be made as to the type of staging each theatre required. Larry said "that a decision was difficult because the committee was split down the middle." [105]

Jocelyn wrote that evening to Sir Laurence, "*This pinpoints our divergence of attitude. I hate the feeling of two camps. All that matters is what will produce the most exciting theatre. It's hard to have those discussions with the architect present. We must establish mutual trust. I am not anti-spectacle. Of course there are plays when spectacle is valid and necessary. It's a question of degree. I think spectacle can always be created, it's one of the easiest things. It's the rest that is difficult.*" [106]

Through this critical time, the Lasdun office reviewed Scheme D and E with other committee members.

27th September 1966: Bill Gaskill
"*He felt Scheme E to be a reasonable compromise though more emphatically single direction and would, therefore, tend to produce a proscenium form of production. He thought that farce would be difficult on this stage but does not think the National Theatre main auditorium should be geared toward farce as in the Comédie Française, but generally felt that it is only LO's view that mattered. He came out quite definitely in favour of Scheme E because it has a far better grip, far better balance of seats, much more interest in the configuration of seats, it was cosier.*" [107]

29th September 1966: Kenneth Tynan, with Kenneth Rae, George Rowbottom and Yolande Bird

"He [Kenneth Rae] would feel cosy in that auditorium. [Ken Tynan] thought it was remarkable how much more effective a grip on the stage was given by Scheme E."[108]

30th September 1966: Meeting with Michael Elliott to Review Schemes

The following day, Michael Elliott observed that "he was in no doubt that Scheme E was superior. He thought the side seats did more than just link the two tiers; he thought they helped to 'suck' the stage into the auditorium. He asked whether we had considered a greater overhang of the upper tier and whether we had considered continuing the top tier down as at Minneapolis."[109]

3rd October 1966: Peter Brook Reviews the Schemes

"Scheme E will make a good house – people all feel comfortable in it – but the stage will have limited possibilities." He considered the useable area of Scheme E would be a narrow band across the centre of the circle. He felt that Scheme A had been dull and conventional, but Scheme B gave evidence of new thought and exciting possibilities of staging, but was uncomfortable for audiences who would feel isolated, detached and withdrawn… an insuperable defect.

He did not understand what E would give that could not be given in a proscenium theatre. He wondered what he could possibly say to Larry, it was really up to the National Theatre. He believed in asymmetry and would like to see the audience crowding in on the stage, arranged in irregular groups one above the other. He thought the German and American idea of large single tiers without gangways to be impossibly dull.[110]

4th October 1966: Peter Hall and Stephen Arlen Meet Lasdun

"PH said he had spoken at length with Peter Brook and they were frankly in disagreement between themselves. PH liked Scheme E. He found the configuration

> "It had marvellous atmosphere; he particularly liked the raised banks of seating to the side. In fact all members of the committee were immensely happy with this concept."
>
> Denys Lasdun quoting Laurence Olivier

attractive and superior to Scheme D. He agreed with DL that it was essential for the geometry of the staging to play against the geometry of the audience.

"He would like to avoid the central gangway in the lower tier and to have vomitories slightly nearer the centre.

"When asked what could be done in Scheme E which could not be done in a proscenium theatre he said that he personally would prefer to direct in Scheme E and he thought that a production could be given a more sculptural quality in Scheme E and could be seen in space.

"Arlen thought that it was wonderful to have the possibility of suggesting infinite distance behind the action. PH did not seem to agree that this was an advantage."[111]

The Olivier Stage (as it was later to be named)

My stage was accepted. The engineers, Flint & Neill, solved the problem of constructing this massive, eccentrically shaped fly tower overhanging the open stage and auditorium – without any visible means of support. It was, in fact, constructed with two massive concrete columns holding up the front corners. Once the concrete had matured, there was an amazing moment when these columns were cut through before being removed. Standing a safe distance back from the stage, we all watched with bated breath. Would the entire edifice collapse on us? To our considerable relief there was no perceptible movement. It was later reported that the massive concrete flytower structure actually lifted a few millimetres when released from its support.

So the stage shape of the Olivier was designed. Fifty-seven years later, it seems to have proved its worth.

A memo from Peter Softley records DL&P's ongoing irritation with the building committee… and with me. I must, of course, point out that at the time of writing, I was only a committee member… I was not appointed consultant (at Lasdun's suggestion) until the following January. He must have recovered his equilibrium by then.

23rd September 1966: Peter Softley Memorandum[112]
"*Comments upon the Building Committee [extracts]:*

3. Committee never at full strength, its attitude varies according to who is present.

4. Committee inconsistent…

5. Committee divided on whether to provide facilities for naturalistic scenery…

8. Technical members assuming role of consultants but working for NT instead of Architect (Pilbrow's project).

9. Advisory committee either to vet Architect's proposals on behalf of the SB[T]B or to advise SBB on correct brief. If the latter, the Architect could be a full member of the Advisory Panel."

26th September 1966: Sir Laurence's Thinking
The ongoing delicacy of the relationship between Lasdun and the committee was exemplified by a letter from Sir Laurence to Lasdun on 26th September.
"*Dear Denys, I don't have to tell you about the pressure that is upon us all to crystallise the plan but because the whole committee is sometimes so extremely hard to get together I am going to have to drive them to a point of definition at this meeting on October 4th.*

"I think, therefore, that the only procedure on this occasion is to ask you to show what models or sketches you wish to show to the full committee, then let me stand up and thank you for coming and get the whole thing tied up without your august presence, as I can see that the probable only way to conclude any matters outstanding is by putting them to the vote.

"Yours ever, Larry" [113]

Lasdun was suspicious and rang Cottesloe, who responded:
"*LO has said his committee was a difficult team to drive and that some members of his committee felt that DL was over-persuasive, too strong a personality, who carried them away and encouraged them to agree to something they afterward regretted."* [114]

Lasdun also reported his conversation with Lord Cottesloe:
"*He [Lasdun] did not see why LO should be so overburdened with a feeling of responsibility since any criticism of the building would tend to fall on the Architect. Neither did he understand LO's preoccupation with what people might think in fifty years' time – he thought the building might be ready to be pulled down by then; Lord C advised him not to tell LO this and in any case he himself thought that the aim was to build something which would be of lasting value like La Fenice in Venice."* [115]

DL&P Final Report[116]
In the DL&P final report, Lasdun quoted Sir Laurence:
"*This auditorium and stage answer everything they have ever asked for in terms of an 'open' solution. It has perfect sightlines, an acting area of the right size, the possibility of enthusiastic members of the audience close to the stage; the possibility of modifying the seating against the stage to amplify the thrust or take a more bland view. It had marvellous atmosphere; he particularly liked the raised banks of seating to the side. In fact all members of the committee were immensely happy with this concept."*

> "He himself thought that the aim was to build something which would be of lasting value like La Fenice in Venice."
>
> Lord Cottesloe, on Lasdun

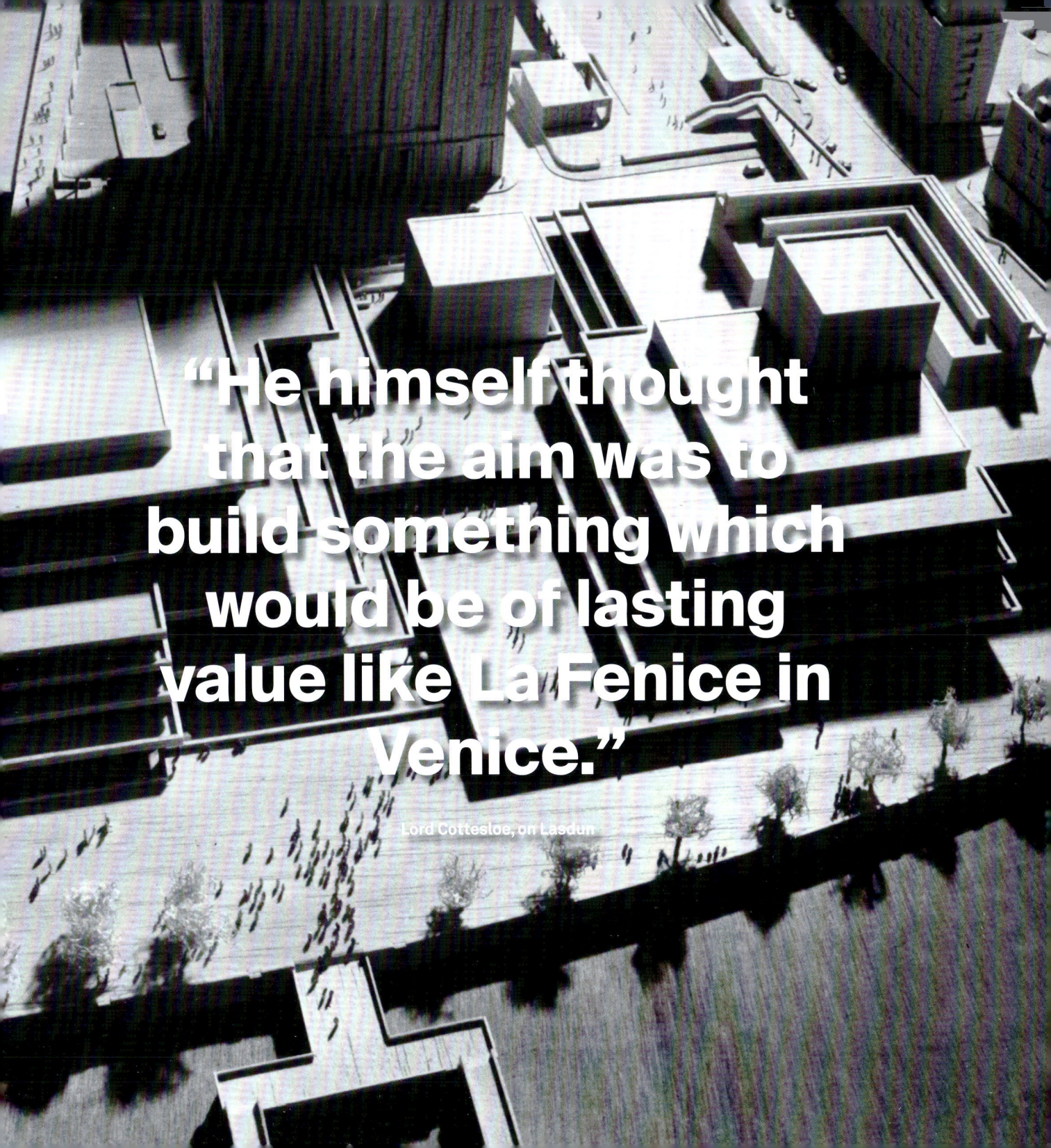

Meeting 27

27th Meeting of The National Theatre Building Committee

10a Aquinas Street, London, SE1
4th October 1966

Present:
Sir Laurence Olivier, Mr. Norman Marshall (in the Chair), Miss Jocelyn Herbert, Mr. John Dexter, Mr. Michael Benthall, Mr. Richard Pilbrow, Mr. Michael Elliott, and Mr. William Gaskill. Mr. Stephen Arlen, Mr. Kenneth Tynan, Mr. George Rowbottom and Mr. Kenneth Rae were in attendance. Mr. Denys Lasdun and Mr. Peter Softley were present by invitation.
Apologies:
Apologies for absence were received from Mr. Peter Hall, Mr. Peter Brook, and Mr. Michel Saint-Denis.

Mr. Lasdun submitted two models, showing different configurations of the audience seating, Scheme D and Scheme E. Both were without ceilings. He said that the ceiling was a major issue of design which would need deep thought. A ground plan, also produced, would show from an operational point of view the further confines of the stage area.

Mr. Lasdun said that in his experience it was often helpful to review the history of a project when an important stage in development was reached. He would, therefore, remind the Committee of certain key moments in the plans for the National Theatre.

In March 1964, when only one auditorium was envisaged; Scheme A was submitted. This attempted to encompass the greatest range possible as between an open and a closed solution. He would define "closed" as a single-direction stage: providing confrontation, and "open" as one, giving the possibility of viewing the action from more than one angle so emphasising its three-dimensional qualities. Scheme A bore, in his opinion, an extremely close resemblance to the Barbican solution which was not surprising as this was a one auditorium project. Scheme A was not received with enthusiasm by the Building Committee and the architects' response had been to search for a one-room theatre with scenic possibilities.

In May 1964, Scheme B was adopted because it had been agreed to build the proscenium theatre as well. Scheme B proposed a dynamic right-angle solution. It was known that more work would have to be done on it; a half-inch model and a mock-up.

From December 1964 to March 1966 all development was held up for "political" reasons.

In April 1966 when it became possible to proceed once more, the considered opinion of the Building Committee proved to be against Scheme B.

A month later Scheme C was submitted which was neither received warmly by the Committee nor produced with warmth by the architects. A decision was, therefore, taken to do more work on Scheme B, but in August, Scheme B was finally rejected on the grounds that 'the physical enclosure of the actors and the audience within a single space was considered too limiting.' In August the Building Committee met and as a result of their unanimity the architects proceeded on the basis of the following nine points:-
1. The seating to be contained within a right-angle and to be arranged in concentric rows.
2. The front row to have a 20'0" radius.
3. The seating to be preferably in a single tier.
4. Two vomitories to be included.
5. Sight Lines to be based on the stage being 2'0" above the floor.
6. The stage to be in sections capable of being raised or lowered so that the profile of the stage can be altered.
7. The fly tower to extend from the front seats to the background wall which should be set well behind the acting area to enable a dark background to be placed far enough back to escape light spill.
8. The ceiling to be designed to include three or four lighting bridges, one of which would need to be against the back wall if the seating is arranged in a single tier.

9. The seating capacity to be not less than 1000.

Mr. Lasdun then stressed that with the exception of one - that of the fly-tower - all the conditions could have been met by modifications to Scheme B. Configuration of the Scheme C seating could be reconciled with Scheme B.

Mr. Lasdun went on to say that Scheme D was generally workable but dull. Scheme E which was preferred by everybody, provided a cosy "armchair" House for the audience that was exciting and that had, through its gesture of angularity, some of the dynamic of Scheme B. Where "circles" would become the obsessive solution in Scheme D, Scheme E would admit, for example, of a pentagonal "stage" (Mr. Lasdun placed one on the model). The blocks of side seats, the "pincers" that gripped the acting area in Scheme E were adjustable, The respective seating capacity of Scheme D and E were 1,038 and 1,171.

Mr. Lasdun concluded by saying that the architects had reached a point beyond which they could not go without further information from the Committee.

After some discussion Mr. Lasdun and Mr. Softley left the meeting.

The meeting then gave further consideration to the models submitted by the Architect, and the following Recommendation was agreed for submission to the National Theatre Board and to the South Bank Board.

"The National Theatre Building Committee unanimously recommends to the National Theatre Board and to the South Bank Board the adoption of a plan for the open-stage auditorium in the National Theatre known as Scheme E.

Recommendations concerning technical facilities will be made after further discussion with the Architects.

The Committee is also considering the Architect's plans for the Proscenium Theatre."

"The National Theatre Building Committee unanimously recommends the adoption of a plan for the open-stage auditorium in the National Theatre known as Scheme E."

The Committee

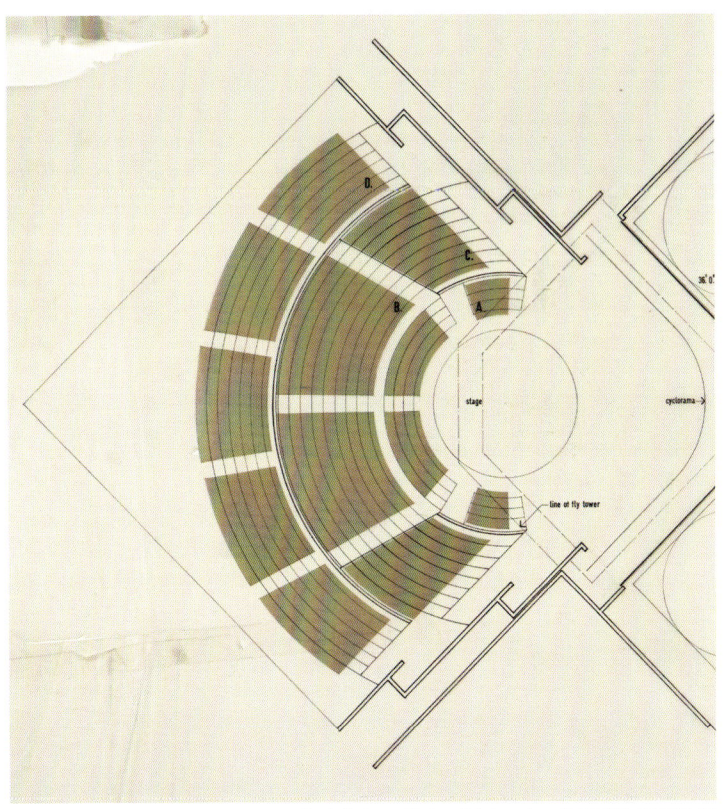

Early Scheme E plan; this is not quite the Olivier as built!

6th October 1966: Sir Laurence to Peter Brook [117]
PRIVATE & CONFIDENTIAL
"My dear Peter,

"I am so dreadfully sorry that my stupid memory should betray me into such bad chairmanship as I showed in Tuesday night. No excuses are really good enough for this mistake but I did have OTHELLO the night before, and I am never anything like on top for a good twenty-four hours after it. It was very kind of you to accept my lapse of memory as a truth and without any apparent suspicions. I do appreciate this more than I can tell you.

"Since you were kind enough to say that whether the rider goes into the recommendations or not you are with it alright providing we have a mock up, I will take advantage of your kindness and not include it in the recommendations with much relief as Lasdun is threatening resignation otherwise.

"It is simply up to me to make sure that the South Bank Board sticks to their guns and insists on the mock up. I think with Chandos's help I can manage this all right.

"What follows will also tally with what I have written to Peter Hall.

"The next meeting will really be all important... Here is the proposed agenda.
1. Configuration of the stage.
2. The amount of flying required.
3. The amount of space behind the acting area on the visible stage and the amount behind that, i.e. the allocation of the amount of space within the limits already given.
4. Whether the stage should be raised two feet, or depressed. (I personally think this is pretty well determined by the line of sight).
5. What exactly do we want from a mock up?

"... Those same people will be only too relieved to get rid of our project from among their problems under the slightest excuse of delay or lack of unanimity. Speaking of lack of unanimity, the points of the agenda that I'm afraid are going to be the crunch are numbers 2 and 3.

"There are some dedicatedly strong opinions on the committee that open stage discipline should be severely imposed by the permanence of the back wall, and there are those also who say let there be such discipline for those who want it and let others have a sense of infinity should they want that, by causing the back wall to disappear.

"This is the real crunch and because I sense that feelings are so high I fear that what I dread most might happen, really that some people will feel forced to resign in order to keep to their principles. This is really why I simply must have your spoken opinion and argument in the Committee on the day of this next meeting.

"It was always a danger, I suppose, in forming as large a Committee as this that such a crunch as this might have to be faced, but I still feel that such a risk had to be taken. I must just rely on the good nature of those whose opinions lose out to stay along and give us the continued benefit of their advice in spite of their principal convictions having suffered a reversal.

"I hope all is going beautifully now for Vietnam[118] for you. Much love..."

11th October 1966: Ken Tynan to Sir Laurence on Scheme E [119]

"We cannot put ourselves in the position of dictating not only to directors on how to direct but to playwrights on how to write them. Suppose Euripides wants Medea carried up to heaven in a chariot, or a modern playwright needs someone to enter by helicopter, who are we to say that they must make do with second best. This is theatrical Calvinism at its very worst. Not content with disapproving of sins, we make it impossible for others to commit them. Permanently roofed, tightly closed in, the result would be a new style for the '70s – the Theatre of Penance."

14th October 1966. Sir Laurence to the Building Committee [120]

"Scheme E became the chosen solution."

Evolved Scheme E plan from 1967 corresponding to model below. Pre drum stage! Compare to the later drawing on p.196

Upper Theatre model, 1967 by DL&P with setting by Jocelyn Herbert

There are two slightly different versions of this model, the photographs often mis-identified. This one, probably part of the original public presentation in 1967, doesn't have what Lasdun called the 'pincers' and are now known as the 'ashtrays,' raised seating blocks on either side of the stalls. They appear in a later model from 1969 (see p.195), suggesting that Scheme E continued to evolve even after it was agreed.

Meeting 28

28th Meeting of The National Theatre Building Committee

10a Aquinas Street, London, SE
17th October 1966, 5:30 pm

Present:
Sir Laurence Olivier, Mr. Norman Marshall (in the Chair), Miss Jocelyn Herbert, Mr. Michael Elliott, Mr. Richard Pilbrow, Mr. Peter Hall, Mr. Peter Brook, Mr. Stephen Arlen, Mr. George Rowbottom and Mr. Kenneth Rae were in attendance.
Apologies:
Apologies for absence were received from Mr. John Dexter, Mr. William Gaskill, Mr. Michel Saint-Denis and Mr. Michael Benthall.

SCHEME E.
The Committee discussed certain points outstanding with regard to the model of Scheme E which had been submitted by the Architects on the 4th October. The following Resolutions were agreed:-

Configuration of the Stage
The Committee noted and accepted that the front, configuration of the auditorium gives freedom for the stage to assume any shape.

They asked that the whole area on each extreme side of the front of the auditorium should be a vomitory so that the front four rows at present offered can be placed over it at any point.

The configuration of the stage is herewith accepted.

The Amount of Flying Required
In the light of Eric Jordan's[121] four points for open-stage theatres the Committee decided that it could not accept the limiting of stage materials to those at present used in front of fire curtains, and requires, consequently, that the whole of the acting area can be screened off by a fire resisting construction.

This will, therefore, necessitate a fly-tower starting from the front edge of the acting area to a back limit described in the next resolution.

In case the above condition should promote an ungovernable sensation of chasm and thereby destroy the feeling of intimacy always aimed at in "The Room", as well as jeopardising acoustics, the Committee suggests that the possibility of some covering composed of mechanical louvers or shutters to seal off this void either totally or in part and so continue the ceiling of "The Room", should be given some study.

The Amount of Space Behind the Acting Area on the Visible Stage
The contour of "The Room" as it is now presented, seems no longer to offer any logical requirement that the confines of the stage at the back should find termination in a corner.

The Committee agreed that there should be a fly-tower capable of containing a cyclorama of radius 40' from the centre of the acting area.

Height of the Stage
The height of the acting area should be studied by the technical committee in the light of trucking requirements.

The Committee then discussed whether a request for a full scale mock up of Scheme E should be included in the resolutions to be forwarded to the Architect. It was agreed that this might create a false impression of uncertainty over the Scheme and that the right to request a mock up was already implicit in previous recommendations submitted.

Mr. Peter Brook said that he would like to record his strong belief that the questions of the ceiling, the fly-tower, the cyclorama and the acoustics were indissolubly linked, and that if a mistake were made in anyone of them the whole theatre would be in danger of being ruined. At worst, the result might be a sort of Hollywood Bowl. The Committee should therefore reserve the right to reconsider the major decisions agreed above, when the consequences were examined in relation to acoustics and the theatre's feeling of intimacy. At all costs a "draughty theatre" must be avoided.

Peter Brook's Warning

Peter Brook's warning was so insightful. Clearly, my enlarged stage and the overarching fly tower magnified the challenge presented to the acoustician, who was yet to be appointed. Only on 14th December was the appointment of an acoustician discussed. However, even after the appointment of Henry Humphries, of the Building Research Laboratory, Lasdun continued to maintain strict control. We consultants were never invited to a team meeting; each discipline was dealt with separately through the architect.

The detailed design of the Olivier ceiling was a case in point. As stage lighting consultant, I was concerned with the placement of the lighting bridges and their adequacy of coverage to the stage. Compromises with Lasdun's concept of the sloping planes of ceiling, with its overall inverted shell-shaping, were negotiated. Their limited width, as they stretched further from the stage, was a real problem. Eventually, I proposed the lighting 'stalactites', vertical 'bridges' that became like 'chandeliers' of stage lighting within the room. But the steepness of the ceiling planes nearest the stage were a problem, too. I would have preferred a less steep angle, which would have lowered the higher sections of ceiling. Only years later did I find that the acoustician would have preferred a lower ceiling height as well!

The moral: open collaboration between all disciplines would have brought an improved result.

However, on 18th October 1966, Softley and Olivier met and Softley reported Olivier's view:

"The stage which the committee as a whole wanted, imposed more limitations than he himself [LO] would have liked. The Committee was his creation, so that he could not complain if he was over-ruled." [122]

It's hard to know what "limitations" Olivier was referring to. The committee had approved Scheme E, which he liked, with the 'Pilbrow' stage that he had approved. Perhaps he was just being tactful with Softley, knowing of his frustration with the committee.

The Storm, directed by John Dexter, opened at the Old Vic on 18th October. Svoboda's designs of multiple-layered

Richard Pilbrow on Olivier stepped lighting bridge

Olivier ceiling with lighting stalactites in 1976

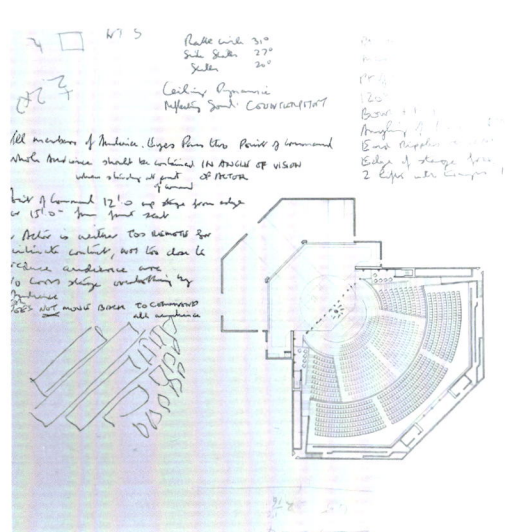

Olivier ceiling exploration

projection screens created one of the most extraordinary productions I had ever seen on any stage. This was setting a very high standard for all of us, and for our new theatres.

South Bank Board Minute 155, 12th October 1966 [123]
"The National Theatre Board's Building Committee unanimously recommends the adoption of a plan for the open-stage auditorium known as Scheme E. Recommendations concerning technical facilities will be made after further discussion with the Architect.

"The Committee is also considering the Architect's plans for the proscenium theatre."

The Council unanimously accepted and approved the Theatre Panel's recommendation. For the GLC, Sir William Fiske added the proviso that the total cost should not exceed the maximum figure of £7.5 million previously specified.

The Chairman said that Detailed Design had taken more time than anticipated, therefore now could not be completed until the end of May 1967. Therefore by the end of November 1966, the following principles must be agreed:

(a) The design of the auditorium and stage of the proscenium theatre.

(b) All the stage arrangements, including the handling of scenery, for the open stage theatre.

(c) Planning of all production departments and scenery docks for the whole theatre.

(d) The front of house for the whole theatre.

Sir Laurence said that, although the time allotted was very short, the Theatre Panel would use their best endeavours to work to the timetable, which was adopted by the council.

Lyttelton Theatre model by DL&P, 1967

On 14th December 1966, the Council agreed that the services of an acoustic consultant were required. Mr. Humphries and the Building Research Laboratory (for a nominal fee of 100 Guineas) were appointed. It was noted that consultants would also be needed on stage and other lighting and on-stage machinery. One name was mentioned for consideration. It was agreed that Mr. Lasdun should consult with Mr. Norman Marshall and Sir Laurence Olivier on this appointment.

South Bank Board Minute 159, 14th December 1966 [124]
"The Council considered Mr. Lasdun's model for the proscenium theatre to which it gave unanimous approval. Mr. Lasdun explained that the theatre re-creates in modern terms the scale of the traditional proscenium theatre: the stage opening is variable from 35 feet to 52 feet; the increase in seating capacity to 850/900 from 700 has been achieved only at some sacrifice of quality of design; pressure for extra seats should be resisted."

The total seating capacity was now about 2250 persons (open-stage 1200; proscenium 850; workshop 200).

Meeting 29

29th Meeting of The National Theatre Building Committee

10a Aquinas Street, London, SE1
3rd November 1966, 5:30 pm

Present:
Sir Laurence Olivier, Mr. Norman Marshall (in the Chair), Mr. Richard Pilbrow, Mr. Michael Elliott, Miss Jocelyn Herbert, Mr. Peter Brook, Mr. William Gaskill and the Secretary. Mr. Kenneth Tynan and Mr. George Rowbottom were in attendance. Mr. Denys Lasdun and Mr. Peter Softley were present by invitation.
Apologies:
Apologies for absence were received from Mr. Stephen Arlen, Mr. John Dexter, Mr. Peter Hall and Mr. Michel Saint-Denis.

```
After the members of the Building Committee
had viewed the new model of the Proscenium
Theatre, Mr. Lasdun said that he would like
briefly to trace the way the thinking on the
proscenium theatre had developed as between
June and November 1966. On the 3rd June the
architects had put forward a model which they
regarded as a starting point for discussion.
It was based on a seating capacity of some
750, and a proscenium width of 40'. In the
knowledge that there would be an open stage as
well, the aim of the architects was to design
a theatre that would admit of the optimum
for proscenium presentation and also for some
degree of flexibility. There would be no apron
to the stage, but there was a suggestion that
it might be advantageous to have a proscenium
opening that could expand. As many people
as possible were to be seated in a central
position, and in order to concentrate the
audience it was thought that there should
probably be a two-tier solution. The seating
was arranged in straight rows. The general
reaction of the Sub-Committee was that 40'
was too wide for the proscenium opening, and
that 30' would be preferable. Doubts were
expressed on the necessity for any orchestra
pit or fore-stage and the architects were
```

asked to examine a solution as between straight and curved rows of seating.

At a meeting on the 21st July, it was learned that pressure was being brought to upgrade the capacity of the proscenium theatre to a minimum of 850. A feeling was developing that the proscenium might be flexible in its width. The idea was introduced that the forward rows of seating should be regarded as "ripple" seats: cheaper seats which would be slightly separated from the main body of the stalls without any feeling of isolation. Mr. Lasdun went on to detail the principles upon which the latest model had been based.

- A seating capacity of 850 plus.
- A proscenium width variable as between 35' and 52'
- A belief that the proscenium theatre must have a dynamic different from that of Scheme E and therefore -
- An attempt to understand in 20th century terms the quintessence of the proscenium format which at its traditional best embraced an hierarchical progression: stage to box to tier. Everything should be geared to the fact that the proscenium was a single-direction stage. The audience should, as it were, be "funnelled" through an aperture and did not need to embrace the stage. Ideally the public should enter the auditorium at a point that visually connects the whole house together.

After discussion the following was agreed:
- The Committee studied a new model of the Proscenium Theatre which, in principle, received its enthusiastic approval and recommendation to the National Theatre Board and South Bank Board.
- The stage offers single directional presentation and the auditorium a capacity of 900.

This was only the second review of Lasdun's proposals for the proscenium theatre. The design was still driven by his conviction that a proscenium theatre was a theatre of confrontation – the opposite to the open stage with its principle of the audience surrounding the stage. The simplicity of the design was initially greeted with enthusiasm.

A More Critical Reaction
Kenneth Tynan wrote to Olivier on 5th August 1966:

"Lasdun doesn't give a damn about the proscenium theatre. He has designed the Denys Lasdun Memorial Theatre... He's a fanatic defending an abstract vision." [125]

The Second Questionnaire[126]
On 21st November 1966, a second set of more technical questions was circulated to the committee regarding Scheme E. Should there be a safety curtain? Should the stage be trapped? Should there be mechanical flying? Was a cyclorama needed? Should there be fixed wagons or not? Should there be a revolve?

1. "In view of the meeting with Mr. Jordan, should there be a safety curtain, which would probably fix the configuration of the stage."

Peter Hall: "Yes."

Michael Elliott: "The answer must depend on two imponderables: what actual limitations on materials would result? What alternatives to a barrier might be possible?"

Peter Brook: "Probably better to have none."

Michael Benthall, William Gaskill, Norman Marshall: "No."

Jocelyn Herbert: "Cannot answer without knowing who Mr. Jordan is and what he said."

2. "Do you consider the stage should be trapped and, if so, with what mechanical devices?"

Peter Brook: "Impossible to answer in theory. Obviously there should be traps with maximum flexibility and largest possible use mechanically."

Michael Elliott: "How can we give a written answer to a huge and complex question that has never been discussed. It is ridiculous. The stage floor must be available from underneath for trapping. What in God's name can one possibly say?"

Peter Hall: "The whole trapped, using portable hydraulic units for maximum flexibility."

Stephen Arlen: "The stage should be an area of absolute freedom."

Jocelyn Herbert: "Yes, the stage should be trapped. If it were possible all over in sections, I imagine hydraulic, but I have not enough technical knowledge to be sure."

3. "Do you have a preference for any particular form of flying, e.g. manual, hydraulic or electro-mechanical?"

Peter Hall: "I am yet to be convinced that hydraulic or mechanical flying are flexible in practical terms, all I have seen are noisy and/or undependable. I favour manual flying."

Norman Marshall: "Although electro-mechanical has been little used yet, I believe this will soon be recognised as the best."

Peter Brook: "I'm not qualified to give an opinion. Many electro-mechanical systems appear to be good but, in practice, do not respond as finely as one would wish."

Michael Elliott: "Without experience or knowledge of either, I suspect there must be advantages. This must be examined, an expert decision must be made."

Richard Pilbrow: "A unique form of mechanical flying has to be developed. An open stage has to provide spot-line suspension capable of lifting substantial weights to very accurate deads with instantly variable speed and variable acceleration and de-acceleration. No mechanical system yet meets these demands."

4. "Any particular views on a cyclorama."

Jocelyn Herbert: "Should be built not an unwinding cloth. A framed cyc, which could be flown in."

Michael Elliott: "Only that it be totally removable."

Peter Hall: "It should not be permanent."

   5.   "Trucking: permanent or ad-hoc?"

Richard Pilbrow: "Trucking must be provided for repertory working and rapid change-over."

Jocelyn Herbert, Peter Brook, William Gaskill, Peter Hall and Norman Marshall: "Ad hoc."

Michael Elliott: "Another vast question. Basically ad-hoc, but upon detailed study there may be good arguments for some permanent provision."

   6.   "A revolve: permanent, as a truck or ad-hoc?"

All responses favoured ad-hoc or a revolve in a wagon.

Peter Hall added: "I am opposed to any machinery that is fixed. It is always in the wrong place. The Stratford sliding stages which cost a mint of money in the thirties, are quietly rotting in the basement!"

Michael Elliott vouchsafed that the questionnaire was "ridiculous – expertise should be sought."

With some embarrassment, I must admit that that expertise was to be me! On 28th November Kenneth Rae confirmed to Sir Laurence that my appointment as theatre consultant was approved, initially for stage lighting and sound and then later for all the stage planning and installations.

Back to Business… Consulting
29th November 1966
Yolande Bird to Sir Laurence:[127]

"*Herewith the photostats of Theatre Projects Consultants' (TPC) contract. It covers any member of the firm, not just Pilbrow. There are no terms of reference for the Technical Sub-committee.*

Its purpose is to sift and discuss technical data and to make recommendations to the Building Committee where different departments are concerned. In view of this, it does not even have a fixed membership. We call on the various National Theatre Heads of Department as, and when, problems relevant to them are discussed."

3rd January 1967
Olivier to Lord Chandos:[128]

"*TPC should be appointed stage consultants. Richard is already lighting consultant. We have frankly been embarrassed by our search for theatre consultants in this country and this hesitancy has caused us to at any rate not close the door on the idea of employing German technicians. I hear that Norman Marshall would advise strongly about going this far afield for our machinery on the grounds of:*

1. *Far greater initial expense.*
2. *Inefficiency due to the problems of obtaining spare parts at the right time and servicing arrangements. Of the list of people who claim the title of stage consultant in this country, his firm (Theatre Projects) have, we are convinced, by far the most qualifications. Can the three month notice period be waived, because Pilbrow has to ramp up his new company?*"

In January, I wrote to Sir Laurence: "*While we don't want a Germanic mechanical miracle, we do want an area with complete and flexible facilities that is labour saving and efficient. BUT this is no ordinary stage. And in nearly every aspect fairly unique problems arise. Time must be allowed for prolonged and detailed expert study.*" [129]

On 3rd March Lord Chandos confirmed TPC's appointment, which was ratified by the Council on 14th June 1967.

Notes on the Informal Meeting of The National Theatre Building Committee

10a Aquinas Street, London, SE1
26th January 1967, 6:15 pm

Present:
Mr. Norman Marshall, Sir Laurence Olivier (in the Chair), Mr. Peter Hall, Miss Tanya Moiseiwitsch, Mr. Michael Elliott, Miss Jocelyn Herbert, Mr. Peter Brook and Mr. Frank Dunlop. Mr. Kenneth Rae, Mr. George Rowbottom and Mr. Richard Pilbrow were in attendance.

Absent:
Mr. Michael Benthall, Mr. William Gaskill, Mr. Michel Saint-Denis, Mr. John Dexter and Mr. Kenneth Tynan were absent.

SUBJECT OF DISCUSSION
The Architect's models and plans for the National Theatre as shown to Press and Public.

OPEN STAGE THEATRE
The feeling was unanimous that this was, generally speaking, very good. The meeting endorsed Peter Hall's "a creative thing"... "the big auditorium has come to a point of originality and strength."

After Michael Elliott had queried the height of the tower, etc, Richard Pilbrow emphasised that the ceiling had not yet been designed. The Architect was conscious that a correct solution still had to be found for this.

Michael Elliott criticised the two points at the side of the stage and, after discussion, it was agreed that efforts should be made to modify the horn corners, to admit better entrances to the actors.

PROSCENIUM THEATRE
The majority opinion was that this had not yet reached the degree of dynamic and excellence required from a proscenium theatre solution.

Peter Hall: "Rather dead." "Conventional and boring... like a shoe box." "Arid." "Mistakedly Puritan." "Too pure geometrically."

Michael Elliott agreed with Peter Hall. "Uninspiring."

Tanya Moiseiwitsch: "Looks a bit like a warehouse or a shoe box... but is it a question of decoration or feet and inches?"

Sir Laurence Olivier: "Germanic."

Norman Marshall: "Dead at sides."

Jocelyn Herbert and Sir Laurence Olivier emphasised that the design fulfilled the brief of enabling every member of the audience to see the stage properly and that this was the most important requisite for the proscenium theatre.

Jocelyn Herbert: "Has answered business of letting people see." "Good that it is adamant and strong."

Peter Hall and Peter Brook criticised the variable proscenium width (32' to 52').

Peter Hall: "I think a proscenium theatre with a movable proscenium is a contradiction in terms." "The essence of proscenium theatre is really the tension between the proscenium width and the auditorium."

Frank Dunlop felt that the theatre was designed for the proscenium at its widest (52'), and that it did not work when the width was reduced.

Richard Pilbrow said that Lasdun had designed it for a width of 44'.

Peter Brook said he felt that the solution lay largely in overcoming the problem of the side walls and their composition. One should think, perhaps, not in terms of plaster or 'pub velour' but of glass or some thing similar.

Richard Pilbrow suggested that a solution might be found if the Architect could design an area of adaptable wall near the stage for times when the proscenium was reduced. Flanged side walls would be an improvement.

This was generally agreed.

There was no general agreement on the question of whether the rows of seating should be curved or straight.

Peter Hall and Michael Elliott tended to be in favour of curved rows of seating.

Jocelyn Herbert, Frank Dunlop and Peter Brook felt that the seating should reflect the configuration of the auditorium.

Frank Dunlop suggested that there might be a solution in seats that would swivel.

Peter Brook suggested that an expert in seating should be consulted.

Sir Laurence Olivier suggested alternative staggering as at Gelsenkirchen.

EXPERIMENTAL THEATRE
Peter Hall had already left the meeting by the time this was discussed. Considerable reservations were expressed about this theatre.

Peter Brook "protested vigorously" against the current rigidity of the design. He believed that an all-purpose flexibility should be part of the basic conception. Unless this were so, productions in the experimental theatre might cost more than productions in the main theatres. The experimental theatre "must be a laboratory". It should have the possibility of making the walls "alive." Actors should be able to make unexpected entrances through apertures in the walls.

Peter Brook was supported by Frank Dunlop who agreed that floor, walls and ceiling should be completely flexible. Regular audience seating was not necessary and should be used only as a definite choice.

This meeting of the building committee included general approval of Scheme E, and ongoing criticism of the proscenium theatre. Some note was taken of the latter concerns during the following months, but the rigidity of "confrontation" remained.

Toward Our National Theatre
In February 1967, the Tory-led GLC proposed that the site of the NT be moved to the Prince's Meadow site, downstream of Waterloo Bridge. After consideration, Lasdun accepted this change and began redesigning the backstage support and front-of-house areas around his theatre concepts. This meant Waterloo Bridge became a pivotal link toward the West End.

In May 1967, an interesting note from Kenneth Rae to Lasdun: "Miss Jennie Lee has been heard to say that terraces as envisaged on the NT are in the wrong climate. Apart from this, she has no reason to believe that the NT will not be built." [130]

9th June 1967: Memo re: Telephone Conversation with Lord Cottesloe with GLC re: Costs
"*Lord Cottesloe phoned re: the meeting yesterday at the GLC with Plummer, Gluckstein, Freeman and Hart. Chandos was present.*

It was very tough going, but the matter will be reviewed in October and we are to proceed to Stage II meantime.

Gluckstein and Freeman are unfavourably disposed on the question of costs. They maintain the building could be cheaper and will find any stick they can to beat the dog to get the costs down.

The most serious aspect in Lord Cottesloe's view is that they have got an idée fixe that the building costs as proposed are of the order of £21 per square foot. This is clearly nonsense because it includes professional fees, road works, abnormals etc. So far as this meeting was concerned, there was absolutely no suggestion that anybody was gunning for the architect.

Later, after the meeting, Lord Cottesloe met Miss Jennie Lee and Lord Goodman separately. They were both furious with the GLC and absolutely on our side, and Miss Lee went on to say that they were obviously cock-a-hoop at the moment at being in power at the GLC and she would see to it that there would be no hurry to hold the meeting with Plummer. She reiterated her determination to get the NT through.

Lord Goodman was equally insistent that he intended to get the NT through, and hinted that maybe HMG, in the end, would have to pay a little more. Lord Cottesloe said he was fine on the brief and that any suggestion of one auditorium would be totally unacceptable to the NT board."

Outline planning permission for the new building was sought on 14th September 1967. Cottesloe rang Lasdun in late October extending his congratulations, but warning: "there will be battles ahead." [131]

In November 1967 Sir Laurence and Lasdun unveiled the new model. Sir Laurence promised: "the finest-looking theatre, the finest-working theatre in the world." [132]

Larger Crisis Continues

Meanwhile, however, the UK economy was in ever deeper trouble. Just as more money was needed, the Wilson Government was staving off disaster by devaluing the pound and introducing wage and price controls. Politics and the economy seemed on the verge of collapse.

How to get approval for the National to proceed in such a dangerous economic environment?

It was clear that the building had to begin construction. It is a (probably unwritten) law of government contracts that, once started, they would have to be completed – even if costs rose substantially.

14th November 1967 Kenneth Rae to Sir Laurence:

"Battle Royal going on between GLC and Treasury. Challenge of devaluation [of the pound]…" "Lasdun's Emporium"… "We're at the rock bottom. LO must speak in support. Visit Lasdun once press conference is over, you must insist upon a Building Committee meeting to review the situation." [133]

21st November 1967 Kenneth Rae to Sir Laurence again:

"The whole project is in jeopardy thanks to devaluation [of the pound] and therefore we have to use all the munitions we can muster. Tyrone Guthrie suggested 'We do not want Great Britain to be branded as philistine as well as bankrupt.' I have grave reservations about the sides of the proscenium theatre, but I think we keep mum on this as Lasdun has assured me that once Wednesday is over the Building Committee will be able to study and make what he calls 'adjustments in planning and design'." [134]

20th December 1967 Norman Marshall to Sir Laurence:

"There are still those who are unhappy about the seating in the proscenium theatre. Unless any suggestions are made now, Lasdun will be able to dismiss them as too late." [135]

On 9th February 1968 Lasdun reported a telephone conversation with Lord Chandos:

"He said firmly that any change to the design and they would be without an architect and back to square one. Chandos suggested that Lasdun made too much fuss about the complexity of the National. He, Chandos, puts up £90m worth of power stations, much more complex (using McAlpine's). DL said a power station is just a shed with complicated machinery in it and we had £5m and not £90m. This was not well received by Lord Chandos." [136]

Other cuts and deferments were necessary when tenders were received in spring 1969. Finally, an acceptable price was obtained from Robert McAlpine and Sons for the reduced scheme. A ceremonial cement-pouring occurred on 3rd November 1969. The contract was meant to be completed in four years and cost £7.5 million.

1st February 1968. Extract from Hansard: [137]

Mr Hugh Jenkins: "While it is very welcome to hear that the Government intends to produce legislation to deal with the matter of the National Theatre, it would give even greater pleasure if one could see some sign of one brick being placed upon another."

Miss Jennie Lee: "… hope that we are now reaching agreement with the GLC, which will mean that at last we shall begin to see the bricks." The National Theatre was at last to get underway.

Studio Theatre

The experimental theatre was based upon the concept of a rectangular room, a black box that was so fashionable in the 1960s, with flexible seating blocks accessed by the public from a balcony running around the room, eight feet above the floor. This was a principle Theatre Projects had developed for the studio theatres of both the Birmingham Rep and Sheffield Crucible, which separated the actor from the audience who entered above, giving the actor all-round access at stage level, It was truly 60's thinking and I knew no better at the time!

11th March 1968: Kenneth Rae to Sir Laurence:
"Re: meeting Jennie Lee, Chandos, Cottesloe. GLC financial limit of £7.5 million. No allowance for inflation. DEFER the Studio Theatre. The shell, you understand, will be there (indeed it has to hold up the roof). If we press for it now we will lose all three theatres." [138]

11th March 1968: Letter from Sir Laurence to all Members of the Building Committee. Private: [139]
"I don't know how much you may have gathered from the press, but not to beat about the bush I have to tell you that things have come to a pretty pass, by which I mean in slightly more dignified language, an impasse.

"I have been before Miss Lee with Lords Chandos and Cottesloe, when it was apparent that the GLC will not go one penny beyond the £3.75 million promised. [The total of] £7,500,000 takes no account of escalation. We are at present asked to guarantee that we have enough money to include any or all inflation. There is no way we can do that.

"The net result, and you know how much it is to my sorrow having to tell you this, is that we are being forced to make economies. There are hidden ones... but there is one that is not at all hidden, the experimental theatre. I am going to have to agree, if we are going to have a building at all, to the scrubbing of any equipment for the experimental theatre. The shell will be there. (Indeed it has to be to hold up the roof.)

"I know how much the experimental theatre means to us all, but I know absolutely that if we press for it now we shall lose all three theatres... two theatres are better than none at all. This is subject to the understanding that should sufficient economies be found, the experimental theatre would be the first to go back."

5th April 1968: Bill Gaskill wrote to Olivier with rightful anger. "I understand about the studio theatre, but it is horrific in its implication. I am just sure there is in that whacking great flytower enough equipment to sink the Berliner Ensemble, and I cannot believe that this is not to be cut out. I just know there is something wrong when it is the experimental theatre which is threatened in this way and I want to register my strong disapproval as a member of the committee." [140]

Change would eventually come. Lasdun, having accidentally (or shrewdly) placed the studio theatre below the Olivier Theatre rear stage, had simply bricked up the empty space. It wasn't restored until September 1972, on Peter Hall's insistence after taking charge of the NT.

31st December 1968: Kenneth Rae to Olivier:
"Lasdun is going to tender. NTBC has had no meeting since 1/26/1968. You can be sure that if the building is a success Lasdun will claim all the credit and if anything goes wrong he will put all the blame on the Committee. It is not long ago since he said 'they are not my plans but your committee's plans.' There should be a BC meeting which has not met since 26th January." [141]

The Last Meeting
There was to be one more meeting of the building committee, the 30th, on 28th January 1969. In the records it is mis-identified as the 28th meeting.

National Theatre in its final location next to Waterloo Bridge. First presentation model, 1967. Note the many differences to the final design

Meeting 30

30th Meeting of The National Theatre Building Committee

28th January 1969 [142]

Present:
Sir Laurence Olivier and Mr. Norman Marshall (in the Chair), Mr. Michael Benthall, Mr. John Dexter, Mr. Michael Elliott and the Secretary. Mr. Anthony Easterbrook, Mr. Coeks Gordon, Mr. Richard Pilbrow, Mr. Rupert Rhymes, Mr. Christian Simpson and Mr. Kenneth Tynan were in attendance. Mr. Denys Lasdun, Mr. Peter Softley and Mr. Harry Pugh were present by invitation.
Apologies:
Mr. Peter Brook, Mr. William Gaskill, Mr. Peter Hall and Miss Jocelyn Herbert.

Sir Laurence Olivier invited Mr. Lasdun to tell the committee about any modifications to the National Theatre since they had been made public in November 1967. Mr. Lasdun said the necessary modifications fell into two groups: those in the first group would have no effect on the theatres in terms of the auditoriums; but were primarily of concern to the South Bank Board and the Greater London Council.
They were:

1. The building of the car park beneath the whole area covered by the theatre instead of only under part of it. This would in no way affect those elements of the building costs which were the concern of the South Bank board.

2. The provision of space for a restaurant should funds be available for it.

The above modifications had, however, led to other alterations:

   Vehicle entrances had been modified.
   The restaurant space was now sited in the previous box office area.

The box office had been resited and replanned in conjunction with the Technical Sub-Committee.

The second group of modifications had been made as a result of a continuing dialogue between the architects and members of the Technical Sub-Committee.

They were:
1. Replanning of the workshop area so as to facilitate a production flow which would be in the correct sequence: Carpenters' shop to paint frame. These had been originally separated by the loading bay.

2. The introduction of mezzanine accommodation in the metal and property workshops. This was an improvement which might prove too expensive when tenders were received.

3. Alterations had been made in the dock area to the Proscenium Theatre and the scene dock for the Open Stage had been enlarged.

4. A proper VIP staircase had been introduced in the FOH. It could also be used by actors for entrances through the auditorium to the Open Stage.

Mr. Lasdun said that there had been most satisfactory consultations with the Greater London council over escape routes and fire regulations; with Mr. Richard Pilbrow over the lighting installations, and with the Catering Consultant over the equipping of the kitchen, the bars and the buffets.

There was no point in the Committee concerning itself with the overall costs at the present time. Tenders would be received in May at which time it might be necessary to discuss economies.

Sir Laurence asked whether any modifications had been made to the plans which would basically reduce the Committee's hopes for the efficient working of either auditorium. Mr. Lasdun reassured the Committee on this point. At the same time he referred to the credibility exercise which had been undertaken to bring the cost of the complex within the agreed sum of £7.5 million, allowing for possible rising costs over four years. As a result, the studio theatre would be unequipped though the space for it would remain. This, however, was public knowledge.

Mr. Softley then demonstrated on the plans the modifications outlined by Mr. Lasdun and pointed out certain other features including:

The FOH entrances, one at pedestrian level and one at car park level.

The two cloakrooms, one associated with each entrance.

The refreshment facilities for the public, ie. bars on two levels and buffet facilities on one level for each theatre.

The separation of box office into advance and performance.

The planning of the kitchen to serve the eventual restaurant and the staff canteen.

The Green Room located behind the canteen and easily accessible to the dressing rooms and the offices.

An improvement to the stage door area to give greater control of access to the building.

The provision of one good size recording studio.

The moving of the Mander and Mitchenson Collection[143] to the office area.

The provision of a projection room from the back of the Open Stage Theatre above the property store.

Mr. Elliott asked whether financial considerations had dictated any concessions on equipment for the theatres. Mr. Lasdun said there was little point in discussing this particular problem until the result of the tenders were available. When they were, it might be necessary for example to overhaul the present balance between audience comfort and equipping the theatres in a sophisticated way.

Mr. Pilbrow informed the Committee that he had revised his earlier opinion on the amount of stage equipment that should be provided for the new theatre. Quite a lot was now projected. It would in no way inhibit the traditional flexibility of English staging and 90% of it was intended primarily to facilitate working the repertory in the most economical way both as regards time and money. While the capital cost would be considerable, it would save a great deal of money in terms of stage staff wages.

Sir Laurence, on behalf of the committee, thanked Mr, Lasdun and Mr. Softley for their most interesting exposition of the plans.

Thus ended the final meeting of the National Theatre Building Committee.

DL&P final model of the National Theatre as it would be built, 1969

Testing the drum revolve outside the headquarters of Mole Richardson in Thetford, Norfolk before delivery to the National Theatre

2.4 Full Scenic Capability

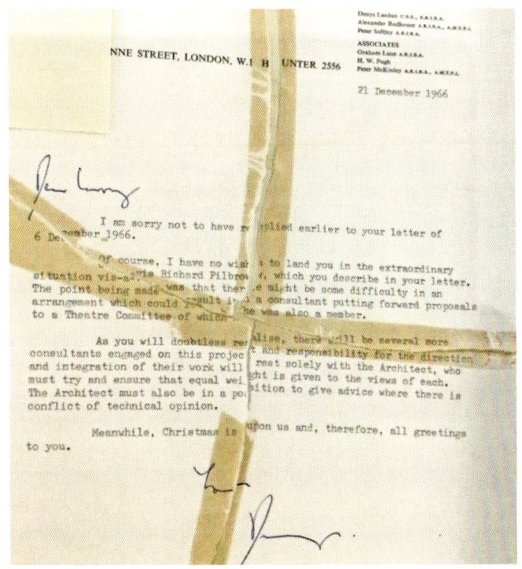

The discovered letter

In February 1967, Richard Pilbrow is asked by Olivier to become the National's technical theatre consultant. With Richard Brett, and in association with the NT staff, the design begins of the Olivier and Lyttelton stages and all their equipment: stage engineering, lighting, and sound, together with planning all the backstage areas with the architect.

It might be noted that the Anglo-British supersonic aircraft Concorde first flew in 1969 and entered service in 1976. These were heady technological times!

"I do remember meetings with Olivier. I remember how much he admired my green suit. I had a green suit with a slightly red line in it. And Larry thought it was absolutely marvellous. [Laughter] He said, 'Where'd you get that – that's a wonderful suit, dear boy.'" [144]
Richard Brett, 2008

In the summer of 2015, I was burrowing through the Olivier Archives in the British Library, when, much to my surprise, I came across a letter from Sir Laurence to Lasdun, dated 6th December 1966.

Sir Laurence: *"Dear Denys, I gather from Kenneth Rae that you have reservations about Richard Pilbrow's attendance at meetings once he is officially appointed as consultant by the South Bank Board. [Richard] is in fact on the staff of the National Theatre. He must, if he is to be any use to us, remain a member of the NT technical committee (which is composed entirely of NT personnel), and attend meetings of the full committee when Norman Marshall and I need him. I have taken Lord Cottesloe's advice on this matter and am assured that what I am suggesting is in no way out of order… he is an expert in several other fields and, as such, I do not wish to be deprived of his views whenever I need them. I feel a little as if, as Surgeon-in-Chief, I were on the Building Board of a Hospital and having presented my anesthetist as consultant concerning that branch of the works, was suddenly told he was not allowed to talk to me any more."* [145]

The apparent reason for this note was that Lasdun and Peter Softley had expressed concern to Kenneth Rae that if I was to become the architect's consultant but remain on the NT technical subcommittee, there would be difficulties. Lasdun on 21st December replied, "I have no wish to land you in the extraordinary situation vis-a-vis Richard Pilbrow. There might be some difficulty in an arrangement that could result

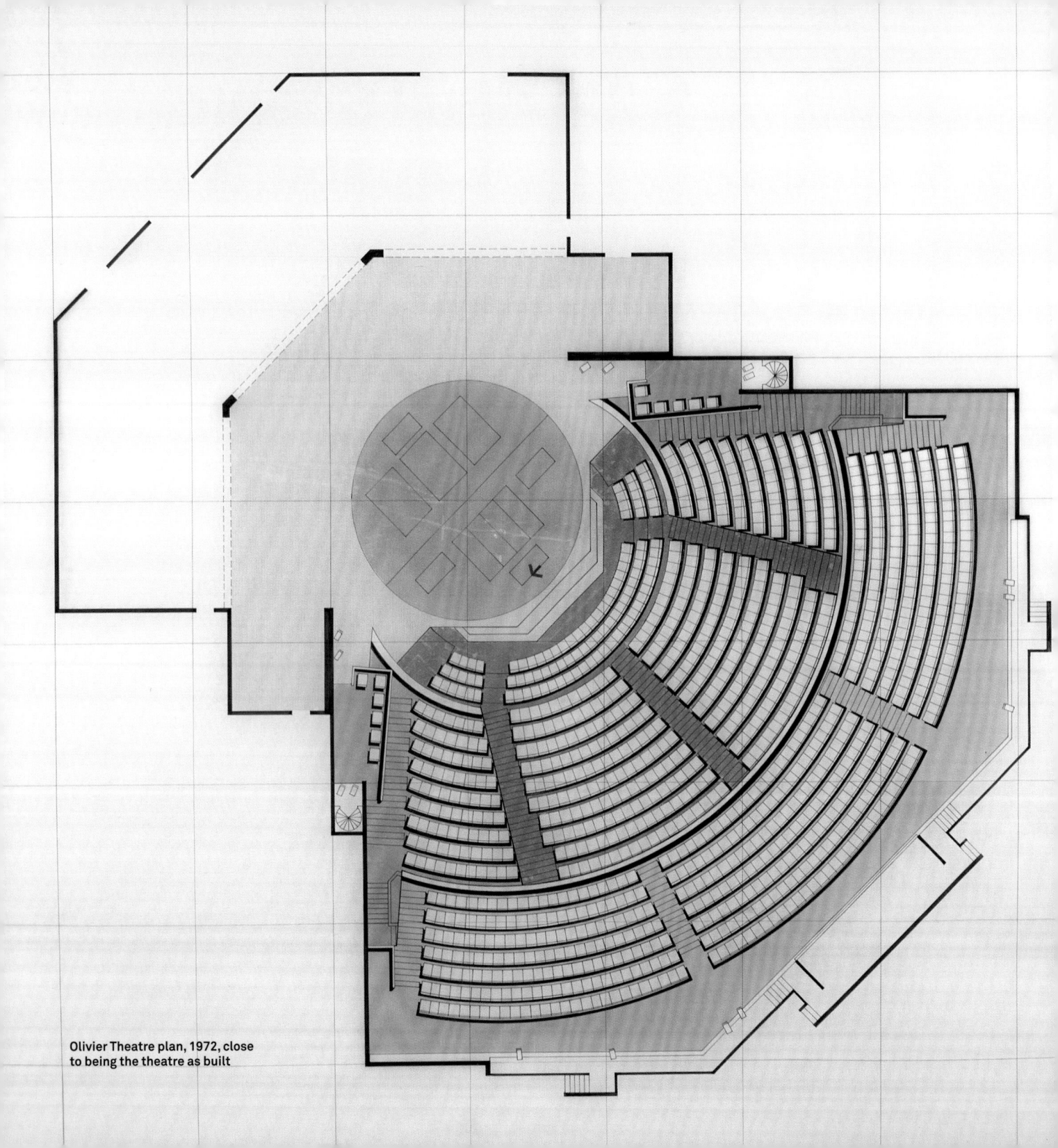

Olivier Theatre plan, 1972, close to being the theatre as built

The later model of the Olivier, 1969, as built complete with the side ashtray seating blocks, again with scenery by Jocelyn Herbert. Compare with p.181. Image © Robert Kirkman FSAI

"Dick, we're offered the National Theatre of Great Britain… now I can offer you a damn pension!"

Richard Pilbrow

in a consultant putting forward proposals to a committee of which he is also a member. There will be several more consultants and the responsibility for the direction and integration of their work will rest solely with the architect, who must try and ensure that equal weight is given to the views of each."[146] This note was at the bottom of the British Library file and is torn into four pieces by, I presume, Sir Laurence. Painstakingly stuck together (at the time, no doubt, by Peggy Gilson, Sir Laurence's ever-patient secretary), but the passing of time had withered the Sellotape into ineffectiveness.

I knew nothing about this controversy but, in February 1967, Sir Laurence called me into his office in Aquinas Street and asked me to become the 'theatre consultant'. He told me that Lasdun had asked that the National appoint an individual to liaise directly with the architects and his choice was to be me.

Sir Laurence asked about my work as theatre consultant on other projects, such as the Birmingham and Leatherhead Repertory Theatres, and I explained my role – trying to assist architects to understand the details of theatre. He asked whether I felt I could take on the NT. I told him that I needed twenty-four hours to consider it.

For some years, I had been concerned about my, and Theatre Projects', expertise in the building and engineering aspects of the theatre-consulting work we were doing. We knew about theatre, but we were very naive about the implications of what we were advising regarding the architecture, the building, and its systems.

I had met Richard (Dick) Brett when we were both schoolboys. I was a new member of the Beckenham Children's Theatre Centre. A group of boys were wiring up the control room of a theatre we were converting from an old church hall. I was 17. Dick was in charge… he was only 11! But, later, from Dulwich College he had gone on to university, studying electrical engineering. After graduating he became an apprentice with the British Broadcasting Corporation. This was during the massive expansion of the BBC's colour TV studios, and Dick had risen to become a senior engineer. We'd remained good friends and he had volunteered, in his spare time, to work with us building Theatre Projects' sound studios in our premises in Neal's Yard, Covent Garden. I was convinced that he was the ideal man to help us turn our advisory service to architects into a professional consultancy. He had always laughed at my offers: "Richard, I work at the BBC, I have a great pension, why would I move to your little firm?"

So now, from the public phone in Aquinas Street, I rang Dick: "We're offered the National Theatre of Great Britain… now I can offer you a damn pension!" [147]

He accepted. We expanded our existing lighting and sound activities and set up a new company, Theatre Projects Consultants. Richard became the first managing director.

Planning Begins

1966 and '67 were exciting times for me with the National. I was responsible for recommending all the lighting designers from the Theatre Projects team to the Old Vic, and for lighting several productions myself. In 1966, during the tensest moments with the building committee, I lit *The Storm*, designed by the genius Czech designer Josef Svoboda. Just weeks after my appointment as consultant, I lit *Rosencrantz and Guildenstern are Dead* with which Tom Stoppard burst upon the theatre scene – first at the Old Vic, then on Broadway at the Alvin Theatre. This was followed by a fabulous *Three Sisters*, another Svoboda design, directed by Sir Laurence, despite the onset of the first of his serious illnesses that pursued him intermittently until his death in 1989.

Each production meant attending rehearsals over several weeks, usually in the rehearsal room at Aquinas Street. Sir Laurence would have lunch most days in his office, of an apple, cheese and a glass of champagne, and I would sometimes drop in and chat with him. Then three weekends of technical dress rehearsals at the Old Vic before opening would follow. Under Sir Laurence, the company at the Vic was family… between dress rehearsals we would eat in the staff canteen or, perhaps more likely, drink in the pub that was conveniently right alongside the stage door on Waterloo Road. The electrics crew in particular, led by Lenny Tucker, with Ronnie Cox, Peter Radmore, Alan Jacobi, Brian Ridley and others, became our close friends.

Dick Brett and I, in close consultation with technical heads, Coeks Gordon and Neville Thompson, stage manager Diana Boddington and general manager, George Rowbottom, began exploring the meaning of Sir Laurence's brief of "full scenic capability."

We set off on a voyage of discovery, designing technical installations that were, for their time, beyond anything ever seen before on the English stage. Indeed some of these innovations set standards that are still hardly matched even today.

The Preliminary Report

I'll start this story of what came next, by quoting my friend Dick Brett:

"I began by drafting our National Theatre Preliminary Report on Proposed Stage Equipment, Lighting, and Sound.[148] It is still a remarkably good document. It begins by listing the influence of key individuals who had worked with the National since its beginnings in 1963: directors Sir Tyrone Guthrie, Franco Zeffirelli, Jacques Charon, John Dexter, William Gaskill; designers Josef Svoboda, Lila de Nobili, Sean Kenny, Tanya Moiseiwitsch, and Sir Laurence himself."

"The three theatres were to work in repertoire – out of 10 to 30 productions that might be available, each theatre should be able to perform every week up to five or eight different productions. This was common practice in opera but unknown in British drama. Everything – scenery, costumes, hair, props, lighting, and sound – must be able to be changed, over two or three times a day, rehearsal to performance, matinee to evening, throughout the year."

The report that Dick and I prepared stated, "It has long been traditional in English theatre that the artist should be suspicious of an excess of technology in the theatre." I certainly held that view. In the West End, every production brought all its own stagecraft needs with it into the theatre. But the more Dick and I examined the challenge of 'rep,' the more impossible that appeared. So, ultimately, our report observed that stage equipment may be required for two reasons:

"To allow the director/designer to design elaborate visual effects or scene changes within a single production, or

To allow rapid and efficient changeover between productions."

The paramount need for the latter drove us toward what was, at the time, a very un-British solution: stage mechanisation.

The report also listed three levels of potential cost: Scales A, B, and C. Scale A offers a level of equipment necessary as a minimum for the theatres (a degree of mechanisation for the open stage theatre, manual operation for the proscenium and minimum for the studio). Scale B adds mechanisation to the proscenium theatre with added facilities throughout, and Scale C adds full facilities to the studio theatre. Needless to say, the minimum Scale A was chosen by our masters… and then further reductions were made over time. Some elements were restored much later in the 1972 budget improvements.

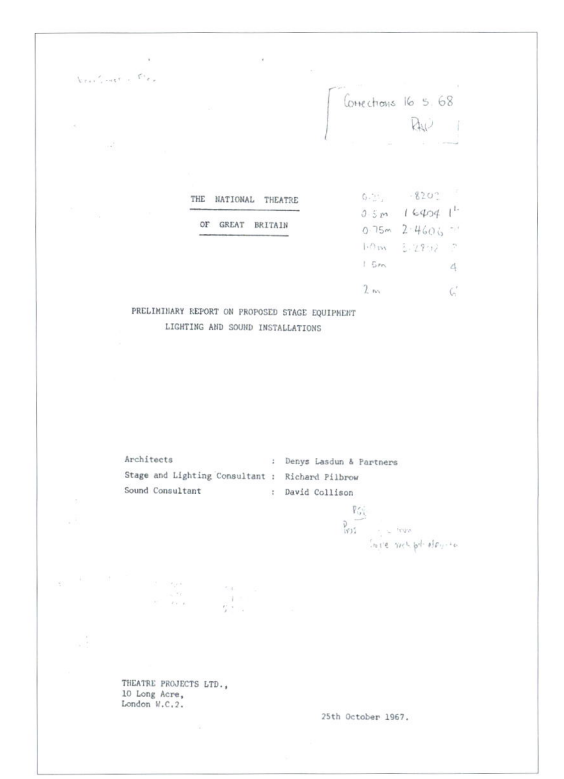

Preliminary Report on Proposed Stage Equipment, Lighting and Sound, October, 1967

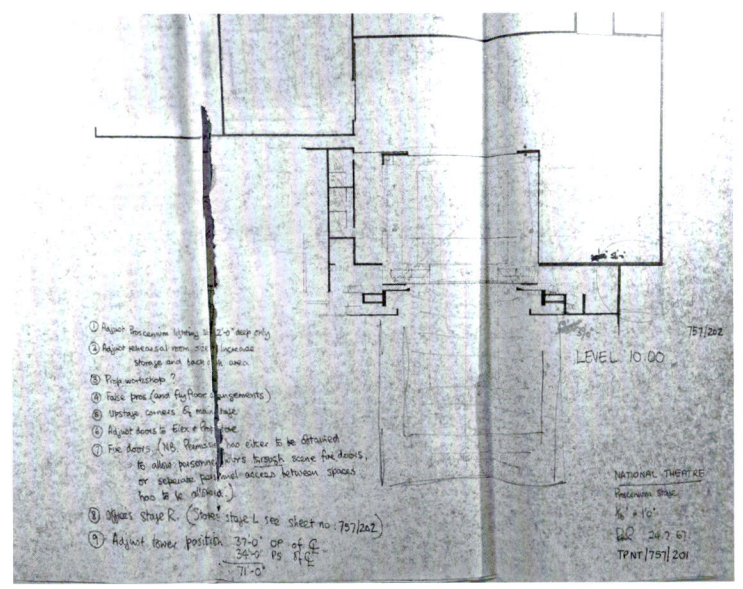

My first Lyttelton sketch, 1967

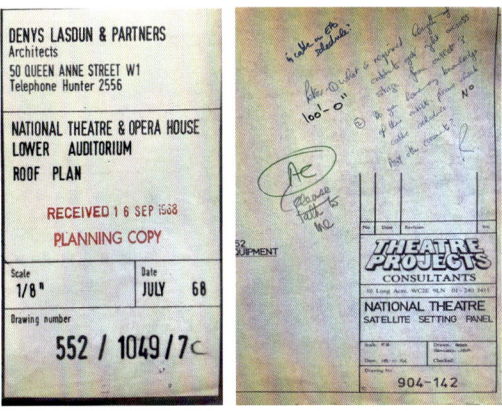

Plans and notes; note one drawing still carrying the name of the by then abandoned Opera House!

2.4 Full Scenic Capability

Lower Theatre: The Proscenium Theatre – The Lyttelton
The proscenium theatre was at workshop (and ground) level. It was to have a main stage supported by side and rear stages, each separated by sound and fireproof doors. A main stage elevator would allow full-stage wagons from the rear or side stages to be sunk flush into the floor onstage. This layout, unique in Britain, was commonplace in Germany and indeed was directly inspired by our experience with *Love for Love* at the Freie Volksbühne in Berlin.[149]

Sir Laurence was particularly concerned about minimising the gap at the front of the stage between audience and actor. The front rows of the auditorium he imagined as 'ripple' seats – low-cost seats for young people and students – to bring energy to the front of the theatre. We struggled with getting the actor as far downstage as possible. We first decided that any potential orchestra pit would be part of the stage itself. Three elevators across the stage front could either form a pit of variable size, a forestage, or be part of the main stage. The fire curtain would be placed on the very edge of the stage. The GLC fire authorities were worried about a potential 'guillotine' danger for the front row of the audience, should they lean forward while the curtain lowered. To overcome their objections, we suggested that the curtain would be in two parts: the lower would rise from below the stage, presumably pushing away any surprised member of the audience, while the top would lower from above, meeting in the middle. A happy consequence of this innovation was that, when open, the height of the bottom section was variable. The entire stage could be raised or lowered, in conjunction with the stage elevators behind, effectively allowing the removal of the stage riser completely or allowing it to be reshaped in any way.

The proscenium was to be quite variable. Its maximum width was to just exceed that of the very front of the then-current Old Vic forestage. (It was anticipated that early shows might transfer from the Vic). But the apparent width and height could be varied to iris in, or open out, the stage opening. Finally, the whole proscenium structure could roll up-and-downstage to provide an optional and variable depth of forestage. If the width of the opening were to be narrowed, the proscenium should be rolled upstage to lessen the negative impact on the side front sightlines.

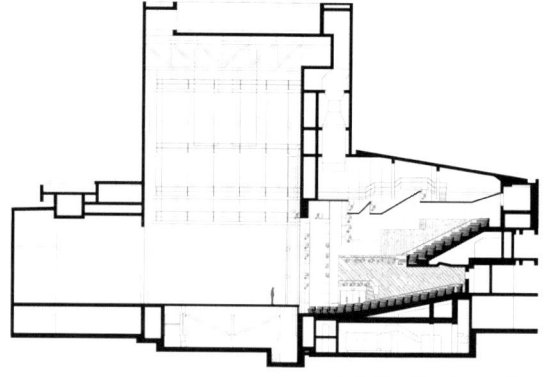

Lyttelton Theatre section

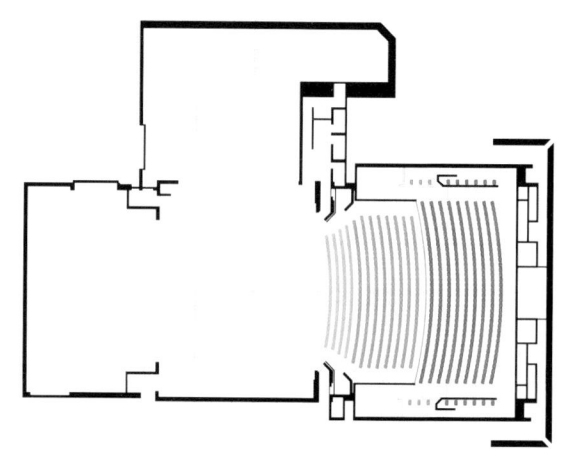

Lyttelton Theatre plan

Main stage scenery suspensions were to be power-operated counter-weights crossstage and side masking pipes with some additional motorised spot lines. Lighting would be short lighting pipes able to be rolled up and downstage between the lines suspending the scenery to wherever they might be required.

The stage floor was to be entirely trapped and most of the subframe removable. The floor could be adjusted in height and raked (angled), together with its subfloor below. A rear stage wagon would contain a revolve that could be set on stage.

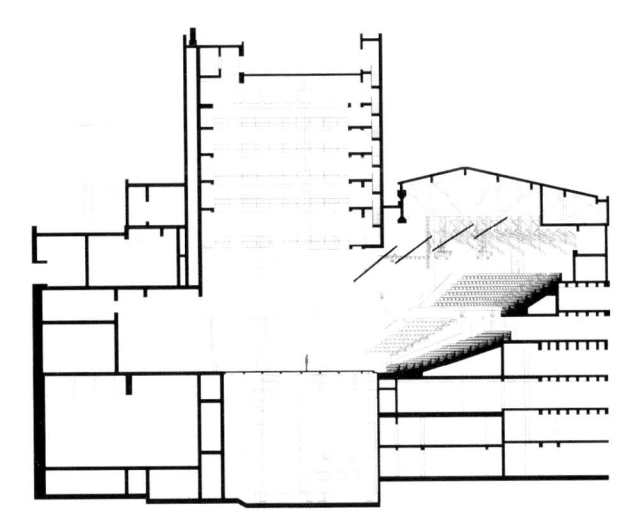

Olivier Theatre section

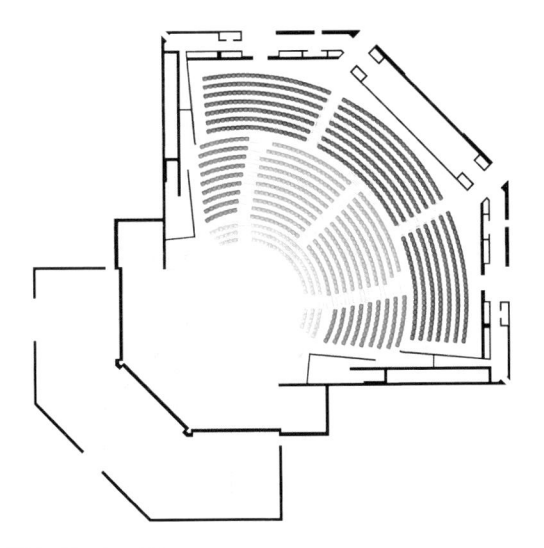

Olivier Theatre plan

Upper Theatre: The Open Stage Theatre – The Olivier

The open stage theatre presented a unique series of challenges. It was to be a modified thrust stage, partially surrounded by audience, backed by a 'space stage' – the whole with (in Sir Laurence's phrase) "full scenic possibilities." It was to allow the impression that while an actor on the thrust was seen to be within the audience's space, he or she could also appear outside the room, remote and far away. This theatre would present unequaled and quite new opportunities to the director. The building committee had been presented with a list of questions about options for staging capability in this space. It was for Dick and me, in close collaboration with key National Theatre staff, to develop specific solutions.

The stage was an eccentric hexagonal shape – the shape I had drawn for Olivier many months before. To the front was the semi-thrust, surrounded by 120 degrees of audience, with the space stage behind. Assuming a cyclorama at the very rear of the stage, this had to be sufficiently wide (120 feet, 36.5m) to enable the stage to be masked from the furthest side seats. Behind the stage were to be rear stages separated by sound – and fire – proof doors, then beyond the rear stages, a scene storage area.

Scenery on such a stage, partially surrounded by spectators, might be of any shape and be hung at any angle. It seemed to require a unique flying solution. Overhead, a 29.4m (96'6") high grid would contain 140 adjustable spot line hooks. Each was to be motor-driven and set in tracks running across the stage beneath the grid. As each hook was double-purchase, an operator could simply slide a hook from left to right anywhere across the stage. Any hook could then be electronically locked to any other hook to lift complex three-dimensional scenic objects.

This was very new thinking in 1967. Power flying then was generally deemed unreliable and dangerous. This installation had to present a new paradigm. The system had to be:

1. Silent
2. Capable of considerable speed variation
3. Able to proportionally accelerate and decelerate
4. Stop accurately at predetermined heights
5. Be absolutely reliable and safe

The use of double-purchase spot lines on sliding pulley blocks was an idea of Dick's from his work at the BBC. Here, though, we had to cope with a vastly greater height to the grid and the added need for total silence, accuracy and safety.

We carried out many experiments with the best flymen on the Old Vic staff. How fast could a human operator move a piece of scenery; how accurately could they stop it? Our new system had to surpass such standards and be absolutely fail-safe. In 1967, computers were still in their very early days. A computer controlling a light's intensity presented one challenge; a computer controlling a crane suspending scenery over live actors' heads demanded a quantum leap forward in safety and reliability.

A quite separate challenge was the nature of the floor: we wanted to be able to create traps anywhere. But with the audience partially surrounding the stage, at what angle should these traps be placed? And how to allow "full scenic possibility"? On a thrust stage, many of the audience are looking down toward the stage; how could the stage floor itself be changed? This was an open stage – there was no house curtain to hide any scene changes from view. How was scenery to be changed? The thrust was set within a wider space stage. How were actors to make entrances without walking long distances from the distant wings?

Dick and I wrestled with these conundrums. We began to think that some form of revolving stage – a drum revolving stage, perhaps like the famous example in the Burgtheater in Vienna – might be the answer. With it, scenes could be brought into view facing the audience, or turned away. Within the revolve, a trapped stage floor could be set at any angle. Furthermore, if the drum contained elevators – as in the Burgtheater – then half the stage could be lowered to the basement, perhaps carrying a scenic floor, scenery, or simply furniture, and then be replaced with a different setting from below.

Everything stemmed from the fact that Sir Laurence, in that private meeting with Michael Elliott and me, had come down firmly for the principle of a stage "in the audience's space, backed by infinity." But then, we wondered, how do you change

Theta–drum diagrams

Author and Richard Brett with a model of the drum revolve

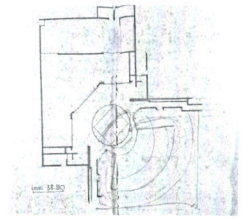

My first Olivier sketch, 1967

scenery in a wide open space? You can bring it down from above, or you can come up from underneath.

To Dick Brett again:[150]
"During the autumn of '67 we did a tour of many theatres in Europe. We went to Vienna, to Mannheim, to Gelsenkirchen, Innsbruck, Stuttgart, Munich. We went to Vienna to look at the Burgtheater drum revolve, a massive revolving structure that contained four rectangular elevators, and to meet Waagner-Biro, the stage engineering company that had built it.

"We were sitting in an open-air restaurant. I took a napkin and drew a circle and then put a line through it. We called it the 'theta drum.' We had been concerned that the area of rectangular elevators within a revolving stage would be too small in our thrust stage. Semi-circular elevators would encompass a larger proportion of the thrust stage. I had the idea that the drum should be like a tin can with the elevators inside. Only the elevators came up to stage level. The tin was hidden. That sounds so simple and so obvious now."

The Olivier Theatre was on an upper floor of the building. All scenery had to be transported from the ground-floor workshop level three stories below. While we planned a large goods lift in the scenery store offstage, our drum could bring full-height scenery from below directly into the middle of the stage. The more we thought about the theta drum concept, the more we liked it. Scenery and actors could come from below. A scenic floor, traps or the elevators themselves could be set at any angle. The front-half elevator of the drum could be set at a lowered level, which would effectively remove the thrust stage shape completely. Just as the proscenium theatre's stage edge could be removed or reshaped, so too could the Olivier's thrust shape tailor to the needs of the designer.

Finally, there was the issue of staging dynamics. This was to be a theatre like no other. We envisaged the flying system allowing scenery, objects, or even people to be moved vertically and horizontally through the stage space. The entire floor could rotate, rise, and sink from view; whole settings could rise from below and spin around to replace the one on stage. Might this create a potential for dynamic staging not seen since the 18th century Baroque theatre?

We met with the top manufacturers of stage machinery in the UK and Europe. The truth was that English manufacturers were used to building equipment for shows, but would be challenged by the need for permanently installed sophisticated equipment that would have to operate reliably for many years.

I remember a heavyset group of engineers from East Germany, led by an interesting man, Klaus Wever. Klaus, a theatre consultant originally from West Germany, had surprisingly crossed over the Berlin Wall to the East, because of his growing dislike of what he saw as resurgent Nazism in the West – an interesting journey in 1967. Klaus' sales director was in my office in Goodwin's Court. I said, "We certainly can't afford equipment from Germany." He said, "Oh, Mr. Pilbrow, Ve have ways to make zat work." I asked what he meant. He said, "Ve vill adjust ze rate of exchange!" Dick and I laughed. The German group, of course, was very serious.[151]

Speaking of serious, back to Dick:
"Then we went out to bid for the equipment for the National. All the Europeans were far too expensive on the drum revolve stage, so it went to Mole-Richardson, which, with Hall Stage Equipment, was one of the two major stage engineering companies in the UK.

"Waagner-Biro was very supportive and they had made us a little model with blue and red elevators and a green half-disc on top. This colour-coding continued into the real thing. Waagner-Biro bid £250,000. The figures we got from Hall Stage and Mole Richardson were much cheaper and they were British. With some misgiving on our part about having to accept the lowest bid, Mole-Richardson got the drum at, I think, a price of £120,000, in around 1971." [Approximately £1.9 million 2022.]

Of course, having the idea is one thing. Building it, quite another!

Concept to Design
After many months mentally wrestling with the problems of these unusual stages, frequent conversations with NT staff, with whom we were working at the Old Vic, and research into what might be our best course of action, Dick and I faced one overriding challenge: this was to be the National Theatre. A theatre for which Britain had been waiting for over a hundred years. It seemed to cry out for the highest quality stages to allow the most ambitious scenography. And as Dick Brett notes that ambition extended to every part of the theatre, visible on-stage and hidden behind it: "The underlying thing throughout all the National was we were creating some amazing innovations – lighting, sound and communications. It wasn't just the drum revolve or flying."

The Olivier:
Cycloconverters and Computers
The design began with the concept that the lifting hoists – a considerable number – were designed to be as simple and cheap as possible, so that the limited funds available could be spent on improved control and drives.

Dick Brett came up with a sophisticated control system that employed computers to control not conventional, expensive DC electric motors, but instead cycloconverters. These control AC motors by changing the frequency of the current. They were not experimental in themselves but had not been used in a theatrical context before. Prototype cycloconverters proved to be very controllable and offered better than 100:1 speed range. With the lifting motors only ever running at a maximum of 500 revolutions/minute, their high-frequency noise was reduced. The cycloconverter also gave full motor torque at standstill, allowing the winding drum to be driven directly by the motor without a gearbox, also helping to reduce noise. The same techniques would be used in the multiple motors driving the drum.

This was all driving the art of stage engineering forward. It was one of the earliest uses of the computer in theatre, with a DEC PCP-11/35 minicomputer plus supporting electronics, much of it custom-made. It was a highly ambitious scheme. This was why, from the outset, Dick and I had stipulated that not less than six months would be required after the completion of the installations to program the computers and cycloconverters, and to train the staff who were to work the stages. That time would ultimately be squeezed down to nothing between the ever-lengthening build and Peter Hall's decision that the only way to get the building open would be to just move in and start using it, ready or not.

Scenery Flying

The flying installation would consist of 127 double purchase hooks hung from tracks running across below the grid and 20 direct lift winches. The full specification required that up to 35 hoists be able to operate together – individually or in groups – at a maximum speed of 2m/sec (nearly 400 ft/min) each carrying a maximum load of 200kg (440lb). Individual deads (stopping heights) would be recorded by moving the hoist to the required position and pressing a button to record that position. This position must be repeated to an accuracy of better than 5mm (quarter of an inch, or one part in 5000). The system would be fully protected against position or velocity errors, overload or slack-wire conditions by monitoring the motion of each hoist every 150ms. Finally, there was to be no manual

Olivier – flying control

Olivier – Grid with lighting windlasses

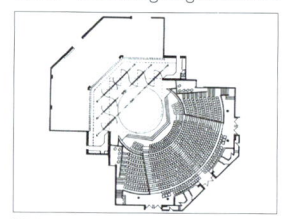

Olivier proposed masking screens

patching of power feeds; the selection of any one of the 150 hoists was to be from a numeric keyboard at the control desk.

Masking Screens

In order to allow the ability to contain the large space stage space that surrounded the thrust, a series of six masking screens were planned. These would fly vertically, track across the stage, and be able to rotate to present an alternate surface. Unfortunately they were lost to cost-cutting. This omission undoubtedly added to the later acoustic problems of the space.

The Richard Brett Theta Drum Revolve

The mechanical concept seemed clear: a 15m diameter, four story tall revolving drum containing two semi-circular elevators and a semi-circular disk that rotated independently on top of the drum. Each elevator was double-decked; the surface was trapped and the substage provided actor access through those traps. The disk also contained traps and the elevator below the disk might be used as an understage level or to drive objects up through the disk. Access for performers was provided through doors and adjustable stairs to the understage level. The drum might be positioned at any angle to the audience and to the access for actors and scenery (at the workshop scenic road level below). The bottom of the drum contained two scissor lifts to provide access to either lowered elevator, irrespective of the drum's angle, from the workshop-level scenic roadway. And of course this could potentially all have stage crew and performers inside it.

The outer drum revolve and the inner split-ring had to synchronise exactly. The split-stages had to lock into position on the drum revolve when they were in the right place, and the drum revolve had to have the capacity to turn very slowly or very quickly, according to the demands of the production. The drum revolve was driven by a number of electric motors attached to wheels on its base, and since no two electric motors functioned identically, it was necessary to compensate for the fractional variations that might occur if one motor was going faster than another.

This is where the computer and cycloconverter system came in. The control computer for the revolve had to be programmed to cover every desirable merry-go-round revolution, from one taking hours to one of a few seconds which might have thrown the actors, giddy and reeling, off-balance, if not offstage. Clearly, safety was of enormous importance and every point of access to the potentially moving drum was tightly controlled, with all the doors alarmed and able to be remotely locked. The operator, positioned on a gallery off-stage right, had a clear view of the drum surface, with video surveillance of the areas inside and around the sub-stage areas of the drum.

The aim was that the two computers, the one for the drum and the one for the flying, could be linked together, so that flown and revolving or rising scenery could be sychronised into a kind of aerial ballet as the different parts of the overall set arrived smoothly in place. It is scarcely surprising to learn that the firm that developed and built the control system, Evershed Power Optics, also specialised in parts of guided missiles.

However, Evershed could not begin to test and programme its control system until every other item of equipment had been properly installed and was functioning correctly. The space in which the drum sat had to be complete... and dry! Water leakage was a problem in the deep basement below the drum. As importantly, the wiring of the installation had to be completed and the control spaces had to be completed, painted, cleaned and air-conditioned before the computers could be installed. This meeting of the building trades, the theatre world and advanced technology presented quite new challenges to all involved.

Lighting in Repertoire and Lightboard
Here was my ultimate personal challenge in my career to date: to design a lighting installation for the new National Theatre. Lighting that could meet the highest international standards for three-dimensional stage lighting... and change over in repertoire from show to show in less than one hour.

Firstly, a layout of equipment – a 'saturation rig' – able to light multiple shows in rep while minimising changeover times and without compromising the quality of the lighting for each show. Comprehensive lighting angles from the auditorium – five lighting bridges, four 'stalactites' (vertical enclosed lighting ladders hung from the ceiling to extend the lighting bridges sideways) and side wall box-boom positions in the Olivier; motorised overhead pipes with winding windlasses to automatically take up cables, and adjustable side-lighting ladders in the Lyttelton. For the '70s, a large number of dimmers (640 in the Olivier, 470 in the Lyttelton) to remove the need to replug lanterns in the changeovers between shows. And a new lighting control system named Lightboard. Dick Brett and I conceived the design in 1969 and Strand Lighting, under chief engineer Martin Moore and a brilliant team, won the contract to engineer and build it. Strand had been Britain's pre-eminent stage lighting manufacturer, but in moving from manual to computer control had somewhat lost their way. Lightboard did much to restore their reputation.

Lightboard could control up to 1000 channels of lights, and supported a multiplexed control highway throughout the theatre for remote control of instruments (pan, tilt, and focus), colour change, and random access projector slide-change and focus. When Lightboard was conceived, the computer had already made possible the memorisation of lighting pictures and the ability to add, subtract, or crossfade from one lighting state to another. Our new system sought to add to this, becoming a 'playable' control to allow multiple lighting states to change and move at different speeds simultaneously. Also, no longer was it necessary to think in terms of single channels for control. Lights could be selected and manipulated by keyboard, singly or with equal access in blocks of light or groups; mixed, interwoven, and freely balanced via multiple control wheels on a 'Lighting Palette' just as a painter mixes their paints. One section of Lightboard was portable and could be used anywhere in the theatre during rehearsals; another allowed any channel to be routed through a sound-to-light device for automatic flashing, synchronised to sound or random modulation. VDU screens showed the status of everything.

I'm going to turn to my friend, lighting designer and programmer, Rob Halliday, to tell the story of Lightboard's development and set its technology in the context of today's electronic devices.

"The specification was issued. Rank Strand, in part, one suspects, trying to reclaim the high ground stolen by Thorn with their succesful Q-File system, accepted it. And then their team of engineers started figuring out how to actually build it.

"It was quite a team. Their leader, chief engineer Martin Moore, had worked backstage at college and later in the West End, running the consoles to replay Richard's design for the musical *Blitz!*, among others, but had also spent time looking after the CDC6600 supercomputers secreted away on Polaris submarines. The people he hired were recent physics or engineering graduates but also lighting designers or console operators for amateur companies, sometimes moonlighting in the West End. They understood theatre, but had the engineering background to apply to solving the problems theatre presented. By the time of the National, that team included David Bertenshaw, Tony Brown, Rick Dines, Vic Gibbs, John Hall, Edwin Lockwood, Tony Payne, John Wright and others.

"Their first problem: how to make a console that could cope with the sheer scale of the National. A Digital PDP-11/05 ran Strand's DDM console built for the Royal Shakespeare Company in Stratford-upon-Avon and installed in 1971; it could control a maximum of 240 channels. The newer, more powerful PDP-11/35 was looking like a good bet for Lightboard (the same computer would go on to run the entire British Air Traffic Control System for many years). However, calculations suggested even that wouldn't cope. For 1000 channels, each channel needed to be refreshed in less than 30 milliseconds for fades to appear

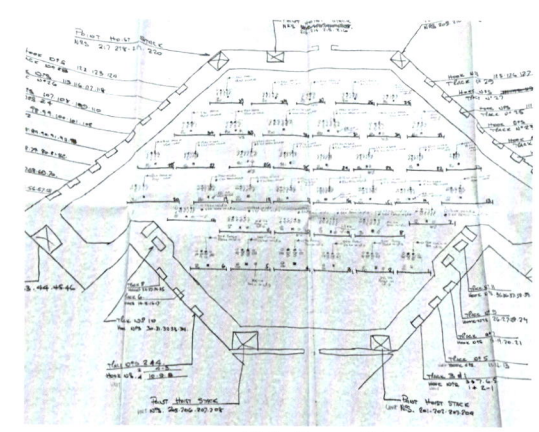

Olivier Theatre lighting outlet layout

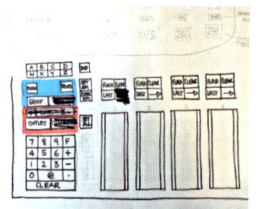

Lightboard – first sketch

Lightboard

step-free; that was also a good timescale for scanning all of the buttons on the console so as to not miss any key pushes.

"Around that, the computer would also have to update the twin displays and the backlights on the keys used to indicate key status, and deal with the stalls control and its display. Plus, there was the complication of those multiple – up to six – overlapping fades with their own times. The 11/35 couldn't do the maths fast enough (just for comparison, it had a processor operating at about 1Mhz, and 64kB of memory whereas a 2023-era iPhone has 512GB of memory and a 3.8GHz processor. And that iPhone cost about $1200; the PDP-11 was about $30,000 in 1973, so perhaps $200,000 now).

"Strand's solution: they designed their own co-processor just to handle the channel processing. A 16-bit hardware processor implemented in Schottky TTL logic, it was power-hungry but fast – a heady 6MHz!

"Software development meant more investment for Strand, replacing the paper-tape systems used to develop DDM with a fanfold paper-tape reader and then, ultimately, with a Plessey disk cartridge, and also purchasing DEC's RT11 operating system. But they didn't want to spend too much, so the development 11/35 was actually one of the two machines that would eventually go to the National. The software was written in DEC assembler code to maximise its running speed; eight man-years of coding, but the final software occupying just 90kB of storage. By contrast, the operating system in that 2023 iPhone occupies about 2.2GB.

"The National Theatre Lightboard did also include a controller for automated moving lights, through a seperate 'PTF' (pan-tilt-focus) control panel. The 1976 installation could only afford to buy twenty remotely-controlled Fresnel spotlights (unheard of at the time in Britain) from the Austrian company Pani, but the systems proved a huge success. A Mark II Lightboard (with colour monitors and more submasters) was later installed in the Royal Opera House, the Deutsche Oper Berlin, the Burgtheater Vienna, the Hamburg Opera and elsewhere." [152]

Lightboard represented a breakthrough. Technologically, however, expensive minicomputers would soon give way to the far more economical microprocessor – the National, particularly on its original schedule, came just too early for this important technological revolution. My Canadian friend Wally Russell, then head of Strand Lighting in the US, called me to ask if he might use the phrase I'd coined, 'Light Palette,' to title a new microprocessor-based control he was building in America. This Light Palette, along with Strand's next British control, Galaxy, took many of the principles Lightboard had established. Indeed, these principles still influence stage lighting control system design today, although the palette's ability to fluidly and simultaneously balance multiple lighting patterns that was achieved with Lightboard sadly seems to have been lost along the way.

More modest lighting innovations pioneered at the National included the centralised control of the functional lighting (working, rehearsal, cleaners and maintained emergency lighting throughout the stage areas). No longer did rehearsals have to wait for people all over the theatre to manually switch off the lights; everything was centrally mastered under the stage manager's control. Also, CCT Lighting manufactured a special version of their Silhouette 1kW zoom profile spotlight. This had a removable gate shutter assembly. It allowed an instrument's shutters to be set to the shape required for one show, then locked. The whole gate could then be removed and used only for that particular show when it returned to the repertoire rather than having to manually readjust the shutters each time. Another time-saver.

Sound and Communications
My partner in Theatre Projects Sound, David Collison, had better tell this story:
"The mixing consoles for the two main auditoria had to be specified – as often happens with large public buildings – some eight years before the equipment was to be installed. One could only guess what technical developments might occur in the meantime and make assumptions. At the time, British theatres did not have sound control rooms, did not employ sound technicians, and mixing desks were a thing of the future.

"When the South Bank Board saw our original budget for mixing consoles, they were horrified. We pointed out that these were based on recording studio mixers (hand-wired in those days before the use of printed circuit boards) with the addition of complicated loudspeaker switching for theatre use. One incensed committee member blurted out, 'This is nonsense. The National Theatre will not be putting on musicals!' Another demanded: 'So why on earth do we need a studio-quality mixer with hundreds of knobs in order to play a baby-crying effect?' Would the audience be able to tell?

"The argument was only won after they were shown pictures of current installations in German theatres and reminded that it was our job to ensure that the flagship theatre of Great Britain was equipped with the latest technology.

"However, my proposal for a recording studio within the complex was turned down on the grounds that recorded music in theatrical productions was prohibited by the Musicians' Union. I pointed out that if music was required for a production, it would be possible to have musicians playing live and piped through to the stage via the control room. More importantly, the sound department (for there would have to be one) would need a soundproof space to record voices and special effects. Some time later, the architect agreed to include about half the space requested as an unfinished storage area, possibly to be converted into a studio at some future date.

"In 1999, twenty-seven years after the theatre opened, the technical manager of sound, Rob Barnard, was given a budget to convert the store room into a studio. At last, the empty cableways to the theatre control rooms we had specified all those years before came into their own.

"The stage communications ring intercom, unprecedented at the time, allowed substations to listen to a mix of the stage manager channel and any one of three other technical channels selected by a rotary switch. Each substation had a two-position switch to connect the microphone either to the stage manager or to the technical channel. The stage manager and the production desk (placed in the auditorium for rehearsals) were able to monitor all the channels and, for cueing purposes or emergencies, the stage manager had a master button to 'crash call' the entire system. There was also a provision for connecting a radio transmitter to any of the channels so that roving technicians could receive instructions via portable receivers." [153]

The other innovation that Dick Brett brought from the BBC was what he called "general facilities panels" (GFPs). Having been appalled by the hotchpotch of electrical boxes of all shapes and sizes attached to conduits and trunking (cableways) cluttering the walls of the prompt corners and running around the stages of existing theatres, he wanted to do something about it. First attempts met with resistance because while electrical contractors installed general lighting and power requirements, sound equipment suppliers liked to be in charge of their own wiring. If the communications or cue light systems came from different companies, yet more electrical installers could be involved. This was a minefield – but with an electrical consultant on staff within Theatre Projects, it proved possible to specify all the electrical work and put it out to bid for a single contract. It was then feasible to install general facilities panels that

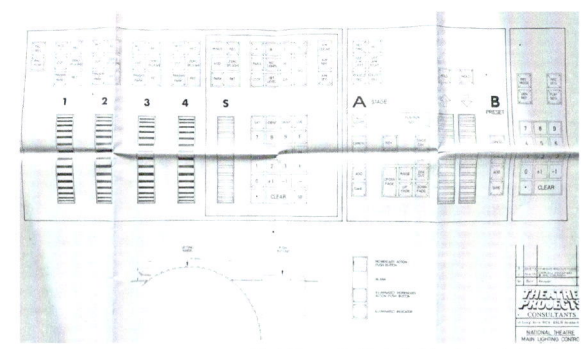

Lightboard's 'Palette': technical drawing

General facility panel   Lyttelton Theatre sound console

brought together what could be six or eight services into one box. Consequently, microphone sockets, loudspeaker outlets, plug-in points for video cameras and monitors, technical power points and cuelights were specified as needed around the stage and neatly incorporated into the general facility panels. These were placed at strategic points around the stage and technical areas. "Limited facilities panels" (LFPs) were sited where only some of the services, e.g., cue lights or loudspeaker outlets, were required. This was an innovation that soon became widely accepted in the British theatre.

These were our plans for realising Sir Laurence's brief for the theatres. Coming to these plans took many months of investigation and design. Today, there are over a hundred boxes of papers of working details from TPC residing in the NT Archives.

But of course, it all needed the backing of those who would ultimately pay for it all, to become reality.

Getting Involved... Politics 1968
A note from Kenneth Rae to Sir Laurence:
> "Pilbrow has cold feet attending the Building Committee if Lasdun is not there. His problem is that he now is a paid Consultant to Lasdun. He will think about it over the weekend and ring me back.

> "The procedure he suggests in his last para [below] is exactly what I hope the building committee decides on the 26th. I suggest that, as soon as possible after L.O.'s return, we ask Dickie to come in and plan our strategy." [154]

Richard Pilbrow to Sir Laurence, 26th January 1968
> "Dear Sir Laurence,

> "Building Committee.
> I'm very pleased to see that there will be a building committee meeting to discuss the whole project, and I would just like to say that I would most urgently like to be in at any meeting. I believe, of course, that officially I have resigned.

> "I suppose I am in a position to explain all the theatrical aspects of the stages as clearly as anyone, and there are some things in our work that I would like the members' opinion on. Incidentally, I would very much welcome an opportunity to go through the whole thing with you, at your earliest convenience.

> "I enclose a copy of the report on the stage equipment, which is slightly more detailed than that in the Lasdun report, which may be of interest to you, or perhaps to Frank [Dunlop]. I also hope that as soon as possible we can start subcommittee meetings, and perhaps discussions with the heads of departments at the Old Vic. It would surely be a very good idea from both the point of view of their practical contribution and morale, to involve everybody as soon as possible.

> "Yours,
> Richard Pilbrow" [155]

The Building Committee's Demise
It's interesting in hindsight that the building committee never did meet again, so never did get briefed on any of our technical plans for the stages. However, the National as an organisation was supportive of our plans.

National Support
In January 1969 Tony Easterbrook, the NT general manager, wrote to Sir Laurence:
> "Memorandum re. level of performance equipment in Olivier Theatre.

> "It is in the nature of this kind of stage that, up to now, scenery has become much reduced because of the difficulty of changing it during the performance. Scenic elements are often either dropped in from the grid or brought from up-stage on trucks. If a grid is to be used (as has been planned) then it seems foolish to restrict such a grid to a proscenium-type grid having its greatest justification when used with objects presented square on to the grid. The grid devised for this stage is inevitably more complex in order to cope with repertory working, but even so is considerably less advanced in design and potential than many such installations found in up-to-date TV studios. We would be very unhappy if economies modified this grid.

> "If the stage is to have on it large scenic elements, then it seems advantageous to install a drum revolve mechanism which will operate large scenic changes mechanically and without necessarily halting the action on stage. Such a drum was proposed by the consultants.

> "Later thinking along these lines has produced a development of the drum which has been called the 'Theta Drum.' Its development is considerably dearer than the drum listed in the consultants original report. Nevertheless it appears that this Theta Drum is the most satisfactory form in that it is the most flexible and capable of handling the most complex types of scene changes.

> "We believe that such a drum together with the grid proposed could make this stage one of the most advanced in the world.

> "I should outline the main changes in the last 12-18 months: Workshop has acceptable limitations. Storage however is inadequate. Foyers: We feel slightly in awe of the architect

here – almost as though we should not express our views about the spaces in which our public live. We are made to feel, perhaps correctly, that the subject of interior decor is the architect's sole prerogative. Proscenium theatre: Development of the proscenium opening. Curve of seating rows is improved. Acting area elevator has been modified.

"Open stage, grid and theta drum. Stage equipment. TPC proposals have been cut by 25% below their minimum 'Scale A'. The result will be marginally better equipped than the Old Vic.

"A suggestion has been made to install the equipment AFTER opening. This would mean closing for SIX MONTHS!

"There may have been economies on the architectural front. We have no means of knowing. Even though it will be hotly denied, the impression remains that in some curious way the shell of the building and outward appearance is sometimes considered more important than its contents. Further economies could make the building a theatrical laughing stock." [156]

Construction Begins

The building and its equipment went to tender in the spring of 1969.

In order to get something, or anything, started, and construction underway, the building contract was in two parts: the foundations and substructure, then the superstructure.

It was during the somewhat frantic rush to complete the substructure documentation that we came across a challenge in the workshop block design. The Olivier Theatre seemed to require a paint frame that might handle a 120-feet-wide cyclorama, perhaps 60 feet high. Originally, we imagined a pit to allow a conventional, albeit gigantic, moving paint frame. The cost of such a pit, excavated into the soft Thames mud below, was prohibitive, so we developed an innovative solution that proved to be very successful: a fixed frame, accessed by several moving gantries, that could carry the painters up and anywhere along this enormous surface.

Olivier Theatre under construction

Further cuts still had to be implemented before McAlpine's was awarded the main construction contract for £7.5 million (£124 millon in 2023 terms), a figure that included no allowance for inflation which was already accelerating upward.

But, at long last, building of the National Theatre began. On 3rd November 1969, the ceremonial cement-pouring was carried out by an unlikely looking group of temporary builders in hard hats… led by Sir Laurence.

Nightmare Time

And then the nightmare really began. The main contractor, Sir Robert McAlpine, seemed to pour concrete well. Denys Lasdun did insist on a few of his board-marked concrete columns being demolished and rebuilt, which may have slowed down the construction's momentum, but essentially it seemed the main contractor felt his work was almost over with the completion of the building's structure. Not so. Any theatre is a complex machine. The National was at that time a uniquely complex machine. And it was to be completed by a host of specialist subcontractors, many of whom had won their contracts through offering overly competitive prices.

Crisis: February 1972

The South Bank Board requested Lasdun's comments on four questions to assist the Paymaster General's case before the Treasury for further money.
1. *If no further money was available, what would be the end of*

the National Theatre project, and in what form would the building be left?

Answer: The building would be a shell without a roof, containing about half of its proper equipment, which would rapidly deteriorate through non-use. No section of the building would be complete.

2. What omission, even at this late stage, could be put back into the project and at what cost?

Answer: Of the sacrifices made at tender stage by way of drastic economy, the workshop theatre, the restaurant, and the sound recording studio could now be reinstated. Reductions had been made by omitting insulation on pipes and ducts, which could result in increase of running costs.

3. To what extent would it be practicable to make purchases now in order to forestall price rises and alleviate unemployment in development areas?

Answer: Most of the large equipment has already been ordered, as it was custom-built.

A schedule of items requiring a decision before the end of April 1972 was organised in two categories: items capable of reducing operating costs (Lower theatre [Lyttelton] power assistance to flying, lighting hoists, mainstage elevator, Upper theatre [Olivier] bar hoists, stage lighting remote control luminaires, CCTV); and desirable additions and improvements (Lower, reduce flying centres to 6", Upper, increase simultaneous flying, masking screens, stage lighting scene projectors, assisted resonance, colour CCTV). Total cost £437,500. [157]

Triggered by the Mid-East oil crisis, 1973-1975 saw a global recession. In the UK, post-war optimism collapsed in the face of the coalminers' strike and the three-day week. With the economy in dire straits, an unaware main contractor, struggling subcontractors, galloping inflation and a disgruntled workforce, progress through 1974-1975 slowed to a snail's pace.

It was to be seven years before the – even then unfinished – building was opened to the public. By then, after strikes, the three-day week, price rises, slowdowns, industrial sabotage and the massive inflation of the early '70s, the cost had risen to £16 million (about £265 million adjusted to 2023).

The horrors of delays meant the drum stage was not fully operational until six years after the 1976 opening, this and other work completed by teams who could only work overnight, after everyone else had gone home. Then, for several years, only the elevators were used to transport scenery from workshop to stage. The drum wasn't used in public until designer Bill Dudley's epic *The Shaughraun* in 1988. An epic embarrassment became, at long last, a rather epic success.

The Building
Parallel to all this technology, the building plan was developing. We were involved with the architects on the relationship between the three theatres, dressing rooms, the two main rehearsal rooms and the metal, carpentry, paint and property workshops, all linked by the huge 'scenic roadway', the Drum Road which ran from the backstage of the Lyttelton, past the load-in, to the understage and the drum revolve of the Olivier. The dressing room block was centrally placed between both stages and rehearsal rooms, with the wardrobe and costume workshops above.

I think we, and the architects, made several planning mistakes. The most serious was that after entering through the stage door, actors and technicians went in one direction to the dressing rooms and stages, while the administrative staff went another. This separation cannot have helped during the later troublesome labour relations that the company experienced.

Secondly, everybody underestimated the need for a much greater staff – creative, managerial, custodial and technical – to cope with the new building and greatly increased level of production activity. Third, the integration of catering and consequential garbage removal was woefully underestimated. For decades, the garbage removal sat alongside the main front riverside entrance – only corrected in the 2015 renovation.

Post Opening
Richard Brett Reports on Progress in 1982[158]

"The Olivier flying installation, which has to be the most sophisticated in the world, is now achieving 97% reliability. With the teething problems eliminated, and the technical team fully trained, malfunctions have only affected fit-ups and rehearsals on very limited occasions (better than 2%) and have not affected performances for periods in excess of eight months.

"Remembering the facilities it offers of providing a sky-hook capable of lifting 200kg at speeds of up to two metres a second and positioning groups of such hoists within an accuracy of 5mm to an almost infinite number of pre-recorded reads, it is time to let it be known that this equipment works and works extremely well.

"What is most exciting is the operators' enthusiasm for the system. The present show *Guys and Dolls* was designed for counterweight flying only, but the cradle capacity was insufficient for the heavy scenery. A total of twenty hoists are used to fly various pieces directly. There are some twelve power flying cues and twenty manual flying cues."

As the head of design, John Bury, said when he first had a chance to use the system: "The sense of controlled power and inevitability of movement is magnificent. It was worth waiting for."

Richard Brett, Now at Theatreplan, Recalls Again in 2013[159]

"I think it's very important to remember that the installation was one of the biggest ones that the contractors had ever handled. The building's main contractor had no knowledge or experience, or wish to know about theatre. He just wanted to pour concrete; in fact at one crisis point I remember the McAlpine's site agent saying, 'If you can't haul it up in a bucket, then we don't want to know!' I think that was after they had ground away excess concrete they had poured in the Olivier rear stage and got concrete dust into the drum revolve electronics!

"Evershed Power Optics, who created the control systems for the drum and the power flying, at least had one chap, Roger Keenan, who saw through the completion of the flying system in the Olivier simply by saying, 'The only way you're going to get this finished is to let me do it. If I need parts, I want the parts. If I need labour, I want it provided – otherwise we're gonna get sued.' It was Roger's determination to deal with it in a proper, technical way that finally completed it. Dr. Ian Young of Evershed Power Optics was the key engineer. He was the man who probably committed most of the sins because his engineering was too clever. 'Oh, don't worry, Richard, we'll do it in the software,' at a time when software was nothing like what we know now. He just got himself into great muddles. Mike Barnett worked on the Lyttelton elevators. And he produced the hydro-screw solution to the Lyttelton elevators, which is a hydraulic system controlled by screw jacks, which Tele-Stage Associates built. It was clever. Mike went on to engineer many major hit musicals.

"As for the drum, in itself it didn't actually suffer huge problems. It was basically successful on its testing. There's a picture of it sitting out in a field with its cover on in the open and spinning 'round at speed. Production manager Douglas Cornelissen and others from the National Theatre thought it was fantastic because it positioned so accurately.

"Of course, the problems of installation were getting the bloody thing in and aligned. Then there were clearly big problems in actually setting it to work. The biggest problem there was that, upon Mole Richardson's recommendation, we had agreed that the wheels would be mounted upside down on the floor. This had seemed like a good idea, but in practice it meant that the load was not being carried evenly by every wheel. As the heavily loaded structural columns went round over the wheels, the bottom frame was flexing.

"It was not a happy period. I go now to meetings at the National and they're held in that same boardroom. I must say, to go into that room is quite scary! I remember how we used to stand outside, nervously – waiting for hours sometimes.

"Although there was little that they could've really done to TPC, other than to have sued us – which I don't think they were ever going to do – it was trying to describe to those people from industry and the board the situation on the technical problems that the contractors were having, and we got no support from anybody. The delays and technical problems were really down to the very poor management by the contractors.

"But we can claim the shape of the fly tower, can't we? And the rear stages. And the general planning we did was brilliant: rehearsal rooms, workshops, scenic roadway!

"And I do remember how well we worked together. I would think things were under control. And then you, Richard, would say to me, 'Oh Dick, what's happened about so-and-so?' And it would be the one thing that I hadn't followed up. That's one of the reasons why we were a good team. For no particular reason, we just happened to question each other about a bit the other one hadn't thought of. I remember that happening on a number of occasions."

Your author remembers very well that nothing worked until the late '70s, but then it was brilliant for twenty years. I took some Canadian clients around the NT in the early '90s. A lad who I'd never met was working the flying control. I said, "How's it going?" Thinking he'd say, "Well, it crashed last week." And he said, "Oh, it's fine." I said, "Well, is it fairly reliable?" He said, "Yeah, yeah." I said, "Well, when does it go wrong?" He said, "What do you mean?" So, I said, "When does it go wrong?" He said, "Oh, I've only been here three years." I've never forgotten that moment.

Drum revolve under construction from above

Drum elevator lowered, 1980

The Olivier, fly tower showing tracked winches

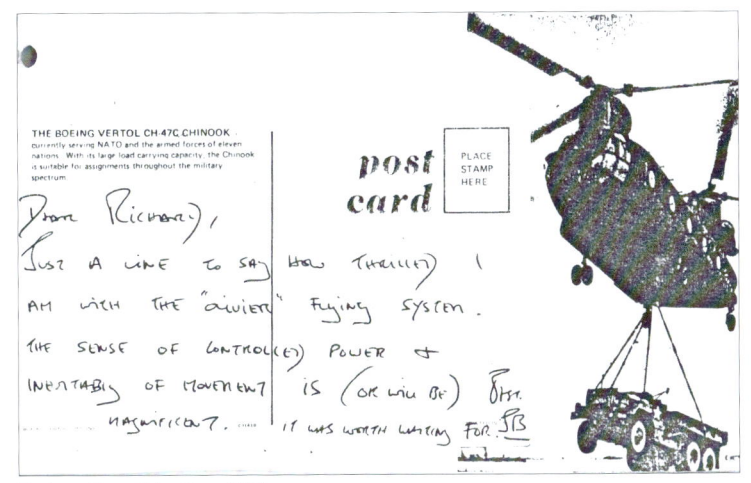

Postcard from John Bury, 1982

Olivier stage from lighting bridge and 'stalactite'

2.4 Full Scenic Capability

North east corner buttresses, 1976

2.5 Getting To The Poetic

"The Prerogative of the Artist"

Denys Lasdun

Meanwhile, Lasdun and his team continued developing the building, of which, of course, the auditoria were only a fractional part.

On his appointment Lasdun had said that, with the "prerogative of the artist," he had to be left alone to create his building. To a very large extent that is what happened. Few within the National organisation knew much about the development of the building overall. We at TPC were involved with the architect in all the backstage and technical planning, but NT staff felt kept on the sidelines as far as the rest of the building was concerned.

Lasdun confessed, frankly, that the struggles over the auditorium designs had been deeply troubling to him, driving him at times into a state of depression. By contrast, the development of the rest of the building was left almost entirely to him.

Interestingly, there appears to be comparatively little documentation about the development of the front of house, which Lasdun later described as his "fourth theatre." For the following section, I must express my gratitude to Barnabas Calder for his insightful, unpublished description of the design process.

"Denys Lasdun was, very clearly, the leader of a talented team. His principal support came from his right-hand man, Peter Softley, who was mainly responsible for the proscenium theatre and all backstage areas. Harry Pugh was in charge of liaison with the consultants and the construction process, while Malcolm Minjoodt was closely involved with Denys as his principal design assistant and his amanuensis, particularly in the early development of ideas. Vital to Lasdun's design process was the creation of models; Bob Kirkman and later Philip Wood led the production of these essential tools in the building design's development.

While we concentrated on the inside of the building, the theatres, Denys Lasdun and his talented team also had to design the rest of the building!

He spoke of "the prerogative of the artist" – to be left alone to create his work, untroubled by the kind of struggles he had endured over the auditorium designs.

"Denys himself said, 'My right-hand man has been Philip Wood, the model-maker. I don't use a scale, a ruler. I have, whatever model we're working with, a scale human being whose eyes are five foot six inches from the ground, just a little silhouette, which I can then move around… I find it gives me a very good guide.' This technique helped produce the strong sculptural effects and three-dimensional interactions of elements in Lasdun's buildings."[160]

The design process of the building might be divided into three stages: first, the initial development, from the summer of 1964 to spring 1965, that culminated in the marvellous model of the combined opera house and theatre presented to the public on 4th May 1965. There followed eighteen months of financial cutting through the rest of 1965 and 1966, until the opera house was deleted and the site moved to the final location on Prince's Meadow in 1967. Planning permission for the amended scheme was sought on 14th September 1967, after which detailed design for tender began.

Winning the Project
During the winter of 2018, I spent time trawling through the voluminous archives of the key participants in the National story: Sir Laurence, the two Peters (Hall and Brook) and, of course, Sir Denys. In the latter files, I found two documents of interest. The first, an undated list of design principles that might have influenced Lasdun's thinking about the design of the whole building. The second, principles that might affect attitudes about the theatre spaces.

Only in late 2018 did I stumble on a series of recordings in the British Library, interviews with Denys Lasdun made in 1997/8, four years before his death in 2001. They include some fascinating and (perhaps surprisingly) refreshingly modest insights.

First about the unique concrete structure and consequent finishes:

"Concrete in the National Theatre was appropriate to a particular task in which I wanted – it must have been what I thought at the time – I wanted structure, surface and space, to be created from one material only, like a church or a cathedral. That particular trio of things could only be done in concrete, in those days." [161]

Second his recollection of the selection process:

"I never asked to go in for the National Theatre, but I received a very well-worded letter from Lord Cottesloe, saying, 'We've been studying various architects' work and we note you haven't put in for it, and we are still trawling and would like you to reconsider whether this wouldn't be something that you might be interested in.' It was rather cautiously worded. I thought, well that's a rather nice way to put it. So, there were a hundred and twenty applications, an enormous amount of speculation and hype in the press as to who was going to get it, which architect would get it, speculation ranging from Philip Johnson round to a very well-known architect in Germany, I can't remember his name [Walter Ruhnau]. All over the place. And so, I queued up, waited my turn, summoned into the room, a biggish room with Lord Cottesloe in the chair, Laurence Olivier, Peter Hall, I think Peter Brook, Lord Chandos, etcetera, etcetera; on the right, theatre and on the left, various important personages, including Steven Arlen, to do with opera. I had submitted a portfolio of the sort of work we did, and was asked, had I ever done a theatre? And the answer was no, I've never done a theatre. And this seemed to have a rather beneficial effect and I realised much later, because this was the National Theatre and nobody knew quite what a national theatre was about, although Brian O'Rorke, don't forget, had done a study earlier on, and Lutyens before that, on different sites. They were terrified of experts, particularly Olivier; he didn't want to be told, 'This is what you've got to do. Here's the theatre I've done in Ontario, whatever, this is what it's about'. That they didn't want. So I said, 'I've never done one, but then I'd never done a university before I did one either and I had never done a college of physicians either, but, somehow, if you are prepared, and you will have to work extremely hard if you have me,' and I spelled it out, I said, 'I've never done one, I'm willing to learn and you will teach me, and if it takes a year, so be it, if it takes two years, so be that, and when you've got nothing more to say, then I want to be left alone to think what is it all about.' Apparently, these were sweet words in their ears. It came very naturally to me because that's the way we worked, it was nothing special, but they were

captivated by somebody they felt they could work with, because none of them agreed with each other anyhow; they all had very differing views. And the next two years were spent unravelling what did they really mean and there is a document which I hold, which I suppose when I'm dead and gone I shall release to the public, of what they all said over two years, fascinating. Some of it contradictory, some of it maddening and some of it so to the point that you had to reread what they said several times until you had got the point. And that is the kind of human relationship out of which architecture can spring, for me." [162]

Third, Lasdun's recollections of the arduous, two-year process of meetings with the building committee. Of his struggle to understand. And, interestingly, one central source of misunderstanding in the design of the Olivier:

"I kept transcripts of every month's meeting, of what Olivier said, what Saint-Denis said, Devine said, Peter Hall, the lot. And I used to take them home and read them, and there were some remarkable statements, simply unconscious statements by somebody, say like Devine – not Devine, this was Saint-Denis, who suddenly said, 'You know, what I'm dreaming about is a space theatre, like a room.' That was probably one of the most highly charged statements that was made during the whole period and I dwelt on it and, in the end, having had to go through the hoops with designing an all-purpose theatre, which is what they all, all governments want, three for the price of one, and dismissing it as not being any good, we then had the long road which lasted eighteen months of searching for what was to be finally the Olivier Theatre. And, indeed, what it is, is a room, but it had to be arrived at from the long haul of discussion, minutes taken, reading them but, you know, I must pay tribute to the man who said, 'I'm dreaming about a room'. It's fascinating. Maybe he didn't realise what he was talking about, that doesn't really matter; it's what he felt he wanted to say. Olivier made some amazing statements, and Peter Brook made amazing statements, I mean statements that I had to dwell on for weeks and weeks and weeks thinking how marvellous they are, what did they really mean?

"So from that point of view, this is a dimension of architecture which very few people know about; they think you have a brief…

Well, who's to say what triggered [the central idea]? Can't tell. You see, I do belong to an old-fashioned school of thought that, for architects, we do try and rationalise every act we do, and the papers are charged with long speeches and discussions about why we did this and why we did that but, in the end, finally, of course, you have to go through the hoops of analysis and everything else, but in the end, it's a mystery.

"And I believe that you have to be unequivocally true to the period in which you seek your living, i.e., from the modern. If you start frigging around with everything else, you end up with postmodernism, which is, you can't dismiss it, but it's not a very profound diet. And a total belief in Eliot's view that we live in historical time and the present; the present is mixed up with the past and you can't separate them, and I believe that to be true. So if that makes me fuddy-duddy, so be it. [Laughs] I have become slightly more tolerant in my old age, but not much.

"What I thrive on is the exchange between a client [and] a user, and this reaches its apotheosis in the long, drawn-out discussions between the theatre committee, the building, Olivier, Peter Hall…" [163]

Ironically Denys, in your author's opinion, actually misunderstood, or misheard, Saint-Denis' comment. The minutes show that what Saint-Denis actually said was, "What I am dreaming about is a space stage that would give a feeling of audience and actor being in the same room." Denys apparently believed he actually called for literally one room – a superficially subtle, but very significant difference. In Scheme B, Denys created a one-room space, surrounded by a concrete balcony. Initially, the committee was impressed by such a radical idea. Only later did doubts about the room's rigidity begin to grow. But Lasdun continued to fight for his concept, despite these growing concerns. Had Lasdun understood more about theatre, had he been more aware of the history of theatre's rich heritage, might he have understood the restrictions of a concrete-locked single room space theatre sooner?

Lasdun then adds a touching tribute to the contribution of his wife Susan, Lady Lasdun, in the creation of the public area carpet and colour scheme. As lighting designer, I was privileged to be part of these explorations, seeking a balance between natural and artificial light, the warmth of the carpet and the almost organic enclosure of the board-marked concrete.

"I ought to say that, although she is my wife, she is also an independent woman of great intellect and sensibility, and frankly has made an immeasurable contribution to my life, particularly as I am constitutionally not a public figure and get awfully het up about anything to do with publicity and the public work and all the rest of it. She guided me through all the ups and downs of what public life involves, which I am ill-qualified, temperamentally and every other way, to deal with. If I can put my foot in it, I certainly do that.

"In the strictly architectural sense, she has always advised on textiles, colours and many other aspects of important buildings like the National Theatre; the carpet for instance, she maintained, after we had been on some other trip to Greece where we saw a kind of heather flower and rocks, she saw the importance of silver grey of the concrete being opposed or complemented by a very subtly mixed carpet which has several colours in it that warmed the concrete. And this was a very skilful operation.

"If you get it, in the case of a concrete building particularly, if you get it too hot then the concrete will look quite different and most unattractive. Whereas since it opened, the theatre, in 1976, the best compliment I can say to her carpet is that when it opened people used to sit on the floor drinking their coffee, because it was so welcoming, warm and friendly. My cynics and, critical cynics I mean, my critics say, 'Well of course they sat on the floor because there weren't enough chairs,' but that's not the truth; the truth is, they sat on the floor because they felt at home. And that's entirely due to her. I could go on a lot about her contribution." [164]

Lasdun's internal notes on the principles of his design written in the late 1960s include:

General Design Principles
(DL&P undated, but maybe 1965/66?)[165]

People live in cities, seek social regeneration. People create occasion. People's ears are stunned by radio and traffic. Families at home have 'the box,' we must offer a different experience. The re-entrant space with the Waterloo Bridge invites. Umbilical cord [of the bridge] Stepping section rationale – weather and terraces, public/private. NT must bridge gap between ivory tower of theatre and daily life. Must not appeal to special literate or cultured class. NT affords glimpse of environment, complete and incomplete, King's Reach, newborn community. Seen by millions of visitors. Building clear on direction. Welcoming hand. Multi-level entrance.

Actor casts spell; invites imagination. Life force. Preservation and change. What public feels on entry must be maintained. Emotional energy not dissipated by interval. Statistical criteria, sight lines, distances do not yield the solution of value judgements.

[Granville] Barker: "A simple living organism – a thing of growth, growing at an uncertain pace, so many influences does it owe to life." Slow liturgical ascent to Level 48. [Upper Theatre] Architecture of contours and terraces. Tradition withers if not nourished. We draw on the past for those values which have meaning for us.

Generated by two prime movers – the nature of the auditoria and service spaces, and the river, its enjoyment; architecture of landscape and anti-form.

Design Principles of Major Spaces (from around 1965)
- Anticipation. Effortless journey to seat. Refreshments.
- Interval. Foyers not large enough so audience loses its identity.
- Must not dissipate atmosphere and concentration build up, but opportunity for a change of scene for those who need it.

Auditoria
- To present and focus upon the scene of the drama. To make audience aware of its corporate identity and shared purpose. Expectancy.
- Complete unobtrusiveness during performance or an extension of stage set/link with reality (P Brook).
- To bring actors and audience into the closest possible relationship.

Stages – Upper Theatre
- *Advantage of sophisticated mechanical handling devices combined with immediacy of one room.*
- *Maximum scope or challenge for directors and designers.*
- *Ability to expand or contract visible setting.*
- *Ability to alter configuration of the stage.*
- *Mechanical aids alleviate difficulty of scene changing without benefit of proscenium masking and curtain.*
- *Flexibility not adaptability.*

Stages – Lower Theatre
- *Intimacy of the best West End theatre, combined with the stage space and some of the equipment of a new continental theatre.*
- *NB. Designed solely for drama, unlike most continental theatres, so without orchestra pit/forestage to come between actor and audience. (Orchestra pit within stage for plays with music.)*

Both stages
- *Properly tuned instruments to ensure audibility, visibility and comfort for every member of the audience.*

Backstage
- *Logistics of repertory working. Civilised conditions for actors and stars. Space for constructing scenery and making costumes so that all aspects of production can be properly coordinated.*

The Building by Lasdun
"… it's at a point in the river… which turns through almost 90 degrees and picks up a panorama of the City of London that stretches from St. Paul's round to Somerset House and on to Hawksmoor's towers at Westminster Abbey. It's a magical position… probably the most beautiful site in London." [166]

"Situating the open theatre in this way [at 45 degrees to the river] involved both a grand gesture and a sculptural response to other points of monumental intensity in the cityscape. The triangular geometry which is felt in every facet and angle of the National Theatre stems, in the long run, from this." [167]

"It is an architecture without facades but with layers of building, like geological strata, connected in such a way that they flow into the surrounding riverscape and city." [168]

View across the river from the terraces - and kite flying! 1976

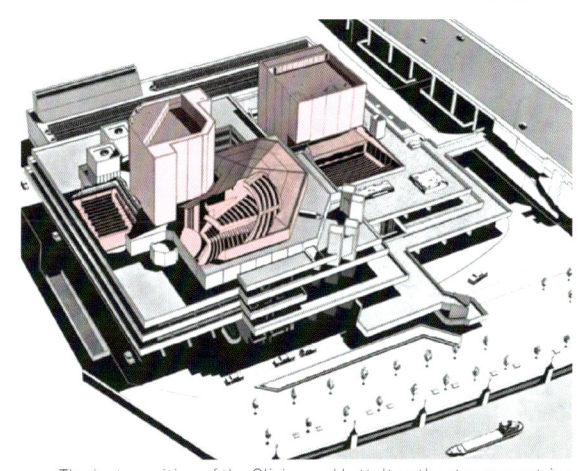

The juxtaposition of the Olivier and Lyttelton theatre geometries cascades out into the public areas; the Cottesloe sits seperately, with its own entrance and foyer spaces

The building exterior expresses the theatres within - the NT in 1976

2.5 Getting To The Poetic

"… I want the feeling that the audience – like the tide of the river – flow into the auditoriums and become a community within them. Then the tide ebbs and they come out into the creeks of the small spaces that are made by all these terraces; because they're not vast terraces, they are very small, human, little places for people to go to. Outside and inside." [169]

The building is plainly born of its time, the 1960s. But Lasdun acknowledged his inspirations: Le Corbusier, Charles Rennie Mackintosh and Hawksmoor, back to ancient Greece and Egypt. The most obvious architectural feature must be the use of exposed concrete. Initially to create a strong and soundproof 'mega-structure,' it was actually only late in the design process that it became clear that this was Lasdun's finish of choice.

The two fly towers dominate. The Lyttelton is virtually a cube, but its apparent weight is diminished by the lower front corners being cut away. The Olivier echoes my stage shape of September 1966; however once that shape was accepted by Lasdun, he harnessed its complexity, signalling the very unusual theatre below and strongly accenting its diagonal axis within the building. In a fascinating manner, the collision between the diagonal Olivier and the rectilinear Lyttelton drives much of the drama that carries through the public parts of the building. The excitement of the whole building lies in the way the horizontal strata are set off against the massive fly towers above that are echoed by the vertical lift shafts in a dramatic composition.

The layers of horizontal strata create the public spaces. As Lasdun described: "My strata are open… you enter the strata. To enter the strata is to penetrate a cave, and to penetrate a cave is to go into a world of special events signaled by the towers." [170]

To your author, the lobbies are extraordinarily successful They echo some of the features of the great theatres of the world, providing carefully calculated changes of scale. Where the geometry of the Olivier meets the Lyttelton, there is a soaring space that rises through multiple levels, becoming the main central concourse of the building. Off this space, toward the Lyttelton, the low-ceilinged lobbies provide places for quieter contemplation and private meeting. After rising, either by elevator or the twin symmetrical stairs that afford brief glimpses back to the main concourse, one reaches a second, grand, three-storey space, the foyer of the Olivier, with stupendous views across the Thames. Access to both auditoria is through confined circulation spaces that, in turn, by contrast emphasise the grandeur of the auditorium within.

The power of the geometry, the beautifully executed, hand-crafted, board-marked concrete, the simplicity of colour, puts all the emphasis on the people who inhabit the space. The exquisitely realised wood graining, almost appearing fossilised in the concrete, gives a strangely organic feel to the wall finishes. Human beings surrounded by "ancient, rugged architecture." A timeless "Fourth Theatre" that strikes a delicate balance between the monumental and the casual. In the climate of the 60s, Lasdun sought a welcoming anti-elitist atmosphere, intended to welcome all, young and old, theatregoer or casual visitor. The roughness of concrete and brick, the comfort of the elegant carpet (designed by Susan, Lady Lasdun), and the open terraces without apparent walls, blur the distinction between indoors and out.

Sir Denys Lasdun at the Royal Society of Arts
25th May 1977 – Edited Extracts

"I shall be speaking tonight as a practising architect, although this must include references to a range of fantasies, feelings, attitudes. These, in my view, nourish the deep levels of action in architecture, particularly when faced with problems as formidable as that posed by the new National Theatre building.

"I have called this an architecture of urban landscape.

"The five acre site stands on part of the river that is known as King's Reach and it is quite one of the most beautiful stretches of the river in London. The theatre is conceived as an extension of the bridge and inseparable from it because I look upon architecture as an extension of the city, indivisible from it. The Olivier fly tower dominates the composition. Inland the building presents a sort of rocky outcrop of stratified concrete and blank fly towers.

"Viewed from the opposite side of Waterloo Bridge, the building presents very marked characteristics. The fly tower of the Olivier is inflected at 45° to Waterloo Bridge with the Lyttelton

Theatre, smaller and lower, modulating the scale of the building to the bridge. The rest of the composition is a series of terraces with minor towers. The terraces are physically connected both to the riverside walkway and to the bridge. During the day, and more so at night, people can be seen inside moving around, so in a sense the building is self advertising.

"Finally, I suppose you might say that it is a building without façades in a normal sense, but with layers of building, like geological strata connected in such a way that they flow into the surrounding riverscape and city. The building is thus an extension of the theatre into the everyday world from which it springs. The basic material inside and out is unadorned concrete.

"Why was concrete chosen? Deliberately, for fantasy reasons. Of course there were practical and structural reasons, but concrete was chosen inside and outside so that it would evoke warm stones, ancient ruins, the non-slick and the permanent, irrespective of whether it streaks, grows warts or has lichen growing on it.

"There is no attempt to apply decoration. It is simply light, space, people, concrete.

"The section builds up step by step from the river to the promenade and finally to the summit of the building – the Olivier fly tower. The Olivier will be the first open theatre in the world to provide the possibility of three-dimensional scenery. This is a considerable technological innovation.

"For me, architecture only makes sense as the extender and promotor of human relations... Architecture as a metaphor for landscape.

"I come now to what I call the 'fourth' theatre. This concerns what theatre was originally about. In addition to the three theatres, there is the whole building and its relationship to the city and the consideration of the theatre as some kind of place where people assemble as a community. In Athens, in the 5th century when drama reached its peak, going to the theatre was not a fringe activity, but central to daily life, the religious life, the economic life of the community.

National Theatre just before opening, 1975

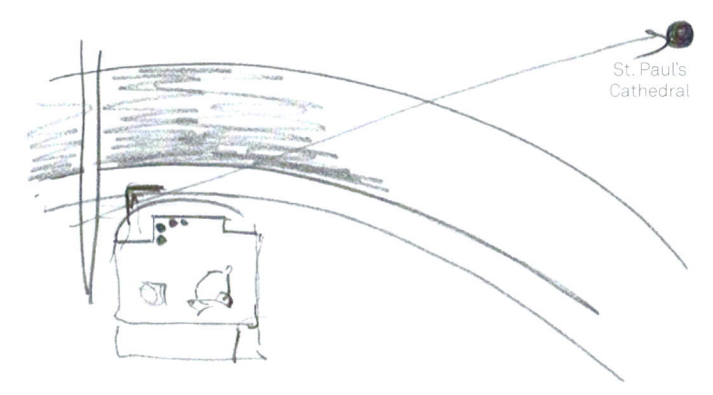

Lasdun sketch of site's pivotal importance

2.5 Getting To The Poetic

A Sense of Theatre

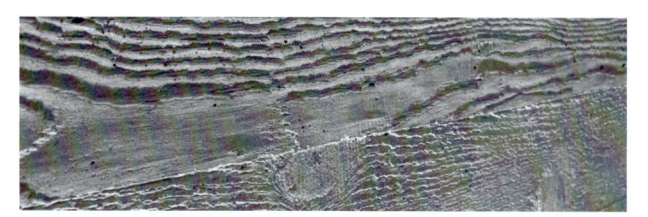

"The question arises, can one recapture this quality in our different and more complex situation today?

"With the street as stage, the city becomes a backdrop. The external terraces of the National provide places for many activities; inside there are also events going on. All these things help to break down the barrier between ordinary people going to the theatre and the past tradition that it was something only for the elite. People sit on the floor and use the foyers like the ancient hypostyle. All the time on different levels there are glimpses of the city beyond and the large cantilevered concrete overhangs keep your eyes focused on the riverscape.

"I have talked about context, assembly and an architecture of urban landscape. These notions take us back to Greece. In Epidaurus there is an exquisite relationship between the setting and the form built at the scale of the landscape, both epic and intimate. It has a sense of belonging to time, place and people."

Denys ends by quoting a Japanese correspondent: *"In its severity of abstract geometric forms and spaces, indicating the numinous of primitive people, those entering unexpectedly encounter the time and space of a kind of ritual. They gaily enter the theatre and go out transformed."*

Architectural Lighting

Denys asked me to work with him on the architectural lighting of the auditoria and public areas of the building. With Tony Corbett (head of a TP subsidiary company, Light Limited), we got involved in the absorbing process of working closely with Denys in revealing his striking wood-boarded, concrete-surrounded spaces with light.

Denys' brief for the public areas was to create what he termed the "Fourth Theatre:"

"It must be space, walls, light, and the ornament is the people moving around in a big, gaunt, bare space, which is beautifully lit and carpeted." [171] Now he saw the audience as the performers. Accordingly, we decided to

> **"To enter the strata is to penetrate a cave, and to penetrate a cave is to go into a world of special events signaled by the towers."**
> Sir Denys Lasdun

Lasdun's Fourth Theatre

> **"It must be space, walls, light, and the ornament is the people moving around in a big gaunt bare space, which is beautifully lit and carpeted."**
> Sir Denys Lasdun

A Sense of Theatre

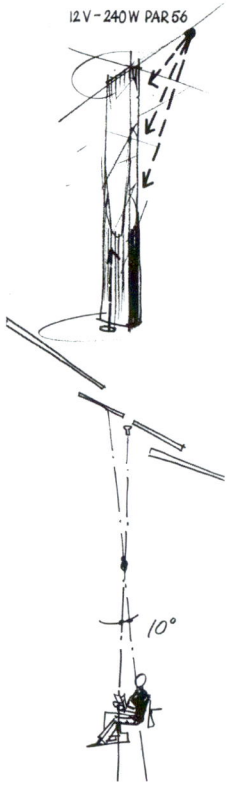

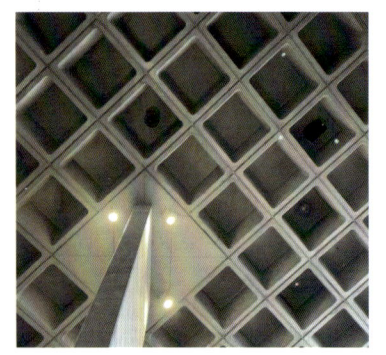

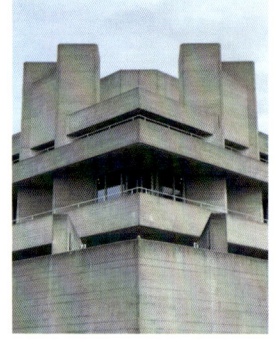

take many of the principles of dramatic stage lighting, and carry them through the public spaces. The lighting was to celebrate the social occasion as its participants became the actors, the public space, their stage.

Lasdun's bold architectural forms provided the impetus. The juxtaposition of the vertical elements, and their visual priority, was the starting point for the design. The massive columns that cut their way, layer after layer, through the building, were to be lit from their base. The light rose with the columns, illuminating the ceiling pads they support, thus making them dominant. Some of the columns were also picked out by glancing beams of light, to edge-light the concrete texture and provide pools of light at their bases. This, for me, was inspired by the theatrical imagery of the sketches of Edward Gordon Craig. Pencil-thin beams emanated from clusters of low-voltage spotlights, making a strong visual statement. Similarly, the vertical plane was emphasised by downlighting the exposed textured concrete balustrades of the staircases. The horizontal bands of concrete were similarly edge-lit to reveal their richness of texture. All the spotlighting was to be of a warm candle-like colour to enrich the atmosphere… candlelight shimmering as if on the walls of a cave.

House Lighting in the Auditoria
The two main auditoria are very different, but the lighting treatment sought to create something of a unified character. A dominant feature of both are the boldly textured fair-faced concrete perimeter walls. These – as in the lobbies – are sharply spotlit to reveal their texture, but with the lights set at a modest level of brightness to create a feeling of warm candlelight. Downlighting in both auditoria is set at approximately ten degrees off the vertical, so the light comes from slightly over the shoulder of the audience when they are seated. All houselighting channels are dimmable, and the intention of lighting the entire audience space was that directors and designers could, if they so wished, extend the effect and atmosphere of theatrical lighting from the stage throughout the entire auditorium.

Exterior Lighting
The aim of the architectural floodlighting was to emphasise the architecture. Rising vertical floodlighting from below the fly towers emphasised their dominant role and accentuated their shape. Originally the lighting was mono-chromatic, echoing the candlelight warmth of the interior, but in more recent years this has been changed to allow the ability to dramatically colour the entire building or even project imagery onto it, though it is notable that the National Theatre team do this with considered restraint and subtlety.

Over the decades various changes have been made to the architectural lighting, initially to increase the functional brightness overall, that while necessary did rather detract from Lasdun's original desire for warmth. The NT Future renovation of recent years has sought to return to the warmth of the original lighting concepts, which were described by a critic in the *Architect's Journal* of 1976 as: "bringing a life to the architecture which I have rarely experienced." [172]

In the summer of 2015, I was amused to find myself in the NT Archive, talking to a young woman. I asked what she was doing. She replied that she was searching the archive for information about the original architectural lighting scheme from 1967. I explained that it had actually been my design, and we talked for a while. I (and I suspect Sir Denys' spirit) would love to see, through the magic of modern technology, the occasional dimming of the new and brighter lighting to more magically create the feeling almost of flickering candlelight that we achieved in Lasdun's 'caves' long ago.

Sir Laurence in the Olivier Theatre
14th June 1978

"The theatre, which opened in 1976, was one of the last major buildings in Britain to embody this view of formal integrity. Designed by Denys Lasdun, it adapted to English conditions the view of his hero Le Corbusier that 'architecture is the masterly, correct and magnificent play of masses brought together in light.' It incorporated other influences, such as the brooding drama that Nicholas Hawksmoor could extract from the mass of a building, and from the interaction of horizontals and verticals. It took from the ancient theatre of Epidaurus in Greece the idea of performance in a landscape, and tried to reinterpret it for a modern, urban, cold-climate setting. There was an underlying belief that modern buildings could and should aspire to stand alongside these great works of the past.

"The National Theatre is constructed around a complex geometry of interlocking right angles and diagonals, and emphatic cantilevered terraces that Lasdun called 'strata,' offset by lift towers and fly towers. There are subtle changes in detail — for example, there are different types of ceiling coffering in the more and less grand areas — the whole then unified with exceptional consistency and few materials: concrete bearing the grain of its wooden boards, blue brick paving, aluminium window frames, a grey-white brick in more functional areas and a purple-brown-grey carpet which, together with the rough grey concrete, contained a memory of the combination of stone and heather at Epidaurus."

Rowan Moore
The Guardian, 5th April 2015

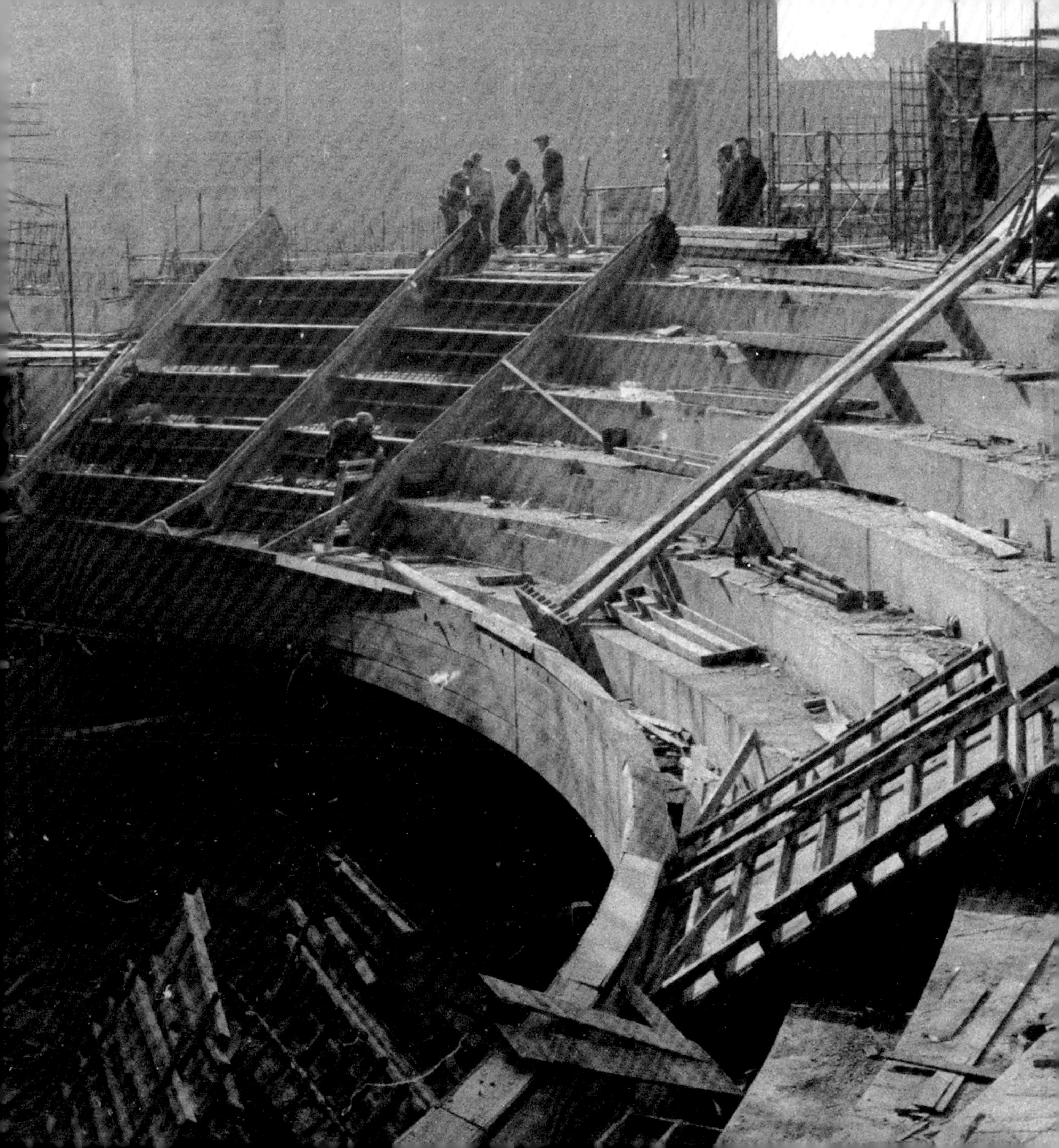

Part Three

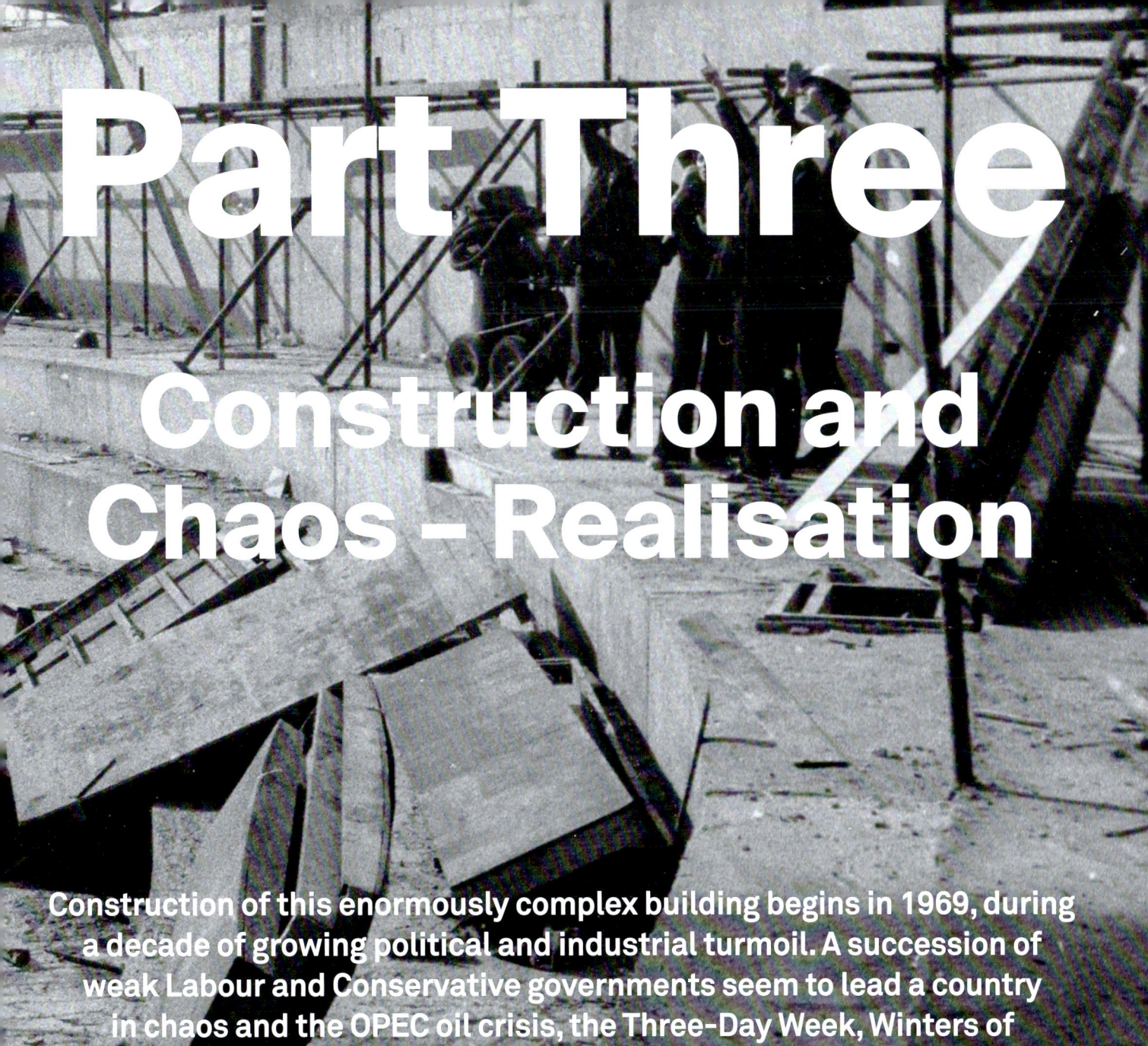

Construction and Chaos – Realisation

Construction of this enormously complex building begins in 1969, during a decade of growing political and industrial turmoil. A succession of weak Labour and Conservative governments seem to lead a country in chaos and the OPEC oil crisis, the Three-Day Week, Winters of Discontent, strikes, and galloping inflation only amplify continuing financial uncertainty for the project. Completion was predicted for 1972 with a public opening in 1973 – that drifted into 1976.

Sir Laurence Olivier and Peter Hall outside the National Theatre, 1973

3.1 Peter Hall Takes Charge and Writes a Diary – Part I

NT Director 1973-1988

Extracts from Sir Peter Hall, *Peter Hall's Diaries: The Story of a Dramatic Battle* (London: Oberon Books, 1983)
(Interspersed with other commentary in **bold purple**)

"[Peter Hall] formally succeeded Olivier in November 1973 when the country was in crisis: The economy was in free-fall because of rocketing oil prices and a succession of strikes meant there were limited fuel supplies. That led, early in 1974, to the imposition of a three-day working week. It was hardly the time to be talking of opening a new National Theatre, then in halting construction. As if that were not enough, Hall faced lingering resentment from some of Olivier's old associates and his initial 1974 season was a string of duds. I remember beginning one review with the words: 'What on earth is going on at the National Theatre?'"
Michael Billington *The Guardian*[1]

Tuesday 25th July 1972
"Denys Lasdun showed me round the South Bank building. Architecturally it is going to be wonderful. It is not palatial, but human. The roof is not yet on and the concrete is raw and rude. But one can feel the intimacy of the place. On the Olivier stage one man could play Beckett, or a hundred men could fight the Wars of the Roses. I was agreeably surprised too with the proscenium theatre. We also heard this morning that the Minister has got the extra money to make possible the studio theatre which had been cut from the plans for economy. It seems I'm winning a first battle – I begin to understand how it could all work. I am tremendously excited."

Peter Hall takes over from Sir Laurence. He asks me to create the design for the studio theatre that he has been allowed to restore to the project. I ask my new colleague at Theatre Projects, Iain Mackintosh, to create the concept design for the Cottesloe Theatre. Building completion is repeatedly delayed, creating immense frustration for Peter and the company, whose plans must be constantly postponed. The building finally opens, at long last, in 1976, but even then nothing is ready. Peter's diary provides a remarkable record of this period; it is interwoven with other contemporary information.

Richard Brett (on the lowered elevator), David Collison, and Richard Pilbrow on the Olivier Theatre drum revolve during construction

Wednesday 9th August 1972
Peter Hall: "Spoke in favour of the Studio Theatre, stressing its importance. It was not intended as a place in which young people might amuse themselves. It was a research facility which was needed by the most creative talents in the theatre. Peter Brook for example was doing his experimental work in Paris – he should be doing it at the NT." [2]

Wednesday 9th August 1972
"The joke is that the South Bank Board cannot avoid having the Studio. Denys Lasdun has built it as the cornerstone of the building. The space has been created by the structure that actually holds up the other theatres."

Wednesday 20th September 1972
Tony Easterbrook to Laurence Olivier: "Studio theatre has a go-ahead. 250 seats average. Estimate cost £337,250. Reduced to £290,000. To be finished to 'rehearsal room standards.'" [3]

Thursday 27th February 1973
"To the South Bank for over two hours of walking round the building. I haven't been since last August. Progress. I think Lasdun's work is triumphant. He has divested concrete of its brutality. It is slender, delicate and in beautiful geometric patterns. I think the theatre is a masterpiece."

Wednesday 2nd May 1973
"The 'topping out' ceremony of the National's new theatre. A fine spring day. The last bit of the roof was ceremonially filled in by the Lords Olivier and Cottesloe, and Larry made a vintage speech about Pagan Ritual, Wotan's and Thor's Day. Then we all had drinks and tramped round the building. It is looking magnificent. The world and his wife were there. Tynan in pink-trimmed blazer. Lord Cottesloe's opening remarks included: 'I am glad we need not carry the ceremony to its traditional conclusion by the sacrifice of the architect.'" [4]

Saturday 7th July 1973
Peter Hall and John Bury came to visit me at the TP office on Long Acre. Aided by the current architectural drawings, I and Dick Brett took them through the planning backstage and introduced the stages: the Lyttelton's flexible proscenium with repertory side and rear stages, and the Olivier's drum revolve and power flying. Peter confessed himself excited by the promised flexibility for three-dimensional, fluid, staging.

Friday 14th September 1973
First meeting of Max Rayne's so-called 'Ginger Group,' intended to speed work up. Max Rayne, Joseph Lockwood (a British industrialist, chairman of EMI between 1954 and 1974), Richard Pilbrow, Richard Brett, J.A. Neil (engineering), Davis Belfield (cost consultants), Harry Pugh and Peter Softley (DL &P), Richard York (NT). Occasionally: Denys Lasdun, Peter Hall.

Friday 21st September 1973
"To George Street for a morning with the building contractors. Rayne in the chair; Joseph Lockwood in attendance. Incredible revelations. Each contractor, under pressure, admits he is behind – but it is because of other contractors, who have let him down. Of course. After a while I wondered how anything ever gets

Lord Rayne, Chairman National Theatre Board, 1971-1988

> "The joke is that the South Bank Board cannot avoid having the Studio. Denys Lasdun has built it as the cornerstone of the building."
>
> Peter Hall

finished, or how any firm ever shows a profit. But this new pressure group of Rayne's first met only last week and already it has started to show some results. The technique is simple. Having discovered which supplier is holding up the contract, Rayne looks up the chairman of the company and then either he, or Joseph Lockwood, or Goodman, or some other heavyweight, rings him up, and says, 'Surely the firm doesn't want to be the one that stops the National Theatre opening as planned, on Shakespeare's birthday 1975? After all, the Queen is booked, and you can't put off a royal personage.' Our orders are leap-frogging to the top of the queue."

Thursday 8th November 1973: The Cottesloe Is Born
Peter Hall to the South Bank Board: "Small theatres with flexible staging and seating, giving an intimate audience/performer relationship, make much innovative work possible. They are the growth area in the theatre today, developing new talent, styles, plays and audiences. The National Theatre must have one in its armoury. John Bury is now working on possible configurations with Richard PIlbrow and the architect to a brief in which seating capacity and fixed installations are secondary to the requirements of flexibility, mobility, and adaptability of the entire area." [5]

Peter came to see me again. He confirmed to me that as a condition of his accepting the leadership position, the studio theatre was to be reinstated. A minimum budget, but with a flat-floor capability; a place for rehearsal, studio experimental performance, and hopefully usable as a TV recording studio, too. He told me that Lasdun says he is "too busy." Could TP help with a concept design for the space? As is usually my habit, I said yes. We had been responsible for the black-box concept intended for the bricked-up space below the Olivier rear stage. Now we were to do something more productive with it.

I had invited Iain Mackintosh to join me at Theatre Projects and he had come on board on 1st October. My acquaintance with Iain goes back to 1961. We met when he was a young stage manager at the Oxford Playhouse, and I was lighting *The Guide*, designed by the famous Australian artist Sydney Nolan. Iain had gone on to run the Prospect Theatre Company, which was an Arts Council-subsidised company but one that had no permanent home. Iain had travelled the UK, and the world, with an acting group, playing every size and type of theatre. This had brought him to the realisation that some theatres seemed to work while others did not. That mysterious and elusive ingredient seemed to lie in the relationship between the actor and the audience. In broad principle theatres of the past, which clustered the audience all around the room in as close a relationship to the stage as possible, tended to be those that more readily sprang to life.

As a producer, I had brought several of Prospect's productions into the West End, most notably *Edward II* and *Richard II*, Ian McKellen's breakthrough success. Iain and I had become friends, and we'd often talked of this quality of theatre that seemed then so alien in those days of 'engineered sightlines.' The then unpopular boxes and balconies of so many West End theatres seemed only echoes of a class-ridden past.

Iain had become involved as an advisor to the Eden Court Theatre in Inverness. He had proposed the addition of boxes 'en-escalier' which would wrap around the central stalls. I went to the opening in Inverness and was immediately struck by the theatre's intimacy. Iain joined TPC, and now I challenged him: "Iain, how about designing a studio theatre for the National over the weekend?" On Monday, he sought me out at the Queen's Theatre, where I was lighting a ghastly ghost play named *Gomes*[6]. At my production desk, he showed me his sketches for what he later came to call a "courtyard theatre".

The courtyard theatre was not a new concept. The Young Vic was the first modern theatre to place a small thrust stage within a space with a surrounding balcony. I'd got on well with the architect, Bill Howell and together we'd developed a slightly larger and more flexible version for Christ's Hospital School in Horsham that opened in 1974.

Iain's sketches seemed exactly what was needed, so we showed them to Peter and John Bury. Iain explained the 18th century antecedents for the concept. Both were enthusiastic, although Peter did say afterward to John, "You must stop that man Mackintosh rattling on about the 18th century."

I introduced Iain to Denys Lasdun. With considerable reticence – who was this upstart addition to Pilbrow's team designing a theatre in my building? – he, too, accepted the concept. Although he did insist that the third level columns – an integral part of Iain's design – were deleted: "Columns are for holding up roofs. I've already built the roof. Take them out."

We had a studio theatre… almost!

Wednesday 14th November 1973
"The South Bank Board meeting was bad. There were imprecise answers to questions about the finishing date of the building and cost. Just an atmosphere of impotent gloom."

Monday 19th November 1973
Ginger Group. Electricians working on a forty-hour week. Seventy men are needed, there are thirty on-site. Power is needed to the drum revolve. Power was provided, but there is water in the drive control room. Lasdun: "Clearly demonstrated that the problem was one of lack of supervision and coordination on the part of McAlpines." The first part of the project – the civil engineering – was OK. But Mr. Neil, the structural engineer, "doubted that. A defeatist attitude has set in." Lasdun: "McA. are searching for trivial issues to build up a case for claims. They must be persuaded to change their attitude." [7]

Monday 26th November 1973
"To the South Bank in the freezing cold to show a group from the GLC around the new building. A general feeling of chaos on the site. And very little is happening. Few workmen about. I now become depressed with each visit. I cannot believe it will be ready as scheduled – or even approximately."

Wednesday 12th December 1973
"South Bank Board at 11.30. Still not clear information about progress on the building. The quantity surveyor talked gloomily, like a sad Lewis Carroll walrus, of possible overspending of half a million, to three quarters, or even a million. Max Rayne sat next to me doodling furiously and muttering that it would be a million and a half. Lord Cottesloe, the perfect English chairman,

"Cottesloe Cockpit": first sketches by Iain Mackintosh, November 1973

Cottesloe Theatre original model, 1973

smiled optimistically at all the bad news, while the members of the Establishment nodded their heads and clucked and tutted about the grave economic crisis facing us, and how this would affect our theatre. They then all left early for a large Christmas lunch with some tycoon or other."

Tueday 18th December 1973
Ginger Group. Peter Softley: "Work now on three-day week."

Wednesday 13th March 1974
"South Bank Board. New target dates for the handing-over of the new building from them to us are the three months from the end of August. Richard Pilbrow came up to me after the meeting and said that from the completion of handover at the end of November, his people needed four months before we could even begin rehearsing. This could be a nightmare. My brain begins to tick. I smell a crisis."

Wednesday 27th March 1974
"Early morning meeting with Richard Pilbrow. Horrifying news. It emerged that it would now be impossible to depend on previews of our productions until the beginning of June '75. So our plans are

in ruins. Our buildup of plays and actors at the Old Vic to a size large enough to occupy the three auditoriums on the South Bank, a buildup already seven months old, is a farce. I was staggered. We shall have to prepare a broadside. I asked for an early morning meeting with Denys Lasdun tomorrow. Why didn't he speak at the South Bank Board meeting the week before last, when he heard them and me say that even with the new dates, showing the building now being delivered to us in the autumn, we could still just make a royal opening in April '75? I had only one immediate thought. We shall have to continue our buildup plans for the rest of this year – it is too late to get out of them: contracts have been made with artists. Then we will stop and start to run down our program until we are given an absolutely guaranteed date for the completion of the building."

Thursday 28th March 1974
"Nine o'clock at Denys Lasdun's. Richard Pilbrow and all my gang present. We wanted to get clear news before today's NT board meeting. Lasdun tried to put all the blame on us. We should not have made our plans, not have started our buildup. Cheek. Anyway, I left some very frightened gentlemen – frightened because they see what I aim to do, which is to disassociate the NT from the architect and from the builders. If there is a national scandal – which I believe there will be – let it rest on the shoulders of those who have produced it."

Wednesday 3rd April 1974
Ginger Group. "Mole Richardson's latest date is disastrous for the NT timetable. TPC's commissioning and training bar chart was considered. McAlpine has appointed a new senior construction executive. Still considering September completion!!!" Flint: "Condensing commissioning through optimism was not realistic." PH considering cancelling all NT actor contracts. Max Rayne: "Arrange advance payment to those contractors with cash flow problems." RP: "Some problems are caused by the fact that all contracts were brought down to the lowest possible price." [8]

Tuesday 9th April 1974
"The South Bank Board met today. Lord Cottesloe, in the smoothest English establishment way, said he quite saw the difficulties of the National Theatre, and if the NT board in their

National Theatre under construction 1969, 1971

wisdom decided they had to run down their present program, of course they would have to. But he did hope that somehow or other they would maintain their program in order to keep the pressure on the builders. He would not admit to the architects or the contractors that the April 23 opening date was off, although in private session he read a letter he is drafting to the Palace to warn the Queen. He pointed out cosily that in fact the Queen had never had a firm date fixed – only 'the spring of 1975.' There was a good deal of talk about Ascot. For if she is at Ascot, she won't open the theatre in June, should that become the first possible date."

Friday 10th May 1974
"Yesterday, while I was going round the South Bank, I ran into a workman who I have several times talked to in the past. He is a theatre fan. He told me that he thought the building would not be finished until 1976, the chief reason being the total lack of supervision or coordination."

Tuesday 11th June 1974
Ginger Group. "Target completion September 7, 1974. Mole Richardson and Hall Stage require 4/5 further weeks. Tele-Stage OK. Crown (electrical) require further 4/5 weeks. Stage floor ready by mid-Dec. Seating by Race; Sir J. Lockwood seeking 'lower price.' Heating is due on by August 1st. Richard Brett reports that Rank Strand installation is 4-5 weeks behind." [9]

July 1974
"On-site, however, the building looked very far from completion. Sections were almost ready, some dressing rooms, parts of the scene dock and workshops, and these were duly admired. The sound 'petals' in the Olivier were slowly being hoisted into

position, The Cottesloe looked like an empty studio. The Lyttelton, closest to completion, still looked like an empty car park. Outsiders, however, could not guess how much of the remaining work was a matter for quick fitting or of more substantial labour. The wires leading from walls could have been quickly connected to boxes of tricks assembled elsewhere, or they could have required the installation of difficult on-site equipment. Journalists were generally of the opinion that the building might be ready by April 1975, but only just, and there was something about the known schedule which seemed a bit optimistic." [10]

Monday 1st July 1974
"Sir Edward McAlpine held a lunch at the Dorchester for all the National Theatre dignitaries. A great deal of jovial establishment chat. I must have heard people offering to 'have a word with' someone at least eight times as a solution to some problem or other. But the atmosphere was good, because news on the South Bank is now promising. McAlpines' speak of the commissioning period for the building beginning in the third week of September. The opening of the theatre in April seems a reality at last."

Thursday 4th July 1974
"This morning we took the press round the new building for the first time, to show progress. Lasdun was brilliant with them. I stressed they were seeing an unfinished building, undecorated and not yet humanised."

Tuesday 16th July 1974
However, there was some serious news discussed at the building progress subcommittee meeting:

"There was a serious shortage of electricians on-site; and that the basic work of installing the main wiring for the Olivier Theatre had been disastrously delayed. Indeed, there was now only about one week to do several months' work. Until the wiring was completed, the equipment could not be properly installed and therefore tested. The chances of opening in April 1975 now looked extremely remote." [11]
At that same meeting, Dick Brett added, "Shortage of electricians. Expert supervision is needed. McAlpine are simply not capable. In the Lyttelton: Race Seating has left the site because McAlpine's were not ready for them." Peter Softley reported that one week was left for several months' wiring to be completed.

Wednesday 17th July 1974
"An emergency meeting with McAlpine's et al because the South Bank is slipping behind again. When Max Rayne gave me the nod, I made my speech about our continuing, big, and expensive buildup at the Old Vic of productions for the new theatre, and because of that our imminent bankruptcy, unless we played there with these productions on time. I pointed out again how delay would mean a scandal, and said again I had every intention that the builders, the contractors, etc., etc., should be involved in the scandal with me. Everybody smiled, but it made an effect."

Thursday 1st August 1974
Letter from Mr. Hugh Jenkins, H.M. Minister for the Arts to Lord Cottesloe [edited for length]: "In my letter of 6th May I promised to let you know that the Government has decided to make the additional funds available to allow the National Theatre to be completed. [This is] on the clear understanding that there would be firm control of all expenditure and the exclusion of refinements which might add significantly to the total cost." [12]

Thursday 15th August 1974
"The preliminary budget for our new South Bank building shows an expenditure of some £5 million a year. The cost of heat, light, insurance and skeleton maintenance staff alone is £1 million a year. Clearly, I am cast as the pilot of the first theatrical Concorde. But then I brighten and reflect that I admire Concorde. It's one of the few beautiful things that our ugly century has produced."

Friday 16th August 1974
"Paddy Donnell had lunch with John Vernon to talk about the BBC coverage of the opening ceremony; in the meantime Kenneth Rae had contacted Martin Charteris, the Queen's private secretary, with the plans for the royal opening. The invitation was still at an informal stage, a matter of penciling in the engagement of 23rd April 1975; the official invitation was to follow in due course to Balmoral, where the Queen was staying. It was never sent.

"Donnell discovered the bad news by accident. He decided to walk over from his office in Aquinas Street; on the way, he met Richard Pilbrow, who told him about the shortage of electricians. The electricians could not cope with the problems immediately arising, and a backlog of work was piling up. Donnell investigated and agreed with Pilbrow that the proposed schedule simply could not be met. Immediately, Donnell returned to Aquinas Street and held back the official invitation to the Queen until the situation could be examined more thoroughly." [13]

Thursday 5th September 1974
Ginger Group. "Softley reported that the pace of work has slackened… lack of skilled labour and stretching of resources. Brett reports: 'Olly wiring is not yet started! Yet is due to be completed 14th September. 12 weeks work to be done in one!' RP reported that there are 28 weeks work to be done in the 19 weeks available." [14]

Saturday 14th September 1974
"Timothy O'Brien and Tazeena Firth arrived to talk about their designs for *John Gabriel Borkman* by Henrik Ibsen [to be performed in the Lyttelton]. Because this is such an entirely new kind of auditorium, with a different focus and a different rhythm, I find it enormously stimulating. For so many years, all my stage work has been based on the principle that less is more, and that colour is distracting and must be used with discipline. Yet sometimes less is less."

Monday 30th September 1974
"At Denys Lasdun's this morning for an unbelievable meeting. Contractor after contractor reported either bad news or no news at all, broken dates or no possibility of knowing when the job will be finished. The handover to us cannot now begin until May and, therefore, an opening before autumn is unthinkable. I banged the table and spoke of my commitments to artists etc. The buildup of the company and repertoire at the Old Vic had meant making commitments to a great many actors, among them Peggy Ashcroft, Diana Rigg, Albert Finney, John Gielgud, Ralph Richardson, and Paul Scofield – all of whose plans were now changed, and that is exactly the same situation I predicted last winter. The water is now getting really rough."

Friday 25th October 1974
"Conversation with Denys Lasdun telling me that a letter was on its way from McAlpine's warning me that criticisms about the delay on the building were emanating from the National Theatre and from me, and that they would take appropriate legal action if this continued."

Monday 28th October 1974
Linklater and Paines [lawyers to McAlpine] to Peter Hall: "We act for Sir Robert McAlpine and Sons… with regard to publicity about the National Theatre. *The Sunday Times* of October 20th, 1974 stated that the National 'simply does not know when McAlpine's are going to finish the monumental building on the South Bank.' As you know, these statements are untrue: McAlpine's work will in substance be completed by the end of December. They are not in breach. We have advised our clients that they could take action, but they have no intention of so doing…" [15]

Tuesday 29th October 1974
"The threatened McAlpine letter arrives – not from them, but from their solicitors. I suppose their motive is to shut me up. If so, it won't work. The building is late and there is going to be trouble. On the other hand, I don't want a Sydney Opera House-type public scandal going on and on and on. It will be damaging to us as much as to McAlpines."

Thursday 31st October 1974
Peter Hall to Messrs. Linklater and Paines: "Thank you for your letter. I find the contents surprising because you appear to be giving me responsibility for statements which you must know are not attributable to me. The question of responsibility for the delay in completion is a matter for the South Bank Theatre Board. But the building is late. Otherwise the National would be occupying it now as planned. The company was originally told to be ready to move in at the beginning of September 1974… I'm afraid that it is an inescapable fact that a series of target dates for completion have not been met… at a meeting on 30th September, McAlpines could nevertheless give no firm indication as to the date on which the building could be ready for the National Theatre to begin its planned program of occupancy. If McAlpines would like to suggest a wording which would

explain the delays, and, more importantly, provide a firm date for occupancy, we would be only to happy to use it." [16]

Wednesday 6th November 1974
Simon Relph [the NT's Technical Administrator 1974-78] to Peter Hall: "Re: Cottesloe Theatre Estimates. We find ourself confused as to exactly how much of the proposed scheme might be included. The basic problem is that to complete the building, architects must be provided with information about the complete design. As we understand it, Theatre Projects have received no fee for their work with the original scheme, and we are now asking them to do more work. In my view, the responsibility lies with the S.B.T.B. As I understand it, both Theatre Projects and the architects have been happy to co-operate." [17]

Thursday 7th November 1974
Removal of limit on contribution to cost of National Theatre:

"In section 1 of the National Theatre Act 1949 (which, by virtue of the Transfer of Functions Order 1965 and the National Theatre and Museum of London Act 1973, authorises the Secretary of State to make contributions not exceeding £5,700,000 in respect of the cost of erecting and equipping a National Theatre), the words '(not exceeding £5,700,000)' shall be omitted, but no contribution shall be made under that section after the passing of this Act without the consent of the Treasury." [18]

Tuesday 28th January 1975
Ginger Group. Peter Softley: "Early August had already slipped by a few weeks." Wiring was ten weeks behind. Lyttelton air inlets delayed carpeting and seat installation – two month's delay. Olly would have the same problem. DL: "It had not been his intention to put signs on the outside of the building". Max Rayne: "The NT needed external signs." Brett: "The NT would be getting a bare-walls building." [19]

Tuesday 11th February 1975
"As we were presented, the Queen asked me when the National Theatre would open. I said I didn't know. The Duke asked me when the National Theatre would open. I said I didn't know. The Queen Mother asked me when the National Theatre would open. I said I didn't know. The Prince of Wales asked me when the National Theatre would open. I said I didn't know. At least they all knew I was running the National Theatre."

Thursday 13th February 1975
Memorandum on 'McAlpine Lunch.' "Peter Hall kept repeating how low the morale of the NT was and he'd had a very depressing meeting with Pinter, Jonathan Miller, et al, who all thought they were going to be sacked. No credibility whatsoever is given to the completion of the National Theatre. He thought it was particularly sad that the money had not been given to complete the Cottesloe Theatre. He and Sir Max both thought that it was the only one of the three that was any good (by that they meant 'popular'). DL exploded at this and said that he and his colleagues had not been sweating their guts out for the last 12½ years to be told that the studio theatre was the most important theatre. Everyone laughed at this and thought DL a joke and told him not to take it so seriously." [20]

Friday 4th April 1975
"Round the South Bank early this morning. The Olivier continues to excite and the Lyttelton is nearly finished. The furniture, the carpets, the lights, the heating are all ready in the offices. Great feeling of lassitude about the place, though."

Friday 11th April 1975
Letter to Richard Pilbrow from Denys Lasdun: "I would like it to be understood that we still expect to maintain full control of all illustrative and descriptive material concerned with the architecture of the building and that this, of course, includes the relationship of stage to auditorium." [21]

Saturday 19th April 1975
Letter from Francis Reid [theatre consultant and lighting designer] to Richard Pilbrow: "Until Thursday last on the South Bank I have always had a feeling that, at best, new theatres were an assimilation of past techniques. The wondrous fact of that new National is that it is a projection forward not only from staging past but from our unrealised dreams of staging present. There are miseries amongst us and principally they mutter about concrete." [22]

Monday 19th May 1975

"My first introduction to the great theatre at Epidaurus. I was overwhelmed by it. The whole day was unforgettable. It's exactly as if someone had said to me, 'The Globe has after all been preserved on the South Bank, come over and have a look at it, then you might understand something about staging Shakespeare.' For here is a Greek theatre, and a masterpiece of architecture as well. Yesterday, the Roman theatre by the Acropolis had left me cold: a brutal confrontation, the audience looking at the performers as their victims. But here, in a Greek theatre, everything grows out of the landscape. The first impression is one of intimacy, yet it holds 15,000 people. The second is one of perfect, simple geometry, yet every geometric calculation is slightly altered in the interest of grace and of humanity. Most extraordinary of all is the way the auditorium grows out of the hillside and, as you sit in it, seems to continue into the landscape, making a whole world of which the spectator feels a part. Why did they site it here? Because for the Greeks the landscape was alive, and full of gods who had a positive relationship with man."

Friday 23rd May 1975

"Took Trevor Nunn round the South Bank. He said to me that if he and I were walking round the building this morning unconnected with it, surely we would say to ourselves, there is no organisation that can possibly take it on at the moment without being crucified by it. I tend to agree with him. The building seems to demand martyrs. And I am going to be very careful not to be one."

Monday 27th July 1975

"Yet there could still be a possibility that the building will not be open for two or three years, that it will be allowed merely to drain away £1/2 - £3/4 million a year, which is what it will cost just to keep it standing empty. It was planned when energy was cheap, and when Larry, the czar of the stage, was determined to design a theatre grander and more beautifully equipped than any in history. This he has done, but it's a legacy which may prove painful in this new age of dear energy and high labour costs. Standards may go, great schemes like the National Theatre may falter, but a little voice inside me still whispers amusedly: All I

Ancient theatre at Epidaurus, Greece. Originally by Polykleitos in around 340BC, although probably smaller, perhaps ending at the first cross-gangway

need to make a play is half-a-dozen people and a space. I don't need the South Bank; perhaps it is already a dodo?

"To a South Bank Board meeting. The usual gloomy recital of stage equipment for the new theatre still nowhere near ready. I got very annoyed and went far too far. I thumped the table and said that if we were now to wait for all the electronic marvels to be finished we might be waiting another two years before we moved on to the South Bank. They were not the essential thing about a theatre. What we wanted was to get in and act."

Thursday 4th September 1975

Special Report on Sabotage at the National Theatre by the National Building Agency. "I have previously reported that various acts of sabotage have occurred on the site. This week we found two more cases, one more serious than the others. Various methods of dealing with this have been discussed: Removal to another site of a suspect (this might result in industrial action), the offering of a reward by McAlpine; the involvement with McAlpine's security department and a police investigation. This method was adopted. Current cases are: sabotage (technical cables cut in lower theatre lighting bridges, SM control room, upper theatre plenum space and control rooms); possible danger to life: metal strap placed to cause blowback of fuse when inserted, cast-iron counterweights placed across top of stairs; accident or vandalism: hose reel turned on to cause flooding, ball valves removed from lavatory cisterns." [23]

Friday 19th September 1975
"Moved into my office on the South Bank. I was very excited. Everything looks wonderful. The river glows outside the window. It is beautiful." **With admin staff all moved to the new building, the Aquinas Street huts are closed a week later.**

Tuesday 23rd September 1975
"The particular rehearsal room in the new theatre that we are using is quiet, has good daylight, height, and is properly warmed. After 21 years of rehearsing in cupboards, leaky halls, and bars smelling of last night's drink and tobacco, at last I am in a place with good conditions. I count this one of the greatest merits of our South Bank building. The work can be created in a proper place."

Friday 10th October 1975
"I was settling down in my office to a session with John Goodwin [Head of Publicity, later editor of Hall's diaries] about the design committee, which was meeting this afternoon, when Larry walked in, looking old and uneasy. He'd asked Denys Lasdun to show him round the new building, so Denys was in attendance. It must have taken great courage on Larry's part to come and see everybody after a year, his appearance so different, feeling so frail, and being the man outside this wonderful place that he has created."

Monday 17th November 1975
"This morning Daniel Thorndike asked Michael Melia, 'Who's there?' and Michael Melia asked the voice to unfold itself. We were rehearsing *Hamlet* in the Lyttelton auditorium, and they were the first actors to speak on a stage of the National Theatre. A thrilling day. Sets and costumes patchy, half-finished, but everything working. The theatre looks well, the actors dominate it easily, and – most important – the acoustics seem to be perfect. I tried experimental lighting cues with David Hersey. What we did would have taken about six hours with conventional equipment. Yet now, on the new computerised board we were able in two hours to dash through various ideas."

Friday 12th December 1975
Your author writes to Sir Laurence with photos of the site and the emerging theatres with "Happy Christmas" greetings.

Monday 22nd December 1975
"News this morning that the Queen doesn't want to open the building until it's all finished, and therefore suggests October, after Balmoral. I can't say I'm sorry about this. It might, I suppose, give contractors and people an excuse for going slower, but then in the past the imminence of a royal visit never did anything to speed them up. I think it's good news. It means the whole place will be well and truly opened and buzzing before we get down to the official formalities."

Tuesday 13th January 1976
"To a Ginger Group meeting. A dozen or so defensive contractors there. It's now clear that what I predicted long ago will happen. We shall be in the new theatre but there will be no stage flying equipment and no stage machinery ready; consequently, our costs will be a great deal more than planned because of the extra stagehands needed. Even so, we must start, we must begin. Truth is, the consultants have had little discipline imposed on them by the South Bank Board to stop them dreaming the most extravagant dreams. I did a little table thumping and then crept off to do [the TV show] *Aquarius*."

Wednesday 28th January 1976
"Denys Lasdun arrived in a great state because he said the curved shape we have given to the Lyttelton stage front ruined the straight lines and angles of his architecture. I explained it was because the stage had to accommodate the productions transferring from the Old Vic without changes being made to them. I soothed him, and said John Bury and I would look into it, but that far more bothering was the problem of getting the theatre finished at all, whatever the front of the stage. This went home with Lasdun and he looked more and more worried. But what can be done? I sometimes feel I am all set up to be a great sacrificial victim: the white temple's first blood. That is not the way I am going to behave. I must believe in my own capacity to succeed. I'm not sure I do any more."

Wednesday 4th February 1976
"Tonight was the acoustics test. The Lyttelton was packed: 700 contractors, engineers and their wives and children, plus a couple of hundred from the theatre. Great excitement. I shall never forget seeing the foyers full of people for the first time.

But the best moment to me was when, at the beginning of the test, Albert [Finney] and Gawn Grainger walked on to the stage and talked to each other deliberately making no sound: a nice start and a big laugh. At intervals gentlemen came on and fired revolvers and let off maroons [fireworks], and others rushed about the auditorium measuring the results. There was singing, and I played the piano for the accounts department in three songs, the lights failed at quarter past ten but Albert continued to tell jokes in the dark. The theatre works. Hearts were high by the end of tonight."

Wednesday 18th February 1976
"A catastrophic dress rehearsal of [Ben Travers' farce] *Plunder* last night in the Lyttelton [All the productions playing at the Old Vic were also being rehearsed on the Lyttelton stage for their opening there in March]. The 30 second scene change took 40 minutes. None of the communication systems is working – no cue lights, none of the flying. You can't time a curtain in or out. The whole situation is horrifying. Shall we make the opening?"

Friday 20th February 1976
"*Hamlet* dress rehearsal in the Lyttelton tonight: 7pm to nearly midnight. Who would have thought a problem in the new theatre would be that the front-of-house doors didn't fit, and that the automatic closing devices made them squeak. We asked for the doors to be fixed last November. Nothing has been done."

Tuesday 24th February 1976
"A ghastly afternoon's rehearsal of *Borkman* in the Lyttelton. The noise of banging and hammering all over the building made it impossible to concentrate. Added to which there was a large electric drill going like a nightmare at the dentist. So the actors were completely inaudible at times. Nothing to be done. The workmen just say, 'If you want the theatre open…'"

Thursday 26th February 1976
"We decided today to go manual with the Lyttelton backstage equipment and bypass the electronic system. This means that over the next months we shall have to install a manual flying system ourselves, line by line. I had a drink with some of the stage crew in the bar. The cry, 'We've gone manual,' was one of jubilation. Power and performance were back where they needed to be, in the hands of the operators, the human touch. All we need is a space, an audience, and some lights. That is all we're going to get in the Lyttelton."

"I sometimes feel I am all set up to be a great sacrificial victim: the white temple's first blood."

Peter Hall

Friday 5th March 1976
"Ran into Harry Pugh [an associate of DL&P], who made an amazing speech to me. It was terrible, he said, that we'd had to endure such difficulties in this run-up to the Lyttelton opening. The contractors and the consultants were all agreed that we must not suffer in the same way in the run-up to the opening of the Olivier. Therefore, he said, they want to test and finish all the equipment there before letting us in. I said this was unacceptable, as I didn't believe that if we gave them more time things would be any more finished. I know there's a report going to the South Bank Board in which they are going to try and bring this one off. But I am not going to let them."

Saturday 6th March 1976
"I talked to Richard Pilbrow and my worst suspicions were confirmed. They are extremely late completing the Olivier. For instance, they haven't yet even started putting in the switchboard, and instead of 30 people working on the stage wiring there are – wait for it – four. So, said Richard, it would be much better if they absolutely finished the Olivier before handing it over to us, but, of course, later than we had planned. I told him if this came up next Wednesday at the South Bank Board meeting, I would oppose it resolutely and there would be a confrontation. He looked rattled.

"The Olivier obviously won't be ready on time. I need this like a hole in the head while we are struggling with moving the Old Vic productions into the Lyttelton for its grand opening next week. If I am not very careful, though, the disgrace will be laid at the door of the National Theatre. It's the fault of the South Bank Board and their contractors. There is clearly a big feud going on between McAlpine's and the architects.

"No one is handling the situation at all properly. We have asked repeatedly for a gang of a dozen men who can go round de-snagging, making lavatories work, correcting doors, etc., etc. McAlpine's have ignored this. Everything is a special job which has to be indented for and go through the office. And costs a fortune. I spent most of the day with my mind seething, wondering what to do. Dress rehearsal of *Happy Days* in the Lyttelton. We had an invited audience of 150. The back of the stalls was like an oven, the front freezing cold; and the play was hardly audible for the din of the air-conditioning – it's like some vast ocean liner at sea. Peggy in fine form, though. I wandered about under the stage after the performance, trying to trace the noises. There appears to be a big, roaring furnace right below the front row of the stalls, and the sound is coming up into the auditorium."

Wednesday 10th March 1976
"Gathering of the South Bank Board to discuss that since the last meeting, a month ago, the delivery of the Olivier to us for rehearsals, etc., has moved from the beginning of April to the end of June, the only explanation being 'electrical difficulties', and the quite spurious argument that the technical consultants don't want the National Theatre staff to go through hell again – they want to finish before we go in. Lord Cottesloe, rather touchingly, in his most Polonius-like way, read out a little prepared speech written in meticulous Etonian handwriting on his own House of Lords notepaper, recording that we must all stand together. He was just about to call the consultants in when I asked if I could have a few moments off the record. I said we were not prepared to accept that the consultants must finish the work first. It was only a way of them giving themselves more time. We had every intention of getting into the Olivier as soon as possible – not, though, to the extent of ruining the plays. If that were to be so, we would stage our planned repertoire in another theatre. But perform we would... The consultants then came in and had their say but it didn't actually mean very much because I had provided a background. The delays and extra labour so far on the South Bank have cost us about £125,000. God knows what the final figure will be.
[The end figure was £377,407. This was paid off over the years, largely by the NT itself, partly by the South Bank Theatre Board, and finally by the Arts Council, whose special grant of £173,597 in 1983 cleared the deficit.]

Monday 15th March 1976
"McAlpine's lunch in the Pavilion Room of the Dorchester: McAlpine father and son; Goodman; Lockwood; Rayne; Cottesloe – the cultural establishment. A good deal of congratulations about having got the building going at last. Cottesloe repeated his joke of last week: 'Well, we're not out of the wood yet, but at least we're in it!' I was there to sour the proceedings by pointing out that if the contractors didn't hand the Olivier over to us by July we were likely to be playing our Olivier repertoire in a tent on the back car park. Some consternation, but the point went home."

Wednesday 17th March 1976
Michael Blakemore presents a paper to a meeting of the Associate Directors protesting what he perceives as Peter Hall's self-serving behaviour as artistic director as well as his diminishing of Olivier's selfless principles over the company's leadership. His accusations are not accepted; Michael eventually resigns.

Monday 29th March 1976
"*Tamburlaine* work this morning with John Bury. Haunted all the time by the problem of scale in the Olivier. We really don't know what the size of things should be in that auditorium."

Monday 12th April 1976
"Lunch meeting to discover how things are progressing with the Olivier. A dreadful atmosphere: smug, hopeless. The news is, of course, worse than we could have expected. In the last month, they have lost a month. What can I do? Play *Tamburlaine* somewhere else? I am very foxed. I must think.

"Peter Softley said two amazing things when I was complaining about air-conditioning noises. I was hearing the air-conditioning, he said, because the theatre was so quiet and had such good acoustics. He also said the actors were hot not because it was hot but because this perfectly designed theatre had no draughts. The perils of perfection! The air-conditioning is noisy. And it is hot."

Wednesday 14th April 1976
"South Bank Board meeting. I asked if we could just be given some firm date – any date – for the Olivier. Silence. Was it, I said, wrong to ask to open on 15th July? Silence. Was I right to ask to open on 15th July? Silence. I have concluded to myself that we shall not be opening *Tamburlaine* on 15th July."

Tuesday 11th May 1976
"Sam Beckett over this afternoon to see the new building. He was thrilled with it, particularly the Olivier."

Friday 14th May 1976
"Working on *Tamburlaine* in the Olivier with John Bury and John Heilpern [assistant on the production]. I yearn for invisible entrances, some way of making actors materialise on to the world. The Barbican is going to be much better than the Olivier from this point of view. But then it should be. John Bury and I saw to that." **[The design of the RSC's Barbican Theatre was the result of a close collaboration between Hall and Bury with Peter Chamberlin, the architect.]**

Tuesday 18th May 1976
"Dinner at Denys Lasdun's. Good food and good company but too many people. Denys at one point became very touchy about his building. I said he mustn't be paranoid – that was just like me. He said I was the last person in the world he would think of as paranoid: I was an extrovert, taking it all in my stride. I suppose that's a tribute to my mask."

Thursday 24th June 1976
First performance in the Lyttelton
"First night of *Blithe Spirit* [Lighting by your author!]. The air-conditioning has broken down and the heat was tremendous. There was about fifty percent less laughter than at any of the previews, so all the actors forced."

Sunday 8th August 1976
"Depressing acoustics tests tonight in the Olivier. The sound was not too bad in the centre of the auditorium but at the sides it was dreadful, and the noise of the air-conditioning is very intrusive… of course."

25th October 1976, H.M. The Queen arrives… in the pouring rain

Friday 13th August 1976
"A date which lived up to its reputation. We were due for our first technical rehearsal of *Tamburlaine* tonight, but Simon came to see me to say the stage staff had refused the ACAS ruling and voted against working in the Olivier while they were on call for the Lyttelton. In the Olivier, nobody but the stage management and production team was there. Kon Fredericks was lurking about under the stage to make sure we didn't rehearse even a cue. I am heartbroken, but we must stand up to the wreckers among them now, or the theatre will not be a place in which to work for the future. If *Tamburlaine* has to go to the wall, it must."

Thursday 16th September 1976
"News that Larry is coming to the first *Tamburlaine* preview tonight. It's all over the papers today that he opened Michael Elliott's new Royal Exchange Theatre in Manchester. Yet he won't come to the Olivier at its opening on 4th October. 'No, no', he says, 'it's your evening – yours and the actors'…"

Thursday 16th September 1976
The first (unofficial) strike of stagehands led by Kon Fredericks, the National's master carpenter and the chief steward of NATTKE (the union representing those working backstage in theatre, cinema and television) over multi-theatre working, causes the loss of four performances. Management gave ground to the demands, but Peter Hall noted he didn't want to work here "unless the bully boys go." [24]

Getting The National Theatre to Function

Richard York, Assistant General Manager
"By the spring of 1972, the NT's general manager, Tony Easterbrook, was desperate that the National Theatre Company was not being consulted about the details of their own theatre. The construction then was up to the Lyttelton Theatre stalls foyer level. There were 1001 details which needed to be resolved. Denys Lasdun's view was strongly that his building had nothing to do with the National Theatre and the National Theatre Board, because they were not the client, and we don't talk to anybody but our clients, who are the South Bank Board. He felt he wasn't able to. That, allied to his prickly temperament, made for no real relationship with the company at all. Tony's idea was that by importing me into his office, as assistant general manager, I would act as liaison.

"I hardly ever met Denys. One did see him from time to time because he was the master amongst his journeyman. With Peter Softley, it took a long time to develop a friendly, reasonable relationship. He was a very nice guy, and tremendously hard-working, devoted to Denys and to the work in hand. Then there was Harry Pugh, who was an easier proposition and a more genial man. He was easy to talk to and sometimes a bit irreverent about his master, which helped oil the wheels. Archie was the clerk of works, I think it was people like Archie who oversaw that quality of the concrete and the detailing, who drove McAlpine's to such high standards. I think it's still one of the treasures of the National Theatre to actually just walk around looking at how beautifully built it is.

"I was actually trying to penetrate the protections of the architectural team and it was three steps forward and two steps back. But they were also up against a very fast ticking clock, and things needed to be decided. They needed information from the National Theatre, whether they liked it or not, and whether they were the client or not.

"A lot of my work involved the loose items of the building: furniture, fittings, and equipment. Or trying to understand things like environment plant, which was a very big investment. There had been no consultation with the National Theatre about the impact of what was being designed in terms of the manpower to run it, the cost of utilities.

> "I think it's still one of the treasures of the National Theatre to actually just walk around looking at how beautifully built it is."
> Richard York

Richard York at The Barbican

"We commissioned our own model of the building, it was in Perspex, so you could actually take in the relationship of different parts of building and the way they were linked together. We began to be able to address things like, where are you going to control the audience, because this free flows through the ground floor to the foyer, but can you shut one off, or do you shut people off from the loos?

"Also, the delivery of goods. You saw where scenery comes into the building and raw materials for the workshops because there was a great big door at the back. But where does staff come in to work in the workshops?

"Catering deliveries were on the front adjacent to the dustbins. Because actually, that was something Lasdun forgot: where are you going to put the waste disposal? The terrible smells of cooking, because they had to put additional ventilation off the kitchen, and the only place to put it was in the north wall and it squirted out over the embankment.

Internal Politics
"The political situation inside the National Theatre was pretty toxic, even in Sir Laurence's time. There was a strong socialist workers party who had taken over NATTKE. They were the heart of the industrial relations at the Old Vic.

"The circumstances in which Peter Hall arrived were unfortunate, and the fact that there were other personnel changes, people felt insecure. Tony Easterbrook was swept away and bully boys came in.

Problems

"This must have been around '73, the shortage of materials. Famously 18 feet of stainless steel tubing, which was said to be on 22 month delivery. The theatre at that point was supposed to be open in 22 months. That was what caused the chairman, Sir Max Rayne, Lord Goodman (who one hardly ever saw) and Sir Joseph Lookwood (who you saw quite often) to decide heads needed to be banged!

"I lasted until '77, until we'd opened the Cottesloe. I was offered a job with the the Barbican. I took it with great relief. Peter went off to do *Aquarius* and make films for weekend television and therefore was just never seen in Aquinas Street. Peter's decision was to be an absentee director. Often, people were summoned to come to his flat in Cromwell Tower [in the Barbican] for meetings, rather than him coming into the office. That left a very sour taste. Larry had been treated very badly by the board. I think Peter had to have been part of that. It was the worst possible moment for him, and it was the worst possible exit for Sir Laurence, who remained a much-loved figure.

Moving In

"Douglas Cornelissen, who had been general stage manager, was the first to move into the building. He was given the role of getting to grips with the realities of servicing the building. I'd spent much of the previous two years taking visitors around and, by that time, we had got a good working relationship going with Lasdun and McAlpine's.

"There were huge deliveries of loose furniture, loose equipment, and lighting equipment. You suddenly realised that this was all on a massive scale compared to the setup at the Old Vic, because we were looking at a repertoire for three theatres. It was an extraordinary increase in activity. And actually you can't just have one photocopier in a building of this size, that, actually each department needed copiers. I have no real recollection of the administrative backups of the South Bank Theatre Board other than the secretary, Mark Harrison, who was a tower of strength but a man overburdened with the minutiae on the one hand, the whole business of signing off vast sums of money demanded by contractors and subcontractors, and, presumably, the design team and the

> **"And then the Queen arrived. On the wettest night in October imaginable. For one of the worst shows, *Il Campiello*."**
>
> Richard York

consultants. We were supposed to get anything above a certain level tendered for. Lasdun's were perfectly capable of choosing the carpet and getting everybody who had a word to say about it to approve it, and to organise the delivery of it. But actually, it came down to saying how many desks and how many drawing boards were needed for the offices. One department was wonderful: wardrobe. It knew precisely what it wanted, not only that but precisely where it should come from, and precisely how much, or how little, should be paid for it.

Opening

"It was the most exciting place to be in London.

"A lot of people were new to the National Theatre organisation, or needed introduction. And there was a huge amount of just sheer administration to make sure that things were arriving on the right day, went to their places at the right time, were taken onboard by somebody, that weren't subsequently nicked, because the building was full of holes. It was terribly hard to secure it properly. Because there were men working overnight, the building never shut down. The taps and shower heads kept disappearing from the dressing rooms.

"There was also all kinds of things that had to be dealt with, like sign posting. Lasdun's sign posting was miniscule. He felt the building would speak for itself. I spent hours going around backstage putting out temporary paper signs.

"And then the Queen arrived. On the wettest night in October imaginable. For one of the worst shows, *Il Campiello*.

"And of course, life then didn't stop because we'd actually opened There was still masses to do.

"Clearly, the public is much more comfortable with the building now; they like going there. I like going there.

Rosie Beattie: A Stage Manager's Story

"The time of actually getting in was extraordinary. I don't think any of us realised at the time that it was a big part of theatre history, because we were all so busy trying to make everything work, get everything right, keep people happy, make sure we didn't lose people… that was a big, big problem. It was just work, work, work, keep going, keep going, keep going, and a great mix of horrors, and then absolute elation. It's only years later, looking back, you think, yes, actually, we were here when all that was happening. It was very wonderful.

"When we moved in, we all got lost. We were opening *Hamlet* in the Lyttelton, and there was this awful noise of drilling coming from somewhere during the final rehearsal, and Peter said to me, 'You've got to go and get this stopped.' Off I went, following the sound of the drilling until, eventually, I was in the car park underneath, and there it was. So I said to the workmen, 'I'm terribly sorry, but would you mind stopping? Because we're right in the middle of the last rehearsal of *Hamlet*.' 'Oh, that's all right with us, love.' Down with the tools.

"I thought, 'Well, I'll probably be in trouble, but what can I do?' Anyway, I looked around and thought, I don't know where I am. How do I get back to the prompt corner of the Lyttelton? Then I saw a bit of daylight, so I climbed my way through the bricks and I came out on the main road. I walked into the stage door and got back to the prompt corner, and all I got was a blasting: 'Where have you been? What do you think you're doing?'

"You couldn't say to actors, 'Oh, will you just pop up to the wig department or costume on the fourth floor?' You'd probably never see them again, they'd get so lost.

"Some of the rewards were wonderful. The second play I did was *John Gabriel Borkman*, with Ralph Richardson, Peggy Ashcroft, and Wendy Hiller. We were in the Lyttelton with the last scene played on a great mound – a John Bury design – where they were dying off at the end of the play. So we got to the end – and then we all looked at each other and said, 'Okay, how are we going to get these people off that mound to take their bows?' Then Ralph Richardson said, 'No problem. We'll just sit on our bottoms and we'll slide down.' I said to one of the ASMs, 'You catch Wendy Hiller. I'll catch Ralph. You catch Dame Peg.' These three wonderful people, very gamely, just sitting down and sliding, and then we sort of propped them up. And you'd take the curtain up and they'd all be bowing.

> **"Actually getting in was extraordinary. Looking back you think, yes, actually we were there when it was happening. It was very wonderful."**
> Rosie Beattie

Diana Boddington – Mentor

"I got to the Old Vic in 1974, and all the stage management were huddled in one dressing room. That was the office. Diana Boddington was the one who'd been working with Sir Laurence, and I used to think, Oh, my goodness, I'm a bit nervous of her. But she was absolutely lovely. But oh gosh, what a character she was. She wore her pinafore dress and her sandals to the last day of working here.

Moving In

"Of course, things had to change when we got here, and there were exciting things: suddenly we got offices and, you know, things were sort of easier in lots of ways, once we got over the shock of the fact that we'd have to walk ten miles a day.

"All the people who came, the posh dinners and escorting the Queen Mother around the building. Meeting Princess Margaret, who was tight as could be, on John Bury's set of *Hamlet*. She was very well gone after her G&Ts in the VIP room, and she insisted on meeting the company at the end of the performance onstage. And John's floor was a typical Bury formica 'slidy' floor, she arrived, and she had her white sandal shoes on, and she just sort of glided from one side of the stage to the other. And she ended up with me, and she said, 'And what do you do?' I said, 'Well, I'm the stage manager.' 'Oh,' she said, 'but you're a girl.' I said, 'Spot-on. I am a girl, yes.'

"Do you think that things have improved over the years? It's difficult to tell, isn't it? They've done so many things to try and change the Lyttelton, and each time they made a complete mess and it doesn't do any good.

"We'd been so used to hearing people in a real, real stew about doing anything in the Olivier. In the early days, we had actors, who had worked in theatre. Then we had a new wave who had done the majority of their work on television. We had to say, 'You have to learn how to use the Olivier, which is a difficult theatre. The very centre of it is the 'Michael Bryant spot' because Michael always found the best place to be and woe betide anybody who tried to get on Michael Bryant's spot. It goes from just below the prompt corner or the OP corner, and the other little entrance there – the very centre of the drum. And if you go too far down, your voice just disappears. If you're too far up, you have to yell. So that is the perfect spot.

"The other thing that I remember was when, eventually, we got to use the drum. The first play was *The Shaughraun*. When it first worked, the tears were just pouring down my face because I thought, I'll never get the chance to use it. We had that lovely Mary Soames as chairperson of the National Theatre, a wonderful lady, and she rang up and said, 'I would love to have a go on this drum revolve.' So she came in and she was like an overgrown schoolgirl, she was so excited about the whole thing. Absolutely fantastic. But then, you know, seeing things like *The Wind in the Willows* it was just utter magic. It really, really was so clever. And once again, we thought, Well, okay, we've waited a long time for this, but it's here. It's happened. Extraordinary".

Laurie Clayton
Lighting Supervisor, Lyttelton Theatre
Longest-serving member of NT staff from 1974 until his retirement in December 2021.

Laurie: Getting in to the building was long hours. You just didn't go home. I can remember coming in before the building was

> "The drum – seeing things like *The Wind in the Willows*, it was just utter magic. We thought, we've waited a long time for this, but it's here, it's happened. Extraordinary!"
>
> Rosie Beattie

handed over, doing *Hamlet* with Peter Hall, before it had even opened at the Old Vic, and putting a trestle table out in the stalls. It was November, it was freezing, everyone had their coats on. Peter Hall demanding to rehearse onstage with lights. We put a rig in, turned it on, David Hersey focused a few things…

Richard: This would've been before Christmas of '75?

Laurie: The rig was being delivered here, and it was stacked in the dressing rooms in boxes. Certain bits of it had to go up and come down again. We couldn't hang anything over stage. There was still a lot of wiring to be done. I can remember the lighting desk just sitting there with lots of cables coming out and days of Martin Moore [Strand Lighting, chief engineer] standing in the back scratching his head, going, 'I hope this works.'

Peter Hall used to smoke. He had a director's chair in the stalls. He was cold, there was no heating, there were no seats, just concrete. And the slots for the air-conditioning, which was not even installed. All the draft was coming from below.

We tried to plan it all in advance, who was going to be where, and at that time the crew was to be expanded. I think I was part of that expansion when I joined in '74. I think at one point there were twenty-two of us to run the Vic and here. Though I did quite a bit in the Olivier, I hung my coat in the Lyttelton. And then we got the Cottesloe as well.

Richard: Yes. That was the last. That was in February '77.

Laurie: At that time, we were also touring a lot of the shows. We toured six productions a year, and we took everything. There were certain shows we couldn't do, like *The Shaughraun*, and *Tamburlaine*, but *Hamlet*, all the shows in Lyttelton were toured. At that time, Peter had done the math; the Cottesloe didn't have to pay for anything because if we did eighty percent of house capacity, it would keep the building open.

Richard: Were you on *The Mysteries*? They were fantastic.

Laurie: I lit those with Bill Dudley.

Richard: Good God. Beautiful.

Laurie: We also had all the foreign theatres of Europe coming here. So we met amazing people from around the world. TNP from Paris. A German company. Swedish. Peter Stein, a couple times. *Summerfolk*. What a nightmare that was. Lots of trees and 20 tons of soil on the stage and a pond.

Richard: What happened when leadership changed? Peter moves on, replaced by Richard Eyre. Did that make an impact on your department?

Laurie: Richard is more of a people person. Peter was a great politician, and I don't think that we would have got the building up without that. To stand on a table the way he did, to shout at everyone and say, 'We are running. I don't care what the consequences.' He was pigheaded, arrogant about it. But we definitely couldn't have done without it.

Richard Eyre came in, and introduced himself, did a big walk around, and had chats with people, going into the bar and talking to people. He was a more visible leader – he did know everyone's name and what they did.

Years later, I toured *Richard III* and *King Lear* with him for the Ian McKellen season. Richard came out to Bucharest. We had the lighting control in Ceausescu's box, and Richard was there, and the silence at the end; you could hear a pin drop. The actors

> "I remember the lighting desk just sitting there with lots of cables coming out... going, 'I hope this works!'"
> — Laurie Clayton

Laurie Clayton

came on for applause, and stood silent, and suddenly the whole place erupted, and the standing ovation went on for – it felt like hours, but it was like ten, fifteen minutes. Richard's there – we're all nearly in tears – it hit the heartstrings, and then Richard's saying, "This is great. This is why I'm doing it."

There was that saying that was coined way back in the '70s, "The National Theatre is yours." It didn't really feel yours. But when Richard was there, it was yours; he listened.

Richard: So, then, Trevor.

Laurie: Trevor Nunn, different again.

Richard: And you did all the changes in the Lyttelton.

Laurie: He always felt that there was a gap between the stage and the audience, especially the circle. He just wanted one big single rake of audience. It was a lot of work, but that work enabled us to do things like update the lighting desk. The control rooms were all changed, so sound did a major reinstall of all their equipment.

Richard: And then the two Nicks arrive. [Hytner and Starr.]

Laurie: Well, Nick Hytner was another people person. He knew everyone's name, and was willing to listen. He was basically

3.1 Peter Hall Takes Charge and Writes a Diary Part I

responsible for the opening up of the building. Now you can't get into the foyers because it's all being used all the time.

Then we got Rufus, and again different. So, it'd be boring if it was all the same all the time, wouldn't it? I could be doing *The Mousetrap*. That seems to be the same – crew are changing on that all the time, and the actors are changing, but that's been going for about as long as I've been here, if not longer.

Richard Brett: A Recollection
"Peter Hall's entirely understandable impatience with the interminable delays was hard to live with. The embarrassment of so much of our design work, with the ambitious stage equipment being unfinished, was a nightmare. Both Richard PIlbrow and I felt ourselves both responsible and at the same time scapegoats for a disastrous situation.

"The state of the nation, the minimal budget provisions and the constant search for savings, the lack of real leadership from the main contractor, McAlpine's, the equipment subcontractors being crippled by their own lowest bid tenders, added up to a nightmare."

Today, in 2023, it's hard to remember how bad those times were.

Dick truly did turn out to be the hero. Despite our work for years trying to design theatre facilities that would lead the world, we had to agree with Peter Hall… bare boards and a passion were all that theatre truly needed.

What did that mean in our massive concrete castle? Stages for the actors to stand on, sufficient lighting and sound, seats, and minimum facilities for the public to get the building open.

In the theatres, Dick took charge. He established a desk at the front of the Lyttelton and was there day and night. He ran the site. "That room must be plastered today! Six pairs of electricians to the second bridge now!" He, with his small team from TPC, drove the completion.

The sound and lighting contractors rose to the challenge, the innovative Lightboard and the sophisticated sound and communications did work as promised. The stage machinery contractors continued to work at nights for months – and indeed years – into the future, toiling at nights when the theatre folk were home in bed. The Olivier power flying was finally commissioned in 1978 and the infamous drum revolve in 1982.

It would be inconceivable today for a consultant to take such an executive role… but Dick made it work. Many men and women of the National – stage managers, technicians, electricians and other staff – worked almost around the clock day after day. The curtain did eventually rise.

I'll let Richard York tell the final nail-biting story… A last word:

The Entertainment Licence
Richard York: "The entertainment licence was entirely my responsibility, to ensure the buildings were licensed for public entertainment. There were two lovely surveyors, Ron and Arthur from the GLC, who liked to come visit for a cup of tea on Friday afternoons, because they both went home through Waterloo station, so it was very convenient.

"Anyway, they inspected us with Conrad, the engineer in the licensing department who was responsible for ensuring that air flowed, and things drained, and all that side of it. They were a really, really good crowd and we got to the opening of the Lyttelton Theatre in the spring of '76. According to Michael Blakemore, Peter Hall slipped in a matinee of Dame Peggy doing his production of *Happy Days*, without telling the rest of the planning committee of the National Theatre or the other associate directors. So that it was a Peter Hall production that actually opened, as the first performance.

"The night before, there had been a number of shortcomings, mostly electrical services, but things didn't meet Conrad's approval. So they said the electrical contractors would work overnight and there was nothing there they couldn't cope with. The following day, the curtain's due to go up at 2:30pm, they will have a meeting in the morning and we will be able to demonstrate that all these things had been tended to. So we all clocked in at

10:00 and it wasn't quite ready, and the clock ticked. At about 12:00, we met again and finally, yes, fine, you can go ahead.

"Arthur looked at Ron and said, 'Have you got the licence form?' Ron said, 'No, I thought you got it.' 'Oh Christ,' they said. 'Well, where do we go to get it,' 'cause actually the GLC wasn't used to licensing theatres because nobody built many theatres at that period in London.

"Anyway, we all trooped along to County Hall and ended up in the director general's office, where fortunately the director general was out to lunch, by this time it was 1:15. But his secretary was still there, and she very kindly said, 'I have those in the safe.' She got them out and she typed up the licence. And, with no mobile telephone, you couldn't just ring Tom Pate, the theatre manager and say 'It's all right, we've got it!'"

> "My heart leaps with joy every time that lovely thing on the South Bank comes within my sights. Am going to try to make another gloating visit this week if possible." [25]
>
> 16th February, 1972: Letter from Laurence Olivier to Lasdun

> "Dick made it work. He was a backstage, and entirely unsung, hero."
>
> Richard Pilbrow

Lightboard with electrician Alan Jacobi, lighting designer David Hersey and son, Dimitri

Lightboard with director John Dexter and lighting designer Andy Phillips during rehearsals for *Galileo*

Richard Pilbrow with Lightboard

Richard Brett on the Olivier grid

3.1 Peter Hall Takes Charge and Writes a Diary Part I

Her Majesty The Queen officially opens the National Theatre, Monday 25th October 1976

3.2 Her Majesty: "Is The Theatre Ready, Mr. Pilbrow?"

The foundation stone for the National Theatre building on the South Bank; the original 1951 foundation stone sits alongside

The Olivier Theatre finally opens in October 1976.

Trail-blazing innovation proves a nightmare and needs a very long, steep climb out of a 'slough of despond' - though in time it will prove triumphant.

The first reactions to the new National Theatre are generally full of praise, though with some noting concerns…

Monday 4th October 1976
After a month of preview performances, the Olivier Theatre finally opens, with *Tamburlaine the Great* directed by Peter Hall.

Monday 25th October 1976 – A Filthy Night
There was pouring rain on the night that the Queen came – at last – to open the National Theatre. All trussed up in black tie, I was in the lineup to greet her, standing next to Denys Lasdun. On turning to me, she said, "Is the theatre ready, Mr. Pilbrow?" Nervously bowing, I replied, "Not quite, Your Majesty." She passed on.

Sir Laurence – An Historic Moment
"The main source of energy flowing that evening was waiting to contribute his brief, and only, performance on the stage of the theatre named after him. Laurence Olivier's absence had been marked since he left the National over two years before. He did not come to the opening of the Lyttelton and declined to speak the prologue to *Tamburlaine* at the first performance in the Olivier. But he could scarcely disappoint the sovereign. With the instinct of a professional, he had got to know the stage, with a little quiet advance practice arranged through the housekeeper, Harry Henderson. 'Every morning at eight he came to the theatre and I let him in to rehearse his speech, with only the cleaners there. He used to ask them if they could hear him all right.' On the night he showed no sign of the serious illness that had plagued him since he left, nor of the mixed feelings he must have experienced on mounting the Olivier stage, with which he now had nothing to do.

'For this moment we must be grateful to the timing and the durable cladding of Mr. Peter Hall's foot when he put it in the door,' he said. His tribute to the architect was fulsome even by his standards: 'Our very eyes and all happy senses will for ever be rewarded by the craft and genius of the actual creator of this situation in which we find ourselves – Sir Denys Lasdun. To those who will follow, I wish joy eternal of all of it.' In actorly style, he thanked the audience 'for your kind attention and for the glory and lustre of your presence. Welcome.' They were the last words he ever spoke from the stage of any theatre." [26]

A Note from actor Gawn Grainger, January 2018
"The 'Sweet Spot' on the Olivier stage is attributed to Michael Bryant, but this is not true. The first person to discover that place on the stage where all the audience can hear you, was Olivier himself.

"He was to make a speech at the grand opening of the theatre and I found out he was coming in early one morning with Kate Fleming, the voice coach. I hid at the back of the circle and watched as he moved from spot to spot with Kate calling out, 'No… No,' then suddenly 'Yes'! He turned and faced the front and tried out a whisper, 'Clear as a bell!' Then he let that fantastic voice of his resound round his building.

"Later on, in *Julius Caesar*, I stole the spot and remember one reviewer saying I was the only one who could be heard.

"I love it as a theatre; I feel now, all these years later, it has grown into a majesty of its own. Now, sadly, all the actors are miked and the romance of being heard has been taken away. They will never know the challenge and the joy." [27]

Some Critical Observations by Kenneth Tynan[28]
Saturday 16th March 1973
A remark by Tynan to a journalist, who didn't use it: "When Olivier asked me to work for him, the National Theatre was merely an idea. Now it is an inspiration. Not bad in ten years. Our welcome to Peter Hall is heartfelt, but we would be more than human if it were not tinged with a distinct overtone of, follow that." [29]

Tuesday 17th September 1974
"I talk to Larry, about the huge theatre exhibition to be mounted at the Hayward Gallery next Spring to mark the opening of the new National Theatre. After discreet consultation with Peter Hall, it has been decided to edit Larry out of the listing of the NT. Fifty-seven pieces are devoted to Barry Jackson's Birmingham Rep; only five to Larry's decade at the National. No mention of his *Othello, Dance Of Death, Long Day's Journey* or *Uncle Vanya*. Nothing about the Shaffer plays, the Stoppard, or any of the non-Larry successes (such as *Much Ado, The Front Page, The Misanthrope, National Health, Equus*, etc.) in which he took such great pride. Nothing but a still from *Three Sisters*; a still from *Flea In Her Ear*, and three costume and set designs by Ralph Koltai. Meanwhile, room after room is devoted to 'Peter Hall's Stratford' – a regime that lasted eight years as against Larry's ten. When I inform him of this by phone, his voice is sombre! 'We really didn't understand P.H,' he says. 'I've never known a man more dedicated to self-glorification. He's rewriting the history of the NT as if it started with his first reading of *The Tempest*.' " [30]

Sunday 9th February 1975
"Supper with Joan Plowright. She fills me in on Larry's state of mind and health. His hatred of P. Hall is now ineradicable and borders on paranoia… He has been appalled by what P.H. has done to the goodwill created by his regime, to company spirit ('It's like a morgue backstage nowadays,' says Joan) and to relationships with the audience. To return to Joan: She says that none of the younger stars with whom she grew up ever wants to work with P. H. again." [31]

Friday 12th September 1975
"I interview Larry for TV, not having seen him for over a year, during which time he has suffered (and nearly died) from a muscular degenerative disease that has robbed his voice of its bass notes. He is frailer than I remember him. He will never appear on the stage again. Over lunch, he chats unhappily about the National, underlining how he laments the fact that under the Hall regime all sense of company solidarity has gone: It isn't a company anymore. They just cast each production from scratch out of *Spotlight*. That wasn't what this National Theatre was created for. That wasn't what we fought for all those years." [32]

Monday 25th October 1976
"The Queen opens the National Theatre. Larry makes a typically florid speech on the stage of the theatre that bears his name, singling out a dozen politicians for praise and not one playwright, actor, or director – except, of course, P. Hall. The choice of play is perverse to the point of madness – a minimal Goldoni called *Il Campiello*: devoid of wit, or warmth, or any kind of excitement. The company shouts, stamps, and runs about, betraying all the signs of panic. The most significant performance was given by a drinking fountain that played throughout the action – quietly pissing on everything we expect of a National Theatre. During the second half, Larry, who was sitting beside the Queen, dropped off to sleep. HRH instantly noticed and directed a beady eye in his direction, fearful that he should topple forward into the acting area, The glare lasted for five minutes until Larry, galvanised by some particularly noisy piece of business, returned to wakefulness. During the interval, Ben Travers said to me, 'If they had to open with a thoroughly rotten play, why couldn't they choose a thoroughly rotten English play?' What a disaster! But will the press record it as such?" [33]

Sunday 3rd July 1977
"Los Angeles. Lunch with Larry: he's here filming *The Betsy* and then going to Brazil for another picture. His energy continues to daunt me. He tells me that he learnt his speech to the Queen at the opening of the Olivier by heart against the advice of Joan, who begged him to read it from notes and not run the risk of drying. 'But,' he says. 'I knew that smarmy bastard (i.e. P. Hall) wouldn't be using notes, and I was damned if I was going to let him outdo me. So I went to the theatre three times, the week before opening, at eight in the morning and rehearsed the speech to the cleaners until I had it word-perfect'." [34]

Drama critic Sheridan Morley, on *Il Campiello*
"There is a number of possible explanations for the presence of *Il Campiello* in the repertoire of the National Theatre at the Olivier. The one I like best is that it represents a complete and never-to-be-repeated mental, physical, and theatrical breakdown on the part of all concerned." [35]

On Olivier: "He's got magic, you see, magic. That's what it's all about."
Peter Wood

Peter Wood on Sir Laurence
Maggie Riley, an actor with the NT company, spoke with director Peter Wood at the end of that memorable Royal opening evening. He talked of the phenomena that some people surrounded by mirrors and the reflections of theatre technology don't count for much, yet one man standing alone on a totally empty stage, can mean everything. "He's got magic, you see, magic. That's what it's all about." [36]

Architect's Journal – 12th January 1977
A Critical Appraisal – Extracts
by Victor Glasstone[37]
"There is our old friend, 'failure of communication.' People in the theatre are, despite their protestations, unaware of their buildings, and therefore inarticulate when briefing their architects. They do not understand how their buildings can assist their own work." [38]

First Impressions in 1976
"By comparison with other new British theatres, the National has a sweep, magnificence, and conviction which makes most others seem almost fiddly and gimcrack… the building is alive and inviting.

"Denys Lasdun expressed the view on a London Weekend TV Aquarius program that 'the building has to be very dense, heavy, because we are protecting The Word from outside noise.' But… the impression is not of denseness or heaviness: It has the lightness of the original model. The external terraces are very appealing in conception, but wet and windswept in normal London weather.

"Sir Denys insisted 'it must just be space, walls, light, and the ornament is the people moving around in a big giant space which is beautifully lit and carpeted.' The foyer of the Lyttelton is beautifully lit, the Olivier less so. A theatre foyer must smell of the theatre. Architectural artifice must create the right mood of anticipation. One of the age-old tricks is a suitably dramatic use of vertical circulation. The foyers of the National occur on a series of interesting and diverse levels, but only once – getting from the Olivier stalls to the circle – is there awareness of people perambulating up and down. The views from the Olivier foyers are magnificent. The Lyttelton foyers are less fortunate… one is barely aware of the river.

"Lyttelton. Praise first. Again, the place is beautifully lit – houselights on. The seats are extremely comfortable. [But] the sound is remote and hollow, from the balcony, one strains. The actor feels far distant, and, in fact, he is. From the proscenium to back wall is 20m. In the immense Drury Lane, seating 2283, it is 25m, as against the Lyttelton's 890. To achieve the audience sitting full square to the stage, the proscenium has had to be made immensely wide, 9.00 to 13.6m. The opening at Drury Lane is 12.8m. As a result, the company is forced into a Germanic breadth of style quite alien to the British tradition of intimacy. This Germanisation is accentuated by the triple proscenium frame, which encloses and distances the actor.

"Olivier. In architectural terms, it is a highly convincing piece of work. But in theatrical terms? To return to the Aquarius interview: 'Out of this came a drawing of a room with a stage in the corner and seats around it.' Which, transcribed, means that after the failure of Chichester and the difficulties inherent in the thrust stage… they decided to opt for corner staging, a form used extensively in the US and found in Frank Lloyd Wright's hideous Kalita Humphreys in Dallas. 'This is where we started… the form of the Olivier generated the whole building. A bowl effect… when you go into that room, it is just you and the stage. Personal relationship is unique to theatres. Make a theatre too big, and you've lost it.' Now, this is where the trouble starts. The auditorium feels immense. And, again, compared to Drury Lane, it is. From the front of the revolve to the back wall is 22m. Drury Lane is 25m. The Olivier seats 1160; Drury Lane 2283. By dispensing with overhanging balconies, the back balcony seats have become a very long way from the acting area. 'It is you and the stage' depends on where you sit. From the centre stalls and the front of the balcony, all is fine. From anywhere else, one is overwhelmed by architecture. The side concrete walls dominate more than the stage. One senses that this will always be a spectacle theatre. Acoustically, too, the variation is prodigious.

"Conclusion. The NT is undeniably an extremely important work. Lasdun is one of our most distinguished architects. Coming 'fresh' to the problems of theatre design he has inevitably repeated many of the errors that someone with more experiences in the complexities of this subtle form might have avoided. The building itself is probably a watershed in postwar British theatre design. 'I don't want anything to come between people experiencing the theatre and your drama,' says Lasdun. But, for my money, the 'architecture,' with its sententious simplicity, does precisely that."

Other Comments from 1976
"I found [the Lyttelton] very drab and rather dreary, dreadfully wide, like all those American stages, and no central aisle, surely a mistake."… "The new National (which everybody seems to hate)"… "A pretty beastly house to work in, I can tell you – awful passages, dressing rooms, endless opening and shutting of doors, no centre aisle, dress circle so high it has no kind of contact with the stalls, dreary buff upholstery…"
Sir John Gielgud.[39]

" 'Comfort' denotes 'respectability', and that spells death to the theatre. Even now, I would be glad to hear that the roof over the stage leaked rain. The theatre, for two and a half millenia, has done its best work as a profession of rogues, vagabonds, and outcasts; the rot set in when they were given votes, and allowed to marry the sons and daughters of respectable people, and the day that Henry Irving got a knighthood, the bell tolled." [40]
Critic Bernard Levin, on the National.

25th October 1976.
The National at last.
Sir Laurence's Welcome

As Brian Benn sees it . . .

"With profuse apologies for the delay, your party will shortly be elevated to this level. In the meantime, Ma'am, I am requested to draw your attention to the large red push-button near your dexter hand : . ."

Brian Benn was a highly experienced project manager with Theatre Projects. Brian was also a key figure in the Theatre Projects Trust/ London Academy of Music and Dramatic Art (LAMDA) Technical Theatre training course that TP ran at LAMDA for over twenty years under administrator (and my personal mentor) Robert Stanton. Brian was a keen cartoonist with a wicked sense of humour

3.2 Her Majesty: "Is The Theatre Ready, Mr. Pilbrow?"

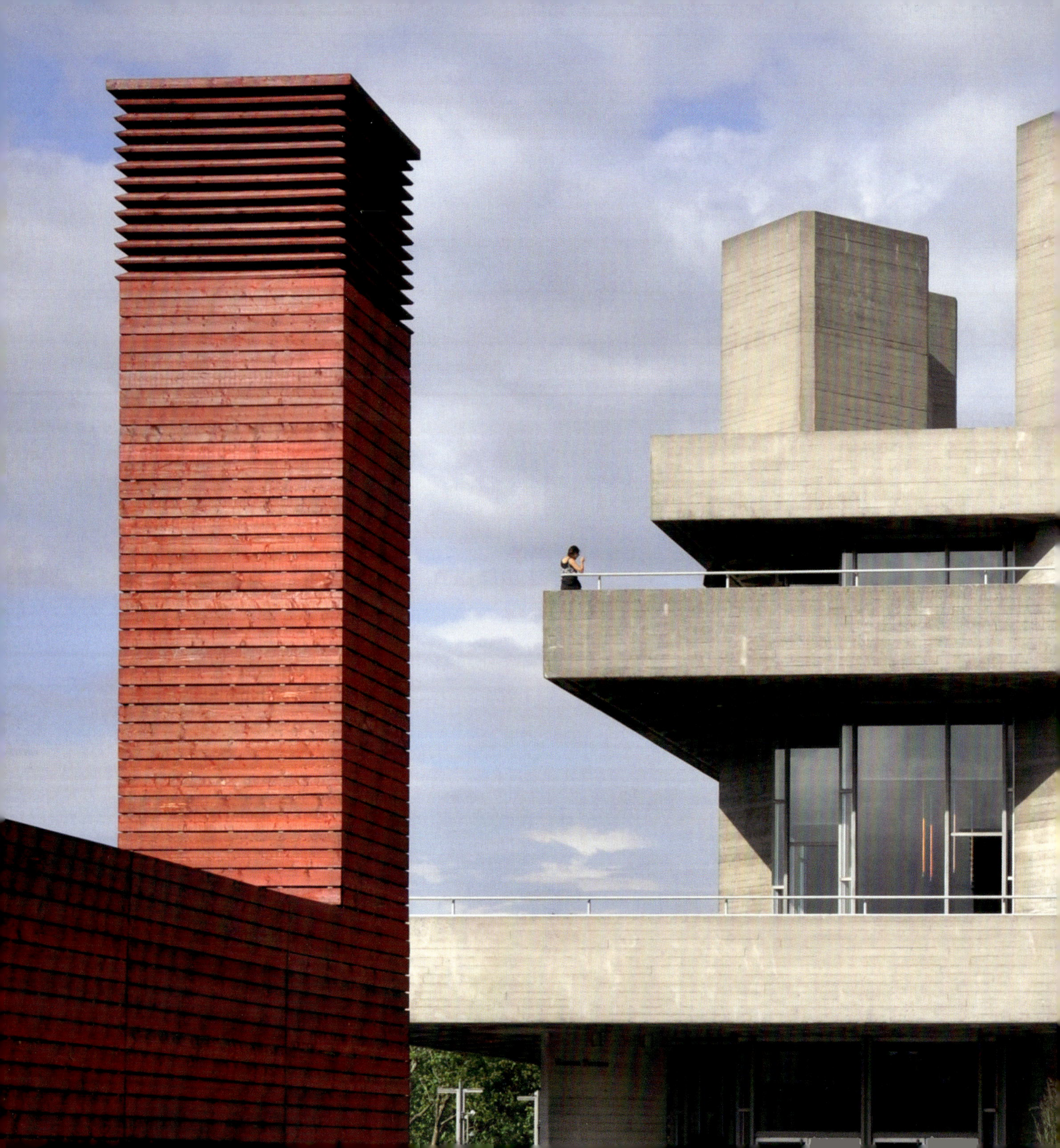

Part Four

Concrete Versus Theatre

Performers, writers, directors, designers and technicians at work. A pictorial record accompanied by interviews with key contributors — a glimpse behind the scenes.

Night view of the National Theatre looking towards St. Paul's Cathedral, 1976

4.1 The Show Goes On

Peter Hall's Diary, Part II, 1976-1988

(Interspersed with other commentary in **bold purple**)

Friday 29th October 1976
"Full houses tonight in the Olivier and Lyttelton. The public has taken the building to its heart. The foyers absolutely packed with people. This is what it is all about. But my God, what a lot of work this place is going to eat up."

Tuesday 26th April 1977
Letter from Peter Stevens to Mark Harrison [Secretary to the South Bank Board]: "I would be grateful if you would add to the matters the National Theatre Board wishes to have raised at the next meeting of the South Bank Theatre Board their very serious concerns regarding the acoustics in the Olivier Theatre."[1]

Wednesday 4th May 1977
Mark Harrison to the SBTB: "It has been reported to the board that in both the Lyttelton and Olivier Theatres a full view of the stage from the front row of the circle is obstructed by the profile of the parapet. The volume of complaints from the public has reached the point where the NT Board finds the situation no longer tenable."[2] This defect was eventually corrected by cutting down the concrete, reducing the height of the balcony rail in both theatres.

Friday 17th June 1977
"To a preview of *The Madras House*. It's caviar to the general, and I don't believe it will be a commercial success. I just hope we get marks for rediscovering a masterpiece. Bill Gaskill has directed it beautifully, and the design really shows what power the Olivier can have, even for intimate, naturalistic scenes."

Thursday 14th July 1977
Letter from Mrs A. to the managing director of the National Theatre: "I regret I found the acoustics, which should have been excellent, abominable. As I am only 35, I feel that deafness is

---

Peter Hall overcomes super-human obstacles, including an incomplete, non-functioning building; inadequate funding; press outrage; and industrial disputes; and wins, over insuperable odds: *Tamburlaine the Great, Amadeus, The Life Of Galileo, The Oresteia, Guys and Dolls, The Rivals, Pravda, Antony and Cleopatra.* **The Cottesloe proves its versatility under director Bill Bryden, with** *Lark Rise, The Mysteries*, **and** *Dispatches.* **Twelve years after opening, the first major use of the drum revolve, in** *The Shaughraun* **with designer Bill Dudley.**

not really a problem anywhere else; for such an expensive, not particularly comfortable theatre, it was extremely annoying." 3

Saturday 20th August 1977
"Read until late… ferreting through a book on Restoration actresses, trying to get a feel of what the theatre was like then. It was a surprise to learn that Restoration playhouses were smaller than the Cottesloe and, as they played mainly in winter, extremely chilly. The audience sat dressed in all their finery, and their warmest clothes: cloaks, surcoats, gloves. Actresses always displayed their shoulders and a good deal of their breasts, and consequently were freezing cold. Important ones, such as Mrs. Bracegirdle, had solo dressing rooms, and the ultimate luxury was to have a fireplace with a sea coal fire. They would then rush from the stage, get warm by the fire, and wrap up their rosy shoulders."

Wednesday 19th October 1977
"Heavy day's *Country Wife* rehearsal. I only did half what I should have done, but I see more and more how performing in the Olivier must be of a public, outgoing nature. It's not a question of being untrue, but of not burying yourself in your fellow actors' eyes. I think this is important for Restoration texts, anyway. Originally, after all, the actors acted on a platform space to an audience of gallants and wits on either side of them as well as in front. There is a sense of representing the audience. It's something to bear in mind for the public style of the play."

Friday 18th November 1977
DL&P memorandum of teleconference, Peter Hall and Lasdun: "[Hall] accepts DL's view that, in its own way, the architectural atmosphere and design of the Olivier is as important to the audience as is Covent Garden or any other theatrical room. The audience must not be deprived of this quality." 4

Wednesday 22nd March 1978
"*Lark Rise* [a play by Keith Dewhurst from Flora Thompson's book *Lark Rise to Candleford*] preview tonight. Much very fine work. And a beautiful environment by Bill [Dudley], the designer, who is a bit of a genius – the whole Cottesloe ceiling has a sky stretched over it. But I have fears. The audience – modern invaders into a lovely evocation of an Oxfordshire village – are expected to stand or walk around for two-and-a-half hours. I think unless Bill Bryden cuts half an hour out of it there will be a new crucifixion, but of members of the public. *The Passion* – for which there were no seats either – rides again."

Tuesday 20th June 1978
"Trevor [Nunn] with me this evening. To my surprise, he arrived early, a habit he is not noted for, and staggered into my office looking very thin and extremely pale. He feels he has to stay for the start of the Barbican; and then, what is he faced with? A still larger organisation, a more difficult industrial situation than at the Aldwych: all the problems that I have.

"We both agreed we didn't anymore want to head huge organisations – we wanted just a simple space and 25 actors. These monsters that we head are having to get bigger and bigger in order to justify their subsidies, and the bigger they get, the less clear they become as artistic enterprises. I ought to leave the National, Trevor ought to leave the RSC, and Brook, Trevor and I ought to start a theatre together. How the hell are we going to do it? The system has often fucked up the individual: Larry, Ralph, and John Burrell by the Old Vic in 1949; Michel [Saint-Denis], George [Devine], and Glen [Byam Shaw] the next year; John Neville by Nottingham – the line is endless. If Trevor and I walked out, would we be beyond the pale? Certainly with the Arts

> "Denys Lasdun's ambitious building has brought off a triumph to confound the sceptics. The huge foyer, with its tables and its Folies-Bergère Manet bars, with its people of all ages and classes walking up and down, listening to music, talking, creates an ambiance of social enjoyment that the French find it easy enough to evoke with their café tables spreading over the Paris pavements, but which has hitherto been unknown in London."
>
> Harold Hobson, *The Sunday Times*

Council – then we wouldn't get money for our new work. Think, think… An exhilarating evening: we looked into the abyss."

Saturday 8th July 1978
"Jacky [Hall's wife] and I drove to Denys Lasdun's beautiful country cottage for dinner. It is, of course, immaculately designed, but homely. The living room has a wonderful doorknob on it, honest iron. From this developed a scene out of Alan Ayckbourn. A screw had come out. So, four times, to the great architect's increasing rage, Sue Lasdun pulled the whole doorknob off and it fell onto the boards with a resounding crash. Denys got pinker and pinker. He kept asking her to be careful and to jam it in. Later in the evening, he pulled it off himself. To anyone familiar with the problems of the National, it was a rich payoff."

Wednesday 12th July 1978
"At the South Bank Board meeting this morning it was implied that the appalling lateness of the stage machinery and its inefficiency was in some way due to the National limiting the access of the technicians completing the job. I banged about a bit, and said we all knew this simply wasn't true. Ulrich [Treasury representative] then declared we should have foreseen that access would be particularly needed by the technicians at this final stage. I replied we should in that case have foreseen it at any time during the last three-and-a-half years, for we were always being wrongly told the technicians were about to finish. From there, I went on to suggest that the clean thing to do was for the South Bank Board to close us down until the work was done. At this, Joe Lockwood thumped the table angrily and said, 'All right, we will close you down.' Ulrich asked how much it would cost. I said in loss of income between £30,000 to £40,000 per week, quite apart from any redundancy payments. We then began a long period of reconciliation, which ended in us all kissing and making up. Max [Rayne] and Victor [Mishcon] arrived late when all the fun was over and we were in a warm glow. Horace Cutler [Conservative Leader of the GLC 1977-81, member of the NT Board 1975-82] said we'd had an excellent argument. Joe Lockwood said I'd been very rude to the Board (this of course with an Establishment grin) but all was now well. A good morning."

> **"It is a relief to be able to report that the new National Theatre feels not like a white elephant or cultural mausoleum: more like a superb piece of sculpture inside which it is possible to watch a play or walk and talk in the lobbies without feeling dwarfed by one's surroundings."**
>
> Michael Billington, *The Guardian*, 12th March 1976

Wednesday 13th September 1978
"The South Bank Board meeting went on and on and on. I dozed at one point. It was like being at a dreadful play, dropping off, and when you wake the play is still as dreadful, still apparently at the same spot, and you don't know how long you have been asleep. The board was making its case against Denys Lasdun and the contractors over the building delays. Arnold Goodman pointed out that history is full of instances of foolish boards and committees and proprietors suing architects or arraigning great artists, but history is always on the side of the artist."

Monday 16th October 1978
Letter from Peter Hall to Denys Lasdun: "Major actors who have spent a lot of time in the Olivier are now saying that they do not wish to act there again in its present acoustics. I am afraid this goes for all ages and all kinds of actors. They don't believe that they're getting through to the audience. The fact that they are, doesn't reassure them at all. They constantly say that they're getting nothing back."[5]

Tuesday 17th October 1978
"Early this morning, my long-delayed and eagerly-looked-forward-to visit to the RSC's new theatre in the Barbican. I think it's beautiful. John Bury and I can be proud. And I am sad Joe [the nickname for the architect Peter Chamberlin] Chamberlin died before it was completed. It's perhaps a little on the wide side, but it has a homely, intimate atmosphere. It lacks the grandiloquence of the Olivier, and that I like. The only problem is that the theatre is buried in the whole bloody complex, and it's going to be a hell of a job to find it. But the theatre will be a marvellous place to stage plays in. They say it will open in the autumn of 1980. I'd

4.1 The Show Goes On: Peter Hall's Diary, Part II, 1976-1988

guess the autumn of 1981 or spring of 1982." [The Barbican Theatre opened on 7th May 1982; the Barbican Centre itself was opened by the Queen on 3rd March 1982.]

Thursday 18th January 1979
"Our directors agreed that the most eloquent use of the [Olivier] space so far has been *The Woman* [designed by Hayden Griffin] and there was a general feeling that the stage was used as it had been designed… but the acoustics are worse than for anything we have done. John Schlesinger said that sitting in the best house seats, he had been unable to hear most of the text."[6]

Friday 26th January 1979
"New York: Dinner with James Levine – the first time I'd met him – and Dexter[7] to talk about me doing some operas at the Met. Levine was late, so we had half an hour on the Shaffer play. Dexter said again that he hated the National, never felt comfortable in it, couldn't bring in the right actors because it would upset the ones that were there already, didn't like the ones that were, and anyway felt the National would put *Amadeus* in the wrong frame for Peter because everything we did got bad notices. I was determined not to get irritated and asked him if he thought *Equus* had suffered by being done at the National, if he had earned less money because of directing it there. But he gave way on nothing. He seemed bent on making me enraged."

Wednesday 18th April 1979 – A Strike Day
"Bill Bundy [NT technical director] isn't in today. Nobody seems to know whether it's because he thinks we are being too tough, or not tough enough. Poor Bill. He gets in a terrible state when choices have to be made; and he hates hurting people. He really cares for those men outside. A brief associates' meeting, bringing everybody up to date. The directors were very unhelpful about scenic compromise. It's always the same. An artist will accept no discipline except his own."

Thursday 19th April 1979
"Bill Bundy came back. He looked really shaken. In some way, I believe, he thinks he is responsible for the strike. He isn't. Ralph [Richardson] told me at lunch today that he drove in the other evening in his car, was stopped by a picket, and wound down his window, expecting a comment or leaflet. 'Do you know this is an official picket?' said the man. 'Yes, I do,' said Ralph in a totally unprovocative way. 'You silly old fucker,' observed the picket. This to a great actor who has provided more jobs for NATTKE[8] members over the years than I have had hot dinners."

Wednesday 6th June 1979
"First night of *Dispatches*. Bill Bryden has done something extraordinary. You feel actually involved in the shit and the curious glamour of war, the horror and the excitement. The language is shockingly real: a fuck in every other line. It's a long way from *Journey's End* [a play about the First World War by R C Sherriff]."

Wednesday 4th July 1979
"Back to the theatre and more grinding away on the budget. The problem is the Cottesloe, which simply cannot sustain a full ensemble of actors and still have low seat prices. Bill Bryden has run the Cottesloe brilliantly, built an audience there, made it a necessary theatre. But, in fact, he has done it with a large permanent company which I should not really have allowed; not because I didn't want it, but because we didn't have the money."

Monday 23rd July 1979
"Finance and general purposes committee meeting. The interest was Denys Lasdun's justification of the IBM building going up next door. If Denys was not a genius architect, he would be a genius advocate. You can see he is not compromising himself, but

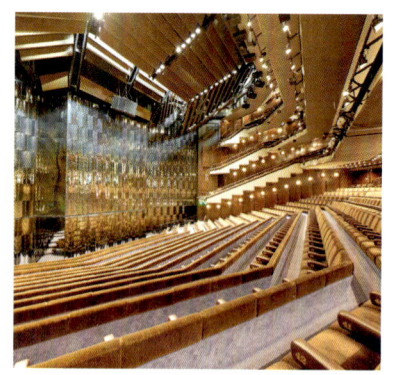

Barbican Theatre, London

Sketch of the Barbican by Elizabeth Bury, John Bury's wife and design partner he is certainly compromising you. He argues that he is creating, in modern terms of course, a piece of Venice by the Thames. He isn't. He is creating a wonderful building for IBM, and the National Theatre loses out."

Monday 1st October 1979
"Found an exquisite picture of the interior of the Warsaw National Theatre in 1790. It's the best representation I have ever seen of the sort of candlelit, crowded theatre that Mozart knew. It's an intimate, magical place, dark, romantic, and very, very sexy."

Monday 8th October 1979
"We have lost the IBM fight. The Fine Arts Commission even commend Denys Lasdun for having put the building so close to us. The very thing we are against, they are for, aesthetically. I think you have to get up very early in the morning to outbox Denys on a matter like this."

Thursday 10th January 1980
"Spent the morning at the Barbican Theatre with Peter Brook and Trevor. It is beautiful, and makes me feel very proud of the work John Bury and I did on its design. It's the best theatre for Shakespeare I have ever been in."

Thursday 17th July 1980
Letter from Harry Pugh to Michael Elliott [NT administrator]: "I confirm that we accept your proposal to consult us on matters concerning the structure of the National Theatre building. I would also confirm our discussion in your office on 23rd June when we agreed that the word structure embraces matters affecting the architectural concept of the building." [9]

Friday 22nd February 1980
Notes on meeting, Lasdun with Jocelyn Herbert and Hayden Griffin. Lasdun said that John Bury has treated the Olivier Theatre as a proscenium all the time, has failed to exploit the dynamic of that stage, and always pushes the audience back. DL will say this to Peter Hall at future meeting. [10]

Monday 1st June 1981
Letter from Lasdun to Max Rayne. Mentions several matters that have been altered – the buffet counter at the Lyttelton Circle, proposal to erect a message centre on the river-facing side of the theatre, and the picnic areas. "I do not understand, therefore, why we have not been consulted on the other equally sensitive matters I have referred to. I fully appreciate that the growth of activities and changing patterns of use are creating needs which the building must be adapted to meet. It is vitally important, however, that this process is properly coordinated so that the public areas maintain their coherence and those architectural qualities which visitors to the National Theatre have come to appreciate." [11]

Friday 23rd October 1981
Letter from Denys Lasdun to Peter Hall: "A final point: You mention loyalties. You, at least, should know that my loyalty is to the architectural integrity of the theatre and it would be disappointing to think that any of your colleagues might think otherwise." [12]

Thursday 28th May 1982
Letter from Lasdun to Lord Rayne: "It is unfortunate that the latest modifications to the Olivier stage should have thrown the Olivier acoustics out of balance again. It is vitally important that any further acoustic treatment should be handled in a way which is sympathetic to the character of the room." [13]

Wednesday 20th October 1982
Notes from a teleconference, concerning the painting of the concrete in the Olivier. DL further went on to say that the world of theatregoers had a very high regard for the Olivier Theatre and such an irredeemable action was most serious. [14]

Friday 22nd October 1982
Letter from Lasdun to Peter Hall, referring again to the painting of the concrete: "It appears that you and [John] Bury have already decided on a course of action involving major changes without consultation with me and are proposing merely to tell me what it is you are going to do. This is in neither the spirit nor the letter of the board undertaking. Since the Olivier Theatre is architecturally, as well as theatrically, a subject of major public interest, I have informed your chairman. I urge you to recognise the importance of discussing the matter with me

before any irredeemable damage is done to the Olivier Theatre, since those involved so far appear not to understand the implications of what they are doing." [15]

Monday 29th November 1982
Letter, Lasdun to Hall: "You mention the colour of the concrete but make no mention of the fact that Bury is choosing a new colour for carpet which it is suggested should be used where necessary in acoustic treatment. Changes of colour, texture, and materials are all matters on which there ought to have been an architectural input before proposals and estimates were obtained from Bovis.[16] Far from your suggestion that I should acquaint myself with your proposals, it is for you to acquaint me since only you know what they are. Only then can it be said that any serious consultation is being sought." [17]

Wednesday 2nd February 1983
Memorandum, Lasdun and Jocelyn Herbert. "She knew about proposal to darken the Olivier. She says she had already protested and that a lot of theatrical opinion, including John Dexter, would rally to prevent this unnecessary damage."[18]

Thursday 24th February 1983
Lasdun to Max Rayne: "We should surely be involved in this reconsideration so that we can arrive jointly at solutions which are compatible with the architecture of the theatre in terms of colour, texture, and material; if there are any specific problems of light spill they should be identified and resolved in ways that will not irrevocably change the character of the auditorium or destroy the underlying continuity of colour and texture which exists between it and the foyers."[19]

Tuesday 12th July 1983
Response from Lasdun to Hall, regarding a letter about why the Olivier needed to be altered: "I do not understand the nature of the visual problem which the third paragraph of your letter attempts to describe. If an individual's concentration varies during a performance, I would have thought that this was more to do with the quality of the production and acting rather than ambient light impinging on peripheral vision. Lastly, you mention that you took a range of advice in order to understand the problems better. It is astonishing, that,

Warsaw National Theatre 1790

knowing our detailed knowledge and concern for the Olivier Theatre, you did not choose to seek advice from us."[20]

Monday 12th August 1985
Rayne to Lasdun: "I am myself a great admirer of your work, but this is not the Royal College of Physicians in Regent's Park, it is a place of public entertainment in a location which still remains remote, arid, and uninviting to the population at large." Also makes a note of surprise that Lasdun is now calling for the exterior of the building to be cleaned, as he had previously suggested that the weathering would add to the effect.[21]

Thursday 15th August 1985
Letter from Lasdun to Max Rayne: "I, of course, accept the need for change. As you say, it would be remarkable if none were necessary – notwithstanding the considerable effort of the building committee, of which Peter Hall was a member, and the theatre administration of the time to get things right. I only ask that such changes as are necessary are accommodated in a way which respects the building both in spirit and in detail and this is in no way incompatible with commercial interest or, indeed, show business, whereas the Ceefax [a teletext display] sign is clearly a hideous afterthought." [22]

Tamburlaine the Great

by Christopher Marlowe
Olivier Theatre – Opening Production
4th October 1976

With Albert Finney
Director: Peter Hall
Production design: John Bury
Lighting: David Hersey
Sound: Julian Beech
Production photographer: Nobby Clark

"Mr. Hall, the director, presented it as a series of poetic arias in symmetrically balanced tableaux. In John Bury's glowing costumes and sets, the eye was ravished. The whole company responded magnificently to this historic occasion. This play does a new theatre proud."
Felix Barker
Evening News, 5th October 1976

"[The Olivier] unlike anything else… created in Britain for the staging of plays, both in scale and in character, a great public space, extrovert and open."
Simon Callow

The Mysteries

by Tony Harrison
Cottesloe Theatre
**25th April 1977 (*The Passion*), 12th December 1984
(*The Nativity*), 19th January 1985 *(Doomsday)***

Director: Bill Bryden
Production design: William Dudley
Lighting: William Dudley and Laurence Clayton
Sound: Chris Montgomery
Production photographer: Nobby Clark
A Promenade Production
Transferred to the then-abandoned Lyceum Theatre in 1985 when funding cuts led to the closure of the Cottesloe

"It was like nothing that had been seen on the British stage, and certainly not the London stage, for some centuries."
Simon Callow

"It's only out of real, heterogeneous audiences that you make real theatre."
Tony Harrison

"How weirdly touching was that group of carpenters explaining the right way to make a cross – and the solemn interplay of miners' lamp-beams. Again, fingers of electric light touched that same nerve."
Peter Shaffer
Telegraph Weekend Magazine, 1988

4.1 The Show Goes On: Peter Hall's Diary, Part II, 1976-1988

Amadeus

by Peter Shaffer
Olivier Theatre
26th October 1979

With Paul Scofield, Simon Callow.
Director: Peter Hall
Production design and lighting: John Bury
Sound: Ric Green
Production photographer: Nobby Clark

"One of the theatrical events of the year."
Milton Shulman
Evening Standard

"I still see the brocaded actors reflected in the shiny blue floor of John Bury's rococo set, and hear the first oboe-note piercing the heart of Paul Scofield's tortured Salieri. He and Peter Hall did me proud."
Peter Shaffer
Telegraph Weekend Magazine, 1988

The Life of Galileo

by Bertolt Brecht
Olivier Theatre
8th August 1980

With Michael Gambon, Michael Bryant
Director: John Dexter
Production design: Jocelyn Herbert
Lighting: Andy Phillips
Sound: Rob Barnard
Production photographer: Zoë Dominic

"Dexter and Herbert had debated the ideal shape of the Olivier stage and auditorium with Denys Lasdun in the 1960s, and would now exploit its epic potential. For GALILEO, Herbert left the Olivier's giant metal shutters visible at the rear of the stage; further downstage stood a screen onto which scene dates/locations were projected. Held on a 'skeletal aluminum framework,' the screen would be raised or lowered into position immediately upstage of the main playing area, which was a raised disc."
Daniel Rosenthal
The National Theatre Story

John Dexter's last NT production. He died in 1990, aged 64. Hall remembers him as "a monster. And a kind of wayward genius. At the National he was trouble, always trouble. I would have a procession knocking on my door, from junior electricians to wardrobe people, saying 'Do we have to have him back? He's so rude. He bullies us so much.' But I thought he was good enough to put up with."

The Oresteia

by Aeschylus (Adapted by Tony Harrison)
Olivier Theatre
20th November 1981

Director: Peter Hall
Music: Harrison Birtwistle
Production design: Jocelyn Herbert
Lighting: John Bury
Sound: Ric Green
Production photographer: Nobby Clark

"Perhaps [Hall's] single most adventurous and completely realised production for the NT and one of the key productions of the post-war period… perfectly suited to Lasdun's vast amphitheatre."
Simon Callow

Guys and Dolls

Book by Jo Swerling and Abe Burrows
Music and lyrics by Frank Loesser
Olivier Theatre
26th February 1982

With Bob Hoskins and Julia McKenzie
Director: Richard Eyre
Musical staging: David Toguri
Scenic design: John Gunter
Costumes: Sue Blane
Lighting: David Hersey
Sound: Derrick Zieba, Ric Green
Production photographer: John Haynes

"One of the best evenings ever spent in the Olivier; it really warmed the place up. I wish that we could make just one musical in this country a tenth as good. I'd even take a twentieth."
Peter Shaffer
Telegraph Weekend Magazine

"I doubt if in its career the NT has given an audience such an unalloyed pleasure."
Milton Shulman
Evening Standard

4.1 The Show Goes On: Peter Hall's Diary, Part II, 1976-1988

The Rivals

by Richard Brinsley Sheridan
Olivier Theatre
2nd April 1983

Director: Peter Wood
Scenic design: John Gunter
Costumes: Bruce Snyder
Lighting: Robert Bryan
Sound: Gabby Haynes
Production photographer: Zoë Dominic

"The best production of this favourite I ever saw. The whole city of Bath seemed to be placed on the stage of the Olivier."
Peter Shaffer
Telegraph Weekend Magazine, 1988

Pravda

by Howard Brenton and David Hare
Olivier Theatre
26th April 1985

With Anthony Hopkins
Director: David Hare
Scenic design: Hayden Griffin
Costumes: Lindy Hemming
Lighting: Rory Dempster
Sound: Nic Jones
Production photographer: Nobby Clark

"A sulfurous and crackling entertainment."
The Observer

"Savagely bitchy and often wildly funny."
Punch

"A big, bristling, biting cartoon. Admirable and courageous of the National to mount this play enshrining a real attack on Press Barons."
Peter Shaffer
Telegraph Weekend Magazine

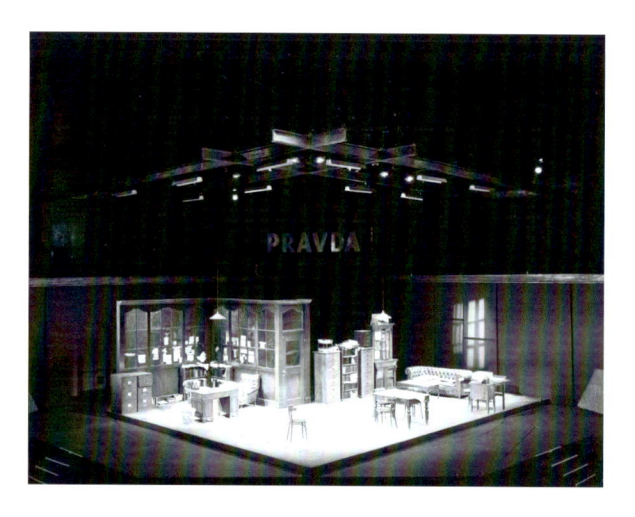

Antony and Cleopatra

by William Shakespeare
Olivier Theatre
3rd April 1987

With Judi Dench, Anthony Hopkins
Director: Peter Hall
Production design: Alison Chitty
Lighting: Stephen Wentworth
Sound: Paul Arditti
Production photographer: John Haynes.

"I believe the fifth act of this play to be the greatest piece of dramatic poetry in our language. Before Judi Dench I had never seen any actress really do it vocal justice. Thank you Peter Hall for the immense humility behind your skill."
Peter Shaffer
Telegraph Weekend Magazine

The Shaughraun

by Dion Boucicault
Olivier Theatre
30th April 1988

With Stephen Rea
Director: Howard Davies
Scenic design: William Dudley
Costume: Liz da Costa
Lighting: Mark Henderson
Sound: Paul Groothuis
Production photographer: Nobby Clark
First use of the drum revolve in a production

"Roll up, roll up, to see the greatest revolving stage on earth. Thrill to the glorious sight of heroes abseiling down the battlements."
Maureen Paton
Daily Express

"Dudley's wonderful setting, utilising all the Olivier's stage, brings into view rocky seashores, barren hillsides, ruined abbeys, crumbling castles and peasant cottages, all backed by a shimmering sea. It is the very stuff of great popular theatre."
Peter Hepple
The Stage

David Hare

Playwright, screenwriter, theatre and film director

Extract from *The Blue Touch Paper*

"The outstanding personal benefit of our years on the road came from the necessity to sit through our own work. There was no way out. Because we were, in the early days, operating the lights or the sound, sometimes stage-managing and even acting, so night after night I would have to watch and listen as speeches, passages, scenes and, on occasions, whole plays lost the battle for attention. Every cough, misplaced laugh and heavy eyelid would strike me to the heart. But as a dramatist who, to the contrary, was committed to believing that the audience's response might well be as significant as the play, I was given a brutal education. It has never left me.

"I was learning that one of the most surprising rewards of theatre is to marvel at how a play may gleam at a different angle according to where and when it's presented.

"In selected parts of the house there was a listlessness, not uncommon in the Lyttelton, which made everyone else conscious they were watching some very small figures shouting at the far end of a very big room.

"A play could be made by its audience and no one else." [23]

> "I kept being told that this man was Machiavellian, and devious, and was a calculating, demonic figure. I just found him perfectly straightforward."
>
> David Hare

David: I didn't know you were ten years with Olivier before you transitioned to Hall. You're one of the few people who straddles the two regimes. Almost nobody was compatible with both. Peter always regretted that he took Michael Blakemore and Jonathan Miller; he wished he had cleaned out, and started again. That was a horrible period, wasn't it?

Richard: Ghastly. David, you started in the most modest of circumstances, writing plays for your own small company, that you also ran. Then you embraced the new, far larger, scale of the National by directing *Weapons Of Happiness*.

David: One of Peter's great things was bringing on younger people. He brought on Brenton, and he brought on me, he obviously brought on Bill Bryden. All his problems, were with his contemporaries… like John Osborne. At the Royal Shakespeare, he'd been incredibly generous to Trevor Nunn, and people in their 20s. Peter, because he himself had been such a prodigy and been trusted to run the Arts Theatre, and then the RSC, had no problem with those of us who were still in our 20s. He expected us to be able to produce first-class theatre.

I was to do *Weapons Of Happiness* simply because Howard Brenton and I had been associated together at Portable Theatre. We were very much the generation of young people that he wanted to bring in to his theatre. The Lyttelton opened first?

Richard: Nothing was ready. We turned the lights on, and we had a floor to stand on, but that was the limit.

David: So, the Old Vic repertoire moved in. All these productions were absolutely fine. *Happy Days* with Peggy Ashcroft. And was it *Eden End*?

Richard: *Eden End* was Olivier's last production as a director for the NT, which I lit.

David: By and large, the repertoire that went into the Lyttelton had all been broken in. I was the first person to do a new production. Hayden Griffin's eyes had lit up at what had been described to him as the potential of the Lyttelton Theatre. So, he had done a bells-and-whistles design, which really intended to knock the audience flat. I would now say it was crazy, in the sense that some scenes were four minutes long, and yet Hayden and I were putting a whole factory on stage, and then sweeping it off. There was a lot of factory scenes, tanks, stuff coming and going, huge portraits of Stalin. Then one of the most beautiful things I've ever seen in a theatre, which was the snow storm at the end, which used a snow cloth and practical snow coming down. Polystyrene snow.

I do remember people saying to me, "Have you been there? Have you looked at the state that theatre's in?" I do remember the first three days of the technical, just watching pieces of scenery get stuck.

Simon Relph [technical director] was, to me, a complete hero. You really felt the whole weight of the business of opening the building was on his shoulders. I remember him at two o'clock in the morning, standing in the middle of the stage, and him just saying, "Don't worry, David, it'll open, it'll just take time."

I do remember everybody being completely exhausted by it all, because we just seemed to be in an endless technical. Terrible, wasn't it? Were you around?

Richard: I was, somewhere, trying to make things work. I was probably hiding.

David: We just heard of you as a phantom that was somewhere in the theatre.

Richard: The Phantom of the National!

David: Exactly. It's a good title, isn't it? I think the character of the National had been determined by the choice to have three auditoria. There is always a lingering nostalgia for Olivier, because he ran one company. What Olivier was trying to work on, was a question of how do you run a company when you've got more than one stage? All his attempt at the Old Vic was about family, wasn't it? That wonderful canteen, the wonderful woman who cooked all that food, and that sort of family feeling, partly because of all those incredible actors that he had. That whole, "I'm the stern father…"

Richard: We all adored the man.

David: Theatre is family and you could see that Olivier was thinking, Well, if we have three auditoria, how do we have theatre as family? I think the problem the National had from the very first day was, you can't. Peter, I think for personal and emotional reasons of his own, was perfectly happy at the beginning with the idea that it should be a department store. Whatever emotional fulfillment Olivier got from leading a company, which obviously he did extremely well, Peter was not really interested in that. He was not a sentimental man at all, whereas Olivier, obviously, was an extremely sentimental man about the theatre.

You had this problem that it was disorienting because you didn't feel that you're all working in the same place. We used to have those fire alarms, where we all had to go out onto the pavement and evacuate the building for security reasons. You'd meet all sorts of people on the pavement, "I haven't seen you, what are you doing?" They'd say, "Oh, I'm working at the National Theatre." The security alerts were great because you'd see a lot of old friends. Then, I believe, there were about four hundred of us, and there are now about eight hundred.

Richard: No, there are over a thousand!

David: Oh fuck! What are they doing, Richard?

Richard: Well, massive education departments and development, raising money, to raise money, to raise money.

David: I do remember when we moved in, there were not

enough people to go in the offices. People would say to you, "Do you want an office?" Now, you can't get an office because every office is jammed with people staring at computers. The character of the National was decided at that fatal meeting at which somebody said, "Don't we have to have a proscenium theatre, as well?"

Richard: It was the South Bank Board decision. Olivier was against it. He wanted everything committed to one theatre.

David: Peter became more and more discontent. Obviously, at the end of his life, Peter would say, "I want to be remembered for the Royal Shakespeare Company, I never had the affection for the National Theatre that I had for the RSC." He regarded that as his monument.

I went to America and came back in 1979; he said, "Will you run the Olivier?" The one thing we understood at once is you've got to have great actors and productions in the Olivier Theatre. It's all Olivier led, the rest is much easier. Partly because, for so many years, the only people who were willing to write for it were me, Howard Brenton, and Peter Shaffer. Most living playwrights would just say, "I don't want to be in the Olivier."

I said, "Well, Peter, I don't understand what the director of the National Theatre is, if he's not the person who's running the Olivier Theatre." He was always trying to hive it off. He then came up with that system of companies whereby Richard and I led a company, Ian McKellen and Bill Bryden led companies. Peter Gill, I think, was leading one, Alan Ayckbourn. Peter was always looking for a way of getting back to a human scale. I do think that Nick Hytner and Nick Starr, by expanding things even more have got it to a point where it almost can only be run by them. There's almost nobody who can manage a theatre on that scale; it's insane. A million pounds a year profit from catering. You really are into some mega-business.

The building that, from my point of view, has weathered extremely well. It looks great from the outside, we know all its problems from the inside. You better than anybody. I always understand that Lasdun had this contract in which no changes could be made without his permission, is that right?

Richard: Well, now it's a Grade II* listed building. It's like the pyramids; you can't officially change anything, except temporarily. So Trevor put in that temporary seating in the Lyttelton for his final season, and Richard Eyre did the temporary arena in the Olivier.

David: Denys was obviously just absolutely committed… The National Theatre was his monument, and he suffered such abuse about concrete and Brutalist architecture. Every time I pass the Royal College of Physicians in Regent's Park, I think it's just a stunningly beautiful building. I always think, "Denys, actually, this is your monument." I talked to Norman Foster – this was in the 90s – and I said, "We have this problem at the National, that it can't be changed without the architect's permission." He said, "I've never heard of such a clause in an architect's contract, ever." Over and over, we were told, "It cannot be changed, Denys won't allow it." Stansted airport is changed all the time, without Norman Foster's permission.

Richard: Every theatre should be allowed to change. But, at the moment, it is stuck in concrete, and it ought to be able to evolve. It'll be another thirty years, I suppose, before that happens.

David, you have said: "A play is never what happens on stage. It's what happens between the stage and the audience. The excitement and fun of theatre is never in the play itself, but in the transaction."

David: I can remember the very first time I went into the Lyttelton, saying, "There is a major problem with the circle in here." There were terrible dead spots in the acoustics. It was always the same. I didn't think of it as an inhuman theatre. I did *Plenty* and Hayden Griffin's design was so fantastic that it just seemed to work. Hayden, in a way, understood the Lyttelton better than anybody. Then we did *A Map of the World* which was a Shavian dialectical play, people stood and made speeches. I remember in the interval, running into [director] Stewart Burge, who said, "I don't get this at all; why are people standing miles apart, shouting at each other? They're meant to be expressing ideas, but whoever shouted ideas." Of course, he was right. We were very, very happy to do *Pravda* in the Olivier. That theatre plays wonderfully with epic style – with an epic actor like Tony Hopkins, who is able to play that size of theatre. He's such a extraordinary figure to look at on that Olivier stage.

Jocelyn Herbert used to drive me slightly mad. There was a play, *Murmuring Judges,* which Bob Crowley designed, and it was, I think, one of the best designs I've ever had for a play of mine. But Jocelyn said, "Oh, at last, the Olivier is completely empty of scenery." Meaning that there was an awful lot of open space. I said to Jocelyn, "So, your idea of a theatre is a place where no scenery is necessary at all?" She said, "Yes, Epidaurus, you know?" I said, "I don't think that can be a long-term solution to the problem of designing for the Olivier; not everything can be done on a bare stage." If you asked what had been the most memorable, the most triumphant uses of the Olivier, you would certainly say *Guys and Dolls*, which had a lot of scenery. You would certainly say *The Shaughraun*, which had a lot of scenery. And *Pravda*, which Hayden designed to the hilt. When Nick Hytner did *Timon of Athens*, it was stunningly well-designed. In every case, there was a lot of stuff on it. It can look great empty, but it also can look great full. I like the Olivier. It's obviously a much more successful auditorium than the Lyttelton, which is very problematic.

Richard: The problem in the Olivier is the circle is too far away.

David: For me, the problem is the air space, and that statistic about there being twice the cubic space that there is in an Italian theatre. From bitter experience, I can tell you that the only thing that makes plays work in the Olivier is story. If I am going to write for the Olivier, I know narrative, narrative, narrative. Howard and I, when we planned *Pravda*, got through the narrative we had planned in the first twenty minutes. We used to talk about, "Throw more story at this, throw more story, throw more story." *Stuff Happens* was a lot of direct address. It's not a picture theatre. You just have to plan story.

I saw Judi Dench, and Bill Nighy, and all these great actors in Chekhov in there. If you put the mature Chekhov plays in there, which depend on mood, you can't create mood in the Olivier, just because the cubic space is so huge. I'm sure they had a lovely production in the rehearsal room, but you put it down in the Olivier stage and it's just miles away, and the audience doesn't feel in relationship to it.

Richard: Every show can be one thing in rehearsal room and

> **"These classically trained actors all glowed in the Olivier. Gambon in *Galileo* was one of the greatest things I ever saw, fantastic."**
>
> David Hare

you put it on any stage, it changes in some strange way.

David: Changes completely. The Olivier always depended on a certain kind of actor who could speak and be heard. Tony Hopkins, Michael Bryant, or Judi Dench, Gambon, obviously. These classically trained actors all glowed in the Olivier. Gambon in *Galileo* was one of the greatest things I ever saw, fantastic. Those actors could deal, but throw an inexperienced actor into the Olivier, it's horrible. The Lyttelton is a more obviously curable thing. You can cure it by making it one space. Getting rid of that balcony, can't you?

Richard: I would reshape the balcony first. The problem is, upstairs, you can't see any seats downstairs. The secret of all Matcham-type theatres, they're all more curvaceous, so you're aware of the multiple levels. The boxes at the side bind the rooms together in those old-fashioned theatres.

David: It's particularly difficult for comedy because actors say you get this delayed reaction: the stalls laughs… and then the circle gets it and the circle laughs. All your timing's all over the place because you can't hold a whole group together.

Richard: That's right. Your phrase: The excitement in theatre, it's in the transaction between actor and audience.

David: Of course. That brings us to the Dorfman [the renamed Cottesloe]. I, personally, think they've ruined it. I think it's ghastly. I don't understand… an experimental theatre? The seats cost £45

David Hersey
Lighting Designer

or something, just to sit in an uncomfortable seat. The whole point of that theatre was meant to be that the National Theatre could let its stays down a bit. And do experimental work. The feeling of it is gone.

You and I both know that theatre depends on a certain rapport, an atmosphere, between the audience and performer. It is possible in different kinds of spaces to do that but, unfortunately, you need different means to do it. What you can do at the London Palladium is very different from what you can do at the Roundhouse.

The National Theatre is lodged in sort of an uncomfortable middle place. What we have not talked about at all is the problem of modern actors' audibility. I had this production, *The Red Barn*, directed by Robert Icke, who is rightly the most admired young director in England. But Robert's attitude is, all that shouting is old-fashioned: I'm not interested in Gielgud, I just want the actors to speak as if they were in a television, and I will mic them. Of course, I've got older, so my hearing is not so good, but I always could hear in the Lyttelton; now I can't hear in the Lyttelton. To me, it seems profoundly unnatural. I think Peter Hall and Laurence Olivier would be absolutely horrified. Now, you can say fashion is changing, but I also feel that the reaching out an actor does to an audience, doesn't happen unless the actor projects. That, to me, is the great mystery and wonder of acting. Those of us who were lucky enough to see John Gielgud saw that John could do that, and you didn't know how he did it. Some of the mystery goes out of acting once you say, "I'll stick a mic on you and then everyone can hear."

I first met Peter Brook when he'd been on that building committee and I was just a student coming down from university. Peter was very generous about seeing young people. I said, "I want to start a theatre," and he said, "Start a travelling theatre, because the thing I have learned by being on this committee is that the shape of the theatre that you are going to make, depends on the work that you're going to do." He said, "Do the work first, and then build the theatre around the work."

Richard: He was probably the sanest voice of the whole group. The trouble was that Denys didn't understand what he was saying!

David is perhaps now best known as the lighting designer of a remarkable run of British musicals, *Evita*, *Cats*, *Starlight Express*, *Les Misérables* and *Miss Saigon*. But the experience to light those shows came from a ten-year period of lighting for the National, RSC and elsewhere. After he arrived in England from America in 1968 I invited him to join the Theatre Projects lighting design team; he took over from me as lighting consultant to the National, remaining in that role for ten years. He gives particular credit to the 1971 production of *The Architect and the Emperor of Assyria* for letting him discover light on stage in a new way.

On the difference between the Olivier and the Barbican:
"The Barbican disappears, the Olivier is always present. The concrete is 'in your face'. Over the years, more and more is covered in black. In the Barbican, as the houselights fade, the theatre recedes into the darkness. You can get a real blackout. The play takes over."

"I remember with fondness *Tamburlaine* in the Olivier. The chaos of opening, but the power of the production."

"Lightboard was a breakthrough. We used all the facilities, but the concept of 'groups' revolutionised the entire process of lighting. I used them all the time, and have done so ever since. It also heralded the start of seriously lighting over rehearsals. We could begin to have fine control over one lamp per channel, and the stalls control was an absolute joy to use – it meant there could be two board ops banging away on the main console and me on the stalls control, just trying to keep up with rehearsals!"

Jason Barnes
Production Manager

One of the longest-serving members of the National, Jason was resident production manager at the Cottesloe Theatre for thirty-two years and 202 productions. At a 2016 celebration of the building's 40th anniversary, he contributed the following:

"I think Bill Dudley is probably the designer for whom I worked most often. Each project needs to start with a napkin and a Biro. Bill would say, 'Here, Jase, I want it like this.'"

"The Cottesloe is the most wonderful space. Iain Mackintosh has talked of proportion and dimension, and those building a courtyard theatre in the future who vary his proportions do so at their peril. A width of 32 feet 6 inches. The first balcony at 8 feet 7 inches, the second 8 feet in total, which equates to 2560 mil and 5 metres on the second balcony. Getting the first balcony as low as possible is absolutely vital."

"An example of where the first balcony level is far too high is the studio at the Curve Leicester, which is 3.6 metres, utterly unreachable, emotionally, spiritually – it's just too high."

"The second-row side seats are fine, but I spent years trying to get the NT box office to print 'Courtyard Playhouse, first level side' on the ticket. Because without that, people have an expectation of looking straight on."

"My favourite shows were *The Mysteries*. On the revival for the millennium after a fourteen-year gap, I was moved to tears and had to leave the auditorium. That was a show I worked on for nearly twenty years."

The Mysteries, 1999 Revival

Howard Davies

(1945-2016) Director

Howard was an associate director of the National Theatre under every artistic director apart from Olivier, until his untimely passing in 2016. But more, it feels like the National Theatre was his home, a place where he made thirty-six, usually acclaimed, productions, from *Cat on a Hot Tin Roof* in the Lyttelton in 1988 to *3 Winters* in the same theatre in 2014. Along the way he teamed up with designer Bill Dudley on the *The Shaughraun*, the first show to exploit the Olivier's drum revolve.

Prior to the National he worked at the Bristol Old Vic, the Birmingham Rep, and at the RSC, where his productions included the original *Les Liaisons Dangereuses*, and his work was also seen at the Almeida, Hampstead, and on Broadway, where he made his debut with *Piaf*.

Howard: Bill Dudley knew that there was this dormant piece of machinery which hadn't been used. That was fantastic because everybody said, "Let's have a go."

It was great because we were the first people to use it. You had to have a kind of Rubik's Cube, three-dimensional imagination to be able to imagine how it would work and, luckily, I've got that. So Bill and I had a lot of fun, but a lot of complexity, working out how to move from one scene to another.

Of course, we had all sorts of technical problems when we got to the tech. Peter Hall was very good, because I remember there was a point in the previews when it all jammed up and came to a grinding halt, and there were also terrorist threats from the Irish. So we had to clear the building one night and wait outside for two hours – we were getting further and further behind in our technical. Peter just said stop stressing. He was totally supportive.

I remember it broke down in one of the previews and there was a moment when the audience had to sit around for quarter of hour. And then somebody shouted, from up above: "This is disgraceful at the National Theatre." The other people around said, "Oh, shut up." And he did shut up, so – it was fun.

Neither of the big theatres, the Lyttelton or the Olivier, quite work. There's a problem between the stage and you, as the viewer, in the Olivier at the back of the auditorium, up at the top. You feel too far away.

It's fine in the stalls. Even in the back row of the stalls in the Olivier, you feel you're there, you're in touch with those actors, but up above – it's even further back and it's a problem.

It requires a choice of play that is rhetorical. It can't just be discursive, naturalistic, or realistic. You can't do that because, basically, actors have got to use their voices to pitch out. Trevor Nunn, when he took over, decided that he was going to use sound enhancement – but for me that's problematic. Also, because of the wraparound nature of the stage, you only get the back of somebody's head unless they're constantly moving, or unless they move far back upstage, which defeats the nature of the stage space. I tried to be very, very bold when I did Chekhov there, because I thought, Oh, this is the most public of his plays. This is the most political of his plays. You know, that'll be fine. In fact, it wasn't fine. We did as well as we could do with *The Cherry Orchard*, but it didn't sit comfortably. When I was doing *Galileo*, Brecht is rhetorical and that sat fine; the debates chucked around in a much more sort of rebarbative way on the stage, which lends itself to that kind of energy.

The Chekhov would have been better suited in the Lyttelton. But the Lyttelton also has its problems. The stage is very, very wide. I love it, because it's got this Cinemascope quality to it. I will never narrow down the proscenium arch, but you have to be quite bold to use something that wide. I again find myself choosing Gorky or Bulgakov there, rather than the more intimate naturalistic plays. Those plays have a kind of sinew to them that for me, made sense in the Lyttelton. And every time I see the Lyttelton closed down, it doesn't work.

It's not an intimate theatre. It is classically based upon a picture frame, but the picture frame is so wide that it has a sort of epic quality to it. So that both spaces seem to require epic theatre, and that leaves the more 20th century discursive naturalistic plays being relegated, if you want to use the words, to the Cottesloe, which is a shame.

But, as you said, theatre people have made it work. Directors and designers have made those spaces work incredibly well. Though I think young directors are afraid of the Olivier. Less so now, because Nick brought in younger directors when he was here and has blooded them on the stage. There is no other theatre like it.

The problem with the circle in the Lyttelton is that it produces two audiences. The people in the circle can't see anybody in the stalls, and the people in the stalls have only got a thin awareness of people above. So when you do anything which earns laughter from the audience in the Lyttelton you get two audience responses. It's interesting because sometimes you get a younger student audience, 'cause it's cheaper seats at the top, and you'll get a big wave of laughter coming from the upper seats and the people who have had a few gin and tonics, are a bit more middle class, a bit less likely to laugh, are silent downstairs.

Richard: The traditional proscenium theatre, the Matcham-type proscenium, linked upstairs and downstairs with the side boxes. You're deeply aware of what other levels are feeling. They made the the auditorium hug the stage.

Howard: But theatres can change with time. Your heart

The Life of Galileo, Olivier Theatre, 2006

doesn't lift if you go and work at the Old Vic now, because it's too big. But if you push out beyond the boxes, you've still got very good sightlines, and if you do that then it will work. But if you take it back to the original proscenium arch, it's a problem.

Richard: I've found the renovation there interesting. Sir Laurence, with Sean Kenny, brought the stage right forward. But he criticised himself about that. I personally preferred it to when they put it back upstage to its historical base.

Howard: No, it's not so good.

Richard: I've never heard anyone else agree with that. [Laughs]

Howard: When we moved *The Iceman Cometh* from the Almeida Theatre with Kevin Spacey, we put it in for a two-month run in the Old Vic. Bob Crowley and I went, "Right, we've got to put the stage right out," which is presumably where Olivier placed it. And it worked. I think the acoustic was fine.

The Almeida is probably my favourite because it's a perfectly intimate, cozy space, and you feel that you're right on top of the actors, so it allows people to engage with the play in a very, very direct and personal way.

The difference between the West End and Broadway is very interesting because the West End has got these old Matcham theatres, which are mostly small. The proscenium is quite tight, and you go to Broadway and all the theatres on Broadway are built for dancing girls. They're very

The White Guard, Lyttelton Theatre, 2010

wide, very shallow, built for cut-out painted scenery. You're close. But it's very wide – it's a different kind of theatre. It was raucous entertainment theatre.

Richard: I've always found those side step-down boxes of a Broadway theatre do bring the audience together.

Howard: They do. They're beautifully designed.

Chichester is too big, and when they were going to redo it, I thought, Oh, that ought to be interesting. They're gonna redo it and then do something radical with it. Well, they haven't.

You take a space and you go, Well, I don't like the space, but I'm gonna work within it and I'm gonna get the best out of it.

I've never worked at the Royal Exchange. I've seen shows there which I've thoroughly enjoyed. It's very strange – you've got this thing which is parked in the middle of that big building. The acoustics are poor. It's quite tricky, especially when it's in-the-round and you can't read somebody's lips if their back is to you. You're struggling.

The actual design of it is very beautiful, but the acoustic is the problem in that building, I think. Acoustics of most modern theatres have been their bane. It's a technology that no one seems to understand.

Richard: Where would you start if somebody said to you, "I'd like a theatre. Would you help us do it? We'll build you a theatre!" [Laughs]

Howard: I'd want to find an old space. When Jonathan Kent and Ian McDiarmid – and Nick Starr, who was working with them at the time – had to leave the Almeida, they converted this bus station into a theatre. It was an impossible space, and the acoustics weren't really good, but the thrill of going into an industrial space which had been converted for you to play with – there's a sort of tangible historicity about it which is thrilling, I think.

The first theatre I worked in was the Bristol Vic, which is gorgeous. You know you walk down the auditorium, and it would creak, because it was wooden and it was old.

It had a history to it, so it felt like an old warehouse itself. Even though it's a purpose-built, wonderful theatre. So, yes, that's what I would prefer to use, a lived-in space.

William Dudley

Designer

Bill has had a remarkable career spanning all genres of theatre – everywhere from the Royal Court to the RSC to the West End; Bayreuth, for the *Ring* Cycle with Peter Hall; the Met in New York; the Royal Opera and ENO in London; Glyndebourne; Glasgow for two remarkable shows with Bill Bryden; *Peter Pan* in a giant tent in Kensington Gardens – and over sixty productions for the National. Some of those have been amongst the National's most memorable, maybe even loved shows: *The Mysteries* in the Cottesloe, *The Shaughraun* which brought the Olivier's drum revolve to life for the first time, and later Tom Stoppard's *Coast of Utopia* trilogy, where Bill pursued his quest to find the best design solution for a show whatever that may be, switching from epic 'real' scenery to versatile, dynamic computer-generated projected scenery and, arguably, starting a new style of design that has been adopted by many shows since.

Plus, during Richard Eyre's tenure, his forthright views on the National's two big theatres rather attracted the ire of the architect…

Discovering the Drum

Bill: We accidentally found out about the drum revolve. I was asked to do *The Shaughraun* in 1986, directed by Howard Davies. I read the script, and then I did independent research on Boucicault. British theatre then [mid-19th century] was happening with a lot of spectacle, and Boucicault was trying to anticipate the movies without perhaps knowing it.

It was somewhat laughed at later, when all the purists, the post-Peter Brook set, pooh-poohed all that. But it was giving people spectacle before the cinema. [J.M.W.] Turner himself painted backcloths at Drury Lane. None have survived, but he is in their account books.

Back to Boucicault. I read the play, and thought, Well, this is meant to be a spectacle. It's like a movie about thirty years before William Edward Freise-Greene, and the Lumiere Brothers. It's staged as spectacle for people who didn't travel so much then. That's what all those dioramas were about, using visual techniques and transparencies and sunrises with miniature lamps and so on. So, we had the revolve and, famously, it didn't work.

I thought this would be a perfect use for this show. Because you've got a castle, and chases, and there's action high up above the stage, and it's risky and melodramatic.

We went down to lunch at the canteen, and there were two blokes sitting there, stagehands. I said, "It's a bloody shame. This show's perfect for it if only the drum was working." They said, "What do you mean? Of course it's working." I said, "Any fool knows that it didn't work." So they said, "Well, it's working now. We are the maintenance team for the revolve. It's part of our duties. And in our spare time we have been quietly working on it since 1976."

I said, "Wow, that's incredible. But nobody seems to know about it." And they said, "We didn't want to tell anybody in case they started using it." That was their actual words. You think, Wait a minute. I'm getting into an alien comedy here. I said, "I won't tell a soul. Is there a chance we could see it demonstrated?" They said, "After tomorrow's changeover, there's a gap between the old set being gone and the new one getting in; we can show it then." I said, "Can I bring a friend?" They said, "All right." I brought down Howard Davies, and we stood there, not on the revolve, but adjacent to it. And it was like standing on the deck of an aircraft carrier because suddenly the ground just fell away very fast. And it was about a forty-foot drop? Voom. And of course, the rest is history.

But, actually the next bit isn't generally known. The guys explained, "Well, the secondary issue is there's a very specific loading, like any piece of machinery, like any crane, and before it pulls out the pins that allows it to move up or down, it weighs itself. You must monitor the weight, every nut and bolt, everything that's going to ride around on it." I think, was it 5.2 tons? So, we went on with the set, and all the props were polystyrene, pasted, painted, and textured up to look like the real thing. It came to the day before the fit-up: they pressed the button and it wouldn't move. A nightmare. They said, "Your set is too heavy." I said, "No, every piece was independently weighed before coming in." They say, "Well, let's have a look down in the bowels." Of course what had the crew done? They put all their spare stage weights on it. They actually stored all the weights and old winches down there, and nobody ever told us that, and I was too stupid to go look. So we cleared everything out, and we pressed the button and it worked – that was a thrill. Joyous, funny, and very Boucicault.

I suddenly saw the real potential of the Olivier. I know about the intrusive concrete curves and all that, and the 'ashtrays' are a bit strange. But one did see the power of the space. I was asked to do a platform performance, and they asked if I would start by coming up on the revolve. It was actually on a Boucicault night, so the lights went down, and I came up sitting by the fire: "Well, hello!" Of course all kinds of purists wailed on us, "You're turning the clock back." I said, "Why assume it's back? This is new stuff." Kinetics on a grand scale.

The sad thing is, the stage is pretty good. The problem is the auditorium doesn't relate to it, it's all too laid-back. When you go in, you think it's a 2000-seater, its volume is massive, and it only seats 1100.

The Lyttelton
'The Odeon,' as we like to call it. Famously the RSC theatre at Stratford was built like a cinema, it had no linking side balconies or boxes. Later they added a line of side balconies,

Photo shoot for *The Shaughraun*, Olivier Theatre, 1988

so 'a titter' could run around the house, which, as we all know, is what brings theatres to life.

In the Lyttelton there is no focus. It's a tough one because you can't really close it down. Yes, there's a big heavy false pros, but that's not it really, is it? Because your seat is here, and the actors are over there. Of course, great productions have been staged there. But people do like a proscenium theatre with a focus.

Then Iain Mackintosh and John Bury – you must have been involved too – came up with the Cottesloe. With the Bill Bryden season, we were about the third production in.

That was the most exciting period of my working life, with Bryden's company. Tight budgets, but fantastic. You never know with Bill, 'cause he did later get a million pounds for the Glasgow show, for *The Ship*, and the second one, which was *The Big Picnic* about the First World War. I did a whole section of No Man's Land about 150 feet long, and the audience glided over it on a moving seating block.

My favourite sort of theatres? Well, there was always a certain handsomeness about the Royal Court when I started there.

Of course I love the Cottesloe, and I thank you all for that.

Michael Blakemore

(1928-2023) Director

Michael first impacted the National Theatre with a stunningly successful play by Peter Nichols, *The National Health*. Three years later he joined Sir Laurence as an associate director, in which role he continued under Peter Hall until 1983. At this point, increasingly uncomfortable about the changes under the Hall regime, he resigned. Michael wrote *Stage Blood: Five Tempestuous Years In The Early Life Of The National Theatre* about his early career and the National. With kind permission from Michael, here are his comments upon the National's new theatres.[24]

"The new building on the South Bank was itself a sort of empire, the largest theatrical complex ever built in Britain, with three theatres, as many restaurants and bars, and a variety of spaces for exhibitions and concerts. I had been taken on a tour of it in mid-construction, when the new theatre was no more than a draughty shell of damp concrete, but could tell even then that the tiers of public spaces facing the river which beckoned you around corners and up staircases would be an astoundingly successful feature.

About the two main theatres I was less sure. Many and often contradictory opinions had been sought during the planning stage, but the sagest counsel had come from Olivier himself. However, he couched it in such quaint traditional terms that the architect, Denys Lasdun, felt free to disregard it: 'No spectator should be further from the focal point of the stage than the length of a cricket pitch.' In the age of the screen close-up no advice could have been more pertinent, but it did not mesh with the architect's vision of a kind of indoor version of one of the great theatres of Ancient Greece, in which spectators had sat in ascending rows of seats scooped out of the curvature of a hill. In Lasdun's Olivier Theatre no second tier would overhang the stalls, but the circle would begin where the stalls left off. Thus in the middle of the 20th century a theatre was being built where a member of the audience in the back row of the upper level was further from the stage than someone in the gallery of Drury Lane, a theatre built two hundred years earlier.

Similarly in the more conventional house, the Lyttelton, architectural theory collided with theatrical horse sense.

> "Theatre takes place within architecture but the two forms are at opposite ends of the artistic spectrum, the one having to do with permanence and timelessness, the other with a celebration of what will pass."
>
> Michael Blakemore

Here the upper level did indeed overhang the stalls, but its incline was so calculated that a spectator, though he had a view of the stage, could see nothing of the patrons sitting in the lower level. The thinking was that this would allow him to concentrate undisturbed on what was happening on stage. In practice it meant that a play in the Lyttelton would address two separate audiences, and in a comedy, where the pleasure of the evening is reinforced by the subliminal signals you pick up from the people with whom you are surrounded, this matters.

Theatre takes place within architecture but the two forms are at opposite ends of the artistic spectrum, the one having to do with permanence and timelessness, the other with a celebration of what will pass. They relate to each other as does the fireplace to the flame, and a splendid mantel or chimney breast means nothing if warmth does not make its way into the room or smoke go up the chimney. Fortunately the space in which a theatrical event takes place is less crucial than the intensity of the event itself and once it has our attention the physical context in which it is happening melts away."

Diana Quick

Actress

Diana is an actor perhaps best known for the role of Lady Julia Flyte in the television production of *Brideshead Revisited*. She received an Emmy and British Academy Television Awards nomination for her work. At the National, she has appeared at the Old Vic, the Young Vic and all three theatres on the South Bank, including in *Tamburlaine the Great*, the show which opened the Olivier.

Working at the National Theatre

"Moving from the Old Vic, with its horseshoe-shaped auditorium, an intimate relationship between stage and audience (despite its scale), acoustic ease, and camaraderie throughout the company from office, to crew, to stage company, into the echoing, concrete, unfinished spaces of the South Bank was stepping into unknown territory for all of us.

"In the Olivier, for *Tamburlaine*, the production involved a lot of people moving swiftly across the rather large distances of the stage, and then almost vying for the one really good spot from which to speak and command the house – that is, stage centre. From this one position it was possible to 'embrace' the house, wide as it was, because you could see everyone even up on the distant tier of the balcony. In any other position on the stage, you were cutting off chunks of your audience.

"Sound in the Olivier was difficult. I've found this to be the case as an audience member – shows which were fairly inaudible, I have been left feeling disengaged because the relationship between stage and audience was not secure; I especially loathe the recent habit of miking performers in both the Olivier and Lyttelton, because it immediately removes that live alchemy where the actor's vocal chords vibrate and transmit sound and meaning and feeling which then resonates directly on the hearer's ear. This is a crucial reason for still going to live theatre.

The Lyttelton

"It was like working in a cinema: so wide, and featureless, with an intimidating lack of centre aisle. We had to learn to stand unrealistically far away from a fellow actor in a scene – it took quite a lot of getting used to – in order not to look as if the whole cast was huddling in a tiny bit of the expanse.

Good Points

"The dressing room block was luxurious for actors used to cramming in to too-few rooms as a matter of course, and it was fun, and good for esprit de corps, to be able to see across to other rooms and engage in dumbshow. The rehearsal rooms were conducive to focused work – big, plain, quiet. The canteen and green room are lavish for those of us used to the cramped basement at the Old Vic.

Other Theatres

"The Manchester Royal Exchange, built to play in-the-round, where that sense of connection with all of the audience to the stage is quite easy to achieve. I've loved playing at the Aldwych and at Drury Lane and a range of older theatres where you feel the auditorium curves the audience towards the stage. Also, of course, there may be an element to those theatres of having been seasoned by many years' playing by accomplished companies: I do believe in the theatre building as being a continuum which becomes 'tuned' by what has taken place within its walls.

"It seems to me that the actor's crucial job is to mold a disparate group of individuals who happen to be in the theatre on any given occasion, into a single entity, so that they can receive the play as a body. Any theatre design has to bear that in mind."

Alan Ayckbourn

Playwright and Director

Alan Ayckbourn's National Service
Sunday Telegraph, **1986**[25]

"It sounds rather rude to say so, since he is not much older than I am, but Peter Hall has always been what I choose to term one of my guardian uncles. During my life there have been several; none, alas, relatives.

He first 'adopted' me as a playwright while I was being very successful (and hence, in the eyes of most critics, rather down-market) in the West End. Peter invited me to write something for the newly built, as yet unfinished, National Theatre South Bank building. He suggested the Lyttelton Theatre.

I gazed at the empty concrete shell of the bare theatre. It seemed similar in scale to the Houston Astrodome – though admittedly lacking some of that vast indoor arena's acoustic intimacy. I was used to working at the time in a 250-seat theatre in the small lecture room of the public library In Scarborough – nobody more than twenty feet from the centre of the action, and to avoid injury would patrons in the front row please keep their feet off the acting area.

So I wrote *Bedroom Farce* for Peter: it seemed to solve the Lyttelton problem by dividing the stage into three smaller stages. The announcement of the play caused a lot of flak. The NT was struggling to establish itself in its new home and was subject to a lot of sniping anyway. If it wasn't the building, it was the productions. Basically, some critics asked what this temple of the arts was doing, presenting this commercial chappie from the West End. The short answer was that it was trying to bring to the place an audience that normally shied away from temples. It isn't, in today's climate, a question people ask; I think I have grown a little more respectable, though that is not what I have striven for.

Then, in 1982, for my first solo voyage, *Way Upstream*, which, thanks to an awful lot of flooding (real boat, real water), almost sank without trace. Ruefully wringing out his wellingtons, Peter asked me for another, and it was as a result of the next success, *A Chorus Of Disapproval*, that he asked me if I would be interested in taking a longer

Alan Ayckbourn © Adrian Gatie

break from Scarborough. He had recently formulated the idea of dividing the National into separate companies.

Would I like to form a group of my own? After twenty-five years, it struck me that a short break from Scarborough, and the Stephen Joseph Theatre-in-the-Round there, might not be a bad idea.

My terms of reference were generous and wide. Three plays, including a new one of my own for the Olivier; and, preceding that, one in the Lyttelton and another in the Cottesloe. The rest – casting, choice of plays – was left up to me.

I started by inviting Michael Gambon out to lunch to see if he would be interested and, if so, what plays he would fancy doing. We are both men of few words and large appetites. Before the soup had hit the table we had fixed the season and set about the serious business of downing the minestrone. We settled on Miller's *A View From The Bridge* (which worried Michael a little because he seemed to recall that the hero had an awful lot of lines) and the 1925 Aldwych farce, *Tons Of Money*. This latter was much more to Michael's taste as he was to play the supporting role of the butler, Sprules, with very few lines indeed. My own new play, after our long association together (since 1974 and *The Norman Conquests*), he agreed to take on trust. The NT contracts department was later quite incredulous. It must have been one of the few instances of a leading actor signing a contract for a play he hadn't read and a part without a name. Gambon is no ordinary star.

After Gambon's genuine 'company' approach agreeing to big and small parts, it was much easier to approach other actors and persuade them to do likewise. We stood a far better chance now of assembling a real company and not a West End two-stars-and-then-the-rest-of-them affair. Before assembling the rest of the company, though, I had the awesome challenge of writing my own new play.

I came up with *A Small Family Business*. With its doll's house set on two floors, it was really the first play I had written that could not be staged in-the-round at Scarborough. It is what I term a light-heavyweight piece. In the Olivier it is difficult to do ethereal plays with delicate messages conveyed by eyebrows; I think you need something with a bit of clout. It was good, as I started to build the company, to bring in actors who had worked with me over the years in Scarborough, many of whom had worked for so long and so hard up there for so little, but all of whom understood and supported the company system. A critic said recently that the acting team seem to bat all the way to number 11. We also bowl a bit, too. Mind you, we had our moments.

Like discovering, as we explored the text more carefully, that *Tons of Money* – to the modern ear and eye – was totally illogical in places. Whatever logic the play had once had seemed to have died with Tom Walls, Ralph Lynn, and Yvonne Arnaud. When you tackle a farce you really earn your money. And the problem is that, beyond a certain level, you can rehearse no further until you have had an audience in to tell you what is funny. We did the equivalent of two weeks' work over six weeks in the rehearsal room and then gained six weeks' experience over nine preview performances in the theatre. Thus, while Gambon contented himself with slowly transforming Sprules the butler into Quasimodo, Diane Bull was developing something equally magical and bizarre as his bent-kneed, myopic, parlour maid fiancée and Polly Adams, as the bemused wife, was holding the whole show impeccably together.

> "I think you have to be very experienced (or bored) before you choose to clothe everyone in polythene bags and set them on a World War II bomb site: it is hard enough just doing the play."
>
> Alan Ayckbourn

A View from the Bridge was almost a holiday by comparison. Being a Cottesloe production (and thus a lower budget) we were obliged to rehearse in church halls in freezing February. We assembled for rehearsal as late as we dared and went home as quickly as we could. Suzan Sylvester, who played the daughter Catherine, fell and damaged her knee and rehearsed with a limp for a bit. We contemplated doing Williams' *Glass Menagerie* with its crippled heroine instead, but she got better.

We were into previews of *A Small Family Business* before the next disaster occurred. We were doing some tidying up sort of rehearsals one afternoon. Gerald Scarfe was sitting in the stalls sketching away bringing out the less fortunate features of Michael Gambon and myself when Michael tripped on a backstage cable severely damaging his ankle. Being the man he is, we stood around for some moments enjoying this latest example of his sense of humour. A few seconds later we realised how serious the injury was. He insisted on playing that night, a sort of one-legged hopping performance. We watched in horror as he turned grey and then yellow with pain. On the following day, he was back again expecting to play. By now the pain of walking was so intense that it was actually difficult to make out what he was saying. Blessedly, he agreed to go home.

The first family broke up after a year – ironically, the victim of its own success. Because *A View from the Bridge* was such an immensely popular show it became inevitable that it should transfer from a small theatre – which it did, in November 1987, to the Aldwych Theatre. For those members of the company who left the National, starting with an Aldwych farce and finishing at the theatre itself, it was a case of almost full circle.

A Small Family Business was recast, with Stephen Moore (another frequent collaborator of mine from *Bedroom Farce* days) replacing Michael. Peter Hall, again, suggested that I might like to do another production, especially since this new group – with the departure of *Bridge* and the disappearance of *Tons* from the repertoire – would only have *Family Business* in its repertoire.

I looked around for another piece for the Olivier. Something big. Something gutsy. My associate artistic director in Scarborough, Robin Herford, who is far better read than I am, suggested *'Tis Pity She's A Whore*. I liked it a lot. It is surprisingly simple and it is also about people I recognise (no dukes, no royalty): corrupt businessmen and difficult teenagers. There is a lot of blood and by the end of the evening very few characters left alive. We are doing it in period. I think you have to be very experienced (or bored) before you choose to clothe everyone in polythene bags and set them on a World War II bomb site: it is hard enough just doing the play.

Besides, I hate monkeying around with other people's plays. I like to think that John Ford wouldn't have gone around putting gratuitous murders into *How the Other Half Loves* either. It is a great company play with everyone getting a look in (before they die) and it reads very fast – less than two hours. A classical play with lots of action with a playing time of around two hours. Everyone in the pub by 9.30pm. What more could you ask for?

I suppose if you work in one place for any length of time, as I have in Scarborough, you begin to wonder if you can manage anywhere else. And faced with an auditorium like the Olivier, you feel – as you would with the man himself – that this is the one to beat. If you can grab and hold an audience in a space that size… Bob Peck once described how, when a big laugh came in that theatre, it was like a shock wave breaking across the stage. The first time he experienced the volume of sound, he involuntarily took a step backwards.

Bedroom Farce, Lyttelton Theatre, 1977

I suppose what I have got from my time at the National Theatre is the excitement of playing in the big league. And a good deal of fun. I have proved to myself that I can play away from Scarborough and win. This time, I have to prove that I can take up the reins again after two years. I think the board there expected that once I had gone they would never see me again. Well, I'm going back. I can't say how things will be once I am there, but they are bound to be different: I dare say we are all in for a few surprises. I hope so." [26]

Simon Callow from *The National: The Theatre and its Work*:
"The actors [in the Olivier] learned to master the particular demands of that theatre (which often meant hitting on the two or three effective parts of the stage and not budging from them), while the parallel group of Lyttelton players learnt a thing or two about the harsh and unyielding acoustics of that place.

No acting style as such developed, though since intimacy was a virtual impossibility in either theatre, an extrovert and public manner, high in energy and physical dynamic evolved, though actors of iron lungs and overwhelming charisma like Paul Scofield or Michael Gambon were able to command a sort of operatic full-throatedness which triumphed over the hard walls and long distances." [27]

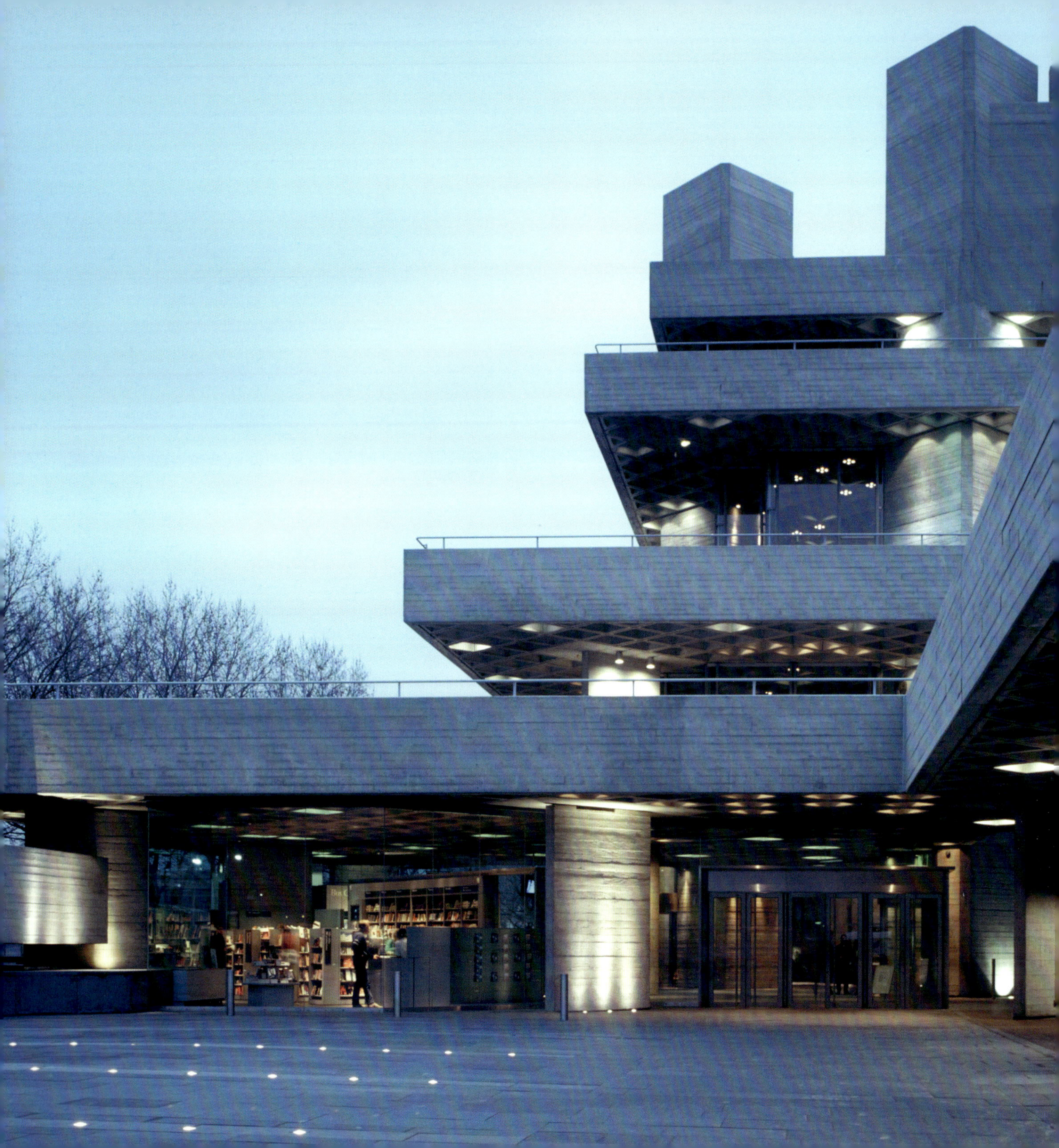

4.2 Richard Eyre
NT Director 1988-1997

"When Eyre took over the National in 1988, the country itself was bitterly polarised after nearly a decade of Thatcherite government. Internally, Eyre inherited an organisation that needed a bit of a shakeup. One of Eyre's least-remarked innovations was to promote women directors. But Eyre also saw that the National was uniquely well-placed to address the state of the nation. The ambition was extraordinary. And never more so than when Stephen Daldry turned Priestley's *An Inspector Calls* into a quasi-expressionist assault on the culture of individualistic greed that was Thatcher's toxic legacy."
Michael Billington, *The Guardian* [28]

I'm grateful to Richard for his permission to reproduce here extracts from his fascinating book *National Service: Diary of a Decade at the National Theatre*.[29] The diary (in black text) is interspersed with extracts from contemporaneous notes from the NT and Lasdun archives (in **bold purple** text).

17th January 1987
"Director Designate of the NT. A bizarre sensation. I don't know whether I expect people to commiserate or congratulate. It's like being in *Metamorphosis*, waking up as Director of the National Theatre instead of as a cockroach."

1st February 1987
"Talk to Bill Bryden [director and NT associate] about the NT. He confirms my sense that it needs to be more about theatre, less about the organisation. It exists to put plays on, and it's defined by the taste and talent of its directors, actors, designers, and writers. A theatre is a theatre is a theatre. People who work in the theatre do it for sentimental reasons: They want a sense of community, of 'family'. They want to share the excitements, to respond to the tensions and

After ten years of Thatcher, twelve years in its new building, both the National Theatre and the Nation felt in need of change.

At the National, a new Director takes charge. Familiar with the building's challenges and determined to tackle them, he soon finds himself in conflict with Lasdun in a battle for change. A taunt of "barbarian" and a new architect follow...

rhythms of putting on plays. The architecture and geography of the NT militate against this. The building doesn't revolve around its stages. They should be the epicentre of the building."

22nd May 1987
"I sat on the Baylis Terrace for two hours until the sun went down with Peter Radmore [head of the NT lighting department], and he spoke with the unelected but unmistakably authentic voice of the theatre's staff. He told me that if I gave them my support I need never doubt that it would be repaid."

11th May 1988
"First night of *The Shaughraun*. Howard's done it beautifully, and Bill [Dudley]'s designed it magnificently, making sense of the Olivier revolve for the first time – and Stephen Rea's wonderful, and I think it'll be successful enough to run it (force majeure) as our Christmas show, which will vindicate the money we've spent on it. So what was born out of chaos will look like policy."

23rd May 1988
Teleconference Lasdun and Eyre: "Lasdun said, with regret that he, Peter Softley and Harry Pugh were appalled at the proposals [to modify the foyers], such as they were and these proposals might be appropriate for a hotel, but not for the NT." [30]

10th June 1988
"Depressing meeting with Denys Lasdun. I tell him I admire the building (as I do) – its nobility, its classicism, its beauty, in fact, I get a thrill out of all its public spaces. But I also say that the Olivier is a difficult theatre to present plays in, which I suppose is a bit like saying that you have a watering can that doesn't hold water, but he doesn't want to discuss it. We work in his building, we know its problems, and so do the audiences. The acoustics are bad because the volume of space is so huge in proportion to the number of people in the audience, and it's enormously difficult to design for. It's an unfocused space: You either leave it bare or create a form of false proscenium, and whatever you do the concrete jaws either side of the stage intrude ostentatiously on the actors'

Peter Radmore (NT 1965-1992)

space. I don't, of course, say all this to Lasdun, but nevertheless he refers to me as a 'barbarian.' In spite of his abuse I can't help liking him and his building. He's still defending himself against the gross and gratuitous abuse he received when the building opened."

14th June 1988
Letter from Eyre to Lasdun: "I am sorry to have engendered a note of acrimony in our meeting on Friday. I think I need to emphasise that I have the greatest respect for your building, indeed, affection for it. I am here as Director because of the building not in spite of it." [31]

4th July 1988
Letter from Lasdun to Lord Goodman: "Like it or not, the building at least speaks with the authentic voice of its time. While it undoubtedly requires maintenance, cleaning, and refurbishment and can accept minor modifications, the proposals may well burden future generations with the task and cost of restoration when fashion changes." [32]

6th July 1988
"Met Maggie Smith and Albert Finney last week… I tell Albert that Peter Brook says that a theatre should be like a violin: Its tone comes from its period and age, and tone is its most important quality. 'Yes,' says Albert, 'and who'd build a violin out of fucking concrete?'"

"Who'd build a violin out of fucking concrete?"
Albert Finney

17th August 1988
Memo from solicitor Paul Herbert to Lord Goodman: [Goodman Derrick & Co are the solicitors Lasdun consulted about his rights as the architect of the NT] Notes that the law on copyright might not be very useful to Lasdun in this case. The drawings and the building are defined as artistic works and it is unclear whether that copyright is still with Lasdun or now with the National Theatre Board.[33]

31st August 1988
Letter from Richard Eyre to Max Rayne: "The Olivier Theatre is universally agreed to be a very difficult theatre to present plays in. We should not be daunted by the fact that the architect has, at least in the past, been intractable. We work in his building, we know the problems, and the audiences are aware of the problems. Fortunately the problems are soluble – with money and with will. With a capital expenditure of no more than the current spending on the lighting board/rig, the Olivier could be immeasurably improved. This is not a matter of arcane aesthetics but of specific design improvements that would make a substantial difference to the experience of the actors and the audience. Moreover, and this should not be taken lightly, it would be cheaper to design for the stage. The application of a thermal lance to some of the concrete interior might cause a tremor in Denys Lasdun's breast; it would cause enormous pleasure elsewhere."[34]

1st September 1988
"Today I am officially The Director. It seems ironical, having been doing the job for at least nine months… I started rehearsing *Bartholomew Fair*, and I knew that I shouldn't be doing it. 'It's a big play for a big theatre,' I tell myself. But I'm doing this play just because the giant mouth of the Olivier Theatre wants to close its jaws on it, and because I can't find a large-scale comedy and none of the directors I've approached wants the Olivier. It's a terrible note to start on."

24th October 1988
Letter from Gavin Stamp [architectural historian] to Lasdun: "I see the *Daily Telegraph* did you proud and put the NT on the defensive, which is good."[35]

8th November 1988
"Meeting with Denys Lasdun. Slight cause for optimism. 'God preserve Prince Charles and God preserve us from his views on architecture,' he says. After Prince Charles's criticisms of the National Gallery extension the architect became a pariah. Denys was upset about a bad review of *Bartholomew Fair* because it said the Olivier Theatre was the culprit as much as the production. Quite unconcerned about whether the review would have hurt me, he wanted me to write and complain about the insult to the architect. Bill [Dudley] and John [Gunter] and I have been talking about how to improve the Olivier and Lyttelton – or as Bill says, 'how to turn it into a theatre.' John's made a model of the Olivier which shows how the acoustics could be improved by cutting down the volume and making it one tier of seating (thereby, of course, making it more like Epidaurus), but we don't show it to Lasdun. He tells us we are 'custodians of the building': we can change the 'fittings' but not the 'room.'

14th November 1988
Letter from Serban Cantacuzino [architect and secretary of the Royal Fine Arts Commission] to Mr. S. Watts (at Lambeth Bridge House): "The Royal Fine Art Commission strongly supported Sir Denys Lasdun's design for the National Theatre when it first saw this in the late 1960s [sic]. It believes that the completed building is a work of great integrity, the interiors of which are as important as the exterior." Emphasises the role that being Grade I listed might play in future protection of the building.[36]

26th November 1988
Handwritten letter from Jocelyn Herbert to Lasdun, attached to a copy of a letter to the editor of the *Illustrated London News* about criticisms of the Olivier: "Dear Denys – Hope you think this is O.K. We mustn't let the Philistines take over."[37]

4.2 Richard Eyre, 1988-1997

2nd December 1988
Reply from Lasdun to above: "Many thanks for writing to the *Illustrated London News*. I only hope it won't discourage them [NT] from using your good self. They badly need your genius in the Olivier. Threats to NT are now receding as I have been asked to examine possible changes, but without damaging the architecture." [38]

4th February 1989
"Howard [Davies]'s production of *Hedda Gabler* has opened in the Olivier. It raises the old questions of how to use that theatre and how to do the classics. The auditorium forces Howard into an expressionistic design and the actors are pulling in the other direction. The NT seems as intractable as ever."

6th February 1989
DL&P Memorandum: "Stuart Lipton [advisor and property developer] said he had been responsible, since his arrival at the NT, for the resumption of dialogue with DL. He now wanted DL to help him by being less confrontational and more sensitive to NT's operational needs. It really was not possible to tell heads of departments that the building would not allow a solution of their problems." [39]

26th February 1989
"The Lyttelton is a big theatre; it needs very strong, clear, large acting that resonates, but at the moment it's imploding."

11th April 1989
"Denys Lasdun did a platform lecture in the Olivier. He announced he had no intention of changing an atom of 'the room' [the Olivier], a space that embraced audience and actors in a unifying hug. He was mandarin, combative, vague, lyrical, and occasionally incomprehensible. But right about fashion and to say about the building: 'It is what it is.' He quoted Arthur Clough: 'Pure form nakedly displayed.' Someone asked him: 'If concrete is the medium of our century and its pure form is nakedly displayed, why was the concrete shuttered and is therefore impregnated with the pattern of a million pine planks?'"

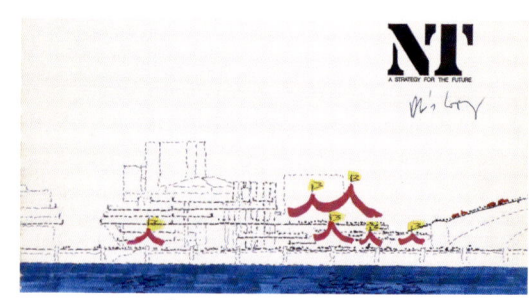

Denys Lasdun's *Strategy for the Future*, 1989

April 1989
Denys Lasdun publishes his guideline document: *Strategy for the Future*. "Since the opening of the National Theatre's South Bank building in 1976 the circumstances under which the National Theatre is required to operate have changed in a number of significant ways. To date, the response to changing needs and financial pressures has been one of expediency leading to haphazard uncoordinated solutions to individual problems as they have arisen, without regard to the architectural integrity of the building or the adverse impression they give to audiences and other visitors to what is, after all, the National Theatre."

The problems listed include: the Lyttelton bookshop, signs, poster panels and leaflet racks, terrace furniture, doormats, general clutter, public toilets, goods and load-in area. It also includes a section on the Olivier acoustics issues. It is recognised that changes will be required from time to time when new circumstances have to be confronted. The proposals outlined in this study demonstrate that the National Theatre building can accept a degree of change to both its front-of-house and backstage areas, while at the same time preserving its fundamental nature and architectural integrity. [40]

14th May 1989
"I went to the ruins of the Rose Theatre, a stone's throw from the Thames, uncovered in excavations for a new office block: mud, a few stone foundations, a hint of wooden columns that look as if they've been chewed by a giant dog, but in spite of it all a feeling of being there in the 16th century. You could feel the theatre: a rough platform, a raked auditorium, a gallery, all

smaller than the Cottesloe. Peter Hall was on hand to say that it proves that Shakespeare was written for chamber theatres. True, but why have we got these aircraft hangars to do the plays in? It's just economics. They're about to fill in the site: a sign of the times, concreting over our history."

11th July 1989 – Sir Laurence Olivier dies, aged 82.
"He [David Aukin – NT Executive Director] told me that Olivier had died and could I come to the theatre straightaway. I knew this was a significant historical moment, but didn't at the time feel anything except mild exasperation and sadness. Only after I had spoken to half a dozen journalists about his legacy and how I didn't really know him, did I start to feel that it was truly the end of an era, the last great buccaneering actor-manager. Brecht said: 'Happy the land that needs no heroes.' Maybe happier perhaps, but duller. Olivier was mercurial, had energy, a remarkable presence, was funny, charming, devious, vain, and occasionally laughably hammy. He willed himself to greatness, but I'm not sure that a 'great' actor is always a good one."

21st October 1989
"[Olivier's Memorial Service in Westminster Abbey] I saw Brian Ridley (who started as an electrician at the Old Vic when he was 16) sitting with a few colleagues from the early days, looking thoughtful and mournful. I caught his eye and he smiled wryly. For me, Olivier was a symbolic loss: the death of a heroic actor of the kind never to be seen again. For Brian it was the loss of part of his youth."

5th December 1989
Letter, Mary Soames [chair, NT Board 1989-1995; Winston Churchill's youngest child] to Denys Lasdun: "You yourself were considerate enough to indicate when you met the board, that one appropriate course might be to entrust the building and its future potential to a new architect, and we have decided that this is the right thing for us to do in seeking the kind of long-term commitment over a period of years which you have given us in the past. I am sure that you know that your place of honour in the history of the Royal National Theatre [the 'Royal' title was added in 1988, but is now no longer generally used by the National] is more than assured." [41]

Brian Ridley

Ian McKellen as Richard III

17th January 1990
"Meeting with Terry Farrell, putative architect for the restoration, renovation, and improvement of the NT building. I say that it's unfortunate that it's practically impossible to see St. Paul's Cathedral from my office without sitting on the window ledge and craning my neck. He explains that it's because the building is aligned at a right angle to Waterloo Bridge rather than parallel to the line of the river."

30th March 1990
Letter, Stuart Lipton to Lasdun: "We are beginning to think about approaching architects for the maintenance and extension works discussed in your brief. We are very keen to keep in sympathy. Could I come to consult with you about potential names?" [42]

20th April 1990
Letter, Lasdun to Lipton: "Any proposed architect must understand the nature of the building and be sympathetic to its architecture and be willing, able and free to work with the spirit of the guidelines. It seems unlikely that architects who are known to be high-tech or postmodern have the necessary degree of understanding and sympathy." [43]

8th October 1990
Letter from [architect] Stanton Williams to Lasdun: "We are aware that you have been consulted about this appointment, but would like to emphasise that we enter

4.2 Richard Eyre, 1988-1997

this engagement with a great respect for the integrity of the building, which we have both always admired." [44]

22nd November 1990
"Playing *Richard III* in the Odéon [in Paris] was the realisation of an adolescent dream – to have a successful production playing in a great theatre in a great city. And it's my favourite auditorium in the world, where I saw Jean-Louis Barrault in 1966."

24th August 1992
"Back from San Francisco where *RIII* was playing. Peter Radmore [NT head of lighting] has died. I thought of him as the conscience of the National Theatre: He believed passionately that it should always aspire to and achieve excellence in all departments, and that it should be a community united by common aims, that it was worth more that the sum of its parts, and that it was an ideal worth devoting his life to. He was exacting, and enthusiastic, and sometimes even exasperating in pursuit of this ideal. When he lit *The Beggar's Opera*, and I pointed out to him that an actor was unlit, he said – with some justification – that the actor deserved to be unlit and would remain so until he started to act better."

16th October 1993
"*Machinal* has opened [directed by Stephen Daldry]. Fiona [Shaw] gives a remarkable performance, and it's an extravagant and fearless piece of staging. Kathleen Tynan says, 'Does Stephen prefer sets to actors? The designers are taking over with an arrogant vengeance. Don't you agree?' I don't. I see it all as a way of making the theatre expressive and using all the tools at your disposal. The important thing is always to hold on to the humanity and the human scale of things – which is what I think Stephen and Ian [MacNeil] have done: in fact the production is about the 'machine' attempting to crush the 'human.'"

19th October 1993
Letter from Lasdun to Lady Soames: "I am astonished and appalled by what has been allowed to be built in the public circulation area immediately outside the Mezzanine restaurant. It is a crude and shoddy intrusion which violates both the language and form of the architecture and, in particular, the diagrid ceiling. Included in the current theatre programme is an announcement of the opening of the new Mezzanine restaurant, designed by restaurant architects Virgile & Stone. It would appear that neither the practice nor the individuals are registered architects and, because of this, the use of the word architect is an offence under the Architects Registration Act 1938." [45]

2nd December 1993
Letter from Norman Lord St. John of Fawsley, Royal Fine Arts Commission, to MP Peter Brooke: "The National Theatre is likely to merit a Grade I listing, like the Festival Hall, and it would not be unreasonable for the local planning authority to take this into account and call in English Heritage when considering any alterations to the exterior or interior of the building. But the London Borough of Southwark shows no inclination of doing this so that the likelihood of further changes, which will compound the damage already inflicted on the theatre, must be of very great concern indeed. Immediate listing would seem to be the only answer." [46]

12th February 1994
"Brian Ridley [chief lighting technician] has died after not many months of a wasting cancer. His death has blighted and blasted the technical staff. None of us can accept the suddenness and the injustice of someone dying so young. And Brian was one of those technicians who made you calmer and more confident. When I was last at the Bulandra Theatre [Romania] I was shown the lighting board by the chief electrician – an antique Strand Grand Master, all handles and brass like a railway signal box. 'How is my friend, Brian?' he asked me. 'Not well,' I said. He looked crestfallen. 'Tell him from me,' he said, 'to get well.'"

17th February 1994
DL&P Minutes of meeting with RFAC: "DL was summoned to Chairman's room for private preliminary conversation. DL outlined bones of the case, expressed his shock and gratitude to Royal Fine Arts Commission for seeing him. Chairman thought the building a masterpiece. Subsequently DL learnt NT and Sir Stuart Lipton had tried to cancel DL's meeting or alternatively to have a joint meeting for a free discussion!

(DL: "Can you imagine Lipton having a free discussion?') What is proposed is a terrible thing to do to this building. Functionally unnecessary and irresponsible. DL said like a puzzle, take away pieces and all disintegrates. DL pleaded for listing and hoped that, if it was listed adequately, this would at least force the NT to have a public enquiry before any destruction. SC [Serban Cantacuzino] said, sadly Grade 1 listing does not give full protection. There was no evidence as far as DL could see for changes to the Olivier and Lyttelton auditoria." [47]

2nd March 1994
Letter from Lord St. John of Fawsley to Lady Soames: "The commission believes that in any alteration to the National Theatre the integrity of the original design should be fully respected and the building treated as if it were already listed." The letter further suggests that service areas can be improved if the NT works with Denys Lasdun. [48]

24th April 1994
"I talked to Mary today about the problems with Lasdun, his opposition to any change. She's very worried about it becoming public: 'We'll be set on at cocktail parties and while we're at the ribbon counter at Harvey Nichols.'"

25th April 1994
"Meeting with the board to discuss funding the redevelopment. We have to grasp the opportunity to renovate, refurbish the building – even to rectify inherent defects. The money is there (from the Lottery) if we can get it. If we don't do it now the building will decay and be unusable (unlicensable) within ten years. It's not at the expense of the art – except that it's going to take a monumental amount of energy to push the plan uphill."

10th May 1994
Minutes of the meeting of the Royal National Theatre Building Development Committee: "The Director said he anticipated a struggle with Sir Denys Lasdun, but had the appetite for a public debate with him about the building, confident that our case for making these changes was watertight. At the moment we were having the debate on Sir Denys' terms and it was important to take the initiative. After spending many years working in this building, he had a personal investment in it and did not take a frivolous view of the building nor of its future." [49]

20th June 1994
DL&P notes on a telephone conversation between Eyre and Lasdun: "When DL said this is mutilation to a major design, he [Eyre] said that is a matter of opinion, to which DL said that is a very architecturally ignorant opinion." [50]

23rd June 1994
Richard Eyre: "There are many criticisms that can be made and have been made of its design, but it is, in my view, indisputable that it asserts clarity of vision, boldness, dignity, and classical simplicity. The changes that we are proposing are essentially remedial. In addition we are continuing to address long-term acoustic defects in the Olivier auditorium.

"It is my unambiguous view that we have an obligation to enhance the enjoyment of our audience and to hand on the building to our successors in a condition that would not require remedial work for another generation. I believe that this can be done without damaging the architectural integrity of the original design." [51]

23rd June 1994
The National Theatre Building is designated a Grade II* listed building by Historic England.

Press release from Department of National Heritage: "National Heritage Secretary Peter Brooke today announced that he has included the Royal National Theatre on London's South Bank in the statutory list of buildings of special interest." From Mr. Brooke: "I am aware that proposals for changes to the theatre are being announced today. My listing decision implies no judgement on those proposals, but I think it is right at this stage to register the building's outstanding architectural quality, so that that can be taken fully into account before final decisions are taken." [52]

26th June 1994
"Denys Lasdun told me that his building was being insulted, vandalised, and mutilated. He said that our plan to remove the walkway – which is self-evidently (and provably) an afterthought, since it entirely blocks the view of the river from the Lyttelton circle level – was like removing a pediment of St Paul's."

14th December 1994
"A salvo from [scholar] Noel Annan in *The Times* about the plan to remove the walkway: 'It is indeed like removing the lower jaw from someone's face. One is reminded of Dean Swift: 'Last week I saw a woman flayed, and you will hardly believe how much it altered her appearance for the worse.'' My, how they must have chortled at the Athenaeum."

15th December 1994
"Noel Annan has appeared on Channel 4 News fulminating about the removal of the walkway. To my intense satisfaction he stood on a balcony that he said 'the vandals' were going to remove. He pointed to a part of the building that no one has ever had any intention of altering in any way, shape, or form, making it transparently clear that he didn't know what he was talking about. But this is the problem: No one will look at the building in detail."

31st January 1995
Letter from Mary Soames to Lasdun: "I am, of course, sorry if I misunderstood the situation with regards to the appointment of Stanton Williams. My memory is clear (and I have checked with colleagues) that their name was referred to you (with those of several other architects) as candidates for consideration and that you did not demur." [53]

2nd February 1995
Excerpts from letter from Richard Eyre to Anthony Hopkins, Peter Brook and others:[54]
"Sir Denys Lasdun's striking modernist design, with its undisguised use of textured concrete throughout, made it a controversial building from the start.

"Since [1976], 12 million people have seen a performance here and many more have visited for backstage tours, exhibitions, platform performances, or foyer music, or to use the bookshop, to eat and drink – or to just sit on the terraces and enjoy one of the best riverside views in central London. I have never doubted that the building fulfils its brief: providing optimum conditions for staging a wide range of drama and accommodating up to 2500 people at any one time. But after 18 years' operation it has become clear that the building is a victim of its own success, and some aspects work less well than others.

"Our master plan [involves] measures drawn by our current architects, Stanton Williams, to improve the building. Amongst other things we want to enlarge the foyers.

"We also propose to demolish the walkway which links the building to Waterloo Bridge and to the South Bank walkway system. This will let much daylight into the foyers and allow freer circulation in the new [pedestrianised Theatre Square]. […]

"You will be aware from recent press coverage that Sir Denys Lasdun has mounted a fierce campaign to combat our proposals. Unless we can unlock this particular planning inertia, the building will inevitably enter into a spiral of decline and be unable to fulfil its primary purpose. […]

"I would like you to write [to the Planning Department at Lambeth Council] to support the principle of [our] being able to change what has become one of our youngest Grade II* Listed Buildings.

> **"A theatre lives in the present. No production is designed to last. In an ideal world, theatres would be demolished and rebuilt in every decade."**
>
> Peter Brook

"If we are unable to move forward, I forecast a dim and dismal future for the building and its foyers."

9th February 1995
Fax, Peter Brook to Richard Eyre: "For Richard to use as he wishes: 'A theatre lives in the present. No production is designed to last. In an ideal world, theatres would be demolished and rebuilt in every decade. A wise architect is one who recognises that a theatre must change and evolve like an airport. His commission can never be to build a monument, nor a memorial.'" [55]

3rd June 1995
"In the evening I had to make a speech at an opening of an exhibition of postwar British theatre architecture in the Lyttelton foyer. I made a feeble speech about the exhibition being a memorial to an epoch of public-funded theatre, but I should have burned effigies of the architects responsible for the calamities."

26th July 1995
Letter from Denys Lasdun to George Perkin, former editor of *Concrete Quarterly*: "Of course concrete properly used is a primitive material. I used it because of a deep desire to return to the basic roots of architecture. I agree with all you say about contrasting it with polished floors, elegant furniture, colour etc. The present colour of the carpet was chosen in conjunction with the lighting. At night it glows and sets off the form and texture of the concrete. Whether concrete is fashionable or not is irrelevant. It is just another building material with its own characteristics and property. It can be primitive and noble." [56]

3rd November 1995
Letter from Lasdun to [NT chairman] Christopher Hogg: "I now wish to put on record that if the porte-cochère is boxed in as proposed and the cathedral window mutilated, it will seriously damage not only the architectural composition of the building but the very quality of the foyer which has been such a success over all these years. Given the possible alternative solution it does seem to me wrong that pressures for revenue should be allowed to destroy the spatial and architectural qualities of a Grade II* listed building, much enjoyed by millions of people." [57]

7th February 1996
Letter from Hogg to Lasdun: "Besides, I emerged from our discussions last November with a feeling that the differences of opinion between us were genuinely and deeply held on both sides and were not going to be easily resolved. So I had accepted the situation, and still do, as one in which reasonable men agreed to disagree." [58]

3rd March 1996
"Michael Coveney thinks that the best thing that could happen in the Millennium is that the NT building crumbles into dust. I've occasionally had the same thought."

14th May 1996
Letter from Lasdun to Chris Hogg: Expresses "disappointment that there will not be any compromise. May I remind you that the Under-Secretary of State, Department of National Heritage has stated that, in the case of a Grade II* listed building, the original architect should be consulted in order to ensure that any alterations are architecturally sensitive to the original design. As you know, no such consultation has ever taken place. It is regrettable that, after all this effort, the board, the management, and your house architects do not appear to understand, let alone value, the architecture of the building." [59]

18th October 1996
Letter from Lasdun to Chris Hogg: "Since the promise of a compromise meeting suggested by Mr Lipton did not materialise, you will hardly be surprised to know that I have sought legal advice from specialist intellectual property counsel. The advice has been most encouraging, alerting me to the fact that the copyright (which I own) in the drawings for the theatre, can and would be infringed in a variety of ways should the board proceed with the changes without my consent. My moral rights would also be infringed by the derogatory treatment which the alterations would represent." [60]

27th November 1996
"A board meeting at the beginning of the week. Much talk about

how to react to Lasdun's threat of litigation. All the board are robust, although Stuart Lipton [property developer] hopes for some face-saving compromise."

9th December 1996
Letter from Lasdun to Chris Hogg: "You do not explain how you plan to achieve your purpose without infringing my copyright. It is quite clear that you do not have a license to use my original drawings to alter or extend the building." [61]

29th January 1997
Letter from Richard Eyre to Clinton Greyn of the Twentieth Century Society: "Your letter has told me nothing that I was not fully aware of. I have an intimate knowledge of the history of the Royal National Theatre, its architectural principles and its aesthetics [Lasdun or Greyn have underlined this final phrase and put several exclamation points after it]. After 15 years working in the building, with all its many virtues and its shortcomings, I am thoroughly acquainted with all the arguments for and against the changes to the building." [62] A note from Clinton Greyn to Lasdun, 13th February 1997, comments that "Trevor Nunn [announced as Eyre's successor] will hopefully prove more sensitive to the building."

11th February 1997
"Second of our regular meetings with the contractors and subcontractors. I told the assembled group (of 15-odd people) that we wanted to keep the theatre open during all the work, we didn't want to lose a single performance. We have to work to non-negotiable deadlines: If we advertise that we're opening a show at 7:30 on such and such a night nine months ahead, we're irrevocably committed to it. So could they work to the same criteria or would it be, forgive me, the see-you-next-Tuesday-John syndrome of the building trade? No, no, no, they guffawed, of course they could hit the deadlines."

18th February 1997
"Denys has complained to Chris Hogg at my reply to a letter from a man in a lobby group called the Twentieth Century Society, who'd written to me in an intensely patronising manner, explaining the aesthetics of the NT's carpet design, as if I had an IQ in the single figures."

12th April 1997
"After some nervousness about whether we would get a preview, we opened *Caucasian Chalk Circle* in the Olivier. The new auditorium – transformed into a theatre-in-the-round – is a triumph: It looks beautiful, it all works, and you can hear. The audience were excited, and so were the actors, who gave a fine performance."

28th May 1997
Letter from Lasdun to Richard Eyre, responding to an invitation from Eyre for Lasdun and his wife to attend a gala at the National marking twenty-one years since the opening. "I understand that the purpose of the event is to raise money for the modernisation of the building. The proposals include serious and unnecessary damage to the architecture of both the Lyttelton front of house and the porte-cochère. Sadly, in the circumstances we feel unable to accept." [63]

Bill Dudley joins in on architecture and Denys Lasdun
"Richard Eyre appointed John Gunter as head of design and me as associate director of design, unpaid. It was just an honorarium thing. John and I and Richard proposed some changes to the building while Lasdun was still alive. Lasdun came with four guys from his office spitting fire. When he came in, Richard was very charming. But Lasdun said, 'I want to know who was responsible for this excrescence at the corner of my building. I'm not going to talk about anything until we've ironed this one out.' So, we go down to the stage door, turn left, and on the corner, under the flying buttresses, someone had extended a little mini wall of bricks. It was matching bricks as well, so it looked like part of the original building.

"I got the giggles. I didn't respect the man, I think he had appalling ideas. He said, 'I want it removed.' So, we went back up to the office and found it was the catering manager trying to hide the dustbins. Because of Lasdun's own mistakes, you turn the corner just as you reach the river, and there are dustbins. The second thing he said, 'Now, what are all those trees doing surrounding my building?' Richard said, 'Well, that's in your original design. We thought they were fine.' He said, 'No. In my contract they were to be chopped down every twenty years.'

"So I said, 'Well, actually the bigger those trees grow the better your building looks.' And he hit the roof again and tore into me. Richard went, 'Oh, Bill.' I wasn't the most diplomatic, but I disliked the man, I disliked his world of architecture. Who was the great French architect? Corbusier. Lasdun worshipped him. I said he should've been strangled at birth. Anyway, the meeting did not go well. He was absolutely infuriated by it. In the following weekend's *Sunday Telegraph* he described John Gunter and myself, as 'two rude stagehands.' He called us both 'stagehands who thought fit to change my building. They are merely temporary curators of my building.' John saw the funny side, but I think Richard was a bit furious about it." [64]

Olivier in-the-round, 1997

The Stanton Williams Renovations
A brief extract from a letter that Richard Eyre wrote in 1994: "When architectural changes were first mooted, the associate directors felt making the Olivier into a single-tier theatre, lowering its ceiling, and bringing in its side walls, must be the fundamental priority of any new scheme. We briefed architects and acoustical engineers to see how the acoustics and the relationship to the audience could be improved in both large auditoriums. Their answer was this: To reduce the size of the Olivier auditorium by lowering the ceiling and raising the seating, making it one level, would require the entire reconstruction of the building, because the Olivier is its epicentre. In the Lyttelton, it is structurally impossible to change the relationship of the circle to the stalls without dismantling the whole auditorium. The auditoriums are what they are. I have long come to terms with this." [65] So instead, in 1997, Richard Eyre allowed the creation of a temporary theatre-in-the-round, for *The Caucasian Chalk Circle*.

Three key changes that were achieved were the removal of the one-way road system around the building, the creation of Theatre Square at the northwestern corner, and the enclosure of the porte-cochère to the front of the building in a glass structure to create a new bookshop and box office. A new access lift was installed to the Terrace Cafe, and reconfiguration of the Cottesloe foyer and changes to the lighting and signage were also undertaken. The glazing line of the Lyttelton foyer was moved outward to relieve audience crowding within; the original line can be seen in the ceiling.

Partial removal of the Waterloo Bridge link that blocks the river view from the Lyttelton foyer was opposed by Lasdun and the issue was dropped.

Making Theatre – A Summation in 1997
"The National Theatre is central to the creative life of the country. In its three theatres on the South Bank in London it presents an eclectic mix of new plays and classics from the world repertoire, with seven or eight productions in repertory at any one time. And through an extensive programme of amplifying activities – platform performances, backstage tours, foyer music, publications, exhibitions, and outdoor events – it recognises that theatre doesn't begin and end with the rise and fall of the curtain." [66]

"The NT is unusual in accommodating almost all production-related activities in-house – from the crafting of performance in rehearsal to the making of scenery, props, and costumes – and the organisation recognises the importance of sustaining these traditional theatre-making skills while hosting the development of new technologies such as video. The extent of this on-site making is key to the culture of the institution, yet largely unseen by the public, concealed within the introverted enclosure of the workshops and elevated offices. There is, however, a growing public interest in the process of 'making theatre', and the 20,000 people a year who now take part in the NT's backstage tours are given a behind-the-scenes view to the stages, workshops, and back-of-house areas." [67]

The David Hare Trilogy:
Racing Demon
Murmuring Judges
The Absence of War

Cottesloe Theatre, then Olivier Theatre
Cottesloe: 1st February 1990

Director: Richard Eyre
Production design: Bob Crowley
Lighting: Mark Henderson
Sound: Scott Myers
Production photographer: John Haynes

"In 1993 David Hare's trilogy about contemporary Britain at the National Theatre showed that a major public stage could be used to address the state of the nation. The staging of Racing Demon, Murmuring Judges and The Absence of War was a defining moment in Richard Eyre's stewardship of the National."
Michael Billington
The Guardian

The Wind in the Willows

by Alan Bennett, from the novel by Kenneth Grahame
Olivier Theatre
1st December 1990

Director: Nicholas Hytner
Production design: Mark Thompson
Lighting: Paul Pyant
Sound: Paul Groothuis
Production photographer: Clive Barda

"An enchanted world for adults and children."
Daily Telegraph

"Some of the most heavenly Englishness, character playing, and sheer theatricality since the RSC's Nicholas Nickleby."
Financial Times

A Sense of Theatre

Angels in America

by Tony Kushner
Cottesloe Theatre
17th January 1992

Director: Declan Donnellan
Production design: Nick Ormerod
Lighting: Mick Hughes
Sound: Freya Edwards
Production photographer: John Haynes

"Angels in America [has] now settled comfortably into the repertory at the Cottesloe Theater, the smallest and most inviting of the three performing spaces at the Royal National Theatre. More than anything else I've seen this trip, it qualifies as the theatrical event of the London season. I was at long last comprehending the remarkable scope and imagination of Mr. Kushner's work. Angels in America has no theatrical precedent that I can think of. It has something of the dark freedom expressed in novels of magic realism, but it's not a novel. It's an occasionally uproarious, often brutal, and sorrowful circus with what might be called novelistic tendencies and a theatrical heart."
Vincent Canby
The New York Times

An Inspector Calls

by J.B. Priestley
Lyttelton Theatre, then Olivier Theatre,
New York and continues to be performed around the world
Lyttelton: 5th September 1992

Director: Stephen Daldry
Production design: Ian MacNeil
Lighting: Rick Fisher
Sound: Paul Groothuis
Production photographer: Ivan Kyncl

"A rep standby miraculously transformed into an urgent expressionistic nightmare."
Michael Billington
The Guardian

"Daldry's vision here owes a great deal to designer Ian MacNeil, whose large Edwardian doll's house, precariously perched amid the smoking rubble of post-Blitz Britain, provides the visual centrepiece of a production that probes insistently at the questions: What do we mean by society? Now, when the lights are raised and Niall Buggy's Inspector Goole points the finger at the audience, we have nobody but ourselves to blame. This is not a comfortable evening. The production – lushly operatic, yet hard as steel – grabs you by the throat and won't let you go. Long may it do so."
Lynn Gardner
The Guardian 2001

Carousel

by Rodgers and Hammerstein
Lyttelton Theatre
1st December 1992

Director: Nicholas Hytner
Production design: Bob Crowley
Lighting: Paul Pyant
Sound: Mike Walker and Paul Groothuis
Production photographer: Clive Barda

"Never before have I been so emotionally overwhelmed by a musical."
Evening Standard

"The most revelatory, not to mention the most moving."
Frank Rich
The New York Times

Machinal

by Sophie Treadwell
Lyttelton Theatre
15th October 1993

Director: Stephen Daldry
Production design: Ian MacNeil
Lighting: Rick Fisher
Sound: Christopher Shutt
Production photographer: Ivan Kyncl

"One of the most devastating theatrical experiences of my life… Never before have the Lyttelton's resources been so thrillingly exploited."
Nicholas de Jongh
Evening Standard

"As it is staged here (using Ian MacNeil's awesome designs), Treadwell's damning expressionist vision of the metropolis can't help but impress itself on you as an uplifting celebration of the vast mechanical resources of the Lyttelton.

"The play is well worth reviving, it's the production that is the masterpiece."
Paul Taylor
The Independent

Stephen Daldry

Director and Producer

Stephen has had quite the career. It began at the Sheffield Crucible with artistic director Clare Venables, then took in the Manchester Library, Liverpool Playhouse, Stratford East and the Edinburgh Festival. He became artistic director of London's Gate Theatre in 1992, then of the Royal Court in 1998, leading the £26million redevelopment scheme that brought architect Steve Tompkins into the world of theatre. He moved into film with *Billy Elliot*, then directed its stage musical adaptation. He was executive director of the London 2012 Olympics opening ceremony, and from 2016 was producer of the television series *The Crown*. His latest work? A stage show based on the television show *Stranger Things*. For the National, he created two seminal productions in the Lyttelton: *An Inspector Calls* and *Machinal*. *Inspector Calls* still tours to great acclaim, more than thirty years after it first opened.

Stephen: I haven't done many shows at the National, but one of the great fun things is to treat the Lyttelton like a found space, because it doesn't work by the normal rules of a theatre. If you're in the circle, you can't see the stalls, so the audience doesn't work as one. It's a cinema. It works on horizontals: right to left, left to right, and back to front. The verticals are irrelevant, which is slightly different from the usual Italian-made theatres. The only saving grace is that it doesn't have a central aisle. The hard thing is you can get a certain amount of energy going in the stalls that is not necessarily shared with upstairs.

In any cinema, the audience will move with the fastest member of that audience. If there are five kids who understand the film up front, on the whole the audience will perceive it. In the theatre, you have to take everybody with you. Of course, a laugh will always start in the stalls, "below the eyeline," as Iain Mackintosh would say. The Lyttelton can do that in the stalls; it's the problem of the upstairs not being connected.

Richard: It did all come from Lasdun. "A theatre of confrontation" was his phrase. That's why it's flat and straight on like that.

Stephen: Yes, but there's a dynamism within that. The seats are straight?

Richard: Virtually. They have a tiny little curve. Larry said that they must be more curvaceous. He was always into curves.

Stephen: The disaster would have been had they put in a bigger curve. Curves are a disaster in the stalls.

Richard: What happened when you moved *An Inspector Calls* from the Lyttelton to the Olivier?

Stephen: I didn't want to move it, because the scale, scope, and language of that show was designed specifically for the Lyttelton. Not just its design, but the placement of the actors in the space, was created for a horizontal language running left to right. Richard Eyre wanted to make some money and the Lyttelton was booked up. Financially, it was the right decision; aesthetically, it was not: we struggled with it in the Olivier. It certainly didn't look or feel as good. The tension, between the theatre and where the actors were in that space, was blurred. It still worked, but only because people had read the reviews. If we'd had opened in the Olivier, we wouldn't have been a success.

Richard: And then you went to theatres all over the world.

Stephen: There are tours right now. But of course what the theatres don't have as it tours is the scope of [the Lyttelton] stage. It doesn't have infinity. In proscenium theatres around the country, there might be twenty seats in the middle of the stalls in which you can pretend that it goes off forever to the left and right. In the Lyttelton, you couldn't see where that sky finished. It made the isolation, of the characters, the house, and the story, feel much more like the language of Beckett. Now it looks like a set.

It's hard to know what you're doing in the Olivier, because everything is geared towards one spot onstage. It's very hard to start a sentence at the same place where you finish it. You have to spray it around and come back. I liked it when Eyre put it in-the-round, but it didn't work because, acoustically, it just couldn't hold up. It wasn't possible to hear what the actor was saying. Everything went up into the tower.

Richard: The circle in the Olivier is awful. You feel a mile away.

Stephen: Yes, you do. But, as an 18-year-old, I have fond memories of those tickets in the circle. Even though, at the back, you feel a long way away, if you get a hit show – where the audience is entirely engaged – you can feel you're in an exciting space. And when you're downstairs in the middle of the stalls, you do feel pretty close. To me, you're quite a happy bunny down there.

If you go to the Globe or the Lyric, Shaftesbury Avenue, nine times out of ten you'll feel like you've had a good theatre experience. Maybe four times out of ten you'll feel like you've had a good time at the Olivier. But when you do have a good time, it's better than the Lyric. That's the contradiction.

Richard: Do you have favourite theatres elsewhere?

Stephen: I like the Swan at the RSC. The theatres based on what you did with the Cottesloe and the Tricycle all work. I love the Crucible Sheffield: I know it's a challenging space, but what's good about it – unlike Chichester and other stages – is that it's a pure space; the math of it is intact, so it does work. There is only one challenge, which is to fill it. If you've got half the house in the Lyric on Shaftesbury Avenue, on the whole you're still having an experience. If you're at the Crucible and you've got half the house, it's half-empty.

> "Everyone can have the same sort of experience, but not the same view. The same view will cripple you."
> Stephen Daldry

Richard: Guthrie reacted against both the Victorian proscenium arch and the modern fan-shaped proscenium auditorium, but what he never got into was multiple levels. What the courtyard rediscovered was that if you stack people up, (a) you get closer and (b) half-empty can appear half-full. It's that simple.

Stephen: It's just about compression. It's an irresistible argument. And it increases capacity. In the old Walter Sickert paintings, there are people almost falling from the balconies.

Richard: That's right. Since the National I have tried to rediscover that old principle. The Olivier and Lyttelton lean back. Good theatres lean forward.

Stephen: I call the others 'blowsy' theatres. Blowsy in that they ask you to lean back, fall away, remove yourself, whereas, actually, all theatre architecture is all about engagement.

Richard: Which is the opposite of the movie house.

Stephen: Because in the movie house it doesn't matter. It's an experience on your own. It's not a collective experience. That's why when the revolution comes, they don't shut cinemas. They shut theatres. Theatre is where revolutions happen.

One great thing about a proper theatre is that the architecture determines price breaks. Not everybody has to have the same view. I'm back to quoting Mackintosh, no theatre will ever work if it doesn't have a significant proportion of the audience below the actor's eyeline. All these repertory theatres that were built and rebuilt in the same style – I'm talking about the West Yorkshire Playhouse. [Now re-named Leeds Playhouse.] Well, that's a disaster, isn't it? It's just a bank of seats.

Richard: The actors are all at the bottom of the pit.

Stephen: They all have to look up – terrible. And I'm not sure of my figures here, but the amount of air the actor has to animate is the amount of oxygen in the building. If you look at the cubic air space of The Old Vic and the Olivier, I believe –

Richard: It's three or four times. Actually the obvious comparison is Drury Lane and the Olivier. Drury Lane has the same volume, and it's got 1000 more seats.

Stephen: The other thing, which we spent a lot of time on at the Court, is airflow. One great problem at the Barbican is that the airflow is against the actor. It isn't taking the words to the audience; it feels like they're being pushed back into your mouth.

Richard: What do you think of the Barbican?

Stephen: I like it, despite the airflow problem. It's not too big. It's not my favourite, but I don't mind it at all.

Richard: I did the technical design of the Barbican too. John Bury and Peter Hall designed the theatre. But those side seats, which we call ski slopes, are not the same as boxes because everyone's looking away from you. They don't do what boxes should do, which is make everyone feel a sense of community. Good theatre should be like a good dinner party. You would never sit everyone on one side of a table, facing the kitchen.

Stephen: Yes. What is the role of the boxes? They're not facing the stage, but they combine everybody.

Richard: They're absolutely vital. A German manager once told me that the golden ring of the opera house is like a rope tying the audience together.

Stephen: The front of house that Lasdun designed was pretty amazing. With some reservations about the later interventions.

Richard: It's wonderful. Fundamental to a lobby space should be those changes of scale, so that you can have a glorious, exciting space while, at the same time, you can have a talk with your girlfriend in a dark corner.

If you were to start again, what would you do? In the '60s there was this great argument: arena, thrust, proscenium. But, nowadays, with the growth of theatres such as the Menier Chocolate Factory and the fringe, our assumptions have shifted. If you built a national theatre tomorrow, where would you?

Stephen: I don't know. Would you start with the old rules that you have described? A proscenium, and then a little bit of this and – I don't know.

Richard: I think you would start with a space that brought people together. That's the fundamental. It's not changed since man sat around the campfire. Have you been to Steppenwolf in Chicago?

Stephen: I have. I remember loving shows there.

Richard: It was inspired by the Broadway model: a close circle with stepping boxes at the side to draw the room together with a variable forestage. It's only 500 seats. It's one of my favourites.

Stephen: I like pop-ups at the moment. There's a company in the States called Pacific Domes. I bought one for Joe Robertson and Joe Murphy to build it in Calais, in the Jungle Refugee Camp. It's called the Good Chance Theatre. You can get 250-300 people in there, and it gets packed. It can go up within a few hours. It's strong enough that you can put in a lighting rig. Bizarrely, the acoustics work. It works as a town hall and a theatre – and if you need to, you can turn it into a dormitory at night. It's a theatre of hope; mobile, responsive and cost effective.

Ian MacNeil

Designer

Ian designed two productions that in many ways shifted perception of the Lyttelton: *An Inspector Calls*, where he commandeered the scene dock on stage left as part of the show, extending the sky off seemingly forever, and then *Machinal*, which used all of the theatre's capabilities to spectacular effect. More recently, he designed the acclaimed revival of *Angels in America* in the same theatre – he seems to be one of the minority that really enjoys the Lyttelton!

Beyond the National, he has designed a huge raft of shows, with one in particular, *Billy Elliot the Musical*, winning him a Tony Award and seen around the world.

Beginnings

People doing theatre in this country are so lucky to have this place. I'm American enough to be furious about the Tory governments that didn't really want it, the wall of indifference and obstruction, and what people did to bloody get it here in the teeth of that opposition. I read Peter Hall's Diaries and the Michael Blakemore book like detective stories; even though it was forty years ago, I'm glued. How can you not be? It's a bloody privilege to work here. The care and civility and passion of people working in this building is the envy of the world.

> "The care and civility and passion of people working in this building is the envy of the world."
>
> Ian MacNeil

The first thing I did at the NT was *An Inspector Calls* – Stephen Daldry and I. We were excited by how big the Lyttelton stage was. *Inspector* was a teeny-tiny house in a vast landscape – what's not fun about that? We skewed it very slightly. The Edwardian proscenium was kinked gently, so that it was slightly off, to disrespect the relentless symmetry of the building.

We took *Inspector* from the Lyttelton to the Olivier. I'd never worked in the Olivier; it was exciting to do a play that felt kind of public and, God knows, the writing is public address some of the time. When you get a show right in the Olivier, it is this public institution, the National, speaking about public things to an egalitarian audience. When it works, it bloody works.

I'm interested in performers. There are people who can play a whole arena in a theatrical way and make you feel like they are talking to you. I respect that in staging and design as well – that people feel like it's for them, as individuals, and collectively.

What's exciting about theatre is to have the very wide aspect, but seize the whole thing and to zoom in as well. Human eyes are more sophisticated than any lens is ever going to be, the human brain is as well – it's a pretty extraordinary thing that we're watching the entire thing all the time, and yet we can elect, with the skill of stagecraft and the performer, to zoom in.

The Olivier circle is simply too far away. We talk about the amount of air that an actor has to animate, and we know that the reason you get excited by an opera singer is because of the physicality of the voice. That's the great secret of the live theatre. But if there's extraneous air, that's a lot of air that some poor fucker has to move so that it actually hits you. I am intrigued with the Olivier's original design. I respect the vomitoria, those frontal entrance run-ups. You have this intense problem where some poor actor has to make an entrance, and you are bored before they've gotten to the place where they can speak a bloody line. They have no attack. That's a real problem. I got really interested in this when we were designing *Everyman*. It's weird that the floor now goes up to these ashtrays, as they're called, because you cannot look at an actor without engaging with them. What am I supposed to be looking at?

You have a lot of work to make human actors look like they're in the right scale onstage. This is a fundamental problem, because what is theatre other than the performer? There's probably a reason Gordon Craig didn't get a lot of shows realised: the pictures were gorgeous but if you put a thing that tall next to the actor – really? For one moment in a show, fabulous. It's an exercise of one's craft to make sure the actors are strong and you've got to rise to that if you're working in these two large spaces.

The Lyttelton is a bit relentless and it's very hard to subvert that. It's like wearing a pair of glasses and the frame keeps interrupting you. The other thing is there is no proscenium in the Lyttelton. A proscenium is a thing that identifies itself; in a great Matcham theatre it just kind of kisses the performer and audience. It's this golden thing, and it gets the angle and the proportions right. The lines wrap around, flinging your eye around to where the performer is.

Richard: To the stage; that's what it's all about. And all the side seats serve to link upstairs and downstairs.

Ian: It's odd to be calling the Lyttelton a proscenium theatre because – to me, 'proscenium' means this object, and the object has been taken away. It's like a picture without a frame, which is not a problem; it's actually very modern: Looming out in the darkness is this rectangle. In a Matcham theatre, you have that golden proscenium which you're puncturing, and the audience feels excited by the actor who actually breaks the membrane, but it's a matter of inches.

Richard: The whole argument, of course, raging here in the 1960s was thrust stages and open stages and arenas and, forty years later, where is that? The argument has almost disappeared.

Everyman, Olivier Theatre, 2015

Ian: But aren't we trying to thrust every show we do? It's been absorbed into the understanding. There was a swarm of unconventional spaces that have been completely co-opted and absorbed into our practice, so we don't use the term anymore. It's always the way with revolutions, you know. We have Tyrone Guthrie to thank for that.

Stephen Sondheim talks about, when you go to the commercial theatre, particularly in America, why do people stand at the end of a show? It's because they're trying to remind themselves that they are at a live event, because that is a precious thing.

Why are the theatres in which you can see other members of the audience so popular? You go somewhere and submit yourself to an experience that involves other people. Why are there all these people? Why are they using their phones? Why is it so uncomfortable? Why is the wine warm? Why does it cost so much? You're thinking, I wish I was at home, watching the bloody telly, and then, halfway through, you're moved. You go in as an individual, you come out as an audience.

It's very moving. – the audience bring it to life. It's the irritation and the kind of humanness of it – your knee brushing against someone else's – that's the spur to engagement. When you go to the movies, you come out lonely, and when you go to the theatre, hopefully you don't. That's the difference.

Mark Thompson
Designer

Mark is one of those designers who seems to effortlessly span genres. He has had remarkable success in the field of musicals, including *Joseph…*, *Charlie and the Chocolate Factory*, *Tina: The Tina Turner Musical*, and the world-wide mega-hit *Mamma Mia!* But the plays he designed alongside those could have been a career in themselves, including productions for the RSC, the Royal Court, the Donmar Warehouse, in the West End, plus more than twenty for the National, including such renowned productions as *The Wind in the Willows*, *The Madness of George III*, *One Man, Two Guvnors* and *Arcadia*.

Mark: A lot of the old Matcham Theatres are horseshoes, which is very embracing, because the stage is the final part of the circle. That's not been found again in modern theatres. If you're sitting in the stalls in the Olivier or Lyttelton, it's a completely different show to the one that you see upstairs. Quite disastrously so, in some ways. If only the Lyttelton had a row of people down the sides, it would've made the whole thing feel more connected. The idea of the concrete, though, that's good; the front of the house has always been quite sexy. When I was doing the NT 50 show –

Richard: A fantastic achievement.

Mark: It was exhilarating. We studied lots of photographs of the area at the time before opening and you realise it was just an old bit of shoreline. It wasn't what it is now.

I don't think all the backstage areas really work. The Olivier isn't properly supported – it's fine if you're doing a Greek play and you don't want any scenery, but you have to be able to bring stuff onstage.

My first show in the Olivier was *The Wind in the Willows*. It was very much written for the drum revolve and the Olivier, but we were only allowed to use one-half of the drum because they couldn't guarantee the other coming up. It was an extraordinary space to work for that show, so it was exciting, and I was young then. [Laughs] The drum was a good idea; the bad idea was that you can't access it. There are only little doors; it is this fabulous bit of machinery stuck in the middle of the building, with

> **"I think it's hard, designing a theatre."**
> Mark Thompson

dressing rooms and corridors all around, and you really want a loading bay, where you can slide stuff in and out of the drum.

But, look, it's easy to – you know – to look back and – it's hard, designing a theatre.

Richard: Have you ever done that?

Mark: No, but I know it must be, because there are too many constraints.

The lighting is a problem in the Olivier because there are all these bridges that are over the point where you want to bisect the circle and you can't because you're not allowed to use that area. So I feel sympathetic.

One of my favourite theatres is the Royal Exchange in Manchester. It was always, How on earth are we going to make this work? During the tech, it always felt anodyne and antiseptic and then, as soon as the people came in, it was so thrilling, because everyone was leaning in and enjoying the piece.

In the Olivier, there's a particular point, if you stand in the middle of the stage, you can sense, this is the most fabulous spot because I've got everyone in my thrall. But, actually, it's not the right place. You need to be further forward because those people are an enormously long way from you. The temptation for designers is to complete the circle and to embrace the enormity of the arena and, actually, that's wrong. You can't do that if you want to be intimate.

Richard: You mentioned the Royal Exchange, people leaning forward. In the Olivier, everyone is sort of laid back.

Mark: It was, presumably, a follow-on from the thrust stages of Stratford Ontario, and Chichester

Richard: Chichester was a big influence. Olivier found it disappointing, and he identified it as the people were too far around the sides, which led to the Olivier plan being 90 degrees as opposed to 180. But the problem was a different one. It was the lack of concentration.

Let's move to the Lyttelton. We talked about its frontal nature.

Mark: That's the theatre no one wants to work in. It's difficult to get directors to want to work there.

Richard: Lasdun came up with the idea of "confrontation" for the Lyttelton, which was the opposite of the Olivier, a theatre of "surround."

Mark: As an intellectual idea, it is quite intriguing, but – well, it doesn't work. It's sort of fine in the stalls but the pitch is too low and, underneath, at the back, the production rows are absolute seats of hell. I hate sitting there. Upstairs, you might as well be in a different building. It's too wide. Why have a theatre that big?

Richard: The two theatres have bred a new massiveness of scenography.

Mark: If you've got an empty model box, it's nerve-wracking if you put a tiny pea in a drum. The temptation is always to enlarge and it and make it touch the sides. It feels that

Henry IV (Part 2), Olivier Theatre, 2005

everything has to be a bit epic. I've seen sets in the dock, even my own, thinking, crikey, this is huge. And then you get it out there, and it's fine.

Richard: The Cottesloe Theatre?

Mark: The Cottesloe is a great space, but the trouble is you want it to be completely changed around easily, and because the turnarounds have to be so quick, you can't do it. Things tend to get stuck in one format.

So what's the book going to be about? Just the National?

Richard: It's the National – and the dichotomy between theatre and architecture.

Mark: To the architect, it's all about the building they're building, not the activity within. They may not understand that the architecture imposes constraints. Good design must come from function. It's a living beast. Things are going to change all the time, and new people are going to want it to do different things. It has to be organic as a building. It has to be able to take on change. which is very hard.

Rick Fisher

Lighting Designer

Rick hails from Philadelphia in the USA, but has been based in the UK for the last thirty years. He arguably became the heart at the core of the UK lighting community while chair of the UK's Association of Lighting Designers. That has continued in the time since, also through his part in establishing and now helping run the backstage lighting charity Backup Tech.

Rick is particularly known for his work with Matthew Bourne on *Swan Lake*, and with Stephen Daldry and Ian MacNeil on the trio of shows *An Inspector Calls*, *Machinal* and *Billy Elliot: the Musical*, which won him his second Tony Award.

Rick has lit twenty-six shows across the National's three theatres since *Peer Gynt* in 1990, including *An Inspector Calls* (1992), *Death of a Salesman* (1996), *Machinal* (1993), *Betrayal* (1998), *Blue/Orange* (2000), *Jerry Springer - The Opera* (2003), *Consent* (2018) and *Middle* (2022).

An Inspector Calls, lit by Rick Fisher

Vincent in Brixton, designed by Tim Hatley

"The National has since shaped so much of British theatre. It added a scale and dimension that can be stunning and has influenced national stagecraft. I always feared that it was not taken seriously as an important and fundamental snapshot of the mood of theatre makers and the aspirations of a particular time in the growth of theatre in the UK. It is important we remember how it emerged."

About the Olivier: "It takes such a long time to get onstage. An entrance there can be epic, but it's very hard to be quick as there is such an acreage of stage to cross. It's all about focus: an auditorium should disappear when the houselights go down. It is hard to be intimate in the Olivier, and also hard to be funny. Yet, *Guys and Dolls* was an epic musical, and funny, too. It was the first time a production in the building finally triumphed. *War Horse* couldn't be staged anywhere else. It was a combination of the Olivier, a brilliant director/design team, and the amazing resources of the NT."

"The Lyttelton, despite the concrete, does disappear with the right show onstage. *An Inspector Calls* was magnificent there, as was *Machinal*. These productions used all the Theatre Projects 'toys' to stunning effect. Yes, it is a very wide space, but it can work."

"The Cottesloe is a wonderful, flexible, people-scale space. I love it. Yes, some of the sightlines are poor, but who cares about comfort?"

"Modern theatres so often seem 'business class' – too comfortable, too laid back, all leaning backward.

"Scale of the human being is so pivotal. Ian MacNeil whose work was so important to *Inspector Calls*, shows this in the musical *Billy Elliot* where he handles change of scale, domestic to epic, and always keeping in mind that the leading character is a child, with such skill."

Tim Hatley

Designer

Tim is another designer who has taken the skills and experience from his training at London's Central Saint Martins College of Art and Design and then from working with the big subsidised companies, the National and the RSC, and carried them into the commercial world.

His recent work in this area has included the hit play *Life of Pi* (which began at the Sheffield Crucible before moving to the West End and then to Broadway, where Tim and projection designer Andrzej Goulding won a Tony Award for their work), and the hit musical *Back to the Future*. Both of those shows combined physical and projected scenery to spectacular effect.

His first appearance in the National's Archive catalogue is as a Design Apprentice; his work there since moving up to the designer role encompasses more than twenty productions, including *Closer* (he also designed the film version of the play), *Stanley*, *Flight*, *Vincent In Brixton*, *Henry V*, *Great Britain* and *3 Winters*.

"The National Theatre Company is the best theatre company in the world. People whinge and whine about the theatres' problems, but nothing is ever perfect in this life. You have to make the best of any situation. Theatre people always do get on with it!"

"The Lyttelton has no sense of enclosure; it's totally flat. Lasdun's theory of "confrontation" was so obviously wrong, all theatres of whatever shape are intended to bring actor and all the audience together. The Lyttelton is a literal box. Try and fight it and you may lose control; if you respect its constraints, you can win. The restraints create a good discipline. It's a nightmare, but a good nightmare."

"The Lyttelton is also too wide. For *Rafta, Rafta*, I used a whole house and revolved it 90 degrees to show it in cutaway."

"A good proscenium theatre should bring actor and audience together. It should draw the audience into the world of play. There should be electricity and energy between actor and all the audience, generating excitement."

"The Olivier is an enormous challenge. The actor seems to have multiple points of command. The ashtrays make a very weird focus. The enormous fan of seating dictates the design onstage and the sightlines are really wide and tough."

"For *Timon of Athens*, I used a large wall placed on the centre of the drum and revolved furniture in and out of sight downstage. For the last act, I stripped the stage almost bare except for concrete 'ruins.' Using the whole empty space is very powerful."

"A design in the Olivier has to drag the audience into the play; everything must come together to create total theatre: play, cast, director, team, set, lighting, sound, audience. If two out of three fail, you are sunk. Most projects actually disappoint. Real success, complete fusion, is seldom achieved; such productions are few and far between. But winning in the Olly is rather delicious!"

"The Cottesloe is absolutely my favourite. There are strong limitations of space and dimension that are all good."

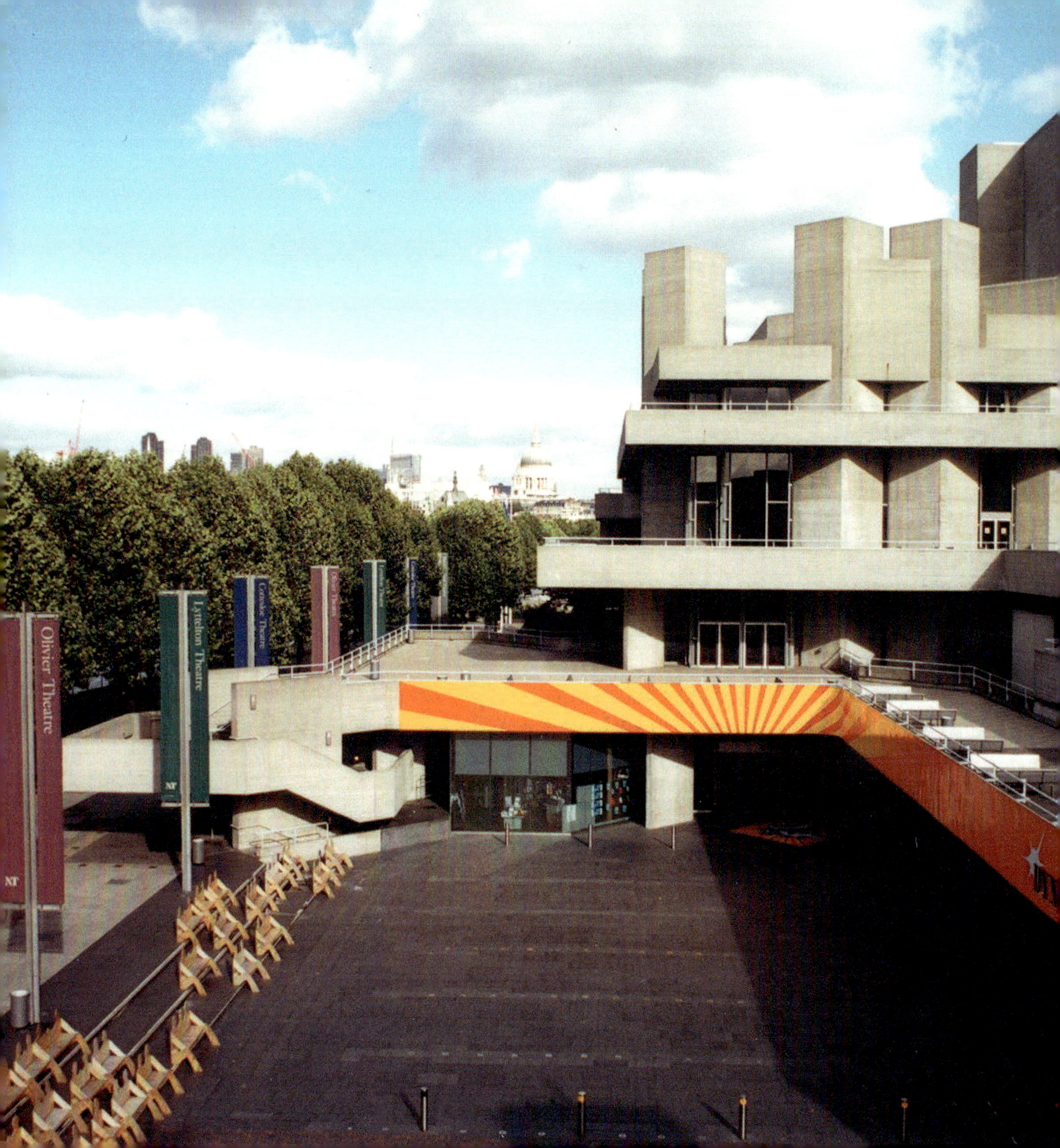
Olivier Theatre
NT
Lyttelton Theatre
NT

4.3 Trevor Nunn
NT Director 1997-2003

As Tony Blair brought change to the country, Trevor Nunn brought change to the National, seeking fiscal prudence and commercial success while admitting to being a caretaker artistic director, in the role to bridge the generations.

Amplification!

Lasdun's passing perhaps allows new opportunities for the building. The Olivier amended; transforming the Lyttelton; adding The Loft. His son, James Lasdun, remembers his father.

"Matters took a very different turn when Trevor Nunn became director of the NT in October 1997. Nunn arrived at the National six months after Tony Blair took office and, exactly like the Labour leader, instantly pursued a policy of fiscal prudence. When I complained, Nunn's emissaries told me it was necessary to balance the books. I never questioned Nunn's credentials as a director. His Stakhanovite workload was also impressive. But Nunn's two prime obsessions as a director are Shakespeare and musicals; and I still believe the latter occupied too much stage time."
Michael Billington *The Guardian* [68]

Trevor Nunn had a remarkable career long before the National. At the age of 24 he became a director of the Royal Shakespeare Company and, under Peter Hall's mentorship, became artistic director in 1968. His influence upon theatre architecture (often in collaboration with his longtime designer John Napier) was significant. The creation of Stratford's mid-scale Swan Theatre in 1986 was a triumph: a demonstration that the RSC could do intimate as well as epic. Twelve years before, in 1974, Nunn had opened the Other Place, a tiny former storeroom in Stratford where young directors could emulate the experiments then being conducted on the London fringe; then, in 1977, he pulled a similar trick at the Donmar Warehouse in Covent Garden, which had been used to store fruit until Nunn and his team spotted its potential.

In 1980 he brought to the stage a gargantuan, garlanded nine-hour version of Dickens' *Nicholas Nickleby;* a year later, in the West End, came *Cats* – an immersive musical spectacular in which the audience sat inside the rubbish tip inhabited by T.S. Eliot's felines (albeit as tunefully reimagined by Andrew Lloyd Webber). *Cats* was, of course, followed by other megamusical hits, such as *Starlight Express* and *Les Misérables*. It is notable how many of those involved with these productions had spent their formative years in the subsidised theatre companies.

Why musicals? "The first proper theatre I saw was pantomime. My theatregoing was always a mixture, going to see classical plays and seeing shows in town. I've never seen any dividing line, and I don't think Shakespeare saw one."

Nunn once compared the job of running the NT to "juggling plates, while riding a unicycle, on a tightrope, over Niagara Falls." "I was *begged* to do it. I was absolutely clear that it was a holding operation. My task was to try to get it on to a financial even keel and to keep all the auditoria flourishing." He adds defensively: "We won more theatre awards than the NT had ever won before, or has done since." [69]

Trevor, in his opening address to the staff of the NT, paid tribute to Richard Eyre and the NT's "unparalleled success." He said he cared most for continuity… "everyone contributes to every show." He quoted E.M. Forster's words: "Only connect" to achieve the "transporting power of live theatre."

Trevor's first production was to be Christopher Hampton's version of *An Enemy of the People* with Ian McKellen.

Nunn used *An Enemy* to confront 20-year-old deficiencies in the Olivier's acoustics, summarised by Richard Cowell of Arup Acoustics during Masterplan discussions in October 1995: "The basic form, with its open stage, provides a fundamental challenge, in that performers turn away from listeners and there are no surfaces close to give early reflections for the support of speech intelligibility… Over the years… performances have been held with deep open staging and reflective surfaces behind… which has been shown to disturb intelligibility." [70]

David Hare had written to Christopher Hogg [chairman of the National Theatre], condemning as "total madness" the

Cats, in performance and during fit-up at the New London (now Gillian Lynne) Theatre, which Sean Kenny helped design. The theatre opened in 1973, the show in 1981; it ran for twenty-one years. Since then the theatre's similarities to the Olivier have allowed it to host a number of transfers from the NT, including *War Horse* and *The Lehman Trilogy*.

Masterplan's failure to tackle the two main auditoria: "If I were a member of the public who… found that after [the NT had spent £40 million] I still couldn't hear in the Olivier circle, or feel close to being in the action from parts of the Lyttelton… then frankly I would think the whole expense… a grotesque waste of public money… When the [Olivier] has a big hit, then the [circle] audience leans in towards the show, trying to pretend they can hear and see better than they can. But at any other time, we are more or less practising a form of apartheid – comfort and pleasure downstairs, horror up. I don't think this is millennially defensible." [71]

"I am one of the few living writers who has been willing to write for the Olivier," Hare concluded, "a theatre where I have been fighting the architecture."

In 2013, Trevor recalled: "I believe that the only person in the country who could have visualised, rationalised and organised the perpetual output of the highest quality in this three-ring circus was Peter Hall. The sine qua non. The guv'nor."

"The Richard Eyre years (1988-97) witnessed a further great leap forward in the programming's daring and identity. Especially during that time, the National presented searing national enquiries, including David Hare's *State Of The Nation* trilogy. The excitement aroused by this new work was palpable. It was a privilege to be part of such a confident and buoyant enterprise.

"For much of a year, I shadowed Richard, observing his extraordinary fleetness of foot in situations of every level of sensitivity. I had agreed to become his successor in the full knowledge that he was an impossibly hard act to follow – but I hadn't applied for the job. No secret was made of the fact that the powers that be had hoped either Stephen Daldry or Sam Mendes would baton-change with Richard; but both young candidates had burgeoning careers in Hollywood and had replied to soundings with a polite 'maybe later.' So I was urged, as somebody with experience, to hold the fort and be a bridge to the future. I agreed to sign up for five years, but I took on the daunting task, thinking of it partly as an honour, yes, but mainly as a duty. At all events, it was clear that I was not being employed as a new broom.

"By the time I was actually doing the job, it was the funding and subsidy issue that loomed largest. Margaret Thatcher's miserable insistence on standstill grants for all arts organisations meant that the Arts Council was disallowed from responding even to the rise in inflation, let alone from considering ambitious creative possibilities. So, in simple terms, it was ticket sales that largely paid for our productions and, therefore, we were under pressure (as commercial theatres are) to be popular if we were not to dwindle.

"At the end of my agreed time, during which we had won a cabinet full of awards, and knowing that our research had confirmed an appreciable expansion of our audience demographic, I could bear the necessity for caution no longer. With some enviably energetic young talents at the National, I set up a season called 'Transformation,' for which we reconfigured the Lyttelton to make a space in which we could do 'events' created by innovators such as Deborah Warner and Matthew Bourne, and for which we also opened a new small theatre at the top of the building [The Loft], presenting new plays by young writers, under the control of young directors. It was also a season for which I managed to establish a seat price of £12. It was a gesture, a hope; the building came vividly alive, the festival atmosphere was pervasive... but there were no flamingoes.

"In the ten years since Nick took over from me in 2003, the range of work has been dizzying and explosive and the popularity factor seems to have doubled, with the £10 seasons, with National shows running triumphantly in the West End and on Broadway, and with the company now televising and filming its work (oh, how I tried), and broadcasting live to cinemas around the world. The National has also won the battle (one that I fought and lost when this brilliant proposal was first made) to be financially responsible for producing its own commercial transfers, ensuring that the profits come back into the National's creative coffers.

"I was similarly delighted that Rufus Norris, a young director whom I have long admired, has been named as Nick's successor. We often hear the dictum that in this country (and especially in the capital) we have the best theatre in the world. Rufus, I know, will continue to open up the building to all, and to surprise everybody with his vision of what is possible; he will do so in the knowledge that at this moment in time, the accolade of 'best theatre in the world' belongs to the National Theatre all by itself. George Bernard Shaw would be speechless." [72]

Some notable moments
November 1997
Cottesloe: *Mutabilitie*, staged in long traverse, but a failure.

December 1997
Peter Pan, a version by John Caird and Trevor Nunn, with sets by John Napier. "Badly over budget of £300,000, cost £600,000!"

March 1998
Not About Nightingales, a previously unseen Tennessee Williams play, directed by Nunn. Designed by Richard Hoover in the Cottesloe in long traverse with "spooky" lighting by Chris Parry. First total triumph of Nunn's tenure. It opens on Broadway in February 1999, winning six Tony Awards.

May 1998
Copenhagen, by Michael Frayn, directed by Michael Blakemore, opens in the Cottesloe, followed by two years at the Duchess Theatre and the Royale on Broadway. It wins the Evening Standard Award for best play. In New York, it wins the Drama

Desk Award, New York Drama Critics' Circle Award, and Tony Award. In Paris, it is awarded the Prix Molière.

September 1998
Cleo, Camping, Emanuelle And Dick, Terry Johnson's play about the making of the Carry On film series, which starred Sidney [Sid] James and Kenneth Williams, among others. "More than 20 years after the first gibes about the Lyttelton resembling an Odeon, William Dudley converted its proscenium arch for *Cleo*. with an art-deco [cinema] façade bathed in an orangey fake-tan glow, framing [a] ruched curtain. This rose to reveal a screen, film of the Rank gong, and a cartoon credit sequence, before the action began in Dudley's cross-sectioned mock-up of Sid's caravan." [73]

October 1998
Helen Mirren and Alan Rickman in *Antony and Cleopatra*, directed by Sean Mathias. "A resounding dud… the verse speaking is mostly wretched. I had one of the best seats. I had just read the play. And I was looking for the subtitles." Paul Taylor, *The Independent*.

"The Olivier is such a horrendous space to work in, but so gloriously huge and impressive. You [know] you're in something grand and fabulous." – Helen Mirren [74]

March 1999
Troilus and Cressida. "Here was verse speaking that was lucid, sardonic and impassioned… a consummate command of verse… in Nunn's hands, the huge Olivier stage shrinks." – *Independent on Sunday*, 21/3/1999.

1999 – Increase of grant by £1 million. Return of three-play repertoire in the Olivier, and a thirty-eight-person NT Ensemble is created. *Troilus* was the first production to use the new Olivier 'environment', its stage expensively reconfigured, and the SIAP acoustic system rebalanced, because Nunn refused to continue directing for an epic space in which he believed directors struggled to achieve any degree of intimacy between actors and audience: "The Olivier is one of the most exciting stage spaces in the world and [also] a pig's ear. There are more rows of seats nearest the stage than the architecture seems to propose. I [had] worked with John Napier on creating a whole range of theatre spaces: at Stratford, we [brought the Royal Shakespeare Theatre stage] about ten feet further [forward] and something absolutely thrilling happened in the '76, '77, '78 seasons. John has got that architectural instinct. [He] found a way of bringing the [Olivier] stage a good deal further forward." *Troilus* convinced Nunn that the Olivier's new stage-to-audience relationship "really did conform to the architectural thrust of the building; [it] brought the circle vastly much more in contact with the stage: the sightline was still absolutely perfect, but [sitting in the circle] it felt like 'We are all one theatre,' not, 'We are on a shelf looking [down] at something remote.' It helped the acoustic enormously."[75]

The redesign covered the three 'ripple rows' of narrow, cheaper seats, without armrests, which Laurence Olivier believed set off the wave of audience response that washes over the whole house; it also ruled out use of the drum revolve, which some considered a waste of the machinery. Stage crews, no longer able to use the drum revolve as a scenic lift for get-ins and changeovers, were obliged to manhandle more set pieces. Several directors and designers later asked, "Why is the Olivier ruined?" [76]

The conversion also cost £250,000 more than first estimated; some of this extra expenditure, and the loss of income from slightly reduced seating capacity, was recovered by cutting production budgets for the ensemble.[77]

Nunn told the board in March 1999 that the redesigned Olivier "environment and the ensemble had generated a sense of a new beginning." His actors wore body microphones for *Troilus and Cressida* and *Summerfolk*, and Ian McKellen said this had brought a huge improvement: previously, "even from some of the most expensive seats," he had found it impossible to hear clearly. Patsy Rodenburg, NT head of voice, worked longer hours with the company, and complaints about audibility had almost completely stopped.[78]

The Daily Telegraph made the use of microphones public, implying, Nunn thought, that amplification had been "imposed by stealth."[79]

"No fundamental change of approach has been embarked upon," he wrote in the next day's edition; there had been no "attempt to conceal this, or mislead audiences, only to find improvement in the ongoing battle with inaudibility." He was conducting an experiment "solely in my own work… not making any demand on other directors to follow my lead." [80]

John Caird did not use microphones on [Edward Bulwer-Lytton's] *Money*, which did attract some complaints about audibility. He said that the *Summerfolk* cast had gone along with the amplification amidst "horror and resentment: 'We are trained actors. We know how to project, and we are wearing body mics and it's the slippery slope.'" [81]

Declan Donnellan, who talked to Nunn about directing an adaptation of *Vanity Fair* in the Olivier, regarded this kind of amplification as "yet another barrier to the audience." [82]

There were no audibility worries in the Cottesloe where Henry Goodman played Shylock in *The Merchant of Venice*.

The Merchant in late November transferred successfully to the Olivier. There, Henry Goodman would get into costume, have his microphone fitted by a sound technician, then take it off and leave it in the wings. "Trevor said, 'Look [mic'ing is] not a dismissal of your skills; it's the acoustic.' In that sense, he was very nice to us. And he should have been tougher; it's our responsibility to be heard and yet to sound conversational. You don't have to walk around with battery packs like in a West End musical." [83]

1999-2000 The Annus Horribilis!
Plans for *Fiddler on the Roof* and a revival of *The Mysteries* are cancelled.

October 1999
Stephen Poliakoff's *Remember This* in the Lyttelton. "One of the worst new works ever staged at the National."
John Peter, *The Sunday Times*.

April 2000
Blue/Orange by Joe Penhall (Cottesloe). William Dudley's boxing ring set inspired by a lecture theatre in Middlesex Hospital. "Best new play since *Copenhagen*."
Alastair Macauley, *Financial Times*.

April 2000
The Villains' Opera, by Nick Dear (Olivier). "Call the police! A crime against theatre has been committed."
Robert Gore-Langton, *Daily Express*.

October 2000
Romeo and Juliet (Olivier). Trevor takes over from director Tim Supple, and has the set repainted. "Where *Troilus and Cressida* was a triumph, this *Romeo and Juliet*, which introduces another new company, is a muddled, mediocre affair characterised by poor verse-speaking."
Michael Billington, *The Guardian*.

November 2000
Peer Gynt (Olivier), directed by Conall Morrison. "What I see at the moment at the National, in the short term is drift and muddle and chaos."
Michael Billington, *The Guardian*.

August 2000
House and Garden by Alan Ayckbourn (Olivier and Lyttelton). An amazing two-play festivity designed to happen in two theatres simultaneously. "We took the National Theatre over, really, for a month or so. And it was a terrific success." [84]

September 2000
Simon Russell Beale in *Hamlet* (Lyttelton). Designer Tim Hatley. Lighting Paul Pyant. "Simon Russell Beale… is giving what may be the most illuminating tour of this theatergoer's lifetime through the murky world of rotten Denmark and the shadow-filled imagination of the unhappy heir to its throne."
Ben Brantley, *The New York Times*.

11th January 2001 – Sir Denys Lasdun dies, aged 86.
"Denys was a great man… very much respected here, notwithstanding our differences. We love his building and will continue to do all we can to make it a fitting memorial."
Christopher Hogg, Chairman, National Theatre

2001
The succession debate. The candidates are: Sam Mendes (film: *American Beauty*) versus Stephen Daldry (film: *Billy Elliot*). Nicholas Hytner: "If you can't do a big play in a big space, [theatre] will fragment. Big actors can put bums on seats for us." [85]

August 2001
All My Sons directed by Howard Davies and designed by William Dudley. Max Stafford-Clark comments: "The NT is ageing, and inside the building it's like a 1960's NHS hospital. And I've no idea what to do about the Olivier."

September 2001
Mother Clap's Molly House directed by Nicholas Hytner. "A level of purely theatrical ambition missing in nearly all the NT's recent new plays." – *The Independent*

Hytner: "The NT has an audience thirsty for adventure, anxious to discuss what it means to be part of a society that's in a state of permanent reinvention, and looking for a really good time. It's a wonderful opportunity." [86]

Hytner interviewed: "Could make this place sing again. Managerially, he appeared slightly immature and naïve, but with the right Executive Director 'could deliver a fantastic five to ten years... and the press would like him.'"

"Is it a pre-requisite of the job to be a white, middle-class, middle-aged, Cambridge English graduate?" asks journalist. Hytner replies: "I'm a member of a lot of interesting minorities."

2001-2002 Donation and Transformation
Nunn had promised that Transformation would be "the most important event in the NT's history," which sounded like hyperbole, before and after the event. [87]

He was adamant that despite abandoning his dream of a full arena conversion, the Lyttelton was transformed; "The buzz was completely different going into that space. It was a perfect scale; it was unifying; [with a higher] stage the improved acoustic seemed to make the whole thing much more intimate." [88]

Mother Clap's Molly House, Olivier Theatre, 2001

Peter Pan, Olivier Theatre, 1997

"As director of the National, and as a director, Richard Eyre had dealt with the strengths and limitations of its auditoriums as best he could. Trevor Nunn was determined to change them. He had altered the Olivier and, in 2001, as he came to terms with the curtailment of his five-year plan, he fought for its two most tangible objectives: reconfiguring the Lyttelton, and creating a fourth auditorium." [89]

"Nunn called an 'equally urgent need for making our stage spaces more desirable... for younger artists, fearful of our big, uncompromising stages.'"

"[NT Chairman] Hogg had insisted that the Board 'retain the right to abort' the Transformation, and in late September, with the post-9/11 war on terror seeming certain to depress the global economy, and, as a consequence, NT Development income, 'the degree of financial risk' was again deemed unacceptable. To abandon the season now would have been humiliating for Nunn; instead, he had to abandon the Lyttelton arena configuration. Its stage would be raised by one metre and fitted with an apron extension; a new, steeply-raked block of temporary seating would be built over the existing stalls, to connect with the circle; this would bring the conversion cost [down to £500,000]. Actors could finally 'feel they were playing to one audience,' and Nunn and [designer] Will Bowen hoped there would still be 'some sense of wrap-around' for spectators; directors approached with the promise of an arena would have to settle for proscenium staging; the Lyttelton would still, in essence, be the Lyttelton."

Deborah Warner said the conversion had created "the theatre that Denys Lasdun should have designed and didn't."

The Transformation cost of £2.5 million was personally guaranteed by Sir Trevor Nunn.

May 2002
In the Cottesloe, Nicholas Wright's *Vincent in Brixton*. Directed by Richard Eyre, designed by Tim Hatley in short traverse with 410 seats, and the wonderful smell of real roast lamb. It is nominated for the Olivier Award for best new play.

August 2002
Tom Stoppard's epic nine-hour trilogy, *The Coast of Utopia: Voyage, Shipwreck, Salvage,* opens in the Olivier with William Dudley's massive video projections and brilliant computer graphics.

Press Release for the Transformation Season[90]
"From May to September the National's most traditional auditorium, the Lyttelton, is being transformed by a sweep of seats from circle to stage to create a new intimacy between actor and audience. At the same time a wholly new 100-seat theatre, the Lyttelton Loft, is being created as a fully flexible space for eight new plays." Trevor Nunn: "I am working for [...] an understanding of the varied potential within Denys Lasdun's famous building."

Both spaces were designed by designer Will Bowen. The Loft was a flexible space that allows the staging and seating to be put in any number of different configurations. Despite its three contrasting auditoria, the National has always lacked one necessary space, a small performance space equivalent to the Royal Court Upstairs or The Gate (both with around 80 seats) where genuinely risk-taking new plays can be presented without reliance on expensive scenic solutions. But the new Lyttelton 650 seat capacity was not economically sustainable, and the original configuration returned for the October revival of *A Streetcar Named Desire*.

The changes wrought by Trevor on both major theatres and to the Lyttelton circle lobby were substantial, but all were temporary... able to be reversed. Thus they did not attract significant opposition.

2003: Nicholas Hytner Takes Over
"There was no way I was going to [continue it]. I think the Loft was great, a real injection of new stuff. [But] the remodelling of the Lyttelton was neither here nor there. If you're [director of the NT], you have to love what the spaces are."[91]

The Loft was a temporary auditorium created in the Lyttelton circle foyer

The Loft – interior

The Lyttelton Transformation – before

The Lyttelton Transformation – after

Play Without Words

The Lyttelton Transformation – view from the circle

Play Without Words. Devised by Matthew Bourne; production design: Lez Brotherston; lighting: Paule Constable; sound: Christopher Shutt. Lyttelton Theatre, 2002

Play Without Words

Oklahoma!

by Rodgers and Hammerstein
Olivier Theatre, West End, Broadway, US Tour
Olivier: 15th July 1998

Director: Trevor Nunn
Choreography: Susan Stroman
Production design: Anthony Ward
Lighting: David Hersey
Sound: Paul Groothuis
Production photographer: Michael Le Poer Trench

"Whatever the reason, the thrills of the evening are inextricably linked to the abiding truthfulness of it. This remains the most rousing and optimistic of shows, but I've never before seen an Oklahoma! where the exuberance of that exclamation point seemed so hard-won. Nunn has done what no one dared dream, paying equal homage to the great outdoors and – in the rapturous world of Rodgers and Hammerstein – to that even greater heart that most of us keep locked within."
Variety

"The encrustations of the years stripped away to reveal its proper colours."
David Benedict
The Independent

Summerfolk

by Maxim Gorky
Olivier Theatre
3rd September 1999

Director: Trevor Nunn
Production design: Christopher Oram
Lighting: Peter Mumford
Music: Steven Edis
Sound: Paul Groothuis
Production photographer: Catherine Ashmore

"With Summerfolk, Nunn's ensemble at the National presents the final production in its year-long season. With each production the company has changed shape and realigned itself – like a kaleidoscope – without losing any of its appeal. It's been fascinating to return and find new depths and talents. With Summerfolk, the six-pack reaches a glowing conclusion. For a year, London has had a local rep company par excellence."
The Independent

"Trevor Nunn's marvellous company has shone throughout the year. There have been exemplary, illuminating productions of Troilus And Cressida and The Merchant Of Venice; and a revival of Candide, which proved that Bernstein's unwieldy masterpiece could actually work on stage; and a night of pure pleasure with Edward Bulwer-Lytton's Victorian comedy, Money."
The Telegraph

"A masterclass in staging, absolutely brilliant."
Howard Davies
Interview with Daniel Rosenthal

South Pacific

by Rodgers and Hammerstein
Olivier Theatre
12th December 2001

Director: Trevor Nunn
Musical staging: Matthew Bourne
Scenic design: John Napier
Costumes: Elise Napier
Lighting: David Hersey
Sound: Paul Groothuis
Video: Tanya Toomey, Dick Straker
Production photographer: John Haynes

"The singing of the matchless score is excellent, however, and the spectacle – all palm trees, whizzing jeeps and spectacular sunsets – is often breathtaking. The show may not be in the same league as the National's earlier musical hits, but at its best, as the song says, it offers some enchanted evening."
Charles Spencer
Daily Telegraph

The Coast of Utopia

by Tom Stoppard
Olivier Theatre
3rd August 2002

Director: Trevor Nunn
Production design and Video design: William Dudley
Video realisation: Dick Straker, Sven Ortel
Lighting: David Hersey
Sound: Paul Groothuis
Production photographer: Ivan Kyncl

"As you might expect, Tom Stoppard's The Coast of Utopia in the Olivier is a bundle of contradictions. Comprising three three-hour plays, it is heroically ambitious and wildly uneven. It opens up the subject of revolution while being politically partial. And it contains passages of breathtaking beauty and surprising ordinariness. But I wouldn't have missed it for worlds and at its heart it contains a fascinating lesson about the nature of drama."
Michael Billington
The Guardian

"Tom Stoppard deserves credit for daring to be big: Clocking in at more than nine hours, his theatrical trilogy The Coast of Utopia occupies historic theatrical ground inextricably linked to Trevor Nunn's production. It's when Stoppard narrows the focus that some of the juice gets squeezed out of a panorama that designer William Dudley's CGI-rich video projections and minimally laden turntable set keep spinning from one hotbed of thought to another."
Variety

Anthony Ward

Designer

Trained at the Wimbledon School of Art, Anthony is another designer whose work freely straddles the subsidised and commercial sectors and genres of theatre, in long-running collaborations with a number of directors.

His work at the National under several generations of artistic director reflects that diversity, including *Napoli Milionaria* in 1991, *Sweet Bird of Youth* (1994), *Oklahoma!* (1998), *My Fair Lady* (2001), *King Lear* (2014) and *Exit the King* (2018).

Anthony: I remember the National opening before I went to art school. I saw the Olivier working full-bore with all three rear stages – three massive sets came out. So not really knowing a lot about theatre then, I was amazed.

Coming here, I felt lucky in that I started with the Lyttelton. As an audience member, sitting in the circle is really unhelpful; you don't feel you're part of the play at all. But I really like sitting in the stalls. However brutal and flat-on the stage is, I feel you can be epic, and have a connection in the stalls.

The Olivier is known as a really difficult theatre, but it is the perfect, perfect theatre for *Oklahoma!* I mean, it was like a gift. I saw the previous revival. I'm not saying it was a bad design – it wasn't – but you sat in the Palace Theatre and you were not on the plains of Oklahoma. But then, you come into the Olivier. You've just got landscape. So I felt I hadn't encountered what was going to be difficult about the space.

I've done three in the Olly. The last thing was *King Lear* with Sam Mendes, that was a classic; I felt I had to embrace the landscape – and the space can do that – but how was I going to produce all those intimate scenes? We came up with a shuttering system that came down at the front of the stage to create a little room. *The Captain Of Köpenick* had a very filmic script. You could have done it with six chairs and nothing else, but we didn't. We took advantage of the drum and it just was all too big and too heavy. It's really tricky designing a play in there.

Every show, every play, every space, has its own dynamic.

> "I have to say the NT is a fabulous place to work. The way everybody handles everything is fantastic. It's absolutely brilliant."
>
> Anthony Ward

Often when a theatre is being built, I find it quite difficult to say, "Well, this is what's wrong with the space." I love going to Glyndebourne, it works great, but I don't know whether I could say why that is. My God, why did people build the Barbican? That's really difficult. I had no intention ever of going to the Globe when it first opened, and then I did and had a fantastic time. I think there's a real energy.

Richard: It's about energy between actor and audience.

Anthony: Yes, absolutely. Absolutely.

Richard: All the audience. It's that collective. But nobody knew about that in the '60s. We had all forgotten that that's how our grandparents built theatres.

Anthony: You can totally understand why it happened. Because they were really trying to go back to Greece and all that. Now everybody loves a found space and atmosphere. We were trying to find the perfect plan, but in actual fact there isn't one.

I still enjoy seeing things in the Lyttelton. Whatever people feel about that space, I think I've seen some fantastic things there.

Richard: If you could somehow connect circle and stalls – it's a lot to do with those concrete side walls, I think.

Anthony: You're right about that. At the same time, there's something reassuring about them. But, over the years, when I sit in either auditorium, I find there's something pleasing – they have become familiar to me.

Richard: You did *My Fair Lady* in the Lyttelton.

Anthony: Trevor's whole thing was we weren't going to put the orchestra in the front of the actors. It's a play with music. The same happened with *Oklahoma!*; the musicians were also behind the set. The side stage was for the travelators. That's one thing about the Lyttelton: please create a bit more space on the stage right. But it was a great space to do that show. Then it went to Drury Lane, which is a nice, big theatre, but I preferred watching it in the Lyttelton to Drury Lane.

If you create something and it works the first time, moving it somewhere is just really difficult – because there's an energy, a dynamic, moving towards an opening night.

Richard: What old or new theatres do you feel relaxed in and enjoy – both as a spectator and a designer?

Anthony: I like going to the Royal Court. It's really cosy, almost tiny. Even then, when you have a really bad seat, sitting right next to the pros, you're thinking, Oh, God. But it's that classic thing, you're right on top of the action.

My Fair Lady, Lyttelton Theatre, 2001

Liolà, Lyttelton Theatre, 2013

Richard: What would you say to somebody if they said, "We'll build you a theatre?"

Anthony: Well, I'd say flexibility. People want very different theatre experiences. I'm not a very progressive designer in terms of seeing space in a different way. But many people are doing that; if the space can be as flexible as possible, that's the great thing. Yet you've still got to build the space, and what does that mean? You build a vast, great, empty volume, and then you have various different shapes of seats or modules or things with which you can do this, do that. That doesn't seem very promising to me. That sounds a little bit like we're putting on a concert somewhere in the middle of a field.

Richard: Theatre architecture is essentially about putting the audience in the right place, and in a dynamic relationship to the performers.

Anthony: At meetings now there's a lot of focus on sightlines. But the truth is actually you can't design it for every single person in the theatre. You cannot do that.

I have to say the NT is a fabulous place to work. The set's all fitted up before it even goes anywhere near the theatre. It's right next to the prop shop, right next to the painters, the workshop. And the way everybody handles everything is fantastic. It's absolutely brilliant.

Peter Mumford
Lighting Designer

Peter trained as a stage designer at the Central School of Art in London, studying under the designer Ralph Koltai. In 1969 he was a founder member of the mixed-media experimental theatre group Moving Being, serving as their designer, lighting and projection designer for all of their productions until 1978.

In the late 1970s, he became a member of the faculty of the London Contemporary School of Dance at The Place, teaching a course relating choreography to visual art and design. During the 1980s, he designed the lighting for a huge number of dance works for companies such as London Contemporary Dance Theatre, Rambert, Second Stride, the Siobhan Davies Company and others.

In 1978 he designed the sets, costumes and lighting for *Parsifal* at WNO, and then expanded into drama in the late 1980s, adding directing shows to his repertoire after that. His work now encompasses all facets of theatre, from the *Ring* Cycle for Opera North through to *King Kong* in Australia (for which he won a Helpmann Award) and New York. At the National, he has lit *The Invention of Love*, *Stanley*, *Summerfolk*, *Vincent in Brixton* and many others across all three of the theatres.

Richard: Your very special shows at the National Theatre?

Peter: *Summerfolk*, in the Olivier; *The Merchant Of Venice*, in the Cottesloe and Olivier; *The Invention Of Love* (Cottesloe, Lyttelton, West End, and Broadway); and *Scenes From An Execution* (Lyttelton).

Richard: What was your first impression of the challenges you faced?

Peter: The Olivier is scary the first time – the lighting rig looks huge, and you don't quite know where to begin. Then you do, and it starts to come under control and, as that happens, it also starts to feel smaller. When you finally achieve a production there that looks good, it's a great feeling. The big difficulty there is the difference from a lighting perspective between the upstage and the downstage area. You can't really cross light downstage, but you can upstage, so you have to make sure that the quality of light is consistent.

Richard: What are the principal problems and opportunities?

Peter: The two most challenging spaces are definitely the Cottesloe and the Olivier. The Cottesloe, obviously, is flexible, so it comes out differently each time, but the lighting angles can be quite tricky because they are very steep in some configurations – but it's an exciting space to make work. I've designed there in most formats. I'd say that one of the most interesting was *The Merchant Of Venice*, which was traverse in the Cottesloe, and then transferred to the Olivier. At the time, one wondered how this could work, a totally different space and scale, but it did, with a bit of redesigning of the set and a wonderful company who just had that play 'inside' them.

I'd just add that I think that having three very contrasting performance spaces is a brilliant idea, especially for a national theatre, because it opens up the possibility to explore theatrical space in so many different ways, and also allows one to choose a space appropriate to the needs of a specific production.

Denys Lasdun 1914-2001

Denys Lasdun passed away on 11th January 2001.

It was unquestionably the end of an era in architecture, and also in the history of the National Theatre. But perhaps also freeing to the National; listed yes, but now at least able to discuss change without incurring the fury of the architect. Nicholas Hytner, the first artistic director to run the company free of Lasdun's watchful eye, initiated the NT Future scheme that saw the biggest changes to the National's environs since its opening. But Hytner had enjoyed the early days of the National as a student; under his tenure elements of the building, including the signage and lighting in the public spaces, actually returned to something much closer to Lasdun's original.

Which perhaps was the point Lasdun had always been trying to make, defending the deliberate permanence of his work against the ever-shifting tides of fashion. His publicly expressed views on the Stanton Williams refurbishment of the 1990s have left us a clear insight into his opinions on this:

Of the Royal College of Surgeons: "It has now become a unique medical precinct. In fact, that's the building which embodies what I deeply feel about architecture. The attitudes that drove that thing into the way it was done is all I can say I've ever contributed. It's a very cherished building isn't it? They love it, yes. Unlike the theatre, which is left like a slum.

"Oh, they're going to move the window; they are filling up, boxing in the porte-cochère with knick-knacks, T-shirts and bookshops; the view of St. Paul's is blanked out. If you read the report that [we] submitted to the South Bank, it describes the design of the theatre at a crucial corner, which is where the building is pointing to Waterloo Bridge and opposite Somerset House, it is a series 'of descending terraces in a rhythm which finally ends at the porte-cochère'. It is utterly clear, and this sensitive bit where it finally anchors itself to the ground is to become a little bazaar. Is that really what you should do to the National Theatre? It's monstrous. When it comes to the cathedral window, again, no explanation given, they're going to bust that open, get rid of it, put a new window some ten feet further out. Why? Presumably to gain a little bit more space in the foyer, either for selling more junk or coffee, or because they say there's a queue. I have been going to the theatre, since I get a free ticket, for over 20 years, I have never seen a bottleneck yet. There's something extraordinary about the whole business.

"Anyhow, they know that if I was to make a public statement, it would be as follows: Yes, I've done a compromise, faute de mieux, to make it a little less awful, but it is awful anyhow. Why do it in the first place? They may or they may not; they may say, blow the whole thing up. There are moments when I think it would be better to blow it up than mutilate it. But we live, don't forget, in the shadow of, what was it, Henry VIII and the change of religion or something, when we desecrated our cathedrals… the Reformation. But you see, we have had something called universal education since then. You would think that there would be some glimmer of what things matter visually or not, but I'm afraid there isn't. I think my faith is in the new generation of young people who are ready to respond to these better values and may want to put it all back." [93]

The Master Builder: James Lasdun on his father [94]
In the summer of 2019, I found this article in *The Guardian* by the novelist and prize-winning poet James Lasdun about his father, written after his death. Entitled *The Master Builder* it is a wondrously intimate portrait of the man with whom I was so privileged to work. Your author, too, has been through the trials of clinical depression. This insight into Lasdun's personal 'black dog,' I find intensely moving. Some extracts:

"Family aside, he lived entirely for architecture. He was consumed by its challenges, obsessed by its possibilities, overwhelmed by its demands. He saw architecture primarily as a sculptural art of space, form and light, with its social aspect always ancillary to that and the technological element of no interest at all. The creation of new, authentic forms, the striking of the 'noble note', as he put it, of true architecture, 'that can modify the consciousness of the user and the passerby', was by this time his exclusive preoccupation. He had close advisers and collaborators, but no close friends. He had no 'hobbies', almost no interests at all outside architecture, other than classical music. He had one preferred style of dressing – cardigan, knitted tie, cords.

"There were ways in which he really was not ideally suited for life as an architect – at least of the large-scale, high-profile public buildings that formed the bulk of his work. Temperamentally, he had a combination of qualities that in a sense could not have made such a career more of a struggle for him. From his mother he seems to have inherited a certain volatility, a choleric mixture of high anxiety, irascibility under pressure, morbid self-absorption, incapacitating depression, and hypersensitivity to any perceived slight.

"He was diagnosed depressive, even (though less certainly) manic depressive, hospitalised occasionally, and dependent on numerous medications all his life. But meanwhile he was jealously protective of his own identity as an artist, and it was simply impossible for him to cede or delegate any of the primary creative aspects of his work to other people, as most architects do. He kept his office tiny so that no part of the design process could ever be far from his personal control.

"To the outside world he gave an impression of charm, exuberant confidence and high functionality. But at home, en famille, he was almost always in crisis, either lying prostrate in a dark room with the same gloomy piece of Brahms playing over and over on the stereo while he alternately brooded in silence and muttered about giving it all up to run a corner tobacconist, or else going off in what he called a 'muck sweat' of stressed-out panic in which he would storm and fret and ventilate his various dreads and suspicions (some of them fully warranted, I hasten to add; others completely paranoid) concerning the fickleness of clients, the pusillanimity of politicians, the treachery of certain of his collaborators, the need to unleash his QC on this or that libelous journalist or broadcaster, and so on.

"For a long time my mother was the only person to whom he fully revealed this side of his nature, the role required of her being to give it her tireless support and to keep its secrets, both of which she did heroically. Later, as my brother, sister and I grew up, we too were gathered into the great turbulent dramas of my father's life. Though he was unfailingly kindly with us – a sort of benign sea-monster he seemed to me as a child, with his purplish face and watery, thyroid-swollen eyes – he was also helplessly self-preoccupied.

"The National Theatre was the background of my childhood, or rather, it was the foreground. The travails of its thirteen-year-long saga concentrated what seemed to be all the most powerful tensions and personalities of the country at large into our household. What Harold Wilson thought, what Jennie Lee or some other minister said, what Laurence Olivier wanted, how the geography of the Thames and the skyline of London were to be accommodated and altered, whether the electricians' union would strike during construction, what to wear for the statutory lunch at Windsor Castle for individuals coming into the public eye – such were the factors determining the tone and texture of my father's life.

"As I look back it occurs to me that with his reality – this tremendous agon thrusting him in and out of the various bastions of British cultural and political life, where the stakes were nothing less than the imposition of his own monumental buildings on to the English landscape and psyche – he had no need for delusion. There was nothing it could add.

"At any rate there was no competing with his struggles. I never minded this, and I have been increasingly grateful over the years that my father was so unremittingly what he was. I certainly couldn't have asked for a better model for what it is to be fully engaged in one's work. Among other useful lessons, he demonstrated that it was normal, even desirable, to feel always somewhat out of one's depth. Though he was good at convincing others of his powers, he had tremendous doubts about them himself.

"He never resorted to easy formulas, never strategically 'chose his battles' as prudent policy recommends, but insisted on fighting them all. His oft-quoted remark to the effect that an architect's role was to give his client 'not what the client thought he wanted but what he never could have imagined existed' could be applied to himself too: he wasn't satisfied with a job until it had brought forth something from himself that he could never have imagined existed."

National Theatre
National Theatre
INSIDE OUT
National Theatre INSIDE OUT
National Theatre INSIDE OUT

4.4 Nicholas Hytner
NT Director 2003-2015

A new Director, one who grew up going to these theatres, takes charge of restoring them, turning to the leading theatre architect of our time to help. Travelex ticket pricing. The Temporary Theatre. NT Live takes the National out to the world.

Plus *Jerry Springer – The Opera; Henry V, His Dark Materials; One Man, Two Guvnors; Saint Joan; London Road; The Curious Incident of the Dog in the Night-Time; Frankenstein; Othello...* and *War Horse*.

"By the time Nicholas Hytner took over the National in April 2003, yet another redefinition of the institution became urgently necessary. For a start, the whole question of 'nationhood' was up in the air. Cultural diversity was also a more vital factor than it had been in the days when Olivier blacked up to play Othello. In addition, Britain was supporting an American invasion of Iraq. It was an inspired idea for Hytner to choose *Henry V* led by the magnificent Adrian Lester, who is a fine classical actor who happens to be black. If ever there was a play for the moment, this was it.

"Hytner was also shrewd enough to recognise the theatre itself was rapidly changing. He encouraged the National to co-produce immersive events with companies such as Punchdrunk and Shunt. He gave Katie Mitchell the chance to freely experiment with video-based work. A succession of plays by Kwame Kwei-Armah, Roy Williams, and Ayub Khan-Din went some way to acknowledging the realities of a multicultural society. And in place of routine obeisance to Broadway's golden oldies, Hytner recognised the emergence of a new kind of music-theatre.

"Not everything has been pure gold: I've felt, in recent years, a nervousness about the great classics. But there have been some outstanding successes – *The History Boys, War Horse, One Man, Two Guvnors* – and two innovations of paramount importance. The first was the Travelex £10 ticket scheme, which brought in new audiences and confirmed the truth of Peter Brook's dictum that 'the future of theatre is cheap seats.' Even more revolutionary is the development of NT Live, which broadcasts productions worldwide from the South Bank. At a stroke, this makes the best work instantly available and rescues the National (and other theatres as well) from the old charge that public subsidy is devoted to supporting the passion of a metropolitan elite.

"Hytner has emerged as a pragmatic visionary who has also helped to change the process by which theatre is transmitted. I realise, of course, that in putting so much stress on Hytner and his predecessors, I am burying the huge contributions made by an army of supportive administrative and backstage staff." [95]
Michael Billington
The Guardian

It must have been some time in 2002. I happened to be at the NT and my old friend Rob Barnard (then the National's head of technical resources) said, "Nick Hytner has heard that you're in the building. He'd like to meet you." I went up to the director's office and met Nick. He said to me, "Richard, I'm going to be the first director of the National Theatre that never met Sir Laurence. You were there. What can you tell me?"

We spent over an hour together. I tried to tell him what life was like at the Old Vic and Aquinas Street. How the building committee functioned. How Lasdun's concrete fortress came to be.

First Year

Nick had determined that the National Theatre deserved large-scale work. Work that would appeal to a broader 'national' public. After a decade of artistic and commercial success for the smaller-scale studio theatres, such as the Almeida and Donmar, it had come to be supposed that quality theatre was only to be found in these small-scale 'fringe' theatres. Nick rejected this notion, and in offering himself as the next director said, "I served my apprenticeship in opera houses, so I learnt early how to manage vast casts on huge stages." [96] In that heyday of English theatre – the Elizabethan age of Shakespeare – while theatre was patronised by the court, it lived or died at the box office. Nick immediately drew parallels between that golden age and Lasdun's theatre on the South Bank. Unlike national theatres in highly subsidised Europe, in England, theatre, far less lavishly endowed, had "to please to live."

Nick stated, "I'm so committed to the idea of a public theatre at the centre of the community. If you can't play to 1100

Nicholas Hytner, Thoughts on the National:
"As a nation we think we know who we are, but we need to find out what we're becoming... so it's a tremendous time to be a national theatre." [103]

"We talk passionately about renewing our audience; we wonder how we could attract a more heterogeneous crowd. We worry about marketing, ticket prices, image. It all matters, but in the end it's only on our stages that we can galvanise new audiences." [104]

"I'm urged on by the example of the first theatres to make the move to the South Bank. The self-confidence of the Elizabethan theatres was nothing to do with their official status – they were daring, disreputable and sceptical of authority. We share with them an audience thirsty for adventure, anxious to discuss what it means to be a part of a society in the state of permanent reinvention, and looking for a really good time." [105]

"We want to make art, and we are in show-business... you start with a vision, and you deliver a compromise. You want a play to be challenging, ambitious, nuanced, and complicated. You also want it to sell tickets." [106]

Jerry Springer – The Opera, Lyttelton Theatre, 2003

people at a time, you can't call yourself a National Theatre." [97]

"I think the theatres on the South Bank are the ideal theatres – they are large, communal, epic; they have narrative as well as intellectual muscle because that is the best way of engaging large numbers of people."

Nick rejected previous criticism of the two large theatres' deficiencies and determined to overcome them. He returned both theatres to their earlier layouts, before the Nunn changes. Then his plan was to cut production costs and ticket prices, and stage work that spoke "to the Nation." He intended to: "examine the constituent parts of its title, and explore both the state of the nation and the boundaries of theatre." [98]

**"Can this cockpit hold
The vasty fields of France?"**
So he opened in the Olivier with *Henry V*, and a rock-bottom budget. Playing Henry was "a fabulous actor, Adrian Lester." Since the production coincided with Britain's highly controversial entry into the Iraq war, it was – to put it mildly – an act of amazing timing… and a sensation. This was joined by *His Girl Friday, Tales From The Vienna Woods*, and David Mamet's *Edmond*, starring Kenneth Branagh. Tickets sold for only £10. To complete that first season, he did loosen the purse-strings to stage Nicholas Wright's *His Dark Materials*, taken from Philip Pullman's epic trilogy of fantasy novels, a wildly successful and controversial work for young adults. An antidote to austerity, this mind-blowing spectacle exploited the Olivier's drum revolve ("a miracle of 1970s stage engineering.") Did it work?… Only just. Nick described the attempt as "an act of reckless folly." Two three-hour plays staged with astonishing panache, almost sunk the enterprise… but theatre people do deliver and so, too, did the incredible NT staff.

Each of the other Olivier shows were budgeted at £60,000, less than half the normal amount. Mark Dakin, head of production, delivered astonishing value. In return, coupled with a £10 ticket, the audience was packed. Thirty percent had never visited the National before. The low-cost ticket scheme was sponsored by the far-sighted Lloyd Dorfman, founder and chief executive of Travelex. His support would in time earn him the honour of having a theatre named after him.

Nick decreed that the Cottesloe should return to its mission of finding new writers rather than stage classics for tiny audiences. Plays from newcomers Owen McCafferty (*Scenes From A Big Picture*, contemporary Belfast), and Kwame Kwei-Armah (*Elmina's Kitchen* – Hackney's murder mile) joined the experienced Michael Frayn's *Democracy*.

And for the often unloved Lyttelton? Kick off with an opera! *Jerry Springer – The Opera*, as lewd as a phallic parade! "Dirty whore, Filthy, dirty, manky, skanking slut whore!" went the lyric, and proved to be another sensation. It accompanied *Three Sisters* and *Mourning Becomes Electra*, the latter with Helen Mirren at the centre of a Howard Davies production.

End of the year: 92% average capacity. A £500,000 surplus versus a budgeted £500,000 deficit.

And successes:

Stuff Happens. David Hare on the politics of the Iraq war.

London Road. A verbatim musical based on the serial murders in Ipswich. Directed by Rufus Norris. "One of the best we ever produced," said Nick.

Richard Bean's *England People Very Nice,* on immigration through the ages.

Dara. Set in Mughal India, adapted from an original play by Shahid Nadeem.

Richard Eyre had introduced Nick to Alan Bennett for *Wind In The Willows*. Their partnership continued with *The Madness Of George III* from the Lyttelton to Broadway and to the silver screen. Then *The History Boys*. "The first preview was the most euphoric night I will ever spend at the National" said Nick. Again, it was an international hit. This was followed by *The Habit of Art,* and *People*.

War Horse

The enormous success of *His Dark Materials* led Nick to search for other, similar material. He found a play adapted from a radio play by Jamila Gavin, *Coram Boy,* that he asked Tom Morris (from the Battersea Arts Centre) as dramaturg to develop it for the stage in the National's Studio worshop, located next door to the Old Vic. This gruesome tale of infanticide in Hogarthian England, directed and designed by Melly Still and set within the musical environment of Handel, was a giant hit in the Olivier for two seasons. Seeing it later, during its too-brief New York run, it proved to be the only theatre experience that reduced me to helpless tears at the end of both acts! Out of its success, Tom was to discover *War Horse*, a young adult novel by Michael Morpurgo about a horse in World War I, Directed by Marianne Elliott and Tom, the stage adaption was to prove a massive, international hit – and a huge money-spinner for the National. Nick admits to his notes upon seeing the first run-through: "too long, too slow, not clear, indulgent… Cut! Cut!" [99]

Other extraordinary successes followed. *The Curious Incident of the Dog in the Night-Time,* the story of a young 15-year old sufferer of Asperger's, told with extraordinary fluidity and sensitivity under Marianne Elliott's direction. Then the extraordinarily comic *One Man, Two Guvnors* by Richard Bean, based upon Goldoni's *The Servant Of Two Masters*, was an update in the style of an Ealing comedy or *Carry On* film, which brought James Corden to international fame. Also by Richard Bean, *Great Britain* told the headline-grabbing story of the *News of the World* and Rebekah Brooks scandal, presented in nail-biting tension with the real verdict's public announcement from the notorious Old Bailey trial – the play could not open (or, indeed, be completed) until the verdict was announced!

Classics followed: *Hamlet* with Rory Kinnear, Bernard Shaw's *Saint Joan* (directed by Marianne Elliott), and *Major Barbara*, starring Hayley Atwell and Simon Russell Beale. Ibsen's *Emperor And Galilean, Women Of Troy* (directed by Katie Mitchell), *Othello* (with Rory Kinnear and Adrian Lester). *Much Ado About Nothing* (with Beale and Zoë Wanamaker), and *Frankenstein* (directed by Danny Boyle).

Nick commented, "The Olivier Theatre is of its time. It is a thrilling place to watch a show if the play, the production and the actors are up to it. I enjoyed wrestling the Olivier to the ground, and the most effective throw was always to work with actors who had the personality and technique to pull 1150 people toward them. But to abandon those actors for an entire evening on what could feel like a football field never did them any favours, so I always advised directors new to the Olivier to think of creating a much more defined acting space within it." [100]

A pivotal development pioneered by the two Nicks (Hytner and his executive director, Nick Starr) was the decision that the National should itself produce or co-produce its own shows when they transferred out of the National. This hugely enhanced the NT's share of any future revenues.

NT Live

Of perhaps even greater import was the decision that the NT should start to broadcast its own live productions for screening in cinemas worldwide. 'National Theatre Live' massively increased the National's reach to an international audience, under the direction of NT's director broadcast and digital, David Sabel. The first production, *Phèdre,* starring Helen Mirren was seen by 63,000 people on one night.

NT Future

The other major occurrence was the 'NT Future' initiative. By the year 2000, the Lasdun building was showing its age. For years, too little had been spent on maintenance and upkeep, and improvements were long overdue. The Nicks determined on a campaign to fund substantial works. Aided by income from *War Horse* and a succesful fund raising campaign, and overseen by experienced theatre architect Steve Tompkins and his team, extensive improvements were begun.

First was The Shed, a new theatre built in Theatre Square in front of and linked to the Lyttelton lobby. Designed by Steve Tompkins, with a bright red exterior within which was a charming small courtyard theatre, reminiscent of the Young Vic. Designed to substitute for the Cottesloe, while it was closed for remodelling, the Shed proved a revitalising shot in the arm to the whole organisation.

All the public areas were renovated, and catering, retail and educational facilities were greatly expanded, particularly opening up the north-eastern riverfront corner of the building to the public. Backstage, a new workshop extension allowed both enhanced operational space (the architects noting that the workshops were "the biggest factory left in central London"[101]), and access for the public to see behind the scenes. A landmark change occurred to the garbage: it disappeared. "All roads led to those bins," Hytner said. "In the end, sorting them out had to be part of an £80m project. Of course, that would never have happened if I'd had to work it all out for myself. But I didn't. That was up to Nick [Starr, now Hytner's partner at the Bridge Theatre] and Lisa [Burger, then the NT's chief operating officer]."[102] The trash, previously located by the front entrance (though interestingly, in a spot that had an external staircase in Lasdun's original building model), was at last removed thanks to some ingenious planning. Of the theatres, the Cottesloe, renamed the Dorfman, saw an increased seat count, a mechanised flooring system, and an improved lobby. The Lyttelton and Olivier remained unchanged, albeit with the theatre technology, including the drum revolve, significantly renovated.

National Theatre – 50 Years On Stage
In 2013, as a celebration of the fiftieth anniversary of the National Theatre Company's founding, Hytner staged a huge presentation in the Olivier and for international television: an epic compilation of fifty years of "Plays, plays, plays."

I went to this historic evening with my old friend, and dear colleague, Dick Brett. At dinner before the show, he told me very quietly that he was suffering from an incurable asbestos-related disease and had not many weeks to live. We then sat watching the extraordinary, star-studded performance together. We were both deeply aware that the occasion was celebrating the theatre that we had both expended so much of our lives to help realise. As the riotous party that followed the show began, I walked Dick to the front entrance of the National. He was tired and needed to get home to rest. We shook hands, embraced, and said farewell.

I never saw him again.

The Shed

NT Future – design team (centre: Lisa Burger, to her left Steve Tompkins and right, Paddy Dillon)

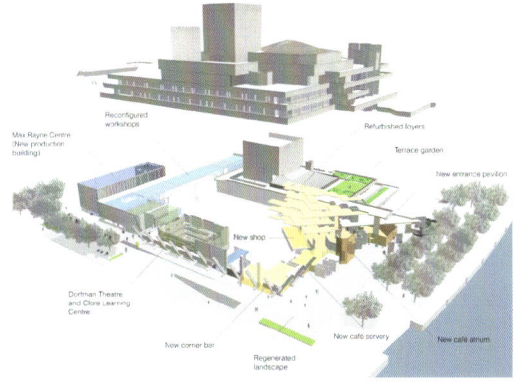

NT Future

4.4 Nicholas Hytner, 2003-2015

Steve Tompkins

Architect

Steve Tompkins is perhaps the Matcham of our generation: an architect who discovered a love of designing theatres and has stuck to it, for each project learning from the one before and along the way befriending those who make shows and learning from them as well. Stephen Daldry found Steve for the late-1990s refurbishment of the Royal Court in London. Since then he and his team at Haworth Tompkins, including particularly Patrick Dillon and Roger Watts, have carried out the redesign of the Liverpool Everyman, the reconstruction of the Battersea Arts Centre, the dramatic reworking of the Theatre Royal Drury Lane, and the design of the Bridge Theatre. For the National, they led the NT Future project, as part of which they designed the temporary Shed theatre.

"The Royal Court was my first major theatre. It was a fine project with a strong leader in Steve Daldry and team with Iain Mackintosh and Theatre Projects."

Steve finds theatre design fascinating: "However hard you work there is always the unexpected – the almost accidental – that sparks a room to life. Our job as theatre architects is to enable that spark of life."

Steve's described his early conversations with Nick Hytner and Nick Starr about their attitudes toward the Olivier and Lyttelton. "We must stop thinking about the two large auditorium as 'problems'. We are going to succeed with more ambitious programming… we won't start by saying our theatres are flawed."

"I tried really hard to understand Denys Lasdun's motivations and priorities in the rebuild. We tried to respect his intentions."

"I had originally thought that the Lyttelton might be 'fixed' by breaking down the side walls and adding linking side seating boxes. Finally we decided that the big theatres were only to be technically renovated."

"The whole of London is now the National Theatre. The NT has three theatre spaces, but extends into the West End with a need for other theatre types for shows to transfer to: the New London (open-stage for *War Horse*), the Apollo (proscenium for *Curious Incident*) and so on."

Royal Court Theatre, London, 2000

The redesigned Theatre Royal Drury Lane, London, 2021

Patrick Dillon on Lasdun

Architect, coordinator of the *Theatre Green Book*

Patrick Dillon was part of the Haworth Tompkins team for the NT Future project. With that completed he left HT and, based on what he'd learnt while studying the history of the building for that project, wrote the rather wonderful book *Concrete Reality: Denys Lasdun and the National Theatre*. He went on to create and coordinate *The Theatre Green Book*, which guides those creating shows and running venues on sustainable practice.

Extracts from *The Hard Solution*, Patrick Dillon interviewed by George Kafka in *The Economist*, May/June 2015:

"The National Theatre was conceived very much as a democratic building, standing out against the previous theatrical tradition that was all about class, status and hierarchy. Lasdun was trying to make a piece of city that would welcome people in."

"Its thinking is entirely classical. Its order, symmetry, and compositional techniques are very much grounded in the classical past. Indeed the finesse with which Lasdun used concrete turned it away from how Le Corbusier had used it: as something to shock, playing up its rawness. Lasdun was doing something different: turning board-marked concrete into a material of great finesse, with great care put into the detailing of the boards' layering, the way they met at junctions and so on. It wasn't about shock tactics at all, but about creating a beautiful and carefully mannered surface. What excited him about concrete at the NT was it being an industrial material, turned into a luxury material by the way it was handled. Through this material the building is at once both a factory and a palace for theatre."

"You see one of the core compositional ideas of the building: the way the axis of the Lyttelton Theatre clashes with that of the Olivier Theatre upstairs. You get this baroque space where different columns and planes are at differing angles to each other, all bathed in light coming off the river to one side, while the diagrid – the concrete waffle slab which runs across the ceiling – picks up all these shadows. It's like being inside one of Piranesi's etchings. It's an absolutely brilliant space, whether you like modernism or not."

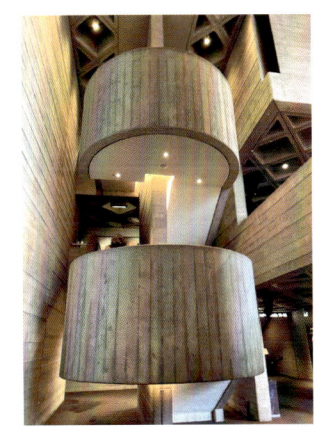

National Theatre foyers and terraces, 2023

"Make people love the building as much as the National Theatre company."

Nick Hytner

NT Future, 2015-2016

Revised porte-cochère and new signage

Lyttelton circle foyer

Dorfman foyer

Max Rayne Production Centre at the rear of the building

Clore Learning Centre

The re-invented eastern corner, bins gone, now part of the journey along the South Bank.

Lyttelton foyer

Photographs by Philip Vile

View from the river, now with sign!

New entrance for the Dorfman Theatre

New workshop and paint frame

New cafe extension

New workshop in the Max Rayne Centre

Dorfman Theatre

The Understudy Pub, in what was once a brick walled corner

All still watched over by Sir Laurence

Henry V

by William Shakespeare
Olivier Theatre
6th May 2003

Director: Nicholas Hytner
Production design: Tim Hatley
Lighting: Mark Henderson
Sound: Paul Groothuis
Video: Dick Straker, Sven Ortel
Production photographer: Ivan Kyncl

"Watching Nicholas Hytner's thrilling new production of Henry V, there are many moments when the drama might well have been written last week, rather than 400 years ago. Traditionalists may bridle, but this is emphatically a Henry V for our times, and one of the most persuasive, and gripping, modern-dress productions of Shakespeare I have ever seen. It is a wonderfully daring start to Hytner's own reign at the National. Rarely has Shakespeare seemed more palpably to be our contemporary, echoing our own doubts, hopes, and fears."
Charles Spencer
Daily Telegraph

His Dark Materials

by Philip Pullman
Olivier Theatre
4th December 2003

Director: Nicholas Hytner
Production design: Giles Cadle
Lighting: Paule Constable
Sound: Paul Groothuis
Video: Dick Straker, Sven Ortel
Production photographer: Ivan Kyncl

"Giles Cadle's designs are literal but satisfying – a grimy bus stop for the Oxford that exists in Will's world. The lights of the Aurora shimmer across the backdrop. The characters' daemons, perhaps one of the trickiest parts to stage, are delicate wisps of puppets, propped on shoulders or swishing along the floor. Hytner, faced with a mammoth theatrical challenge, seems to have pulled it off."
Madelaine North
The Independent

"This is an almost faultless piece of theatre."
Jeremy Austin
The Stage

"Giles Cadle's designs make extensive use of the Olivier's drum revolve, with witches and bears inhabiting its upper regions and Oxford colleges and consistorial church courts rising from its lower depths."
Michael Billington
The Guardian
The Stage

The History Boys

by Alan Bennett
Lyttelton Theatre
8th May 2004

Director: Nicholas Hytner
Production design: Bob Crowley
Lighting: Mark Henderson
Sound: Colin Pink
Video: Ben Taylor, Dick Straker
Production photographer: Ivan Kyncl

"Behind the almost ceaseless laughter lies a hymn to the joys of language, intellectual exploration, and inspirational educators.

"Nicholas Hytner's production also contains a clutch of fine performances. Richard Griffiths is overwhelmingly moving as the unfashionable Hector, whose love of the boys embraces their bodies as well as their minds.

"In short, a superb, life-enhancing play."
Michael Billington
The Guardian

Saint Joan

by Bernard Shaw
Olivier Theatre
4th July 2007

Director: Marianne Elliott
Production design: Rae Smith
Lighting: Paule Constable
Sound: Paul Arditti
Production photographer: Kevin Cummins

"Elliott's production not only dramatises but truly visualises his words: she shows he really was writing for the theatre as well as for people who prefer to read his loquacious, pre-emptive prefaces.

"In Saint Joan the battle scene features a tremendous rearing-up of the revolving stage: It becomes like the lid of a gigantic box, with bodies sliding helplessly down it. Joan's dissent really has rent the world.

"Anne-Marie Duff is the person to persuade you that this rending was possible. She's a marvel: fiery, straightforward, as skinny as a 10-year-old, narrowly focused, adorable, maddening. Paule Constable's extraordinary lighting is instrumental in establishing Joan's power. She arrives on a dusky stage in a nimbus of white light; she leaves by way of a re-creation of a Fox Martyrs' picture, arms outstretched, made rosy – as if post-orgasmic – by the flames that engulf her. GBS is a dramatist worth staging."
Susannah Clapp
The Guardian

War Horse

by Michael Morpurgo, adapted by Nick Stafford
Olivier Theatre then fourteen countries worldwide
Olivier: 17th October 2007

Director: Marianne Elliott and Tom Morris
Production design: Rae Smith
Lighting: Paule Constable
Video: 59 Productions
Sound: Christopher Shutt
Puppet Design: Basil Jones and Adrian Kohler
(Handspring Puppet Company)
Photographer: Simon Annand

"Genius isn't too strong a word to describe this astonishing production."
Daily Telegraph

"The most moving and spectacular play in London."
Sunday Express

"If ever a piece of theatre worked magic then it must be War Horse."
Evening Standard

London Road

by Alecky Blythe and Adam Cork
Cottesloe then Olivier Theatre
Cottesloe: 7th April 2011

Director: Rufus Norris
Production design: Katrina Lindsay
Lighting: Bruno Poet
Sound: Paul Arditti
Production photographer: Helen Warner

"This production is one of the most exciting experimental pieces the National has ever presented. Doubters can be assured there is no 'cashing in' on the tragedy, rather a deep, abiding sadness that it happened at all, and even a slight, knowingly shameful admission that something good has come out of it: a reborn community and a renewal of civic pride in an area that became unjustly known as a red-light district when Ipswich Town left Portman Road for a new stadium elsewhere."
Michael Coveney
The Independent

"This miraculously innovative show finds a new way of representing reality. Rufus Norris's production and Katrina Lindsay's design also deftly evoke the community's transition from a period of terror to one of entrapment."
Michael Billington
The Guardian

One Man, Two Guvnors

by Richard Bean
Lyttelton Theatre
17th May 2011

Director: Nicholas Hytner
Production design: Mark Thompson
Lighting: Mark Henderson
Sound: Paul Arditti
Production photographer Johan Persson

"The result, a kind of Carry On Carlo, is one of the funniest productions in the National's history… the National, in taking on an old Italian play, has not only improved Goldoni but also struck gold."
Michael Billington
The Guardian

"It's a rich, slow-spreading smile, like butter melting in a skillet over a low flame. And whenever it creeps across James Corden's face in the splendidly silly One Man, Two Guvnors which opened on Wednesday night at the Music Box Theater, you know two things for sure: You're in for trouble, and you're already hooked. Struggle as you will, there ain't nothing you can do about it."
Ben Brantley
The New York Times

The Curious Incident of the Dog in the Night-Time

by Simon Stephens, from the original book by Mark Haddon
Cottesloe Theatre
4th July 2012

Director: Marianne Elliott
Production design: Bunny Christie
Lighting: Paule Constable
Video: Finn Ross
Sound: Ian Dickinson
Production photographer: Manuel Harlan

"Believe the buzz. The Curious Incident of the Dog in the Night-Time is spectacular, like Cirque du Soleil with brains. Under Marianne Elliott's imaginative direction, a brilliant design team allows us to inhabit the boy's consciousness on a terrifying journey that begins with the death of a dog and ends with his discovery of the power of his own mind."
Marilyn Stasio
Variety, reviewed in New York

"The Curious Incident of the Dog in the Night-Time was one of the most original shows and startling successes at the National last year."
Susannah Clapp
The Observer

Othello

by William Shakespeare
Olivier Theatre
16th April 2013

Director: Nicholas Hytner
Production design: Vicki Mortimer
Lighting: Jon Clark
Sound designer: Gareth Fry
Production photographers: Johan Persson, Philip Carter

"These days it's becoming hard to write about the theatre without praising Nicholas Hytner. Can't he do something wrong so that we critics can start looking less like courtiers?

"His latest crime is to direct a terrifically exciting, exceptionally coherent Othello. Its triumph depends on tremendous performances by Adrian Lester and Rory Kinnear. It also depends on Hytner. Time and again his abrasive modern stagings have shown Shakespeare to be urgent."
Susannah Clapp
The Guardian

The Silver Tassie

by Sean O'Casey
Lyttelton Theatre
15th April 2014

Director: Howard Davies
Production design: Vicki Mortimer
Lighting: Neil Austin
Sound: Paul Groothuis
Production photographer: Catherine Ashmore

"The Silver Tassie is now most famous for being rejected by Dublin's Abbey Theatre. Howard Davies's superb revival turns this verdict on its head. It's the expressionism that now seems tremendous. With the most startling explosion I have ever heard in the theatre, domesticity is blown apart. You watch the walls come down; the smell of frying meat gives place to whiffs of gunpowder. In a ruined church, battle-torn soldiers gather. Here the language is incantatory or snarling. Neil Austin's lighting drizzles despair on to Vicki Mortimer's impressive design."
Susannah Clapp
The Guardian

Nick Starr
NT Executive Director, 2002-2015

Nick was executive director of the National from 2002 to 2015, having originally joined the press office in 1987 and worked as assistant producer then head of planning under Richard Eyre before becoming executive director of the Almeida. After leaving the NT, he and Nick Hytner created the Bridge Theatre next to Tower Bridge. These are notes of our conversation:

About NT Future
"You play the cards you're dealt. The National Theatre's theatres were there, they are what they are. When we took over, Nick Hytner and I saw that our job was to create exciting productions."

"Steve Tompkins, our friend and architect, wanted a crack at improving the Lyttelton, but we said no."

"Under Trevor Nunn, far too little had been spent on the building's maintenance, probably less than £250,000 per annum, so we increased it to £2 million p.a. and uncovered a £15 million shortfall of needed maintenance. We needed to make a big decision: Go for £83 million!"

"We determined to go for bigger public, backstage, and educational space. Changing the theatres themselves was not our priority."

"We couldn't start a major fund-raising campaign by announcing that our theatres did not work. We had to prove their success first."

"Being in receipt of public funding bestows a heavy responsibility."

The Bridge Theatre
"Our new project is a commercial theatre, south of the river, by Tower Bridge. Commercial theatre has virtually abdicated responsibility for new work. We are determined to fill that gap."

Theatre Design
We discussed how a vibrant emotional charge can be engendered by the interaction between the actor and all of the audience. Nick recalled that *Curious Incident of the Dog in the Night-Time* began in the Cottesloe, moved to the Apollo then the Gielgud Theatres, and then to the Ethel Barrymore Theatre in New York City – the show improved with each larger seat count.

We discussed the National Theatre Building Committee. How it was only after the National was completed that I'd come to realise that the dimension to the furthest distant seat was less important than the need for intimacy and compression. We talked of the nightmare of the opening period. Peter Hall forced the building to open. None of our innovative equipment was completed, and our reputation was in the mud. But, eventually, the stages did work. And the equipment was finally successful.

I explained that since the days of the National, Theatre Projects had always sought to lead on the design concept of both the stage and auditorium. Nick exclaimed, "You are the architect of the interior!" "Yes," I admitted, "we probably are... but, rather understandably, the architect seldom wants to share that credit!" Nick: "So the architect only does the decoration!" I replied, "Well, he does create the whole building that hopefully stands up, and is waterproof! But that is a real challenge for us, as theatre designers, in selling this concept of our authorship of the theatre space! Architects would much rather it was kept a secret!"

Vicki Mortimer
Designer

Vicki trained at the Slade School of Arts. Her work since has spanned drama (with shows for Emma Rice's Wise Children, Chichester, Shakespeare's Globe, the Almeida, the Young Vic and in Japan, Sweden and New York) and opera for the Royal Opera, the Vienna Staatsoper, the Salzburg Festival, the Berlin Staatsoper, ENO, the Lyric Opera of Chicago and Glyndebourne.

For the National, her shows have included *Follies*, *The Silver Tassie*, *The Threepenny Opera*, *Cat in the Hat*, *Three Sisters* and *The Last of the Haussmans*. She is an NT Board member.

Richard: Where did you work first at the National?

Vicki: In the Cottesloe. I did a play with Katie Mitchell, *Rutherford and Son* in 1994. The content lent itself well to an end-on approach and it suited the material nature of that theatre, which, at the time, was still quite a grubby-metal-and-tired-upholstery environment.

I do remember the sense of coming into a space that had a very loyal audience. You had to design a sort of sightline triangle; you had to contain all of your key action there. Katie, at that time, was fond of a square-on set. If you were doing a room, it had to look like a room. It couldn't be a theatrical cheat. But, of course, neither corner we were looking into was available for activity. It was a design challenge.

Richard: What happened next?

Vicki: I think it must have been taking *Three Sisters* into the Lyttelton with Katie again. The Lyttelton is the one, I think, where, atmospherically, the auditorium is hardest, because it feels the coolest – a bit dusty. It's something to do with that disconnect between upstairs and downstairs, but also that cinematic thing. It's an uncompromising shape, all straight lines, which, when you walk in there as a designer, you think, Oh, brilliant. But, actually, you have to work much harder to step over the edge of the stage, to get the audience to feel that you're coming toward them. It means that as an audience member you have to really lean in to have access to what's happening; that can be quite hard, because it feels like there's a big volume of space around the audience as well. It does feel as if everything's really a long way away. One of the greatest pleasures I've had working there was *The Silver Tassie*, because we were able to use the rear stage in a way that really benefitted the play. It was tenement, battlefield, and hospital, and then a sort of social club. But we were able to quite literally explode the tenement building, blowing it apart so the tenement itself created the bombed-out buildings of the trenches. It could give an audience an experience that was incredibly rich and true to what O'Casey was trying to say – because *The Silver Tassie* is a really, really messy play, but messy because it's got this passionate anti-war content.

Of course, it's true that all of the actual playing, the scene, still has to happen within a very small strip of stage. In a way, there's no bad theatre space. It's just another kind of set of conditions.

Richard: I like the way you said that. No bad theatre spaces.

Vicki: But if you genuinely treat every space as a found space, I think you just go, Well, this is the space I'm in. How am I going to make this play work in here? Most designers are, by nature, flexible thinkers. You might say, Oh I wish I had a bit more wing space but, actually, if you haven't, then you do something else, don't you?

Richard: And the Olivier?

Vicki: I enjoy enormously doing things in there. I'm about to do *Threepenny Opera*. I still don't understand how this room works and still haven't got the whole architecture in mind yet. Storage, obviously, becomes a big part of any design there, because, compared to the stage area, the storage is small.

Othello was a puzzle because it's a play made up of scenes between very small groups of people, and they are very rarely public. There are two-handers and three-handers. It became clear that we had to bring all those private scenes into the middle, into the container. The bottom line was, How do we get every single scene to sit on exactly the same sweet spot? The idea of alternating trucks really became a solution.

Richard: Tell me other theatres that you love, hate, enjoy.

Vicki: It's not really ever about the building, I don't think. The people who work in a building make an enormous difference in how willing or happy one is to work there. I wouldn't say I like the space, but the people at the Young Vic make it a really fabulous place to work. It's confined but, at the same time, there's again that sort of inequality between the number in the pit, and in the upper level, you're sort of up against a wall with very few people upstairs. People have responded to the space very cleverly. It means a massive investment of time and effort has to go into auditorium design each time, and there's nothing wrong with that.

I still wonder why there's such a liking for a horseshoe arrangement of people. I certainly enjoy sitting in those side seats because I can see the workings, but for an ordinary theatregoer it seems like an odd position. Sightlines are on your to-do list every day when you're a designer. I have a secret enjoyment when I'm making theatre projects that include a partial sightline, because that's part of our experience in life. Making completely democratic sightlines seems to me a shame, but also impossible. It's never democratic.

Richard: We in the theatre design business would say that a theatre with perfect sightlines is going to be damned boring. In fact, it's called a cinema. The people to the sides spark life into the room.

Vicki: Yes, absolutely. It makes you feel like a community watching something, rather than individuals. Somewhere like Glyndebourne provides a unified, yet diverse, set of positions that you can sit

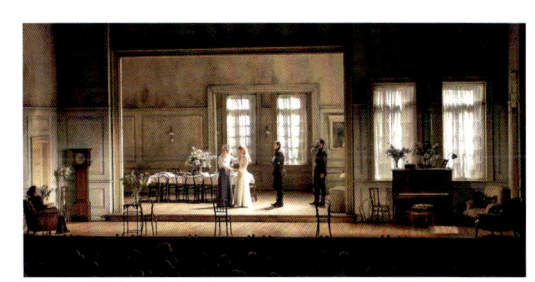

Three Sisters, Lyttelton Theatre, 2003

in, and that feels to me probably the best formula. It's a warm environment, which helps hugely.

Richard: How about the new Stratford?

Vicki: The Swan works well, because it's just what it is. You accept whatever its faults are. Whereas the new main house and the temporary space felt like you were just designing in the problems. Also, those stages were built when the expectation was that we would all be performing epic theatre, when the resources were such that you could have a huge company and the actors were your scenery. But we can't afford to do that anymore. There must have been a tipping point where scenery was cheaper than hiring actors. Those spaces don't work, because you need a winning formula between the scale of the performance and the number of people watching. That's partly because we are used to proximity so much, aren't we?

Richard: You can't put people in a football stadium to enjoy a play.

Vicki: We want to be close to live performance. And at stadium rock performances, those screens are enormous.

Richard: In live theatre it doesn't really work too well. Of course, the whole world now is video, because they're videoing everything [for programs like National Theatre Live]. That's a whole new ball game. Ninety percent of our audiences are going to see plays on the screen.

Vicki: I also feel that as a designer, there's an agenda that I need to address. We have to pay attention to what we want design to look like on screen.

Bob Crowley

Designer

Bob was born in Cork, Ireland and trained at the Bristol Old Vic Theatre School. While lists of awards can't tell you everything about a person, his seven Tony Awards, three Drama Desk awards and his Olivier award, all for best set design, do tell you he's been pretty succesful since.

Like others he balances his work on plays, opera and ballet with the commercial world of musical theatre, becoming Disney's go-to designer for a run of shows including *Aida*, *Mary Poppins* and *Tarzan,* which he also directed, and also designing shows such as *Once* and *An American in Paris* in New York and London.

Before that, he created a series of acclaimed shows for the RSC, including *The Plantagenets*, and Howard Davies' original production of *Les Liaisons Dangereuses*; for ENO (Nicholas Hytner's production of *The Magic Flute*); the Royal Opera (*La Traviata*) and the Royel Ballet (*Alice's Adventures Underground* and *The Winter's Tale*). For the National, he has designed more than twenty productions, including *Ghetto*, *Carousel*, *The Madness of George III* and *The History Boys*.

Richard: Have you got favourite theatres?

Bob: I love the Royal Court. The audience-actor relationship there is exquisite. I love the Royal Opera House. I really love the Olivier.

I was a student of stage design at the Bristol Old Vic Theatre School. Our tutor brought us to London, we put on hard hats, and they brought us into the National in 1974. I'll never forget walking into the Olivier, which was still just a concrete shell, but all the flying lines were in. All the lighting bars were on the floor, and there were no seats, there was no purple carpet, there was nothing, just the raw concrete space, and I've never forgotten it.

To this day, I go to the Olivier expecting something wonderful. I'm always interested to know what people are going to do with it. The minute you walk into the Olivier, you begin to think anything can happen there, and I just get excited every time.

I think people put too much scenery into the Olivier. That's my biggest caveat. If you trust the space... I talked to Jocelyn Herbert a lot about this.

Richard: She was very supportive of Lasdun.

Bob: She was, and she was very supportive of me, in my younger years at the National. I began very much as a minimalist. I used to be known as Fight-for-a-Chair Crowley. One actor called me that because there was nowhere to sit onstage. But I do know that the Olivier works best when you find an object, or just one piece of scenery, or one pillar, and you just put it in the right place, and you put the actor in the right place. If you do it with enough confidence – and you need great actors, of course – then the Olivier is a brilliant space.

It's tough sitting up in the circle. I do go up and sit in the back because that's where I started off. I remember, quite vividly, seeing wonderful, wonderful productions up there. It's not true that if you sit in the bad seats you don't have a good experience.

Richard: And the Lyttelton?

Bob: I can't say I have the same affection for it. The problem is the circle; it's very separate from the stalls. You're unaware that there's a dress circle over your head. But, like any theatre space, it depends on what's happening on the stage. There are moments when it's the most brilliant space. Famously, I did *The History Boys*, which worked brilliantly.

Richard: A lot of your colleagues, say: script, actors, space: "Our job is to make it work."

Bob: And not to show off too much. It's to make the actor feel secure, and make the playwright feel that he or she's being heard.

Richard: Have you worked in the Cottesloe?

Bob: I have, yes. Very happily. The first show was *A Midsummer Night's Dream* with Paul Scofield. I had a lovely time there.

Richard: There's something magical about the lobby spaces.

Bob: The spaces are lovely, and the cathedral window upstairs is beautiful. You never feel like you're in a foyer. There's always air outside and balconies on a summer's night; there's no better place to go to. There's leg room and the best programmes in the world.

The National was criticised, wasn't it? Initially, it was unloved. I think the perception of it began to change when the Barbican opened. I never fell in love with that building – and to work there was very difficult because you were underground. It became known as the bunker.

If you find you're in the wrong row there, God love you, then you have to walk another mile to get to two rows in front of you because there's no centre aisle. The other problem is the architecture of the foyers. No matter how marvellous the experience I've had there as a theatregoer, the architecture manages to act as some kind of wipe. As I emerge, the experience isn't supported. It deteriorates very quickly.

I worked in the Royal Exchange, which I loved. Again, it has an excitement about it when you walk into the building and you see that brilliant juxtaposition of the Victorian architecture and this beautiful space age modular floating thing. There's a sense of ritual about it. You go into a big theatre, you expect

The History Boys, Lyttelton Theatre, 2004

something different to walking into the Royal Court or the Donmar. It's like church. I'm a lapsed Catholic, and I replaced my religion with theatre, but I still love 'smells and bells.'

Richard: The theatres of the West End? Any strike you as better, worse, horrid, interesting?

Bob: I like Wyndham's very much. It's a beautiful theatre. I do love the Aldwych. But maybe I associate theatres with great experiences. I used to come up from Bristol, and I'd queue at, like, eight in the morning, and get the day seats. I saw *The Trojans*. I saw *Travesties, Nicholas Nickleby*. My love of the theatre is absolutely linked to what I saw there.

So you came out of that whole post-war kind of era of optimism, didn't you, where anything was kind of possible.

Richard: Guilty. Yes.

Bob: You've nothing to be guilty about with The National Theatre. I think it's one of the greatest institutions. It's a privilege to work there. It's something in the DNA of that building that makes you want to go back there again and again and again and again to watch. But the people here, the work ethic here – you have the best seamstresses, and the best wigmakers, the best sculptors, the best prop makers, the best scene painters. It's brilliant.

Marianne Elliott

Director

Marianne was the director of a series of remarkable shows for the National Theatre, including *War Horse* (co-directed with Tom Morris), *The Curious Incident of the Dog in the Night-Time* and *Angels in America*.

She is also the daughter of my friend and collaborator Michael Elliott, who was on the NT Building Committee and then went on to help create the Royal Exchange in Manchester. Despite a very theatrical family heritage (her mother was the actress Rosalind Knight, her maternal grandfather the actor Esmond Knight) she has said she "hated" the theatrical profession as a child and "used to ask her parents not to talk shop."

Despite that ambivalence, she did study drama at Hull University, but then went to work as a casting director and drama secretary at Granada Television. But perhaps the pull was too strong: in 1995 she began to work at the Royal Exchange, and in 1998 became the company's artistic director. In 2002 she moved to become associate artistic director at the Royal Court in London; in 2006 she joined the National and began that run of shows. Since stepping away from the NT in 2017 and establishing her own production company, her productions have included a new production of Sondheim's *Company*, with the central character re-imagined as a woman.

Richard: I adored *Husbands & Sons* [a combination of three D.H. Lawrence dramas, produced in conjunction with Royal Exchange Theatre and presented in the Dorfman Theatre]. Why didn't you want to do *Husbands* in the Olivier?

Marianne: Because I wanted to portray the deep amount of feeling and subtext above and beyond what is actually said by the characters. The Olivier is not the best place for a lot of subtext. I also wanted to deal with the intimacy of the stories, to be as close to the actors as I could.

It would have been easier to stage it in the Lyttelton: I would have had three sections of the stage being the three houses, and I could have blacked out or gauzed out two of them. But I felt that you needed to be in the same room as the characters. You needed to feel totally surrounded by that environment. Because the Lyttelton stage is raised up, it feels like you're looking at something on a platform.

I like the Olivier; it is is a fantastic space. You can make incredible visual statements quite simply there. It's wonderful to be able to play on such a grand scale. There's a clear link from the actor to the audience. It sometimes feels like the performer is in the lap of the audience, so it breaks through any kind of proscenium arch framework. For something like *War Horse*, it's much more immediate than the proscenium arch. The only thing about the Olivier is that you have to know where the focus is, and, as a director, how to control that focus. Where is the audience meant to be looking at any time?

It's not a place of great agility, not a lively place. It can be difficult there to move from scene to scene to scene. But you can feel very connected to strong visual epic storytelling.

Richard: For *War Horse,* you had a strip of cyclorama, with lights below, that brought the whole room down in scale.

Marianne: The theatre is too high. You always need to articulate the space, either bring it down with a cyc, or have a row of chairs in a square, or have a very particular playing area, or have a set that clearly tells you where you're meant to be looking but isn't too sprawling. With *Saint Joan*, we just put a platform within the large stage. It looked like a piece of burnt wood. It was a square; we had chairs on either side, and, upstage of that, a sort of burnt wall of trees. That was the way we tried to articulate the space.

Richard: The circle seems far away?

Marianne: Yes, it feels very far away. It doesn't feel as connected.

Richard: People have said to me that it's a long way to get onstage. But defining the space…

Marianne: It does help. Or you make a virtue out of the fact that you've got very long entrances. Again, in *Saint Joan*, her very first entrance was through a door, which we put as far upstage as we possibly could. It was a long, long, long, long, entrance, which was full of impact. But the space is not agile. You can't just turn up onstage quickly.

Richard: For *Husbands & Sons* in the Cottesloe/Dorfman, you raised the whole floor, which was very effective.

Marianne: Bunny Christie designed it and she has worked in the Cottesloe a lot, so she knows the pitfalls. Raising the floor really, really helps. It's not really a theatre designed to be in-the-round, because the acoustics aren't in-the-round. I like in-the-round because every seat has an individual experience with the story being told. I also love that you're so close to the actors and there is nowhere for the actors to hide. It's not about illusion; it's the absolute craft of the acting. That is something that theatre does better than any other art form.

Richard: *The Curious Incident of the Dog in the Night-Time*? I'm sorry I didn't see that at the National, because you went from the Cottesloe to the West End.

Marianne: We had to basically rethink it entirely. We were going from a space where you felt like you were inside Christopher's head to a space where you were watching Christopher's head more objectively. We put Christopher in a box for the proscenium arch in the West End; at the Cottesloe,

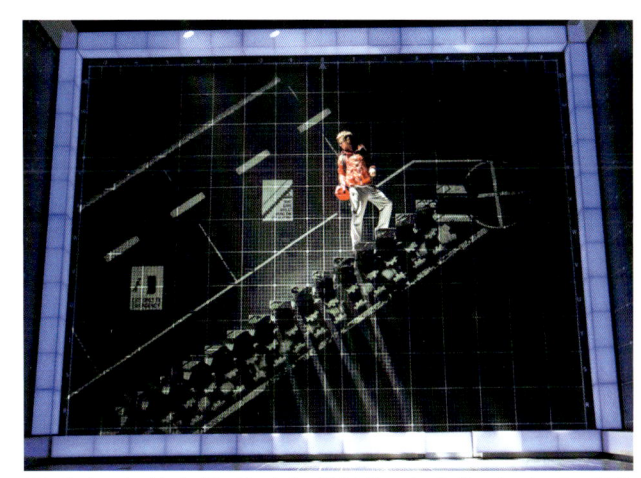

The Curious Incident of the Dog in the Night-Time, Apollo Theatre, London, 2013

we had no box. The audience looked down and, therefore, we had just the floor and would project on that. We didn't have any of the walls or the sides.

Richard: What do you feel about the Lyttelton?

Marianne: The Lyttelton is the trickiest space, because it's very wide and the stage is very high. And there is very little wing space and very little space upstage. It can, at its worst, feel a bit of a lecture hall, but it's been flexible and eclectic in what it can produce. I chose to do *Angels in America* there: I felt it should be there because you can enter and exit without being seen. You can have walls, you can fly things and people, and you can lower the stage.

Richard: Tell me about other theatres. Ones that you hate, or love.

Marianne: Well I don't like the West End much, because of cramped foyers, very few toilets, not very comfortable seats. And you often can feel very distant from the acting on the stage. I do like the Royal Exchange. I like the Royal Court. It just feels quite intimate, doesn't it? Acoustically, it's a bit more difficult than one imagines. But then theatres always are, aren't they?

Bunny Christie

Designer

Bunny trained at the Central School of Art. Her first design for the National was *The Mother* in 1986. She has since designed across all three theatres at the NT, as well as devising shows in the NT Studio. Those productions have included *The Red Barn*; *Husbands & Sons*; *People, Places & Things*; *Emil and the Detectives*; *Children of the Sun*; *The White Guard*; *Dealer's Choice*; *Elmina's Kitchen*; *Baby Doll* and *The Curious Incident of the Dog in the Night-Time*, which also transferred to the West End and then to Broadway.

Beyond the NT, her work has included shows for the Donmar, the Almeida, the Bridge, ENO, the Royal Opera, Houston Grand Opera, Chicago Opera, LA Opera and in the West End and on Broadway, those productions including *Made In Dagenham*, *Ink*, *Heisenberg* and *Company*, for which she won Olivier, Tony and Critics' Circle awards. She designed all of the productions of Eve Ensler's *The Vagina Monologues* from its British premiere at the King's Head to performances at the Royal Albert Hall raising money for women's charities worldwide. She received an Honorary Doctor of Letters from her home town's university, St. Andrews, and was awarded an OBE for services to the theatre industry.

Bunny: In the Cottesloe – and I know that space really well – there are problems. For the last few things I've done in there, I've raised the floor a lot, because if you sit in the balconies, you're disconnected from the action. Some of the sightlines are really bad. I've watched shows on those high side seats, and I couldn't be bothered trying to see; I sat back and thought, I'll just listen, like a radio play. We didn't solve it, but it really helped to raise the stage. For *Husbands & Sons*; we've raised the stage about four feet.

Richard: I'm worried that the new seats upstairs, added for the renovation, are the worst in the house.

Bunny: They've tried to make them really high. Because when you go up to the gallery in old theatres, the seats are steeply raked, and they work because you can see right over people's heads. It feels really scary, but you can get a good view. Of course, people lean over the balcony and then you can't see over their heads, and then there are lamps and loudspeakers along the balcony fronts. Do these things have to be this big?

The other thing that drives me nuts: when they did the new renovation, I thought, they'll change where the dock door is. It's tiny, so everything has to be built in tiny sections. A lot of money was spent on the front of house, the bars, and the ladies' toilets, which is lovely. But nothing for the crew and for designers.

Richard: What are your favourite theatres? Do you have any that particularly wow you to work in, or to see a show in?

Bunny: Of course, the Dorfman/Cottesloe is great to work in. Part of that is because you are designing the auditorium. It's the same with the Young Vic. There's something exciting in that, although it's irritating that we have to spend hours designing the seating, trying to get the right number of seats in, and the fire exits. It is unrecognised, unpaid work because you have to do all that before you design your set. And that eats up days and weeks of your life.

I'm really happy I did something in The Shed, just after I'd done something in the Lyttelton. As designers, the fun is really doing the big stuff and then doing some nice tiny thing in a few square feet.

The White Guard, Lyttelton Theatre, 2010

I first started going to the theatre properly in Glasgow, the Citizens. It was magic. The scale of it was lovely. It sat in the middle of a wasteland of the Gorbals, and it was like a little jewel. It was this magic place with beautiful, beautiful people on stage. I think we forget that sometimes, the glamour. I don't mean glamour in terms of richness. I mean the glamour of actors on the stage, of beautiful people saying beautiful things. This was why theatres weren't ordinary places, isn't it? They gave people places to go that felt luxurious and lovely and special. You can get that from a black studio theatre space because it feels full of expectation. It doesn't feel like a conference hall or a business centre.

Richard: In the Lyttelton, what are the good things, what are the bad things?

Bunny: When I did *The White Guard* there, I used all the stage machinery. That was amazing. I suggested, "We could have something that looks like a huge big box set that miraculously disappears into the rear dock and reveals something else. And we could have something on the forestage lifts that comes up and is a really small space. But we'll never be able to afford that." The director Howard Davies said, "Let's just ask them." We went into Nick Starr's office and I described to him what we were looking at. Nick said, "Let's make it happen."

Just like that. The crew were really great. It was really good collaboration of those who know that theatre really well, rather than me coming in and saying, "This is how it has to be."

Richard: How do you feel about upstairs?

Bunny: Well, it feels like the balcony's too far away. It's fantastic sitting in the stalls.

Richard: Lots of people complained about the disconnect. And the Olivier – what do you feel?

Bunny: Every time I design for the Olivier, I find it really, really difficult to get focus. The scenery feels like it's got to be so far upstage that you're just doing a kind of backdrop or something. It's very wide, and it doesn't feel very flexible. When you put scenery on the drum of the Olivier, the audience seems too far away. I want the balcony closer. There are also funny things about where you can fly, where you can't fly. It drives me nuts. I have found it the hardest place to design for. I've seen some great shows in there. But, again, you feel miles away when you're sitting upstairs. I don't know how many shows Paule Constable has done in there. She very sweetly said to me that she thought she'd probably only got it right, like, three times.

Alex Jennings

Actor

A three-time Olivier Award winner, for *Too Clever by Half* (1988), *Peer Gynt* (1996), and *My Fair Lady* (2003), Alex is the only performer to have won in the drama, musical, and comedy categories.

He has worked extensively with the Royal Shakespeare Company and with the National Theatre, playing more than twenty roles at the company from the 1989 production of *Ghetto* onwards.

He played Prince Charles in the 2006 film *The Queen*, and Edward VIII in the Netflix series *The Crown*. His other film appearances include *The Wings Of The Dove* (1997), *Bridget Jones: The Edge of Reason* (2004), *Babel* (2006) and *The Lady in the Van* (2015) in which he portrayed the playwright Alan Bennett.

Richard: What was the first moment for you when the NT moved into the big concrete fortress?

Alex: *Hamlet*, with Albert Finney, and *Tamburlaine*. 1976. I was in my late teens. I was thrilled by the building, and, later, by getting the opportunity to work there.

Richard: What was your first engagement at the National?

Alex: Nick Hytner's production of *Ghetto*, the Joshua Sobol play. It was in the Olivier. I've always loved the challenge of it: you may be able to say many things about me, but you can hear me. Then I worked with Trevor Nunn but we were suddenly being mic'd. It was a production of *The Relapse*, and I was playing Lord Foppington. Brian Blessed was in it, and I didn't quite understand why Brian Blessed and Alex Jennings should be mic'd. It didn't make me happy.

As an audience member, I find the Lyttelton more difficult because of the width and letterbox aspect of it. If you're onstage at the Lyttelton, as opposed to the Old Vic stage, you absolutely feel that.

Albert Speer [by David Edgar] was an amazing production, brilliantly designed, and brilliantly directed by Trevor Nunn. As a performer, you're very much affected by the design that is behind and around you.

Richard: Have you played the Cottesloe?

Alex: I've only been allowed in there once; I'm too loud! *Collaborators*, which I did there, had a slightly odd audience permutation, in long traverse. It transferred to the Olivier rather well, because it was a big, very theatrical piece.

Richard: Other theatres around the country?

Alex: I always loved the old theatre at Stratford. I don't know what the problem with it was. The Old Vic in Bristol is just perfect. I'm also excited by the challenges of completely different spaces. The Theatre Royal Drury Lane: you just have to get it out there. I did *My Fair Lady* there. Terrifying, absolutely terrifying. The gap between the orchestra pit and the audience starts miles away. But I did grow to love it.

My fear is that actors are becoming less equipped to embrace those spaces. Because one watches so much on the small screen, as we do now, that it's changing the nature of what we're being asked to do. You still need some equipment that you can call on. Sometimes you're working, having a conversation with a particular actor, and you can't actually hear what is being said to you.

Neil Austin

Lighting Designer

Neil is a lighting designer who, in a way, spans generations at the National: early in his career, while working with lighting designer Mark Henderson, he would recreate Mark's work for director Howard Davies as the productions toured or moved to new theatres. More recently he has lit shows for Howard, notably *The White Guard* (for which he won his second Olivier award), *The Cherry Orchard* and *The Silver Tassie*.

His first production at the National was the co-production of *Further than the Furthest Thing* in 2000, and he has returned many times in the almost quarter-century since, for productions including *The Cherry Orchard*, *England People Very Nice*, *Henry IV*, *Our Country's Good* and *Thérèse Raquin*.

He became a regular at the Donmar Warehouse during Michael Grandage's tenure there, notable productions including *Frost/Nixon*, *Parade*, for which he won a Knight of Illumination Award, and *Red*, which won him his first Tony Award for its Broadway transfer. His second came for *Harry Potter and the Cursed Child*, seen around the world. More recently his productions have included Marianne Elliott's *Company*, and Disney's *Frozen*, working once again with director Michael Grandage and designer Christopher Oram.

I interviewed Neil at the lighting designer's 'office' – his production desk in the Garrick Theatre, where he was lighting *The Winter's Tale* for Kenneth Branagh. Some highlights from that conversation:

"Despite the spaces the NT is a great place to work. My first experience of theatre was at the age of 8, I was blown away by *Hiawatha* in the Olivier. It is such a huge auditorium: after experiencing the West End, I was amazed. The weirdness compared to what I knew of theatre. The 'Olly' and 'Cott' were so different to anything I knew about. The impact! Made it all a new experience. Unrecognisable as a theatre."

"My first new show at the NT was *Henry Four, Part One And Two*, for Nick Hytner. It was very daunting, but ultimately successful."

Lighting in the Olivier

"Now there are so many moving lights. The marvellous speed of access to them gives you a powerful sense of real control."

"Downstage of the drum is still a problem area. Lighting-wise it's a no-mans-land. Lighting in 3D so far downstage is very hard, yet all directors want to be there."

"If you stand at the centre of the drum everything makes sense, it seems the focus of all lighting and indeed of the entire house."

"The Olly seems to breed a style of lighting with broad brush strokes."

"I recently did *Our Country's Good* with an amazing cyclorama in the Olivier, backlit in blue and frontlit in red with twenty-eight Source Four spotlights pin-spotting details in the Aboriginal artwork – it was beautiful."

"I love the Lyttelton… in the stalls. But the circle is horrid and feels completely disconnected. I saw *One Man, Two Guvnors* from the second row of the circle, and was very aware of two audience reactions, one at the top and one at the bottom."

"The Cottesloe has been my least successful lighting experience, but of course, it's the best for audiences."

London's South Bank in March 2020, showing the remarkable changes that have taken place in the area - and across London - in the half century since the National was built

4.5 Rufus Norris
NT Director 2015-2025

"Rufus Norris, when he takes over in April 2015, will inherit a bustling institution. But he – and one hopes next time it might be 'she' – will also have to confront a lot of questions. What is the job of the National Theatre? How can it truly represent a country that is now one of the most cosmopolitan on earth? Given the existence of the peripatetic National Theatre of Scotland and National Theatre Wales, is it effectively the National Theatre of England rather than of Great Britain? Are there still more ways in which new technology can be used to broaden its appeal?" [107]
Michael Billington
The Guardian

The National Theatre today has more than fulfilled the dreams of its supporters, and has evolved as the world around it has evolved. Superb productions and amazing stagecraft reach out, via NT Live, to a worldwide audience, while full houses, remarkable initiatives in education and audience involvement, and a newly revitalised, functioning, greener, and ever-more-popular building attract the public throughout the day.

During Rufus Norris' leadership the National faced some of its toughest times, but survived, and evolved. Amazing possibilities await. Rufus has said: "I go to the theatre to be moved," and has worked to ensure that is true of all who come to enjoy a show at the National.

Rufus became the National's sixth Director in March 2015, the first since Sir Laurence to have trained as an actor.

Brought up in Africa and Malaysia then the UK, he trained as an actor at RADA before turning to directing. In 2001 he won the *Evening Standard* Award for Outstanding Newcomer with David Rudkin's *Afore Night Comes*. Between 2002 and 2007 he was associate director of the Young Vic. He made his National debut with *Market Boy* in 2006, becoming an associate director of the company in 2011.

The job then took on is probably the toughest in British theatre – and would only become more so as Covid arrived.

Rufus does seem to have mastered the challenging Olivier stage. His colleague and friend, the lighting designer Paule Constable, has said that she thinks "the most consistently exciting director in the Olivier is Rufus, who has found a way to make it work as a storytelling space." Rufus is flattered by the comment but gently brushes it aside: "I don't think it's something I'm aware of, or necessarily agree with – we've had so many great artists work in that theatre." But he is very aware of its challenges – or, at least, its perceived challenges. "The width and depth of the Olivier may feel imposing at first, but it is a space I enjoy directing for. In spite of its size, when all the elements of acting, directing and design come together perfectly, it can be an incredibly intimate theatre. It does have the luxury of being able to both accommodate huge sets, but also of withstanding a stripped back, almost barren stage. But I think it demands that directors and designers think of it in 3D, even when the staging isn't in the round." He also notes that the relationship between stage and audience is a tough one to understand when putting a show together in the rehearsal room. "The specific challenge – which is what really makes it unlike any other space – is the combination of the fan of the audience and the audience effectively being in three parts – the stalls, the raised stalls and the circle. To play to all three inclusively while creating a holding frame visually is very particular and very tough to rehearse. Every show in there needs respacing and reconfiguring when you get into the house. You have to make the audience join with the show."

Under Rufus' tenure, the Olivier did return to an in the round format for a while as theatres tried to reopen post-Covid, the additional seating on stage counter-balancing the need to leave seats empty to provide social distancing between audience members. "That structure came out of necessity – the need to seat the audience in a safe way. It's not the first time we have had the audience on stage in the Olivier, but it was really fantastic to see how theatre makers pivoted work they had been planning to make in one form to accommodate this new set-up."

A quirk of Rufus' time at the National is that while he has directed in the Olivier and the Dorfman (with *London Road* even starting in the smaller space then transferring to the larger one), he has never directed a play in the Lyttelton. "That's definitely not from design," he says, "more about opportunity: we've had some wonderful directors and work scheduled in there during my time as Director." He feels the Lyttelton is almost the reverse of the challenge of the Olivier: that at first glance it does not seem challenging. "The wide-openness of the Olivier is really breath-taking the first time you see the theatre, probably the hundredth time too. By contrast the Lyttelton can feel pretty straight forward at first glance. It's not – but actually, no theatre space is ever straight forward. With the Lyttelton, I think the sheer width and depth of the stage can surprise theatre makers. It asks for you to be creatively canny and not make assumptions about how that space works – and I think that presents huge opportunities in the ways you can use it. Do I regret not working in there? Of course. It's really just been about the way the planning has evolved, but in truth perhaps there is something about the sort of work the Olivier responds to that is closer to my personal taste and, perhaps, strengths." Perhaps that is the very bold stagecraaft I think the Olly and the Lyttelton have bred in Britain.

He is aware that there are those who feel that theatres need to change, but does comment that change isn't always for the better: "the height added at the Young Vic means it has lost some concentration; a theatre is a container of acoustic energy, but more importantly of human energy; it needs a lid!" But he also explains that he does "think all theatre makers should be able to work with what they are presented with – though I imagine at different points in our careers many of us would have something we would like to change about the space we are working in at that moment! While I enjoy the flexibility of somewhere like the Dorfman and having more of a say in where the audience is, there is something rather focusing and strangely creatively liberating about having constraints presented to you. And if you regularly work in a space, you can become familiar enough with it that you can challenge those perceived constraints. That's a confidence that probably then carries through to rehearsals and working with the rest of the creative team."

As has become traditional, Rufus will complete two terms in office: "the time has flown by. It's such a huge organisation with a huge reach and it's something that any Director wants to live up to; the job carries enormous responsibility and privilege, which I feel keenly." His era included the unexpected challenge of Covid: "a challenge that as an organsisation, and as a sector, I think we really rose up to meet. It is of huge importance to the economic and cultural health of the country to ensure theatre's survival – and to ensure it can flourish right across the country. For the National it brought forward initiatives that we'd already been looking at, such as the National Theatre at Home programme making productions available online; that allowed us to connect with audiences outside London in a different way, and to share our work on a much broader scale. But it also allowed some of the seeds we have been sowing for a long time to start to come to fruition, particularly our work with the theatre makers of the future at the New Work department and with our Learning team as the pandemic began to subside. So many young people missed out on those first steps into the industry during those two years; we want them to have confidence that theatre has a place for them and that it is an industry that is valued."

As Michael Billington asked earlier, are there ways of broadening the theatre's appeal, even beyond a building? Under Rufus, the NT has encouraged new technologies but has also led many stunning people-oriented initiatives. Expanding NT Live, new schools activities with streaming video resources, even including kids' participation in writing and performance, 'Let's Play,' 'Connections,' 'Theatreworks' training, the sensational community-based 'Public Acts,' combined with increased touring are making the NT a truly national theatre for everybody.

> "Theatre is the ultimate collaborative art. What's a theatre? It's a story house. It's where we tell stories, and everybody and everything that is involved in making theatre is in service to that story."
>
> Rufus Norris, *The National Theatre: A Place for Plays*, a symposium held at the National, 30th October 2016

NT Staff on the terraces of the building, 2019

Everyman

Late 15th century play newly adapted by Carol Ann Duffy
Olivier Theatre
22nd April 2015

Director: Rufus Norris
Scenic design: Ian MacNeil
Costumes: Nicky Gillibrand
Lighting: Paul Anderson
Sound: Paul Arditti
Video: Tal Rosner
Production photographer: Richard Hubert Smith

"Norris's virtuosic production that captures both the frantic dizziness of a money-driven world and the beckoning finality of death."
Michael Billington
The Guardian

A bold, bracing start from Norris. Amen to that."
Financial Times

"Rufus Norris, the National Theatre's new boss, kicks off his tenure with an Everyman for everyone. This is one of Britain's oldest extant plays zapped into the 21st century with a plain-speaking adaptation by the nation's poet laureate, Carol Ann Duffy. Norris directs with the eye-popping flair of an opening ceremony, centering on a commanding Chiwetel Ejiofor performance as the universal Everyman. Spectacular, straightforward and, alright, a little bit sentimental, it's impossible not to like – even if it's hard to love. What's a national theatre for if not for this? Who's it for if not for all of us?"
Variety

Husbands & Sons

by D.H. Lawrence adapted by Ben Power
Dorfman Theatre
19th October 2015

Director: Marianne Elliott
Production design: Bunny Christie
Lighting: Lucy Carter
Sound: Ian Dickinson
Video: Tal Rosner
Production photographer: Manuel Harlan

"To make an audience feel it is watching not just one uncurling episode, but an entire way of life: this surely is what directors and playwrights often wish for. It is what adapter Ben Power and director Marianne Elliot have pulled off."
The Guardian

"The audience sits on all four sides of Bunny Christie's terrific domesticity-in-triplicate set and Marianne Elliott directs the enterprise as if it were a great piece of music (there's haunting use of a song on the gramophone), replete with shifting contrapuntal moods and orchestra colours."
The Independent

"Marianne Elliott's production is engrossing and elegant, snapping out of the domestic realism with moments of contemplative beauty and symbolism."
CultureWhisper

wonder.land

by Damon Albarn & Moira Buffini
Olivier Theatre, after opening at the Manchester International Festival
Olivier: 23rd November 2015

Director: Rufus Norris
Scenic design: Rae Smith
Costumes: Katrina Lindsay
Lighting: Paule Constable
Video: 59 Productions
Sound: Paul Arditti
Production photographer: Brinkhoff/Mögenburg

"Norris directs this show with extraordinary visual flair. Rae Smith's set deploys shape-shifting, almost hallucinogenic abstract visuals that beautifully evoke something of the infinite realms of digital reality. Wonder.land manages to convey on stage something of the simultaneously colliding and dissolving frontiers between the real world and cyber space in a way contemporary theatre rarely manages."
The Telegraph

Ma Rainey's Black Bottom

by August Wilson
Lyttelton Theatre
26th January 2016

Director: Dominic Cooke
Production design: Ultz
Lighting: Charles Balfour
Sound: Paul Arditti
Production photographer: Johan Persson

"A marvellous revival of August Wilson's tale of a blues legend and her band in 1927 Chicago."
The Telegraph

"Dominic Cooke's production of Ma Rainey's Black Bottom, Wilson's 20's drama, is terrific. And tremendously welcome at the National. The 'mother of the blues' is played by Sharon D Clarke with imperious splendour. She is like a liner, cresting waves of sycophancy, riding the roll of the blues."
The Guardian

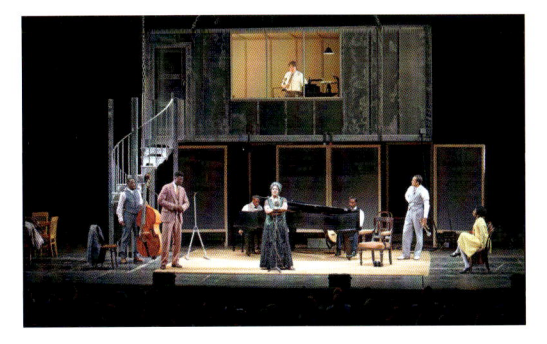

Les Blancs

by Lorraine Hansberry
Olivier Theatre
22nd March 2016

Director: Yaël Farber
Production design: Soutra Gilmour
Lighting: Tim Lutkin
Music and Sound: Adam Cork
Production photographer: Johan Persson

"This most humane and disturbingly beautiful of productions demands that its audience continue to wrestle with the intractable issues that lie at its heart."
The Telegraph

"Lorraine Hansberry's death at age 34, left her play Les Blancs unfinished. Completed by her ex-husband, it's an extraordinary piece – more didactic than dramatic, perhaps, but a cross-section of colonialism that presents the situation from all sides. Angry but even-handed, the monumental simplicity of director Yaël Farber's staging creates a space for careful reflection of a delicate issue – and on the National Theatre's main stage, that feels momentous in its own right."
Variety

The Threepenny Opera

by Bertolt Brecht, music by Kurt Weill
Olivier Theatre
18th May 2016

Director: Rufus Norris
Production design: Vicki Mortimer
Lighting: Paule Constable
Sound: Paul Arditti
Production photographer: Richard Hubert Smith

"I'm not sure that Norris's production makes a case for The Threepenny Opera as a masterpiece outside of the songs, but I did have a fantastically good time: a gleeful gob in the eye of gentrifying London."
Time Out

"I've never before seen a London staging of Threepenny that came so naturally by the sour sardonicism of this collaboration between Bertolt Brecht and Kurt Weill from 1928."
The New York Times

The Deep Blue Sea

by Terence Rattigan
Lyttelton Theatre
1st June 2016

Director: Carrie Cracknell
Production design: Tom Scutt
Lighting: Guy Hoare
Sound: Peter Rice
Production photographer: Richard Hubert Smith.

"Cracknell's production shows Rattigan as an inheritor of Ibsen's mantle, a visionary about the circumstances that imprison people."
The Guardian

"It's a beautifully judged, exquisitely sad production that remains faithful to Rattigan's period setting, but subtly enhances it with Peter Rice's remarkable ambient sound design, which makes Tom Scutt's yawning, semi-translucent block of flats set feel like a huge, lonely living creature, a giant shadow of McCrory's phenomenal Hester."
Time Out

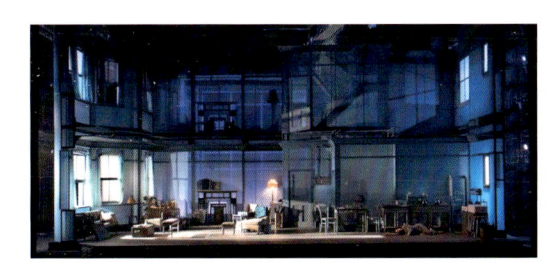

Amadeus

by Peter Shaffer
Olivier Theatre
19th October 2016

Director: Michael Longhurst
Production design: Chloe Lamford
Lighting: Jon Clark
Sound: Paul Arditti
Production photographer: Marc Brenner

"Stunning piece of theatre."
Michael Billington
The Guardian

Longhurst's remarkable achievement is to have turned a straight stage play into an epic piece of music theatre. I have seldom seen as confident a melding of speech and song, music and image."
The Independent

"A note-perfect production by rising director Michael Longhurst that gives it a fresh, vital and musically inventive new reading, one which fully confirms its classic status."
The Telegraph

"When the acting, Longhurst's stage direction, Simon Slater's musical direction and the Sinfonia all merge in the final Requiem sequence, the drama becomes as towering as the music."
Financial Times

Angels in America

by Tony Kushner
Lyttelton Theatre
11th April 2017

Director: Marianne Elliott
Scenic design: Ian MacNeil
Costumes: Nicky Gillibrand
Lighting: Paule Constable
Sound: Ian Dickinson
Production photographer: Helen Maybanks

"The prime impression is of Kushner's conviction that, although we live in dark times where both God and Marx are dead, there is always hope in the instinct for survival and the tenacity of the human spirit."
Michael Billington
The Guardian

"The most intelligent, provocative and affecting drama of my lifetime, and this production [by Marianne Elliott] overflows with its brilliant daring. But if ever there were a time when we needed to understand our devils and wrestle an angel for a blessing, it is now."
Los Angeles Times

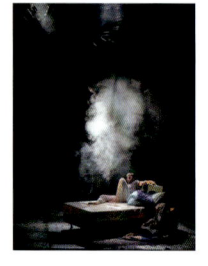

Network

by Paddy Chayefsky, adapted by Lee Hall
Lyttelton Theatre
11th April 2017

With Bryan Cranston
Director: Ivo van Hove
Set and Lighting design: Jan Versweyveld
Costumes: An D'Huys
Video: Tal Yarden
Music and Sound: Eric Sleichim

"This version of the Oscar-winning Network is an almost total triumph. Bryan Cranston brings a wiry magnetism to the role of the TV news anchor, Howard Beale. Ivo van Hove and his designer, Jan Versweyveld, have also transformed the National Theatre's normally inflexible Lyttelton stage into an extraordinary blend of television studio and public restaurant. The success of the show lies in its capacity to use every facet of live theatre to warn us against surrendering our humanity to an overpowering medium, whether it be television or invasive technology."
Michael Billington
The Guardian

Follies

Book by James Goldman,
Music & Lyrics by Stephen Sondheim
Olivier Theatre
22nd August 2017

Director: Dominic Cooke
Production design: Vicki Mortimer
Lighting: Paule Constable
Sound: Paul Groothuis
Production photographer: Johan Persson

"The National Theatre's production, plopping itself into the Olivier, and leaving in its wake a churning, frothing mass of excitement and audience expectation. This isn't just triumphant, it's transcendent."

"Dominic Cooke's production showcases Follies as a classic of musical theatre just as much as the show itself showcases the classics before it. The result is some Platonic ideal of Follies – and 2 hours 15 minutes of goosebumps."
Tim Bano
The Stage

The Lehman Trilogy

by Stefano Massini, adapted by Ben Power
Lyttelton Theatre
then London, New York, Los Angeles and elsewhere
Lyttelton: 7th April 2018

With Simon Russell Beale, Ben Miles and Adam Godfrey
Director: Sam Mendes
Scenic design: Es Devlin
Costumes: Katrina Lindsay
Lighting: Jon Clark
Video: Luke Halls
Sound: Nick Powell
Production photographer: Mark Douet

"What an astonishing evening! Spanning 150 years and running three and a half hours, Stefano Massini's play traces the trajectory of western capitalism by following the fortunes of a single family. Sam Mendes's production uses just three actors: Simon Russell Beale, Ben Miles and Adam Godley. The result is an intimate epic that becomes a masterly study of acting as well as of the intricacies of high finance. The joy of Mendes's impeccable production lies in watching the actors at work as they switch genders and ages to evoke multiple characters."
Michael Billington
The Guardian

Rae Smith

Designer

Rae indelibly stamped her mark on the history of the Olivier stage with her remarkable design for War Horse, *which has since been seen all over the world and won her the Olivier, Tony, Drama Desk and other awards. As always, creating that design was the result of years of work on other shows, stretching back to 1985 and encompassing everywhere from the Tron in Glasgow to the Royal Exchange to the Metropolitan Opera in New York.*

Her first show at the National was The Visit *in 1991, and her sixteen productions since then have included* Street of Crocodiles, Saint Joan, The Light Princess, wonder.land, The Seafarer *and* This House.

Rae: I wasn't a theatre baby. My starting point was I wanted a fine art career. I wanted to do something that involved people working together. I had a naïve idea that if I did theatre, I could use all the things I liked: drawing, painting, making 3D things, a multidisciplinary artistic pursuit. I went to about twelve schools before I did my A-levels. So it was instilled in me to make friends everywhere I went. That was a sort of childish notion that I had, and it continues to be true.

My first job was design assistant at the Glasgow Citizens Theatre. When I was at my first year at art school, there were third-years who I adored; one of them was Kenny Miller, who's a very flamboyant guy from Manchester. It was in the '80s, so there was a lot of gay politics about coming out; gay nightlife wasn't restricted to just gay men. As a woman, I could infiltrate the grandness of the gay mafia in the theatre, not by stealth but just by having fun. The theatre version of that was the Citizens Theatre, run by Giles Havergal and Philip Prowse.

Kenny invited me to work as his assistant at the Citizens Theatre. I ended up working for Greg Smith, the designer who headed the Lyceum Edinburgh – another beautiful Matcham theatre – so I started painting his scenery. I just lied my way into my paint job. I said I could paint canvas flats for a pantomime, and I couldn't. I'd never used rabbit-skin glue in my entire life, so my first day at work was phoning up a scene painter friend, and, in hushed tones, getting him to tell me exactly how to do it. I'd never been so nervous or neurotic, having to live a lie, mixing the glue with the paint powder, and hoping it went off properly, so when it dried all the paint didn't come off. Thank goodness it all worked, and I actually could do it. And the painting looked lovely in the end.

Richard: Nothing like being pushed off a cliff, to see if you can fly, is there?

Rae: No, no, there isn't, and sweating about half a stone off having lied your way into a job. White lies about my skill set.

Richard: It's all right. Some of us live like that. We're never going to be found out.

Rae: The imposter syndrome. I still have it.

Richard: Let's cut to the National. Shall we start with the Lyttelton?

Rae: It's a mystery, the Lyttelton. It's like a television box without the editing that television gives you, because all the seats have a different perspective and, as you know, the stalls and the balcony are completely different experiences. Acoustically, it's a challenge as well.

At a lecture on Lasdun in 2015, there were a load of

architects. The chief architect fidgeted all the way, actually walking out when I was talking. He was so not interested in a theatre designer's opinion about what works and what doesn't, theatrically. Yet the building is there not because of any other reason than people coming to the theatre and being in the same space as the actors. The fundamental things that we wrestle with in those spaces are big issues and should be listened to, even if they're a bit boring.

Richard: They're not boring at all.

Rae: Well, not for us, because we inherit the end result. In the Lyttelton, we inherit the strange perspective of every seat being a different sightline. We inherit that you can't hear very well. We inherit the lack of offstage space on either side. You try ever so hard, every time you work there, to give it some clarity, but you can't. What is the most helpful thing I can do? Build something that projects the voice back out into space. Use the panoramic downstage area as effectively as possible. Use the big open space of it all. There has been a habit of building loads of architecture in that space, not that you need it. Every time I'm in there, part of my subconscious goes, Well, how can we make this into Frank Matcham?

Richard: Tell me about the Olivier.

Rae: It's a really tough space. I start with Olivier himself and his projection ability. When I said you have to inherit the experience of the space, that's what I meant: him, his voice, the old rep-style actors who could project up to the gods. It takes a certain kind of vocal training.

The problem is putting people in the right place so you can hear and see them, not building too much scenery around them because it dwarfs their physicality. Of course, you wouldn't have that with a Matcham. When we did *War Horse*, I thought, Oh, my God, it's not an interior space at all. It's an exterior space. It's a landscape of the mind. If you allow your mind to gallop around, unfettered by walls and doors, and you work with actors who can walk into a space and not be seen until they enter the room, as well as a director who sees it in that way, then it's a brilliant space to work in.

> "I mean, I love Frank Matcham's proscenium arches. I love, love, love, love, love, love, love, love them, because the proportion is right. There's a sense of beauty about them."
>
> Rae Smith

Richard: You did something really clever in *War Horse* by dividing the space vertically. That screen, with the lights above and below, was brilliant, because there's something wrong with the scale of the whole thing.

Rae: Scale is one thing you have to wrestle with in there. I would think about that Edwardian idea of the self, inside a room downstage centre, inside a hall. It's a bit like the Houses of Parliament. You always have a room where one fellow can dominate an argument and you have the landscape, the British Empire behind it. It's very prescriptive in its scale, height, and width. It's a type of imperialist realism, scale-wise, that gives a momentous picture in a very intimate portrait. I love it.

Richard: That's fascinating.

Rae: *War Horse* was an accidental design in the sense that I tore a big bit of paper out of my sketchbook because I didn't want a square in there, and that became a cloud. It also became something you looked inside, like a view. It was also an adventure in projected scenery, because that was as quicksilver as it could get.

The first time I made a show in the Olivier was *Saint Joan* with Marianne. It used a simple square platform that turned around. I remember putting the square onstage and Nick Hytner rightly saying, "No, bring it downstage, because that's your hot spot." We positioned it exactly where he said, and the simple raised stage – using the landscape with blasted trees surrounding it and the actual dock door – became the cathedral. It was really effective, and it was a very happy experience because of Nick Hytner saying, "It's looking good. Just do that." That's what I mean about received knowledge. If he hadn't said that to me, if he hadn't worked on all those shows, if he didn't feel it was his place to say something – one simple instruction was the difference between it being successful and not successful. There is a scary feeling when you're in there that if you haven't got it, it's gonna kick your ass.

Richard: The Cottesloe?

Rae: Love, love, love it; love, love, love it. I mean, I was lucky enough to do the last show in the Cottesloe, *This House*, which is about Parliament. It had a hundred and twenty scenes in Act I and fifty-seven scenes in Act II, and they were all played within eight seconds of each other. So, it had to be something that was story-told in the space. It was perfect for them; we basically built the House of Commons in the Cottesloe, just the benches, and it was amazing fun.

Richard: Other theatres, anywhere else in the world you love or hate?

Rae: I like the Met. I love it.

Richard: It's amazing, isn't it? It's so huge, but it works.

Rae: It's an extraordinary space. Big, extraordinarily ridiculous for one person to stand on that stage and be heard and seen, but it does happen. A real kind of challenge for a designer, I must admit. I'd like another few goes there!

What do you think of the Dorfman? Do you think it's changed for the right reasons?

Richard: On the whole, it's fine. I like the new red walls. We

War Horse, Olivier Theatre, 2007

were against it being all-black from the outset, but that's what Peter Hall and John Bury wanted. The modernisation is, on the whole, good. Theatres have to turn into shopping malls, I suppose; that's life. One reason that prompted this book is they've spent – what is it now, £90 million? – and they're not allowed to touch the two theatres.

Rae: They're not allowed to touch the Olivier and the Lyttelton?

Richard: No, because they're national monuments, Grade 2* listed, both of them. That, to me, is just absurd; the inside of every theatre must change over time. Almost all old theatres have been knocked about and rebuilt.

Rae: Hypothetically speaking, if we said, "This is what we would like it to be; this is what you architects have done wrong; we want it to be changed to this," it would be nice to hear their feedback. Would they say, "We don't care. It's a national monument," or "We do want it to work for an audience, so everyone enjoys it. But it's fine the way it is." We're talking about putting theatre on, not creating mausoleums of someone's great genius.

Jon Clark
Lighting Designer

Jon trained as a theatre designer rather than just a lighting designer, graduating from Bretton Hall with a first-class degree. That perhaps helps us understand his goal of using light to define shape and control space, almost architecturally, rather than simply illuminating each scene.

This approach seems to have found favour with directors including Stephen Daldry (for whom he has lit *The Jungle*, *The Inheritance* and the new stage production of *Stranger Things*), Sam Mendes (the National's production of *The Lehman Trilogy*), Jamie Lloyd and Katie Mitchell.

Like most lighting designers, he spans a range of production genres, having lit plays, operas, musicals and dance. He is an associate artist of the RSC, and has reached the milestone of twenty-five productions at the National, including *Othello*, *Amadeus*, *The Motive and the Cue* and *Dear England*. These are notes from our conversation:

Olivier Theatre
"… is a vast space with a remote and seemingly laid-back audience. The circle is so far away and of enormous width, it has a very remote feeling. The central question is how to relate to the human scale of the actor. *The Beaux' Stratagem* used a big chunk of architecture in the middle, but it felt isolated and remote."

"The space can be helped by layering lighting vertically. Light has a very long journey from source to stage. To avoid the floor being too dominant we use side light but these far-away sources draw the eye out."

"I'd like to face the Olly with a bare stage and just use light – Svoboda style."

"Can the Olly do anything except epic? You can't fight the volume, you must celebrate it."

Lyttelton Theatre
"I enjoyed lighting *Women of Troy* in there. I love the pros light slots with low angle cross light potential, but they do create a dark brown frame emphasising the gap between stage and audience, which can feel very remote."

Favourite Theatres
"The Young Vic for its containment. *Streetcar* with that revolving set, was irritating on video, but far better on stage contained by audience. The new egg crate grid gives good access but is very chunky and creates obstructions. Lyric Hammersmith feels like home! Royal Court… wonderful proportions."

Not So Good Theatres
"RST, something went very wrong with the new space. The temporary Courtyard was distinctly better. Too narrow, high and steep with too many terrible seats. I did *Lear* in the Courtyard, which then transferred. Not so good."

Lighting Ambitions
My ambition is for light to model the actor in exquisite detail, and then move them in time."

Ben Power

Former Deputy Artistic Director, Playwright

Ben studied English at Cambridge University. After collaborating with Rupert Goold's Headlong company, he became an associate director of the National in 2011, going on to write for the company an adaptation of Ibsen's *Emperor and Galilean*, a new version of *Medea* which starred Helen McCrory, and *Husbands & Sons* which condensed three works by D.H. Lawrence into a single play. Ben's adaptation of Stefano Massini's 2013 play *The Lehman Trilogy* opened at the National and has also been seen in the West End, New York and Los Angeles.

Alongside this work, Ben oversaw the National's temporary space, The Shed, from 2013 and was the National's first deputy artistic director in 2014 until 2019.

Richard: What do you feel about what Lasdun left you?

Ben: It's so hard to answer objectively, isn't it? One takes the building, warts and all, because of the magic that's now written in the walls. Do you know, the speech at the end of [Alan Bennett's] *The Habit of Art,* when he quotes Ronnie Eyre (director) talking about closing the National, opening not as a theatre but opening as a bingo hall, a pool hall, and an ice skating rink, and letting the edges be knocked off it by use, and then Bennett says, "It's plays that do it."

I always think new theatre buildings are so hard to connect with, and this is why found spaces feel so vivid and vital: they bring their own texture. But I do love all of this building. I find the Lyttelton extremely difficult; one is always immensely grateful to have a design which overcomes the challenges of the space. We're in a moment where there's a great divide between directors who say, "I absolutely don't want to work in the Lyttelton" – Rufus has never directed in Lyttelton – and an increasing number who say, "I think the Olivier is impossible. I don't want to go there. I want to control the image." For an emerging generation of European-influenced directors, the 'mess' of the Olivier, because of the number of different viewpoints, of the scale – they don't like that. You go, "Yeah, but it's really difficult [in the Lyttelton]," and they say, "Oh, no, no, but it's fine because I can…" It obviously doesn't work because they don't quite appreciate the challenges, the width.

Richard: I didn't see *The Deep Blue Sea* [in the Lyttelton] yet. I talked with Giles Havergal about it, and he said, "But isn't the play meant to be set in a little room? Not in a gilded cage like a palace!"

Ben: It just about holds, but it is stretched. You feel the strings of the play vibrating because they're stretched so far across this room. It just about works, but that's because of the intensity of performance and because the set is completely beautiful. If it moves over the river [to the West End], the set would have to be much narrower and that would only help. The play is an absolute masterpiece.

I find it very hard not to love the Cottesloe/Dorfman completely. It's gorgeous, everything that one would want in a theatre. I can't imagine ever getting bored of it. It's hard to imagine a play that you couldn't stage in there.

Richard: Criticisms from designers – quite legitimate – are the poor sightlines from the sides when you're in an end-stage condition. But it goes with the concept.

Ben: But I've had wonderful nights up there, high on the sides in the Cottesloe..

Richard: It's because it's contained. It's contained with people.

Ben: Exactly, and you get the feeling of a 'bear pit.' That feels a bit extreme as a way of describing it, but that shared feeling overrides any other sense.

Tell me, is the story true about the Olivier circle, that the original design was a single rake of seats and that the break came in to accommodate the control rooms?

Richard: No. Denys' original design was for an absolutely square room – literally, a square with a stage there and seating, literally, in straight lines, but it would have been perfectly frightful. He came up with this concept after two months. He had said he wanted a year to accumulate all the dreams of everybody, and then he had to be left alone to design the building. So, we were warned. [Laughs] But this is where it started, with a concrete balcony.

Ben: Oh, wow. There is nowhere in the world, I think, like the first fifteen rows in our theatre. When an actor comes down and talks to you – he walks down, Rory Kinnear in *Hamlet,* coming down and down until you think, Stop, you can't come any further, and he just comes further and further and further until he's just talking to you like this. It's just mind-blowing. I suppose that those big gestural, choreographed shows like *Oresteia* or *Guys and Dolls*, that opened the theatre up – and must be felt, from all points in the house, like you were a part of something – because of the scale. But we struggle with that now, I think. I think it's rare to see a show that manages that.

Richard: It's interesting that outdoor-like productions – *Oklahoma!* or *War Horse* – were fantastic. It's when you have a set with a room that it gets really tricky.

Ben: So true. When you're looking for plays, the challenge of finding repertoire for the Olivier is so difficult. You could program the Lyttelton and the Dorfman from now until the cows come home. What are the plays that need the Olivier, that are going to be opened up by the Olivier? It is so difficult to find them. You want plays that are big. Anything that's even remotely human-sized is really difficult. But I do love the vastness of the Olivier's stage, open to the back shutter.

Richard: It's easy to fill it with too much scenery. In many ways, restraint is terribly good.

Ben: That's right. That was Nick's light bulb moment: "We will get better shows if we reduce the scenic budgets. It will mean that they'll put less stuff in there and the shows will get better." I think that was part of the rationale; we were spending half a million on shows and no one's coming to see them for most of the year, and we're charging £80. If we charge £12, £10, and give designers £100,000, suddenly you've got plays that are alive because they're much simpler; you've got two chairs and great performers. That's it. Get on with it.

We're in an interesting moment; after years of neglect of the drum until Nick [Hytner] reclaimed it for *His Dark Materials* the Olivier really works if we use every aspect of it. Right now, we've retreated from that; a lot of its recent use has just been dropping part of the stage or using it as a lift. I did an Ibsen play, *Emperor and Galilean*, with [director] Jonathan Kent and [designer] Paul Brown. The use of all levels of the drum, and properly switching and exchanging parts, was really magnificent – and on a tight budget.

Richard: I'm pleased they've rebuilt the flexible forestage. One reason for the drum was to parallel the Lyttelton, where you could take the stage riser out of the way. But with the drum, too, you could set the front elevator down at auditorium level and build the stage in any shape you like. Now you'll be able to do that and use the vomitoria. That's good because one of the problems is getting on and off stage.

Ben: It's a huge problem with new plays in there. You commission a play, and they write it, but they haven't taken account of that problem with entrances.

Richard: The voms will help. The other reason behind the drum was that we knew how big the space was: you could put the drum anywhere you'd like, add a bit of scenery, and people could pop out from behind it, without having to walk from over here.

Ben: That is so fantastic, to create a fast entrance point. It's brilliant. Somebody needs to do a big drum design again.

Paule Constable
Lighting Designer

Paule is a hugely prolific lighting designer. Her lighting work spans all of the genres from *War Horse* to the reinvention of *Les Misérables* to her many collaborations with Matthew Bourne. Her run of shows at the National began with *His Dark Materials* and now stretches to over fifty productions, including *Follies* and *The Ocean at the End of the Lane*; she is an associate artist of the company.

She is also a powerful campaigner and advocate for causes that concern her, including improved sustainability in production and better care of freelance theatre workers.

As you can see, Paule is one of the busiest lighting designers on the planet. Well, she is brilliant too. She has been my guide and mentor through putting this book together.

Richard: Tell me about your relationship to the National's stages. You have had great success on all of them.

Paule: Richard, firstly you must stop apologising for them! All of you made three remarkable stages in a quite remarkable building for a quite remarkable company that I feel privileged to be part of.

But yes, I do have a complicated relationship with the Olivier in particular. It is a really, really hard space. There are so many practical challenges – the vast 'dementor' space upstage that just seems to eat the action, those concrete pincers, the challenge of simply getting onto the stage quickly – you wonder why those existing voms at the front aren't used…

Richard: I think that is partly about the changes that have happened to the stage over the years, lifting it up and moving it forwards…

Paule: Then there's that circle, which feels so distant and remote. And the overwhelming impact of the floor, which is always very present. Nothing is easy in there. But on the other hand, I have made *Follies* in there, and *Saint Joan*, and *War Horse*. It puts you on your mantle – when it works, it is exciting. Different people have tried to deal with it in different ways over the years. Nick Hytner tried to control it. Others think the way to deal with it is to stuff it full of scenery and be damned. Rae Smith, and Melly Still on *Coram Boy*, have both opened it out instead, celebrated the epic quality it has. I think the most consistently exciting director in there is Rufus, who has found a way to make it a storytelling space.

I think what I've learnt is that you can't be passive in there, you can't be back foot in there – and I think that's actually what I love about it.

Richard: The Lyttelton?

Paule: I think the challenge is its very flat, very frontal design – there's a lack of any sense of perspective, and it can feel like watching a tennis match, your head moving from side to side. What does work is massive architectural settings – brutalist design meeting brutalist architecture, perhaps?

I do think Ian MacNeil managed to almost reinvent it, with *Inspector Calls* and then *Machinal*. And I think Bunny Christie, particularly with *Burnt By The Sun*, and Vicki Mortimer, with *Silver Tassie*, are both designers who have really wrestled with it. And of course there have been lots of experiments with it: the Lyttelton Transformation season, which I lit *Play Without Words* as part of, was certainly a bold endeavour.

Richard: And then…

Paule: The Cottesloe? It's interesting, isn't it, because its transformation to the Dorfman is one of those changes where you wonder if it has actually been improved, a bit like the changes at the Young Vic – a theatre I grew up in and adore and think was a space of a perfect scale. The Dorfman feels smarter, but has it lost some of that funky informality it used to have, tucked away around the corner, almost its own little world apart from the rest of the building. I wonder if a lean-forward theatre has become one in which you instead lean back?

But – we will still make it work.

I have a Josef Svoboda quote I use when I'm feeling a bit miserable: "When I sit alone in a theatre and gaze into the dark space of its empty stage, I'm frequently seized by fear that this time I won't manage to penetrate it, and I always hope that this fear will never desert me. Without an unending search for the key to the secret of creativity, there is no creation. It's necessary, always, to begin again, and that is beautiful."

I think what you, Lasdun, all of you gave us were spaces that perhaps we need to fear, a little, but that also challenge us – because that challenge is what can bring out the best in us, the theatres giving us something to react to, a blank canvas rather than no canvas at all. We don't always succeed, but when we do – and by we, I mean everyone, the teams making the shows, everyone working in the building who are always so wonderful and supportive and amazing, the freelancers and suppliers who coalesce around it – really remarkable things happen.

Richard, you and I have spent so much time talking about how you felt you somehow failed, yet we all have amazing relationships with these theatres, and we love them; they've taught us a huge amount, and continue to do so, and the influence of that has spread far beyond the NT. To create a national theatre that's done that for as many generations as it has, and will continue to do, is quite the opposite of a failure: it is an extraordinary success.

Last Nights at the National: *Small Island*
Rufus Norris' production of *Small Island* adapted by Helen Edmundson, based upon the novel by Andrea Levy, marked for your author yet another advance in wrestling with the challenges of the Olivier that emerges triumphantly.

The moving tale of immigration from the Caribbean into post-war Britain, it interweaves several protagonists' stories to stunning effect. The epic power that can be evoked in the Olivier is more than matched by the intense intimacy of each individual's struggles for survival in a racist society… a truly shattering contemporary problem for today. A National perspective upon a vital and international problem.

Rufus' design team, Katrina Lindsay (set and costumes), Jon Driscoll (projection), and Paul Anderson (lighting) create a constantly shifting world of powerful imagery. Skeletal settings and simple suggested environments stimulate the audience to use its own imaginations to become one with the action; the breadth of vision of the Olivier stage sets a nationwide perspective of changing times that can ingeniously close into the most intimate detail. And, for once, the very vastness of the Olivier auditorium gives these deeply personal dramas a universal significance.

Michael Billington, in *The Guardian*, wrote: "This feels like a landmark in the National's history." A landmark indeed. A universal call for tolerance and empathy to a nation passing through deeply troubled times. A clarion call for a new theatre… with a story of hope.

Translations
Brian Friel's amazing play, directed by Ian Rickson, is set in the remote Donegal countryside in 1833. The evocative setting by Rae Smith, with lighting by Neil Austin, exactly captures the very best of the Olivier's unique qualities. Rae places the scene, a country 'hedge' school, far down-centre for this powerful and intimate drama, while surrounding it with an evocation of the remote Irish landscape that stretches seemingly to infinity. A deeply tragic human story set within an entire epic world foreshadowed by its imminent danger of collapse. Magical theatre.

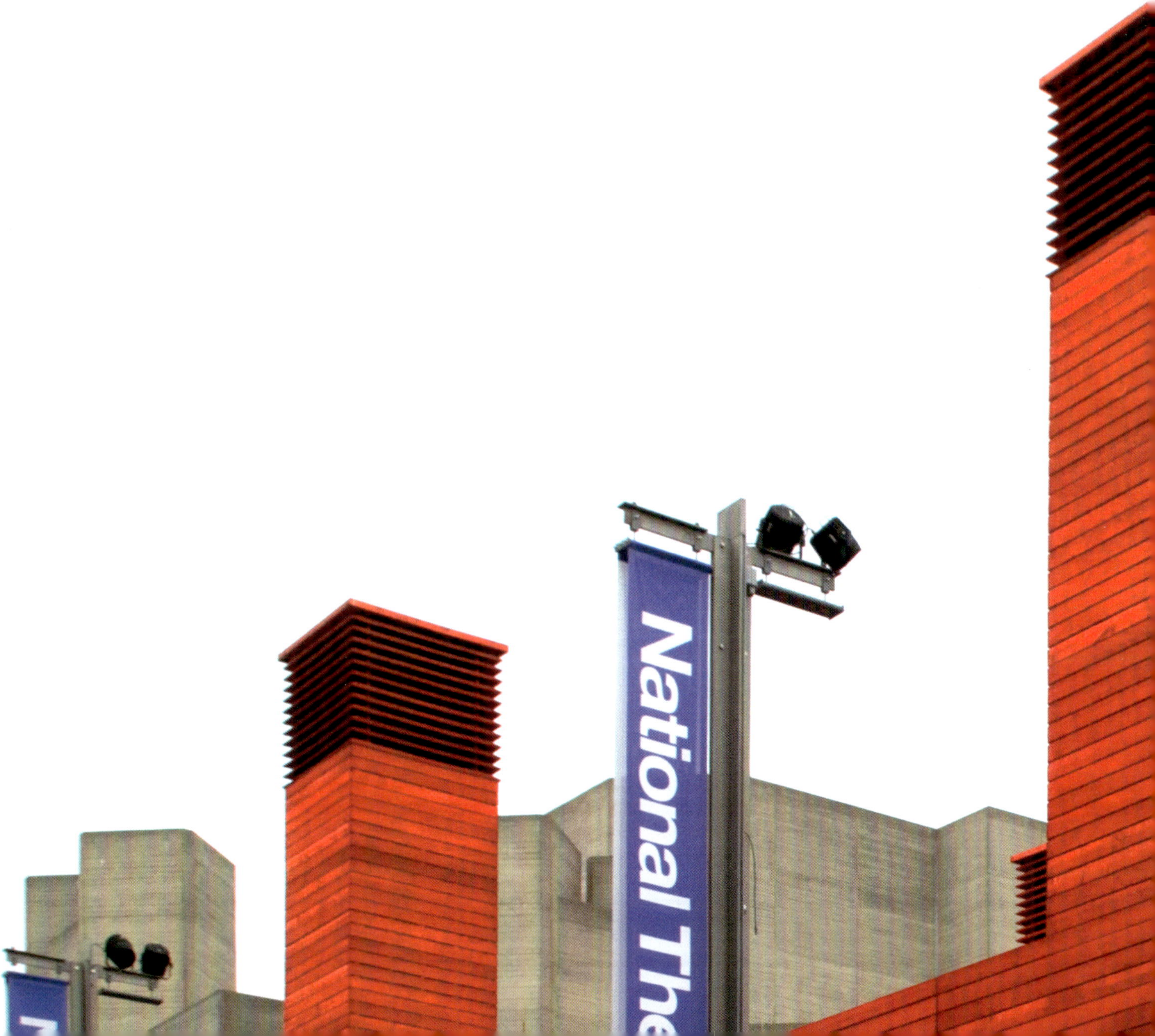
National The

Part Five

Five Decades of Theatre Design and Architecture

The National has grown up. Meanwhile the world of theatre has changed. Donmar, the Almeida, the Menier Chocolate Factory; the work of Kneehigh and Punchdrunk; the Tricycle, the Royal Court and the National's own temporary Shed, have brought a new dynamic of intimacy and flexibility more akin to the Cottesloe/Dorfman than the National's larger spaces. Yet the Olivier and the Lyttelton have opened new horizons for stagecraft. The design of theatres emerges as a collaborative process.

Olivier Theatre, 1976

Olivier Theatre, 2021

Although they have not been able to change the fundamental architecture, theatre people have certainly evolved the space. Note how the stage has extended forward and upwards, how elements of the concrete at the sides and on the circle front have been covered for both visual and acoustic purpose, and how the theatre technology – lights and loudspeakers – have become less concealed. Practical changes include new access walkways along the front side walls.

5.1 Our Theatres Examined in a Changing World

The National Theatre in 2017

As Lasdun's building has grown in popularity, professional opinions of the principal theatres have ebbed and flowed. The emergence of the fringe and new approaches to theatre-making have revolutionised styles of production. Outstanding productions and a sense of theatre have established the National Theatre Company as a national treasure with a worldwide reputation.

Change, Growth, Development

Six artistic directors – so far – have struggled with the vagaries of the National's theatres. Each had their share of failures and triumphs. Each has sought to make changes to Lasdun's unyielding concrete.

Peter Hall began his tenure by lifting the Olivier stage some 18 inches… an alteration that remains today. Richard Eyre was determined to make changes to both the Olivier and Lyttelton. He was frustrated by the durability of the concrete and the cost of change, but also by Lasdun's open hostility. Grade II* listing in 1994 brought such ambitions to a halt. Later Eyre was to achieve a temporary improvement by converting the Olivier into a theatre-in-the-round stage. However, the consequent seat loss meant this change was a short-term one.

Trevor Nunn sought help from his long-time designer, the brilliant John Napier. They first altered the Olivier by lifting the stage further and moving the whole downstage over the front stalls 'ripple' seating. This covered the drum revolve, making it inoperable; and a huge new lighting bridge around the rear of the acting area further limited staging opportunities. In his last year, Trevor initiated, and personally paid for, a 'Transformation' of the Lyttelton. Initially he sought to convert it into an arena, but the budget limited his options to simply raising the stage, adding an apron, and levelling the auditorium into a single tier, with the addition of temporary seating on scaffolding. Again seat count was diminished by the covering, and so loss of, the rear stalls.

Nick Hytner took a boldly different approach. He revelled in the epic qualities of both the houses, and determined to restore them… In fact, back to the Peter Hall configuration. A bold new production policy, and a revolutionary Travelex sponsored low-cost ticket scheme, worked. A series of smashing productions brought unprecedented artistic and commercial success to the National.

Olivier Theatre

Comments 1976 – 2023

"Sitting in the Olivier auditorium one feels at the centre of more than the National Theatre… the Olivier is cosmic… theatric mundi, theatric orbit, theatric vitae humane (the theatre of the world, global theatre, the theatre of human life)."
Mark Girouard
Architectural writer,
The Architectural Review, January 1977

"Architects think the Olivier is beautiful. And it is. You will also get actors who say they like it. Standing in the middle of that stage they feel fantastic. It's wonderful because it feels intimate. But the actor plays to the stalls, the expensive seats, and forgets three quarters of the theatre. What is so elusive is that nobody quite knows why they are not having a good time."
Declan Donnellan and Nick Ormerod
Making Space for Theatre, 1995

"If you stand on the stage of a 'proper' theatre, there is a circuit of energy flowing out to the audience and back to the performer again. Here the circuit wasn't completed. The energy going out of me did not come back. Instead of being recharged, like a dynamo, I felt like a battery, running down."
Albert Finney
From Peter Lewis, *The National, A Dream Made Concrete*, 1990

"It is an exciting, vibrant sort of space, with a certain magic about it, but it seemed extremely tiring to work in."
Denis Quilley
From Peter Lewis, *The National, A Dream Made Concrete*, 1990

"The huge sweep of the Olivier is frightening at first sight. You have nowhere to hide. It's like a wild animal – you wonder how you're going to control it. It makes you work very hard, using the full range of your voice. But when it's full of people, it can become almost intimate, unlike the Lyttelton. That has none of the contact, physical and emotional, that you get from a traditional proscenium theatre. The hardest thing to play there is comedy."
Michael Gambon
From Peter Lewis, *The National, A Dream Made Concrete*, 1990

"You step on the stage and it feels as though it seats 3000 people – and it only seats 1200. So there's an awful lot of empty air, per member of the audience and per actor onstage."
Roger Allam
Actor

Cottesloe/Dorfman Theatre

Comments 1976-2023

"The Cottesloe is the beating heart of the National."
Ronnie Mulryne and Margaret Shewring,
The Cottesloe at the National, 1999

"It is beyond argument that, for the practitioner, the Cottesloe is the most successful space of the NT's three auditoria. It combines the characteristics most sought by actors and directors: intimacy, good acoustics, lack of pretension, and flexibility of staging."
Sir Richard Eyre

"Our favourite space [is] the Cottesloe. The Cottesloe provides an intimacy (in terms of the distance between the actor and the audience) and it provides an epic dimension as well. It's actually a big stage, and the nature of the space and its flexibility allows you to use the theatre in an epic way, but maintaining an intimacy which we believe theatre absolutely requires."
Declan Donnellan and Nick Ormerod
Making Space for Theatre, 1995

"The Cottesloe offers a particular intimacy. No pause dies. Laughter is infectious and sustained, whereas in larger auditoria laughter often dwindles away like water into sand."
Sir Trevor Nunn
The Cottesloe at the National, 1999

"The Cottesloe is a strong space. There are tensions across the space, which derive from its architecture. It holds its performers in three dimensions, offering a sculptural space to the designer."
Alison Chitty
Designer
The Cottesloe at the National, 1999

Lyttelton Theatre

Comments 1976-2023

"One of the most devastating theatrical experiences of my life… Never before have the Lyttelton's resources been so thrillingly exploited."
Nicholas de Jongh
about *Machinal*, Oct 1993

"The Lyttelton has its problems. It is an extremely audience-unfriendly auditorium. The main problem is that there is no visual or easy aural connection between the stalls and the circle. You can sit in either one and not be aware of the other. In the old Matcham theatres laughter runs round the auditorium like wildfire because the side boxes conduct it. Those boxes are crucial. It's such a pity that the horseshoe and centuries of experience have been neglected."
William Dudley
Designer
Making Space for Theatre, 1995

"It was like exchanging a horse-shoe for a shoebox. The stage felt very wide and the auditorium felt very deep and I didn't feel like me at all."
Albert Finney
From Peter Lewis, *The National, A Dream Made Concrete,* 1990

"The Lyttelton is jinxed with a chilling auditorium and a stage of excessive dimensions, with a reputation for swallowing plays whole."
Michael Radcliffe
British Theatre Design: The Modern Age, 1989

"If you sit in the circle in the Lyttelton, you're completely unaware of there being anyone in the stalls at all except in a comedy you hear this laughter coming from somewhere underneath you."
Roger Allam
Actor

Lyttelton Theatre

Cottesloe/Dorfman Theatre

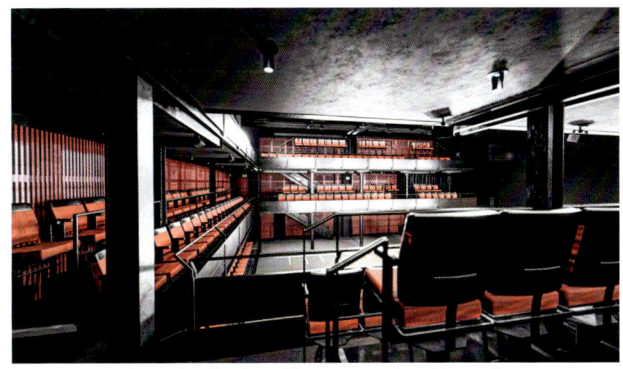

Cottesloe/Dorfman Theatre - rendered image from laser scan

NT Future
The 'Two Nicks' determined to bring overdue improvements to the National's building and facilities. Under the leadership of NT CEO Lisa Burger, architect Steve Tompkins and his team, led by Patrick Dillon, completed a fascinating survey of the physical plant and fabric of the National entitled the *Conservation Management Plan*.

They then decided upon a plan of major renovation and expansion, with a new building, the Max Rayne Centre, incorporating new office and workshop space and a new paint frame, added at the rear in the most obvious external change to the National since its opening. A high level walkway allows the public to view the activity in this workshop. The public areas were extensively refurbished, with a foyer window in the centre of the building moved outwards and facades in the north-east corner opened up to provide new catering facilities. The two main auditoria received technology upgrades, while the Cottesloe was modernised and its seat count expanded, changing its name to the Dorfman Theatre in recognition of a major donor; adjacent areas were adapted to provide new spaces for education or other uses.

The Shed
One of the most striking, albeit temporary, elements of NT Future was the Shed. Designed by Steve Tompkins, it was a 225-seat courtyard theatre on two levels, made in raw steel and plywood, with a bright red, rough-sawn timber exterior to complement Lasdun's board marked concrete. The Shed proved to be an inspiring addition to the National complex.

Today
Rufus Norris inherited a work in progress. His own projects have often brought the Olivier to thrilling and spectacular life. In the Lyttelton, other directors have increasingly seemed to grasp the wide-open challenge to achieve some stunning theatre. 'A Sense of Theatre' can triumph over concrete.

In the 2020 pandemic, the Olivier was once again successfully adapted to in-the-round form, pragmatically optimising seat count to include Covid-driven social distancing. In 2022 another experiment saw the Lyttelton changed to a traverse format, with two single rakes of seating, one rising over the familiar auditorium, the other over the stage. Experimentation, though always temporary, continues at the NT!

The Shed interior

The Shed interior

Michael Billington

Michael is a British author and arts critic. Drama critic of *The Guardian* from 1971 until 2019 – "Britain's longest-serving theatre critic" – and still writing for the newspaper today, he is the author of biographical and critical studies relating to British theatre and the arts. Most notably, he is the authorised biographer of the playwright Harold Pinter.

Michael: Of the new building I remember the opening day, when we saw *Happy Days* in the afternoon in the Lyttelton, and then *Plunder* in the evening. We saw *John Gabriel Borkman* and John Osborne's play, *Watch It Come Down*. That was the first week.

My first impression was of the size of the public space, because we were so used, and we still are, to cramped lobbies, where you jostle, and push, and shove. To walk into a building with that sort of vast arena, where you could mingle and move around – that was a first, and it still hits me whenever I go.

Richard: Lasdun's greatest achievement was his fourth theatre – as he called it.

Michael: The Lyttelton was the first space we saw, which wasn't the best advertisement for the National. But my first impression was it was rather impressive. The limitations of the Lyttelton have grown on me over the years, but the first time, it seemed big, wide, handsome, and it could shift from Peggy Ashcroft, alone on the stage with *Happy Days* – she didn't get lost in that space – to *Hamlet* with Albert Finney a couple of months later.

The more one goes to the Lyttelton, the more one sees it's very hard for directors to handle. Once or twice I've seen designers who didn't know how to design for it.

My impression is Rufus only worked in the Olivier and the Dorfman. I think it's fair that the National does have a proscenium theatre. I just wish it had fewer straight lines, was slightly more curved, horseshoe shaped.

Richard: Denys took it into his head that this was to be a 'theatre of confrontation'. Nobody ever argued with him. I was just doing the technical work, but the Lyttelton really isn't a proscenium at all. The great proscenium theatres are surrounded by audience. They hug the stage.

Michael: That's right. No, it feels geometric. Mathematical really. And designed more quickly than the others.

I remember Peter Hall was getting very incensed by this time wasn't he? I think it was in that first year of the Olivier he said, "It's like working in a village hall." That phrase stuck in my mind, because what he meant was that nothing worked, and if you want to bring on any scenery, you had to shunt it on by hand, because the opulent machinery didn't work.

Richard: Nothing was finished. It was like driving a Jaguar without wheels.

Michael: Peter felt he had been given this hopefully sophisticated, ultra-sophisticated machine, and as you say, it didn't function. He felt angry about that, as you know.

Richard: He was very angry.

Michael: But the first impression of the Olivier was *Tamburlaine*. I thought it was spectacular as a space, and I still do. I love sitting in it. It made it feel it is your space. I think directors don't always know how to use the space,

5.1 Our Theatres Examined in a Changing World

but that's a comment not on the design, but on the state of direction. There was a very good production of *Les Blancs*. The director really knew how to use the circularity of the space, to use entrances, to use the auditorium.

Richard: That was very good, and simple. You don't actually need to fill the Olivier with lots of scenery. People have, and sometimes successfully, but you don't need to.

Michael: And then we move into the Cottesloe, which they opened with *Illuminatus*, Ken Campbell, a day-long event. I just got so tired, I didn't stay the whole day. But again, the immediate impression was a friendly one, and it remained so over the years.

Richard: The Cottesloe remains very much loved…

Michael: I think actors like working in smaller spaces.

Richard: They do, and of course, that's what's happened in our theatre. Theatres like the Almeida and Young Vic.

Michael: And the Donmar, exactly. We talk a lot about flexibility, because the Cottesloe has always been so flexible, hasn't it? You could clear the space. As Bill Bryden did. You could create a mini-proscenium if you wanted to.

Richard: Yes, it really has worked. Theatre Projects have now designed twenty or thirty courtyard theatres around the world.

Michael: Stratford is not one of yours? What they have done is they've got two theatres, which are too similar. There is one in the main theatre, around the same principle anyway. There is no feeling of contrast, so therefore directors and designers are losing the opportunity to use perspective and framed proscenium arch productions.

Richard: The Royal Shakespeare is important in this architectural story, because it was the Elisabeth Scott theatre, where the architectural press adored the building, while the theatre people always loathed it. They fiddled for forty years, and every few seasons, a little bit had been added, but it took eighty years to knock it down and build a new one. I'm not sure of the parallels to the National story. We'll have to wait.

Michael: I think it is good to tinker with the National, but I would just say, the overwhelming impression was a delight that it was there, and it worked. I mean Peter Hall says this quite well in his diaries, doesn't he? He talks about one Saturday, when he says, he looks around. There are three shows playing. The building was brimming with people. He said this is what they were aiming for.

It still seems to me to set an example that going to the theatre for a member of the audience should not be a trial. It should be something that is relatively comfortable to achieve, and you should be able to do all these things like park, eat, have a coffee, meet friends, and see a play. But you try that in the West End, and you're up against so many obstacles. So the National remains a beacon of how theatres could operate. The other thing that's always hit me in contrast to some American cultural palaces is this vitality during the day. I remember years ago being invited to meet the director Peter Sellars in the Washington Kennedy Center. He said, "Let's meet at two on a Wednesday afternoon." So I turned up at two and there was this empty cathedral, foyer is empty. Only a box office clerk. The whole great edifice is dead until seven in the evening. Yet, the National is always alive. I think it's been even more alive recently. I noticed because of those desks they have now got in the main foyer. A lot of people there with laptops. I teach American students, some of them with lodging nearby, and it became their library.

Richard: It's packed all the time. At ten in morning there will be 200 people in the lobby. And then 100 school kids will come in, sit on the floor and have their lunch. It's fabulous.

Michael: It's also the natural place for meeting. I thought to fix up a meeting with a director. Where shall we meet? National Theatre, it's the obvious place just to have a coffee and to chat.

Richard: Lasdun created the capability to have that activity, because the Building Committee had nothing to do with the public areas. That really had his complete carte blanche.

You have the lofty spaces and squashed spaces, and that's what lobbies should offer. The great classic lobbies do that. You can go and hide with your girlfriend in a corner, or you can celebrate.

Michael: I've often wondered, how many marriages have broken up because of the National Theatre, because of people making assignations, with people they shouldn't be meeting; it's really a perfect place to meet.

Richard: Tell me about other theatres. Does your heart lift at some and drag a little at others?

Michael: I think the Young Vic is a good space. It's intelligently used. It is generally flexible, and there is always an element of mystery and surprise when you go in. Under the David Lan regime; he changes the space almost every production, and that's exciting.

Richard: Audiences love that.

Michael: The original Tricycle was one of yours? Again a very simple courtyard space, wasn't it.

Richard: Yes, it really was beautiful.

Michael: I go there with pleasure. I think there are some successful smaller spaces. I like the Donmar. The Almeida. I think one sits there with pleasure, because it keeps the sort of rough rawness of the building.

Richard: That's important. Places have to have memory, don't they, I think theatre architecture is about much more than technical sightlines, acoustic issues, it's atmosphere. Peter Brook says the most important thing in a theatre is atmosphere.

Michael: Well Peter, with the Bouffe du Nord he found it. I'm not a great fan of most West End theatres, the Haymarket is an obvious exception. It's a beautiful space.

I find the Crucible in Sheffield has a welcoming quality. I mean it's very hard to disassociate the theatre from the work, because you know, the Crucible has had a distinguished line of directors and the work has been first rate, so one goes there with pleasure.

Richard: That's right. How do you find the Barbican?

Michael: With difficulty. [Laughter] That's always a cheap answer. I don't know. There is too much space above the stage, isn't there? I mean there's nothing wrong with the stage, but it seems a huge volume.

Richard: The balconies are both claustrophobic and vertigo-inducing.

Michael: It depends where you sit, I get my seats in the seventh row and I have a good time, but I teach American students, and I insisted that they go there. I said, "You've got to go to the Barbican and you've got to see the RSC. Go to see Antony Sher in *Henry IV*, So they dutifully go and because they've booked far too late, they got seats up in the top level, towards the side. I've never had such an angry group of students, who said that from those top side seats they, A, they could see right into the wings. They could see everything the stage manager was doing. B, They couldn't see the whole stage. The sightlines were absolutely appalling. So next time, I insisted they've got to have seats in the stalls. Otherwise, you just turn them off the whole experience. It's not a friendly space. Those automatic doors closing you in. There is no escape now. The Olivier feels intimate. The Barbican doesn't.

Richard: How do you react to the growth of NT Live and all that, the video versions of everything?

Michael: NT Live is a great idea, a revolutionary thing about the theatre that's happened in my lifetime. Because obviously the objection to theatre was, it was only available to the few. Now it is available to pretty much anyone who wants it in most parts of the world. I think it's just fantastic. I don't go much to NT Live, because I've seen the shows. I go quite a lot to Opera Live. The Royal Opera House or the Metropolitan. I find the experience utterly delightful. I think that the availability of theatre is astonishing.

Giles Havergal

Director

"I learnt the most from Giles Havergal, who gave me my first job at the Citizens Theatre, Glasgow. On most evenings, Giles instinctively stood at the front of his theatre with the humblest employees, the ticket-takers, welcoming the audience as if they were part of his company. Everything was contained within that one old building, and the crown touched the feet so to speak; the governor walked amongst us, all of us, knew us all by name. I relate this tangential history of Mr Havergal as he seems to me always to have been the finest director of a theatre I have ever encountered, because he made a true circle of the audience and artists, inspired I propose by the architecture of his old theatre." [1]

Mark Rylance, Actor. First artistic director of Shakespeare's reconstructed Globe Theatre.

Giles is a theatre and opera director and actor, teacher, and adaptor. He was artistic director of Glasgow's Citizens Theatre — a fine example of the traditional style of theatre design the National rejected — from 1969 until he stepped down in 2003, one of the theatre's triumvirate of directors alongside Philip Prowse and Robert David MacDonald.

Richard: I'm writing this book about the confusions that exist between theatre and architecture. I find both the big theatres at the National somewhat flawed; however, forty years on, the National Theatre Company is incredibly successful – I think the moral is that theatre people make things work!

Giles: So you might say that if we're going do a theatre, you can give us a building that doesn't work at all, and we'll make it work. I suppose that probably is true, but I can't help thinking that isn't quite right at the National. I'm amazed that the audience still goes to the Olivier, really, because it's such a disconcerting experience. You kind of don't want to look at anything, unless it's on a colossal scale.

Why was it that there was clearly no problem with the architect who built the Citizens Theatre Glasgow, a perfect auditorium? There are theatres up and down the country. I take it mostly old, or is that being fuddy-duddy? Are there some modern ones, where you just go, whoop?

Richard: No, there are no modern theatres as good as the best of Matcham. Campbell Douglas was the architect of Her Majesty's, which is what the Citz in Glasgow used to be called. I'd never heard of him.

Giles: Was it because in those days there were many more theatres being built and pulled down or burnt down? It was much more of the stock and trade of a specialist architect, "I do churches. I do theatres," whereas now it's Zaha Hadid turning her guns on the idea of a theatre. Isn't it now architects suddenly going, "Theatre?" And theatre design should be such a specific trade.

Richard: Yes. That is a very large reason. There were architects who specialised in building theatres. So, if you were an owner and you wanted a theatre, you wouldn't dream of going to…

Giles: … the person that was building the town hall.

Richard: It wouldn't occur to you. You'd go to a theatre architect. But the other thing was that there was a solid tradition that had evolved since Shakespeare. It really began with the Elizabethan theatre, which evolved, up until the late 19th century. If you wanted a theatre, you wouldn't dream of making it triangular or concrete. You would respect the theatres that worked. A theatre architect built what he knew would work, and the owner would demand that, too.

Giles: It was a much more artisan concept. It had to look nice from the outside, but it didn't have to be an architectural gem. It had to fit in with the high street in which it was being built.

Richard: That's correct. There was an evolving tradition in specialist theatre architects, and owners, who knew what they wanted, which generally was as many seats as possible on a tiny site. That was the brief.

Giles: But isn't it odd that so many worked? I mean, the other theatre I work in, which is also 1878, is the Grand Theatre, Leeds. I only do opera there, but I take it it works for plays as well.

Richard: Amazingly, yes. I mean, it's one of those wonderful cross-over theatres, magical.

Giles: Theatre Royal Glasgow is another.

Richard: But what is that magic? They were brilliant at condensing, collecting and creating a room that wrapped the audience and the artists together. Michael Elliott, the director whom I worshipped, said that the audience should be wrapped round the artists like a scarf round your head on a cold winter's day. It's a lovely phrase.

Giles: Yes. It's lovely. And that's what he did at the Royal Exchange. So, what're you asking me?

Richard: Clearly the Citizens is an amazing part of your life, and, as you said, it is a beautiful space.

Giles: I've just been looking this morning at a documentary that went out on the 70th anniversary of the Citz moving to the Gorbals theatre. In it, Philip Prowse says, "I was taken up there to see the theatre, and I just thought it is the most beautiful, the most excellent drama theatre in the country." And I was hooked. And when people said to me after my 28th or 30th year, "Why are you still here?" I just used to take them in and show them the auditorium, and just say, "Well, there's the answer."

Citizens Theatre Glasgow in 2014

Of course, the secret was you could do an epic, *Tamburlaine* and things like that. We did things like pushing the stage through the proscenium arch over the orchestra pit, so there was a sense of the epic, but you could also do Pinter. You could do tiny, tiny things. And I don't know another theatre where you could do both really easily. You can do a one-man show there no problem, and when you want to open it up and do the big guns, to do your Marlowe or your Shakespeare or Schiller, you can do it.

Richard: The Cottesloe is a small space and can be extremely intimate, but can be epic as well. That's a lot to do with the verticality, I think that that's very important.

Giles: Papering the walls with the audience, yes.

Knowing I was going to be talking to you, I wondered where 'in-the-round' fits into this conversation. I take it that the agony between the architect and the demands of the theatre really becomes public when you're trying to build something like a pros arch or a thrust. If you're in the round, your problems are, well, not exactly solved, but you have whole different sets of problems.

Richard: So much in theatre design is related to how many people have to be seated in the auditorium. A hundred people is one thing; a thousand is totally different.

Giles: I think the Orange Tree – which is one of Iain and yours, isn't it? I think that's lovely.

Richard: Lovely, yes. Small is beautiful.

Giles: Small is beautiful, absolutely.

Now when I work at ACT, when I work at RADA – I do everything in the round now. It's just so easy. You just put the chairs out, let them sit there and get on with it.

Richard: Then there's the whole Guthrie influence with the thrust stage.

Giles: What's your view on that vis-à-vis the conflict between architecture and theatre?

Richard: I think that the form of the theatre, the actor-audience relationship is quite separate. I mean, you can have a wonderful thrust-stage theatre or a lousy thrust-stage theatre.

Giles: The point you're really making is that surely there must be some symbiosis between architecture, and that's where you come in, isn't it?

Richard: That's meant to be our role, yes.

Giles: Isn't this the point that you're making, that a theatre is not the place to go to for a star architect, because a theatre is basically a practical building and that actually for Leicester Council to go to that very grand guy who was completely wrong – they should've got Joe Soap from up the road who's a good theatre architect.

Are there the equivalent of Mr. Campbell, who built the Citizens? Are there jobbing architects who you now would say, "I've got this friend. He's not at all famous, but he lives in Montreal, and he is really good at theatres"?

Richard: There are. I've worked with probably a hundred and fifty architects, and there are maybe four or five…

Giles: I take it that's your job. If the architect gets it wrong, you've got to come up with a design. You've got to do the architect's job.

Richard: Architects rather like to be told their buildings are great successes. The fact it wasn't them that actually designed the room, that's easily forgotten.

Giles: What did happen between the temporary theatre in Stratford and the permanent one, which now exists? Why did one work and the other not? I've been to both, so I know. Somehow that first one I thought, "Oh, God, this is gonna be terrible," but it sort of worked. But by the time I went to the second one, every seat – I sat in two different seats at the matinee, in the evening, and they were both no good.

Richard: It's very complicated. But in principal it's the completely opposite situation. This was not the architect going off on an architectural folly. It was the theatre that wanted something mistaken.

Giles: More seats?

Richard: I believe the theatre consultant should've said, "You can't do it." I call the form a 'narrow-bodied' courtyard. It's like the Cottesloe, narrow galleries and a thrust stage. I think you can possibly go to maybe six – or seven hundred.

Giles: I mean, there're a lot of seats in which you really can't see.

Richard: Can't see anything, and it's really cleverly worked out to optimise the view, but they're still horrible seats.

The fascinating thing is you look at the Globe, which I call a wide-bodied courtyard.

Giles: The real Southwark Globe?

Richard: Yes, the real Globe works in many ways amazingly well, because it's wider. You get to the question of what would you actually do with the Olivier. To me, the Olivier, the stage is interesting, but it's set in a football field of an auditorium. You want to take all that audience and bring everyone up, forward and closer to the stage.

Giles: Yes. Actually, the Lyttelton, the same. If you're in the circle of the Lyttelton, you are a long way from the stage. Downstairs is not too bad, actually. Even at the back downstairs you feel involved.

I saw *One Man, Two Guvnors* from there, and it didn't work. I was upstairs, and I was with another theatre director. We both said the press were in row six downstairs, and I'm sure it was fantastic, but it really didn't work from above. I mean, brilliant bits, of course, but as an evening – it was all going on 'over there'.

But then are we all going to be saying that this thing we have called drama cannot be played to these very big numbers? See, where does that leave Her Majesty's or the Haymarket?

Richard: Her Majesty's is a wondrous theatre. I've spent many years there, both as a stage manager and as producer.

Giles: Could one ever do plays at Her Majesty's? I saw *Amadeus* there, didn't I, or is it too big?

Richard: It's on the edge, isn't it, but you can go with a big-ish play.

Giles: But then why, with these examples of big auditoriums that work – why are they constantly building big auditoriums that don't work. I mean, Leicester – how big is Leicester?

Richard: Leicester's 900. But, the problem with Leicester – I mean, it's the dressing-room access thing, and the ridiculous lobby going all round everything. But the two auditorium are both poor as well. The larger space is a poor imitation of the Lyttelton, and the smaller of the Cottesloe. In both cases the balconies are too high and remote.

Theatre Royal Haymarket, London, in 1994

Her Majesty's (now His Majesty's) Theatre, London, in 2010 - where your author took his first professional job in theatre

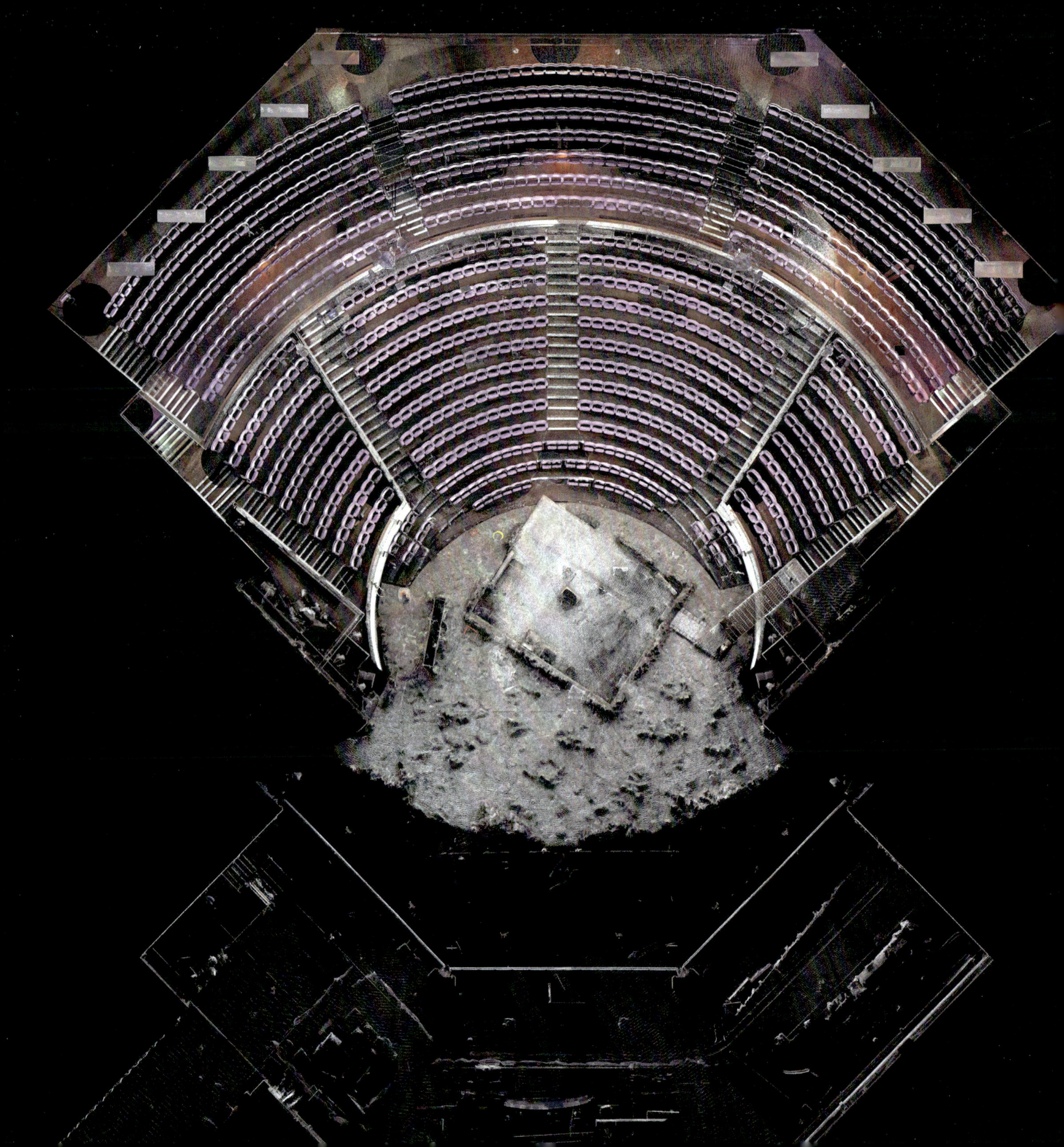

5.2 The Shape of Theatre

The Dorfman - laser scan

The National was an attempt in the 1960s to create a theatre of the future. Then our theatrical heritage, represented by the West End, seemed only old fashioned. Today, the essential ingredient of live performance, an intimate actor/audience relationship, looms larger. Ever-growing competition from other media and the explosion of the fringe and other forms of dramatic storytelling make re-examination of the form of theatre newly relevant. Comparative theatre studies have served to guide theatre architects since the 18th century. Today new technologies allow ever more detailed appraisal of the shape of theatres intended to create a more dramatic future.

Comparative Studies
It was in 1767 that Frenchman Pierre Patti first wrote on theatre architecture and published comparative plans of contemporary theatres. This was followed by Dumont in 1774, and over a hundred years later Edwin Sachs with his three encyclopedic volumes: *Modern Opera Houses and Theatres*. Leading theatre architects during the late 18th century were specialists, specialists in designing theatres, and they diligently studied the work of their peers.

The success of the work of Matcham and Phipps in the UK, Fellner & Helmer in Europe, McElfatrick, Lamb and Krapp in the USA, all attested to the benefits of expertise. They followed the well-worn path of tradition, but at the same time embraced changing building technologies, growing market demands, and the evermore pressing dictates of fire and safety regulation. The result, theatres that even today are admired for their intimacy, atmosphere, and even acoustics half a century before formal science in that elusive skill emerged.

The So-called 'Modern Era'
In Part 1.2 we saw how, in the latter years of the 19th century, a reaction to the then perceived frivolous Victorian period of architecture produced change. Led by Wagner, the 'new theatre' movement sought pure frontal sightlines and eschewed decoration. 'Engineered theatre' replaced intimacy and atmosphere. From the early 1920s, modernism, coupled with the impact of cinema, contrived to make frontally oriented theatres with minimal decoration almost universal. Then came the global destruction of World War II.

The Sixties
The post World War II period was one of slow recovery from the impact of war and austerity. But by the 1960s a new

Exterior of the National Theatre, view from the west, 2008

optimism and exuberance had taken hold. Rebuilt cities seemed to offer a new hope; tired and run-down sections of those cities seemed ripe for the developer's wrecking ball. In London ancient areas such as the Covent Garden Market saw plans for wholesale demolition, to be replaced by dreams of a new commercial and tourist 'paradise' of soaring skyscrapers and modern architecture. Thankfully that new world failed to materialise before public tastes changed.

In 1962, Sir Laurence led a small group of actors to West End theatres to conduct an experiment for the new National Theatre for which planning was about to start. He would stand onstage, in the New (now Coward) Theatre, Wyndham's and others, while we acolytes would run out with tape measures. How far away might an audience be placed before they were beyond his visual, aural and emotional grasp? He came to a conclusion: anyone seated more than 19.8m, 65' away could not enjoy a quality experience. That dimension set the parameters that dictated the Olivier and Lyttelton theatres. Otherwise those West End theatres attracted only condemnation: the dressing rooms were squalid, the bars preposterously inadequate, and the loos… disgusting.

Of their architecture, we took little notice. It was to be another thirty years before the virtues of that Matcham-led period began to be appreciated. For your author it was to be a decade before he awoke.

A New Architect
When the search for an architect for the National began, the post-war building of theatres had just begun. And with very mixed results. The lessons of tradition had been lost and the general opinion about architecture amongst the building committee members was a low one. The recent early regional rep theatres were deemed to be barely adequate and there was a general desire for new beginnings.

Denys Lasdun seemed to fill the bill… An architect of obvious skill, he professed to be quite innocent about theatre and eager to learn from the committee of 'experts.'

What could go wrong?

Lasdun did begin by briefly examining a few existing theatres. The company were playing at Chichester and the Old Vic. Committee member Michel Saint-Denis was involved in the emerging Vivian Beaumont Theater in New York. Germany, coming to the end of their astonishing post-war building boom, had built dozens of theatres; one, Gelsenkirchen, had attracted acclaim. Lasdun created scale drawings of all these, but the committee's focus was upon the new.

So followed twenty-four months of discussion. As Lasdun acknowledged in a 1996 interview: "None of them agreed with each other anyhow, they all had very differing views. Some of it contradictory, some of it maddening, and some of it so to the point that you had to re-read what they said several times until you had got the point."

But our new architect, albeit eager to learn, could also misunderstand. It is a cliché to say that a little knowledge can lead to error. Coupled with a sense of over-confidence, quite natural in an architect of principle, mistakes could be rendered into concrete. Confusion in the client body was unlikely to help.

Lasdun seized upon a phrase of Saint-Denis' that in fact, according to the minutes, he misheard. Saint-Denis is actually reported as saying: "What I am dreaming about is a space stage that would give a feeling of audience and actors being in the same room."

Thirty-four years later Lasdun remembered, "Saint-Denis, who suddenly said, 'You know, what I'm dreaming about is a space theatre, like a room.' That was probably one of the most highly charged statements that was made during the whole period, and I dwelt on it, and in the end, having had to go through the hoops with designing an all-purpose theatre, and dismissing it as not being any good, we then had the long road, which lasted eighteen months, of searching for what was to be finally the Olivier Theatre. And indeed what it is, is a room, but it had to be arrived at from the long haul of discussion, minutes taken, reading them, but you know, I must pay tribute to the man who said, 'I'm dreaming about a room'. It's fascinating. Maybe he didn't realise what he was talking about, that doesn't really matter; it's what he felt he wanted to say."

But Lasdun decided upon this concept, not of 'a feeling' but of a literal 'room' (Scheme B) after only two meetings of the committee. He persisted with it for two years, despite increasing criticism until, quite reluctantly, abandoning it after the committee rejected his concept in the summer of 1966.

Unchangeable Theatre
The National is made of concrete, a material that gives strength and density, and in the public areas, a quite wonderful character from the wood-grain texture.

But theatres need to change. In Shakespeare's time, the first Rose was replaced after five years by the second, for apparently quite mundane reasons: to increase the audience head count, and the needs of backstage storage. The first Globe burnt down in 1613, and was replaced by an improved second theatre a year later. This began a pattern of continuing replacement that lasted four hundred years. Almost all theatres were regularly destroyed and rebuilt, or at least had their interiors regularly remodelled.

Theatre is the most mercurial of the arts. The building that houses it must change over time as the demands of writers, directors, artists, and the fickle public changes. Art simply does change… continuously.

The Olivier Theatre
Throughout the deliberations about what became the Olivier Theatre, it was referred to as the Open Stage. Sir Laurence's hope was for a Chichester-style thrust stage, but modified. He disliked audience to either side of him, looking across the stage to each other, so he stipulated that the seating should extend no further than 118 degrees around.

Lasdun's fixation upon a room led to the stage in the corner of a square room. The demands of stagecraft (for which your author drew the initial concept plan) opened one corner of that room to a world beyond. The result is a very large space with side walls fundamentally at right angles to each other and a very long distance apart. The geometry of Lasdun's faceted ceiling, coupled with the large stage and fly tower (for which I was also responsible), results in an enormous volume, far greater than ideal for a space intended for drama and the un-amplified human voice. Within this over-large space the audience is spread quite widely and, in particular, the circle is overly far from the stage, making the space even larger. 1100 people are in a volume as large as the Theatre Royal Drury Lane, which seats a thousand people more.

The resultant 'modified thrust stage' is today's Olivier. The flexible wide-open stage that surrounds the foreshortened thrust allows exceptional opportunity. Stripped bare for Greek tragedy or filled with an evocation of war in the trenches of the Somme, it allows powerful visual effect. Tightly focusing on the actor on the semi-thrust can achieve a brilliant balance: stories told by actors within a panoramic world, perhaps unlike any other theatre.

The whole *can* spring to life – executed with sufficient flair and brio, a sufficient Sense of Theatre can win… or upon occasion, lose.

The Lyttelton Theatre
Lasdun's idea of a 'theatre of confrontation' was an architectural conceit. Without input from the building committee, and in reaction against their confusing advice, Lasdun alone decided that this was to be the opposite of the open stage Olivier. He (and it must be added, apparently our distinguished committee) was unaware of how the design of proscenium theatres had gradually evolved over three hundred years. He saw physical confrontation to be the way forward. Straight rows facing a wide, flat-sided stage, and an anonymously dark coloured, adjustable, proscenium. Despite murmurings of discontent from the committee, Lasdun elected for bare-concrete side walls, and an almost straight, distant, circle that divides the audience into two; those above and those below. Again, the exceptional width of the room, the parallel concrete side walls, the distant circle, and the multiple overhead lighting bridges that break up the ceiling, all contribute to making a challenging acoustic environment. Long rows of continental

seating without aisles, and no seating on the side walls, militate against an easy sense of audience community.

Influenced by architectural trends from the 1930s, such as Elisabeth Scott's Shakespeare theatre in Stratford, both theatres ignored the challenge of audience-to-audience awareness and audience-actor intimacy.

Silence and Acoustics
Several of the interviews throughout this book have touched on the complex sound and acoustic issues. Styles of performance and actors' vocal abilities, of course, change over time – as do audience's ability to listen. In the 1970s considerable efforts were initially made to achieve a quiet environment. The concrete construction was intended to create a solid low noise environment; with quiet air-conditioning, and low-noise stage equipment. Unfortunately, as technology has changed, background noise has increased. The introduction of moving lights added the noise of fans and motors, the use of large-scale projection brought even noisier video projectors, and more recently, changes in stage mechanisation have led to an even higher 'noise floor.' All these things militate against actor audibility. Sound designer Paul Arditti, in an October 2018 letter[2], reiterated his plea to his fellow designers to take a more aggressive stand against excessive equipment noise. Silence, and darkness, are both key starting points in creating a sympathetic and intimate storytelling environment.

The Olivier and Lyttelton Compared
The following pages compare the scale of the Olivier and Lyttelton to two traditional West End theatres of similar seat count. Of course, the Olivier was intended to be a new and very different type of theatre, a 'modified thrust stage.' Modified in two ways: first by having the audience surround of the stage reduced to 118 degrees from an actor standing at the 'point of command,' as opposed to 180 degrees of, say, the full thrust as at the Sheffield Crucible. Second by surrounding the thrust with the capability of a 'full scenic environment'. The reduction of surround led to a flattening of the Olivier stage compared to a full 'Guthrie' thrust. While the Olivier stage edge is able to be reshaped as a production may require, it is today often

made even flatter than in the Lasdun drawing below. But the examinations overleaf look at how an audience might be disposed around a stage whatever the shape. While four levels of seating would be unacceptable today, a tighter multi-level audience surround with side ledges might enhance intimacy and improve acoustics.

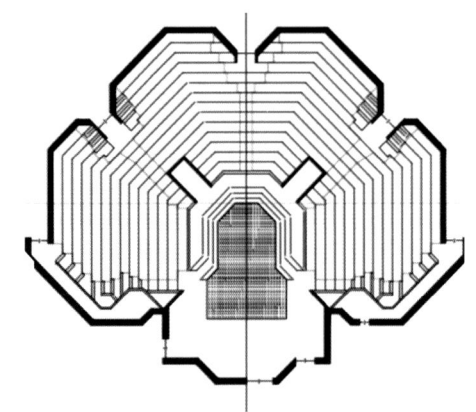

The Crucible, Sheffield

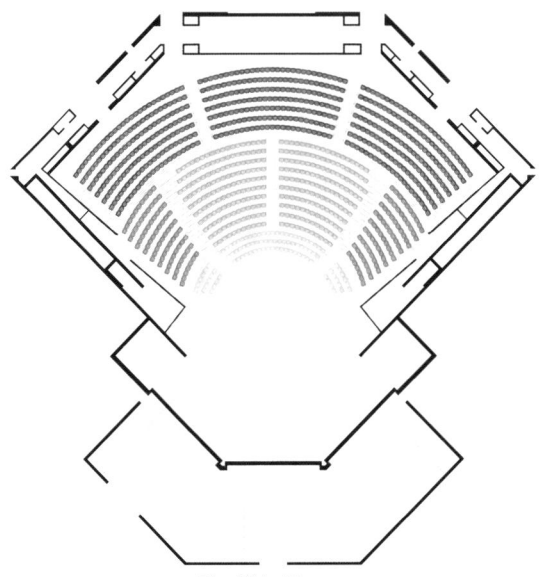

The Olivier Theatre

5.2 The Shape of Theatre

Olivier

These 3D laser scans illustrate the Olivier Theatre and compare it to a 'classic' West End house, the Novello by W.G.R. Sprague from 1905, previously known as the Strand Theatre. Both seat an almost identical quantity of around 1100 people. The difference is immediately apparent.

Whatever powerful visual impact the Olivier possesses, the acoustics remain a real challenge. The vast volume, the distant walls and lack of any reflective acoustic surfaces within a reasonable distance of the performers, present huge problems. As actors move about the vast stage, obviously turning in many directions, the acoustic effect of the reflective surfaces (already compromised by distance) changes. The huge near-stage ceiling panel reflects an actor's voice to the circle, when he, or she, is standing downstage centre, but that reflection is immediately lost as they move upstage. The same surface however brilliantly reflects the sound of the audience back to themselves, accidentally, if quite pleasantly, raising the audience's pre-show anticipation.

Various methods of amplification support have been tried and rejected. Extensive efforts have been made to encourage actors' vocal training, which has often made significant improvement. But finally, most productions in recent years have employed amplification with personal radio microphones, a development regretted by many actors but generally accepted as unavoidable.

Olivier   Novello

Olivier
capacity 1160

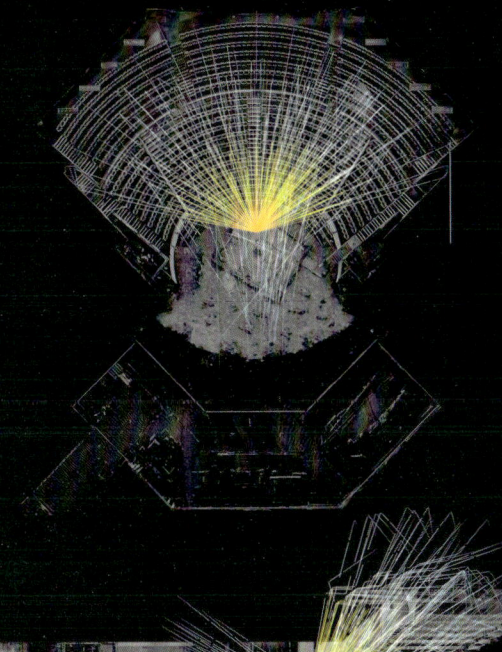

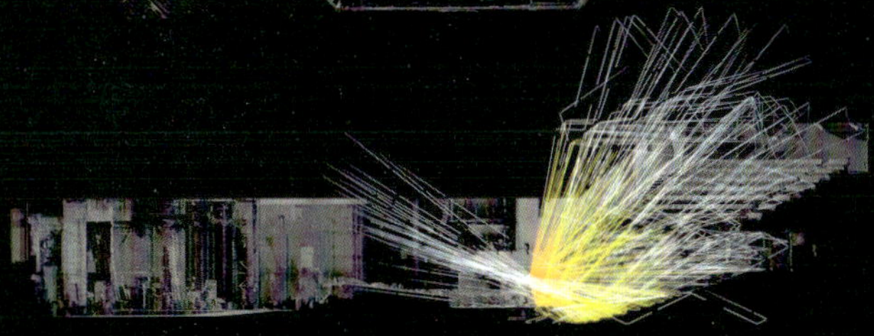

Axonometric View
The Olivier and Novello have comparable seat counts but very different spatial characteristics. The Olivier is larger in plan and occupies a bigger volume. The furthest seat is 25m (82ft) from the stage and there is 10m³ (353ft³) of volume per seat. The furthest seat in the Novello is 23m (75ft) from the stage and there is 5m³ (176ft³) of volume per seat.

The volume per seat has implications for the room's acoustics

Novello
capacity 1105

Acoustics
"Where the Olivier went wrong acoustically, it was the wrong shape to start with, and it could never work. That's completely inherent to the shape of the room, so getting back to the theatre consultant, the acoustician, the architect starting off together. That's really important, because the acoustician can stop that initial framework being all wrong."
Richard Cowell, Acoustician

Olivier – distance to stage

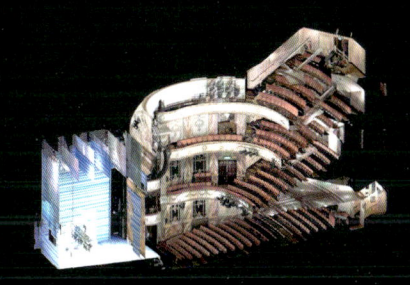

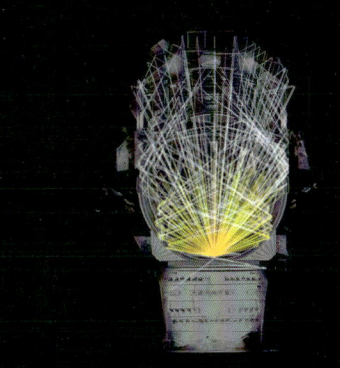

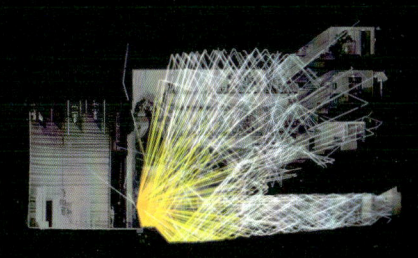

Novello – distance to stage

Lyttelton

These 3D laser scans illustrate the Lyttelton Theatre and compare it to a 'classic' West End house, the Noël Coward from 1905, also by W.G.R. Sprague and previously known as the Albery, and before that the New Theatre. Both seat 900-or-so people. The difference is immediately apparent.

Lasdun's theory of confrontation created a flat, two-level auditorium that divides the audience into two. The almost straight circle and lack of side boxes make the room seem more cinema than theatre. The traditional form that had evolved in the 19th century from the Elizabethan, then Georgian, courtyard theatre into the splendid intimacy of Matcham and Sprague, whose auditoria seem almost to hug the performer in three dimensions, was lost.

The Lyttelton's stage, unique in Britain, has both full-size side and rear stages, the latter with a disk-revolve wagon. The fully trapped floor is also four elevators. The three to the front can create an orchestra pit, whilst the fourth allows the whole stage to be raked or lowered to orchestra stalls level. A two-part safety curtain both rises and falls allowing the stage height to be modified for a production.

The width of the proscenium was derived from the width of the forestage in the Old Vic under Sir Laurence. A false proscenium, adjustable in height and width and able to be moved up and down stage was intended to provide enhanced flexibility, but the stalls seating width militates against narrowing the opening very far. This flexibility coupled with the side and rear stages has made the Lyttelton a theatre capable of considerable spectacle, yet small scale drama can feel overwhelmed by the theatre's flatness and excess width.

Tight vertical sightlines to the stage edge make advancing the actor through the proscenium almost impossible, again a consequence of the almost straight circle front. Thus a powerful characteristic of a more conventional proscenium theatre, crossing the line of the proscenium and advancing into the audience, is lost.

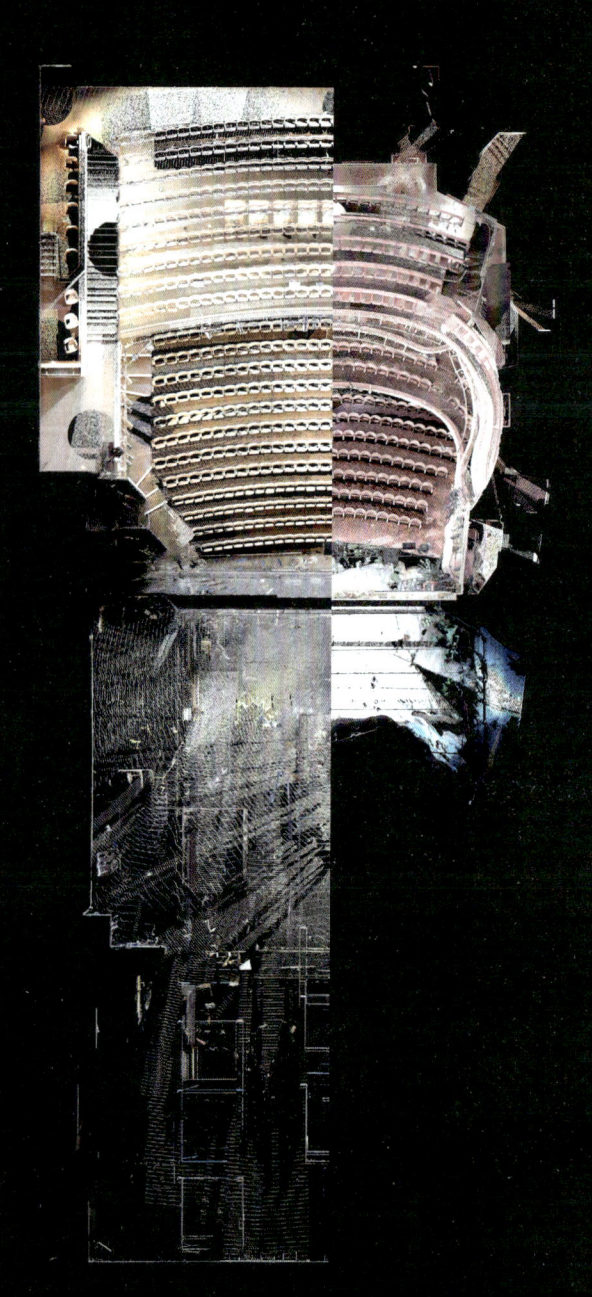

Lyttelton   Noël Coward

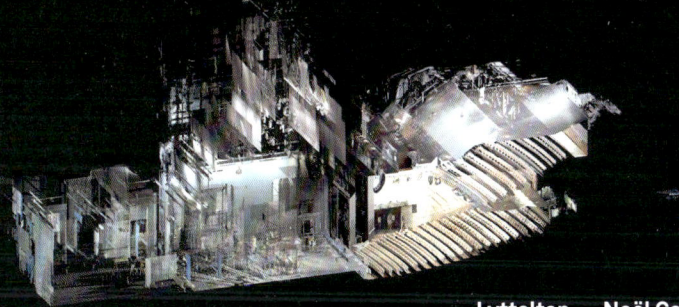

Lyttelton
capacity 897

Noël Coward
capacity 952

Lyttelton stage, view from the stalls

Noël Coward stage, view from the stalls

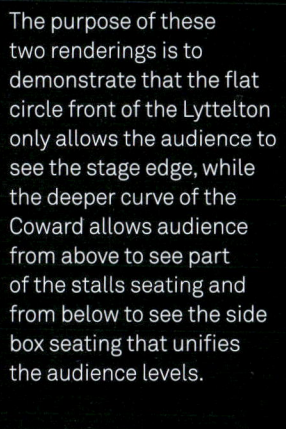

Lyttelton auditorium, view from the circle

Noël Coward auditorium, view from the circle

The purpose of these two renderings is to demonstrate that the flat circle front of the Lyttelton only allows the audience to see the stage edge, while the deeper curve of the Coward allows audience from above to see part of the stalls seating and from below to see the side box seating that unifies the audience levels.

The almost straight circle and seating rows of the Lyttelton target the downward sightline to the stage edge. Audiences' peripheral vision is filled with the almost black proscenium and board-marked concrete sidewalls. The Coward allows the actor to break through the line of the proscenium and still be seen advancing into the audience chamber. The actor in the Lyttelton is confined behind the flat stage edge.

Denys Lasdun's preliminary sketch for Genoa

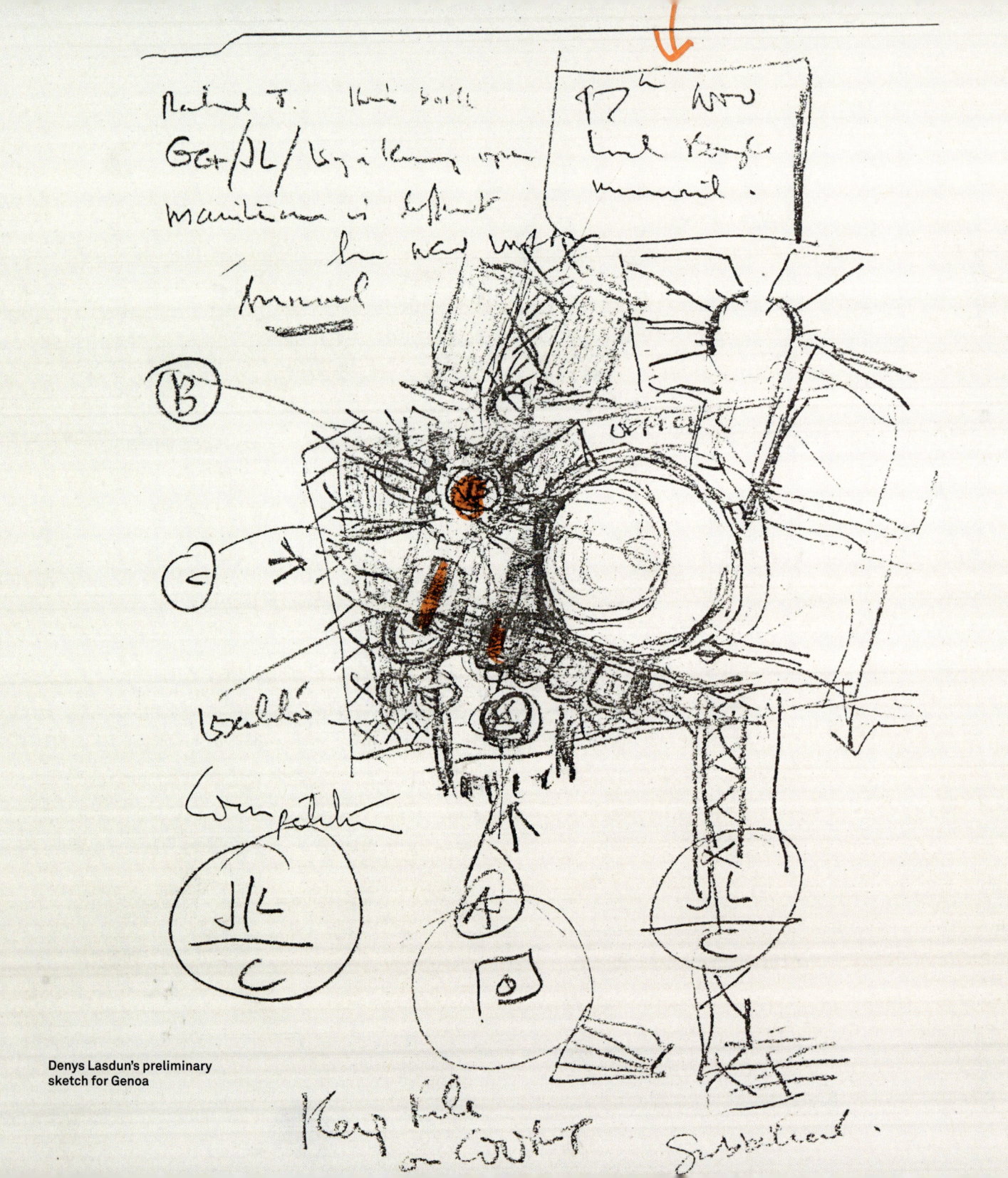

5.3 Genoa: A Design Revolution

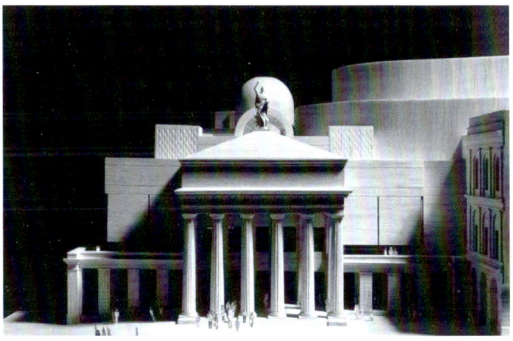

The pronaos surviving from the earlier Genoa opera house incorporated into Denys Lasdun's proposed scheme

Five years after the National opens, a reconciliation – and a new adventure.

Denys Lasdun initiates an historic innovation: a new collaboration in theatre design.

A little history is made, though sadly not actually built, in Italy.

Five years after the tempestuous 1976 opening of the National, an Italian tempest irrupted over theatre architecture in the Lasdun office. Public awareness of the lasting success of Matcham-style boxes and balconies begins to be recognised only after 1980 with the successful reopening of the Theatre Royal Nottingham. The Manchester Royal Exchange and London's Young Vic fuel enthusiasm for something new. What was to come in theatre architecture?

Since that wet and bedraggled night at the Olivier Theatre when Her Majesty arrived to open the National, Sir Denys – as he had become – and I were not friends. Despite a good working relationship over the stages and architectural lighting, our relationship had soured over the Olivier fly tower, which he had only reluctantly accepted; but, in his eyes, a more egregious sin had been that the press was crediting one of my team, Iain Mackintosh, with the design of the Cottesloe Theatre.

Denys was furious. We were accused of deliberately seeking to undermine his position, and for a while there was even talk of legal action between DL&P and Theatre Projects.

So I was surprised when, in 1981, he invited me to his office. I was pleased, but curious.

We met and he invited me to sit down. "Richard," he said, "you and I have not always seen eye to eye. I've been giving this a lot of thought. With the National at last finished, I think I've worked out what you do! You know about theatre, I am an architect. Would you care to join me in collaborating on an international competition for an opera house to be built in Genoa?"

I was delighted. But I explained that, for me too, the NT had been a massive learning experience. We did know about theatre; indeed, I thought that I had, quite recently, stumbled upon a very fundamental principle of theatre design… that the audience play a vital role, and that the relationship between actor and audience was central. Accordingly, we at TPC had begun to initiate our design concepts with simple sketches for the architect that began by exploring that fundamental principle of audience participation and intimacy, to help our colleagues set out on the right path.

So what was an opera house? A place for musical theatre; of lots of music and lots of theatre. The Royal Opera House Covent Garden had been our kindergarten, its classic Italian Opera principles lay at the heart of all opera worldwide. Might a resurrection of the classic opera house be the key to a new model?

I'd had an early-learning crash-course in opera operations on a large scale. In 1961 my friend Bill Bundy, Technical Director of the Royal Opera House (and later of the National), had employed us as they began their exploration of how to modernise that magnificent theatre in Covent Garden. We reported directly to Sir John Tooley, the General Director. It was a six-month adventure, studying every aspect of this massive operation: large-scale opera and ballet in repertory. No architect had yet been appointed and we were to explore the preliminary options for expanding the site into the neighbouring, still operating, fruit and vegetable market. Our study was a day-and-night round the clock activity examining every aspect of operations. Our most significant contribution was persuading the powers that be to cancel the demolition of the neighbouring historic Floral Hall, and convert it to an extended foyer-space as an elegant lobby extension, to be surrounded by a hugely enlarged side-stage, scene-dock, load-in and storage area.

The original National project on the South Bank had included an opera house, before Theatre Projects had become involved. A sketch design was prepared by DL&P with input from representatives from Sadler's Wells Opera. The DL&P scheme was for a three-level proscenium theatre with wide, deeply curved, overhanging stepped balconies, of which glimpses can perhaps be caught in the famous photograph of discarded models of the National. It promised, I fear, problematic acoustics and sightlines. Perhaps fortuitously, the Treasury deleted this from the NT project to reduce the capital cost.

After a productive meeting in Genoa with our hoped-for future Italian colleagues, we agreed with the opera company that we should adopt the classic horseshoe model inspired by the founding opera tradition of the original Genoa Opera House by Carlo Barabino in 1828.

With support from Bill Bundy of the Royal Opera House, from the American acoustician Russell Johnson, and aided by a young architect in our office, Paul Jenkins, we began to developed a classic five-level horseshoe opera house of 2000 seats with balconies subtly inclined toward the stage. The original classic Italian horseshoe, like La Scala, had horizontal balconies with raked stages. The 20th century however had brought flat floor stages and seen several rebuilds after World War II, but two examples, in Munich and Dresden, gently sloped the sides of the horseshoe downward toward the new stages making a subtle but significant side sightline improvement.

Our Team consisted of:

Contractor Impresa CATTANEO Emilio & Figlio

PROGRETTO ARCHITTECTONICO
SIR DENYS LASDUN CBE RIBA In collaborations con
DOTT. ING. MARCO, DASSO DOTT. ARCH. ALBERTO PONIS

IMPIANTI TERTRALI
RICHARD PILBROW FRSA, RICHARD BRETT B.Sc (Eng)
of Theatre Projects Consultants Ltd.

TECHNICA ACUSTICA
RUSSELL JOHNSON B.ARCH of Artec Consultants

I'm going to invite our project designer, now retired, Paul Jenkins, to describe the development of Genoa in partnership with Denys Lasdun & Partners.

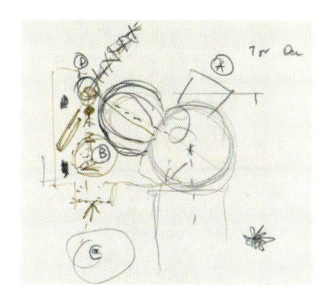

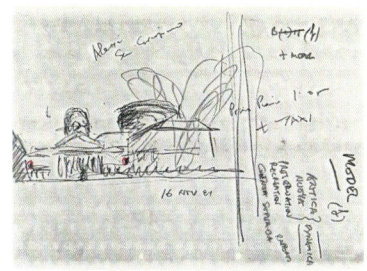

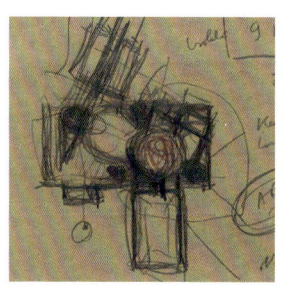

"The Genoa opera house was originally built in the late 18th century to a design by Carlo Barabino (1768-1835) and was one of the great opera houses of Europe.

"The building was bombed by the RAF in 1944-ish, destroying the auditorium and stage but the portico (the Pronaos) facing the small square it fronted survived, again another key component of the later scheme. It is possible that the bombardier on the bomber was none other than a colleague, I remember only as Stefan [Kuszell], a Polish exile and Lasdun's right hand man on the project. On one trip he showed us his air force log book in which he was on a raid over Genoa the night the Opera was bombed; they missed the docks but dropped the bombs on central Genoa instead!

"Move on thirty years and the site was still empty; Genoa was a poor city post-war and unlike Milan who rebuilt a replica of La Scala quickly, Genoa waited for three decades before starting the process. By then the memory of the Barabino house was lost, the opera company had been performing in a converted cinema for a generation. The city appointed Carlo Scarpa the doyen of Italian cultural architecture to design a modern opera house fit for the new era. Scarpa got the project to scheme design stage, and then died. This left the city with a buildable scheme but wanting an eminent architect to carry it to a conclusion.

"They set up a design and build competition, I think with five original entrants. The team we worked with was Cattaneo, a contractor, who had a Genoa office but were based in Bergamo. Cattaneo hired a notable local architect to assist them, Alberto Ponis. Alberto realised this was too big for him alone so he asked Lasdun to join him in the project. Alberto had worked for Lasdun in London and was obviously trusted by him.

"Lasdun then asked you to help, thinking he would just be dealing with you personally. We brought in Russ Johnson, Alberto brought in some eminent German structural engineers and Italian M&E. So the team was complete.

"The expectation of the client was that the new proposal would build on Scarpa's project. This had a huge 2000 seat single tier auditorium, fairly traditional Italian stage house and a rather uncomfortable relationship to the Galleria and Pronaos. Lasdun's first step was to reject the existing scheme, I think this was a condition of him joining the team, in favour of an idea for more integration with the urban context. This decision adds to the complexity of the site, but I think was a key to the appeal of Lasdun.

"You came back from your meeting and briefed Dick Brett who briefed me. I was just 27 and still cutting my teeth at TP; this was my first big break. In true TP tradition I was thrown in the deep end. As I recall we had a brainstorm with you, Russ, Dick and me. It was obvious that the site was going to be very complex as it was really too small for a modern opera house. So, we set about working out how to put the theatre together.

"The stage was a full three wagon affair, rear and side stage wagons at stage level and in the basement with huge and complex lifts and multi-function wagons. The load in was one level down and the rehearsal room on the roof. Dick and I went off to Munich to study Helmut Grosser's [Germany's senior Technical Director in Munich] containerised scenery handling system which we adopted for the design. This created a monstrous volume which Lasdun decided to wrap in a massive cylinder of stone like a renaissance fortification.

"The auditorium was a pretty simple decision; as Russ pointed out, when in Rome do as the Romans do. If you are building an opera house in Italy for an Italian opera company performing the classical Italian repertoire you had better have an Italian Opera House. A decision strongly endorsed by the opera company later.

"So, I drew a very simple classical five tier house with very shallow three row balconies and a big high level volume to overcome the traditional shortcoming in Italian opera houses: reverberance. The plan was very rational based on circles in squares, very Sacred Geometry and in line with Lasdun's rational approach. It had the benefit of having a much smaller footprint than the Scarpa scheme which allowed Lasdun to create an extension to the galleria from the centreline of the portico with the auditorium on one side and the foyers on the other.

"The orchestra pit was a multi-form system, a big deep overhang Bayreuth-style Wagnerian option, an open Verdi style and the extended forestage potential with all its sightline problems. We also had a tilting stalls lift for flat floor use, a mechanised Vienna ballroom/promenade.

"Come the day when we had to present this to Lasdun, you were unable to make the meeting so Russ and I went with my A3 sketches and some doodles from Dick. I recall the meeting well. We sat at the meeting table in Lasdun's office with just him and Stephen. After the pleasantries and his obvious displeasure that it was not you presenting to him I launched into my pre-prepared spiel. Then Russ flipped the drawings face down and took Lasdun through the issues related to the acoustics of opera and the stage/auditorium junction. After ten minutes he turned the drawings back over and I explained these were 'illustrative' and took them through the rational.

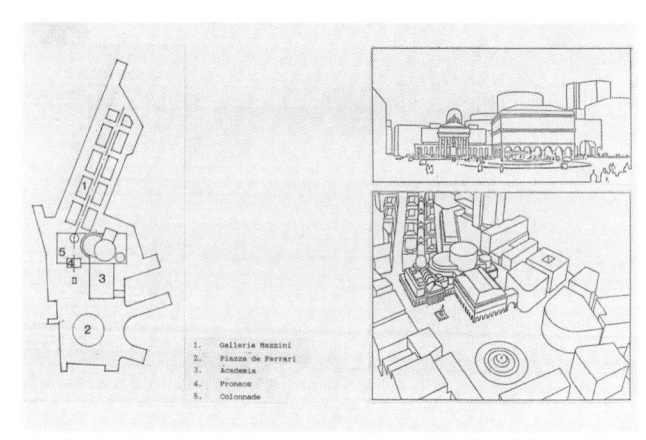

Lasdun drawings showing the new opera house within the existing buildings

Stefan pointed out that the smaller volume and footprint allowed Lasdun to pursue his urban idea and the principle of the scheme was sold.

"I continued with the development working within the context of his architectural vision; concrete balconies obviously, rational and expressed services and custom seating to deal with the acoustic and side balcony problems, an open lattice ceiling with lighting bridges and a huge lifting chandelier, opening into an acoustic chamber above.

"The process of developing the design was surprisingly collaborative: they adopted my proposals and incorporated them into their drawings! Time for the competition was tight, and Alberto realised they wouldn't have a rational scheme so came to TPC's office in Langley Street and he and I spent a day pouring over historic plans to come up with a suitable grand staircase and bridging approach. Again, Lasdun incorporated this into the scheme without argument.

"The competition was in two stages. Our scheme was radically different from the competition. Ours was however the favourite with the opera company and we progressed to the second stage, with Aldo Rossi as the lead architect for our competitor. This was not great news as he was the darling of the Italian post modernists and a new generation architect while Lasdun was a foreigner leading a foreign team and seen as an older generation architect. What did the English know about Italian Opera anyway? So we dug deep into the technicalities of the very complex stage arrangements, the tight sightlines, which had to be illustrated in detail, and the need to present everything in Italian (we hired an Italian architecture student to translate and label up all our drawings).

"In the middle of this stage there was a public meeting at the temporary opera house where the two schemes were presented by two very eminent advocates, both Italian architectural critics of opposing views. Bruno Zevi, a great writer on the modern movement and a supporter of a more rationalist approach to architecture who was a friend and supporter of Lasdun, and Paolo Portoghesi, an architect and professor who favoured a more organic Baroque approach and supported Aldo Rossi. It was, by Alberto's account, an electrifying debate lasting long into the night with the opera fans shouting over the speakers that they wanted their new opera house, the pros and cons of the diverse architectural approaches of two world class architects being dissected and discussed by two internationally famous architectural theorists and critics.

"The detailed design complete, the stage two submission had to be delivered. I was dispatched to Bergamo with the negatives on a passenger seat next to me. They were to be printed and signed by the principles of each consultancy company involved as this was a full tender submission for construction. There was no way you, Lasdun and Russ were going to travel to Italy just for the signing so I was delegated with the job of forging all three signatures on over 900 prints, which took most of the night before the deadline. Another sign of Lasdun's trust I guess.

"The triplicate packages complete, Alberto and I were driven with the documents in the Cattaneo's company limo from Bergamo to Genoa, Verdi blazing on the sound system, Italian pastries and coffee on tap, with a chase car in case of accidents. We delivered the documents to the central post

Views down into Lasdun's Genoa auditorium

office to be officially date stamped then headed for a blow out Genoa lunch before I flew back home.

"Despite the support of the opera company we didn't win. The reasons were analysed at a thank you lunch in Genoa which Cattaneo flew the UK team out to once we heard the bad news. The chairman gave a very generous thank-you speech where he insisted it wasn't our work but intimated that he had greased the wrong wheels and apologised for his error! But I suspect it was largely because Rossi and the majority of the jury were ardent members of the communist party, who controlled the city authority. The jury was a fix.

"Still it was one of the great projects I worked on at TPC."

There I'll end Paul's recollections. The Opera Company loved our scheme. But alas, Italian politics stood in our way. In the final competition we came in second place, and a more politically acceptable architect, Aldo Rossi, won. Rossi's design was for a single-level, super-cinema version of a 2000 seat auditorium. The opera company, and the press exploded in a very Italianate fury.

A DL&P file memorandum tells the story. "The competition became of national interest, which attracted the Rome socialist and communist parties and their party architects: Aldo Rossi, Paulo Portoghesi and Carlo Aymonino. The former as designer, the latter as jury assessors, you pat my back and I'll pat yours… New conditions were added in phase 2, which could favour the Rossi project."

5.3 Genoa: A Design Revolution

From *L'Espresso*, Genoa, 8th April 1984: "The horrible solution (plan by Aldo Rossi, Ignazio Gardelle and Angelo Sibella) is based on falsehood… to this hypocritical outside corresponds an equally shameful inside, where the old hall with boxes is replaced by a 'stadium' that offends its memory." Of the scheme by Lasdun and his local collaborators, Marco Dasso, and Alberto Ponis, the writer continued, "It is enough to consider it masterly and we know that it was most appreciated by experts free of prejudice. Technologically perfect, it is strictly modern yet respectful of the original design of Barabino. The most qualified members of the jury voted for this plan to the end. Our local partners phoned up London to ask Lasdun's reaction. 'No comment' was his very British answer."

I wrote to Sir Denys on the 19th of March 1984:

"Dear Denys, I've just had a glance at the Rossi scheme for Genoa that your office kindly passed to us. What can one say? It seems sad for us, but a damn tragedy for them.

I trust this finds you well. With every best wish, yours, Richard."

Denys Lasdun wrote in the introduction to our scheme: "The Opera House demands of the Senate and People of Genoa something more than a pale copy of the past or a thin distillation of a few meagre 'primary elements.' It needs to express the complexities of modern ideas and modern living in ways that have been found acceptable to the 20th century. It needs to draw on a wide vocabulary of forms which are both archetypal and contemporary and use these forms in the service of a fully thought out and integrated expression of the Opera house's functions. Central to the functional requirements is the provision not only of a superb auditorium for opera, but a stage offering maximum flexibility combined with the minimum essential requirements for international standards. This will promote new possibilities in the dynamic stage of opera for the 21st century. It is from the above hypothesis that we will begin."

A note from a sympathetic friend in Genoa: "I heard that four people voted against [Rossi]: the chief engineer of

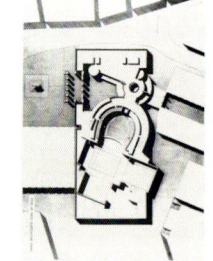

Section through the proposed Genoa opera house, showing the complex sub-stage machinery, and the smaller theatre below the main house

Plan showing theatre and surroundings

Commune, the Scenographer, the Theatre Superintendent and an expert in technical installations. It seems that in their opinion the project will not work. I'm sorry for Genoa, for architecture, and for you. It could have been rewarding to have in Italy a good building of yours."

A last word from Denys to the team: "I am convinced (and not only myself to tell the truth) that our project is the moral winner of the competition. In fact one has achieved a product of the highest architectural merit which is the unanimous consensus of connoisseurs. I feel obliged to thank you and your collaborators for the results, since the project has achieved a magnificent milestone image of my firm."

Five decades later, this Italian adventure seem prescient indeed. Denys's invitation for us to join his team was a pivotally important one. His was the first such request from a leading architect since we had begun to initiate stage and auditorium design for our architects. In the five decades that followed many others joined his ranks: Lord Foster, Frank Gehry, Michael Hopkins, Barton Myers, César Pelli, Renzo Piano, Christian de Portzamparc, William Rawn, Moshe Safdie, Snøhetta, Michael Wilford and others. All have sought our services to collaborate in designing some great theatres.

Denys proved himself to be a quite remarkable innovator. Hitherto he had perhaps seemed averse to collaboration. But by his action on the Genoa adventure he proved himself capable of far-sighted co-operation, welcoming open theatre design partnership in a

Genoa, auditorium design by Aldo Rossi, as built

Lasdun's design for Genoa. An alternative version adds a traditional central Royal box

manner that would prove to be the first of many such in the future and setting a trend for teamwork between theatre and architecture for decades to come.

A final comment on the winner from Carlo Zevi: "It's hard to find a more jumbled series of gruesome and totally useless styles clashing with each other. It's not just a matter of academic retrology or futile 'post modern' irresponsibility. With one shot they succeeded in producing a contemptuous theatre and defacing Genoa's heart…"

The Bastille, Paris
We had one final adventure with Denys Lasdun. Another competition, this time an open international challenge for a new grand opera to operate alongside one of the world's most beautiful houses, the 1875 Garnier Opera, named after its brilliant architect, Charles Garnier.

I had some foreknowledge of this project. The brief was prepared by Michaël Dittman, a director and assistant to Rolf Liebermann, artistic director of the Paris Opera. Michaël was, I believe, of German descent and enjoyed stage machinery.

During the late seventies he visited my office in London several times. He traversed the world visiting recent opera houses and essentially picked all the parts he liked for his new 'super-facility'. For better or worse this resulted in a brief for a massive building, which would pack the Bastille site end-to-end, leaving little room for anything but an outer skin for architecture. However we joined the competition… with 757 other competitors!

Helped by Paul Jenkins, Dick Brett, and the DL&P team, a scheme was assembled, but we were all less than optimistic. Our project did indeed disappear and a young Uruguayan-Canadian architect, Carlos Ott, won. The project opened in 1989 with the second flexible theatre deferred to a future date. The Bastille has a huge cinema-style 2700 seat auditorium, facing the largest stage on earth, built in sixteen lateral sections on multiple levels with correspondingly large support areas.

I visited the Bastille several times. I once asked the technical director his thoughts on his theatre. He replied "As a theatre technician I'm proud. As a taxpayer of France I'm appalled."

Theatre Royal Nottingham renovation,
Charles J. Phipps 1865, renovation RHWL
with Theatre Projects, 1978

5.4 Designing Theatres

Ken Dodd welcomes the first audience to the newly renovated Theatre Royal Nottingham

My experience as a lighting designer and a producer opened my eyes to the totality of theatre, but most vitally, to the realisation that the relationship between actor and audience lies at the core of live theatre. This chapter will follow my journey of quite personal discovery, and provide a scrapbook of many projects across the world that represent examples of theatre-led designs – putting people first.

This experience was amplified by my working with Denys Lasdun. I was aware that my naïveté as a member of the building committee and indeed as consultant had failed to provide a fine architect what he really needed: guidance beyond the purely technical. His first request was about "the nature and anatomy of theatre" to which he never received a clear reply. It took me years and a dozen projects to begin to understand what he'd really needed.

The Theatre Royal Nottingham, the backstage and foyers updated for modern working but the auditorium restored rather than dramatically changed, was pivotal. It began the belated process of opening my eyes.

Theatre Design – A Personal Learning Experience

The design of theatre had always fascinated me. At age 11, I created a theatre space in my parents' Victorian house. I spent countless hours poring over my model theatre. At boarding school, age 15, I'd converted an abandoned barn into a theatre. While at drama school, I'd ridden my motorbike across Germany to Vienna, to visit the new theatres that were already being rebuilt after the destruction of World War ll. Theatres seemed uniquely fascinating things: places where stories were shared, art was created, magical webs were spun.

I'll begin this chapter about our changing world of theatre design by examining some pivotal mentors.

On 7th February 1978, comedian Ken Dodd opened the newly renovated Phipps / Matcham / Renton Howard Wood-designed Theatre Royal Nottingham. For three hours, Dodd, a hilarious comic, held the audience in hysterical laughter. The theatre's all-embracing architecture placed every person in his grasp. Thus began my awakening. This was actually the quality Sir Laurence had sought: audience embrace of the performer.

The New Amsterdam, New York. The world's first 'Broadway' theatre, 1903 – restored 1997. Original architect: Herts & Tallant. Restoration architect: Hardy Holzman Pfeiffer Associates.

Stephen Joseph

Aspiring to be a director, having endlessly read Edward Gordon Craig's *Master of the Art and Science of the Theatre,* I studied stage management at the Central School of Speech and Drama. The founder of the course was Stephen Joseph.

Stephen was a tall, inspiring, firebrand of a man; a passionate enthusiast for theatre but, in particular, arena, theatre-in-the-round staging, which he'd experienced while studying in the States. He was impassioned by the purity and simplicity that he saw there, seeing it as the essence of theatre: actor and audience together, without the distraction of scenery. In 1955, he was attempting to start his own theatre-in-the-round, presenting Sunday night performances with professional actors at the Mahatma Gandhi Hall in Euston. I began to stage-manage and light some of his shows… always on a very tight shoestring.

After battling with the establishment for many years, Stephen made a decision. "I look forward to going to an innocent place, such as Scarborough, where people who come to the theatre are not theatregoers."[3] He did establish his own arena stage theatre in Scarborough, Yorkshire. He invited me to be his first stage manager, but an offer of an assistant stage manager job in the West End seemed more alluring. Scarborough eventually became a success. Sadly, Stephen was to die at the age of 49, but his legacy has continued under the direction of Sir Alan Ayckbourn, the incredibly prolific dramatist and the director of the Stephen Joseph Theatre for so many years.

Sean Kenny

Sean was a particularly charismatic, short, stocky Irishman, with a supreme gift of the blarney, a scene designer who had studied architecture under Frank Lloyd Wright in the US. He rocketed to prominence with his designs for Lionel Bart's *Oliver!* – the first show to expose the bare walls of the theatre and the lighting rig (designed by John Wyckham) in the West End. I met Sean on Lionel's next megamusical, *Blitz!*, that depicted onstage the bombing of London in World War II. I lit this production, which was probably the most sensational spectacle ever seen on the London stage, before or since! Sean taught us that nothing was impossible. In *Blitz!*, his set consisted of moving towers representing three-storey houses that, being motorised, perambulated around the stage to create different street vistas of London under fire. For me, this moving architecture later directly inspired the moving towers of box seating that we employed at Christ's Hospital in Horsham, and in the multiform Derngate Theatre in Northampton which was to prove a breakthrough in flexible theatre design.

Frank Dunlop

Frank Dunlop called me a few days before the Young Vic Theatre was due to open under his direction. "Richard, I have a lighting problem… We don't have any!" I jumped into a cab, and hurried down to The Cut. It was true. The new theatre, on a shoestring budget, had forgotten to order any lights. I rang Fred Humphries at the Theatre Projects lighting rental store in Neal's Yard and ordered an immediate vanfull. Crisis averted.

I knew Frank as an associate director to Sir Laurence at the NT. His new theatre fascinated me. Influenced by Frank's enthusiasm for the Elizabethan theatre, particularly Henslowe's Fortune, it had a small thrust stage that unlike any other of this form at the time was set within a surrounding balcony, 'courtyard-style.' The architect was Bill Howell. I got on well with Bill, and we resolved to work together in the future…

Some months later, we were commissioned to design a new theatre for a school, Christ's Hospital in Horsham. The client wanted a derivative of the Young Vic, but with the ability to change from thrust to end stage, all utilising student power.

Influenced by my *Blitz!* experience, I suggested that one end of the rectangular galleried room should be made with movable towers that could lengthen or foreshorten the room and, if removed, could create an open end stage or proscenium.

Importantly, with a third of the audience seated in the gallery, reconfiguring the downstairs seating to change the actor/audience relationship was simply made less labour-intensive.

Some time later, the RSC toured into the theatre, loved it, and used it as a model for the Swan Theatre in Stratford.

Harold Prince

In 1962, I met Hal Prince, Broadway's most successful producer/director in history, as his projection consultant to the musical *A Funny Thing Happened on the Way to the Forum*. This was designed by my friend Tony Walton, with lighting by the legendary Jean Rosenthal and was my first venture onto the Broadway stage. Hal invited me to become his London producing partner with that show. It was followed by many others, including *Fiddler on the Roof*, *Company*, *Cabaret*, and *A Little Night Music*. On Broadway, I lit for Hal the musical, *Zorba* and, later, in the '90s, his epic revival of *Show Boat*.

I learnt two important lessons from Hal. The first, as producer, was an insight into the complexity of creating a production; I moved from simply lighting to responsibility for the financing, casting, publicity, and every other detail of the production. But most important was the lesson to be learnt from the audience. Without the audience's participation, you had nothing. With *Fiddler*, which ran for five years at Her Majesty's Theatre, I spent many hours in the top stage-left box, watching the audience; laughter, silence, the wiping away of a furtive tear... This was theatre and I met the cream of Broadway designers, writers, directors, and technicians. My eyes were opened far beyond any parochial English experience of the stage. All these amazing lessons fed into my theatre designs.

Russ Johnson: Acoustician Extraordinaire

It was in New York in the early 1970s that a Canadian friend, theatre consultant and entrepreneur Wally Russell, introduced me to Russell Johnson, who was then an unemployed

Russell Johnson

Harold Prince

acoustician. He had been project manager for the acoustics firm Bolt, Beranek and Newman on the notorious acoustic disaster Avery Fisher Hall, in New York's Lincoln Center. Russ was deeply bruised by the experience but, in his bones, he felt he knew what had gone wrong. The hall was simply too big, and the scheme had been compromised by a late change in the design brief, adding more seats. The consulting team had been too weak and had acquiesced to this deterioration caused by the client, leading to an international fiasco.

Contrary to all accepted opinion, he was convinced that most acousticians were wrong. His secret: that people hear because they have two ears, and they are on the side of their head! Most of Russ' peers did esoteric calculations about volume and reverberation times. Russ did not believe in pseudoscience, he believed that theatre architecture, and thus acoustics, must work by reflecting sound into our ears!

Russ sought side reflections of sound into the human ear; I was seeking to rediscover side boxes of audience seating to restore the intangible psychic connection of energy created by a three-dimensional audience wrapped about the performer. Bingo! We clicked.

Russ completed a circle for me. Spaces that wrap the audience around the performer as intimately as possible, are rooms that come to life. Acoustics, sightlines, and emotions fuse together to make great rooms for lively theatre and music and for human communication. Russ died in 2007. His legacy in acoustics will not soon be matched.

Beginnings In Theatre Design

It was, if memory serves, during the summer of 1970 that while on holiday on the Hebridean Isle of Coll, one sunny morning my sound partner David Collison and I set out to draw, at full scale, in the sand on the beach below my house, the ground plan of the Olivier Theatre. Upon completion, we climbed the prominent hill above the beach and looked down. My heart sank... my stage, coupled with Lasdun's auditorium, seemed to be awfully large. Yet it was already being cast in concrete.

I seemed to have fallen into theatre architecture almost by accident. The phone had rung, an architect would ask, did we know about theatre, and I would reply in the affirmative. We would meet and look at the architect's developing plans... working with architects, many of whom became good friends: Roderick Ham, Peter Moro, and others. The rules of the 60s were simple: good frontal sightlines to a proscenium stage. It was our job to make that stage the best possible within the confines of the budget, put the lights and loudspeakers in the right places, ensure the dressing rooms were adequate, and that the box office had not been forgotten.

My first big project was the new Birmingham Repertory Theatre. There, the client had requested a 900-seat version of their beloved old Rep from 1920 that seated 284 on a single steep, rake plus a high balcony for 170 - so double the size. That great English director from between the wars Basil Dean (who later, in his 80s, became a mentor of mine) had been an advisor to Sir Barry Jackson on the original design. This time, architect Graham Winteringham simply designed a bigger version with 900 seats now entirely on a single rake. I'd added a large stage to match, a studio space and support facilities. The result seemed gargantuan. For the very first season, the company extended the forestage into the auditorium, seeking to connect to the audience who seemed so far away. Perhaps theatres could not simply be expanded like balloons.

Michael Elliott and Richard Negri

My closest friend in theatre, and constant inspiration, was director Michael Elliott. We'd worked together since 1959, had both been on the National Building Committee, and together had encouraged Sir Laurence into breaking out of the concrete-

Richard Negri

Michael Elliott

galleried stage that Lasdun had designed, which seemed such a straightjacket to the imaginations of future theatre makers.

The last season of the Old Vic Company, under Michael Elliott, had been a great experience. Afterward, Michael, turning down Sir Laurence's invitation to join him as his deputy at the National, determined upon creating his own theatre company away from the West End. He decided upon Manchester as a suitable home. While the company would initially be housed in the Manchester University Theatre, we began to explore a new concept for a theatre of our own. TP's first in-house architect was Eric Jordan, who joined us after retiring from his post as head of the theatre division of the Greater London Council. He was a world-renowned expert on fire safety and sightlines in theatres and I knew he could add the theatre architectural experience we needed.

Richard Negri was both a brilliantly original designer and an extraordinary, religious, introverted human being. Michael, Richard, and I, worked together on many notable productions, from *Brand* (starring Patrick McGoohan) for the 59 Theatre Company at the Lyric Hammersmith, the production that really launched all our careers, to Vanessa Redgrave's sensational debut in *As You Like It* for the RSC in 1961.

For the Old Vic Company season, Richard designed an extraordinary forestage and proscenium. The stage's curved front contained a concave lowered section that created a kind of substitute for the Elizabethan inner stage, a place for

5.4 Designing Theatres

extremely intimate scenes but now, uniquely, in the lap of the audience. The proscenium was a series of three circular arches consisting of bands of aluminum, making the entire portal like a tunnel, drawing in the audience. The outer ring, which concealed my new semi-circular lighting bridge, was a dark brown colour, matching the auditorium. Upstage was an almost black arch, while between was a strip of shiny aluminium. This reflected any colour of light that might be onstage, seemingly drawing the atmosphere of the stage out into the auditorium. For *Peer Gynt*, both the yellow sands of the desert and the icy wasteland of Norway seemed to spread into the audience. Even the movement of actors onstage might produce a shimmer of reflection akin to flickering candlelight, linking stage to audience. It was an astonishingly powerful effect, achieved with such simplicity – another lesson.

Richard's theatrical vision was an inspiration to all of us. He had turned his back on the pressures of commercial theatre and had become head of the Wimbledon School of Art – England's top theatre design school. There, each year, he and Michael had experimented on three-dimensional theatre forms employing different actor audience relationships, but each one surrounded by various clusters of audience on two-level, movable, scaffold towers. Using student actors from Central School, single acts of different plays during a single evening would be presented in different configurations.

From this experimental research for our new project in Manchester, under the leadership of Negri, Eric Jordan and I began to develop a revolutionary idea for a completely new kind of theatre.

In 1971, Michael and I drafted its manifesto:

"Nearly all the theatres we possess in this country were built in the 19th century, or follow their design. Because all our childhood experience of theatre, and our fathers', and their fathers', was in these buildings, we think that their shape IS theatre. The opposite is the truth.

"The blank wall of the curtain, across an orchestra pit, sealing off the world of the stage from the auditorium, does not even

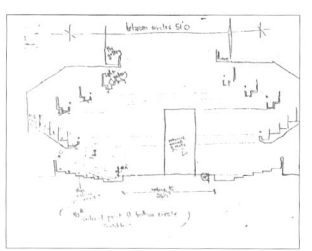

Manchester Theatre Project section

The Old Vic Negri stage

belong to the 18th century. In the theatre of Congreve and Goldsmith the boxes and the audience went far beyond the edge of the stage. But before the Restoration in this country, and the Renaissance in Europe, no theatre had ever been in this shape at all. The theatre of 5th century Athens, where European drama was born, and the Globe Theatre on the South Bank of London's Thames, where English theatre was born, were entirely different.

"In all theatre known to man before the Renaissance, the play took place in some sense AMONG the audience. Not because they knew no better – a tradition doesn't live for 2,000 years without purpose – but because it was thought to BE theatre. Like cabaret in a modern restaurant, like a preacher in a congregation, like an orator on a soapbox, they felt that the closest connection with a group of people must be from a place AMONG them. Or rather, they didn't think, it never occurred to them that it could be any other way.

"All that time has taught us about the use of scenery, and now of electricity, we must be grateful for. Our theatre must have at least as much visual potential as the Victorians', but we will not pay so high a price for it. We will not seal off the actor like some infectious disease behind a glass wall. We know that by having him in some sense AMONG us, we shall most feel his presence...

"First, I suppose, must be the tiny space that the theatre auditorium occupies. Normally 70' is thought to be the maximum distance at which an actor can command a member of the *audience. The furthest member from the stage in THIS theatre is 30' away – and that in a theatre of 750-800 seats could not be thought possible if it had not been done.*

"Secondly, the audience is wrapped around the main action like a warm scarf round the head in cold weather. Nothing could be so intimate. And INTIMATE is what EVERYBODY wants a theatre to be.

"Thirdly, beyond the stage that is cocooned by the audience there is another area. The stage is open at one side to a large 'mysterious' area from which actors will emerge, and scenery, into the central stage. Here are the mysterious distances, the bright scenery, which penetrate right into the audience.

"But most exciting of all, fourthly, that 'mysterious' area SURROUNDS the audience! That will put us IN the action, in a way that makes Cinerama look like a peep-show. Are we on a desert island? Are we in a forest? The trees can lean into the auditorium from every side, but disappear in a flash.

"Intimacy, spectacular scenic effects, real drama – it will be vital, alive, a place where theatre happens, and is known to happen. What else is commercial success?

"We believe that this theatre will attract the best actors, the best directors and designers, and the largest audience, long after we are forgotten."
Michael Elliott & Richard Pilbrow (1971)

A brilliant young architectural firm, Levitt Bernstein Associates, was selected to turn the concept into a reality of steel and glass. The now-famous Royal Exchange was born. The theatre, looking like a lunar module, is suspended – because the floor couldn't take any additional weight, let alone its 150 tonnes – from the massive side columns of the great Exchange hall that it sits at the centre of.

The most intimate, yet epic, theatre in the world, it seats 750 people, all within only 9 metres (29.52 feet) of the centre of the stage! Fifty years later, the Royal Exchange remains one of Britain's leading theatre companies.

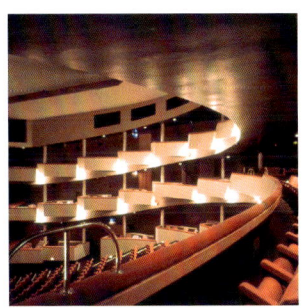

Eden Court Theatre, Inverness, opened 1976, shown in 2019

Royal Exchange, Manchester, opened 1973

Iain Mackintosh

Iain Mackintosh was a co-founder of the Prospect Theatre Company, an Arts Council-subsidised operation that toured the UK and internationally; it had no permanent base. I'd met Iain at the Oxford Playhouse in 1961, when we were both very young. We met again when, as a producer, I presented some of Prospect's shows in the West End, amongst them *Edward II* and *Richard II*, Ian McKellen's first starring West End roles. They were enormous successes and took London by storm.

While continuously touring, Iain had come to realise that some theatres, irrespective of their size, worked – and some did not. Some sprang instantly to life, while others remained inert and impervious to excitement. Iain had invested a lot of time trying to work out why. The quality seemed dependent upon the actor-audience relationship, and the finest theatres of Victorian/Edwardian England exemplified the best of these. The boxes and balconies of tradition created theatres that most readily sprang to life.

Iain got a chance to experiment with this as an advisor to the Eden Court Theatre, being built in Inverness and due to open in April 1976. Designed by architects Law & Dunbar-Naismith, the building was to house all types of performing arts, from opera to popular music, concerts, ballet, modern dance, drama, and films. Iain had suggested that the 800-seat proscenium theatre should have step-down boxes 'en-escalier' along the sides of the room, joining the circle to the stage, and that was what was built. I visited, and was impressed.

Iain told me that he was getting tired of constantly travelling; I invited him to join Theatre Projects Consultants as our theatre design guru, and he accepted.

Three weeks after Iain began, Peter Hall asked me whether Theatre Projects might design a studio theatre for The National: "Lasdun tells me that his team are too busy." Over a weekend, I passed the task to Iain, and the Cottesloe concept – called the 'Cottesloe Cockpit' on Iain's original sketches – was born.

A Last Lesson: *I'm Not Rappaport*
I was to produce the New York hit *I'm Not Rappaport* in England. It was to open in June 1986 in my least-favourite theatre, the huge single-level, steeply raked 900-seat Birmingham Rep, but I was still confident the play and our wonderful star, Paul Scofield, would triumph. How wrong I was.

Herb Gardner was a playwright of sensitivity and humanity, capable of droll humour. The play centres on Nat, a cantankerous octogenarian, an unregenerate socialist of the old school, and Midge, an ailing black apartment superintendent, who spend their days kibitzing on a park bench in New York's Central Park.

We assembled a wonderful cast. Paul was to play Nat, and Howard Rollins, a brilliant young actor, Midge. Dan Sullivan had been the original director in Seattle and on Broadway; Herb was closely involved throughout.

Paul Scofield, clearly one of Britain's outstanding actors, was, from the outset, deeply sensitive about not being Jewish. He was trying to assume a role unlike any he had attempted before. Herb and Dan spent hours in conversation with him at his beautiful home in Sussex.

Rehearsals were tense. Paul continued to find the role a challenge. The first night in Birmingham was, frankly, a disaster. In the huge auditorium, our heroes' delicate, witty banter fell very flat. The comedy took place in total silence. At the end of the evening, Paul was deeply disturbed.

Next morning in my hotel, I was rung by Ros Chatto, Paul's agent.

Birmingham Repertory Theatre, Birmingham UK, after renovation.
Architect: Graham Winteringham

Apollo Theatre, Shaftesbury Avenue, London UK

I'd known Ros for decades. "Richard," she began, "we have a serious problem: Paul is unable to play this part." I extemporised – clearly, last night had been a low point, but eventually he would find his way and be wonderful in the role. "No, Richard," she returned. "You don't understand. He cannot play the role. He cannot continue. This has never happened in his career. You know what a man of integrity he is. He cannot carry on."

This was serious. I had to remind Ros that we had a contract. Breaking it would carry very serious consequences.
"I'll send you a doctor's certificate later today. I'm sorry Richard, that's it."

We had a major crisis. Scofield was not a lightweight who might easily change his mind. We knew how hard this would be. But Dan and Herb both agreed that Paul, with his extraordinary talent, would ultimately find himself and be a great Nat.

Via Ros, I persuaded Paul that we should at least meet to talk. Dan tried hard to convince Paul that there was hope. But Paul was adamant. Finally, after many hours of stressful conversation, I came up with a compromise. We respected Paul's position, but we could not just shut down the production and throw everybody out of work. I, as producer, would guarantee that, after he gave us three more weeks to try to make the show work, if Paul was still unhappy, I would close the show with no recriminations.

Next, we spent a week in the far more intimate Theatre Royal Brighton. The show was better. The following week, we opened at the Apollo Theatre on Shaftesbury Avenue, a beautiful Victorian playhouse with seventy more seats than the much physically larger Birmingham but on three levels, creating a wraparound intimate auditorium. The same play, the same production, the same Tony Walton setting, costumes, lighting, cast… and an absolute triumph! The audience rocked with laughter, was overcome by emotion, the critics raved. Paul received some of his finest reviews. The Daily Mail proclaimed, "A joyous shout of triumph." "A superb performance from Paul Scofield," declared The Guardian. "A rare chance to see one of our most elusive greats, Paul Scofield," wrote Time Out.

Most importantly, Paul was a superb Nat. For him, it had been like climbing Everest, but he was happy. The show ran at capacity for the contracted six months. We had a hit.

This experience vindicated my theory of intimacy in an auditorium. A high quality production of a wonderful play with a fine cast in two auditoria. One, archetypical of the '60s – symbolic of everything in theatre architecture that I had come to despise. The other a perfect example of the lesson I had learnt from the past: the superiority of an intimate, wraparound, three-dimensional auditorium… the lesson of back to the future!

Innovations: The Design of Theatre Space

In the almost fifty years since Lasdun's National Theatre building opened, theatre design has changed. Criticism of the two large theatres, coupled with praise for the intimacy of the Cottesloe, opened my eyes to the evident challenge. At the same time, the fame (or notoriety) of the National began to send me on what became an international journey as a theatre design consultant, eventually travelling around the world many times. This led to many opportunities assisting architects in exploring the design of more intimate, human-scale, theatre spaces.

What we had to explore was how to make theatres more liveable. How to rediscover theatres that might respond to Sir Laurence's heartfelt dream: spaces where an actor might feel "marvellous". Our focus was on artistic and architectural issues – the design of theatre space.

My work as a stage manager, lighting designer, and West End producer had led me to the realisation that three-dimensional theatres of the past, with balconies and side-boxes that bring the audience into a close and vibrant relationship to the performer, possess virtues that were lost during many years of modern 20th century theatre architecture. Finally, with the renovation of the 19th century Theatre Royal, Nottingham, came my realisation that such traditional spaces brought actor and audience member into a lively, interactive interconnection that is fundamental to the truly living experience essential to all forms of live performance.

From the courtyards of Shakespearean England, the early opera houses of Italy, and the corrales of Lope de Vega's Spain, three-dimensional theatres evolved that sought to optimise the relationship between actor and audience. Theatres grew in size, but always strived to retain this intimacy. In the cultures of the Far East, similar courtyard theatres developed in India, China, and Japan, with stage and auditorium united in a single congruent space.

Since 1978, my work at Theatre Projects has led to innumerable theatres around the world being inspired by these classic principles of physical and acoustic intimacy and enhanced actor/audience participation.

In recent years, the world of theatre has undoubtedly changed. The popularity of smaller more informal fringe spaces, and of environmental theatre has had incredible impact. The

Performer in the embrace of the audience: Royal Lyceum, Edinburgh, UK in 2018, architect C.J. Phipps

"A piece of theatre changes completely according to the space it's in – a fact to which I have become increasingly sensitive, having spent most of the last twenty years on tour. This has often been a dispiriting experience: the increasingly prevalent cultural 'administrators' have tended to impose on us their latest 1500-seat concrete bunkers, built to survive nuclear holocaust, replete with sleep-inducing armchairs. At the National we have one vast space, the Olivier, which demands the energy of plutonium just to get things across to the front row and is extremely constraining in spite of its size, and the Lyttelton with its audience cut in half on two shelves."
Declan Donnellan
Director

"One of the best kept secrets in the theatre is the frequency with which architectural design totally frustrates the intentions of the artists for whom the work is ostensibly undertaken. It is one of theatre's great ironies that those who design its stages and auditoria, no matter how distinguished they may be as architects, are often baboons when it comes to creating a space in which actors and audience can happily cohabit." [4]
Charles Marowitz
Introduction, *Accommodating the Lively Arts* by Martin Bloom

"Theatre exists in the mind of the audience. The horseshoe shape of the Bristol Old Vic meant the audience could see you and you could see them... Architecture is empowering the audience."
Tom Morris
Artistic director, The Bristol Old Vic Theatre [5]

advances in media, the Internet, and the music industry have all pushed the boundaries of performance. Massive spectaculars exist alongside the smallest-scale studio work.

But where actor meets audience remains, for me, the centre of live theatre design. For any stage shape, for any size of audience, this lively dynamic brings theatre to life.

What makes live theatre unique? It is this simple fact: a live performer meets a lively participating audience. No two performances are ever the same. The actor constantly adjusts his performance according to the circumstances and atmosphere surrounding that performance. A rowdy Saturday night differs from a subdued Monday evening.

A successful theatre brings audience and actor together. The collective energy exuded by an audience is optimised in direct relationship to how aware each individual is of the others around them.

The magic of theatre design lies in capturing this energy – this collective life force – emanating from every human being, individuals transformed into that wondrous beast: the audience.

Lively theatre – people matter

Collaborative Theatre

Since that meeting in 1982 with Denys Lasdun, when he sought our collaboration for the Genoa opera house, our world of theatre design has been quite different.

We began consulting on the technology of the stage. The National Theatre had made it evident that technical advice was actually insufficient. To create a new, vibrant lively human-scale theatre, we had to influence the architecture. And this influence had to be welcomed by the architect and be the outcome of true collaboration.

One challenge is that there is no one type of theatre. Theatre may be needed for drama, opera, ballet, water spectacle, commercial promotional events, business conferences and numerous other variations. For each I have come to believe there is an approach that can make for success in the fullest sense of the word.

The key lies in a phrase from Mark Rylance: "congregate play."

From 1978 onwards, the team at Theatre Projects and I have sought to design three-dimensional theatres – theatres on multiple levels that seek to wrap the audience as tightly as possible around the house, in boxes and balconies. Experience derived from working on renovating some beauties of the past also enriched our thinking.

The following pages illustrate this with a range of projects that differ widely in their design, but which in each case was the result of a collaboration between theatre and architect. They are located around the world. Usually they are new buildings, but sometimes they are redesigns of existing ones. In every case they have demonstrably enriched the audiences they serve with 'lively theatre.'

Ahmanson Theatre, Los Angeles, USA – before

Ahmanson Theatre, Los Angeles – after.
Architect Welton Becket Associates (1967 original), Ellerbe Becket Architects (1994 redesign).

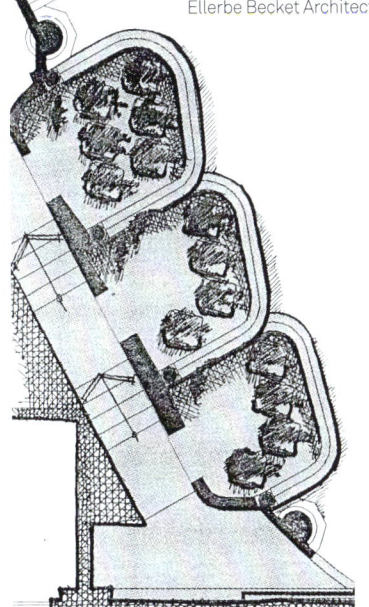

Ahmanson Theatre: TP box concept sketch

5.4 Designing Theatres

Drama

Steppenwolf Theatre, Chicago, Illinois, USA
Dolby Theatre, Los Angeles, USA
Royal Court, London, UK

A proscenium for drama is what many think of as a 'traditional' theatre; such theatres can range enormously in scale but the best, regardless of size, link the audience to each other and to the performers on stage.

Examples abound in the UK, the skilled work of specialist theatre designers such as Matcham, Phipps and others, who understood this vital connection. They are exemplified by the likes of the Royal Lyceum in Edinburgh and many in London's West End. Some, such as Nottingham's Theatre Royal and the Royal Court in London, have been sensitively renovated.

In America, what I call a 'Broadway' theatre is characterised by a wide, shallow stage with one or two balconies close to that stage and step-down boxes on either side, the first of which was probably the 1903 New Amsterdam in New York. Before then, American theatres were generally closer to their English counterparts, with a more horseshoe-shaped auditorium. The difference was often driven by a very practical problem: the standard New York plot ratio! Fire destroys theatre less often now but sometimes nature intervenes in other ways, such as at San Francisco's Geary, restored after an earthquake.

A modern version of the Broadway model inspired Steppenwolf in Chicago but, proving it can scale up, also the Dolby (originally Kodak) Theatre, which hosts the Academy Awards each year (drama about drama!), the Disney Theater in the Dr. Phillips Performing Arts Center in Orlando, and others.

Steppenwolf Theatre, Chicago, USA, architect James, Morris & Kutyla

The Geary (now Toni Rembe) Theater, San Francisco, as restored after earthquake damage; original architects Bliss and Faville, restoration architects Gensler and Associates

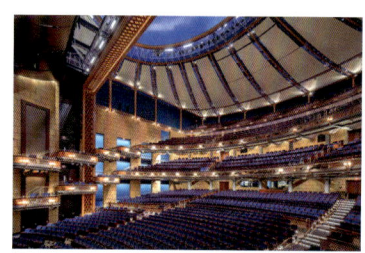

Disney Theater, Orlando, Florida, USA, architect Barton Myers Associates/HKS/Baker Barrios Architects

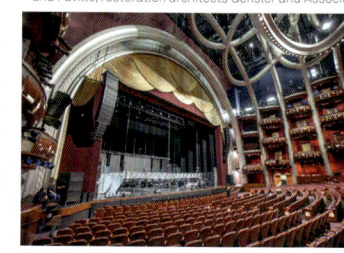

Dolby (Kodak) Theatre, Los Angeles USA, architect Rockwell Group/Ehrenkrantz Ekstut Kuhn

Theatre Royal, Nottingham, UK, architects C.J.Phipps and Frank Matcham, renovation by Renton Howard Wood Levin

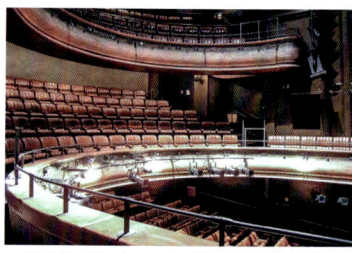

Royal Court Theatre, London, UK, architect Walter Emden, renovation by Haworth Tompkins

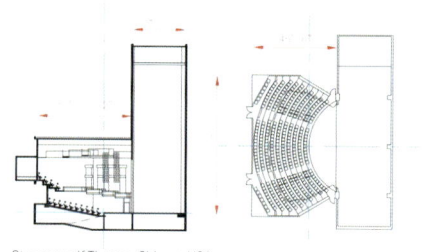

Steppenwolf Theatre, Chicago USA

Dolby (Kodak) Theatre, Los Angeles USA, final section

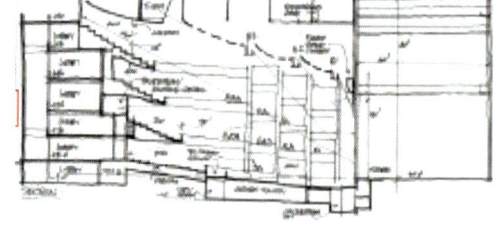

Dolby (Kodak) Theatre, Los Angeles USA, TP Concept Sketch

Three-Dimensional Intimacy

The Royal Exchange, Manchester, UK
Walt Disney Concert Hall, Los Angeles, USA

Designed by Richard Negri, the Royal Exchange was the outcome of a multiyear partnership with director Michael Elliott. It resulted in the world's first and most intimate multilevel theatre-in-the-round, which opened in 1976. It accommodates 750 people within 29 feet (9 metres) of the centre of an arena stage.

Beyond drama, the symphony hall – a theatre for music – has evolved. Led initially by the architect Hans Sharoun in Berlin, his Philharmonie (1963) became the world's first concert hall-in-the-round with 'vineyard' seating. This was inspiration for the Walt Disney Concert Hall in Los Angeles by Frank Gehry. This combines the intimacy of a surround hall for a more intimate audience experience with flexible staging opportunity.

Royal Exchange, Manchester, UK, as in 2009, architect Levitt Bernstein Associates

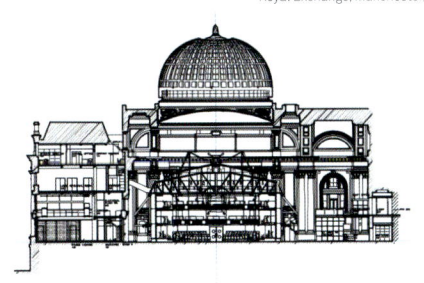

Royal Exchange: section through Exchange building and theatre module

Royal Exchange: exterior of theatre module within hall, as in 2009

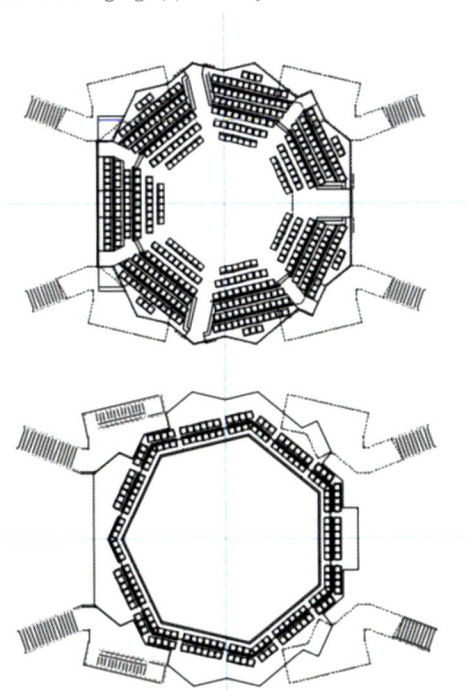

Walt Disney Concert Hall, Los Angeles, USA

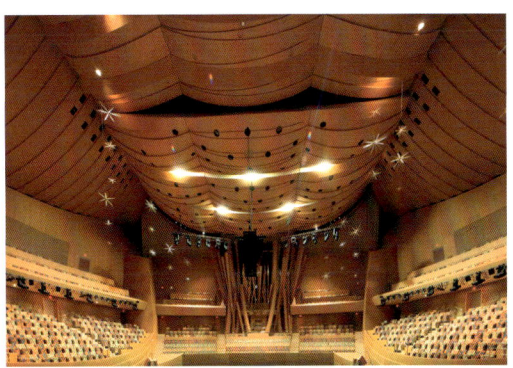

Walt Disney Concert Hall, Los Angeles, USA, architect Frank Gehry

Royal Exchange Theatre: plans at 1st and 2nd levels

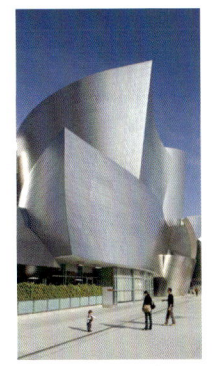

5.4 Designing Theatres

Courtyard Theatres

Christ's Hospital School, Horsham, UK
Polonsky Shakespeare Center, Brooklyn, New York, USA
Wyly Theatre, Dallas, Texas, USA

Christ's Hospital was based upon Frank Dunlop's Young Vic Theatre. Christ's and the NT's Cottesloe Theatre introduced the modern courtyard theatre, which has been widely imitated around the world, most recently with the Polonsky Shakespeare Theatre Center for Theatre for a New Audience in Brooklyn, New York. Christ's also inspired The Royal Shakespeare's Swan Theatre that led to the new RSC theatre in Stratford-upon-Avon, as well as TP's Chicago Shakespeare Theater. The Wyly Theatre in Dallas is a new, uniquely flexible version, allowing not only the central courtyard to be reconfigured, but also the surrounding balconies to be flown out leaving a 100 foot (30.5 metre) square, entirely clear space that can even be opened to the outside world.

A theatre that can be opened to the outside world has multiple benefits; both ecologically and dramatically. From natural ventilation to linking a dramatic story to the outside world, a natural or urban environment.

The original Tricycle Theatre, London, UK, architect Tim Foster of Tim Foster Architects

Wyly Theatre, Dallas, USA

Mid and bottom: Christ's Hospital School, Horsham, UK, architect Bill Howell of Howell Killick Partridge and Amis

Wyly Theatre, Dallas, USA, side windows revealed, architects Rex/OMA

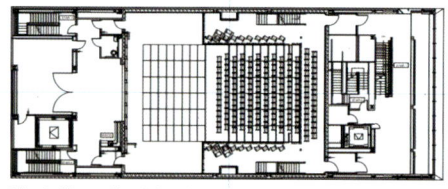

Polonsky Theatre, New York – plan

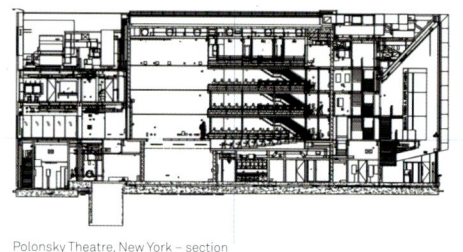

Polonsky Theatre, New York – section

Left and above: Polonsky Theatre, New York, USA, architects H3 Hardy Collaborative Architecture

The Courtyard Expands

The Bridge Theatre, London, UK

Upon leaving the National after twelve triumphant years, Nick Hytner and Nick Starr built the first new commercial theatre in London for many years, beneath a residential development on a spectacular site overlooking Tower Bridge. To design their Bridge Theatre, , which opened in 2017, they turned to Steve Tompkins, Roger Watts and the Haworth Tompkins team.

An attractive, open, airy foyer leads down to the theatre below. Described as "a completely new design approach" it is, in fact, a very large Cottesloe. Because it is located below residential accommodation, the height is limited to 30 feet (9.14 metres). This presented some limitations to the stage, but proved a virtue for the auditorium since the floor to floor dimensions of the three balconies are extremely compact, the first priority of the courtyard form. The entire theatre was pre-fabricated offsite by stage engineering specialist Tait then installed into the empty building space.

The constant issue in judging a theatre is form versus seat count. To me, this form may have its limits. I've found The Bridge in end stage/proscenium form (950 seats) overlarge; the stage simply seems too far away and I found hearing difficult from the rear stalls and balcony. However in thrust form (900 seats) the theatre works far better, and in promenade (an audience of 1075) for the Hytner productions of *Julius Caesar* and *Midsummer Night's Dream* – the format of *The Mysteries* rediscovered – it was absolutely thrilling.

In discussing the design of The Bridge, Steve acknowledges the influence of the Young Vic and recent courtyard spaces: "We looked at courtyard spaces and chamber opera houses where everybody is tapered around the walls in narrow galleries." The undoubted success of The Bridge is yet another demonstration that people-oriented theatre spaces possess a unique quality that encourages the theatrical event to spring to life. It is the most recent evidence that for lively theatre to more readily succeed, an encircling audience simply works.

Nick Hytner welcomes his audience

The Bridge Theatre, London, UK, architect Haworth Tompkins

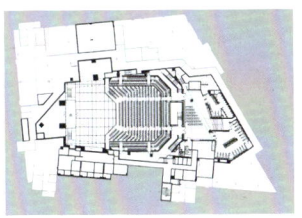

The Bridge Theatre – stalls plan, proscenium layout

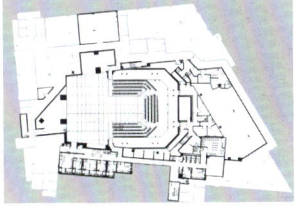

The Bridge Theatre – stalls plan, thrust layout

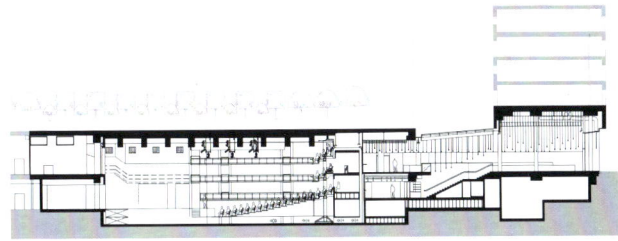

The Bridge Theatre – section. Drawings courtesy of Haworth Tompkins

5.4 Designing Theatres

The Thrust Stage

Crucible Theatre, Sheffield, UK
Chicago Shakespeare Theater, Chicago, Illinois, USA

The Sheffield Crucible is a real Tyrone Guthrie/Tanya Moiseiwitsch theatre. Colin George, director of the Crucible, wanted a true thrust. He commissioned the pair, fresh from the completion of the Guthrie Theater in Minneapolis (their third thrust, after Stratford, Ontario and Edinburgh) to advise him.

Guthrie, who was disappointed by the asymmetric auditorium introduced by the architect in Minneapolis, insisted on returning to a symmetrical space, with a narrow thrust, surrounded by a lower 'moat' and two vomitoria. The Guthrie stage concept makes the stage a crossroad at the core of the theatre. The overhead eggcrate bridges allow stage lighting from multiple angles.

The Chicago Shakespeare uses almost an intersection of forms, placing a flexible thrust stage within a courtyard-form auditorium.

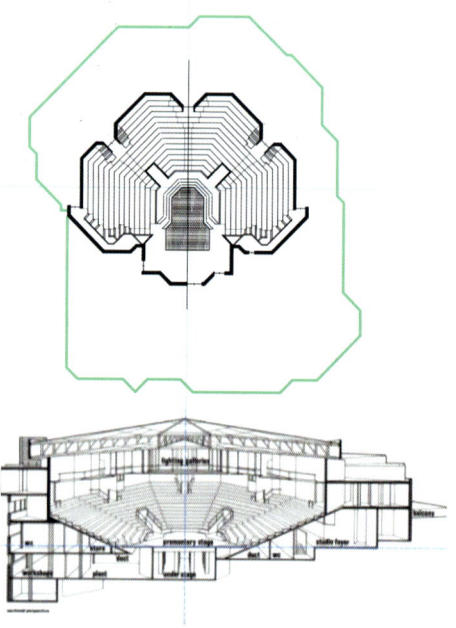

Crucible Theatre, Sheffield: plan (showing auditorium within building) and front elevation

Crucible Theatre, Sheffield, UK, architect Renton Howard Wood Levin

Chicago Shakespeare Theater, Chicago, USA, architect Kuwabara Payne McKenna Blumberg Architects/DLK Architects

A Sense of Theatre

Arts Centres

The Esplanade Arts Centre, Singapore
The Arts Commons, Calgary, Alberta, Canada

Arts centres are a uniquely important investment for communities determined to jump-start advances in the arts – and perhaps manifestations of what the London National Theatre Opera House scheme could have been.

Singapore began for Theatre Projects with a study of performance types across South-East Asia. Sadly, the smaller theatres, specifically intended for East/West performance were deleted, the government preferring the two main halls for music and lyric theatre as a desirable first phase. Phenomenal success is now leading to expansion.

For Arts Commons in Calgary, Alberta, TP's first project in North America, our study of the community indicated the need for a high-quality flexible concert hall, with two drama theatres.

The 750-seat Max Bell has a variable proscenium. A lesson from the Lyttelton lay in the flexibility of the pros. Moving the entire structure of the side boxes of the forward part of the auditorium enables the stage width to vary and the forestage to advance or retreat. Then, the ultimate in intimacy: a small semi-circular courtyard, the Martha Cohen.

Esplanade Concert Hall, Singapore, Esplanade – Theatres on the Bay, architect Michael Wilford & Partners/DP Architects

Esplanade Lyric Theatre, Singapore, architect Michael Wilford & Partners/DP Architects

Max Bell Theatre, Arts Commons, Calgary, Alberta, Canada, architect Raines Finlayson Barrett and Partners

Martha Cohen Theatre, Arts Commons, Calgary, Alberta, Canada, architect Raines Finlayson Barrett and Partners

The audience applauds: curtain call at the end of a performance at the Esplanade Lyric Theatre

5.4 Designing Theatres

Opera

Winspear Opera, Dallas, Texas, USA
Den Norske Opera, Oslo, Norway
Glyndebourne, Sussex, UK

The magnificent Winspear Opera House in Dallas, Texas, in many ways an evolution and realisation of the auditorium outlined for Genoa, is part of perhaps the ultimate arts district – a bigger version of London's South Bank of which the National is a part – where for over thirty years outstanding arts facilities have been built: a major art museum, a world-class symphony hall and the Wyly drama theatre.

Other opera houses that exemplify TP's approach include the architecturally stunning Den Norske Opera, in Oslo Norway; the Niarchos Cultural Center, home of the Greek National Opera, in Athens, Greece; and the exceptionally intimate Glyndebourne Opera set in the lush green fields of Sussex, England.

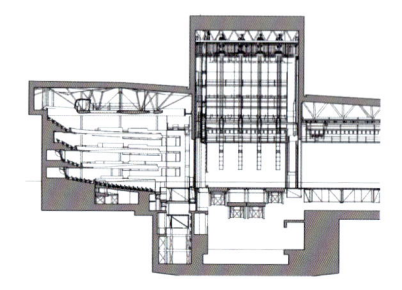

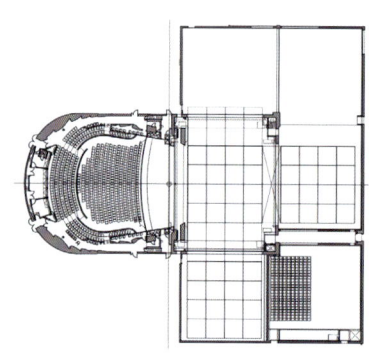

Winspear Opera, Dallas, Texas, USA, architect Foster + Partners/Kendall Heaton Associates

Niarchos Cultural Center, Athens, Greece, architect Renzo Piano Building Workshop/ Betaplan

Glyndebourne Opera House, Sussex, UK, architect Michael Hopkins

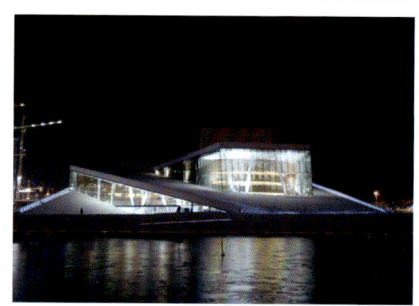

Den Norske Opera, Oslo, Norway

Den Norske Opera, Oslo, Norway, architect Snøhetta

Den Norske Opera, Oslo, Norway

A Sense of Theatre

A New-Style Multipurpose Hall

Belk Theater, Charlotte, North Carolina, USA and others

Multipurpose halls are commonly found across the United States. Cities require a hall for performances ranging from symphony, opera, ballet, and large scale touring Broadway shows to local school assemblies. Such halls had third-rate reputations thanks to their overlarge auditorium with their usually super-cinema style, wide fan-shaped seating on one-or-two levels.

I knew that almost all the classic opera houses of Europe housed a wide range of musical and social events. My realisation was that reconfiguring multifunction halls with three-dimensional auditoria would yield a quality that would improve their acoustics, sightlines, and theatricality. The Belk was TP's first large-scale multipurpose hall in the US. Similar approaches in Cincinnati Ohio, Dayton Ohio and Madison Wisconsin have created large theatres that are equally successful for symphonic music as well as opera, ballet and Broadway touring theatre.

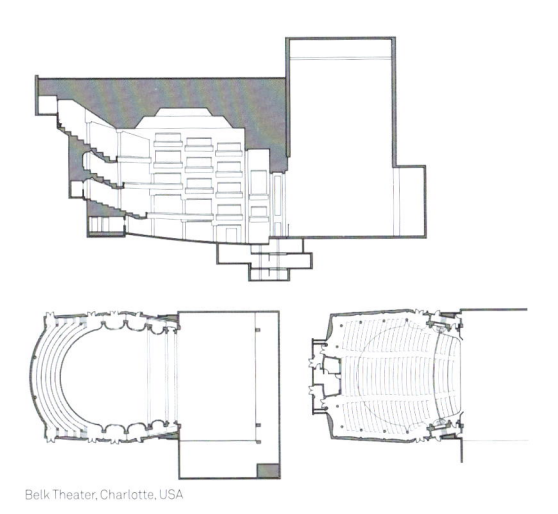

Belk Theater, Charlotte, North Carolina, USA, architect César Pelli Associates/Morris Architects/Middleton McMillan

Kauffman Center, Kansas City, Missouri, USA, architect Moshe Safdie Architects

Mead Theater, Schuster Performing Arts Center, Dayton, Ohio, USA, architect César Pelli Associates/Morris Architects/Middleton McMillan

Aronoff Center for the Arts, Cincinnati, Ohio, USA, architect César Pelli Associates/GBBN Architects

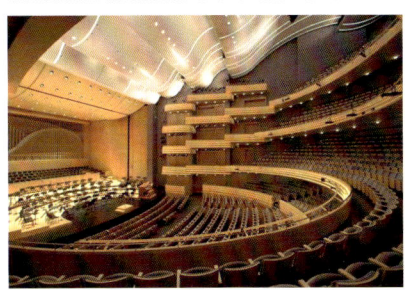

Overture Center, Madison, Wisconsin, USA, architect César Pelli Associates/Potter Lawson & Fladd Architects

Belk Theater, Charlotte, USA

5.4 Designing Theatres

The Multi-Form Hall

Derngate Centre, Northampton, UK
Steinmetz Hall, Orlando, Florida, USA

Flexible staging and changeable actor-audience relationships were pioneered in TP's courtyard theatres. For Northampton's Derngate Centre, Richard Brett and I extended this concept to a larger scale that allowed a 1500-seat room to convert from full symphony hall to opera/lyric theatre to a flat-floored arena, employing movable audience towers and seating banks on air castors. This created an enormously successful, heavily utilised and popular venue that has been in constant use since 1983.

Theatre today seeks both flexibility and intimacy. History so clearly shows us how the past has evolved. The root of theatre is the courtyard, the demands of larger audiences and more elaborate staging led to the world epitomised by Matcham. But the committed proscenium restricts flexibility. A return to the modern courtyard, typified by Derngate, points the way to a new future.

"The dawn of a new age of entertainment architecture."
Architects' Journal, UK.

Movable architecture can work. My last example opened in 2022. Another symphony hall that changes from concert hall to opera house with the capability of transforming from raked seating to a flat-floor hall: the 1700-seat Steinmetz Hall. This is the latest addition to the Dr. Phillips Center for the Performing Arts in Orlando, Florida by architect Barton Myers. It combines the finest of modern symphonic acoustics with flexibility of form perhaps not seen since the classic Renaissance opera houses of Europe.

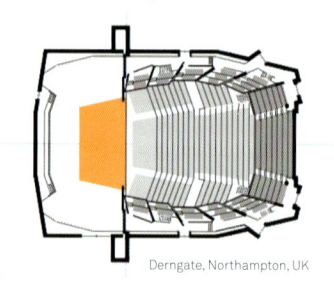

Derngate, Northampton, UK

Steinmetz Hall, Orlando, Florida, USA, architect Barton Myers Associates/HKS/Baker Barrios Architects; proscenium mode

Derngate – stalls

Derngate – flat floor

Derngate, Northampton, UK, architect Renton Howard Wood Levin

Derngate - proscenium

Derngate - symphony

A Sense of Theatre

Creating Spaces to Unleash Imagination

Flexibility, Economy, Intimacy, Theatricality
The threads linking all these projects are fourfold. First, flexibility to offer new possibilities of stagecraft to directors and designers and new experiences to audiences. Second, economy. Modern technology can assist in providing high-quality, cost-effective operations. Third, yet of greatest import, intimacy. Above all else, live performance demands intimate contact between the artist and every member of the audience. Lastly, theatricality. Three-dimensional spaces for performance that congregate actor and spectator in lively juxtaposition to each other are spaces that readily spring to life, ready to support that explosion of energy that makes live performance so irresistible.

Theatre Technology
Theatre technology advances exponentially. The National's innovations have been followed by countless more: air castors, fibre optics, motion control, moving lights, LEDs, video, and movable architecture. From the simple courtyard to the most complex water spectaculars technology has allowed the creation of spaces where anything is possible.

Feasibility
Before you can even design the performane space, you have to understand what it is for and how it exists within its local cultural environment. Sometimes that is in cultures with rich performance traditions. Sometimes that is in communities where few precedents exist. In almost every country, satisfying different historical/cultural traditions is essential. Being a consultant demands listening, patience and understanding. The aim should not be to export some uniform set of imperialistic prejudices; we are seeking to harness our experience to uncover the deepest aspirations and dreams of those wanting to create this new place. The intention is never to build a performance space for us, but to create a livable space for those who will own it, run it and use it.

However, a pivotal issue, always, is the project's fundamental feasibility. Our conviction, that theatre is a uniquely human-oriented art form, must be balanced against the need for the essential activity within to be sustainable – financially and practically – and for it to fit seamlessly with the local arts ecology. Here I must pay tribute to another TP colleague, David Staples, managing director of the group from 1986 to 2018.

David first joined us for an extraordinary venture involving a chain of arts centres across Iran, which sought to bring into harmony the ancient traditions of Iranian art and Western performance. David, with exceptional skills in arts management and leadership, rapidly pioneered new and imaginative ways to uncover the essence of a client's true needs to ensure that the program for a new centre was both imaginative and practical. The details of every building project must be firmly based on a clear understanding, at every level, of the implications of those details upon operations long into the future.

Collaboration
It is perhaps a surprise but an architect alone, especially a famous architect, might find the challenge of theatre design very hard. Frank Lloyd Wright designed elegant buildings, but woeful theatres. The world's most famous opera house, by Jørn Utzon in Sydney, is famed for its stunning roof and silhouette but houses third-rate performance spaces. Theatre requires collaboration.

Theatre Projects has collaborated successfully with dozens of architects around the world to realise newly dynamic spaces for music, dance, and theatre. These include Brian Avery, Norman Foster, Tim Foster, Frank Gehry, Hugh Hardy, Hertzog & de Meuron, Michael Hopkins, Rem Koolhaas, Levitt Bernstein, Barton Myers, Terry Pawson, César Pelli, Renzo Piano, Fred Pilbrow, Christian de Portzamparc, William Rawn, Nick Thompson and Clare Ferraby of Renton Howard Wood Levin, Moshe Safdie, Snøhetta, Steve Tompkins, Michael Wilford, Keith Williams, of course Denys Lasdun, and others too numerous to list. The TP design team over the years has been led by myself and Iain Mackintosh with architect/designers Eric Jordan, Paul Jenkins, Tim Foster, Neil Morton, Anne Minors, Peter Lucking, Brian Hall, Cy Almey, John Runia, Carol Allen, Athos Zaghi, Mark Stroomer, John Coyne, and Scott Crossfield. Over the years we have worked with acousticians too numerous to list here – ensuring the optimum acoustic for any chosen performance demands the closest collaboration with architect and theatre designer. Through all of this, teamwork is fundamental.

The theatre designer's creed: actor and audience, human-scale, bold vision, advancing technology, and relentless attention to every detail. Unleashing the imagination of theatre-makers of the future.

From the past: a theatre for people

5.5 Theatres for People

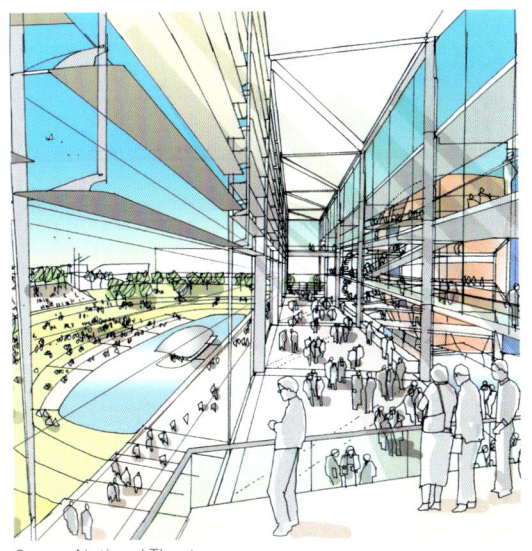

Cyprus National Theatre

Sir Laurence pleaded, "cannot we concentrate on making a place where the actors feel marvellous?"

At the National, it eluded us all. At Nottingham, my eyes were opened. In the decades since I think I have come to understand, and to be able to help architects understand.

So perhaps a real example, showing how that hypothetical sense of theatre was brought to a real new theatre.

What is that 'magical' formula that brings theatre to exuberant life?

In 1966, when I joined the National Theatre Building Committee, I was a 33-year old lighting designer in London and on Broadway, a producer in the West End, and a fledgling theatre consultant. In the latter role, I was concerned with the stage and its technology. My thoughts about auditorium design were rudimentary. Sir Laurence had asked for his theatre to be a place where his actors would feel wonderful. Over the next decade my focus entirely changed as I began to realise how such an ambition might be realised. After fifty years working with architects around the world, I came to a realisation: that theatres 'spring to life' in direct relationship to the intensity of the relationship between actor and audience but also between all parts of that audience.

That great period of theatre architecture in the early 20th century was a product of gradual evolution that placed humankind at its centre. Peruse new theatres in architectural magazines and countless bizarrely shaped projects will appear. Theatre makers will often overcome what the architect has wrought, but the essence of a successful theatre stems from the life naturally generated within the space.

There are some fundamental principles that may lead toward a more lively space, as at the National Theatre of Cyprus, designed by my son Fred Pilbrow for KPF Architecture. It shows a people-oriented space may be embellished by shape, form, structure, acoustics and integrated services, all merging to create opportunity for that 'sense of theatre' to flourish.

Here, really, are the key things I've come to understand about theatre design.

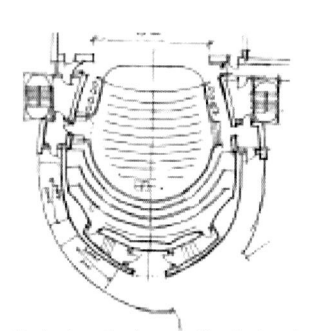

Evolution of a theatre: The National Theatre of Cyprus. Theatre Projects sketch

Concept to architecture, sketch by Fred Pilbrow

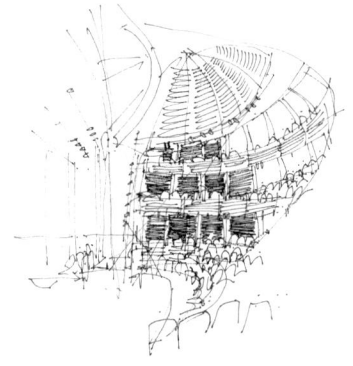

Congregate our audience, surround and contain them

Actor and Audience

The first requirement of theatre is to foster the relationship between actors and audience. A performance is intended to unite an audience. Individuals enter a place and, providing the event works and the relationship is established, the public becomes veritably one. That's why the great moments in theatre take place in laughter or silence – when the audience reacts together.

One begins to see how a slope, a hemicycle, a certain seating density, a continuity between auditorium and stage are required to foster this relationship. The crucial factor is atmosphere. If a theoretical theatre is built – a sort of beautiful geometry – the result will be a place unsuited for theatre. To build a theatre, one must always start out from the feeling of being human. In the end there is only one criterion: that which fosters this relationship. Then everything else falls into place.

Therefore the question: how should a theatre be built, cannot be solved by relying on formal data. Spectator and actor must coexist within a single space that surrounds and unites them. This space has to be friendly yet demanding; neither cold, nor sterile, nor abstract. It ought to stimulate the imagination without telling any story.[6]

The heart of theatre is the place where performer meets audience – the auditorium. Other parts of a theatre building are important, but it is in the auditorium that the success or failure of the whole will lie. Any examination of theatre architecture must start here, at the centre. Are there universal qualities that might guide us in our search for new and lively places of performance?

Intimacy and Energy

With the human being as storyteller, be it by song, dance, musical instrument, or spoken word, and the human audience as spectator, it follows that the ground rules of auditorium design must stem from the fundamental characteristics of the human body. The human ability to project the voice, and perhaps more subtly, to project the personality; the human ability to perceive facial expression or gesture from afar will set the parameters of the performance space.

Performer/Audience Relationships

Every book on theatre design has diagrams illustrating standard actor-audience relationships. Audiences are placed in front of, on either side of, or around the stage, which is labelled proscenium, thrust, traverse or arena. Few of these examinations ever consider the performer-audience relationship in three dimensions, yet that is vital in understanding how an actor relates to their audience. An actor should inhabit the centre of the theatrical world not just in plan but also in section. The most common error in theatre design is insufficient attention to the space in elevation.

An actor standing on a stage platform above their audience is in a relationship of commanding their attention. A politician rousing a crowd knows the control that is derived from a soapbox. An actor performing at the lower level of a steeply raked auditorium is below their audience, who look down on the performer, observe them, just as a group of students may observe a lecture.

For live theatre to achieve a balanced audience in section, half that audience should be below the actors' eye-line. Subtle adjustment of stage height can be very significant. A low stage in a small auditorium brings audience and performer psychologically closer together, but in a larger theatre a low stage will make the performer more remote. Raising the actor places him more positively in the audience's focus.

It is vitally important that every part of an audience

is brought together closely in plan and section. Nothing is so subtle as a theatre in section. Every inch counts. An extra inch of elevation at the lowest level may add several feet to the topmost tier. An orchestra stalls seating rake that is too steep forces any balcony above to be higher than it otherwise would be. Too high a balcony separates the audience vertically into different groups that will be disconnected from the performer and from each other. Acousticians may seek to lift a balcony to allow more sound to penetrate below; done to excess this can destroy a theatre's overall cohesion. A study of late 19th century theatres is illuminating. The theatres of Matcham and McElfatrick were devised with almost fiendish ingenuity. Every tier is subtly shaped with the front sides drooping downward and the rear sides upward to optimise sightlines. Each level carefully limits the view from the extreme seats. If every seat had a 'perfect' view, the theatre would significantly increase in size – and likely prove a failure.

The more balconies there are in a theatre, the closer to the stage will be the furthest seat. However there are objections to seating that is too high. The old 'Gods' or 'Peanut Gallery' carry connotations of social or racial inferiority from the days when the top levels of seating were the province of the poor and under-privileged. Balconies bring people closer to the stage. This is the highest priority. Front rows are prime rows. More balconies bring more prime rows.

Side Wall Boxes
Linking levels together is vitally important, both visually and psychologically. Audiences must be aware of each other and aware that they are all 'together.' Side wall boxes or 'ledges' play a fundamental role. Only a few faces on the side walls will provide a psychological link between levels, and between player and spectator. The height of boxes is pivotal. Ideally the performer might be able to touch those in the near stage boxes. Side boxes are the umbilical cord that encourages the baby to come to life, binding player to spectator, and level-to-level of audience participation.

The finest auditorium will involve compromise. Some seats will be to the front. Seats to the side will enjoy a different, but often closer, view. They will bring the theatre to life. Good design means achieving the best balance. Every seat will have a different, and unique, sightline to the stage. An 'ideal' theatre might be compared to a dining room table. You must sit around the table to experience a sense of togetherness.

Viewing Distance
You can't see the features of an actor's face if you are more than about 65 feet (19.8m) away. You can't really appreciate gesture from more than about 120 feet (36.6m) away. For drama the former dimension should be a limit, for musicals and opera or ballet, the latter. If the stage is a width of say 45 feet (13.7m), that will dictate how many people can be seated on one level with reasonable viewing conditions. The aural equation is more complex. Firstly an actor's ability to project the voice varies greatly dependent upon their skill and upon the type of material being performed. But electronic amplification of sound, even if it is perceived as undesirable, is possible, and to an ever higher standard.

But what of the completely intangible? What of the projection of the human spirit – or personality? How can this be measured? Some performers clearly do have greater power of projection than others. Unforgettable experiences are often the product of a great actor, musician or dancer whose personality and power, whose 'life-force' seems to strike you to the heart even across considerable distances.

Teamwork

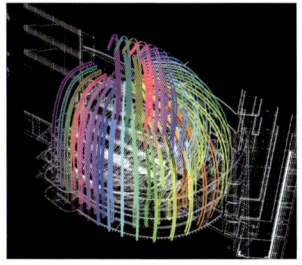

Architecture to enfold audience

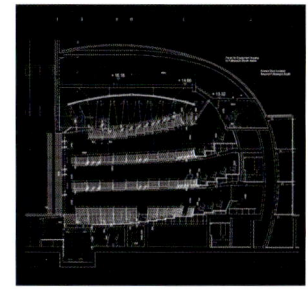

Integrate structure and services

A cauldron-like space

5.5 Theatres for People

Good sightlines, intimate acoustic

One space: intimacy, curves, verticality

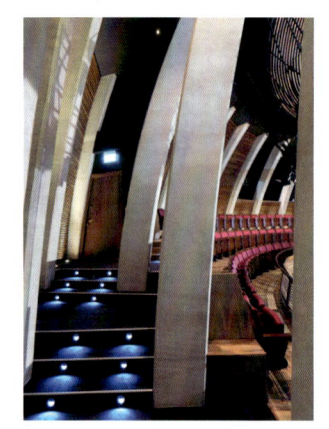

Structure to embrace and frame space

Open and welcoming exterior

There are no simple answers. This power of personality is heavily dependent upon the actor, the type of performance and the nature of the occasion. A dramatic actor is seldom able to overcome a vastly overlarge space. But a 'star' can rise upon occasion above an unsuitable situation, and an audience can thrill to a famous performer or to a much-heralded event. A rock-and-roll superstar, albeit supported by all the paraphernalia of modern technology, can overwhelm tens of thousands. On the cinema or video screen a different type of star personality exerts their animal magnetism through the medium of the camera's lens.

For live performance to exert its power, audiences must see, hear and feel the performer, but also reciprocate their feelings and response. For this communion to occur, visual intimacy must be as intense as possible. Acoustics must be optimised. For emotional energy to be kindled and to burst into flame, it must be fed with the emotional oxygen of the clustered audience, embracing the performer as tightly as possible in the coitus of performance. A noted American scholar of theatre history, Professor Franklin J. Hildy of the University of Maryland, who served on the advisory committee of London's Globe Theatre, has suggested criteria for theatre auditoria design. "Let there be no dead space in a theatre. Wherever one looks in a historic theatre auditorium there are signs of life or the potential for life. Within each audience member's range of vision while watching a play, there are other audience members to look at. Even doors, like those found at the end of every aisle in Wagner's famous Festspielhaus in Bayreuth, Germany, suggest the potential for life to arrive at any moment. Following World War II, however, economics, combined with the proliferation of cinemas, inspired some theatre practitioners to ask that the modernist aesthetic of neutral space be applied to theatre architecture. This, it was argued, would put all the audience's focus onto the stage. Ultimately it worked against the social nature of live theatre. Live theatre's social nature turns out to be one of its most essential characteristics."[7] Second, Hildy writes, the colour black is anathema in an auditorium; it creates negative, rather than positive, space. Third, let the auditorium be known again as 'the house' as it has for generations. Yet our National Theatre is today a place of concrete disguised by black serge. Is this the most suitable house for our drama?

A 2005 thesis, *Theatre Architecture as Embodied Space: A Phenomenology of Performance*[8] by a German-born scholar Lisa Marie Bowler explores: "what makes a theatre feel like a theatre."[9] I admit that I'd never heard of phenomenology. It is a science-based philosophy developed by a German, Edmund Husserl, at the turn of the 20th century. It can be employed to describe space and the experience of that space – moment by moment – on the spectator. Bowler uses it to describe theatre space.

Initially, I was suspicious. The paper seems pretentious and overly academic. Upon reflection, a series of quite interesting issues emerged – issues that might appear self-evident, but are pertinent to anyone contemplating a theatre.

"An actor walks into a room, and the room changes."[10]

"A theatre building as it is experienced in performance is a radically different perceptual entity than the same building when it is dark and empty."[11]

Undoubtedly true.

"The basis, or origin, of the stage's aesthetic transformation lies not in the space of the stage itself nor in the dramatic text, but in the shared

space of stage and auditorium, or more precisely, in what happens in this shared space." [12] "The effect of intimacy created by a concentrated, cauldron-like space created on the basis of the principles – one space, intimacy, curves, verticality and decoration – far outweighs the disadvantages of not all seats having equal view of the stage." [13] "If the space of a theatre is to be experienced as a shared space, however, it is important that one be able to see others sharing in the experience." [14] "The architectural principle of 'enwrapment' ensures that spectators do not lose contact with each other as they focus on what is happening in the performance area." [15]

"A group of cognitive scientists measured spectators' responses to different types of theatre spaces and they came to the conclusion that an environment which provides sensory stimulation increases the engagement of the audience with the theatre event." [16] "The experience of watching theatre is still too often understood to be a passive state, rather than an activity involving multiple perceptual channels." [17]

"What this suggests is that the experience of perceiving a space happens not just through visual or aural or kinetic channels, but is also emotional. A space is known by registering its affective and emotional effects, that is, by attending to how it feels." [18]

"Theatres are built but once finished do not 'act' as they are supposed to. Some do work well but are never loved by those who work in them or come to visit them. Others fail outright. The fact is that the undertaking of building a theatre cannot be reduced to a formula that will definitely work."

Peter Brook was one of the most outspoken enemies of this functional approach. He argued that the only way of arriving at a shape or a constellation that works is through experimentation in the space itself, taking into account the very specific situation and the relationship between performers and spectators. [19]

Economics v. Art
It seems self-evident that more seats must mean more tickets sold, more income and in consequence more profit. But this oversimplification is in most circumstances simply not true. For a seat to possess any value it must be sold to the public.

One of the oldest rules of the theatre manager's book (perhaps dating back to Aeschylus) is that a shortage of seats is the best guarantee of success. The seat that is unobtainable is the seat that everybody wants to buy. Rarity value is close to priceless in 'show business' and has been through the centuries. A 'Sold Out' sign is worth all the advertising one could buy.

Sense of Place
A theatre must be a 'place'. It must have a sense of having been lived in. A place maybe of comfort, perhaps memory, perhaps exhilaration. But it should be a place that possesses character. Hopefully the clustered audience will make an enormous contribution to preparing the atmosphere of the room for performance. But architecture and interior decoration will, and must, play a vital role.

Human Space, Densely Clustered, Intimately Spectacular
The human essence lies at the heart of lively theatre. Styles of presentation may change, competition from new forms of entertainment will proliferate, but the human constant remains. Wonderfully spectacular, or essentially simple productions may take the stage, but an auditorium that welcomes, that thrills, that binds artist and audience together will last long into the future.

Collaboration

Exterior with a sense of drama

Preparation for the event to come

Audience tightly clustered

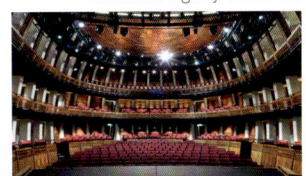

The end result: the stage in the warm embrace of the auditorium

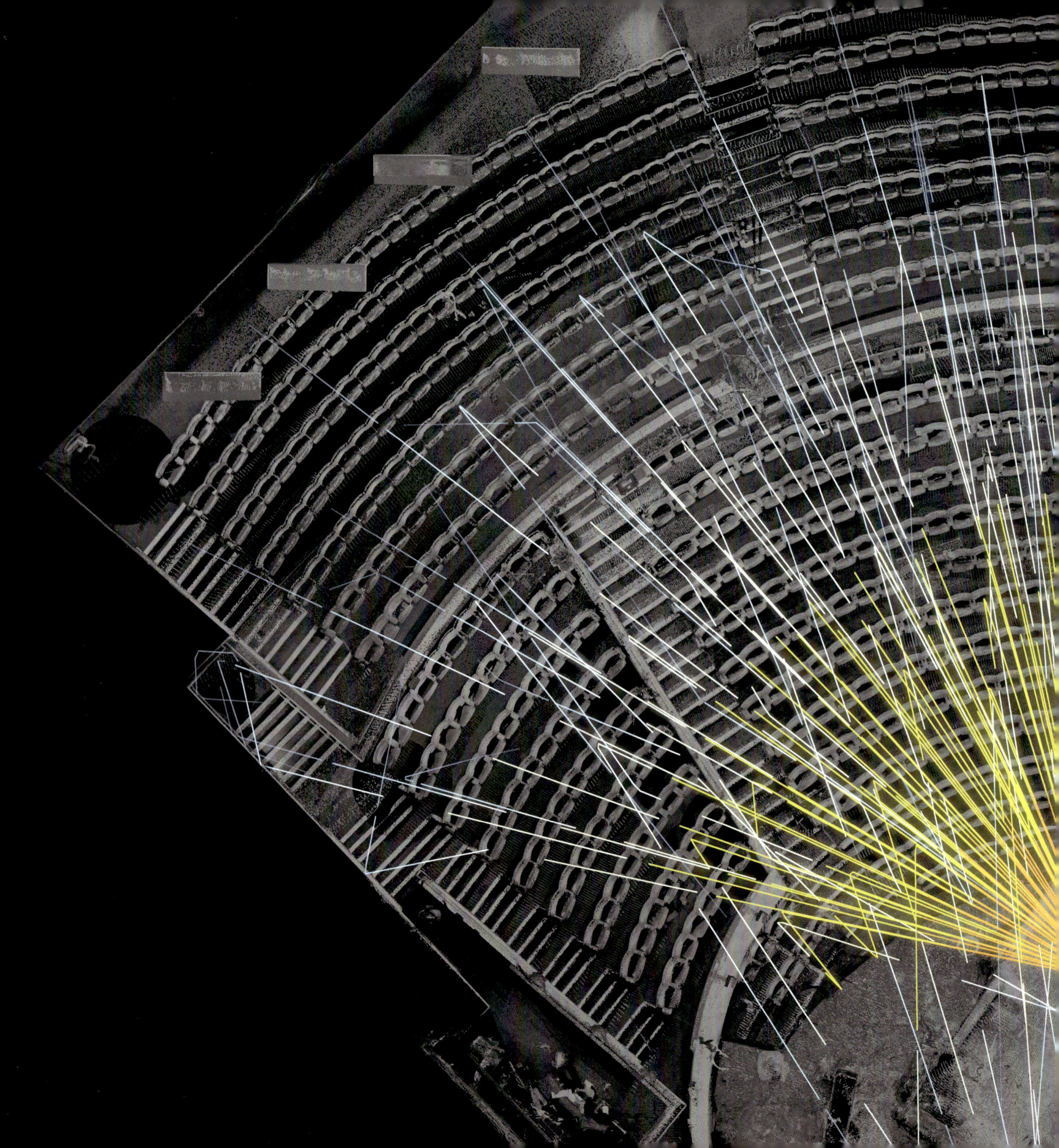

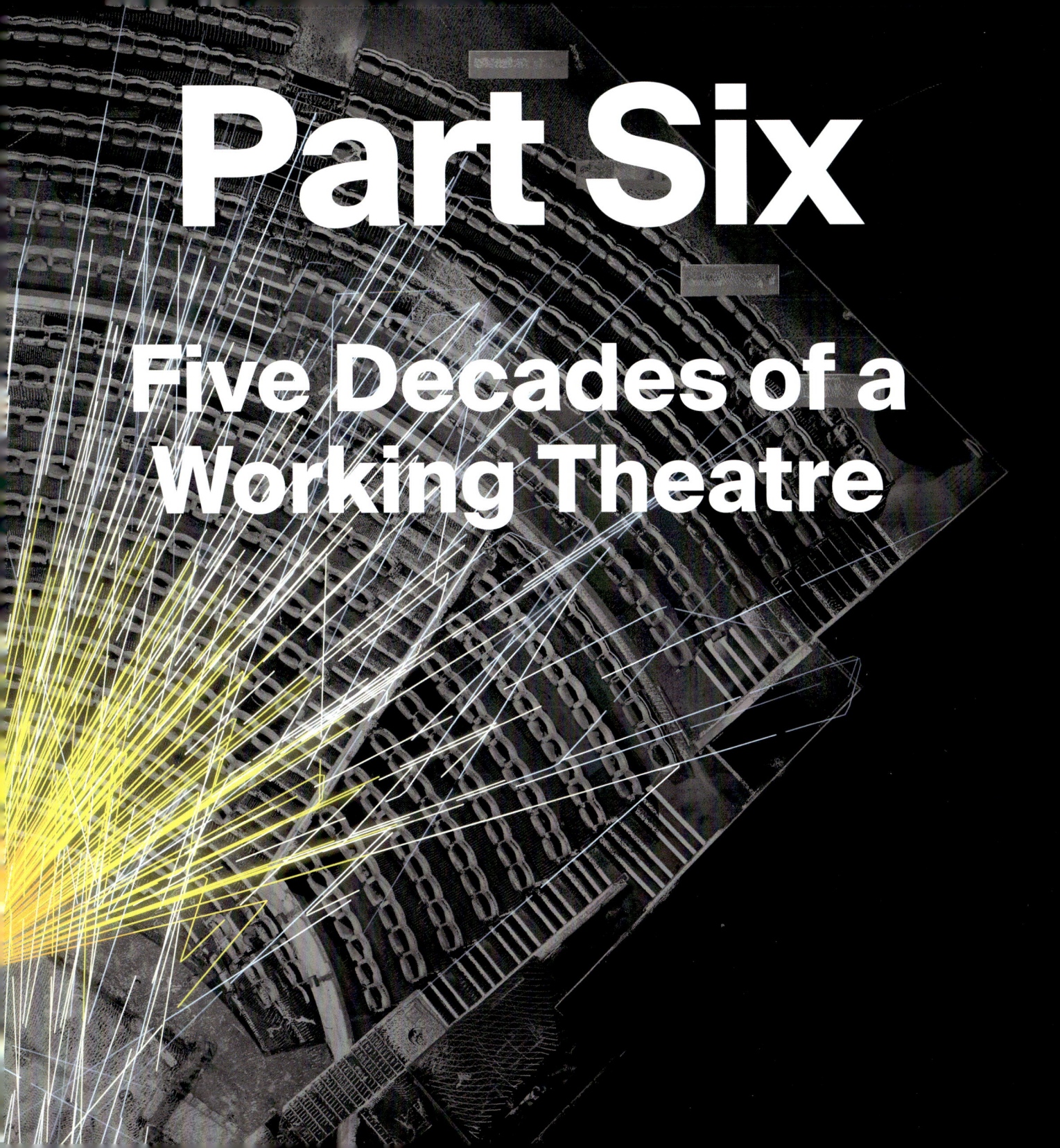

Part Six

Five Decades of a Working Theatre

The Olivier Theatre during the fit-up for the 1999 Ensemble Season

6.1 Fifty Years of Performance Design

Lyttelton Theatre, showing front of house lighting positions

The National has fostered remarkable designs on its stages, thanks to the facilities and the supportive, creative environment it offers. A chance to consider just some of that incredible work.

A theatre without shows is just an empty space.

The three theatres at the National have rarely been empty: since opening they have offered a breathless schedule of "plays, plays, plays," many with remarkable performances. But many also remarkable to look at.

Among its countless revolutions, the National Theatre arguably created a revolution in production design in the UK. By giving designers facilities, opportunities and a freedom – the "right to fail" often mentioned in connection with the National – from the pressures of commercial theatre, shows have been made that perhaps could not have been made anywhere else. The brilliant *War Horse* ended up being a commercial hit, but would any commercial producer have dared make it?

The National's supportive environment has allowed entirely new design approaches to be pioneered – think of Bill Dudley's projection work on *The Coast of Utopia*, a design discipline that is now almost a standard part of shows. And it has allowed successive generations of designers to hone their craft – lighting designer David Hersey credits the early NT production *The Architect and the Emperor of Assyria* as the show that really taught him to see – before applying those skills elsewhere.

Let us take a tour through some examples of the remarkable design work that the NT has enabled.

For these photographs I am indebted to Philip Carter, who had taken over the mantle of 'technical photographer' in the 1980s, moonlighting from his NT day jobs of production book-keeper, technical scheduler and creator of the theatre's system for repertoire planning and more. He has created an amazing record.

Olivier Theatre

The Relapse, 2001 Director: Trevor Nunn, Designer: Sue Blane, Lighting: Paul Pyant

Coast of Utopia: Shipwreck, 2002 Director: Trevor Nunn, Designer: William Dudley, Lighting: David Hersey

Anything Goes, 2002 Director: Trevor Nunn, Designer: John Gunter, Lighting: David Hersey

The Bacchai, 2002 Director: Peter Hall, Designer: Alison Chitty, Lighting: Peter Mumford

His Dark Materials, 2003 Director: Nicholas Hytner, Designer: Giles Cadle, Lighting: Paule Constable

Cyrano de Bergerac, 2004 Director: Howard Davies, Designer: William Dudley, Lighting: Paul Anderson

Henry IV Part 2, 2005 Director: Nicholas Hytner, Designer: Mark Thompson, Lighting: Neil Austin

War Horse, 2007 Director: Marianne Elliott, Designer: Rae Smith, Lighting: Paule Constable

Fram, 2008 Director: Tony Harrison, Designer: Bob Crowley, Lighting: Mark Henderson

Fram, 2008 Director: Tony Harrison, Designer: Bob Crowley, Lighting: Mark Henderson

Mother Courage, 2009 Director: Deborah Warner, Designer: Tom Pye, Lighting: Jean Kalman

Emperor and Galilean, 2011 Director: Jonathan Kent, Designer: Paul Brown, Lighting: Mark Henderson

Olivier Theatre

Fela! 2011 Director: Bill T. Jones, Designer: Marina Draghici, Lighting: Robert Wierzel

The Cherry Orchard, 2011 Director: Howard Davies, Designer: Bunny Christie, Lighting: Neil Austin

Edward II, 2013 Director: Joe Hill-Gibbins, Designer: Lizzie Clachan, Lighting: James Farncombe

James III, 2014 Arena format. Director: Laurie Sansom, Designer: Jon Bausor, Lighting: Philip Gladwell

Behind the Beautiful Forevers, 2015 Director: Rufus Norris, Designer: Katrina Lindsay, Lighting: Paule Constable

Our Country's Good, 2015 Director: Nadia Fall, Designer: Peter McKintosh, Lighting: Neil Austin

Amadeus, 2016 Director: Michael Longhurst, Designer: Chloe Lamford, Lighting: Jon Clark

As You Like It, 2016 The Forest, Director: Polly Findlay, Designer: Lizzie Clachan, Lighting: Jon Clark

Salome, 2017 Director: Yaël Farber, Designer: Susan Hilferty, Lighting: Tim Lutkin

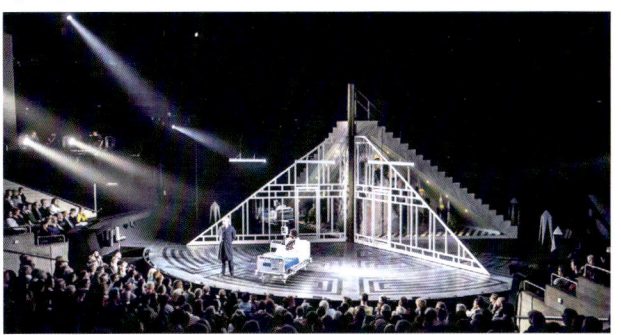

Twelfth Night, 2017 Director: Simon Godwin, Designer: Soutra Gilmour, Lighting: James Farncombe

6.1 Fifty Years of Performance Design 437

Lyttelton Theatre

No Man's Land, 2001 Director: Harold Pinter, Designer: Eileen Diss, Lighting: Mick Hughes

Pillars of the Community, 2005 Director: Marianne Elliott, Designer: Rae Smith, Lighting: Chris Davey

Rafta, Rafta, 2007 Director: Nicholas Hytner, Designer: Tim Hatley, Lighting: Hugh Vanstone

Present Laughter, 2008 Director: Howard Davies, Designer: Tim Hatley, Lighting: Hugh Vanstone

Happy Days, 2007 Director: Deborah Warner, Designer: Tom Pye, Lighting: Jean Kalman

Burnt by the Sun, 2009 Director: Howard Davies, Designer: Vicki Mortimer, Lighting: Mark Henderson

Children of the Sun, 2013 Director: Howard Davies, Designer: Bunny Christie, Lighting: Neil Austin

From Morning to Midnight, 2013 Director: Melly Still, Designer: Soutra Gilmour, Lighting: Bruno Poet

Liola, 2013 Director: Richard Eyre, Designer: Anthony Ward, Lighting: Neil Austin

Three Sisters, 2003 Director: Katie Mitchell, Designer: Vicki Mortimer, Lighting: Paule Constable

Dara, 2015 Director: Nadia Fall, Designer: Katrina Lindsay, Lighting: Neil Austin

Lyttelton Theatre

Light Shining in Buckinghamshire, 2015 Director: Lyndsey Turner, Designer: Es Devlin, Lighting: Bruno Poet

The Motherfker with the Hat, 2015** Director: Indhu Rubasingham, Designer: Robert Jones, Lighting: Oliver Fenwick

Jane Eyre, 2015 Director: Sally Cookson, Designer: Michael Vale, Lighting: Aideen Malone

The Red Barn, 2016 Director: Robert Icke, Designer: Bunny Christie, Lighting: Paule Constable

The Deep Blue Sea, 2016 Director: Carrie Cracknell, Designer: Tom Scutt, Lighting: Guy Hoare

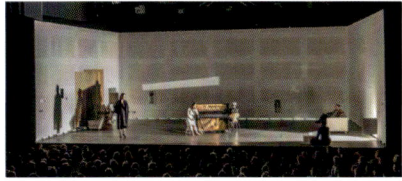

Ma Rainey's Black Bottom, 2016 Director: Dominic Cooke, Designer: Ultz, Lighting: Charles Balfour

Hedda Gabler, 2017 Director: Ivo van Hove, Designer: Jan Versweyveld, Lighting: Jan Versweyveld

Angels in America, 2017 Director: Marianne Elliott, Designer: Ian MacNeil, Lighting: Paule Constable

Angels in America, 2017 Director: Marianne Elliott, Designer: Ian MacNeil, Lighting: Paule Constable

Network, 2017 Director: Ivo van Hove, Designer: Jan Versweyveld, Lighting: Jan Versweyveld

The Lehman Trilogy, 2018 Director: Sam Mendes, Designer: Es Devlin, Lighting: Jon Clark, Projection: Luke Halls

6.1 Fifty Years of Performance Design

Cottesloe/Dorfman Theatre

Stanley, 1996 Director: John Caird, Designer: Tim Hatley, Lighting: Peter Mumford

Syringa Tree, 2002 Director: Larry Moss, Designer: Kenneth Foy, Lighting: Jason Kantrowitz

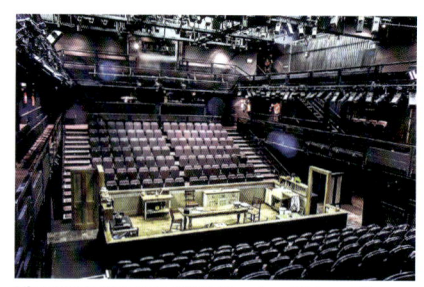

Vincent in Brixton, 2002 Director: Richard Eyre, Designer: Tim Hatley, Lighting: Peter Mumford

Fix Up, 2004 Director: Angus Jackson, Designer: Bunny Christie, Lighting: Neil Austin

The False Servant, 2004 Director: Jonathan Kent, Designer: Paul Brown, Lighting: Mark Henderson

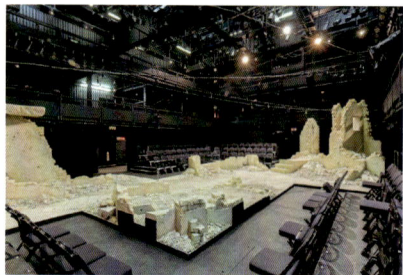

Paul, 2005 Director: Howard Davies, Designer: Vicki Mortimer, Lighting: Paule Constable

Tristan and Yseult, 2005 Director: Emma Rice, Designer: Bill Mitchell, Lighting: Alex Wardle

President of an Empty Room, 2005 Director: Howard Davies, Designer: Bunny Christie, Lighting: Mark Henderson

The Seafarer, 2006 Director: Conor McPherson, Designer: Rae Smith, Lighting: Neil Austin

The Overwhelming, 2006 Director: Max Stafford-Clark, Designer: Tim Shortall, Lighting: Johanna Town

A Sense of Theatre

Maurice Pinder, 2007 Director: Sarah Frankcom, Designer: Ti Green, Lighting: Mick Hughes

Landscape with Weapon, 2007 Director: Roger Michell, Designer: William Dudley, Lighting: Rick Fisher

Or You Could Kiss Me, 2010 Director: Neil Bartlett, Designer: Rae Smith, Lighting: Chris Davey

London Road, 2011 Director: Rufus Norris, Designer: Katrina Lindsay, Lighting: Bruno Poet

The Hard Problem, 2015 Director: Nicholas Hytner, Designer: Bob Crowley, Lighting: Mark Henderson

People, Places and Things, 2015 Director: Jeremy Herrin, Designer: Bunny Christie, Lighting: James Farncombe

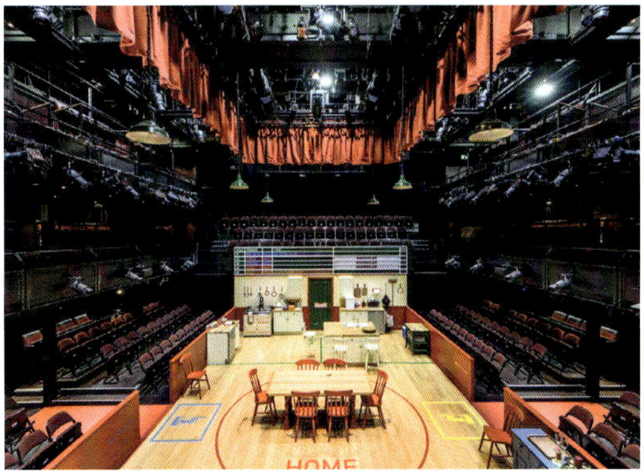

Rules for Living, 2015 Director: Marianne Elliott, Designer: Chloe Lamford, Lighting: Neil Austin

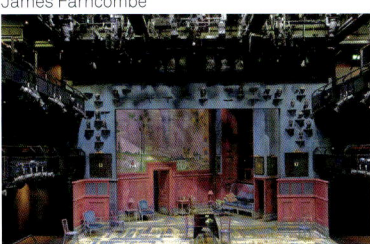

Evening at the Talkhouse, 2015 Director: Ian Rickson, Designer: The Quay Brothers, Lighting: Neil Austin

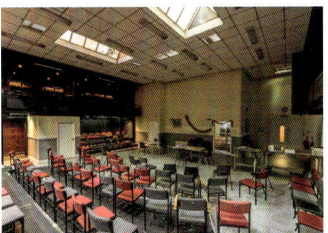

Love, 2016 Director: Alexander Zeldin, Designer: Natasha Jenkins, Lighting: Marc Williams

The Flick, 2016 Director: Sam Gold, Designer: David Zinn, Lighting: Jane Cox

6.1 Fifty Years of Performance Design

The Olivier Theatre: view down to the stage from the high in the fly tower, looking down on *Danton's Death*, 2010

6.2 Technical Evolution

The grid above the Lyttelton Theatre stage

The National's technical resources were cutting edge in their day, but constant production leads to wear and tear, and technology marches ever on.

How did those pioneering installations fair? And has the National continued to innovate as the time came to replace them?

Rob Halliday offers a summary of the many ways the National's technical facilities have evolved over almost five decades.

It's a scary yet exhilarating place to be, living on the cutting edge – and that's exactly where the technical facilities of the National Theatre were at the time of its opening, Richard Pilbrow having grasped not just the challenge of the plan to present multiple shows in rep, but that the building presented a perhaps once-in-a-lifetime opportunity to embrace technology as a way of doing things better, rather than just repeating what had gone before.

As we've seen, that didn't always go according to plan. The reasons for this are many and various. With the National a headline British project, British contractors were chosen even if in some cases companies from other countries might have been better qualified to deliver these incredibly complex pieces of machinery. And the timing of the creation of the National straddled technological revolutions from other industries, the complex electronic control systems for flying and lighting specified just a little too early to take advantage of the coming micro-processor technology.

Plus: all involved were inventing much of the future of technical theatre as they went along, at a time of dramatically rising costs, political unrest and constant pressure to get things done. This was bespoke, cutting edge, unique equipment. It needed time to be installed properly, made to work, refined. Delays and then Peter Hall's decision just to move the company in and start performing meant it didn't get it. Both Concorde and the Boeing 747, technological pioneers from the same era, got time for testing and polishing before the public were allowed on board.

To the credit of all involved, no one gave up on the things that didn't work immediately. Writing about the National's technical infrastructure on the tenth anniversary of the building's opening for *Cue* magazine, Bob Anderson noted that "the technical contractors who had taken great risks to design the new equipment faced greater costs and delay trying to finish and carry out tests while the theatres were in use. Inevitably there had not been sufficient foresight to entirely eliminate mistakes, and these had to be faced and remedied. Luckily most contractors completed their obligations without excessive delay and the management, the South Bank Theatre Board, were eminently fair in paying additional costs." [1]

The Passing of Time

As Bob Anderson also noted, "maintenance was recognized as a special problem at the National," the complex and in many cases unique systems "expected to require more attention than could be provided by operational staff or maintenance contracts." Within a couple of years of its opening, the NT had established a systems engineering department, intended to keep systems functioning, create backup systems for when they didn't, and update to new technology as it appeared and funds permitted. Technology never rests, so the work of this department and its descendants has basically never stopped throughout the building's life. It probably never will.

Olivier Theatre
The Drum

"In about 2012, it was discovered that the Olivier's drum revolve was basically falling to pieces," noted Mylan Lester in 2017[2]. He and Steve Colley formed the heart of the stage engineering and rigging team that had been involved in a series of projects to rejuvenate the NT's stage machinery, even before the big NT Future building upgrade project that began in 2015. "Various reports were commissioned, one of which pretty much said put it on bricks and run away," Lester continued. "The trouble is, if you take it away you're just left with a really big hole in the middle of a really big stage!"

The drum's core structure was a massive lattice of steelwork, most clearly seen in the publicity picture taken by its original manufacturer, Mole Richardson, when they assembled it in their car park prior to packing it up for delivery to the National (p,194). "It was an amazing concept that, mechanically, was slightly ahead of its time and electronically, in terms of its control system, was way ahead of its time," Lester adds. "Over the years it had also just suffered from wear and tear, running on an uneven surface, mis-loading, over-loading and just generally being abused."

It had also gone through periods of almost falling out of fashion, seemingly unloved during some eras of the National's history, or its use complicated by changes made to the Olivier stage by different directors or designers. Peter Hall had raised the whole stage by about 300mm quite early on, necessitating all manner of changes to the drum's mechanics and safety systems, and extended the stage forward of the drum in a way that quickly became permanent. Richard Eyre tried the Olivier as a theatre-in-the-round for a while. Trevor Nunn and John Napier shifted its height again. The arrival of Nick Hytner as artistic director seemed to bring a change of attitude. He'd made use of it on one of the earliest shows he directed for the company, *The Wind In The Willows*, and dramatic use of it in one of his earliest as the artistic director, *His Dark Materials*, which had triggered an earlier round of restoration work. "Nick Hytner and Nick Starr, then executive director, had an overarching view that the National Theatre should invest in itself properly, not just in putting on plays," notes Rob Barnard, one of the managers for the NT Future project, but also someone who had been with the building from the very beginning, starting as an installation technician during construction, later a member of and ultimately heading the sound department. "They had a much broader vision, and that meant we were able to rebuild." [3] It helped no doubt that during Hytner and Starr's tenure, the National had a number of productions which went on to hugely successful commercial lives, notably *War Horse*, which provided the organisation with some extra spending money.

The result for the drum, as Mylan Lester recalls, was that "it was decided to repair it properly, at which point we put together how much it was going to cost and how we were going to do it – how long it was going to be out of action for. But the theatre didn't close: for the shows they programmed over that period, the creative teams were just told there was no drum. And so beneath the shows we lifted the whole hundred-and-sixty odd tons of the drum, which includes the counterweights for the elevators, 6mm. That doesn't sound like much but 6mm or 6m is still lifting, to within an accuracy of less than a quarter of a millimetre over the whole 12m diameter. Then we chopped out and replaced the entire bottom 4 feet, and increased the number of wheels up to seventy." Working with the specialist entertainment company Tait, new drives and controls were installed under the watchful eye of Tait's Kevin Taylor – who has a remarkable connection with the drum, his father having worked for Tele-Stage, another of the original suppliers to the National, as the drum was first brought to life.

The drum is perhaps haunted by one mis-judgement in its original design: just how much weight it would be expected to carry, particularly as scenery evolved from wood to steel construction. Its design allows just five tonnes per elevator, and as Paul Handley, the National's Production and Technical Director, notes, any amount of scenery plus a full company of actors can quickly get you close to, or even over, that limit – a particular challenge with long-standing directors and designers who remember putting more weight on it in times past when the rules were less rigidly enforced. He also notes the difficulty of explaining just what this unique piece of machinery can do, particularly to directors and designers new to it: "one more visionary director was actually canny enough to drag her writer in to look at the drum before he'd even started the play he'd been asked to write – and actually that's inspired, because of course he walked in there and went, oh my God, this is incredible!"

More recently, lack of use during the Covid shutdown period has taken its toll on what is now a fifty-year-old structure, with the National pondering once again whether to attempt to rejuvenate it, whether a bigger, perhaps even total, reconstruction is needed, or whether new scenic techniques, particularly video, have changed the need for it. But that central problem remains: it really is the very heart of the Olivier Theatre.

Power Flying

The Olivier Theatre's power flying system was unique at the time the building opened, and remained unique throughout its working life. There is an old theatrical joke about providing a 'sky hook' to solve difficult or impossible rigging challenges, but the Olivier system provided just that: a series of individual hooks which could be easily repositioned across the stage and could then be synchronized to operate together in different combinations to lift scenery of any shape or at any angle – silently. It was "a vastly ambitious thing to do, really state of the art," according to Roger Keenan who helped create the system while working for a company called Evershed Power Optics in the 1970s. Mark Ager, co-founder of the company Stage Technologies that would

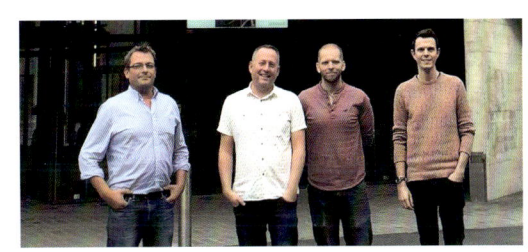

NT Lighting Team, 2017: L-R, Matt Drury, Paul Hornsby Marc Williams and Daniel Murfin

help establish power flying as the norm in theatres in Britain and across the world from the early 1990s, has noted that "so many of the modern concepts of power flying systems – playbacks, deads, timed and synchronized cues – existed in this pioneering system. It was an amazing feat of engineering at the time, and the start of a journey to automation in the theatre."

So successful was this system that replacing it has proved problematic, a new system installed in the mid 2010s replaced by an altogether different system, from Tait, in early 2023. This offers sixty winches installed around the Olivier fly tower, their cables running up to the grid, onto moveable trolleys then down to new hooks. These are rated to lift 250kg rather than the old 200kg, and to lift people as well as scenery. A new control system finally allows full programming and integration of flying and drum – quite a change from the previous drum control system, where everything was run manually during the show, and from the original drum control, where rotation fell under the control of the stage team but up/down movement was considered to be elevators and so had to be operated by the building's engineering and maintenance department!

Lyttelton Theatre

In the pros-arch Lyttelton, the power flying system originally intended for the theatre was abandoned very close to opening on technical grounds; a standard manually operated counterweight flying system was installed instead, and this system remains in place today. However modern health-and-safety requirements have brought changes above the Lyttelton stage: in a comprehensive survey of the theatre's grid, it was discovered that many of the roof beams being used to hang individual hoists for heavier show elements from were actually close to their load limit doing their real job of holding up the roof. A space-frame system was therefore installed across the grid, to allow these loads to be removed from the roof beams.

At stage level, the National continues to make use of the hydraulic systems that allow the Lyttelton's stage to be tilted to a rake, the three elevators across the stage front, and the rear stage wagon with a built-in revolve that can track from the rear scene dock onto the stage as required. All, by legend, suffered from water damage when the water tank used to float a boat on stage for Alan Ayckbourn's play *Way Upstream* burst. All were serviced and fitted with new control systems during NT Future and remain in use.

Cottesloe / Dorfman Theatre

The little Cottesloe has perhaps had the biggest transformation: it is the only one of the three to have changed name, to the Dorfman, after long-time NT supporter Lloyd Dorfman.

Always a hugely adaptable space, the desire was to make it quicker and easier to make those changes, and in particular to allow it to transform into a flat-floored space during the day for use by the NT's Learning department. Architects Haworth Tompkins and theatre consultants Charcoalblue designed a new seating system that allows the seats to fold down into boxes mounted onto moving elevators that can give steep – or shallow-raked seating to an end stage, or a flat floor to allow any other configuration of the space. In a nice touch of continuity, the new seating was built by Race, the company that supplied the NT's original seating back in 1976.

Charcoalblue and Haworth Tompkins also designed a second row of high seats to be installed around the balconies, allowing their occupants to see over those in the front row and giving a useful increase in both seating capacity and audience density; these replaced the previous leaning rails. Some, however, feel that all of these changes together have altered the theatre's innate character rather more than might be expected from what feels like relatively subtle shifts.

What hasn't changed is the separate identity of the smallest theatre, which has its own entrance around the side of the building, quite separate from the main river-facing foyers. In 1976 the public pathway along the Thames ended at the National, so a trip to the Cottesloe meant walking past the bins that lived at the National's north-east corner. Now the river bank has been extended outward and that pathway continues on past the Lasdun-designed IBM building next door (this now undergoing massive change despite its listed status, IBM having moved out) and on to the Tate Modern gallery; the National has responded by filling this corner with new restaurants and coffee bars.

With space in the existing building at a premium, a new Haworth Tompkins designed building, the Max Rayne Centre, was added behind the National's south-east corner. This houses production offices, new workshop space and a new paint frame; a big window at one end allows the public views in to what were once very private workshops, and inside a new high-level walkway allows visitors to walk through the workshops should they choose. As seems to be the new way, perhaps since the opening of Leicester's Curve theatre in 2008, the public are encouraged to discover how theatre is made, rather than just seeing the end result on stage. Another new structure, the Deck, an events space intended to help balance the books, was squeezed in to the upper terrace on the building's north-east corner next to Olivier's roof.

Lighting

The pioneering Lightboard – the 'Total Control System' as it was known by its manufacturer before it gained its final name – is felt by many to have helped shape the way lighting for performance is created to this day, long overnight sessions lighting an empty stage replaced by daytime rehearsals with the cast on stage, everyone working together to create the show. "Lightboard heralded the start of seriously lighting over rehearsals," recalls David Hersey, who lit many of the early shows in the new National Theatre complex and has returned to the National countless times in the years since.[4]

Lightboard was typical of the innovation at the NT: a remarkable device, right at the edge of what was technologically possible at the time yet with some functionality unmatched by its successors. The desire was to create the best – interestingly, it now seems impossible to find out how much it actually cost! But the rapid advance in computer technology meant that within ten years it had to be replaced, the DEC PDP11 minicomputer it relied on no longer supported by its manufacturer. So far ahead of its time was it that when the National came to replace it, they couldn't actually find a product that did everything it could do, particularly controlling the twelve automated moving lights that had been installed as part of the Olivier's permanent rig. The National opted for the best they could get – Strand's Galaxy, in many ways Lightboard's direct descendent but engineered around the newer microprocessor technology – then built their own control system to run those moving lights.

The lighting rig continued to evolve gently for the next thirty years, adopting moving lights as they became readily available commercial products rather than the original custom-engineered devices, and moving through two more generations of control systems, Strand 500-series, and then ETC's Eos family of consoles[5]. As lighting rigs have grown more complex, so the role of controlling – 'programming' – those rigs has become more demanding, with the National establishing a team specialising in this area and bringing in new tools, such as pre-visualisation of lighting, where useful.

At the same time, what evolved perhaps more than the equipment itself was how designers used it and, particularly, the angles of light they wanted to achieve and so where they wanted to rig lights. This is most obvious in the Olivier, where early pictures show the curved 'jaws' of the side boxes that wrap around the stage fully visible in light concrete, while current pictures show them covered in dark material and hidden behind lights. Ten years after the building opened, a new overhead upstage lighting walkway – 'Bridge 5' – was added to the Olivier to assist with changeovers between shows by providing walk-on access to focus lights; moving lights now provide a better solution, and that bridge has gone. The Olivier's core overhead rig now consists entirely of moving lights, the realisation of a dream Richard Pilbrow talked about when designing the place but which was then unachievable. And technology offers possibilities unimaginable in 1976: during 2022 and 2023 the National added remotely controllable followspot systems, either by human operators (the Spot Me system) or performer tracking (Zactrack) that can share positional data with both lighting and sound control systems to allow lights or sound to follow performers automatically as they move around the stage.

Since about 2016, the big shift has been sparked by the rapid evolution of lighting technology from traditional incandescent tungsten lightbulbs and arc discharge bulbs to new, more efficient LED-based lighting fixtures. The National as an organisation under Hytner and then Rufus Norris, encouraged by the passionate environmental beliefs of one of its associate artists, Paule Constable, has focused increasingly on sustainability and its environmental impact, making a commitment to achieving net zero carbon across the organisation by 2030. By 2023 Matt Drury, the NT's Head of Lighting since 2012 (and only the fourth person to hold that role in the National's entire history, after Lennie Tucker, Peter Radmore and Mark Jonathan – there have been fewer heads of lighting at the National than artistic directors) was proud to announce that all of the National's production and houselight systems, as well as the lighting around the exterior of the building and in many of the foyer spaces, were entirely LED, aside from a few special cases (such as followspots) where suitable LED replacements weren't yet available . This transition has also involved upgrading wiring and control systems, quite a challenge in a building made of unyielding concrete and Grade II* listed.

This last brings added complications: replacing the houselights in the Lyttelton involved creating custom LED fixtures that provided a suitable warm light onto the concrete surfaces while at the same time visually resembling the original fixtures. In the Olivier the new LED houselights successfully recreate the 'fingers of light' across the textured concrete side flank walls of Richard's original design.

For the most part, all of this work has been carried out while performances have continued on the National's never-ending production schedule, installing temporary systems while parts of the permanent system were replaced. Covid brought many challenges to the theatre world, but did finally force a break in that performance schedule while allowing work updating the building to continue.

Critically, as ever, the NT's aim remains the same as it has always been: to give those making shows the best possible tools to deliver on their ambitions, or on their dreams. Lighting designer James Farncombe notes how after working at the National several times he "came to appreciate how we benefit from three rigs that have been developed over years, shifting with trends and technology, discoveries and improvements made by four decades' worth of lighting designers and lighting staff – there is a real sense of heritage there." [6] American lighting designers brought up in the commercial world of New York theatre tend to look around in bewildered wonder when they visit the National – "they own all these lights?" asked one. They do. And that freedom to just create light has, arguably, led to the remarkable lighting seen on the National's stages, and the other stages inspired by the work at the National, in the decades since the building opened.

Sound

The National's influence on the profession of sound designer is just as strong, with the list of former NT sound staff reading like a who's who of British sound designers. "I think the National helped change the landscape," comments the NT's current Head of Sound and Video, Dominic Bilkey, "because what was pioneering in the building when it opened was the concept of a sound department that did designs, and of speakers in the roof and on stage and in other places, not just on the pros – things that were quite rare at the time. So you got to the point where directors had a relationship with a sound designer – it wasn't just 'can someone bring me some sound effects' – and wanted to work with them again, which led to people who worked here leaving to help establish that profession. But equally, I think it's healthy that people come in to work with us, when you don't just have an insular world but where people bring in ideas from outside. And where we all get on board and engaged to deliver something amazing – but where we all know, and accept, it might fail. That's the key thing here – it can fail." [7]

"That should be written in stone for any subsidised theatre," adds Paul Handley. "The right to fail." [8]

As with lighting, the original specification for the National's sound systems was written by a pioneer in the field, TP's David Collison. "It was Altec and Tannoy loudspeakers everywhere, Amcron power amplifiers, a control desk from a company called Alice, who I think built broadcast sound desks," recalls Rob Barnard. "Enormous tape playback machines that when you pushed the button went CALANK – it's a good thing they were in the control rooms!" [9] The sound positions stayed behind glass until Richard Eyre's famous production of *Guys and Dolls*, when Derrick Zieba won the fight to move the desk and operator into the Olivier's auditorium where they have remained ever since – though in the Lyttelton the sound desk remains in a control room – with a power-operated lowerable window – except for particular shows.

The NT's sound team has also adopted new hardware as it appeared – those big open-reel tape machines replaced by cart machines, then digital samplers; the beautifully engineered analogue Cadac mixing consoles which moved from studios into musicals then became the hubs of the Olivier and Lyttelton sound systems for years before the National became an early adopter of the DiGiCo digital mixing desks: "The DiGiCo console in the Lyttelton is one of the first generation of the SD7 flagship desks," notes Bilkey. "Inside it's all labelled in pencil; all the connectors have the marks of the person who assembled it."

Part of the challenge facing the National's sound team has always been that they have been involved in trying to overcome the acoustic challenges of the venues, particularly the Olivier. All kinds of attempts have been made to tame this, including physical acoustic treatments (most noticeably around the circle front, the raw concrete there now almost entirely hidden) and electronic aids, including for a while during the Richard Eyre-era, the SIAP acoustic enhancement system ("all the speakers are still up in the roof disconnected – the Olivier is a bit of a graveyard of sound history," Bilkey comments.) Nowadays there seems to be a general acceptance that radio microphones provide the best solution, though it is by no means a rule and is ultimately up to the creative teams of each show. The NT continues to experiment with new audio technologies as they appear to help with this, including the object-oriented systems that allow sounds to accurately track the position of performers in space.

Sound also faces the same challenge as everyone else when trying to update the listed building and its infrastructure. Dom Bilkey: "Some of the sound positions are still driven by the original 100V line cabling, because it runs through conduit cast into the concrete – it's there until the world ends! Sometimes you find yourself stripping back layers trying to work out what's going on, sometimes you find it's easier to just add another conduit and start again. That costs a little bit more – but it also helps futureproof things for the next ten or twenty years."

Video
The freedom to experiment in the NT's supportive environment, and that right to fail, helped build the disciplines of lighting and sound design, but it arguably also helped establish theatre's latest design discipline, that of video/projection designer. Some of that came early on in support of an established scenic designer, William Dudley, as he moved from pushing the physical possibilities inherent in the National's stages in his drive to bring the Olivier drum to life for *The Shaughraun* in 1988 to experimenting with an entirely different type of design that he felt could free him from those physical limitations with the computer generated scenery for Tom Stoppard's *The Coast of Utopia* in 2002. The team of Dick Straker and Sven Ortel worked with Dudley to realise that vision in terms of projection and playback; the trio would go on to use similar techniques for the 2004 Andrew Lloyd Webber musical *The Woman in White*.

In 2006 another pair of video designers, Mark Grimmer and Leo Warner of 59 Productions, first worked at the National on *Waves* with director Katie Mitchell. They remember that from that moment on "the NT has always felt like a place where innovation was cherished and ambition was nurtured."[10] That nurturing led those designers to create, amongst other work, the video element of *War Horse*. And the establishment of this new design discipline has led to video becoming almost a standard element in theatrical design not just at the National, but everywhere.

Around The Outside
The original building lighting scheme included lighting for the exterior, but the equipment used tended to be unreliable. In 2004 a new system was created allowing the river-facing parts of the building to change colour using LED technology, and for text or artwork to be projected onto the Lyttelton fly tower. This has been expanded and revised in the years since, supported by lighting manufacturer Philips/Signify. The NT now often takes on particular colours to celebrate particular events much as the Empire State Building does in New York. What Lasdun would think of this often bold use of colour on his building is hard to imagine, but it is always done with restraint and elegance, making the National as distinctive a part of the London skyline by night as it is by day. (What he would think about now having his name emblazoned on the side of the building, as the title of a new restaurant within the NT, is another question entirely!)

Beyond The Building
The NT building has always supported the work of the NT company beyond the building itself – it was always intended as a base from which traditional tours would be sent out and that continued. Later the acclaimed, much emulated NT Live broadcasts, designed to simulate the experience of going to the theatre by having the broadcast appear at just certain cinemas just once on a specific date and time, carried NT productions to the world. Of course they were actually recorded, which turned out to be invaluable as Covid hit, allowing the NT first to continue to connect with its audiences, then to generate some ongoing financial support, as the building was forced to close down. During the later lockdowns, the Lyttelton was effectively turned into a movie studio for a filmed production of *Romeo and Juliet*.

The National was quick to reopen for live audiences as lockdown eased – that fundamental flaw of the Olivier, its excessive volume of air per audience member, suddenly seen as an advantage – only to be shut down again by successive coronavirus waves. By early 2023 live performance was fully back, but not quite as before: the rep system which the NT has always operated, with its constant changes between shows, judged too expensive as the organisation recovered from two years of shutdown. Individual shows now sit on each stage for continuous runs of a few months. Might that become the new normal?

If it doesn't always feel like the technology of the National Theatre is quite as uniquely on the cutting edge as it was in 1976, that's arguably because so many of the things it pioneered have become standard, become commonplace. But keep this in mind: the National never set out to be cutting edge for the sake of being cutting edge. It set out to make available the best possible tools to allow those working there to make the best possible shows. And that, really, is exactly what it is still doing today.

Olivier Theatre set for
the Royal Opening, 1976

6.3 Acoustics

DL&P model of Olivier Theatre ceiling reflectors

The acoustics of both the Olivier and Lyttelton theatres have been problematic from the outset. Research, enquiry and experiment have attempted many solutions. Finally the position has been reached where sound amplification of the actor's voice is most often employed.

This is surely a sad state of affairs for the National Theatre in the land of Shakespeare.

In the same way that Theatre Projects would now always aim to be involved and helping shape an auditorium from the earliest moments of its design, so too do acousticians since it is far easier to work with a space that is acoustically sound than to attempt to fix a dfficult space later.

Unfortunately that was not the case at the National Theatre. With very little discussion, Henry Humphries was appointed as the acoustician, but was only paid a nominal fee and, sadly, passed away before the National opened. Look at the faceted panels that form the Olivier ceiling and you can easily assume the design was acoustically driven, but in fact it was more visually led. Plus the design of both rooms and their hard concrete construction has resulted in two spaces that seem to fight an actor's voice rather than carrying it easily to the audience.

Precisely defining the problem is, of course, hard. And it has changed over time: performance styles change. Actor's skills change – a young actor who has grown up performing for the television camera is quite different from the likes of Sir Laurence who grew up in the theatre. Though he only ever performed there once, there is a sense that the theatre that carries his name was very much designed for his style of performance – one that is perhaps now gone. Plus of course audiences change: once you are used to the presentational sound of cinema or the ability to set the volume you choose when watching at home, are you prepared to put in the effort to really listen?

Theatre makers, as ever, just try to solve the problems. Not being allowed to radically change the two big theatres, they have tinkered, adding acoustic materials, electronic systems and now, most usually, the kind of actor-worn radio microphones established in the world of musical theatre.

Paul Arditti

Sound Designer

Paul is a British sound designer, working mainly in the UK and US. He specialises in designing sound sytems and sound scores for the theatre. He has won awards for his work on both musicals and plays, including Tony, Olivier, and Drama Desk Awards. He spent an early part of his career at the National before moving to the Royal Court and then becoming independent. He is now an associate of the National.

Richard: When did you start at the NT?

Paul: 12th August 1985. It was my 24th birthday. I found myself working with Peter Hall who was known as a quite tricky director, but I've always quite enjoyed tricky directors.

Richard: So talk about the Olivier.

Paul: I think from day one, directors have been aware of the challenges acoustically. All sorts of things have been done, including raising the level of the stage and adding acoustic absorption to the back dock doors, the doors at the back of the stalls and circle, the concrete surface on the front of the circle, and what I call the proscenium concrete bits. The result of all these interventions is that echoes have been tamed, but the auditorium has now been dampened to the point where the acoustic voice is barely audible without help.

There have been electronic interventions at certain times. A SIAP system used a lot of microphones, electronics, and speakers to try and increase the amount of sound reaching the auditorium. That system didn't last very long. A later system for when radio mics are not employed used a rifle microphone stage left to feed sound to the raised section auditorium left, and another microphone stage right to the section on auditorium right, so when an actor is pointed away from you, you have more of a chance of hearing what he or she is saying.

But those things are all sticking plasters, really. There are major problems to do with the dimensions in terms of the length of the audio reflections; the large expanses of very reflective material, like concrete; the height of the fly tower; and the size and openness of the 'proscenium.' None of the things you expect to enjoy in a Matcham-style theatre are present. Trying to get an actor audible from the stage into the auditorium is difficult enough when we're also trying to put musicians and actors in all sorts of places throughout the massively wide space. It's really tricky. Parts of the auditorium get very different shows. Everyone talks about the difference between the stalls and the circle. The circle is so far away and so high. The raised seating at the side is the most problematic place, because the angle is so oblique, It's almost impossible to take those seating blocks into consideration. You're rarely looking at the thing that the designer intended you to look at, which is tricky because there are such a lot of seats there. So, as sound designers, we can at least make sure those areas are covered with speakers so that anything that's played back or amplified can be heard there. In a way we have the same problem acoustically, as visual designers have visually. Some things we do are creative, but much of what we do as sound designers is remedial. No audience should be expected to put up with the shortcomings of the auditorium. If there is a way we sound designers can help cure it, then we should do it.

Richard: On the National, we didn't have one meeting with architect, acoustics, and theatre consultant together. For example, the ceiling planes are the wrong angle.

Paul: Yes, they are. That's why there are problems in the front rows of the circle; there are very unhelpful echoes.

In the Royal Court Theatre, at the beginning of a performance, when an actor comes onstage and starts speaking, you sit back in your seat because, if anything, that person is louder and clearer than you expect, and you can hear their breath and them scratching their head… it's a small theatre, and the acoustics are amazing. In the Olivier, the opposite happens. The houselights go down, an actor comes onstage and starts speaking and you lean forward, because you can't quite hear what they're saying, it seems to be such a long way away, so much further than would be suggested by what you can see, and there's a disconnect between what you see and what you hear. So what we have to do is to try and counterbalance that. But acoustics have been a black art in the way that sound design has been a black art for a long time. If sound designers cock it up, it only lasts for the period of that production, whereas acoustics last for as long as the theatre does.

It is amazing when you look at those theatres built 150 years ago, how in the complete absence of any form of amplification and with the necessity of getting as many people as possible into the auditorium, they built auditoriums – and they are called auditoriums for a reason – to get that sound, to all those seats. If you look at some of those Matcham theatres – where the stage is in relation to the proscenium, the angle of the proscenium, the angle of the header above the proscenium, the degree to which seats overhang each other – there was no way he could even sketch the travel of sound on his plans, yet he nevertheless knew the materials, the dimensions, and the angles he was using were probably going to work. Where did we go wrong with the Olivier? Lasdun wanted it to look like one of the most acoustically perfect theatres in the world and yet he made one of the acoustically worst theatres in the world, so there's definitely a disconnect there somewhere.

Richard: Speaking of technology, there are all us lighting people making noises that you weren't used to.

Paul: Yes, this is my particular bugbear. In the Olivier, the noise level gradually crept up as more and more moving lights were used. Nick Hytner, in around 2011, said, "Okay, it's too noisy in here. I want all the lights that make a noise removed." He has the power to do that, and the Olivier became very quiet again. But now we have video projectors and the noise is going up again. Most people don't realise that, even using microphones, raising that noise floor takes the dynamic range away. It's very difficult when there are 300 fans all cooling their respective machines.

Richard: Talk about the Lyttelton.

Paul: When I first started there in the '80s, there was never a question of miking any actors. Nowadays, most plays even without music are miked, which perhaps says something about the style of acting. But the acoustics depend massively upon the set. You can say that about every theatre, actually, but the larger the theatre, the more that matters.

I think the width of the proscenium is a problem. Just in terms of focus. And, again, it creates a building with parallel concrete sides an uncomfortable distance apart for echoes. In some seats, particularly at the front of the circle, if an actor turns in a certain direction you get strange echoes.

The Cottesloe/Dorfman has always been a wonderful theatre

> "I'm a fan of smaller theatres and better sightlines."
> Paul Arditti

The ceiling reflectors above the Olivier Theatre auditorium

for me. It's what we call as dry as a bone. Wherever you point a speaker, the sound will go there and stop which is exactly what you want. So you can focus sound just as you focus lights. There are very few acoustic problems to overcome.

The recent refurbishment – I'm going to be controversial here – hasn't, to my mind, been successful. They've added seats, but they've added them underneath the balconies. Where there were one or two rows, there are now three or four without great sightlines, and certainly not great for hearing. We're now trying to put tiny little speakers under balconies to squirt the sound to these new seats. It's not really a problem for spoken dialogue, because it's a small room, more for sound effects. It's also spoilt the feeling of the theatre. Now it's 'proper.' I'm cross about that. It was my favourite theatre in the world, now it's been compromised.

Richard: Theatres elsewhere?

Paul: Most West End theatres seem to me to be not fit for purpose anymore. Too uncomfortable to sit in or to work in, but survive because they are too beautiful to knock down.

If you're building a proscenium arch theatre, you do need to take into consideration the size of that space. For a house that does plays, there is an upper limit of the size of the room, which is more to do with hearing an actor on the stage than if you can see them. Places like the Royal Court, which is 450-500 seats, are beautiful places to see and hear actors. While I'm not saying that all theatres should be tiny, I don't want to be always doing remedial sound design. I'd like to be able to watch actors doing their stuff without microphones stuck on them. I'm a fan of smaller theatres and better sightlines. I also like Iain Mackintosh's courtyard designs, again, there's a maximum size. The new Royal Shakespeare Theatre at Stratford seems to go beyond the maximum size. If you go beyond a certain size, the building is too big. The thing about the old Stratford theatre was that the circle was miles back and the back of the circle even worse. But those seats are where we all began to experience Shakespeare, and they're the ones they've gotten rid of...

Richard Cowell
Acoustician

Richard trained as an architect, interning with Mies van der Rohe's office, before becoming an acoustician. He worked at Sound Research Laboratories at the time of the National's opening. He became one of the founders of Arup Acoustics.

Richard P: Did you know Henry Humphries, the original NT acoustician?

Richard Cowell: I knew Henry, but not very well, before he died in about '74, '75. The NT was left acoustician-less.

I was asked to do a few acoustic measurements. This was just before opening. I found how difficult and unworkable the Olivier was.

The issues in the Olivier were sizable. The Olivier is ten cubic metres per seat, which is about the right sort of volume for a concert hall rather than a theatre. And you lighting chaps had just taken up all the surfaces that we could've used. Unlike the Sheffield Crucible, which is smaller, and then Chichester, a little bit bigger, they got to a size where if you're out on the open stage, the reflections arrived late, so you get this foggy sound, which worsens when you're turning away from the audience.

Richard P: To the best of my memory, I don't believe we ever had a team meeting with Lasdun, Humphries, and TPC.

Richard Cowell: The divide-and-rule approach.

Then we got to *Volpone,* and we got these headlines; acoustics were all over the press. We were immediately into a 'defend the new theatre' mode. And so, we then embarked on a seat by seat analysis of each of the complaints.

I was thinking that there were some fundamental issues with this theatre. It was going to be an uphill struggle to hold this thing together. So, we put in a microphone by the side of the stage to pick up the voices facing laterally. And then pumped a little sound over a reinforcement system, which was so low in output that you couldn't describe it as an amplification system. I always described it as an enhancement system.

We went through a phase where Richard Eyre was in New York, in the Beaumont Theater, and they'd had an artificial reverberation system. He came back and declared that we were having one, too. But the problems here were quite different. My advice was to be very cautious about it all. Trevor Nunn just stuck radio mics on the performers. But when Nick Hytner came in, he had a complete review of the whole story.

We spent time with Jeannette Nelson, when she came in as voice coach, and I think we managed to demonstrate that two-thirds of the difficulties of the theatre were resolved by voice coaching. I produced a checklist for each part of the organisation to deal with – in other words, the acoustics needed so much management to get good results. You had to take the production policy, you had to take the designers, you had to take the directors, and you had to take the operations and management. Each of them had a checklist of how to deal with this.

Richard P: I was talking to Jeannette. She was saying that most difficulties have been removed by a conscious effort, and they still do have voice rehearsals several mornings a week.

The fundamental problem of the Olly is the right angle: your walls are not sending the sound into the room, they're sending the sound into the back corners, aren't they?

Richard Cowell: We actually went through every surface in the theatre. This wall was helping some and damaging others. You finished up with an incredible chessboard guess at the best balance within all of these things. Because we had covered the balcony front with carpet, in a huge fight with Denys, in order to deal with the focusing effect on the first seating plan. The minute we removed from the balcony the high-frequency reflections when people move forward on the stage, that front overhead panel suddenly became a very useful reflector because the sound travelled up, and it was actually now hitting the audience.

So, you've got all these combinations of positioning on stage, whether it's working in this position or that position. And the

Victoria Palace: reflection from boxes to stalls

Lyttelton: zero side reflection to stalls

variety of listening positions and the variety of surfaces, and the echo, and the foldback, and everything, all of this stuff, it was an absolute nightmare, frankly. It was a nightmare to get a balance.

Richard P: Now those angles of the ceiling panels, lighting-wise I had always wanted them to be less steep. I had always wanted to bring the whole ceiling down.

Richard Cowell: That would've been wonderful. It would've made a huge difference. Well, it's interesting, because one of the things the Olivier does do, if you go in there for a performance, the aural sense of anticipation is fantastic. Because those ceiling panels are all just chucking your own audience noise back at you. That's worth bottling!

Richard P: So, what about the Lyttelton?

Richard Cowell: We had a similar situation with the complaints from performers. They weren't getting the sound back, and I was yet again cursing the lighting designers. There were many fewer risks in the Lyttelton because it is more conventional geometry. You had to do something a bit silly to have regular complaints. There were a few rather poor bits of set design, where a lot of the volume behind the stage was allowed to get active, acoustically, and then roll into the auditorium and mess up the articulation.

The background noise from the ventilation needed a lot of attention. In both theatres, we were struggling – and probably continue to do so now – with technical noise from lights, from hoists, it just goes on and on and on.

William Sickert, *The Old Bedford*, 1895

6.4 Theatre Makers and Architecture

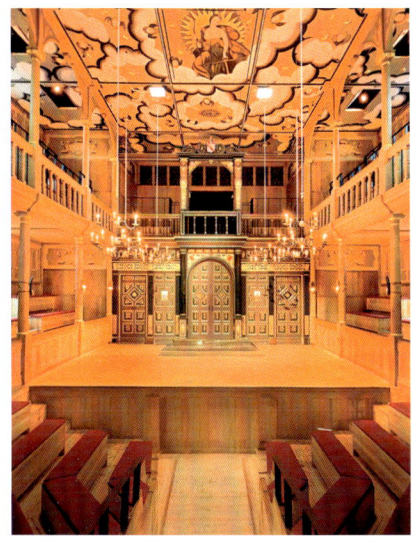

The Wanamaker Playhouse at Shakespeare's Globe

In 1946 Sir Laurence Olivier wrote: "The edifice itself is important, but that is nothing compared to the people who are to be concerned with operating such a theatre. It is the human material that matters most – the administrators, directors, playwrights, actors, stage managers, designers, painters, technicians and musicians."[11]

Almost fifty years in Lasdun's building has proven Sir Laurence's wisdom. Let that human constant reign supreme. Theatre makers must speak out loud and clear about the essence of theatre – communication between human beings – to find a new level of collaboration between theatre design and architecture.

Four times in less than a century, Britain attempted to build a National Theatre. The one finally created has been dogged with – at best – some controversy.

It was noticeable that while the original building committee included many fine minds of theatre of the time, there was only one actor – Sir Laurence himself. It is interesting to consider what might have resulted if there had been more opinions from those who actually use theatres as their tool for connecting to their audiences. And interesting, now, to consider whether later generations of theatre makers have come to any better understanding of how performance spaces actually work!

Foreword from the book *London Theatres*[12]
by Mark Rylance – an extract:
"In my experience, the best of these old theatres always have some circular device in their ornate ceiling. If there wasn't a circle, I knew we would have a difficult time. It wasn't just that the acoustics were problematic but it was going to be harder to convince the audience that they were in the same room with us. We would be perceived to be masters at the head of passive diners. I feel the greatest theatres always have the irrational curve of a circle in their seating and design. Why?

"Most years I go walking in the mountains with my brother and a group of friends. When we light a fire at sunset, we roll rocks around to sit on and intuitively create the earliest storytelling theatre known to man. The centre is where the heat is and that heat spreads fairly to each walker sat round in a circle, as do the stories of the day's sights, the jokes, hopes and remembrances, the songs, and sometimes the dance, more to keep warm, I must confess, than to represent any dying fawn or lovesick swan. There is a shared experience. The fire and story both share the centre. Our faces are lit alike by the imagination and the red glow of the flames."

Mark Rylance
Actor

Mark has enjoyed an esteemed career on stage and on screen since making his professional debut at the Citizens Theatre, Glasgow in 1980.

He won the Academy Award for Best Supporting Actor and the BAFTA Award for Best Supporting Actor for his portrayal of Rudolf Abel in Steven Spielberg's *Bridge of Spies* (2015). He is also the winner of two Olivier Awards and three Tony Awards.

Mark was the first artistic director of Shakespeare's Globe in London, from 1995 to 2005.

Mark had just come from a meeting at the Globe Theatre, discussing possible changes to the theatre after twenty years. In particular the decoration of the entire auditorium he felt was needed so that it presented a completely encompassing unity with the decorated stage and tiring house. The historic evidence suggests that the whole of the original Globe interior was a richly decorated space. These are my notes on our conversation:

Globe Theatre, London

The Olivier is problematic. Mark wondered whether making it a single tier house would help? I expressed my doubts, saying the auditorium needed to be in a closer and in a more vertical relationship to the stage. (Mark said that in *Countrymania*, the Goldoni play he performed in the Olivier in 1987, he once played to fifty-seven people in the stalls!)

However spectacle can win out in the Olivier. He cited the recent *Follies*.

Rufus Norris is a good friend. Mark loved his production of the play set in India: *Behind The Beautiful Forevers*.

The Lyttelton is a barren, square space with a remote and isolated circle.

Acoustics in both theatres are poor. The need for amplification in both spaces is a terrible curse.

Both spaces seem to work best when they are fully opened up to give a panoramic vista. He mentioned *Happy Days*.

Surely the Olly and the Lyttelton must be one day be redeveloped. "Your book must make this point." Every theatre must be able to evolve. Anything Mark can do to petition, or lobby for change in the National's theatres, he would.

Mark loves the exterior and the public areas of the NT. The board-marked concrete makes it seem almost natural… A hard shell to protect the places of performance. But the interiors should be soft, pliable, and malleable, like the soft centre of a chocolate.

Michael Grandage

Director

Michael is a British theatre director and producer. He was an actor before becoming artistic director of the Sheffield Theatres from 1999 to 2005. From 2002 to 2012 he was Artistic Director of the Donmar Warehouse in London. He is currently Artistic Director of the Michael Grandage Company.

Michael: You're working on the premise that our National Theatre certainly has one very successful small auditorium, but two troubled large ones?

Richard: Yes, I am. But the NT Company is the most successful theatre company in the world. So the truth is, and this is not a truth I like very much: an architect can do what the hell he wants, and we theatre people will make the result work!

Michael: Or whether the brand of a company isn't about the building. When I started at the Donmar, I took on a company from Sam Mendes. It was in such a good place critically, I was able to hit the ground running. But the thing that interested me quite quickly was, are we creating a Donmar aesthetic? I worked with [designer] Christopher Oram on that first season. And so we created a style of presentation that I think wasn't dependent on a small three-sided auditorium. We put the Donmar into the West End, but it was still a Donmar production. The National Theatre is the most successful theatre company in the world, but maybe it's a successful company in spite of its building.

I started going to the National in the late 1970s, and so I was seeing great theatre in a building… I, at that time, was nowhere near sophisticated enough to know whether the building itself was working. It just felt like a great place to go. We'd all go there, like we'd go to temple on Sundays. It was this concrete temple. It appealed to my, what I now realise is, an aesthetic. That sort of 'Bauhaus', big, monumental stuff. I love all that.

Richard: What were those early productions?

Michael: I saw John Dexter's *Galileo* on the Olivier stage, which was one of the first times I'd seen two people on a

> **"I think Sheffield is still, to this day, the most liberating stage I've ever worked on in my life."**
>
> Michael Grandage

very large space facing each other. I thought, "My gosh, he's put two people navigating this space in those scenes… And then, separate from that, he's put the great anointing of the Pope scene, with all its splendour." When you think, shouldn't the theory be that that stage lends itself only to the great robing of the Pope sequence? And yet, I was aware that it also lent itself to two people just talking to each other, as long as you create enough space between them. I learned when I was at Sheffield on that extraordinary, huge thrust stage that Tanya Moiseiwitsch had designed with you. I realised, when we did *As You Like It*, that it's better for you not to say, "I love you," between Rosalind and Orlando together, but actually putting them on a diagonal, with one at the top end of the stage, and one at the bottom of the stage, and her shouting… not shouting, even, just going, "I love you." Somehow, the entire auditorium… we felt it meant more.

Danton's Death, Olivier Theatre, 2010

I remember Victoria Hamilton, who played Rosalind, said, "I cannot tell you as an actor how thrilling it is running towards the person you're supposed to be in love with, and feeling the wind rush through your hair." She said, "You can't do that on small stages." And yet everybody says the only place to do great theatre is in small spaces. But having done five years at the Crucible, and only one production on the Olivier, *Danton's Death*, which was not successful at all, I do think bigger stages offer a different thing, not worse, necessarily, just different.

My experience with the Olivier stage was we had the most wonderful, extraordinary, rehearsal period, where I thought it was coming alive like nothing I've ever seen in a rehearsal. And then we put it on the Olivier stage.

First of all, I didn't really know where centre was. When we got to the guillotine scene, we put it up high and we created something. As you know, nine times out of ten, when you move from rehearsal room onto the stage, the physical design takes it that next step towards creating something even more special. That was one of the few occasions… And it was Paule [Constable] doing some beautiful lighting, and Christopher [Oram] doing a perfectly good design, beautiful costumes and all that, but somehow, when we put it on stage, it seemed to dissect the stage rather than bring it to life.

The only problem I feel about the Lyttelton as a theatregoer is, now, in my older age, I actually can't sit in the middle of rows. I have to sit on the end of a row. Well, if you sit on the end of a row, you really are on the periphery of the action. When you're on the very end, that huge, wide stage is over there. But somebody has to sit on the ends, and I happen to be the person.

Richard: I talked to Stephen Daldry, who thinks the Lyttelton is one of the greatest theatres, because, of course, of *Inspector Calls*. He had the time of his life.

Michael: I have seen some of the great evenings on the Lyttelton stage. Nick's [Hytner's] *Carousel* was possibly the greatest night I've ever had at the National, which maybe says that it's good for musicals.

Richard: The size of the two big theatres has bred a whole new scenography, hasn't it?

Michael: One of the interesting things, you don't need to do full on naturalistic. Bunny Christie is a particularly great example of a set designer who can do a sort of spare naturalism with all of those Howard Davies Russian pieces, that works very well in the Lyttelton.

Is the premise, though to talk about how theatre wins? Somehow, what you're saying is in spite of all the faults, architectural or otherwise, of those two big theatres, somehow, when you put something good on it, the evening wins.

Richard: If it is sufficient theatre, it wins. Yes. I'm calling the book *A Sense of Theatre*, which is a phrase George Devine coined.

Michael: What did he mean?

Richard: It means that there's a spirit that animates everything to do with the theatre, from the man pulling the ropes on the curtain, to the prop girl, to the actors and actresses. It's theatrical, in the best sense of the word, not the 'lovey' sense of the word.

Michael: It's a beautiful phrase. It's a poetic phrase. What you represent for me as a director, you lighting designers and designers. When I was coming into the theatre, you were regarded as technicians. I'd say, 'Well, no, they're not. They're poets, like everybody else.' Like writers, they have to be poets, otherwise they can't do it.

Richard: That's the sense of theatre.

Michael: I think that's an important definition. I always say we are the interpretive artists with a very big creative brief. Because the creative artist has to be the writer who wakes up and writes what is in their head, and we interpret it, but we interpret it with a phenomenally creative brief. Which is why 'a sense of theatre' is such a beautiful phrase… the theatre at its best, is sort of poetic.

Richard: Tell me more about Sheffield.

Michael: I think Sheffield is still, to this day, the most liberating stage I've ever worked on in my life. Because what you all got right, that maybe is problematic in the Olivier, is that you got the ratio of stage to audience dead right. All of those people just crowd down from the top to the bottom enough for them never to feel like it's a vast way away. It's always close.

Richard: You just lean forward like that. A good theatre, you lean forward.

Michael: You lean forward in good theatres, and sit back…

Richard: The Lyttelton, you tend to lie back.

Michael: It's a wonderful thing that happens at Sheffield. I found the whole design ratio, and also the genius of having those lights up in the roof that come on like a sort of canopy. I cut my teeth on Shakespeare up there. I thought, celebrate the diagonal.

Richard: That was central to Guthrie's thinking. He saw the stage as a crossroads.

Michael: That's right. With the voms coming up.

Richard: Chichester's a bad imitation.

Michael: Really not good.

Richard: It's too flat.

Michael: Shallow.

Richard: Fat and flat. Except, of course, it has worked.

Michael: Yes, it has. It's a beautiful looking building, from the outside.

Richard: Your favourite theatres?

Michael: I think the Crucible's probably my favourite. As a theatre goer, I love the Almeida. I think that's an interesting space. The Donmar, obviously, is a tricky space, but a beautiful one, if you get it right, because you're wrapped around. But I would obviously say that, because they're the two theatres I've run. Outside of those two theatres, I am a huge fan of West End architecture and I won't get on the bandwagon that is diminishing, I detect, at the moment. There was a bit of moment where everybody was bashing them, saying they're not fit for the 21st century.

Richard: Nick Hytner was a bit rude about them, wasn't he?

Michael: Yes, but Nick was trying to say, "I'm building a new one, and therefore the way I'm going to promote my new one is by attacking all the ones that are out there." Which is a way of marketing yourself. He's quietened down now, and eventually, he'll be the first to say how good they are when somebody says, "Can we transfer one from your theatre into one?"

No, I think if you get what's in them right, they're the most wonderful buildings. Those wonderful Sickert paintings, where you see people hanging over each other, they tell you everything you need to know about the sweaty, beautiful nature of inside a theatre building.

And why I'm here with a company now, [in the Wyndham's with *Red*[13]] is because of, in the early '80s, when I was a student at drama school … the West End had a very cheap student scheme.

I think we're blessed with some of the most beautiful theatres, here, in the world. And when you think that the West End is an entity, so hundreds of thousands of people a night are pouring in. Then you've got this vibrant off-West End group, the Donmar, and the Almeida, the Tricycle [now the Kiln]. Then you've got our National. When you join it all up as a theatre ecology…

Richard: It's phenomenal.

Michael: We should be very proud of that, because there's nothing else quite like it. The same exists on Broadway, but there it's much more about money. Broadway looks at that Broadway community and then puts a figure on it, and then says to its city, "Look what we are creating in revenue. You have to take that seriously." Sometimes, I think we should do a little more of that here, because it would be a very good case to government about why the arts really do need support.

Richard: So, if somebody gave you a piece of land and said, "Build a theatre," what would you do?

Michael: That's interesting. It goes back to what you were saying at the very beginning, I suppose, about the National and how it survives in spite of its building. A little bit of me goes, I don't know what I would build physically, because theatre for me… Sheffield taught me that it's a community theatre, with two universities and a big community. The Donmar is the exact opposite. There was no community. It's a Covent Garden little studio that will attract people from anywhere and everywhere towards it. So they were two very different things.

The first thing I would do is work out what you want to achieve in terms of getting to what kind of audience, because the perfect example, look what they've done at Glyndebourne. It's an absolutely exquisite theatre in a field. All the world comes to it, so it's got no community that it plays to, except the opera community. I would happily do something like that if I thought all the people in the world would come to it, but in order to do that you have to put something in them that people want to see.

There's a wonderful moment in *Red*, and I'd forgotten about it, but having had the first preview last night. Rothko says to the assistant, "Tell me what you see, looking at that painting," and the boy goes, "Give me a second." And then he really looks at the fourth wall, which hasn't got a painting on it, so he's looking out at us in the audience, standing at the front.

He looks out, in the moment he takes to think, it's obviously silent, and we're just looking at his face. I thought, "This is extraordinary," because we're all kind of sitting on top of him all the way up, like a wall almost, and it just went completely silent. And to hear 700 people… no cough, nothing. Not a movement in a seat. They all just sat there, breathlessly waiting to hear what his verdict would be, and he was looking at us. He just stood there looking at us. I thought, you can't get that dynamic in many theatres. Not all the way up in the circle and the balcony.

Richard: That's very profound.

Michael: And somebody standing on the edge of the stage just looking at us, as if looking at a painting, and we are the painting looking back at him. And then the word that comes out of his mouth is, "Disquieted. That's what I feel." And you go, "It's interesting, because we're a little disquieted by you looking at us."

Richard: That's magic.

Simon Russell Beale

Actor

Simon is an English actor, author and music historian.

Born in Penang, Malaysia and educated at the Guildhall School, St. Paul's Cathedral School and the University of Cambridge, he has gone on to be described by *The Independent* as "the greatest stage actor of his generation." He has won the Laurence Olivier Award for Best Actor, and was knighted in 2019.

Simon: It's deep in my heart, this building. I don't know quite how that happened. Well, I do know; I was doing great shows with great colleagues, but the actual building, itself, I have great affection for. Every time I see it from the other side of the river, there's a little bit of my heart that leaps, especially since they started lighting it up with beautiful colours. I just love it. It's so exciting.

Richard: Late in his life, Lasdun did some sketches of a possible renovation, and he added flags and a cafe along those front terraces by the Lyttelton.

Simon: It looks uncelebratory during the day. Whereas at night it glistens.

Richard: He had this theory that the concrete would turn white as it got older, but of course it didn't. When it rains, it turns dirtier.

Simon: And you get little drips down the thing. But I have an immense affection for it. I think one of the big triumphs is the dressing room courtyard.

Richard: I wanted a little park at the bottom. [Laughter]

Simon: Absolutely right, we should be able to have access to that bottom level, have chairs and be able to smoke down there.

Richard: Because it's the extract from the car park, you can't do that.

Simon: But, it's completely sensational, because it's both private and public, and communal. It's the actor's private place.

So you can stand without your shirt on in the window and shout across at somebody. I always think of a Neapolitan courtyard. You know about the banging of the glass, don't you? We do it on the final call for the press night. So "Ladies and Gentlemen, this is your beginner's call for *Othello*, your half hour call for press night". So you've half an hour. Therefore, it's usually five to seven, so the other actors are just coming in for their half. You've got three casts all together. It's about the only time virtually everybody performing that night is in their dressing rooms. So you've got every dressing room occupied.

It's like Ralph's Rocket [an early NT tradition instigated by Ralph Richardson, of launching a rocket firework on the opening night of each show, sadly long lost], and specifically for press night. When we did the 50th Anniversary party, Nick Hytner said to me, and to David, who was stage managing – he said can you make sure everybody is in the dressing rooms for the beginner's call.

So the message went around to everybody to participate in their dressing room. "Ladies and Gentlemen, your beginner's call for the 50th anniversary". And the banging started. It was unbelievably moving. That night, you looked around the square, and you saw Judi Dench, Maggie Smith, Michael Gambon, Ralph Fiennes. Nick Hytner happened to be in the dressing room I was sharing with Roger Allam, and we were banging on the window. Nick cried. There is a photograph – he managed to organise it so that there was a photograph from every side. So we got everybody, and you can point them all out. All banging on their windows. So, that is the psychological triumph of this building. I love that. It is the place where you can relax and find yourself.

Richard: Were you ever discomforted finding your way about the building?

Simon: I can't remember now. I must have been. The other thing is that I don't mind the backstage of theatres being crap. It's never worried me – you know, I think it's almost part of the magic that you have a really glossy front, and backstage is…

Richard: But windows. You do like windows.

Simon: Of course. But the other great triumph is the two rehearsal rooms. All actors need is natural light and air. That's all you need. You go to the Barbican, and you've got rehearsal rooms seven floors below ground. It doesn't matter what the building is like, and how crap it is, as long as you've got some access to light.

Richard: It's a horrifying thing, but there are still architects, and some very famous architects, who think, why would actors need daylight? They're only in for a few hours… it's bullshit. [Laughter]

Simon: The idea that actors only spend the hours of performance in the theatre. I heard somebody recently talking about renovating a regional theatre. Apparently some person said, "Oh, the number one issue was wanting a bed in a dressing room, but surely this is a work place." And you think, well, obviously you haven't played Hamlet twice in one day. [Laughter]

The thing about private space. I remember when Nick Hytner at one point, wanted to open up access – a very modern thing – to everything. He had the sudden realisation that there were bits of this process that we go through, all of us, not just actors. We have to be private. The idea of the public being able to come in to watch rehearsals is an absolute nightmare. How do you get Helen Mirren to make an absolute ass of herself.

On the stages themselves, I love being up there. I absolutely love it. The last play I saw though, was miked. Again, this is one I blow hot and cold about. I don't know whether I command that stage as well as I'd like to. But I have seen actors command it brilliantly. I saw Kenneth Branagh do *Edmond* beautifully, and it was technically astonishing what he did, he just filled that space. I do realise that talking sideways is tricky. But once you obey the rules, it's a bit like verse speaking really; you can do a lot. And you can also be very quiet. As long as you take the audience down with you, you can be very quiet.

So I have a huge affection for the Olivier. The miking thing, when Trevor first introduced it for straight plays, I had very mixed feelings. But seeing a show two weeks ago, which was *Les Blancs*, I thought it was fine. The problem is, that it didn't apply to everyone. There are just occasional moments where somebody is facing on stage, and you don't know where the voice is coming from.

Richard: So many different things have happened. I mean, actors, many don't have that sort of capability that I think you were taught thirty years ago.

Simon: But it's not just the capability. The requirements of the last hundred years, about what is natural, and what is convincing, have changed. Principally, presumably, because of cinema. Now when you go to memorial services, you regularly have now a recording of the actor who's died. Both Alan Howard and John Whitmore were sitting with Nick, and we heard John Gielgud do "Ye Elves", from *The Tempest*. He consciously used every single note in his toolbox. He just said I'm going to give you a virtuosic display of how to use the human voice. Up, down, loud, right, left. I mean it was breathtaking.

Also just literally in the last ten years the presentation of literary text has changed in terms of the visual impact of a play. I mean people now also very often expect – Rufus is the past master of this – expect a particular type of collaborative visual impact. I can't quite describe it. It's not a designer saying this is a very beautiful thing I've presented. It's to do with a sort of a more 'poor theatre' type of story telling but with all the ingredients of expensive theatre. [Laughter] Obviously *The Threepenny Opera*.

Richard: I saw it last night. Poor theatre. It's wonderful, just tacky old bits of backstage.

Simon: And extremely expensive!

Richard: Yes. [Laughter]

Simon: I think certainly things happened with the *War Horse* puppet thing. The visual impact is leading the production – or at least it's equal to the verbal.

Richard: You're evoking the imagination, aren't you, in the audience?

Simon: *Everyman*, for Rufus, was about getting an emotional reaction out of the audience, from something, not naturalistic, but visually beautiful. The Olivier lends itself very well to that. Because it's sort of open-ended. The Lyttelton, I have much less affection for. I don't know why; it seems a bit boring. [Laughter] Everyone loves the Cottesloe, or Dorfman.

Richard: Do you?

Simon: Oh yes, I mean any play that Nick said would you like to do this, I said can I do it in the Cottesloe?

Actually except for *Lear*, but Nick didn't allow Shakespeare in the Cottesloe. Then I thought, let's be the complete opposite and do it in the Olivier. It's like I bypassed the Lyttelton. I said, okay, if we can't do it small, let's do it whoppingly big. But the Cottesloe is always great. Always. It's just perfectly made. Whereas there is something about the Olivier, you're like, "Wow!" I mean *Much Ado About Nothing*, for instance. I think it was one of the most beautiful shows I've done in my life, and that was in the Olivier. And I convinced myself that it couldn't possibly be in the Lyttelton. It wouldn't have had the same impact.

Richard: So the Lyttelton. The complaints are it's too wide, but then other people say, well, that's its virtue; it's so wide. Everything is a panorama. But the other big thing is the circle being so disconnected.

Simon: Famously, yes, the worst acoustic is the second row of the circle, isn't it?

The dressing room courtyard

Banging on the windows

Richard: That's right. But it's the disconnect. And the blank side walls, where, of course, our ancestors would have put people in boxes. But some people love it. Designers and directors love it more than others.

Simon: Perhaps they're more in control of it. I mean it's lovely to play. I mean it's not a problem to play. It's easier to play than the Olivier.

Richard: Is it?

Simon: Oh yes. I'm not doing down how tricky the Olivier can be.

Richard: Is that more than the spread of the room?

Simon: I've done more in the Olivier than anywhere else. And I was aware that when I got back to the Cottesloe from *Collaborators*, I'd got in the habit of swinging from side-to-side.

Richard: Right. Other theatres in your career, what sticks out, good, lovely, horrible, any favourites, unfavourites?

Simon: Well, as I said, backstage in the Barbican, is a disaster. Sorry. But I like the Barbican auditorium. I also like being in the audience in the auditorium. Also, I don't know why I'm such a lightweight, but I love the doors closing. [In the Barbican, each seating row has its own door and they are synchronised to close together as a show starts]. I love it. I just love it. It's like being in a Rolls-Royce.

6.4 Theatre Makers and Architecture

I could be talking as if I'm completely audible most of the time in the Olivier, and most people are going, I can't understand a word he says. I've no idea.

Richard: Somebody might tell you. [Laughter]

Simon: Well, they might. I should talk about speed, because I do tend to speak very fast sometimes. And my notes from the voice department were always about saying things too fast.

You know, I get the sense that the Olivier is a much more intimate theatre than the Lyttelton, and much more community-based. One is embraced.

That leads into what I was saying that you can take them down with you. Because I flatter myself, I think we made *Much Ado* work emotionally for the top [of the theatre], as well as the bottom. There is one particular occasion when Benedict – there is a lovely scene with Beatrice right at the end. And he says, "How doth your cousin?" And she goes, "Very ill." And I say, "How are you?" And she goes, "Very ill, too." And Benedict replies, "Serve God, love me, and mend." And I always wanted that to land. And it's such a beautiful – you know, Shakespeare at his simplest best. You know, those four lines of all, "How are you doing". And I remember me and Zoë [Wanamaker] trying to, as I say, take the audience down step-by-step through that "How are you? Not very well. How's your cousin? Not very well." But being conscious that rather than doing it straight ahead to the stalls, definitely doing it up there, the last lines. "Serve God, love me, and mend." So with any luck, they got the emotional impact.

There's nothing more powerful than standing in the Olivier by yourself. Even visually, I think, a little human being. But you have to pitch up.

Now, I want to know what Richard Eyre said!

Richard: Well, Richard, of course had a real love/hate relationship with Denys because he had these terrible battles. He tried to make architectural changes. Denys called him a barbarian very publicly. It was in the papers. Denys and Richard fought, seriously fought. [Laughter] But then Richard says, *Guys*

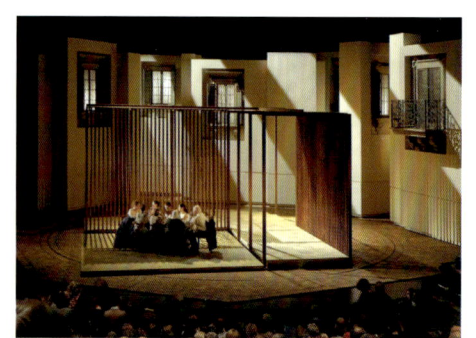

Much Ado About Nothing,
Olivier Theatre, 2007

The Lehman Trilogy,
Olivier Theatre, 2018

and Dolls, I'm never going to do anything better in my life. So he's critical, but loves it.

Simon: But Peter [Hall] must have loved the building, didn't he?

Richard: He was so overwhelmed with just the challenge of getting the place open, and the opposition, the union strikes, and political opposition. But only Peter actually could have opened this place. There were times in the early days when it was touch-and-go whether it was going to be finished.

Simon: What did Nick Starr say?

Richard: They made the decision not to fight the theatres. They made the decision that they would make the company a bigger success than it was, and they didn't want any hint of controversy about architectural issues. So they decided to go with them, and do brilliant work in them. I also think Nick Hytner was pretty fond of them both.

Simon: Nick was very keen on the idea of part of the National remit is that they should do big public plays.

It's getting more and more difficult – because of the expectations of what good acting is, I think it's getting more and more difficult now. All the rules are changing.

Richard: Simon, thank you very, very much.

A Sense of Theatre

Dame Judi Dench

Actor

Does Judi really need an introduction? She has lit up stages and both small and large screens for decades now.

Her professional debut was in 1957 with the Old Vic Company; with them she appeared in roles such as Ophelia in *Hamlet*, Juliet in *Romeo and Juliet*, and Lady Macbeth in *Macbeth*.

Over the next two decades, she established herself as one of the most significant performers in theatre, at both the National and the Royal Shakespeare Company. I had the delight of working with her as she stepped outside those companies to play Sally Bowles in the original London production of *Cabaret* in 1968 – she gave a wonderful performance.[14]

While she has continued to appear on stage – most recently in *The Winter's Tale* for Kenneth Branagh, with whom she has long worked – she has also received critical praise in television, for series such as *A Fine Romance*, and on the big screen whether playing M in every James Bond film between 1995 and 2015, or in *Shakespeare in Love*, for which she won the Academy Award for Best Supporting Actress, or *Mrs Brown*, *Chocolat*, *Iris*, *Mrs Henderson Presents*, *Notes on a Scandal* and *Philomena*, all of which she received Oscar nominations for.

Judi: We never used microphones. Well, certainly not all the time I was there. But we did for *A Little Night Music*. That's slightly different. A musical, You have to do that. Something hidden in your wig.

Is it because people don't project any more? I don't know. I don't believe it's insurmountable. I can't think we did all those plays there in all that time and… Maybe there were lots of complaints that we never knew about!

Richard: There always have been complaints. And they've kept trying to fix the acoustics, without real success.

But may I ask you about your impressions of the NT? You walk onto the Olivier stage for the first time. It's formidable, isn't it? But it can be thrilling.

Judi: Yes it is. But I don't ever remember it, strangely, being a frightening space. Never. I never remember thinking, "God, this is big." But then, if you've played Dallas, the State Fair Music Hall[15], and played *Hamlet* on it!

Richard: You've done that?

Judi: Yes, with the Old Vic tour. I suppose nothing is large after that.

Richard: That is very true.

Judi: I'm really interested to know, do people permanently complain? Or is it a question of the fact that actors' projection today isn't adequate?

Richard: I think it's both. They've fiddled with the acoustics constantly. And each generation has tried to improve it, without complete success. They did get it quite a lot better, I think, under the Two Nicks [Hytner and Starr]. But partly because they concentrated on voice training. I'm told that they held class every day.

Judi: All those warming up things we used to do. It was wonderful. I loved it, the Olly. And it was perfect for *Antony And Cleopatra*. Wonderful. It suddenly, at one point, seemed to open right out.

Richard: Often, when the stage is opened right out or when it's quite sparsely decorated, it's more powerful.

Judi: It is, it is.

Richard: No one's ever done a better *Oklahoma!*

Judi: And that revolve… I think we used the revolve in *A Little Night Music*. Oh that was such fun, all that. What fun it was.

Richard: So your highlights?

Judi: Doing *Absolute Hell* in the Lyttelton. I adored it. I just adored it. I believe it's being done again.

It's a divine play. I had the best time. I just remember being… we couldn't get off the stage. Well, not that Greg Hicks' character and mine wanted to be off the stage. We were just on stage all the time. But I can remember, at one point, being on our hands and knees behind the bar, saying, "How can we feel so drunk when we're drinking water?" And we were, we were drinking gallons of water. But it was a wonderful feeling, like being very drunk. It was glorious, I loved it. That was the Lyttelton.

The National is a warren of corridors. I remember also being in *Antony and Cleopatra* and Alan Bennett was doing *Down Cemetery Road* in the Cottesloe. I came out of my dressing room and he came out of his. I immediately said, "Alan!" We got together, talk, talk, talk, and as I put my foot onto the stage of the Cottesloe Theatre, I thought, "I've had my call. I'm not even meant to be in this theatre. I'm meant to be in the Olly!"

Richard: It can get confusing. But the dressing rooms around the courtyard…

Judi: All around the courtyard, you see everybody getting ready. I love that. Love it. I remember when the Japanese were there. Gambon was in the theatre and so was I. I got into my dressing room and all the Japanese were getting ready for a matinee all the way along here. It was completely silent. And they were, you know, absolutely quiet. People were handing things out and they were offering things and putting things on and making up… and I looked up and saw Gambon out of his

"*A Little Night Music*. Oh that was such fun, all that. What fun it was."

Judi Dench

dressing room, you know, watching, and I was watching. And he saw me, and said, "Doesn't it make you feel like a pile of shit?"

Richard: It's very nice, that feeling of community.

Judi: Except if you're doing the play that goes on longest. As you see the lights going off all over the world. And, you suddenly think, "Oh, everybody's gone home. They're all going home now. I'm practically the only light left on."

But, the rehearsal spaces, I like them. Those big rehearsal rooms. I loved them. I find it easy that the play transforms from those rehearsal rooms onto the stage. That's not always the case, I think. But I loved it. I love Linda, Vincent all being at the stage door in that time. So, it was kind of a continuance of it all.

Richard: Other theatres, outside the National? Do you have some that spark your excitement?

Judi: Because of being with The Vic from 1957, of course, I simply dote on it. Love The Vic. You get very upset when you go back and they've done things and blocked up doors. I remember at The Vic there was a wonderful stage manager called John Way, who used to make beer, and his beer was in the OP-side prop room. And once during a performance of *Henry VI,* they all burst their, I knew nothing about beer, but they all popped their corks. We all heard. I don't think the audience did, but we all did. And then of course, they changed the stage door at the Vic.

Richard: Yes, that's horrid. You come in the wrong side.

Judi: You have to go in the Waterloo Road side!

Richard: And the pub used to be next door.

Judi: Yes, next door!

Richard: Other favourites?

Judi: The Haymarket. Beautiful. They've had to put in a new staircase, I believe. What I loved about those old stairs is that they were worn down. Worn and polished and so beautiful.

I loved that room, that I was lucky enough to be in, where Sir John [Gielgud] spent some nights during the war. A beautiful dressing room. And a wonderful stage and the actual auditorium and everything. Yes, I love that. Love it.

Richard: The West End theatres tend to grip you, the audience.

Judi: Yes. Well, if they like you. You know The Palace, which was built, wasn't it, as an opera house. And it had all those mirrors around it. That's a beautiful theatre, except when you have those remarks as you get people walking past your dressing room window. I remember that remark, somebody reminded me of it the other day, of me hearing that person saying, "Judi Dench in *Cabaret*? Nobody'll go to see that dear, no one!"

Richard: Have you played at The Swan?

Judi: The Swan in Stratford? Yes. That's quite hard. We did *All's Well* there.

Richard: How do you feel about the thrust stage?

Judi: Well, the thing is, you can't fly anything, which is a pity. So it limits you.

Richard: There are huge arguments over the National as to whether the actor wants the audience in front of him or...

Judi: Or beside him or...

Judi Dench and Patricia Hodge rehearsing *A Little Night Music* at the National, 1995

Richard: Olivier felt blocked by those behind him. He didn't like Chichester at all.

Judi: No.

Richard: That went far too far around.

Judi: Well, that's like 'Lighthouse acting', isn't it. You have to share the joke. I mean, you start there and you have to move it around, it's really hard.

But you adjust to it, don't you? But that kind of promenade thing, it's like the hanamichi in a Japanese theatre. It's hard, I mean, I don't know whether that's good for the audience. I think it's quite distracting to look over and see people facing you on the other side.

Richard: That's what Olivier was concerned about.

6.4 Theatre Makers and Architecture

Judi: I think it's distracting.

Richard: That's why the Olivier is fundamentally ninety degrees.

Judi: Yes, yes. Yes, I love that. *Little Night Music* was wonderful. Didn't feel big at all.

Richard: That's wonderful. Back to theatres. Just for a moment. Other countries? Anything strike you about New York or anywhere else?

Judi: I remember the Fenice. We did *Romeo and Juliet* with Zeffirelli there. And we went up an hour and a half late 'cause of a gondola crush. Came down something like one o'clock in the morning. Oh, and it burnt down after that.

Richard: Yes, it did.

Judi: But it's been rebuilt.

Richard: Have you been back?

Judi: I've been back to see it.

Richard: They've done an exquisite job.

Judi: Yes, people just sitting, looking at the theatre architecture. You never get that.

Richard: It may be the most beautiful theatre in the world.

Judi: I think so. Well, certainly that I've ever been in.

The Barbican... I didn't like it because the cart kept breaking down in *Mother Courage*. I don't like going to a theatre, where you have to press a button in order to get in, which you had to. I don't like a theatre where you're all on different floors and have a lift to get to the stage. Where is the feel, where is the community? I don't know how you remain a company. Being on stage is fine and the house is fine, but it's not a theatre I would ever want to go to again. Not ever.

A Little Night Music as part of the *50 Years On Stage* gala, Olivier Theatre, 2013

Richard: It's so often forgotten, creating a backstage community. I always think one of the mistakes at the National, that I was part of, you come in the stage door, then the actors all go there, and the office workers all go up there, and they never meet again, and that's very sad.

Judi: It's a great pity.

Richard: It led to the industrial problems that Peter suffered.

Judi: Yes, I bet it did. You go down that long corridor and then quite suddenly you're in a separate place. Absolutely, Richard, I quite agree.

Richard: We now always try to create a back stage 'hub', which is, dressing rooms, rehearsal room and the admin all together.

Judi: It's interesting, I never really thought about it, about that thing of how important it is to have a kind of unity backstage as such. That's why the National is lovely. It's also got that very nice restaurant, and the bars and things like that. That's very nice and that you can look out. You know there's a great communion between actors. I love that.

When I was at the National, I got my DBE and Tony Hopkins birthday was all on the same day. So there was a lot of singing that night, that was so nice.

A National Theatre Platform Performance

25th October 2016
Architect Steve Tompkins and lighting designer Paule Constable – extracts[16]

Steve: By accident or design, the Olivier and the Lyttelton have grit in plenty. They are very particular personalities aren't they, but actually at least they have personality.

None of the great and good of the theatre world could actually agree from one week to the next about what Denys should be designing and what his priorities were, so to actually produce this extraordinary synthesis, not only of the auditoria, but of all the wider complicated relationships with city, with society, with the idea of what a National Theatre building should be and how it should relate to a different sort of society emerging from the strictures of the post-war years. To me it's a miracle that he didn't get anything else wrong. He got so much right about this building.

Lasdun talked about public life and energy around the building, day and night; he talked about the building as a catalyst, other things happening over the years. So I like to think that he would have been quite pleased the way the building has become animated in the time since it was finished.

Paule: Olivier's concern at the very early stage about not knowing what the theatre wanted to be, is actually a typical thing for us as theatre makers. We fear the permanent, because we never make anything that's permanent. I think the relationship between architect and theatre maker is so fascinating: so often you're making things that are permanent, and we're making things that aren't, and somehow finding a common ground is extraordinary and frightening.

Steve: The architect's DNA is programmed to solve problems and iron out the problematic when actually, it's the problematic that make theatrical space so intense, so beguiling. As architects we need to learn to make unfinished theatres in the confident knowledge that we are then in the hands of theatre makers like you guys, who can complete them in different forms for every production, every evening. For the other intangible is the live performance itself, which we can never predict.

> "I can take any empty space and call it a bare stage. A man walks across this empty space whilst someone else is watching him, and this is all that is needed for an act of theatre to be engaged." [17]
>
> Peter Brook, 1968

Paule: Making theatre isn't about control, great theatre is about imagination, possibility. We all want a personal relationship with what we're looking at, what we're experiencing. And I think that's true of the architecture as well.

Steve: The great legacy of Denys Lasdun is that despite the critique of the building, sometimes feeling monumental, sometime hermetic, actually it's a very broad framework of freedom for theatre makers. All that's needed is the confidence that it is a thick-skinned building, it can take some insouicence, it can take a bit of cheek, it can take a kicking, because it's strong, it's confident in its own voice, so I'm really cheered by the fact that theatre makers are taking on these spaces, wrestling them to the ground, and forcing, beautiful intimate, vibrant productions out of them… sometimes kicking and screaming, but actually they are themselves beautiful spaces and will live on as a masterpiece, an extraordinary piece of work.

The Missing Theatre project by the designers organisation Scene/Change[18] during the Covid pandemic

6.5 Theatre In Challenging Times

The third decade of the 21st century brought turmoil the likes of which had perhaps never been seen before. Brexit came first, the politically motivated decision to separate a country from its closest neighbours. Then a pandemic shut down the entire world. Then a faltering recovery in the face of an economic crisis, and new wars in Europe and elsewhere.

It has been a difficult time to be a theatre maker, or a theatre.

Covid

The National Theatre has always been buffeted by the winds of the world around it. Lasdun's considered, concrete architecture was robust enough to withstand the shifts in public opinion led by Prince, now King, Charles as they swung against the building then back around in favour of it. All of the theatre's artistic directors have had to deal with times of financial turbulence, of tensions with funding bodies and ultimately the government. The vote for Brexit in 2016, coming into effect early in 2020, had an impact on every organisation that exists as part of a larger world, whether that be science or the arts.

But all of that was nothing compared to the arrival of Covid-19, the coronavirus, in early March 2020.

As with many things that at first seem to be surprising, shocking and new, history reveals that they are not. The Shakespearean age was interrupted by the 1665 bubonic plague that sent our players out into the countryside and closed their then newly established London theatres. The 1917 Spanish flu pandemic caused fifty million deaths. Hong Kong had battled with the SARS pandemic in 2002. But the remarkable thing this time was that this was a pandemic for our global, inter-connected age. The virus spread rapidly around the world. On 12th March, Broadway announced the abrupt closure of all of its theatres. Four days later, just an hour before curtain up time, UK theatres started to close, with all officially shut down by the Government on 20th March as the entire country was ordered to stay at home.

For the first time since it opened in 1976, the NT building was completely shut down.

The NT company quickly did what theatre people have

always done: improvised. Its collection of performances filmed for the NT Live one-off broadcasts over the years suddenly took on new value, rebranded *National Theatre At Home* and made available online for free (with the agreement of all who'd first made the shows) for anyone who needed a distraction from lockdown. They were a good distraction – but also a reminder that a performance on a screen, or particularly a performance watched alone or even in a small group, is not the same as a performance watched live in the company of others.

Above all else, we are social animals. Our very essence is our ability to communicate with each other. Our sweetest moments are together. The intimacy of physical contact. The gathering of family. The clustering of friends to share stories. That is the magic of theatre.

The coronavirus, with its potential to spread without apparent symptoms and without physical contact, was scary. Before the invention of vaccines, our only defence against such pandemics was separation, isolation, the avoidance of touch – seemingly the absolute opposite of what we most fundamentally crave. That's what we did this time, too, hiding behind masks if we did briefly venture out. But in remarkably quick time, science provided the solution that let us, falteringly at first, but with increasing confidence, return to a more familiar life.

Post-Covid
If 2022 felt like the start of a post-Covid era, it also saw the return of something that I had seen before in my lifetime but hoped never to see again: war in Europe. The horrors of the Russian barbarism that has engulfed Ukraine stunned all sentient human beings. How is it possible? But then one remembers that history never stops. Humanity has always survived – though increasingly, we seem to be rather pushing our luck.

Covid and the economic crises that followed it have been unprecedented in what they have revealed: injustice, intolerance, inequality, rising autocracy and other cascading problems. As theatre struggles to recover it faces doubtful audiences, city centres sometimes devoid of urban workers, gutted tourism. Individuals and organisations, striving to resolve problems, face reduced finances and, often, staggering debt.

These difficult times have stripped the rosy glasses off our eyes. Age-old realities must now be faced. Black lives do matter. Freelance workers require greater equity. Global warming demands urgent new initiatives and more sustainable approaches to everything. We need a more egalitarian, fairer, caring society.

In our world of theatre, remarkable initiatives emerged. Social media expanded theatres' horizons; rehearsals via Zoom have expanded into techniques that allow remote lighting and technical rehearsals to span the globe, while streaming has allowed theatres to connect to far-flung audiences. New connections are being explored between theatre makers and people of all ages and ethnic groups beyond any traditional or established boundaries.

Theatre will recover. As our rogue and vagabond ancestors have taught us, tough times call for even more robust responses.

The National Theatre Post-Covid
The National survived. It figured out how to reopen – the vast space and huge volume of air per audience member of its two bigger auditoria perhaps a virtue in this situation, its air handling fitted with upgraded filters and run in full fresh air mode not only during but for hours before and after each performance. The Olivier was reconfigured to an in-the-round format but with seats left empty to keep audience members distanced from each other. It got one show open, on 21st October 2020; on the 4th November 2020 it was forced to shut down again as the next wave of the virus hit. But it just kept coming back, albeit changed in one key way: playing in rep, different shows on different nights that has been a feature of the National since it began, was too expensive. It went, and at the time of writing has not come back.

Like many other arts organisations in the UK, the National Theatre had, over the years, been forced to reduce its reliance on government funding as that funding was progressively cut. Instead it came up with other ways to earn income – increasing audience sizes, sponsorship, commercial transfers of successful shows, perhaps most famously, *War Horse*. Immediately prior to Covid, eighty-five percent of the NT's income was self-generated.

That meant the pandemic, with no performances and no income of any kind, immediately presented a huge problem, the NT losing seventy-five perent of its income overnight. Despite reacting quickly to control costs, including through job losses of up to thirty percent of the theatre's permanent staff and 400 casual staff, it quickly faced a multi-million pound deficit.

In December 2020, the NT received a £19.7million loan from the Culture Recovery Fund set up by the UK Government's Department of Digital, Culture, Media and Sport – a scheme which in total provided £1.57billion to help support culture and heritage organisations in the aftermath of Covid. But while welcome it was a loan, not a grant. Like all loans, it will have to be paid back – affecting the NT's finances, and so potentially its work, for years to come.

Eras Ending, Eras Beginning

It took more than a hundred years of effort to get the National Theatre established, more than ten years to get its building built. But the organisation has now existed for sixty years; it has occupied that building for close-on fifty. The National Theatre, company and building, look to the future, as it always has. But it also now has its own remarkable history, one that shapes and defines it in so many ways.

Past, present and future intersected at a company meeting on 16th June 2023. It had been called for Rufus Norris to announce that he would end his tenure as the National's sixth Artistic Director at the end of his second term, in 2025. But it also provided a moment to reflect on all the people who helped shape the National through its history as the company were also told of the passing of Leonard Tucker,[19] the National's original chief lighting electrician at the Old Vic and then the South Bank, a few days before. One more link to the company's foundations had been lost.

The National will move forward, as large organisations do. Judgements will be formed on Norris' tenure. Some felt that as the first non-Oxbridge graduate to run the company, he lacked a depth of knowledge of the wider classical repertoire. Others felt that there had been no era-defining show – by which perhaps they really meant big commercial hit – of his era, no equivalent to *War Horse* or before that *Guys and Dolls*, or *Amadeus* or *Equus*. Norris himself rightly points to his success in opening up the organisation to new voices, and providing an outlet for new writing and new plays many directly born from the nation the National serves: the *Death of England* trilogy, the musical *Standing at the Sky's Edge*, the verbatim play *Grenfell*, an intersection of football, theatre and the state of the nation in *Dear England*, or *Nye* which looks at the creation of the UK's National Health Service. Plus of course he led the National through the Covid pandemic, navigating unprecedented times.

At the time of writing it is not known who will succeed him, though the rash of other directors quitting their jobs suggests there will be much jockeying for this position – an affirmation that the National is still a peak those who make theatre want to summit. Whoever it is, they will find an organisation of people ready and willing to follow their lead, a building that provides them an enduring home, and of course three theatres full of particular challenges but also, as so many shows have proven over the years, also offering remarkable opportunities – indeed, very much defining what the National Theatre is.

Though there are other, later theatres that take the lessons learnt from the creation of the National, the National's three auditoria have proven themselves to be very much places for plays – places for audience and actors to gather together, even in challenging times.

Thoughts from the Pandemic

Paule Constable – Lighting Designer

Richard: How did the plague hit you? (We believe that Shakespeare went home and wrote *King Lear*!)

Paule: I sat in the uncanny silence and gardened for five minutes and then I started to witness the disintegration of this beloved world of theatre – and saw that the entire freelance community were being silenced, ignored, hung out to dry. So I became a key participant in creating Freelancers Make Theatre Work.[20] We opened Pandora's Box! Whether it will make a difference in the long term I have no idea – but the balance of power in our industry is so skewed. We do little to value the work that all freelancers contribute. That has to change…

We face global warming, video streaming, freelance neglect, scared audiences… And the need for a hug. Right now we are living under a government who are wilfully mistrusting of the arts in general. With Covid and now Brexit ripping our industry apart I cannot believe that they have any understanding of what we bring – either to the exchequer or to the mental health and the well-being of so many. We have to fight for our lives now. So more than ever we have to be relevant. Theatre had become – in many ways – entertainment. But we have to find our voice, we have to fight and question and we have to know what we are doing and why. That has never been more important. In the short term, there are huge challenges – we are all feeling brittle, exhausted and overwhelmed. That makes for a volatile workplace. I have found myself angrier than ever and have let that anger affect the people I value the most. I wish there were some way to collectively acknowledge the grief we are suffering after these two years – so we can move through that together. I feel the aspiration for change and the realities of a post-Covid workplace are contradictory. There are companies and buildings trying to do better – and many who aren't. How do we tackle this? I don't know, but if anyone has any thoughts I would love to hear them.

Tim Hatley – Designer

The National Theatre should be the heartbeat of the nation's theatre – a place for designers, writers, directors and actors of all walks of life to experiment and grow, and to allow the next generation to learn the craft of making theatre. This is more important now than it has ever been, and I believe is the key to keeping theatre alive in this country.

The huge success of the NT Live broadcasting to live audiences in cinemas globally is brilliant. Although as an audience member it is not as powerful as experiencing a performance live, in these post Covid-times I am sure we will be seeing this medium being pushed further and further. If it enables people around the world to experience our world-class theatre – this can only be a good thing.

Bunny Christie – Designer

2020 was devastating for a lot of freelancers in all areas of theatre making. I particularly worried about theatre builders, painters, propmakers, costume and wig makers. Fabric shops going bust. Banks foreclosing on small businesses vital for us making shows and creative people making a living and supporting their families with their talent. I'm concerned that theatre buildings and production companies receive much-needed money from Government but that doesn't then reach the people making the product. This time has exposed so much inequality in our business.

The best thing to come out of the year for me professionally was the founding of Scene/Change, a collective of theatre designers campaigning for better fees and conditions and accessibility to design. It's been a fantastic thing to have a support group of generous designers at all stages of our careers.

Bob Crowley – Designer

The post-pandemic future of the theatre? I think it's too soon to imagine what will happen, except to say that resilience, tenacity, blind faith and pure cock-eyed optimism have been the foundation of surviving in the arts thus far… and hopefully will see us through to a new exciting future. I have to believe this.

Peter Mumford – Lighting Designer

At the beginning of 2020 I was I was directing and designing my concert staging of *Die Walküre* in Lisbon when Covid erupted big time. I had a hundred-piece orchestra all tuned up and the principals ready. Thirty minutes before the dress rehearsal, the Government shut us down; I was on a plane home the next day. After that all planned projects went down like skittles both for me and all my compatriots and a pretty barren eighteen months followed – a quite extraordinary experience unlike any other in my career.

I guess I was more fortunate than most as many of the European opera houses struggled on with huge support from their governments. We reopened The StaatsOper in Vienna with a restaging of *Madama Butterfly* in August 2020, and then *Peter Grimes* at Teatro Real in Madrid. I returned to my studio home and directed and lit (with projection) on a double Zoom connection with a monitor in the auditorium (with me on it!!) and a mobile phone to my assistant. It was a great success and well received.

The pandemic has certainly had the effect of bringing our theatre working communities together. We have however learnt how little the cultural aspect of our society is regarded by our government. I've always known that Britain is a country with an amazing output in terms of art and artists, far less appreciated at home than globally. So although I don't have high hopes, I would like the return of theatre to somehow play a significant role in the rebalancing and restoration of society as a whole, because that is the raison d'être of art – to mirror society and show people something new and revelatory.

David Hare – Playwright

There's never been a building in Britain which caused as much controversy as the National Theatre, the brutalist cathedral on the South Bank. Denys Lasdun had earlier designed the Royal College of Physicians, tucked away in the corner of Regents Park, like an early maquette but on a far more human scale. Because it was hidden behind trees, he'd got away with it in the fickle court of public opinion. In the face of a dirty culture war, Lasdun understandably became both paranoid and martyred, a miserably unhappy figure, defensive to the last, and bewildered that no one could see how elegant at least the public face of the National was, with its gorgeous layered foyers offering a quiet place for students, scholars and friends to spend all day. Now, with brutalism back in fashion, we can see that this is architecture which was built to last. In it, the National Theatre, under successive directors, offered us all some of the greatest theatre-going nights of our lives. A good part of the credit must go to the man who designed the space.

British theatre won't recover from Covid without the emergence of a major playwright. It's only a great writer, writing from the heart, who makes the theatre reach outwards into the whole of society, not just to aficionados. In the 20th century we had Brecht and John Osborne and Samuel Beckett and Eugene O'Neill who all radically changed the art form, and put it right at the centre of the culture. That hasn't happened so far in the 21st. No writer has yet had that impact. We can all make shows, but what we need is plays – and specifically plays which non-theatregoers feel they want to see.

Rufus Norris - NT Director, speaking an April 2021

I think if you look through history, these periods of challenge often lead to revolution or evolution. There was a plague in the late 16th century that meant that the players had to leave London and tour round, they went to a place called Stratford, a young man went to see a play there and that's how Shakespeare met theatre. Another plague later on meant that Shakespeare had to sit inside and write sonnets and *King Lear*; when the Puritans lost their control over entertainment, there was a thirty-year period where there were no plays and at the end of that women went on stage for the first time; and the Arts Council was formed out of the Second World War.

So in each period like this where we're going through tremendous difficulty, aspects emerge… I don't know whether this is the beginning of a new form – we'll find out.

With theatre having long faced criticism for failing to reach a broader audience, with many simply unable to afford tickets, the coronavirus-forced closures may have fast-tracked a new way of bringing plays to people.

And if the pandemic has made "all the world a stage" - perhaps Shakespeare would approve.

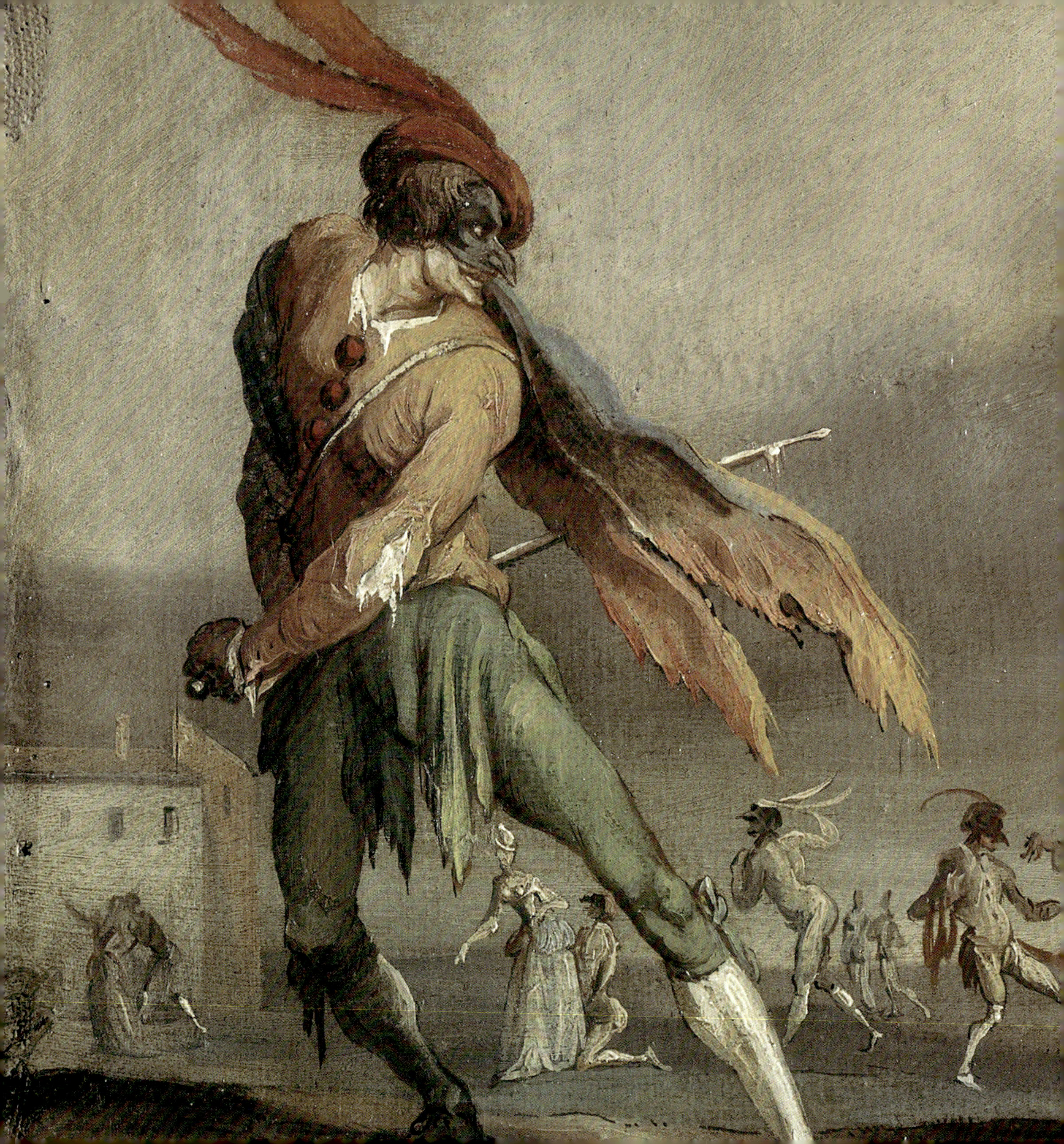

Part Seven

Finale

A Personal Conclusion

Now to finally complete this book. After seeking opinion about the National from so many others, so many participants in its success, it's time to express an opinion… My own.

There is no one sort of theatrical experience. Theatres for drama, theatres for musicals, theatres for music, theatres for spectacle, theatres for circus… Each require stage, auditorium, backstage, lobbies, theatre technology… even if only two boards and a passion. Audiences may surround the actor, or the platform may surround the audience. Whatever the actor/audience relationship, for spontaneous combustion to occur this relationship must excite.

Sixty years of theatre has left me with the conviction that for theatre architecture to ignite, the physical relationship that binds every audience member into a collective, and that collective to the performer, is pivotal.

There is a fundamental energy that runs throughout nature, through all living beings. Ancient philosophies of every kind have recognised it: Chinese Qi, Aka to the Egyptians, Prana to the Hindus. Most recently, the new-found science of neuroaesthetics has identified the mirror neuron, elements in our brains that radiate and receive input from others around us. Our social connections are vital. We share stories, we feel sound and movement within us, we empathise with drama that surrounds us. Billions of brain cells interact with billions of others creating powerful experiences within our heads.

We love to be entertained in a crowd. We are immediately stimulated by the presence of other people around us. Theatre is about participation: living actor and lively audience. Theatre architecture is about creating that combustion chamber.

The reputation of Lasdun's building has grown over the years, particularly as the popularity of the South Bank has risen. Architects are revered members of our society and Lasdun, clearly a man of great integrity, was one of the most original of his generation. Yet, from the evidence of the building committee minutes, he failed to follow his own announced timetable of twelve months "during which the architect must absorb your wants but also your dreams," after which he had to be left alone to design the building, "and that would be done without their interference." For the Olivier, his "stage in the corner of a room" was conceived within four months of his engagement, and remained an 'idée fixe' through another year of debate. The design of the Olivier Theatre (Scheme E) was finally resolved only after heavy pressure from the building committee. The Lyttelton arrived: a theatre of confrontation that demonstrated a lack of awareness of historical precedent, even in the face of client concerns. The public areas were Lasdun's unfiltered creation, for which he does deserve enormous credit. But a National Theatre, a theatre for drama, in which the unamplified voice cannot be heard, and in which emotion is hard to evoke, has problems.

Sir Laurence, at the very first meeting with Lasdun, said "how can we get the atmosphere of an old theatre in a new one? Plaster and wood is better for voice." Lasdun responded by talking of "engaged intensity" rather than any pastiche of the past. But his solution led to two overlarge theatres, made largely of concrete and stainless steel. Yes, we sought a 'new' theatre for our future, but was this the right direction, or did our architect simply not understand the subtlety of creating 'lively' theatre?

In his foreword to this book, Richard Eyre asked "[This book] deals with matters that haunted my waking and sleeping hours for years, but its appeal is much wider than that: It addresses a problem that applies to almost all bespoke theatres, galleries, museums, cinemas, and concert halls. How does a committee of professionals, expert in their own fields, sanction spaces so ill-suited to the art form that they are designed to serve?"

How did this distinguished group of theatre makers, most of them directors (notably, Olivier was the only actor), find it so hard to give our talented, but inexperienced, architect adequate guidance? An architect, no matter how talented, needs guidance, and Olivier's chosen committee should have provided that wisdom. Instead it contributed confusion rather than clear direction.

Lasdun was brilliant, richly influenced by architectural history: Le Corbusier, Hawksmoor and Mackintosh, but he was unaware of the heritage of theatre building and seemed unable to understand the often incoherent advice that theatre folk were trying to give him.

I admit to prejudice. But working with so many architects: Frank Gehry, Norman Foster, Rem Koolhaas, Barton Myers, and many others, has led me to this view. The most brilliant architects must come to understand this interdependence of architecture and performace for a useful, lively theatre to emerge.

The design of a theatre represents a singular, and often misunderstood challenge to any architect. No other type of building presents such a conundrum. No other building exists only to provide a frame for continuous creative activity of another art form: theatre. And yet theatre itself is a creative endeavour that exists only in relationship to its audience.

A piece of sculpture, or art, or even music may exist in a vacuum. Theatre entirely depends upon the participation of an audience. An audience that exerts a powerful, and constantly changing influence in real time upon the artist.

Theatre is live storytelling to lively participants. A living actor meets a participating audience of fellow human beings.

Humanity – human scale – lies at the core of theatre. Thus architecture must provide a place; a "house" for theatre to ignite and for uniquely human interactivity within.

At the National, within the magnificent, popular building that houses a theatre company that is internationally renowned, the two main stages are hard to ignite.

And yet… both of those theatres have hosted superb productions. They have elicited memorable stagecraft that has supported thrilling experiences, from today's *Lehman Trilogy*, *Network* and *Follies*, to yesteryear's *Guys and Dolls*, *War Horse*, *Oklahoma!*, or *The Shaughraun*.

Architect Steve Tompkins described both major auditoria as having "grit in plenty," to encourage theatremakers to rise above their limitations. They certainly have done on so many occasions. A sense of theatre, employed by generations of brilliant theatre people, has created the world's foremost theatre company.

"Humanity – human scale – lies at the core of theatre. Thus architecture must provide a place; a 'house' for theatre to ignite and for uniquely human interactivity within."

But the theatres could be better. Will posterity one day say, "Enough", and seek to make improvements? I believe it might. Just as Elisabeth Scott's theatre, after decades of tinkering, was finally rebuilt, so one day, the National's two principal theatres will be changed. But let the RSC example at Stratford sound a warning. Even the most skilled theatre makers and architects can make mistakes. The future must proceed with extraordinary care.

The Olivier is the toughest challenge. Its allusions to classical Greece lend it an inevitable grandeur. But maybe within its too-distant walls the opportunity might be taken to add extra seats. The Lyttelton is a lesser challenge. Resorting to our English traditions; reshaping the circle, and adding audience instead of concrete along the sides of the house might dramatically improve the space for lively theatre.

Paule Constable speaks passionately about imagination, about unleashing possibilities as yet undreamt of. Steve Tompkins has written: "If theatre architecture is to evolve, we will need to become more experimental, more informed, more responsive, more communicative, and more aware of the real lives of our completed buildings."

An architecture that more readily binds players and spectator together might better aid audience and actor in that magical process.

My friend and colleague Gene Leitermann in his book *Theater Planning* suggests:
"Another reason for the interest in theatre design is the fascination that the theatre building itself elicits. Michel Foucault (1926-1984), a French philosopher, cited the

theatre as an example of a heterotopia – a space that is simultaneously both mythic and real. The overlapping of real and mythic space within a theatre can be expanded upon: the theatre building exists, in physical space, in relationship to a city or landscape. The stage (or performance area) is a physical space in which the actors move; it exists within the theatre building and in relationship to the audience area. The scenographic space occupies the physical stage space and suggests a fictional space in which the characters of the play live. Layered on the scenographic space is the dramatic space created by language and theatre craft. This dramatic space encompasses both the space in view of the audience and the fictional world 'off stage.'

"We may never articulate this overlapping of real and fictional space, but we are instinctively aware of it. And we understand that somehow the fictional space is always a latent presence. Perhaps that's why even an unused theatre building anticipates the performances that could take place. And why, once occupied, a Theatre is changed by the performances it houses."

Stories underpin our lives. Others' laughter calls on us to smile, tears makes us weep… Theatre might be described as a machine to make us feel. The physical placement of people in our audiences – so they both embrace the performer and encourage a collective response more easily – can underpin those reactions.

Mark Rylance has spoken eloquently of the need to act with his audience, how a circular room enfolds our spectators into becoming that living beast: an audience.

Sixty years of studying theatre, and working upon their design, sixty years of lighting and producing theatre, made one thing very clear to me. It is the audience that brings theatre to life, it is the audience and its energy that inspires performers to attain ever greater heights. The design of the House can powerfully assist in igniting the theatrical event: actor and audience together. Denys Lasdun's 'Fourth Theatre' – the public areas – will remain his magnificent memorial for many ages.

Here, theatre lovers for generations will gather to ready themselves to join in the communion of storytelling.

As time passes, the building itself appears to grow in stature. What are those qualities it possesses that are so perennially fascinating?

From afar, Lasdun's open terraces juxtaposed by the powerful verticals of elevators and stage fly towers present an imposing prospect. Evocative of a battleship or medieval fortress, yet one that seems more open and welcoming the closer the visitor approaches. This timeless evocation is amplified by the detailing and texture of the materials with which the building is made: the blue-brick paving, the fossil-like textured board-marked concrete, the heather-coloured carpet, which are supplemented by the slit-like openings that afford glimpses from one space to another. Enlivened by shafts of candle-coloured light, the muted colours of the interior are animated by the people as they, in Sir Denys' prophetic description, ebb and flow through the building.

At the heart of London, the National stands above a significant turn of the River Thames like a timeless monument. It seems to have been there forever. At night the light from within acts like a welcoming beacon signalling the arts. Once inside, the textured walls and diagrid ceilings seem to protect the visitor like the encompassing boundaries of a cave. On multiple, overlapping terraces the public seem to be stars in their own drama.

But the centre of this magnificent building, the two main auditoria, where actor and audience meet, offer both unprecedented opportunity and challenge. The smaller Dorfman continues to be a place of vibrant, lively, intimate, action. Might the two large houses, the Olivier and Lyttelton, one day be transformed to become places that more readily spring to vibrant life?

We will see.

Richard Pilbrow
17th September 2023

Harmony

A quick sketch of an idea...

7.1 A Personal Conclusion

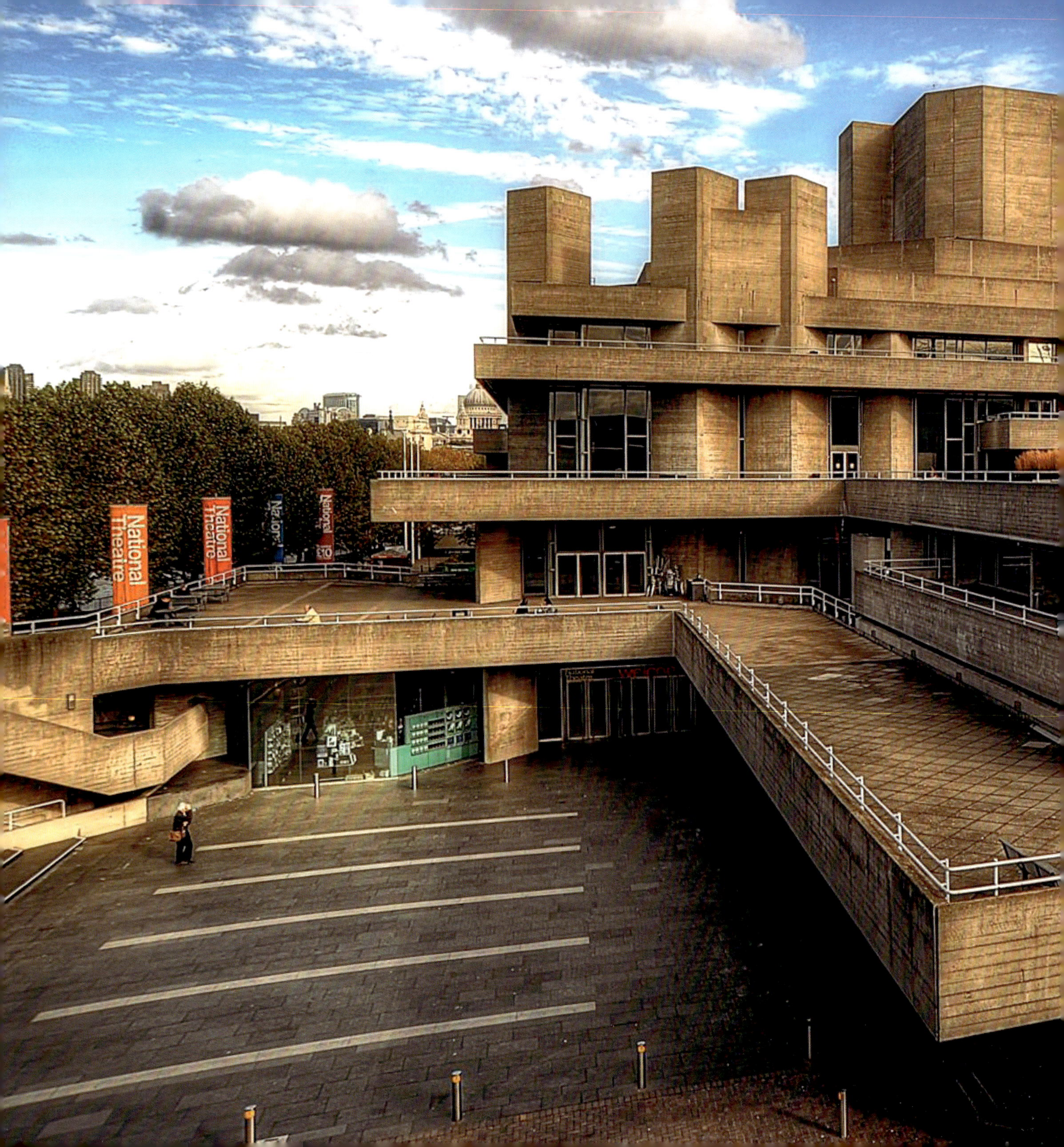
National Theatre
National Theatre

Appendices

Author's Note and Thanks

Central to this book are the minutes of the National Theatre Building Committee, which met from January 1963 to January 1969. The task of the committee was to prepare the brief for the proposed new National Theatre, to assist in the selection of the architect and to collaborate with the architect on the design of the building. Of the thirty meetings listed, some seven appear to have left no records.

These minutes have not previously been published in full. They are quoted here verbatim, without editing. The minutes were originally prepared in longhand by Yolande Bird, secretary to the National Theatre Board. After transcription, she distributed drafts to the participants, inviting comments before their finalisation. In 2015, Yolande told me that the minutes were seldom modified.

For the commentary between the notes of each meeting, I have drawn upon my personal papers, recollections and other documents: the minutes of the South Bank Theatre Board; the National Theatre Archive, which includes 110 boxes of archives presented to the NT by Theatre Projects Consultants; archives of Sir Laurence Olivier, held in the British Library; and archives of Sir Denys Lasdun & Partners, held by the Royal Institute of British Architects at the Victoria and Albert Museum. I have also drawn upon the work of other writers that are listed in the appendix, and upon personal interviews with some of the artists who have generously shared their stories about making the National Theatre a special place.

Soon after the delayed 1976 opening my life designing theatres took me overseas, most particularly to live in the US. I have therefore often turned to the words of others to keep me connected to the National Theatre and theatre in Britain. In particular I must mention five writers: The late Richard Findlater, the late Irving Wardle, Michael Coveney, Michael Billington and my colleague at Theatre Projects, Iain Mackintosh. I had the pleasure of briefly knowing Richard Findlater when he was with *The Observer* and as a young producer I was highly influenced by his seminal examination of the British theatre, *The Unholy Trade*. Irving Wardle was a long-term acquaintance. His book on Devine, *The Theatres of George Devine*, particularly opened my eyes to the complexities of the interplay between three giants who figure in this story: Devine, Olivier and Guthrie.

Michael Coveney edited *Plays and Players* before becoming theatre critic for the *Financial Times*, *Observer*, and *Daily Mail*. He has been a window for me into what's on the London stage during the years of my self-imposed exile. Michael Billington, as theatre critic of *The Guardian* between 1971 and 2019, has also been a link for me into British theatre. His book, *State of the Nation* (2007) has been a revelation. His insights into the subtleties of theatre, set within the social story of British society, have been my guide.

Iain Mackintosh has been a colleague for over fifty years. His insights into the difference between 'live' and 'inert' theatre spaces, attracted my attention when, as a producer, I brought some of his productions into the

> "Plays plump, plays paltry, plays preposterous, plays purgatorial, plays radiant, plays rotten, but plays persistent. Plays, plays, plays. The habit of art."
>
> Alan Bennett, Playwright

West End of London. Iain's book *Architecture, Actor and Audience* remains the classic text on theatre design.

I have drawn from three histories of the National; *The History of The National Theatre*, by critic John Elsom, partly based on investigations by journalist Nicholas Tomalin, published in 1978; Peter Lewis' *The National – A Dream Made Concrete*; and Simon Callow's *The National – The Theatre and its Work*, which contains insights that can only come from the pen of a fine writer and a brilliant actor. I'm deeply grateful, too, for the National's own story by Lynn Haill and Stephen Wood on the NT's website.

I'm grateful indeed for permission to quote extensively from *Peter Hall's Diaries: The Story of a Dramatic Battle*, thanks to the blessing of Lady Nicki Hall and James Hogan, head of Oberon Books. Also to Richard Eyre for extracts from his *National Service: Diary of a Decade at the National Theatre*, and Michael Blakemore for extracts from *Stage Blood*. I am honoured that director Richard Eyre contributed the foreword.

I must acknowledge my debt to four people who have written definitively about the National Theatre and Denys Lasdun. First, Daniel Rosenthal, whose *The National Theatre Story* is a brilliant, encyclopaedic study. Then, architectural historian Barnabas Calder, whose unpublished thesis on Denys Lasdun and the National's design gestation is a fascinating document, as is his book *Raw Concrete: The Beauty of Brutalism*. Next, Patrick Dillon, who led the NT Future architectural team for architects Haworth Tompkins, and who has created a fine book, *Concrete Reality,* about the building he had come to so admire. Finally, admiration and gratitude to Nicholas Hytner, whose book, *Balancing Acts,* tells the behind-the-scenes story of his time of leadership at the National and proves he is a masterly writer as well as one of the finest theatre producers/directors of our time.

Through my subsequent experience with many, many architects I came to realise that Denys Lasdun was unique. I sensed, from the beginning, an earnestness and an integrity, which I sought to understand. I was also, at his request, his lighting designer in the public areas of the building, which gave me some insight into his thought processes in this 'Fourth Theatre.' I'm grateful to William J.R Curtis' magnificent work *Denys Lasdun – Architecture, City, Landscape,* which reveals Lasdun's deepest motivations.

My thanks to Lisa Burger, until May 2022 joint chief executive director of the National, who has offered me her constant support. Thanks to her, the National has opened its doors, allowing me to wander at will in a way I've not known since those fraught days of final construction. She was supported by a great team that includes Donna Parker, NT board secretary. Lisa's successor, Kate Varah, continued that support in the book's final stages.

There are over a thousand people whose dedication brings the National Theatre to life. It is impossible for me to list all those to whom I am indebted, but I must extend thanks to a few very special people: Alan Bain, digital drawing and design; Rob Barnard, head of technical resources (semi-retired); Philip Carter, IT/photographer; Matt Drury, lighting; Paul Jozefowski, NT Future; Paul Handley, production and technical director; John Langley, external relations; Erin Lee, head of archive; Jeanette Nelson, head of voice; Sarah Corke, acting head of publishing; Harry Scoble, ex-head of publishing; and Jonathan Suffolk, ex-technical director. Last, but not least and, in actuality when visiting the building, first: the wondrous gatekeeper of the world's greatest theatre, Linda Tolhurst, heroine of the stage door.

The resourcefulness of my research assistant, Acatia Finbow, amazes me, while at Theatre Projects, my friend and colleague John Runia is a constant source of guidance.

And finally, a tribute to my partners in this venture. Firstly, my son Fred Pilbrow. A brilliantly successful architect, he and his colleagues at Pilbrow & Partners, especially graphic designer Flora Cox, have brought architectural wisdom and brilliant design skills to this book. Secondly, Rob Halliday, whose love of the National and keen editorial eye have been an invaluable combination. To all, I must extend my heartfelt thanks.

RP

Epilogue: Richard Pilbrow 1933-2023

Richard passed away on 6th December, 2023, peacefully, at home, surrounded by family.

To those of us who'd been working with him on this book, this wasn't unexpected – he had been battling a pretty intense cancer since the middle of the year, and it had been clear for the previous few weeks that he wasn't winning that battle. But it was nonetheless a shock, since Richard had always been one of those presences that felt like it would be here forever. This didn't just feel like the end of a life, but the end of an entire era of theatre history given how much he had crammed into that life. Of the three leading characters in this story, Olivier left his mark on theatre history with his performances and through the creation of the National. Lasdun's memory lives on in his timeless buildings across London, elsewhere in the UK and Europe. But Richard's extends not just to the thousands of performance spaces he was involved with, but the inspiration he provided to so many others who make or work in theatres - worldwide.

There will always be that question, when an author passes away just before his book makes it out into the world, of proprietary: how much was this actually the book the author intended against how much had it been changed once they were no longer around to keep an eye on it. When Richard passed, the book was in that awkward publishing phase, between the moment an author decrees the words finished and when it becomes an actual finished book – the phase of polishing and proof-reading and pictures and making sure it all fits together as a whole. All of us involved with it – Rob, Fred, Flora, Acatia – had been working with him on this for a long time, and so were very clear of what he wanted to achieve and what we still had to do to deliver that. Richard saw pretty close to final proofs of the book you are reading now. He was happy with it, and every revision since has been accompanied by the question, what would Richard do?

For their part we must thank the invaluable fresh eyes brought to the final proof reads by Jules Lauve, Dawn Chiang, Robert Bell and Iain Mackintosh, all of whom have known Richard long enough to know both how he thinks and how he speaks. And we must also thank Dan, Nadia and Rebekah at the NT Archive, our wonderful indexer Christine Shuttleworth for the order she found in the words, and the team at Unicorn for all they taught us about the world of books. And of course Molly and Abigail, who were very sure to be sure we heard Richard's opinions right to the end!

Richard also lived to see the tremendous support for this book, both from the companies and individuals who have supported its creation, and to the many who supported it via the Kickstarter campaign. This, we think, really fascinated him: the ability to directly connect a project with those it interested. How different his theatre-producing days might have been had this been available then! On his behalf, we thank everyone who has been part of making this long-held dream of his into a reality.

We realise that the world is now suddenly split in to two groups: those many who knew Richard, through working with him or just meeting him somewhere along the way, and those who will now never have the chance to do so, never get to experience his remarkable fascination with the world and desire to always move things forward, make things better. The countless tributes which appeared on the internet after his passing are a great insight, particularly the thoughts shared by his daughter Daisy. Plus inevitably, because he was an unstoppable writer, he'd also already recorded his own history, candidly and with sometimes searing honesty and openness, in his previous book, *A Theatre Project*. While it was never planned as such, it makes a remarkable companion volume to this, a wider-lensed view of the same period in British theatre history.

Most importantly, his legacy lives on very particularly in the remarkable National Theatre.

History never rests, of course. A few days after Richard's passing, the world lost another link in the National's history with the passing of director Michael Blakemore. But there also came the announcement of the start of the next chapter in the National's future, with the appointment of Indhu Rubasingham as its seventh Director. Richard, we suspect, will be cross to have missed out on that – and would have been excited to see what this next chapter brings.

Rob & Fred, 19th December 2023

489

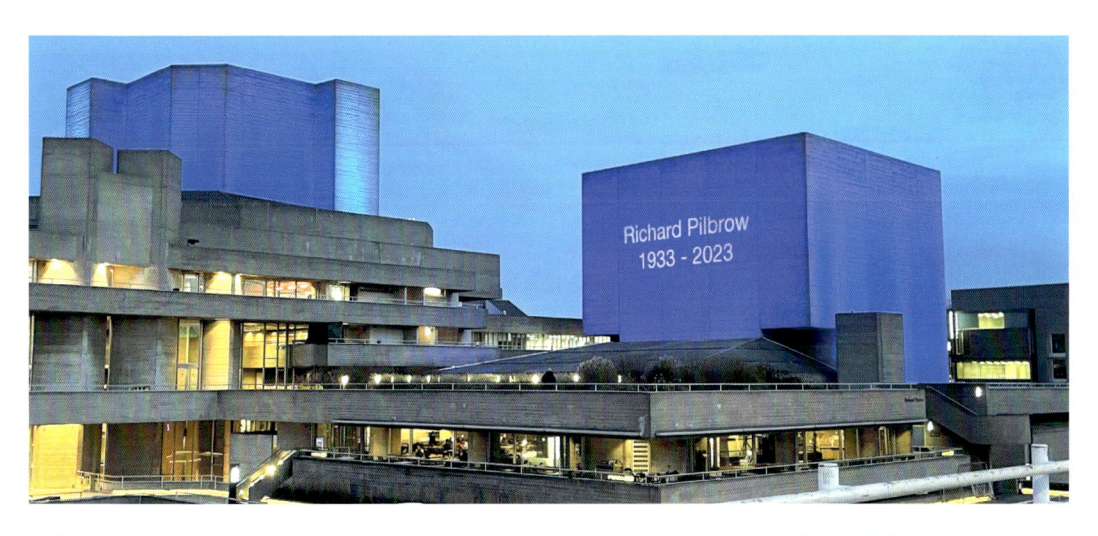

The National Theatre Building

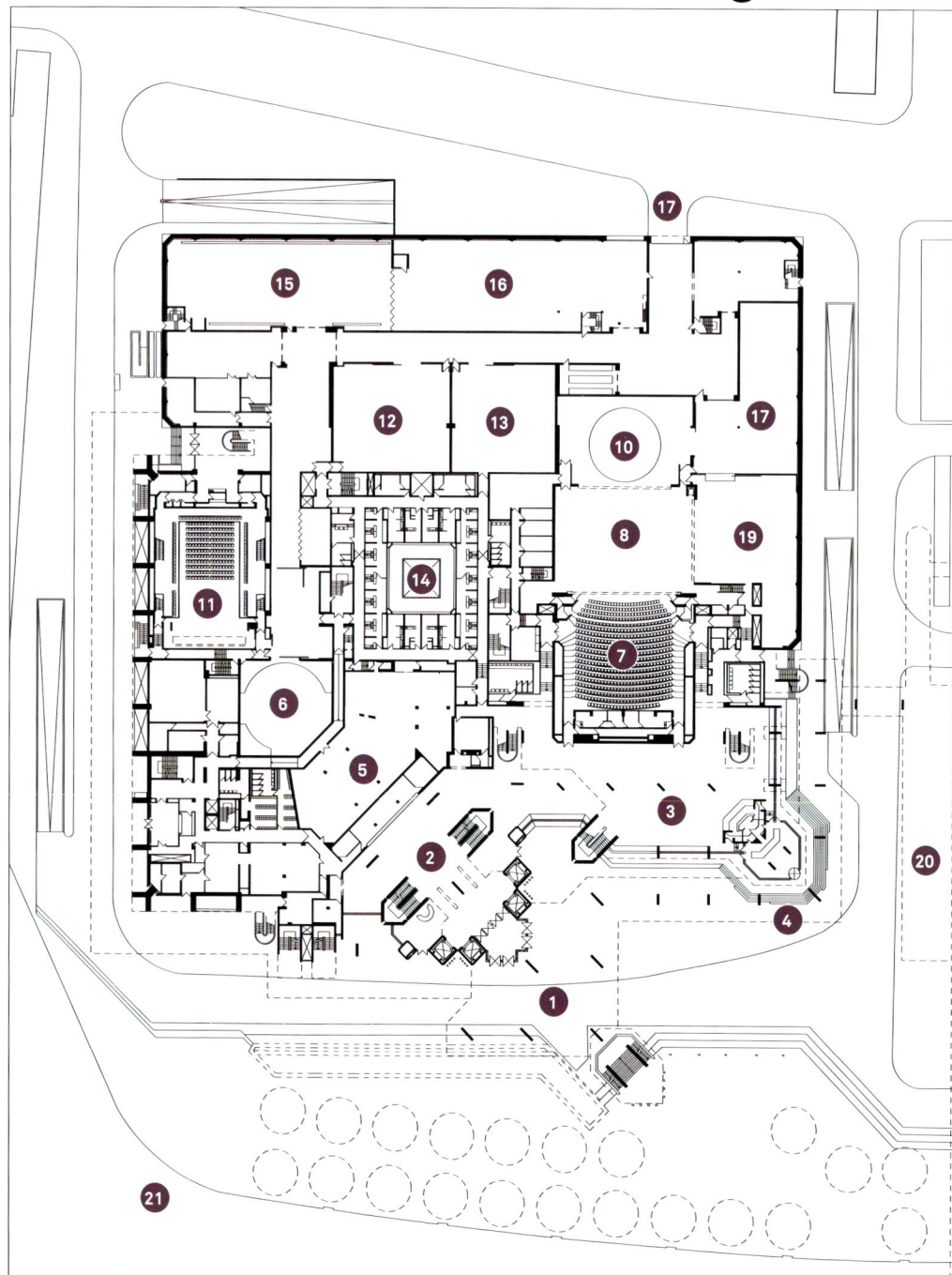

1. Porte-cochère, later part enclosed
2. Main entrance; Olivier foyer above
3. Lyttelton foyer
4. Original box office, later coffee bar
5. Olivier Theatre (beneath seating)
6. Drum revolve substage
7. Lyttelton Theatre
8. Lyttelton stage
9. Lyttelton side-stage
10. Lyttelton rear-stage with tracking revolve
11. Cottesloe, later Dorfman, Theatre
12. Rehearsal room
13. Rehearsal room
14. Dressing room light well
15. Paint frame and workshops
16. Workshops
17. Workshops
18. Dock door
19. Technical offices and stores
20. Waterloo Bridge
21. River Thames with 1976 embankment line

Note: In this section north is used to denote facing the River Thames for simplicity, though the National actually faces approximately north-north-west.

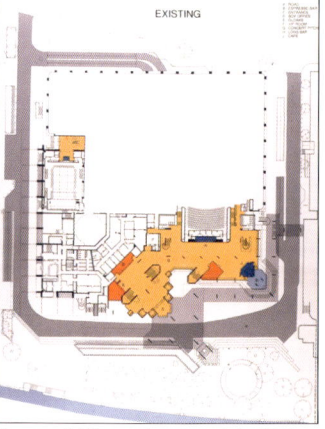

National Theatre building and environs, 1976, drawn by Haworth Tompkins prior to the NT Future project

Stanton Williams drawing of the NT in 1976: note the road around the building

A Sense of Theatre

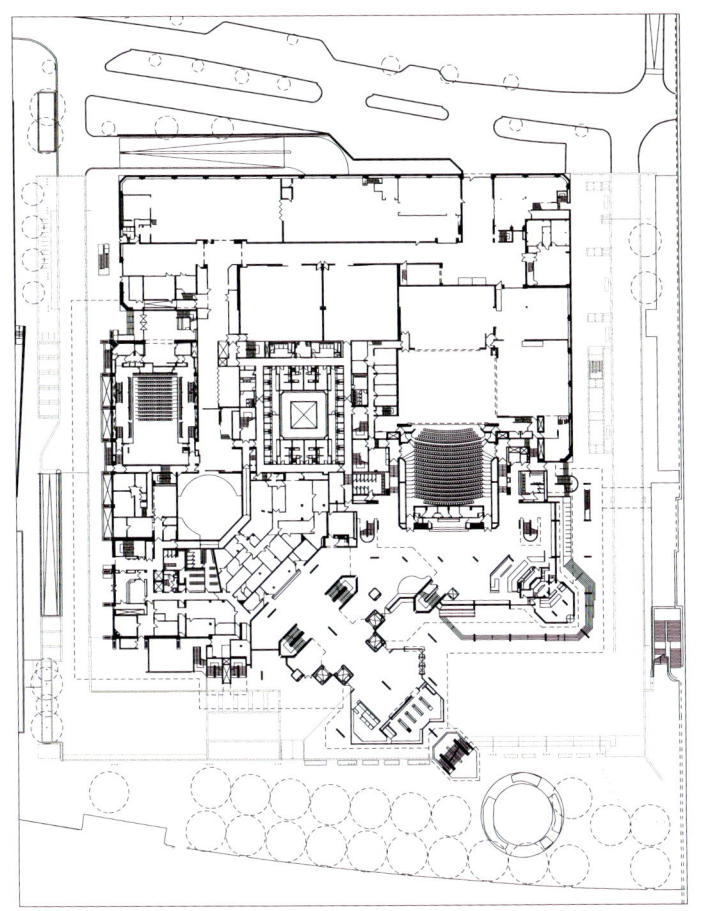

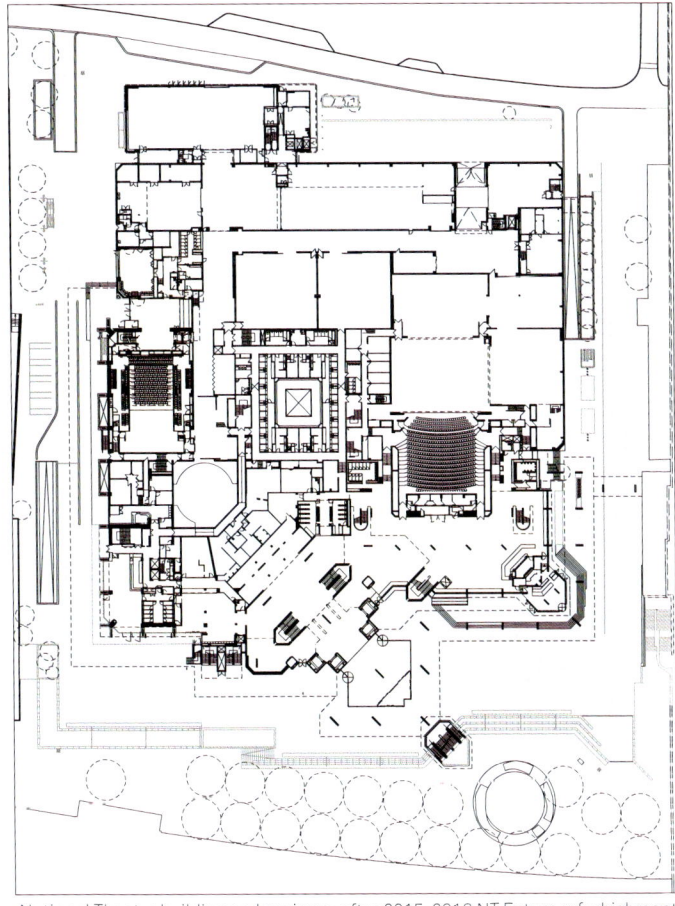

National Theatre building and environs, after 1997 refurbishment

National Theatre building and environs, after 2015-2016 NT Future refurbishment

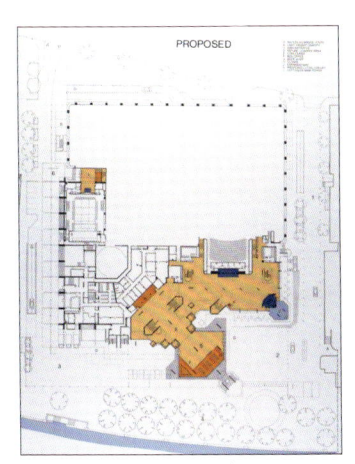

Stanton Williams 1997 scheme: road removed

Since 1976 both the National Theatre building and its surroundings have evolved. In 1976 the river cut back sharply in to the building's east side; that line is later pushed outwards to become part of the Jubilee Walkway as Lasdun creates a sibling building next to the National for IBM in 1978.

An early change not visible on these drawings is the installation of an illuminated, scrolling sign to promote the building which originally carried no signage to identify it.

The first major changes come in 1997, when architects Stanton Williams fill in the porte-cochère and remove the road that originally encircled the building, creating an outdoor space called Theatre Square. This scheme also sees the ground floor glazing in the Lyttelton foyer pushed outwards to increase internal space.

In the 2015-2016 NT Future scheme, architects Haworth Tompkins re-work the porte-cochère, reconfigure glazing in the centre of the building to mirror Lasdun's original eastern glazing line, and rework the east side of the building to create new public spaces and restaurants. A new workshop building is added to the rear of the National, with revisions to the area around the Cottesloe. And - forty years after opening - the building gains signs identifying it as the National Theatre!

The National Theatre Building

National Theatre, view from the front (looking across the River Thames), 2018 on, terraces of the IBM building (also designed by Denys Lasdun) to the left. Note The Deck, a self-contained structure used for events on the top terrace on the building's east side (left of the drawing), designed by Haworth Tompkins, prefabricated off-site and installed in 2018.

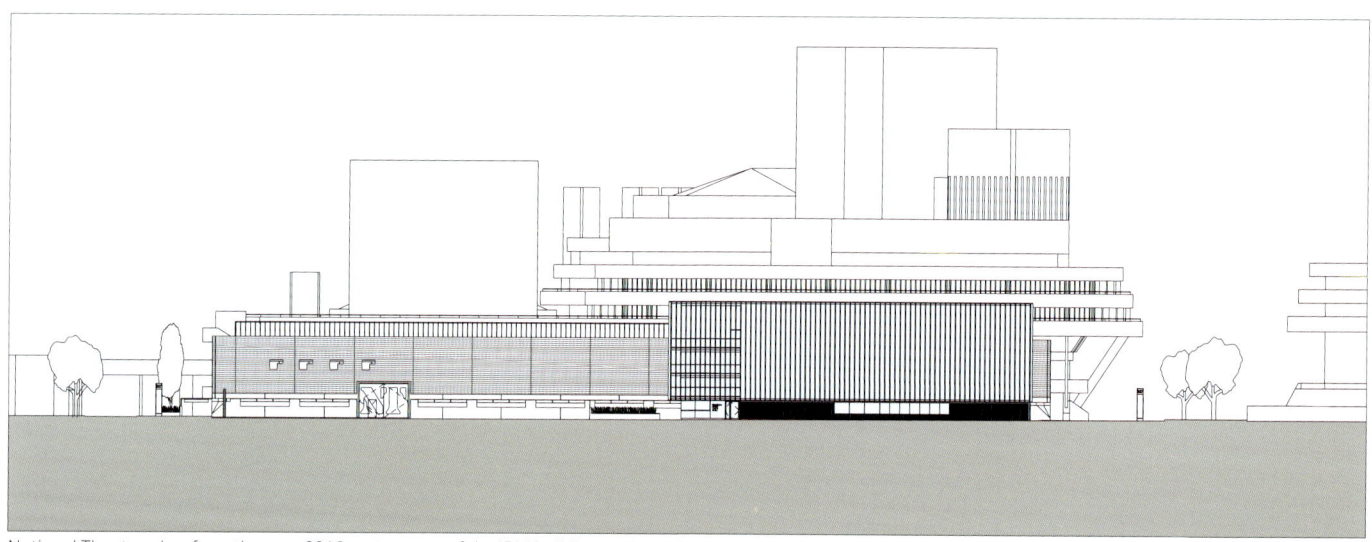

National Theatre, view from the rear, 2016 on, terraces of the IBM building to the right. The structure on the left is the Max Rayne Centre, designed by Haworth Tompkins and added as part of the 2015-2016 NT Future scheme to provide additional office and workshop space including a new paint frame that replaced the original; this also led to the removal of the distinctive tall triangular skylights for the original paint frame in the south-east corner of the workshop block.

National Theatre, view from the east (Tate Modern side), 2016 on.
Yellow shading indicates changes in the 2015-2016 NT Future scheme.

National Theatre, view from the west (Waterloo Bridge side), 2016 on;
this is the view seen in many photographs throughout the book.

Cottesloe / Dorfman Theatre

Lyttelton Theatre

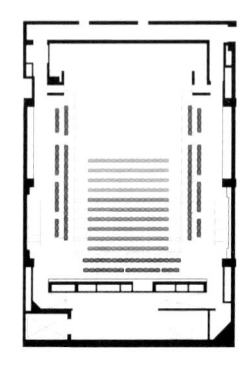

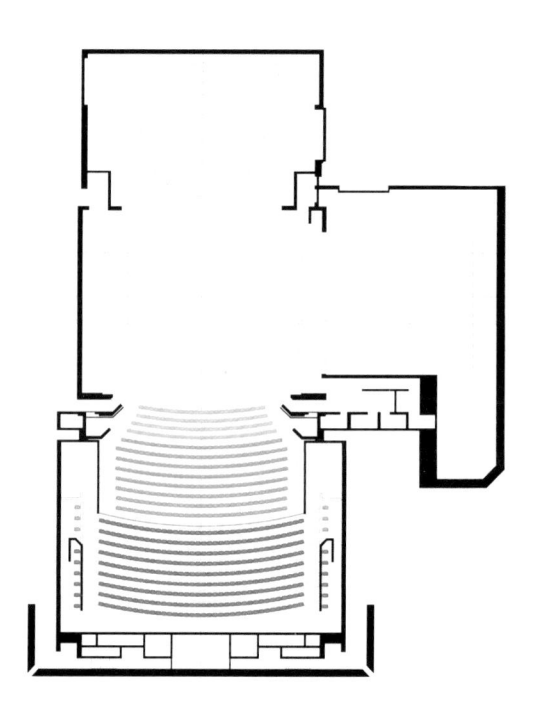

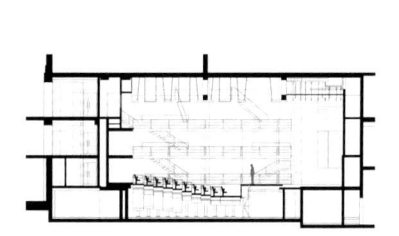

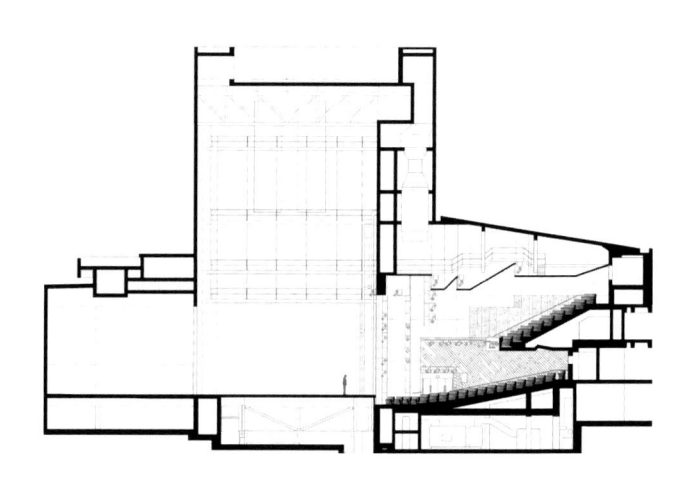

1 2   5   10   20 m

Olivier Theatre

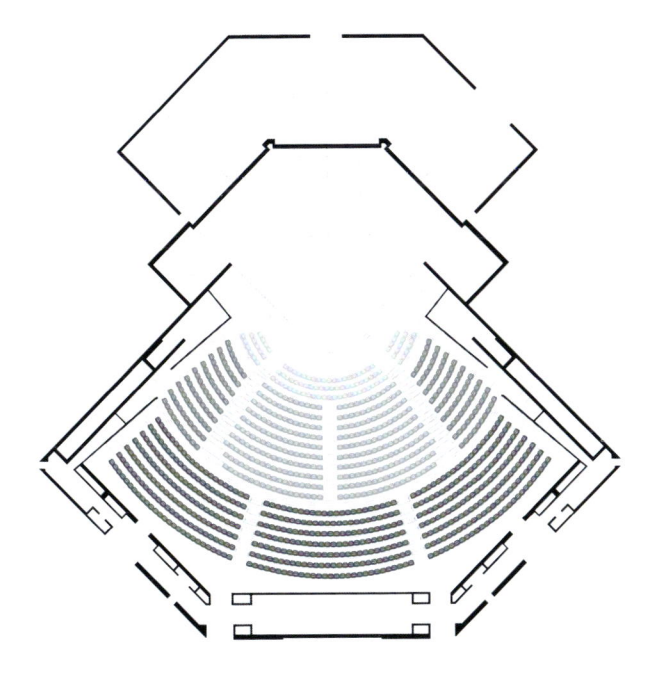

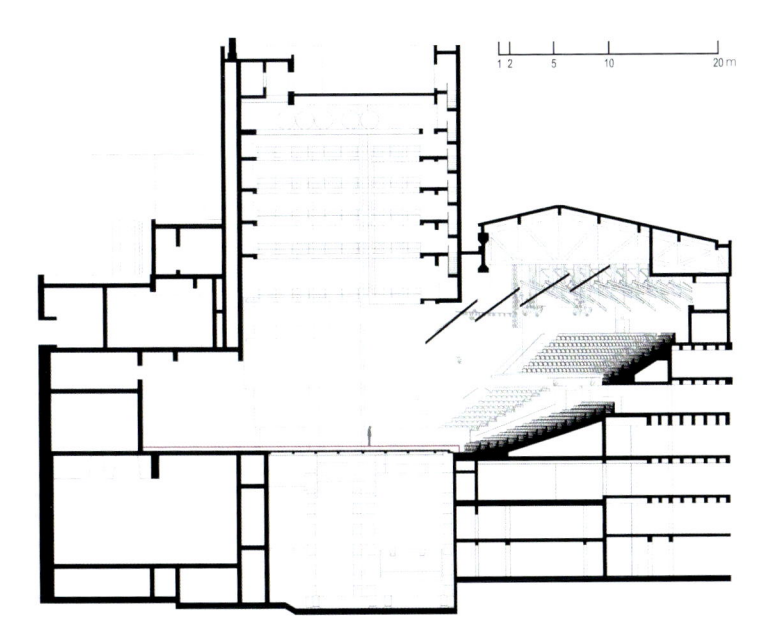

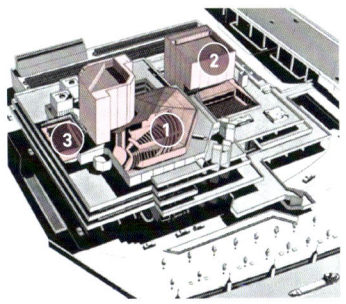

1: Olivier Theatre, 2: Lyttelton Theatre, 3: Cottesloe / Dorfman Theatre

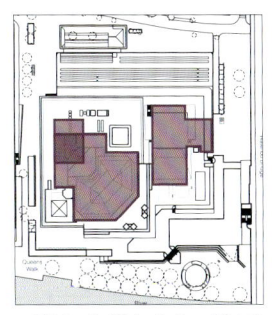

Olivier (left), Lyttelton (right), Cottesloe (tucked under Olivier) on site plan

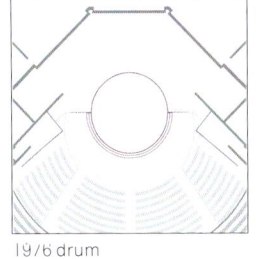

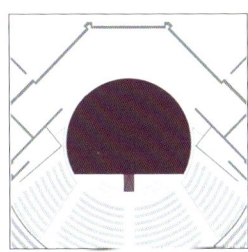

1976 drum

1976 straight – opening gala

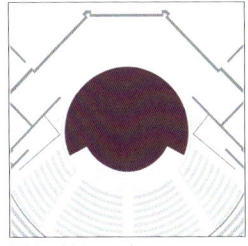

Mid-1980s and current

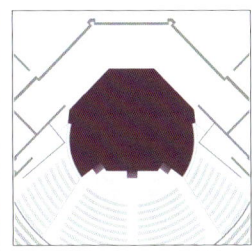

Mid-1980s show, straight front

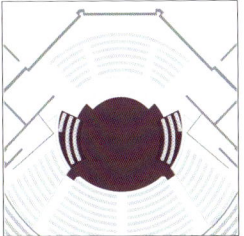

1997 In the round

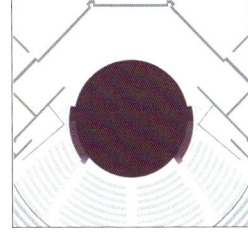

1993, 1995 then early 2000s

The main drawings show the theatres as they opened. The Olivier stage has evolved in terms of its height and front edge; the purple line on the section shows the 345mm higher stage level installed under Peter Hall and still in use today. See p.497.

The National Theatre Building

The Design Evolution of the Olivier Theatre

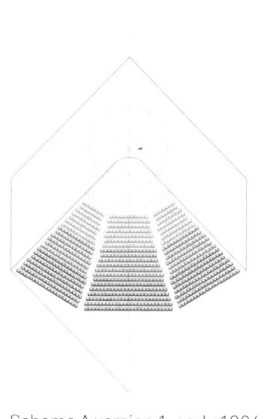

Scheme A version 1, early 1964

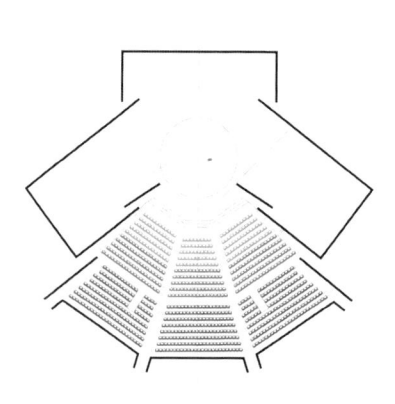

Scheme A version 2, early March 1964

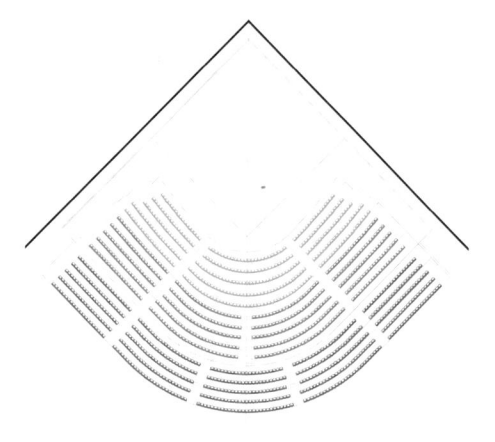

Scheme B, late March 1964, still being discussed as the National Theatre-Opera House model is shown to the public in 1965. This includes a balcony that surrounds the stage

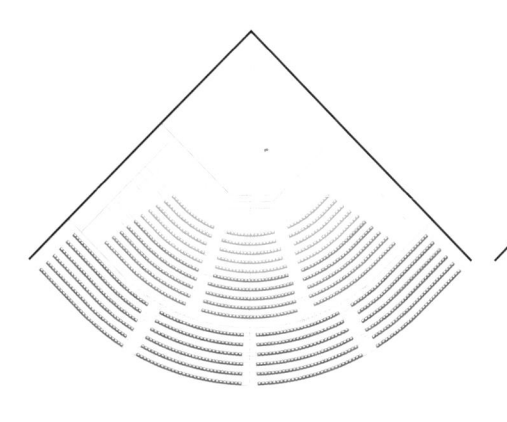

Scheme C, May 1966, after the cancellation of the Opera House

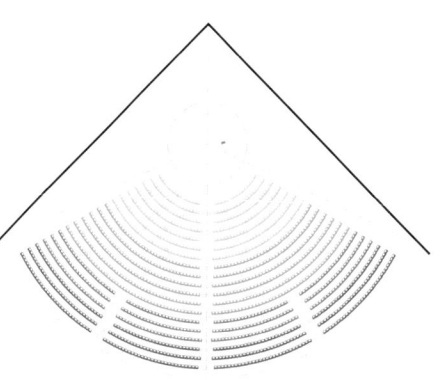

Scheme D, August 1966, single seating level

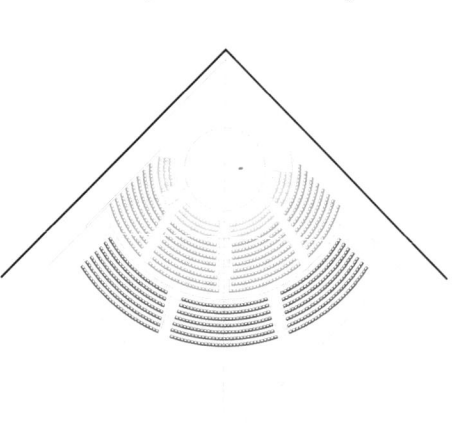

Scheme E, August 1966, stalls and circle seating with raised seating on either side of the stalls between those two levels. Earlier versions have more aisles in the circle. With further revisions, particularly to the sides, this becomes the Olivier Theatre

The design of the Upper Theatre - which became the Olivier Theatre - as it evolved through six versions (two variants of Scheme A, then Schemes B to E, the final design) between 1964 and 1966. Scheme E is then subtly altered, adding the raised side seating 'ashtrays' to create the Olivier as built (previous page). These new drawings are matched in scale as closely as possible based on seat size. The theatre's design is often said to be inspired by the Greek theatre at Epidaurus, but also by discussions about having the stage and the audience in a single room, and by Laurence Olivier's desire not to have audience members behind him as happened in Chichester. This aspiration becomes increasingly diluted over the years as the front edge of the stage is moved forwards.

A Sense of Theatre

The Ongoing Evolution of the Olivier Stage

Note: these are representative shows with suitable images available, not necessarily the first or only ones to use these stage configurations

The Olivier Theatre stage has ebbed and flowed over the years. At opening, the front of the drum revolve was notionally the front of the stage but as planned you could drop the revolve to give a flat floor then construct any shape forestage you liked, as happened for the Royal Gala Opening (p.257). Note there the space from the drum to the front row of the three rows of low-priced 'ripple' seats which have no arm rests, and that the stage sits below the side concrete jaws. In 1980 Jocelyn Herbert is building up and forward for *Galileo* - the stage now above the bottom of the jaws and right up to the front row.

By the mid-1980s an almost permanent forestage slightly lower but to about this line is almost standard, perhaps to give somewhere for the actors to go as the now-functional drum drops behind them. This 'Hall Floor,' 345mm higher than the original stage, becomes the standard stage level, covering the original upstage truck winching system. For some shows, straight or faceted fronts return. In 1993, Jocelyn Herbert returns and takes the stage up and out further still, half way up the jaws and over the ripple seating. Others follow. For Richard Eyre's 1997 in-the-round season this is the front line used. Under Trevor Nunn the stage stays high and over the ripple seats; the drum is out of use.

Nick Hytner pulls back to the mid-80s line and height, though with the sides extended further forward to the edge of the jaws, and the jaws masked; this becomes the norm. 2023 sees a surprise return to the very original line, the front of the drum, perhaps to better let the show then transfer into a proscenium arch theatre?

1980:
L: Fit up for *Galileo*, des: Jocelyn Herbert, line of drum visible, stage level below side jaws

R: *Galileo* set floats forward of and above the stage

1988/1990:
L: *The Shaughraun*, des: William Dudley, drum in use

R: *Racing Demon*, des: Bob Crowley, similar line but straight front edge

1993/1995:
L: *Square Rounds*, des: Jocelyn Herbert, higher and even further forward

R: *Women of Troy*, des: Iona McLeish, same front line, not quite as high

1997/2002:
L: In the round season, 1997; view towards auditorium

R: 2002: Trevor Nunn and John Napier come up and out further; drum out of use, temporary revolve installed

2011/2023:
L: *Emperor and Gallilean*, des: Paul Brown; Hytner era, back to mid-80s configuration, drum back in use

R: And back to the beginning: *The Witches*, des: Lizzie Clachan, fit-up, 2023

The National Theatre Building

Bibliography

Adams, Joseph Quincy: *Shakespearean Playhouses: A History of English Theatres from the Beginnings to the Restoration* by Project Gutenberg [eBook].

Bennett, Alan: *The Habit of Art,* Farrar, Straus and Giroux; Reprint edition. Billington, Michael: *State of the Nation.* Faber & Faber, London, 2007.

Blakemore, Michael: *Stage Blood: Five Tempestuous Years in the Early Life of the National Theatre.* Faber & Faber, London, 2013.

Bloom, Martin: *Accommodating the Lively Arts*, Smith and Krause, Lyme NH, 1997.

Bowsher, Julian: *Shakespeare's London Theatreland*, Museum of London Archeology, 2012.

Brook, Peter, *Threads of Time*, Bloomsbury Methuen Drama, 1998. [eBook]

Brown, John Russell, *The Oxford Illustrated History of the Theatre*, Oxford University Press, 1995.

Calder, Barnabas: *Committees and Concrete: The genesis and architecture of Denys Lasdun's National Theatre* [PhD Dissertation].

Calder, Barnabas: *Raw Concrete: the Beauty of Brutalism,* William Heinemann, 2016.

Callow, Simon, *The National: The Theatre and its Work*, Nick Hern Books & National Theatre, 1997.

Coleman, Terry: *Olivier*, Bloomsbury, London, 2005.

Coleman, Terry: *The Old Vic.* Faber & Faber, London, 2014. [eBook]

Cook, Judith: *The National Theatre,* George G. Harrap & Co, 1976.

Courtney, Cathy editor: *Jocelyn Herbert, A Theatre Workbook*, Arts Books International, London. 1993 [eBook]

Coveney, Michael: *London Theatres*, Forward by Mark Rylance. Frances Lincoln, London 2017.

Craig, Edward Gordon: *On the Art of the Theatre*.

Dillon, Patrick: *Concrete Reality*, National Theatre Publishing, 2015.

Ellis, Ruth: *The Shakespeare Memorial Theatre*, Winchester Publications, London,1948.

Elsom, John & Tomalin, Nicholas: *The History of the National Theatre*, Jonathan Cape, London, 1978.

Eyre, Richard, *National Service: Diary of a Decade at the National Theatre*, Bloomsbury, London, 2003.

Eyre, Richard. *What Do I Know*, Nick Hern Books, 2014 [eBook].

Fair, Alistair: *Modern Playhouses – An Architectural History of Britain's New Theatres, 1945-1985*, Oxford University Press, 2018.

Fair, Alistair, C. Alan Short: *Peter Barrett, Geometry and Atmosphere*, Ashgate Publishing, 2011.

Fay, Stephen: *Power Play: The Life & Times of Peter Hall*, Hodder & Stoughton, London, 1995.

Gaskill, William: *A Sense of Direction*, Limelight Editions, New York, 1990.

George, Colin: *Stirring up Sheffield*, Unpublished manuscript.

Glasstone, Victor: *Theatre Architecture in Britain*, RIBA Journal 50 (1968).

Goodwin, Tim: *Britain's Royal National Theatre, The First 25 Years*, National Theatre with Nick Hern Books, 1988.

Hall, Peter: *Peter Hall's Diaries: The Story of a Dramatic Battle*, Oberon Books, London, 2000; first published Hampshire Hamilton, 1983.

Hall, Peter: *Making an Exhibition of Myself*, Oberon Books, London, 2000; first published Sinclair-Stevenson, London, 1993.

Haill, Lyn, ed: *Olivier at Work*. Nick Hern Books/NT, London, 1989.

Haill, Lyn, ed and Wood, Stephen: *Stage by Stage*, National Theatre Publications, London, 1998.

Hare, David: *The Blue Touch Paper. A Memoir*, W.W.Norton & Co. [eBook]

Harwood, Ronald: *The Faber Book of Theatre*, Faber & Faber, London, 1993.

Holden, Anthony: *Laurence Olivier*, George Weidenfeld & Nicholson, London, 1988.

Hytner, Nicholas: *Balancing Acts – Behind the Scenes at the National Theatre*, Jonathan Cape, London, 2017.

Joseph, Stephen: *Actor and Audience*, in *A Brains Trust* ed. by Stephen Joseph, Manchester University Press, 1964.

Lasdun, Denys, ed: *Architecture in an Age of Scepticism*, Heinemann, London, 1984.

Lasdun, Denys: *A Language and a Theme, The Architecture of Denys Lasdun & Partners.* RIBA Publications, London, 1976.

Leacroft, Richard: *The Development of the English Playhouse*, Methuen, London, 1973.

Lewis, Peter: *The National, A Dream Made Concrete*, Methuen, London, 1990.

Littlewood, Joan: *Joan's Book*, Methuen, London, 2003-2016. [eBook]

Kennedy, Dennis: *Granville Barker and The Dream of Theatre,* Cambridge University Press, 1985.

Mackintosh, Iain: *Architecture, Actor and Audience*, Routledge, London, 1993.

Mackintosh, Iain: *Theatre Spaces 1920-2020*, Methuen, London, 2023.

Miller, John: *Ralph Richardson: The Authorised Biography*, Pan Books, London, 1996.

Mulryne, Ronnie, and Shewring, Margaret, eds: *The Cottesloe at the National: Infinite Riches in a Little Room*, Mulryne and Shewring, Stratford-upon-Avon, 1997.

Nightingale, Benedict: *Great Moments in the Theatre*, Oberon Books, London, 2012. [eBook]

Olivier, Laurence: *Confessions of an Actor*. Weidenfeld & Nicholson, London, 1982.

Olivier, Laurence: *On Acting*, Weidenfeld & Nicolson, London, 1986.

Olivier, Richard, and Plowright, Joan: *Olivier at Work: The National Years*, Nick Hern Books & National Theatre, London, 1989.

Olivier, Tarquin: *My Father Laurence Olivier*, Headline Book Publishing, London, 1992.

Pilbrow, Richard: *A Theatre Project*, Plasa Media, New York, 2011.

Purdom, C. B.: *Harley Granville Barker, Man of the Theatre, Dramatist, and Scholar*, Greenwood Press, Westport CT, 1956.

Ratcliffe, Michael: *Plays in British Theatre Design: The Modern Age*, ed. John Goodwin, George Weidenfeld and Nicolson, London, 1989.

Rokison-Woodall, Abigail and Hytner, Nicholas: *Shakespeare in the Theatre*, Bloomsbury Press, London, 2017. [eBook]

Rosenthal, Daniel: *The National Theatre Story*, Oberon Books, London, 2013.

Rosenthal, Daniel, ed: *Dramatic Exchanges: The Lives and Letters of the National Theatre*, Profile Books, 2018.

Theatre Projects Ltd: *National Theatre Preliminary Report on Proposed Stage Equipment, Lighting and Sound*, 25th October 1967, unpublished report.

Trussler, Simon: *Cambridge Illustrated History: British Theatre*, Cambridge University Press, 1994.

Wardle, Irving: *The Theatres of George Devine*, Faber & Faber, London, 1978.

Whitworth, Geoffrey: *The Making of a National Theatre*, Faber & Faber, London, 1951.

Ziegler, Philip: *Olivier*, MacLehose Press, London, 2013. [eBook]

Credits & Archives

Photographs and Images

I am grateful to many people who, guided by my associate Acatia Finbow, went to considerable trouble to locate drawings and photographs and put me in touch with the photographers. I thank all these talented artists or permission to reproduce their work.

Particular thanks to Chris Arthur and Philip Carter, who captured the magic of the National from inside the National across different generations, to Philip Vile for his photographs of the building as it is today, to Catherine Ashmore for always being there to find the perfect picture to tell the story, and to Ian Grundy for his remarkable photgraphic record of seemingly every other theatre in the country!

Thanks also to James Lasdun for permission to use drawings and other material from his father's archive, held by RIBA.

While all reasonable efforts have been made to obtain clearances, not all of the original sources could be located. Any omissions and errors of attribution are unintentional and will, if notified in writing to the publisher, be corrected in future editions.

Archives

The Theatre Projects Consultants Collection – one hundred and two boxes of extraordinarily detailed papers and drawings documenting TPC's work on the National Theatre – is held by the National Theatre Archive in London. It can be searched using their online catalogue and viewed at the Archive, located in the NT Studio building next door to the Old Vic (this building originally constructed as the Old Vic Theatre Annex in 1957 to designs by architects Lyons Israel & Ellis, to provide workshop, wardrobe and storage space), on request. If you have any interest in the history of the National, the NT Archive is a wonderful day out.

Further information about many of the technical innovations created for the National can be found in the Backstage Heritage Collection archive at www.theatrecrafts.com, which includes a full set of *TABS* magazine which did much to document the new theatres built during the 1960s, '70s and '80s.

Your author's personal archive has been presented to the Theatre Collection at Bristol University, one of the world's largest collections of theatre history and live art.

Photo credits are also available online at www.asenseoftheatre.com. Images are identified left-right, top-bottom across the page.

Cover: The National Theatre, 2016 © Philip Vile, courtesy of Haworth Tompkins.

War Horse, National Theatre, 2008 © Brinkhoff/Mögenburg.

Inside cover: Actor Sir Laurence Olivier, director of the National Theatre, and architect Denys Lasdun view a model of the proposed theatre (designed by Lasdun) on show in London, 29 December 1967. Keystone/Hulton Archive via Getty Images.

Introduction Section:

p. viii Lucian Msamati as Salieri in *Amadeus*, Olivier Theatre, 2017. © Philip Carter.

p. ix Richard Eyre, from the subject's archive.

p. xii The cast of *Guys and Dolls*, Olivier Theatre, 1982. © Donald Cooper.

p. xiii Richard Pilbrow, from the author's archive.

p. xiv The Olivier Theatre under construction © J.E. Rackham Photography. Reproduced by kind permission of Carole Ellis, courtesy of the National Theatre.

p. xvii Richard Brett with a model of the Olivier Theatre drum revolve, from the author's archive.

p. xviii - xix Exterior of the National Theatre, 1976. Photograph by James Holmes, courtesy of the National Theatre.

p. xx Interior of the Olivier Theatre. Photograph © Paul Karalius on behalf of Push The Button.

p. xxi The Olivier Theatre in situ at the National Theatre, courtesy of Haworth Tompkins.

Contemporary drawing of the plan of the Olivier Theatre by Pilbrow & Partners.

Contemporary drawing of the cross section of the Olivier Theatre by Pilbrow & Partners.

p. xxii Interior of the Lyttelton Theatre. Photograph © Paul Karalius on behalf of Push The Button.

p. xxiii The Lyttelton in situ at the National Theatre, courtesy of Haworth Tompkins.

Contemporary drawing of the plan of the Lyttelton Theatre by Pilbrow & Partners.

Contemporary drawing of the cross section of the Lyttelton Theatre by Pilbrow & Partners.

p. xxiv Interior of the Cottesloe/Dorfman Theatre © Philip Vile.

p. xxv The Cottesloe/Dorfman in situ at the National Theatre, courtesy of Haworth Tompkins.

Contemporary drawing of the plan of the Cottesloe/Dorfman theatre by Pilbrow & Partners.

Interior of the Cottesloe Theatre, 1977. Photograph by James Holmes, courtesy of the National Theatre.

Drawings showing variations of stage and seating in the Cottesloe Theatre. Courtesy of Iain Mackintosh/ Theatre Projects.

p. xxvi View into the Lyttelton foyer at the National Theatre at the time the building opened. © Chris Arthur.

p. xxvii The foyer areas at the National Theatre in situ, courtesy of Haworth Tompkins.

Public space at the National Theatre, 2023 © Rob Halliday.

View of the National Theatre foyer, 1976. Courtesy of the National Theatre.

View of the National Theatre foyer, 1976. Courtesy of the National Theatre.

View into the National Theatre foyer around 1997. © Morley von Sternberg, courtesy of Stanton Williams.

p. xxviii Drum Road – backstage corridor at the National Theatre, 2023 © Rob Halliday.

The stage door at the National Theatre, 2023 © Rob Halliday.

The Max Rayne Centre, 2023 © Rob Halliday.

Corridor around the drum at the National Theatre, 2023 © Philip Carter.

Dock door at the National Theatre, 2023 © Rob Halliday.

p. xxix Rehearsal room at the National Theatre, 1976. Photograph by Doug McKenzie, courtesy of the National Theatre.

View into the National Theatre dressing rooms, courtesy of Haworth Tompkins.

Part One

p. 0 - 1 Cover of *Drama*, July 1924, issue 40, showing W.L. Somerville's design for an auditorium for the National Theatre. Produced by the British Drama League.

p. 2 The Old Vic Auditorium © Philip Vile, courtesy of the Old Vic.

p. 4 Harley Granville Barker by Frederick Henry Evans, 1890s © National Portrait Gallery, London.

Title page of William Archer and Harley Granville Barker's *A National Theatre: Scheme and Estimates*, published by Duckworth Press, 1907.

p. 7 William Somerville's submission to the competition for the National Theatre, 1924. Reproduced by kind permission of the Somerville family.

Bromide postcard of Lilian Baylis, by Vandyk, c.1920. © National Portrait Gallery, London.

William Somerville's submission to the competition for the National Theatre, 1924. Reproduced by kind permission of the Somerville family.

p. 9 Sir Edwin Lutyens's design for the National Theatre in the original South Kensington site. c.1937.

Bernard Shaw and National Theatre architect Sir Edwin Lutyens, 1939. Hutton/Picture Post/Hulton Archive via Getty Images.

Bernard Shaw and Geoffrey Whitworth laying the foundation sod, 1938. Photographer unknown.

p. 10 Proposals for the National Theatre, c.1943 by Sir Edwin Lutyens.

Edwin Lutyen's 1944 design for the National Theatre on a site between Hungerford Bridge and Waterloo Bridge.

p. 11 Ralph Richardson as Peer Gynt, Old Vic Theatre, 1944. Photograph by John Vickers © Bristol University/ArenaPAL.

Laurence Olivier as Richard III, 1955. © Moviestore Collection Ltd/Alamy Stock Photo.

p. 12 Brian O'Rorke's plans for an open stage at the National Theatre, SMNT-floor-plan 2. Courtesy of the National Theatre.

Edward Brian O'Rorke, 1940 © RIBA Collections.

Brian O'Rorke's plans for an open stage at the National Theatre (Detail), SMNT-floor-plan-2. Courtesy of the National Theatre.

National Theatre Sketch, Brian O'Rorke, 1946, SMNT/11/26/7. Courtesy of the National Theatre.

p. 14 The foundation stone of the National Theatre, 1951, from the author's archive.

p. 15 National Theatre director Peter Hall, standing outside the theatre's new home on the South Bank in London, 1976 © PA Images/Alamy Stock Photo.

Mock Funeral for the foundation stone of the National Theatre, given by Kenneth Tynan and Richard Findlater, 1955, photographer unknown. © Look and Learn/Peter Jackson Collection.

p. 17 Chichester Festival Theatre exterior, 1962. © Historic England Archive.

Chichester Festival Theatre auditorium, 1962. © Historic England Archive.

p. 18 Detail from *Performance at a Country Barn*. Aquatint by W.R. Pyne after John Wright, c.1780. © The History Emporium/Alamy Stock Photo.

p. 19 Detail from *Performance at a Country Barn*. Aquatint by W.R. Pyne after John Wright, c.1780. © The History Emporium/Alamy Stock Photo.

p. 20 Successful Design, Stratford Theatre Elevations, c.1876. Courtesy of the RSC.

Stratford Theatre auditorium plan, c.1879. Courtesy of the RSC.

p. 21 Shakespeare Memorial Theatre, 1932, photograph by Leo Herbert Felton © Architectural Press Archive/RIBA Collections.

Shakespeare Memorial Theatre, photographer unknown.

Elisabeth Scott, image originally published in *Architect's Journal*, January 1928 © RIBA Collections.

p. 22 Shakespeare Memorial Theatre, Stratford, 1974, from the author's archive.

The Swan Theatre, Stratford-upon-Avon, 2023: Photograph by Lucy Barriball © RSC.

p. 23 The Royal Shakespeare Theatre, 2010 © Peter Cook.

p. 25 Illustration from a medieval musical manuscript. Le Labo – Cambrai, manuscrit 126, f° 53 r. © SCP, le Labo – Cambrai.

p. 27 The Swan Theatre, by De Witt. Illustration by Arnoldus Buchelius in his manuscript Adversaria. Courtesy of Utrecht University Library, Ms 842 (7 E 3), fol. 132 r.

Portrait of Richard Burbage (1573-1619), oil on canvas, artist unknown © Dulwich Picture Gallery/Bridgeman Images.

p. 29 Interior of Shakespeare's Globe Theatre, South Bank, London, 2005. © Bob Masters/Alamy Stock Photo.

Reconstructed view of the Rose Theatre, Phase I, by C. Walter Hodges, 1990. © Estate of C. Walter Hodges/Museum of London. Reproduced by kind permission of the artist's family.

Reconstructed view of the Rose Theatre, Phase II, by C. Walter Hodges, 1990. © Estate of C. Walter Hodges/Museum of London. Reproduced by kind permission of the artists' family.

p. 30 Conjectural drawing of the second Globe Theatre, 1614 as drawn by Richard Leacroft (1914-1986). Figure 29 in his book *The Development of the English Playhouse* (Methuen Drama, 1988).

Cutaway model of Inigo Jones's 'Indoor Theatre', made in 1974 by John Ronayne. Courtesy of John Ronayne.

p. 31 Frontpiece to a book by Francis Kirkman, published 1662, republished 1672, reprinted 1809. Venue disputed, V&A catalogue indicates Red Bull Playhouse, London, others suggest possibly Salisbury Court London. © Victoria and Albert Museum, London.

Drawing of an unidentified playhouse, almost certainly the Theatre Royal on Drury Lane, London (1674) by Christopher Wren. Reproduced by kind permission of the Warden and Fellows of All Souls College, Oxford.

p. 32 The Theatre Royal Drury Lane, Sir Christopher Wren, 1674. Conjectural scale reconstruction based on the longitudinal section, as drawn by Richard Leacroft (1914-1986). Figure 63 in his book *The Development of the English Playhouse* (Methuen Drama, 1988).

p. 34 Riot at Covent Garden Theatre in consequence of the managers refusing to admit half-price in the Opera of Artaxerxes, 1763, maker unknown © The Trustees of the British Museum, London.

David Garrick, 1770, by Thomas Gainsborough © National Portrait Gallery, London.

p. 35 Reconstruction of the Theatre Royal Bristol, James Paty, 1764-6 as drawn by Richard Leacroft (1914-1986). Figure 76 in his book *The Development of the English Playhouse* (Methuen Drama, 1988).

p. 36 Scale reconstruction of The Theatre Royal, Drury Lane, designed by Robert Adam, 1775 as drawn by Richard Leacroft (1914-1986). Figure 83 in his book *The Development of the English Playhouse* (Methuen Drama, 1988).

Etching depicting a scene from *The School for Scandal*, 1777, maker unknown.

Inside view of the Theatre Royal Drury Lane from the stage; altered & decorated in the year 1775. Engraving from Robert and James Adams, Architects, 1776 © British Library/Granger.

p. 37 Scale reconstruction of The Theatre Royal, Drury Lane, Henry Holland, 1794 as drawn by Richard Leacroft (1914-1986). Figure 92 in his book *The Development of the English Playhouse* (Methuen Drama, 1988).

p. 38 Drury Lane Theatre from The Microcosm of London, R. Ackerman, 1808-1811, in the collection of the British Library.

p. 39 Edmund Kean as Sir Giles Overreach in *A New Way to Pay Old Debts*, George Clint. England, 1820 © Victoria and Albert Museum, London.

Bucks have at ye all, pub. by William Holland, 1811 (coloured etching) City of Westminster Archive Centre, London, UK/Bridgeman Images.

p. 41 The Palais Garnier, Opera of Paris, interiors and details © photogolfer/stock.adobe.com.

Bayreuth Festspielhaus, interior of auditorium © Lebrecht Museum & Arts/Alamy.

p. 42 *The Old Bedford*, Walter Sickert, 1895. Walker Art Gallery/National Museums Liverpool © National Museums Liverpool/Bridgeman Images.

In the flies at the Drury Lane Theatre, in the *Illustrated Sporting and Dramatic Times*, 26 January 1884.

p. 43 Henry Irving photograph by Herbert Rose Barraud. Public domain.

Ellen Terry as Lady Macbeth, John Singer Sargeant, 1889 © Tate, London.

Self-portrait of Edward Gordon Craig, 1923. Reproduced by kind permission of the copyright holders, Edward Gordon Craig estate.

Image made by Edward Gordon Craig, for the publication *Scenes*, 1907. Reproduced by kind permission of the copyright holders, Edward Gordon Craig estate.

p. 44 Set design for *Orpheus and Eurydice* Act II at Hellerau Festspielhaus, 1912. Courtesy of Bibliothèque de Genève.

The Kunstler Theatre, Munich. Stage with setting by Julius Diez for Reinhardt's *Twelfth Night*, 1909 as drawn by Richard Leacroft (1914-1986). Figure 208 in his book *Theatre and Playhouse: An Illustrated Survey of Theatre Building from Ancient Greece to Present Day Playhouse* (Methuen Drama, 1988).

p. 45 Cambridge Festival Theatre, c.1928. Photograph by Scott and Wilkinson for *Stage Lighting* by Harold Ridge (1920).

Photograph of the model for Total Theatre Project for Erwin Piscator, Berlin, photographer unknown, view from the front into the auditorium, 1927. Bauhaus-Archiv, Berlin. © Groupius: DACS.

The Pictures postcard, printed by The Carlton Publishing Co.

p. 46 The Stephen Joseph Theatre, Scarborough. © James Drawneek/Stephen Joseph Theatre.

The Crucible Theatre, Sheffield: the auditorium, 1971. Photograph by John Donat © John Donat/RIBA Collection.

p. 47 A view of the redecorated Birmingham Repertory Theatre, 1953 © Trinity Mirror/Mirrorpix/Alamy.

The New Birmingham Repertory Theatre © Richard Glover.

Thorndike Theatre, Leatherhead, Surrey, the auditorium. Architect Roderick Ham. Photograph by Fox-Waterman Photography Ltd © RIBA Collections.

Billingham Forum Leisure Centre, Billingham, County Durham: the auditorium of the Forum Theatre. Architect Alan Ward of Elder Lester and Partners. Photograph by Dennis Wompra Studios © RIBA Collections.

p. 48 'Engineered' Theatre, photographer unknown.

Cologne Opera House and Theatre, opera auditorium. Photograph by Elke Wetzig, reproduced under Creative Commons licence CC-BY-SA-3.0. https://commons.wikimedia.org/wiki/File:Oper_K%C3%B6ln_Zuschauerraum_2010_7610.jpg

Mermaid Theatre, Puddle Dock, City of London: the auditorium. Photograph by Colin Westwood © Colin Westwood/RIBA Collections.

p. 49 Images of Sir Laurence Olivier, backstage at the National Theatre from the author's archive.

p. 50 Exterior of the Old Vic, 1963 © Chris Arthur.

p. 51 Sir Laurence Olivier leaning out of the window of the temporary headquarters of the National Theatre, 7 August 1963 © Keystone Press/Alamy.

p. 52 Old Vic Theatre, across the auditorium © Chris Arthur.

Old Vic Theatre auditorium, from the stage © Chris Arthur.

Old Vic auditorium ceiling © Chris Arthur.

Back to Methuselah from the lighting desk, Old Vic, 1968 © Chris Arthur.

p. 53 Exterior of the Aquinas Street rehearsal rooms © Chris Arthur.

Rehearsal Room at Aquinas Street. Photograph by John Haynes, courtesy of Bridgeman Art.

Old Vic fly floor © Chris Arthur.

p. 54 Russian programme for the National Theatre touring production of *Othello*, 1965, from the author's archive.

p. 55 *Hamlet*, Old Vic, 1937, photograph by Angus McBean. © Harvard Theatre Collection, Houghton Library, Harvard University.

Peter O'Toole as Hamlet and Max Adrian as Polonius in *Hamlet*, cartoon by Bill Hewison © Punch Cartoon Library/TopFoto.

Uncle Vanya, Old Vic, 1963, photograph by Angus McBean © Harvard Theatre Collection, Houghton Library, Harvard University. RNT/PR/3/2. Courtesy of the National Theatre.

Michael Redgrave as Vanya and Laurence Olivier as Astrov in *Uncle Vanya*, Old Vic, 1963, photograph by Angus McBean © Harvard Theatre Collection, Houghton Library, Harvard University. RNT/PR/3/2. Courtesy of the National Theatre.

p. 56 Robert Stephens and Laurence Olivier in *The Recruiting Officer* by George Farquhar, 1963 © Lewis Morley/Science Museum Group. Image from the collection of the Yale Centre for British Art.

Royal Hunt of the Sun, Old Vic, 1964, photograph by Angus McBean © Harvard Theatre Collection, Houghton Library, Harvard University.

Royal Hunt of the Sun, Old Vic, 1964, photograph by Angus McBean © Harvard Theatre Collection, Houghton Library, Harvard University.

p. 57 John Stride as Valentine, Laurence Olivier as Tattle, Joyce Redman as Mrs Frail and Robert Land as Scandal in *Love for Love*, Old Vic, 1965. © Zoë Dominic. RNT/PR/3/15. Courtesy of the National Theatre.

Ensemble of *Love for Love*, Old Vic, 1965, from the author's archive.

John Stride as Rosencrantz, Edward Petherbridge as Guildenstern and Graham Crowden as the Player in *Rosencrantz and Guildenstern are Dead*, Old Vic, 1967.

Photograph by Anthony Crickmay. RNT/PR/3/24. Courtesy of the National Theatre.

Two images of the staging of *Rosencrantz and Guildenstern are Dead*, Old Vic, 1967, from the author's archive.

p. 58 Sir Laurence Olivier © Zoë Dominic.

p. 59 Old Vic stage from the stage left wing © Chris Arthur.

p. 60 Rupert Rhymes © Chris Arthur.

Tom Gillon, property master for the National Theatre at the Old Vic © Chris Arthur.

Pat Leighton working in the box office of the National Theatre at the Old Vic © Chris Arthur.

Michael Gambon © Chris Arthur.

Ronald Cox and Leonard Tucker working on something unknown for the National Theatre at the Old Vic © Chris Arthur.

p. 61 Lynn Holm and Jennifer Careth applying wigs backstage at the National Theatre at the Old Vic © Chris Arthur.

Fred Taylor, Master Carpenter for the National Theatre at the Old Vic © Chris Arthur.

Diana Boddington, Stage Manager for the National Theatre at the Old Vic © Chris Arthur.

Roger Ramsdell, Painter for the National Theatre at the Old Vic © Chris Arthur.

Harry Henderson, Housekeeper for the National Theatre at the Old Vic © Chris Arthur.

Ernie Davis working at the stage door of the National Theatre at the Old Vic © Chris Arthur.

p. 63 Making up backstage at the National Theatre © Chris Arthur.

Geraldine McEwan, Robert Long, Jacques Charon and Laurence Olivier © Chris Arthur.

p. 64 Michael Bogdanov rehearsing in the Young Vic, 1978 © Donald Cooper.

Part Two

p. 66 - 67 Front: Malcom Minjoodt, Philip Wood, mid: Peter Softley, Theo de Rouw, rear: Denys Lasdun and 'The Scrapheap' of discarded models for the National Theatre, models made by Robert Kirkman and Philip Wood. Photograph by Behr Photography © RIBA Collections.

p. 68 The Festival of Britain South Bank Site and environs, Lambeth, 1951. Source: Historic England Archive, EAW035662.

p. 69 Drawing of the County of London Plan, 1943.

p. 71 Copy of a National Theatre letter to Denys Lasdun from Yolande Bird, assistant to Kenneth Rae, 18 March 18 1964, from the author's archive.

p. 72 Sir Laurence Olivier © Zoë Dominic.

Norman Marshall by Howard Coster, 1933 © National Portrait Gallery, London.

Peter Hall in 1962. Photograph by Gordon Goode © Folger Shakespeare Library. Negative No. 7 of Job 1384, taken 5/14/1962.

p. 73 Peter Brook, photograph by Angus McBean, 1947 © Harvard Theatre Collection, Houghton Library, Harvard University.

George Devine, c.1962 © Sandra Lousada/Mary Evans Picture Library.

Michel Saint-Denis rehearsing at the Old Vic School, 1961 © Sandra Lousada/Mary Evans Picture Library.

John Dexter © Roger Mayne Archive/Mary Evans Picture Library.

p. 74 William Gaskill, by Roger Mayne, 1960 © Roger Mayne/National Portrait Gallery, London.

Michael Elliott, from the author's archive.

Michael Benthall, courtesy of SWNS.

Roger Furse, photographer unknown.

Photo Credits 501

p. 75 Sean Kenny, 1963 © Lewis Morley/Science Museum Group.

Tanya Moiseiwitsch photograph by Frances Goodman, 1947. © National Portrait Gallery, London.

Richard Pilbrow, from the author's archive.

Jocelyn Herbert, 1962 © Sandra Lousada/Mary Evans Picture Library.

p. 76 Kenneth Peacock Tynan photograph by Ida Kar, late 1950s © National Portrait Gallery, London.

Stephen Arlen, 1966. *Evening Standard*/Hulton Archive via Getty Images.

The Fourth Lord Cottesloe, reproduced by kind permission of Hon. Elizabeth Duncan Smith.

Oliver Lyttelton, 1st Viscount Chandos, by Elliott & Fry, 1956 © National Portrait Gallery, London.

p. 77 Denys Lasdun, 1985 © Tom Evans.

Peter Softley, captured on film by David Collison, from the author's archive.

Harry Pugh, captured on film by David Collison, from the author's archive.

Richard Pilbrow photographed in 1973. Evening Standard/Hulton Archive via Getty Images.

Richard Brett, from the author's archive.

David Collison, from the author's archive.

Iain Mackintosh, from the subject's archive.

Bob Anderson, courtesy of Theatre Projects.

John Pilcher, from the author's archive.

p. 79 Interior of the Old Vic Theatre, London, 1962 © Chris Arthur.

p. 80 Interior of the Chichester Festival Theatre, 1962 © Historic England Archive.

p. 81 Plans for the Chichester Festival Theatre, 1963. West Sussex Record Office, CFT 1/1/1/1/2.

p. 82 La salle Jean Vilar du Théâtre National de Chaillot, 1963. Photographer unknown.

La salle Jean Vilar du Théâtre National de Chaillot, 2009. Photograph by Patrick Berger, reproduced under Creative Commons licence CC-BY-SA-3.0. https://commons.wikimedia.org/wiki/File:Chaillot_-_Salle_Jean_Vilar.jpg

p. 83 Stage and Auditorium of the new permanent theatre of the Stratford Festival Theatre, 1957. Photograph by Herb Nott & Co Ltd. Courtesy of the Stratford Festival Archives.

Interior of the Vivian Beaumont Theatre, New York. Image by Glenda Altarejos, reproduced under licence CC BY-SA 4.0. https://en.wikipedia.org/wiki/File:Vivian_Beaumont_theater_interior.jpg

p. 85 Two images of the Interior of Nottingham Playhouse, 2018 (top), 2010 (bottom) © Ian Grundy.

p. 91 The Old Vic stage from the fly floor, 1963 © Chris Arthur.

Prompt corner at the Old Vic Theatre © Chris Arthur.

Prompt desk at the Old Vic Theatre © Chris Arthur.

p. 93 Musiktheater im Revier, Gelsenkirchen, Germany © Michael Rasche.

Interior of the Chichester Festival Theatre, 1962 © Historic England Archive.

p. 94 Map of South Bank c. 1960, reproduced with the permission of the National Library of Scotland.

p. 95 Plan for a production of *Hamlet* at the Old Vic, 1963, by Sean Kenny. Reproduced by kind permission of Mac Kenny.

p. 100 Photograph of Denys Lasdun in front of flats he designed in the East End of London, 1952 © Nigel Henderson Estate/Tate.

p. 103 The table plan for the Arts Council architect interviews for the National Theatre, October 1963, courtesy of the National Theatre.

p. 104 Denys Ladsun, c.1968. David Farrell via Getty Images.

p. 105 Lasdun's first sketch of 'The Room'. Reproduced by kind permission of James Lasdun.

p. 110 The Interior of the Stratford Festival Theatre, Ontario, Canada, 1982. Photograph by Jane Edmonds. Courtesy of the Stratford Festival Archives.

Interior of the Theater am Schiffbauerdamm, Berlin, Germany © Moritz Haase.

p. 112 Denys Lasdun's plans of the Vivian Beaumont Theater, New York © Lasdun Archive/RIBA Collection.

Denys Lasdun's comparative section drawings of Chichester, the Guthrie Minneapolis, the Beaumont New York, Gelsenkirchen and the Old Vic © Lasdun Archive/RIBA Collections.

p. 113 Denys Lasdun's plans of the Chichester Festival Theatre © Lasdun Archive/RIBA Collections.

Denys Lasdun's sketches of the Guthrie Theatre, Minneapolis © Lasdun Archive/RIBA Collections.

p. 114 Denys Lasdun's Scheme A for the Upper (later Olivier) Theatre at the National Theatre © Lasdun Archive/RIBA Collections.

p. 115 George Devine, 1958, photograph by Ida Kar © National Portrait Gallery, London.

p. 118 Denys Lasdun's Scheme Av2 for the Upper (later Olivier) Theatre at the National Theatre © Lasdun Archive/RIBA Collections.

p. 120 Main hall of the Berliner Philharmonie © posztos/Shutterstock.com.

p. 121 See p. 114.

p. 123 See p. 118.

p. 124 See p. 114.

See p. 118.

p. 126 Peter Brook, photograph by Douglas H. Jeffery. UK, 20th Century © Douglas H. Jeffery/Victoria and Albert Museum, London.

Early scheme model of the Olivier Theatre, c.1960.

Photograph by Behr Photography. Model by Robert Kirkman. © Lasdun Archive/RIBA Collections.

John Bury, 1961 © Sandra Lousada/Mary Evans Picture Library.

Peter Hall: Photograph by Reg Wilson © RSC.

Lasdun's first sketch of 'The Room. Reproduced by kind permission of James Lasdun.

p. 127 Section of Denys Lasdun's Scheme B plan for the Upper (later Olivier) Theatre at the National Theatre © Lasdun Archive/RIBA Collection.

Denys Lasdun's Scheme B plan for the Upper (later Olivier) Theatre at the National Theatre © Lasdun Archive/RIBA Collections.

p. 129 Colour version of Denys Lasdun's Scheme B plan for the Upper (later Olivier) Theatre at the National Theatre © Lasdun Archive/RIBA Collections.

p. 130 See p. 127 lower.

p. 132 Denys Lasdun's site study sketch for the National Theatre © Lasdun Archive/RIBA Collections.

Denys Lasdun's site study sketch for the National Theatre © Lasdun Archive/RIBA Collections.

p. 133 Denys Lasdun's site study sketch for the National Theatre © Lasdun Archive/RIBA Collections.

See p. 127 upper.

p. 135 See p. 127 lower.

p. 136 See p. 126 2nd image.

p. 138 Denys Lasdun site sketch for the National Theatre © Lasdun Archive/RIBA Collections.

Denys Lasdun initial sections for the National Theatre © Lasdun Archive/RIBA Collections.

p. 139, **p. 141** See p. 127 lower.

p. 141 See p. 127 upper.

p. 142 Article on the evolution of the National Theatre designs, *The Sunday Times*, 21 February 1965. Courtesy of *The Sunday Times*.

p. 144 Denys Lasdun site model for the National Theatre showing the Theatre and Opera House, 1965. Model by Robert Kirkman / Philip Wood © Lasdun Archive/RIBA Collections.

p. 146 Discarded models or 'scrapheap' of the Royal National Theatre, South Bank, London in Lasdun's model studio, photograph by Behr Photography © RIBA Collections.

p. 147 Key to the 'scrapheap' image © RIBA Collections.

p. 148 Poster for the National Theatre's 1965 visit to Moscow, courtesy of the National Theatre Archive.

p. 151 See p. 129.

p. 153 See p. 129

See p. 127 upper.

p. 156 Denys Lasdun Scheme C model section for the Upper (later Olivier) Theatre at the National Theatre © Lasdun Archive/RIBA Collections.

p. 157 Denys Lasdun Scheme C for the Upper (later Olivier) Theatre at the National Theatre © Lasdun Archive/RIBA Collections.

p. 158 See p. 129.

p. 160 See p. 157.

p. 162 Jocelyn Herbert © Sandra Lousada/Mary Evans Picture Library.

p. 163 Denys Lasdun's plan of the Lower / proscenium theatre stalls, National Theatre © Lasdun Archive/RIBA Collections.

p. 164 Denys Lasdun's drawing of the Lower/proscenium theatre with parallel walls, National Theatre © Lasdun Archive/RIBA Collections.

Denys Lasdun's drawing of the Lower/proscenium theatre with fan layout, National Theatre © Lasdun Archive/RIBA Collections.

See p. 164.

Denys Lasdun's drawing of the Lower/proscenium theatre circle, National Theatre © Lasdun Archive/RIBA Collections.

Denys Lasdun's section drawing of the Lower/proscenium theatre, National Theatre, London © Lasdun Archive/RIBA Collections.

p. 165 See p. 129.

p. 167 See p. 127 upper.

p. 172 See p. 157.

Denys Lasdun's Scheme D plan for the Upper (later Olivier) Theatre at the National Theatre, London © Lasdun Archive/RIBA Collections.

p. 173 Theatre Projects plan of Upper (later Olivier) Theatre with the Old Vic stage overlaid, 1966, from the author's archive.

p. 174 Denys Lasdun's Scheme E for the Upper (later Olivier) Theatre, early drawing with hand sketches of possible fly tower shape overlaid © Lasdun Archive/RIBA Collections.

Denys Lasdun's Scheme E plan for the Upper (later Olivier) Theatre at the National Theatre © Lasdun Archive/RIBA Collections.

p. 177 Model of the South Bank, London showing the proposed National Theatre and Opera House next to County Hall, seen from above © RIBA Collections.

p. 179 See p. 174 lower.

p. 180 Sir Laurence Olivier, in his office at the National Theatre, February 4th, 1965. Cleland Rimmer/Evening Standard via Getty Images.

Peter Brook in Glasgow, 1988 © PA Images /Alamy.

p. 181 Upper Theatre public drawing, 1967. Source TABS vol 26 no. 1 March 1968. © Lasdun Archive/RIBA Collections.

Model of Upper (Olivier) Theatre at the National Theatre © Lasdun Archive/RIBA Collections.

Denys Lasdun's initial 1967 model of the Olivier Theatre, London, model by Robert Kirkman and Philip Wood, photograph by Behr Photographers © Lasdun Archive/RIBA Collections.

p. 183 Lighting bridge in the Olivier Theatre, from the author's archive.

Auditorium and ceiling of the Olivier Theatre © Richard Einzig/Arcaid Images.

Early sketch of the Olivier Theatre ceiling, from the author's archive.

p. 184 Model of Lower/proscenium (later Lyttelton) Theatre revealed by architect Denys Lasdun and Laurence Olivier. Courtesy of British Pathé still 188.

p. 191 Denys Lasdun, first publicly shown model of the National Theatre on its final site next to Waterloo Bridge at the Arts Council, 1967 © Guardian News & Media Ltd 2024.

p. 193 Denys Lasdun, final exterior model of the National Theatre on its final site next to Waterloo Bridge, 1969, model made by Philip Wood © Lasdun Archive/RIBA Collections.

p. 194 The Olivier Theatre drum revolve erected for its first test outside the headquarters of its manufacturer, Mole Richardson, in Thetford, Norfolk, from the author's archive.

p. 195 Letter from Denys Lasdun to Sir Laurence Olivier, 21 December 1966. Reproduced by kind permission of James Lasdun.

p. 196 Designs for the National Theatre: plan of the Olivier Theatre stage and auditorium, 1972 © Lasdun Archive/RIBA Collections.

p. 197 Model of the Olivier Theatre as built, with set design by Jocelyn Herbert, 1969 © Robert Kirkman FSAI, courtesy of the National Theatre.

p. 199 (Bottom left) Author's first sketch of the Lyttelton Theatre, from the author's archive.

(Top right) Preliminary Report on Stage Equipment, by Theatre Projects, from the author's archive.

(Bottom right) Plans and notes from Denys Lasdun & Partners and Theatre Projects Consultants for the National Theatre, from the author's archive.

p. 200 Drawing of the centre-line section of the Lyttelton Theatre as at 1976, drawing by Pilbrow & Partners.

Drawing of the plan of the Lyttelton Theatre as at 1976, drawing by Pilbrow & Partners.

p. 201 Drawing of the centre-line section of the Olivier Theatre as at 1976, drawing by Pilbrow & Partners.

Drawing of the plan of the Olivier Theatre as at 1976, drawing by Pilbrow & Partners.

p. 202 Diagrams for the Olivier Theatre drum revolve, drawn by Tim Foster, from the author's archive.

Author and Richard Brett with the original drum revolve model built by the stage engineering company Waagner-Biro, from the author's archive.

Author's early sketches of the Olivier Theatre, from the author's archive.

p. 204 The power flying control console in the Olivier Theatre, from the author's archive.

Olivier Theatre grid with lighting windlasses, from the author's archive.

Diagram showing the Olivier Theatre proposed masking screens (never implemented), from the author's archive.

p. 206 Lighting outlet layout for the Olivier Theatre, from the author's archive.

Author's early sketch for Lightboard group master (palette) controls, from the author's archive.

Lightboard in the Lyttelton Theatre at the National Theatre © Chris Arthur.

p. 208 Theatre Project's sketch of Lightboard main control panel, 1973, from the author's archive.

General facility panel for the National Theatre, from the author's archive.

Original sound control in the Lyttelton Theatre, from the author's archive.

p. 210 The Olivier Theatre under construction, c.1972. Photograph by J.E. Rackham

Photography, reproduced by kind permission of Carole Ellis, courtesy of the National Theatre.

p. 213 The Olivier Theatre drum revolve in construction from above, 25 July 1974. Photographer Unknown.

The Olivier Theatre drum revolve, one elevator lowered, 1980 © Philip Carter.

The Olivier Theatre flying system hooks, 2010 © Philip Carter.

Postcard from John Bury to the author, 1982, from the author's archive.

The Olivier Theatre, view to the stage from the lighting from one of the lighting stalactites, 1976 © Chris Arthur.

p. 214 Buttresses on the east side of the National Theatre looking towards the River Thames, 1976 © Richard Einzig/Arcaid Images.

p. 215 Denys Lasdun, 1985 © Tom Evans.

p. 219 Exterior of the National Theatre from Waterloo Bridge, 1976. Photograph by James Holmes, courtesy of the National Theatre.

3D diagram of the National Theatre, 1976, by Roy Castle.

National Theatre seen from the north-east, 1976, photograph by Donald Mill © RIBA Collections.

p. 221 Aerial view of The National Theatre, 1975 © Skyscan.co.uk.

Denys Lasdun orientation sketch for the National Theatre site. Reproduced by kind permission of James Lasdun.

p. 222 Designs for the Royal National Theatre, South Bank, London: north-west elevation, drawing dated November 1968 © RIBA Collections.

Exterior of the National Theatre from the ground floor, 1976 © Chris Arthur.

Board-marked concrete at the National Theatre © Rob Halliday.

National Theatre: the bustling foyer of the Lyttelton theatre, 1976, showing the original glazing line. Photograph by John Donat © John Donat/RIBA Collections.

p. 223 National Theatre: The Lyttelton foyer seen from outside at night, 1976, showing original glazing line. Photograph by Donald Mill © RIBA Collections.

p. 224 Two images of the auditorium of the Lyttelton Theatre, 1976, images courtesy of the National Theatre.

Diagram demonstrating the architectural lighting scheme for the foyer columns and the houselights in the Olivier Theatre. Reproduced by kind permission of Theatre Projects.

Two photographs of the National Theatre foyer areas c.1976 © Chris Arthur.

Slit window above the concrete base of the National Theatre, south-west (workshop) corner © Rob Halliday.

Photograph of the National Theatre ceiling showing the diagrid © Emily Halliday.

Exterior corner of the National Theatre, art direction by Ben & Leo Halliday © Rob Halliday.

National Theatre, seen from the south-west showing workshops and Lyttelton and Olivier fly towers, 1976. Photograph by Eric de Mare © RIBA Collections.

p. 226 Laurence Olivier in the Olivier Theatre, 14 June 1978. Photograph by Arnold Newman, reproduced by kind permission of the artist's estate.

p. 227 The Lyttelton foyer looking west from the highest foyer level, 1976. © Chris Arthur.

Part Three

p. 228 – 229 Olivier Theatre circle in construction, c 1972, photograph by J.E. Rackham. Reproduced by kind permission of Carole Ellis. NT Building-325-in construction, courtesy of the National Theatre.

p. 230 Sir Laurence Olivier and Peter Hall inspect the site of the National Theatre, 2 May 1973. Evening Standard/Hulton Archive via Getty Images.

p. 231 Peter Hall: Photograph by Reg Wilson © RSC.

p. 232 Olivier Theatre drum revolve under construction showing Richard Brett (on the lowered elevator), David Collison and Richard Pilbrow (on top disk) © Philip Sayer.

p. 233 Lord Rayne, 1960. Photograph by Rex Coleman for Baron Studios © National Portrait Gallery, London.

p. 235 First sketches of the Cottesloe Theatre dated by Iain Mackintosh, 10 November 1973, labelled "Cottesloe Cockpit: Infinite Riches in a Little Room." Theatre Projects Consultants Collection at the National Theatre Archive.

First model of the Cottesloe Theatre, from the author's archive.

p. 236 Two images of the National Theatre under construction, c 1970 and c.1972. Photographs by J.E. Rackham. NT Building-290-in construction and NT Building-301-in construction. Reproduced by kind permission of Carole Ellis, images courtesy of the National Theatre.

p. 240 Theatre of Epidaurus. Photograph by Carole Raddato. Reproduced under Creative Commons Attribution-Share Alike 2.0 Generic licence. https://commons.wikimedia.org/wiki/File:The_great_theater_of_Epidaurus,_designed_by_Polykleitos_the_Younger_in_the_4th_century_BC,_Sanctuary_of_Asklepeios_at_Epidaurus,_Greece_(14034893682).jpg

p. 244 Official opening of the Royal National Theatre, South Bank, London, 25 October 1976: the Queen, Prince Philip and other members of the Royal family being greeted in the foyer. Photograph by Peter Baistow © Architectural Press Archive/RIBA Collections.

p. 245 Richard York by Peter Bloomfield © Barbican Archive.

p. 247 Rosie Beatty, from the subject's archive.

p. 249 Laurie Clayton, from the author's archive.

p. 251 Alan Jacobi, David Hersey and son Dimitri with Lightboard in the Olivier Theatre, c.1978 Photographer unknown.

Director John Dexter and Lighting Designer Andy Philips with Lightboard in the Olivier Theatre during the making of *The Life of Galileo*, 1980 © Zoë Dominic.

Richard Pilbrow with Lightboard in the Lyttelton Theatre, c.1976. Photograph by Philip Sayer.

Richard Brett in the Olivier grid, c.1976, from the author's archive.

p. 252 Her Majesty the Queen arriving at the National Theatre, 25 October 1976. Ron Galella/Ron Galella Collection via Getty Images.

p. 253 The 1976 Foundation Stone at the National Theatre today; it sits next to the 1951 Stone. © Rob Halliday.

p. 257 Lord Laurence Olivier giving the opening speech from the stage at the National Theatre, 25 October 1976. Central Press/Hulton Archive via Getty Images.

Cartoon by Brian Benn, from the author's archive.

Part Four

p. 258 - 259 National Theatre Roofscape with the Shed temporary theatre. Reproduced under Creative Commons licence CC-BY-SA-4.0.

p. 260 National Theatre view towards St. Paul's Cathedral, 1976 © Richard Einzig/Arcaid Images.

p. 261 Peter Hall, 1977 © Allstar Picture Library Limited/Alamy.

p. 264 Barbican Theatre auditorium from the side. Photograph by Peter Dazeley from his book *London Theatres* (Frances Lincoln, 2017).

Barbican Auditorium © Dion Barrett.

Sketch of the Barbican Theatre by Elizabeth Bury for Bamber Gascoigne's *World Theatre: An Illustrated History* (Little, Brown and Company, 1968). Reproduced by kind permission of the artist.

p. 266 Premiere of the opera *Pirro* by Giovanni Paisiello at the National Theatre, Warsaw, 1790. National Museum of Warsaw, Poland © Album/Alamy.

p. 267 *Tamburlaine the Great*, National Theatre, 1976. Photograph by Nobby Clark/Popperfoto via Getty Images.

(Need to check final order) James Grant as Peter, Karl Johnson as Jesus, Edna Dore as Mary and Brian Glover (above) as God in *The Mysteries: The Passion*, National Theatre, 1985 © Donald Cooper.

Joe Duttine as Jesus in *The Mysteries: The Passion*, National Theatre, 1999 © Donald Cooper

p. 268 Simon Callow as Mozart and Paul Scofield as Salieri in *Amadeus*, National Theatre, 1979 © Donald Cooper

Michael Gambon as Galileo Galilei and Nicholas Selby as Sagredo in *The Life of Galileo*, National Theatre, 1980 © Zoë Dominic. RNT/PR/3/171. Courtesy of the National Theatre.

Staging for *The Life of Galileo*, National Theatre, 1980 ©Zoë Dominic.

p. 269 *Oresteia* chorus in rehearsal, National Theatre, 1981. Photography by Nobby Clark/Popperfoto via Getty Images.

The cast of *Guys and Dolls*, Olivier Theatre, 1982 © Donald Cooper.

p. 270 Set design by John Gunter for *The Rivals*, Olivier Theatre, 1983 © Zoë Dominic. RNT/PO/5/118. Courtesy of the National Theatre.

Set design by Hayden Griffin for *Pravda*, Olivier Theatre, 1985 © Group Three Photography. RNT/PO/5/142. Courtesy of the National Theatre. Reproduced by kind permission of Christine McDougall.

p. 271 Anthony Hopkins and Judi Dench in *Antony and Cleopatra*, Olivier Theatre, 1987 © Reg Wilson/Shutterstock.com.

Two images of the set designed by William Dudley for *The Shaughraun* showing the drum revolve in use, Olivier Theatre, 1988 © Philip Carter.

p. 272 David Hare at the premier for *The Reader*, December 2003. Photograph by Patrick McMullan via Getty Images.

p. 276 David Hersey c.1976, courtesy of the subject.

p. 277 Jason Barnes. Photograph by Martin Smith/Origin8 Design, courtesy of the ABTT.

Poster for production of *The Mysteries* at the National Theatre, 1999, designed by Michael Mayhew. RNT/PP/2/4/218. Courtesy of the National Theatre.

p. 278 Howard Davies © Ivan Kyncl/ArenaPAL.

p. 279 *The Life of Galileo*, Olivier Theatre, 2006 © Catherine Ashmore.

p. 280 *The White Guard*, Olivier Theatre, 2010 © Philip Carter.

p. 281 William Dudley, 2005. Photograph by Richard Finkelstein.

p. 282 *The Shaughraun*, Olivier Theatre, 1988, photo call showing set. Photograph by Michael Mayhew, courtesy of the National Theatre.

p. 284 Diana Quick, 2009 © GL Portrait/Alamy.

p. 285 Alan Ayckbourn © Adrian Gatie

p. 287 The cast of *Bedroom Farce*, National Theatre, 1977. Photograph by John Haynes. RNT/PR/3/108. Courtesy of the National Theatre.

p. 288 Exterior image of the National Theatre c.1997, porte-cochère filled in as part of the 1997 refurbishment by architects Stanton Williams. © Peter Cook, courtesy of Stanton Williams.

p. 289 Richard Eyre during rehearsals for *The Changeling*, 1988 © John Haynes, courtesy of the National Theatre.

p. 290 Peter Radmore, c.1965 © Chris Arthur.

p. 292 Cover of the *Strategy for the Future* document by Denys Lasdun and Partners, 1989 © Lasdun Archive/RIBA Collections.

p. 293 Brian Ridley © Chris Arthur.

Sir Ian McKellen as Richard III, 1995 © John Haynes.

p. 299 The Olivier Theatre set up in the round, c.1997 © Philip Carter.

p. 300 The cast of *The Absence of War*, Olivier Theatre, 1993 © John Haynes. RNT/PR/3/411. Courtesy of the National Theatre.

Richard Briers as Ratty and Adrian Scarborough as Norman, *The Wind in the Willows*, Olivier Theatre, 1990 © Clive Barda/ArenaPAL.

Set by Mark Thompson for *The Wind in the Willows*, National Theatre, 1990 © Philip Carter.

p. 301 Stephen Dillane as Prior Walter and Nancy Crane as the Angel in *Angels in America*, Cottesloe Theatre, 1993 © John Haynes.

Diana Kent as Sheila Birling and Kenneth Cranham as Inspector Goole in *An Inspector Calls*, Lyttelton Theatre, 1992 © Ivan Kyncl/ArenaPAL.

p. 302 *Carousel*, Lyttelton Theatre, 1992 © Clive Barda/ArenaPAL.

Machinal, Lyttelton Theatre, 1993 © Ivan Kyncl/ArenaPAL.

p. 303 Stephen Daldry, 2016 © Associated Press/Alamy.

p. 306 Ian MacNeil, Photographer unknown.

p. 307 Chiwetel Ejiofor in *Everyman*, Olivier Theatre, 2015 © Philip Carter.

p. 308 Mark Thompson, 2014. Tim P. Whitby via Getty Images.

p. 309 *Henry IV, Part 2*, Olivier Theatre, 2005 © Philip Carter.

p. 310 Rick Fisher. Photograph by Ken Howard.

An Inspector Calls, Lyttelton Theatre, 1992 © Philip Carter.

Vincent in Brixton, Cottesloe Theatre, 2002 © Philip Carter.

p. 311 Tim Hatley, 2012 © Dan Wooller/Shutterstock.com.

p. 312 Royal National Theatre, exterior, c.2000. Photographer unknown. Courtesy of the National Theatre.

p. 313 Trevor Nunn, 2013 © WENN Rights Ltd/Alamy.

p. 314 *Cats* in performance at the New London Theatre, 1981. Photograph by Reg Wilson © Cameron Mackintosh Ltd.

Cats fit-up at the New London Theatre, 1981. Photographer unknown, courtesy Cameron Mackintosh Ltd.

p. 318 *Mother Molly's Clap House*, Olivier Theatre, 2001 © Philip Carter.

Peter Pan, Olivier Theatre, 1997 © Gautier Deblonde.

p. 319 Two images of The Loft, National Theatre, 2002 © Philip Carter

p. 320 The Lyttelton Theatre before the Transformation season © Philip Carter

The Lyttelton Theatre during the Transformation season 2002 © Philip Carter.

Four images of the set by Lez Brotherston for *Play Without Words*, National Theatre, 2002 © Philip Carter.

p. 321 Set by Anthony Ward for *Oklahoma!* Olivier Theatre, 1998 © Philip Carter.

Cast of Summerfolk, National Theatre, 1999 © Catherine Ashmore. RNT/PR/3/525. Courtesy of the National Theatre.

p. 322 *South Pacific*, Olivier Theatre, 2001 © Marilyn Kingwill/ArenaPAL.

The Coast of Utopia: Voyage, Olivier Theatre, 2002 © Ivan Kyncl/ArenaPAL.

Will Keen as Vissarion Belinsky and Guy Henry as Ivan Turgenev in *The Coast of Utopia: Voyage*, Olivier Theatre,

2002 © Rowena Chowdrey/ArenaPAL.

p. 323 Anthony Ward. Photographer unknown.

p. 324 Martine McCutcheon as Eliza Doolittle in *My Fair Lady*, Lyttelton Theatre, 2001 © Michael Le Poer Trench/ArenaPAL.

Liola, Lyttelton Theatre, 2013 © Catherine Ashmore.

p. 325 Peter Mumford, courtesy of the subject.

p. 328 Fire Garden installation at the National Theatre, 2012 © Ludovic des Cognets.

p. 329 Nicholas Hytner, 2015, photograph by David Levene © David Levene, courtesy of eyevine.

p. 330 *Jerry Springer - The Opera*, Lyttelton Theatre, 2003 © Philip Carter.

p. 333 The Shed at the National Theatre, designed by Haworth Tompkins, c.2013. Reproduced under Creative Commons licence CC BY 2.0.

The NT Future design team, photograph by Peter Guenzel c. 2016.

Diagrams from the NT Future document showing areas of the building to be modified, courtesy of Haworth Tompkins.

p. 334 Steve Tompkins, from the subject's archive.

Royal Court Theatre, 2000 © Andy Chopping, courtesy of Haworth Tompkins.

Redesigned Theatre Royal Drury Lane, 2021 © Philip Vile, courtesy of Haworth Tompkins.

p. 335 Three images of the foyers of the National Theatre © Rob Halliday.

Exterior image of the National Theatre © Rob Halliday.

p. 336 Entrance to the National Theatre post-2016 © Philip Vile, courtesy of Haworth Tompkins.

Lyttelton Theatre circle foyer © Philip Vile, courtesy of Haworth Tompkins.

Dorfman Theatre foyer © Philip Vile, courtesy of Haworth Tompkins.

Max Rayne Building © Philip Vile, courtesy of Haworth Tompkins.

Clore Learning Centre © Philip Vile, courtesy of Haworth Tompkins.

Re-invented north-east corner of the National Theatre post-2016 © Philip Vile, courtesy of Haworth Tompkins.

Lyttelton Theatre foyer © Philip Vile, courtesy of Haworth Tompkins.

p. 337 Exterior of the National Theatre entrance © Philip Vile, courtesy of Haworth Tompkins.

Entrance to the Dorfman Theatre © Philip Vile, courtesy of Haworth Tompkins.

Workshops at the National Theatre © Philip Vile, courtesy of Haworth Tompkins.

New café with amended glazing line reflecting Lasdun's earlier glazing line to the west © Philip Vile, courtesy of Haworth Tompkins.

Workshops in the new Max Rayne Centre at the National Theatre © Philip vile, courtesy of Haworth Tompkins.

Interior of the Dorfman Theatre post-2016 © Philip Vile, courtesy of Haworth Tompkins.

The Understudy Pub in the National Theatre's revised north-east corner (compare with p.214) © Philip Vile, courtesy of Haworth Tompkins.

Statue of Laurence Olivier as Hamlet outside National Theatre, by sculptor Angela Conner © Chris Arthur.

p. 338 Adrian Lester as Henry V in *Henry V*, Olivier Theatre, 2003 © Tristram Kenton.

Cast of *Henry V*, Olivier Theatre, 2003 © Philip Carter.

His Dark Materials, Olivier Theatre, 2003 © Philip Carter

Anna Maxwell Martin as Lyra Belacqua, Dany Sapani as Iorek Byrnison and Dominic Cooper as Will Parry in *His Dark Materials*, Olivier Theatre, 2003 © Ivan Kyncl/ArenaPAL.

p. 339 The cast of *History Boys*, Lyttelton Theatre, 2003 © Ivan Kyncl/ArenaPAL.

Anne-Marie Duff as Joan of Arc in *Saint Joan*, Olivier Theatre, 2007 © Kevin Cummins. RNT/PR/3/682. Courtesy of the National Theatre.

Saint Joan, Olivier Theatre, 2007 © Philip Carter

p. 340 Two images of *War Horse*, Olivier Theatre, 2008 © Philip Carter.

The cast of *London Road*, Olivier Theatre, 2011 © Helen Warner.

p. 341 James Cordon as Francis Henshall and Suzie Toase as Dolly in *One Man, Two Guvnors*, Lyttelton Theatre © Johan Persson/ArenaPAL.

The Curious Incident of the Dog in the Night-Time, Cottesloe Theatre, 2012 © Manuel Harlan/ArenaPAL.

p. 342 Olivia Vinall as Desdemona and Adrian Lester as Othello in *Othello*, Olivier Theatre, 2013 © Johan Persson/ArenaPAL.

Two images of the cast of *The Silver Tassie*, Olivier Theatre, 2014 © Catherine Ashmore.

p. 343 Nick Starr photograph by Sarah Lee. Courtesy of eyevine.

p. 344 Vicki Mortimer © Pamela Raith.

p. 345 *Three Sisters*, Lyttelton Theatre, 2003 © Philip Carter.

p. 346 Bob Crowley, 2012 © WENN Rights Ltd/Alamy.

p. 347 Set of *The History Boys*, Lyttelton Theatre, 2004 © Philip Carter.

p. 348 Marianne Elliott © Helen Maybanks/ArenaPAL.

p. 349 *The Curious Incident of the Dog in the Night-time*, at the Apollo Theatre, London, 2013 © Marilyn Kingwill/ArenaPAL.

p. 350 Bunny Christie, 2018. © PA Images/Alamy.

p. 351 *The White Guard*, Lyttelton Theatre, 2010 © Catherine Ashmore.

p. 352 Alex Jennings, 2015 © Associated Press/Alamy.

p. 353 Neil Austin, image from the subject's archive.

p. 354 Aerial view of the South Bank site, March 2020 © Above All Images.

p. 355 Stage and film director Rufus Norris in central London after being named as the new artistic director of the National Theatre, 2013 © PA Images/Alamy.

p. 357 The people of the National Theatre, 2019 © Cameron Slater, courtesy of the National Theatre.

p. 358 Chiwetel Ejiofur in *Everyman*, Olivier Theatre, 2016 © Philip Carter.

Anne-Marie Duff as Lizzie Holroyd in *Husbands & Sons*, Dorfman Theatre, 2015 © Manuel Harlan/ArenaPAL.

p. 359 *wonder.land*, Olivier Theatre, 2015 © Brinkhoff/Mögenburg. Costumes by Katrina Lindsay.

wonder.land, Olivier Theatre, 2015 © Tristram Kenton.

Ma Rainey's Black Bottom, Lyttelton Theatre, 2016 © Philip Carter.

The cast of *Ma Rainey's Black Bottom*, National Theatre, 2016 © Philip Carter.

p. 360 Two images of *Les Blancs*, Olivier Theatre, 2016 © Philip Carter.

Rosalie Craig as Polly Peachum and Rory Kinnear as Macheath in *The Threepenny Opera*, Olivier Theatre, 2016 © Philip Carter.

George Ikediashi as the Balladeer and Rory Kinnear as Macheath in *The Threepenny Opera*, Olivier Theatre, 2016 © Richard Hubert Smith.

p. 361 *The Deep Blue Sea*, Lyttelton Theatre, 2016 © Richard Hubert Smith.

Helen McCrory as Hester Collyer in *The Deep Blue Sea*, Lyttelton Theatre, 2016 © Richard Hubert Smith.

Lucian Msamati as Antonio Salieri with members of the Southbank Sinfonia in *Amadeus*, Olivier Theatre, 2016 © Marc Brenner. RNT/

Photo Credits 505

PR/3/867. Courtesy of the National Theatre.

p. 362 Cast of *Angels in America,* Lyttelton Theatre, 2017 © Philip Carter.

Amanda Lawrence as the Angel in *Angels in America,* Lyttelton Theatre, 2017 © Philip Carter.

Andrew Garfield as Prior Walter in *Angels in America,* Lyttelton Theatre, 2017 © Philip Carter.

Two images of the set for *Network,* National Theatre, 2017 © Philip Carter.

Bryan Cranston as Howard Beale in *Network,* Lyttelton Theatre, 2017 © Philip Carter.

p. 363 The ensemble of *Follies,* Olivier Theatre, 2017 © Philip Carter.

Follies, Olivier Theatre, London, 2017 © Johan Persson/ArenaPAL.

Sarah Marie Maxwell as Young Solange, Emily Langham as Young Carlotta and The Cast in *Follies,* Olivier Theatre, 2017 © Johan Persson/ArenaPAL.

Two images of *The Lehmann Trilogy,* Lyttelton Theatre, 2018 © Philip Carter

p. 364 Rae Smith © Sandra Lousada/Mary Evans Picture Library.

p. 366 *War Horse,* Olivier Theatre, 2007 © Philip Carter.

p. 367 Jon Clark, 2019. David M. Bennett via Getty Images.

p. 368 Ben Power, 2013 © Bill Knight.

p. 370 Paule Constable © David Monteith-Hodge.

Part Five

p. 372 – 372 Exterior of the National Theatre including The Shed temporary theatre, c.2013. Used under Creative Commons licence CC BY 2.0.

p. 374 The Olivier Theatre, c.1976 © Richard Einzig/Arcaid Images.

The Olivier Theatre, 2010. Photograph © Paul Karalius on behalf of Push The Button.

p. 375 Exterior of the National Theatre in 2017 © Chris Arthur.

p. 377 The Lyttelton Theatre, c. 2010 © Paul Karalius on behalf of Push The Button.

The Dorfman Theatre, from the author's archive.

Laser scan render of the Dorfman/Cottesloe Theatre. Courtesy of Ryan Metcalfe/Preevue, reproduced with permission from the National Theatre.

p. 378 Two images of the interior of The Shed temporary theatre, National Theatre c. 2013 © Philip Vile.

p. 379 Michael Billington, 2016 © GL Portrait/Alamy.

p. 382 Giles Havergal, 2019, photograph by Paul Stuart © Paul Stuart.

p. 383 The Citizens Theatre, Glasgow, 2014 © Tommy Ga-Ken Wan.

p. 385 Theatre Royal Haymarket, London, 1994 © Ian Grundy.

Her Majesty's (now His Majesty's) Theatre, London, 2010 © Ian Grundy.

p. 386 Laser scan of the Olivier Theatre by Pilbrow & Partners.

p. 387 Laser scan render of the Dorfman Theatre. Courtesy of Ryan Metcalfe/Preevue, reproduced with permission from the National Theatre.

p. 388 Exterior of the National Theatre, view from Waterloo Bridge, photograph by Man Vyi in 2008. Public domain.

p. 391 Comparative drawings of the Olivier and Crucible Theatres, from the author's archive.

p. 392 Comparison of the Olivier Theatre and Novello Theatres by Pilbrow & Partners.

p. 393 Isometric scan of the Olivier Theatre by Pilbrow & Partners.

Isometric scan of the Novello Theatre by Pilbrow & Partners.

Acoustic plan of the Olivier Theatre, drawing by Pilbrow & Partners.

Acoustic plan of the Novello Theatre, drawing by Pilbrow & Partners.

Acoustic section for the Olivier Theatre, drawing by Pilbrow & Partners.

Acoustic section for the Novello Theatre, drawing by Pilbrow & Partners.

Point cloud image of Olivier Theatre showing distance to the stage by Pilbrow & Partners.

Point cloud image of Novello Theatre showing distance to the stage by Pilbrow & Partners.

p. 394 Comparison of the Lyttelton Theatre and Noël Coward Theatres, drawing by Pilbrow & Partners.

p. 395 Isometric scan of the Lyttelton Theatre by Pilbrow & Partners.

Isometric scan of the Noël Coward Theatre by Pilbrow & Partners.

Lyttelton Theatre stage from the stalls, drawing by Pilbrow & Partners.

Noël Coward Theatre stage from the stalls, drawing by Pilbrow & Partners.

Lyttelton Theatre auditorium from the circle, drawing by Pilbrow & Partners.

The Noël Coward Theatre auditorium from the circle, drawing by Pilbrow & Partners.

p. 396 Denys Lasdun, sketch proposal of the Carlo Felice Opera House, dated 17 November 1981 © Lasdun Archive/RIBA Collections.

p. 397 Denys Lasdun, stage 2 exterior model of Carlo Felice Opera House competition, Genoa © Lasdun Archive/RIBA Collections.

p. 399 Denys Lasdun, four sketch proposals of the Carlo Felice Opera House, dated from 16 November 1981 - 1 January 1982 © Lasdun Archive/RIBA Collections.

p. 400 Denys Lasdun's plans for the Carlo Felice Opera House in situ © Lasdun Archive/RIBA Collections.

p. 401 Two models of the proposed auditorium for the Carlo Felice Opera House, Genoa © Lasdun Archive/RIBA Collections.

p. 402 Rendering showing section of the proposed Carlo Felice Opera House including studio theatre beneath main theatre auditorium and complex sub-stage machinery © Lasdun Archive/RIBA Collections.

View from above plan of the proposed Carlo Felice Opera House site © Lasdun Archive/RIBA Collections.

p. 403 Teatro Carlo Felice Opera House as built to the designs of Aldo Rossi, photograph by Maurizio Beatrici. Reproduced under Creative Commons licence Attribution-Share Alike 4.0 International licence. https://commons.wikimedia.org/wiki/File:Teatro_Carlo_Felice_Interno1.jpg

Auditorium model with set dressing of Denys Lasdun's design for the proposed Carlo Felice Opera House © Lasdun Archive/RIBA Collections.

p. 404 Theatre Royal, Nottingham, 1978, courtesy of Theatre Projects.

p. 405 Ken Dodd at the Theatre Royal, Nottingham in 1978 © Mirrorpix.

p. 406 The New Amsterdam Theatre, New York c.1997 © Whitney Cox.

p. 407 Frank Dunlop, 1981, photograph by Allan Warren. Used under Creative Commons license CC-BY-SA-3.0. https://commons.wikimedia.org/wiki/File:Frank_Dunlop_Allan_Warren.jpg

Sean Kenny, 1963 © Lewis Morley/Science Museum Group .

Stephen Joseph, c.1960 © Scarborough Theatre Trust/Stephen Joseph Theatre.

p. 408 Russell Johnson, courtesy of Artec Consultants Inc/Arup.

Harold Prince, from the author's archive.

p. 409 Richard Negri, from the author's archive.

Michael Elliott, from the author's archive.

p. 410 Concept for the Manchester Theatre Project, from the author's archive.

The Old Vic Theatre proscenium, 1962, from the author's archive.

p. 411 Eden Court Theatre, Inverness, as in 2019. Reproduced by kind permission of LDN Architects and Mark Hopton.

The Royal Exchange Theatre, Manchester © Joel Fildes.

p. 412 The Birmingham Repertory Theatre © Richard Glover.

Apollo Theatre, London © Kirsty McLaren/Alamy.

p. 414 Royal Lyceum Edinburgh, 2018 © Tommy Ga-Ken Wan.

Pit boxes & gallery. Etching by George Cruikshank from *My sketch book*, 1834 © British Library/Granger.

p. 415 The Ahmanson Theatre, Los Angeles before renovation (original 1967 design) © Adrian Velicescu.

Interior of the Ahmanson Theatre, Los Angeles © Vladimir Perlovich.

Concept drawings for the Ahmanson Theatre boxes, courtesy of Theatre Projects.

p. 416 Steppenwolf Theatre, Chicago.

Geary Theater (now the Toni Rembe), San Francisco, auditorium as at c.1996. Photograph by Marco Lorenzo © Chicago History Museum, Hedrich-Blessing Collection.

Walt Disney Theater, Orlando Photograph courtesy of the Dr. Phillips Center for the Performing Arts.

Interior of the Dolby (formerly Kodak) Theatre, Los Angeles © Mike Hume.

Theatre Royal Nottingham © Ian Grundy.

Royal Court Theatre, 2004 © Ian Grundy.

Section drawing of the Steppenwolf Theatre, Chicago, courtesy of Theatre Projects.

Plan of the Steppenwolf Theatre, Chicago, courtesy of Theatre Projects.

Section of the Dolby Theatre, Los Angeles, courtesy of Theatre Projects.

Concept drawings for the Dolby Theatre, Los Angeles, from the author's archive.

p. 417 The Royal Exchange Theatre, Manchester, 2009 © Ian Grundy.

Plan drawings of the Royal Exchange Theatre, Manchester and first and second seating levels, courtesy of Theatre Projects.

Section drawing of the Royal Exchange Theatre, Manchester 'pod' inside the Exchange Hall, courtesy of Theatre Projects.

Royal Exchange Theatre, Manchester, theatre module inside the Exchange Hall, 2009 © Ian Grundy.

Walt Disney Concert Hall, sidewalk view from southeast corner. ART on FILE via Getty Images.

Walt Disney Concert Hall interior, 2012 © SiliconValleyStock/Alamy.

p. 418 Tricycle Theatre, London © Steve Stephens

Two images of Christ's Hospital School, Horsham, from the author's archive.

Interior of the Wyly Theatre, Dallas © Iwan Baan.

Exterior of the Wyly Theatre, Dallas © Rob Halliday.

Section drawings of the Polonsky Theatre, New York, Courtesy of Theatre Projects.

Interior and exterior of The Theatre for a New Audience at Polonsky Shakespeare Center © Francis Dzikowski/OTTO.

p. 419 Auditorium of The Bridge Theatre, London, from the stage, 2017 © Philip Vile.

Stage of The Bridge Theatre, London, 2017 © Philip Vile.

Plans for The Bridge Theatre stalls, London, courtesy of Haworth Tompkins.

Plans for The Bridge Theatre circle, London, courtesy of Haworth Tompkins.

Section drawing of The Bridge Theatre, London, courtesy of Haworth Tompkins.

p. 420 Crucible Theatre, Sheffield, © John Donat/RIBA Collections.

Plan and elevation drawings for the Crucible Theatre Sheffield, courtesy of Theatre Projects.

The Chicago Shakespeare Theater. Photograph by Vito Palmisano.

p. 421 The Esplanade Concert Hall, Singapore © Tim Griffith.

The Esplanade Lyric Theatre, Singapore © Rob Halliday.

Max Bell Theatre, Calgary © Richard Schick.

Martha Cohen Theatre, Calgary. Photograph courtesy of Theatre Projects.

The Esplanade Lyric Theatre, Singapore during performance © Rob Halliday.

p. 422 Winspear Opera House auditorium, Dallas © Rob Halliday.

Section and plan drawings of the Den Norske Opera, Oslo, courtesy of Theatre Projects.

Exterior of the Stavros Niarchos Foundation Cultural Center, Athens © Michael Denance.

Interior of the Stavros Niarchos Foundation Cultural Center, Athens © Michael Denance.

Glyndebourne Opera House auditorium © Richard Davies.

Interior of the Den Norske Opera, Oslo © Erik Berg.

Exterior of the Den Norske Opera, Oslo © Erik Berg.

p. 423 Belk Theater, Charlotte © Timothy Hursley.

Section and plan drawings of the Belk Theater, Charlotte, courtesy of Theatre Projects.

The Mead Theater, Schuster Performing Arts Center, Dayton © Andy Snow.

The Kauffman Centre, Kansas City, by Brit By Birth - Own work. Licensed under Creative Commons licence CC BY-SA 4.0, https://commons.wikimedia.org/w/index.php?curid=97345290

The Aronoff Center, Cincinnati © Steve Bullock, courtesy of Ducharme Seating.

Overture Center for the Arts, Madison, 2004 © Jeff Goldberg/Esto.

p. 424 The Steinmetz Hall in the Dr Phillips Center for the Performing Arts, Orlando, courtesy of Theatre Projects.

Stalls of theatre set-up at the Derngate, Northampton, photographer unknown, courtesy of Theatre Projects.

Flat-floor setup, Derngate, Northampton, photographer unknown, courtesy of Theatre Projects.

Plan drawing of Derngate, Northampton, photographer unknown, courtesy of Theatre Projects.

Event set-up, Derngate, Northampton, photograph by Martin Charles, 1984 © Lasdun Archive/RIBA Collections.

Proscenium set-up, Derngate, Northampton, photographer unknown, courtesy of Theatre Projects.

Symphony hall set-up Derngate, Northampton, photographer unknown, courtesy of Theatre Projects.

p. 426 Detail from *Comedy in the Country, Tragedy in London*, by Thomas Rowlandson. London, 1807 © Victoria and Albert Museum, London.

p. 427 Conceptual drawing for National Theatre of Cyprus, courtesy of Pilbrow & Partners.

p. 428 Sketch of National Theatre of Cyprus, courtesy of Theatre Projects.

Sketch of National Theatre of Cyprus by Fred Pilbrow, courtesy of Pilbrow & Partners.

Sketch of National Theatre of Cyprus by Fred Pilbrow, courtesy of Pilbrow & Partners.

p. 429 The architectural team working on the National Theatre of Cyprus, courtesy of Pilbrow & Partners.

Three CAD design images for the National Theatre of Cyprus, courtesy of Pilbrow & Partners.

p. 430 Four images of the National Theatre of Cyprus, courtesy of Pilbrow & Partners.

p. 431 Design team for the National Theatre of Cyprus, courtesy of Pilbrow & Partners.

Four images of the Interior of the National Theatre of Cyprus, courtesy of Pilbrow & Partners.

Part Six

p. 432 - 433 Laser scan of the Olivier Theatre by Pilbrow & Partners.

p. 434 Fit up in the Olivier Theatre c.1999 © Philip Carter.

p. 435 Lyttelton Theatre, showing front of house lighting positions © Philip Carter.

p. 436 *The Relapse*, Olivier Theatre, 2001 © Philip Carter.

Coast of Utopia: Shipwreck, Olivier Theatre, 2002 © Philip Carter.

Anything Goes, Olivier Theatre, 2002 © Philip Carter.

The Bacchai, Olivier Theatre, 2002 © Philip Carter.

His Dark Materials, Olivier Theatre, 2003 © Philip Carter.

Cyrano de Bergerac, Olivier Theatre, 2004 © Philip Carter.

Henry IV, Part 2, Olivier Theatre, 2005 © Philip Carter.

War Horse, Olivier Theatre, 2007 © Philip Carter.

Fram, Olivier Theatre, 2008 © Philip Carter.

Fram, Olivier Theatre, 2008 © Philip Carter.

Mother Courage, Olivier Theatre, 2009 © Philip Carter.

Emperor and Galilean, Olivier Theatre, 2011 © Philip Carter.

p. 437 *Fela!* Olivier Theatre, 2011 © Philip Carter.

The Cherry Orchard, Olivier Theatre, 2011 © Philip Carter.

Edward II, Olivier Theatre, 2013 © Philip Carter.

James III, Olivier Theatre, 2014 © Philip Carter.

Behind the Beautiful Forevers, Olivier Theatre, 2015 © Philip Carter

Our Country's Good, Olivier Theatre, 2015 © Philip Carter

Amadeus, Olivier Theatre, 2016 © Philip Carter

As You Like It, Olivier Theatre, 2016 © Philip Carter

Salome, Olivier Theatre, 2017 © Philip Carter

Twelfth Night, Olivier Theatre, 2017 © Philip Carter

p. 438 *No Man's Land*, Lyttelton Theatre, 2001 © Philip Carter.

Pillars of the Community, Lyttelton Theatre, 2005 © Philip Carter.

Rafta, Rafta, Lyttelton Theatre, 2007 © Philip Carter.

Present Laughter, Lyttelton Theatre, 2008 © Philip Carter.

Happy Days, Lyttelton Theatre, 2007 © Philip Carter.

Burnt by the Sun, Lyttelton Theatre, 2009 © Philip Carter.

Children of the Sun, Lyttelton Theatre, 2013 © Philip Carter.

From Morning to Midnight, Lyttelton Theatre, 2013 © Philip Carter.

Liola, Lyttelton Theatre, 2013© Philip Carter.

Three Sisters, Lyttelton Theatre, 2003 © Philip Carter.

Dara, Lyttelton Theatre, 2015 © Philip Carter.

p. 439 *Light Shining in Buckinghamshire*, Lyttelton Theatre, 2015 © Philip Carter.

*The Motherf**ker with the Hat*, Lyttelton Theatre, 2015 © Philip Carter.

Jane Eyre, Lyttelton Theatre, 2015 © Philip Carter.

The Red Barn, Lyttelton Theatre, 2016 © Philip Carter.

The Deep Blue Sea, Lyttelton Theatre, 2016 © Philip Carter.

Ma Rainey's Black Bottom, Lyttelton Theatre, 2016 © Philip Carter.

Hedda Gabbler, Lyttelton Theatre, 2017 © Philip Carter.

Angels in America, Lyttelton Theatre, 2017 © Philip Carter.

Angels in America, Lyttelton Theatre, 2017 © Philip Carter.

Network, Lyttelton Theatre, 2017 © Philip Carter.

The Lehman Trilogy, Lyttelton Theatre, 2018 © Philip Carter.

The Lehman Trilogy, Lyttelton Theatre, 2018 © Philip Carter.

p. 440 *Stanley*, Cottesloe Theatre, 1996 © Philip Carter.

Syringa Tree, Cottesloe Theatre, 2002 © Philip Carter.

Vincent in Brixton, Cottesloe Theatre, 2002 © Philip Carter.

Fix Up, Cottesloe Theatre, 2004 © Philip Carter.

The False Servant, Cottesloe Theatre, 2004 © Philip Carter.

Paul, Cottesloe Theatre, Cottesloe Theatre, 2005 © Philip Carter.

Tristan and Yseult, Cottesloe Theatre, 2005 © Philip Carter.

President of an Empty Room, National Theatre, 2005 © Philip Carter.

The Seafarer, Cottesloe Theatre, 2006 © Philip Carter.

The Overwhelming, Cottesloe Theatre, 2006 © Philip Carter.

p. 441 *Maurice Pinder*, Cottesloe Theatre, 2007 © Philip Carter.

Landscape with Weapon, Cottesloe Theatre, 2007 © Philip Carter.

Or You Could Kiss Me, Cottesloe Theatre, 2010 © Philip Carter.

London Road, Cottesloe Theatre, 2011 © Philip Carter.

The Hard Problem, Dorfman Theatre, 2015 © Philip Carter.

People, Places and Things, Dorfman Theatre, 2015 © Philip Carter.

Rules for Living, Dorfman Theatre, 2015 © Philip Carter.

Evening at the Talkhouse, Dorfman Theatre, 2015 © Philip Carter.

Love, Dorfman Theatre, 2016 © Philip Carter.

The Flick, Dorfman Theatre, 2016 © Philip Carter.

p. 442 View down the inside of the Olivier Theatre fly tower, 2010 © Philip Carter.

p. 443 Fly bars below the Lyttelton Theatre grid, 2014 © Philip Carter

p. 445 The National Theatre Lighting Team. 2017 © Rob Halliday.

p. 450 Fisheye shot of the Olivier Theatre and ceiling, 1976 © Chris Arthur.

p. 451 Model of Olivier Theatre ceiling reflectors, photograph by A. Kuszell.

p. 452 Paul Arditti © Sarah Alford-Smith.

p. 453 Sound baffles in the Olivier Theatre © Philip Carter.

p. 455 Victoria Palace Theatre, London © Ian Grundy.

Laser scan of the Lyttelton Theatre by Pilbrow & Partners.

p. 456 *The Old Bedford*, Walter Sickert, 1895. Walker Art Gallery, National Museums Liverpool. © National Museums Liverpool/ Bridgeman Arts.

p. 457 Interior of the Sam Wanamaker Playhouse at Shakespeare's Globe, London. Reproduced by kind permission of Peter Dazeley.

p. 458 Mark Rylance, 2015 © Gary Doak/Alamy.

The Globe Theatre, London © Bob Masters/Alamy.

p. 459 Michael Grandage, 2018, photograph by Marc Brenner. Reproduced under Creative Commons licence CC BY-SA 4.0 https://commons.wikimedia. org/wiki/File:Michael_ Grandage_2018.jpg

p. 460 *Danton's Death,* Olivier Theatre, 2010 © Philip Carter.

p. 463 Simon Russell Beale, photograph by Ian Gavan via Getty Images.

p. 465 Aerial image of the dressing room courtyard at the National Theatre. Taken from Google Maps.

p. 466 *Much Ado About Nothing*, Olivier Theatre, 2007 © Philip Carter.

The Lehman Trilogy, Lyttelton Theatre, 2018 © Philip Carter.

p. 467 Dame Judi Dench, 2017 © Malcolm Park Editorial/ Alamy.

p. 469 Patricia Hodge and Judi Dench in rehearsals for *A Little Night Music*, National Theatre, 1995 © Sasha Gusov/ ArenaPAL

p. 470 Dame Judi Dench performing *A Little Night Music* as part of the *50 Years On Stage* gala, 2013 © Catherine Ashmore.

p. 472 The Scene/Change *Missing Live Theatre* installation at the National Theatre, 2020. Photography by Seamus Ryan.

p. 473 The #scenechange *Missing Live Theatre* installation at the National Theatre, 2020. Photography by Seamus Ryan.

Part Seven

p. 478 – 479 *Masks of the Commedia dell'Arte: Capitan Spezza Monti and Bagattino* © Photograph Scala, Florence.

p. 483 *Masks of the Commedia dell'Arte: Franca Trippa and Frittellino* © Photograph Scala, Florence.

Composite image showing the Olivier Theatre with side audience boxes, from the author's archive.

Appendices

p. 484-485 Exterior of the National Theatre in 2007 © Al Richardson.

p. 489 A memorial to Richard Pilbrow at the National Theatre, 8 December 2023 © Matt Drury.

Richard Pilbrow on Waterloo Bridge overlooking the National Theatre while it is under construction, 1974. Evening Standard/Hulton Archive via Getty Images.

p. 490 Drawing of the National Theatre as in 1976, courtesy of Haworth Tompkins.

Drawing of the National Theatre as in 1976, courtesy of Stanton Williams.

p. 491 Drawing of the National Theatre as in 1997, courtesy of Haworth Tompkins.

Drawing of the National Theatre as in 1997, courtesy of Stanton Williams.

p. 492 Front elevation of the National Theatre as in 2018, courtesy of Haworth Tompkins.

Rear elevation of the National Theatre as in 2016, courtesy of Haworth Tompkins.

p. 493 Side elevation from the east (Tate Modern side) as in 2016, courtesy of Haworth Tompkins.

Side elevation from the west (Waterloo Bridge side) as in 2016, courtesy of Haworth Tompkins.

p. 494 Contemporary drawings of the Cottesloe/Dorfman Theatre: plan and section, drawings by Pilbrow & Partners.

Contemporary drawings of the Lyttelton Theatre: plan and section, drawings by Pilbrow & Partners.

p. 495 Contemporary drawings of the Olivier Theatre: plan and section, drawings by Pilbrow & Partners.

3D diagram of the National Theatre, 1976, by Roy Castle.

National Theatre with theatre locations overlaid, courtesy of Haworth Tompkins.

Contemporary drawings of variations in the Olivier Theatre stage front edge since 1976, drawings by Pilbrow & Partners.

p. 496 Contemporary drawings of the six schemes (A v1, Av2, B-E) during the development of what became the Olivier Theatre at the National Theatre, drawings by Pilbrow & Partners.

p. 497 Load-in and set for *The Life of Galileo*, Olivier Theatre, 1980 © Catherine Ashmore.

The Shaughraun, Olivier Theatre, 1988 © Philip Carter.

Racing Demon, Olivier Theatre, 1990 © Philip Carter.

Square Rounds, Olivier Theatre, 1993 © Philip Carter.

Women of Troy, Olivier Theatre, 1995 © Philip Carter.

Olivier Theatre in the Round, 1997 © Philip Carter.

Olivier Theatre with temporary revolve, 2002 © Philip Carter.

Emperor and Galilean, Olivier Theatre, 2011 © Philip Carter.

The Witches fit-up, National Theatre, 2023.

p. 528 Rob Halliday, courtesy of the subject.

Fred Pilbrow, courtesy of the subject.

p. 529 Richard Pilbrow, on the River Thames opposite the National Theatre, 2010. Photograph by Robert Bell.

Back Cover

Olivier Theatre drum revolve under construction showing Richard Brett (on the lowered elevator), David Collison and Richard Pilbrow (on top disk) © Philip Sayer.

Richard Pilbrow on Waterloo Bridge overlooking the National Theatre while it is under construction, 1974. *Evening Standard*/Hulton Archive via Getty Images.

Other Books By The Same Author

Stage Lighting Design: The Art, The Craft, The Life
(London: Nick Hern Books)
nickhernbooks.co.uk/stage-lighting-design

A Theatre Project
(New York: PLASA Media, Inc)
atheatreproject.com

Stage Lighting
(London: Cassell), out of print

Walt Disney Concert Hall: The Backstage Story (with Patricia MacKay)
(Cambridge: Entertainment Technology Press Ltd)
etbooks.co.uk

The National Theatre: A Place for Plays (editor)
(Cambridge: Entertainment Technology Press Ltd)
etbooks.co.uk

Author Website:
richardpilbrow.com

Endnotes

These Endnotes are also available online at www.asenseoftheatre.com. Richard passed away before these endnotes were finalised. A few sources that he held only in his memory are therefore currently unknown. These are identified as 'Unconfirmed source.' As they are identified they will be added to the online Endnotes.

Part One
1.1 - The Quest for a National Theatre

1. Granville Barker adopted the hyphenated form Granville- Barker after his second marriage and retirement from active production, to become an author of such works as *Prefaces to Shakespeare*.
2. William Archer and Granville Barker, *Scheme and Estimates for a National Theatre* (London: Duckworth, 1904), title page.
3. Dennis Kennedy, *Granville Barker and the Dream of Theatre* (Cambridge: Cambridge University Press, 1985), p.2.
4. Archer and Barker, p.36-37.
5. Kennedy, p.192.
6. Archer and Barker, p.xxi.
7. Ibid, p.xviii.
8. Winston Churchill, quoted in Geoffrey Whitworth, *The Making of a National Theatre* (London: Faber, 1951), p.57.
9. John Elsom & Nicholas Tomalin, *The History of the National Theatre* (London: Jonathan Cape, 1978) p.41.
10. Whitworth, p.71.
11. Ibid, p.73.
12. Ibid, p.86.
13. Ibid, p.83.
14. Ibid, p.96-98.
15. Terry Coleman, *The Old Vic: The Story of a Great Theatre from Kean to Olivier to Spacey* (London: Faber, 2014), p.64.
16. *The Unknown Granville Barker: Letters to Helen and Other Texts, 1915-1918*, ed. Simon Shepherd. (London: Society for Theatre Research, 2021).
17. Whitworth, p.148.
18. Whitworth, p.149.
19. Kennedy, p.200.
20. Ibid, p.200.
21. Ibid, p.201.
22. Ibid, p.201.
23. Letter from Granville Barker to Viscount Esher, 24 February 1943, in C.B. Purdom, *Harley Granville Barker – Man of the Theatre, Dramatist and Scholar* (Cambridge, MA: Harvard University Press, 1956), p.269.
24. Sir Edwin Lutyens in *News Chronicle* 31 October 1938, in Daniel Rosenthal, *The National Theatre Story* (London: Oberon Books, 2013), p.26.
25. Whitworth, p. 210.
26. Michael Billington, *The State of the National: British Theatre since 1945* (London: Faber & Faber, 2007), p.9.
27. Minutes of the Executive Committee, papers of the Shakespeare Memorial National Theatre, 21 November 1945. National Theatre Archive, closed file.
28. Minutes of the 1st Meeting of the Joint Council of the SMNT & Old Vic, 13 February 1946, papers of the Shakespeare Memorial National Theatre. National Theatre Archive, SMNT/1/6/8.
29. Irving Wardle, *The Theatres of George Devine* (London: Faber & Faber, 1978/2010), p. 96.
30. Ibid, p. 97.
31. John Miller, *Ralph Richardson: The Authorised Biography* (London: Pan Books, 1996), p.123-4.
32. Wardle, p.107.
33. Peter Lewis, *The National; A Dream Made Concrete* (London: Methuen, 1990), p.11.
34. Wardle, p.136.
35. Wardle, p.136.
36. Wardle, p.136-8.
37. Whitworth, p.232.
38. Purdom, p.279.
39. Purdom, p.269-270.
40. Whitworth, p.238.
41. Rosenthal, p.31.
42. Unconfirmed source, possibly SMNT/6/3/11.
43. Letter from Cecil Masey to Kenneth Rae, 13 November 1948, papers of the Shakespeare Memorial National Theatre, National Theatre Archive, SMNT/6/3/2.
44. Minutes of the 27th Meeting of the National Theatre Building Committee, 14 April 1950, papers of the Shakespeare Memorial National Theatre. National Theatre Archive, SMNT/1/6/11.
45. Minutes of the 36th Meeting of the National Theatre Building Committee, 27 July 1954, papers of the Shakespeare Memorial National Theatre. National Theatre Archive, SMNT/1/6/11.
46. Minutes of the 35th Meeting of the National Theatre Building Committee, 22 April 1954, papers of the Shakespeare Memorial National Theatre. National Theatre Archive, SMNT/1/6/11.
47. Ibid.
48. Buckingham Palace to Lord Esher, 1 December, 1952. OV/SMNT/24/11/1952.
49. Minutes of the 37th Meeting of the National Theatre Building Committee, October 27 1954, papers of the Shakespeare Memorial National Theatre, National Theatre Archive, SMNT/1/6/11.
50. George Bernard Shaw, quoted in Rosenthal. p.37.
51. Minutes of the 17th Meeting of the Joint Council of the SMNT & Old Vic, 2 March 1951, papers of the Shakespeare Memorial National Theatre, National Theatre Archive, SMNT/1/6/8.
52. The same Frank Dunlop who, while at the School became assistant to the designers Motley and years later became the creator of the Young Vic Theatre.
53. Author's correspondence with Frank Dunlop, 2 February 2019, personal archive.
54. Wardle, p.140.
55. Ibid.
56. Letter from Lord Esher to Kenneth Rae, 20 September 1957. National Theatre Archive SMNT/2/2/2.
57. Philip Ziegler, *Olivier* (London: MacLehose Press, 2013), p.222.
58. John Barber for *The Daily Telegraph*, 7 December 1957, in Rosenthal, p.40.
59. Terry Coleman, *Olivier: The Authorised Biography* (New York: Henry Holt & Company, 2006), p.318.
60. Felix Barker in the *Evening News*, 10 March 1960, quoted in Rosenthal, p.42.
61. Letter from Laurence Olivier to his son, Tarquin, quoted in Rosenthal, p.44.
62. A personal note: This rent was exorbitant. The normal commercial rate was 20%, while at Her Majesty's for *Fiddler on the Roof* I paid Prince Littler 17.5% of the gross for its five-year run.
63. Peter Hall, in Richard Eyre, *Talking Theatre: Interviews with Theatre People* (London: Nick Hern Books, 2009), p.41-2.
64. Felix Barker in the *Evening News*, 10 March 1960, quoted in Rosenthal, p.42.
65. Rosenthal, p.53.
66. Rosenthal, p.46.
67. Minutes of the 32nd Meeting of the Joint Council of the SMNT and Old Vic, 21 March 1960, papers of the Shakespeare Memorial National Theatre. National Theatre Archive, SMNT/1/6/8.
68. Memorandum from Tyrone Guthrie, papers of the Shakespeare Memorial National Theatre, 9 May 1960. National Theatre Archive, SMNT/1/5/6/1.

1.2 - Playhouse Design and the 20th Century

69. 1st Meeting of the National Theatre Building Committee, January 3, 1963. National Theatre Archive, closed file.
70. Marian J. Pringle, *The Theatres of Stratford-on-Avon, 1875-1992: An Architectural History* (Stratford-upon-Avon: Stratford-upon-Avon Society. 1993), p.22.
71. Iain Mackintosh, *Architecture, Actor & Audience* (London: Routledge, 1993) p.102.
72. Pringle, p.22.
73. Ibid, p.28.
74. This theatre, based upon Wagnerian principles, was to also inspire the Birmingham Repertory Theatre (1912) and the Goodman Theatre in Chicago (1927).
75. A story surely repeated at the world-famous Sydney Opera House.
76. Pringle, p.42.
77. Mackintosh, p.104.
78. Ruth Ellis, *The Shakespeare Memorial Theatre* (London: Winchester Publications,1948).
79. Pringle, p.44.
80. Ibid, p.50.
81. Peter Hall quotes on Chicago Shakespeare Theater website. https://www.chicagoshakes.com/your_visit/theater. Accessed 13 Feb 2019.
82. Adrian Noble, conversation with the author, summer 1991.
83. John Russell Brown, *The Oxford Illustrated History of Theatre* (Oxford: Oxford University Press, 1995), p.173.
84. Richard Flecknoe, *A Short Discourse of the English Stage*, 1664, quoted in Joseph Quincy Adams, *Shakespearean Playhouses: A History of English Theatres from the Beginnings to the Restoration*, 1917.
85. Joseph Quincy Adams, *Shakespearean Playhouses: A History of English Theatres from the Beginnings to the Restoration*, Kindle Edition. Accessed 1 February 2019
86. The shape of the stage in the Elizabethan theatre is the subject of controversy. The remains of the Rose Theatre clearly show a trapezoidal thrust stage rather than the square or rectangular one of tradition. Speculation continues as to whether the thrust stages of the Globe and others might not have been such a shape. Discovery

and excavation of The Curtain in 2016 has thrown another surprise into the discussion.
The Curtain stage appears to have been a rectangle 14 metres wide and only 5 metres deep, much wider than had been previously considered.

87 John Stockwood, Sermon Preached at Paule's Cross, 24 August 1578.
88 Thomas Middleton, *The Roaring Girl*, 1611.
89 The drawings were identified by Iain Mackintosh in the September 1973 issue of *Tabs*, this view endorsed by Professor John Orrell in *Shakespeare Survey*, 1977 and *The Theatres of Inigo Jones and John Webb*, (Cambridge: Cambridge University Press, 1985.
90 Sam Wanamaker (1919-1993) was an American actor who moved to England in 1952. Having run the Liverpool New Shakespeare Theatre (demolished in 1976 after a fire) and worked at Stratford-upon-Avon he formed the Shakespeare Globe Trust in 1970 to recreate the Globe on Bankside as close as possible to the original site. Thanks to his tenacity the rigorously researched Globe opened in 1997, sadly three and a half years after his death. Doubters who thought it a theatrical theme park were proved very wrong by the success of Mark Rylance's opening seasons.
91 The re-imagined Globe on Bankside had been more than twenty-five years in the making when it opened in 1997. Mackintosh and Orrell had persuaded Sam Wanamaker and his architect Theo Crosby to include alongside it an empty shell intended for a rebuilt Phoenix Theatre, modified only to meet present-day safety regulations. Wanamaker died in December 1993, Crosby in September 1994; the Globe opened in 1997 with Mark Rylance
as artistic director and Crosby's assistant Jon Greenfield as executive architect. Dominic Dromgoole had succeeded Rylance in 2005 when the Globe was persuaded by Gordon Higgott and others that the drawings were not of the Phoenix and were much later and so needed further modifications to make the connection with Shakespeare. The resulting Wanamaker Playhouse opened in 2014.
92 Prescot was instigated by Matthew Jordan and Elspeth Graham of Liverpool's John Moores University. The team included two veterans of the Globe, architect Jon Greenfield and master carpenter Peter McCurdy who built both the Globe and the Wanamaker, along with Nicholas Helm. A re-creation of a frons scenae derived from that shown in the Cockpit-in-Court drawings was created for Shakespeare North and installed for a season in 2023.
93 *History of the Theater*, edited by Oscar G Brockett (Boston: Allyn and Bacon, 1968), p.271.
94 Richard Southern, *The Seven Ages of Theater* (New York: Hill & Wang, 1961), p.239.
95 Diary of Samuel Pepys, 8 May 1663, https://www.pepysdiary.com/diary/1663/05/08.
96 Colley Cibber, *An Apology for the Life of Colley Cibber: With An Historical View of the Stage in His Own Time*, ed. B.R.S. Fone (New York: Dover Publications, 1756, 1967/2000), p139.
97 Ibid, p. 301.
98 Iain Mackintosh, p.16-18. All five paintings are illustrated in *Hogarth, France and British Art* by Robin Simon, 2007.
99 Arthur Murphy, *The Life of David Garrick* (Dublin, 1801), p.381.
100 Count Francesco Algarotti, *Essay on the Opera*, 1755.
101 Mackintosh, p.36.
102 George Saunders, *A Treatise on Theatre*, 1790.
103 Richard Cumberland, *Memoirs, Volume II* (London, 1807), p.384.
104 *The Torrington Diaries*.
105 Benjamin Dean Wyatt, *Observations on the Design of the Theatre Royal Drury Lane*, 1813.
106 Mackintosh, p.42.
107 My own Methodist grandfather reportedly never set foot in a theatre … "dens of the devil."
108 Mackintosh, p.43.
109 Edward Gordon Craig, *On the Art of the Theatre*, (London: Heinemann, 1911/1957), fifth edition, p.138.
110 Mackintosh, p.45.
111 Hiram Kelly Moderwell, *The Theatre of Today* (London: John Lane, 1914), https://Archive.org/details/cu31924027208416
112 Architect: Renton Howard Wood Associates. Theatre Design: Tanya Moiseiwitsch. Theatre Equipment: Theatre Projects Consultants.
113 This moat was often filled in in later years to extend the stage.
114 Alistair Fair, *Modern Playhouses: An Architectural History of Britain's New Theatres, 1945–1985*, (Oxford: Oxford University Press, 2018).

1.3 - A Company of Players

115 Richard Olivier and Joan Plowright, *Olivier at Work: The National Years* (London: Nick Hern Books & National Theatre, 1989), p.18.
116 Michael Billington, *The National Theatre at 50: Michael Billington's view from the stalls*, in *The Guardian*, 18 October 2013.
117 Source unconfirmed.
118 Philip Ziegler, *Olivier* (London: MacLehose Press, 2013), p.275.
119 Simon Callow, *The National: The Theatre and its Work* (London: Nick Hern Books & National Theatre, 1997), p.16.
120 Ibid, p.6.
121 Olivier & Plowright, p14.
122 Ibid, p.11.
123 Ibid, p.18.
124 Ibid, p.19.
125 Ibid, p.24.
126 Ibid, p.54.
127 Ibid, p.56.
128 Ibid, p.58.
129 Ibid, p.58.
130 Ibid, p58.
131 Ibid, p.71.
132 Ibid, p.81.
133 *The Guardian* "To the Old Vic, A son," issue unconfirmed.
134 Frank Dunlop, 16 December 2016, interview with the author.
135 Frank Dunlop letter to Denys Lasdun. 21 May 1968. Lasdun Archive, RIBA Collections, LaD/165/2.
136 Notes on a Teleconference with Frank Dunlop, May 23, 1968. Lasdun Archive, RIBA Collections, LaD/165/2.
137 Callow, p.34.
138 Billington, *The National Theatre at 50*.
139 Callow.

Part Two
2.1 - Beginnings. Finding an Architect: Meetings #1-14

1 South Bank Theatre and Opera House Board, Terms of Reference, 13 August 1962, papers of the South Bank Theatre Board. National Theatre Archive, closed files.
2 Philip Ziegler, *Olivier* (London: MacLehose Press, 2013), p.251.
3 John Elsom and Nicholas Tomalin, *The History of the National Theatre* (London: Jonathan Cape, 1978), p.168.
4 Minutes of the 27th Meeting of the National Theatre Building Committee, 15 April 1950. National Theatre Archive, SMNT/1/6/11.
5 Minutes of the 27th Meeting of the National Theatre Building Committee, 14 April 1950. National Theatre Archive, SMNT/1/6/11.
6 Terry Coleman, *Olivier: The Authorised Biography* (New York: Henry Holt & Company, 2006), p.341.
7 Ziegler, p.292.
8 Unconfirmed source.
9 Ziegler, p.293.
10 Laurence Olivier letter to Peter Brook, 6 August 1962, Olivier Archive, British Library, Add MS 80367.
11 Denys Lasdun, *Architecture in an Age of Scepticism* (London: Heinemann, 1984), p.137.
12 Note that this offered the committee just six weeks to complete the Brief for the NT. Surely a ludicrous proposition!
13 Royal Institute of British Architects.
14 South Bank Theatre Board.
15 London Academy of Music and Dramatic Art.
16 Basic Requirements Document, 25 October 1963, Lasdun Archive, RIBA Collections, LaD/157/1: "A main or large theatre, seating about 1000, and adaptable so as to offer two features:
An amphitheatre with an apron or peninsular stage (not a theatre 'in the round'); and a proscenium arch or stage.
A small theatre, seating about 400, mainly for experimental purposes.
Opera House: A new opera house, seating about 1600, and comprising one auditorium only. Some form of adaptability would not be ruled out, account being taken of the traditional features, namely, stage, orchestra and audience." Hand written note: "Note by RA Lynex for use at interviews with Architects, 25.10.63"
17 Unconfirmed source.
18 The architect who had been responsible for the previous, most recent design on the South Bank.
19 Sir Hubert Bennett (1909-2000), head of the L.C.C.'s architects department 1956-1971, succeeding Leslie Martin.
20 Herbert Morrison (1888-1965), Labour politician, Cabinet minister and Labour Leader of the L.C.C. Prime mover of the Festival of Britain, 1951.
21 Minutes of the First Meeting of the Council of Management, South Bank Theatre and Opera House Board, 16 January 1963, South Bank Theatre Board papers. National Theatre Archive, closed file.
22 Letter from Sean Kenny to Laurence Olivier, 2 July 1964. Laurence Olivier

Archive, British Library. Add MS 80354
23. Table of Appointments for Interview, South Bank Theatre Board, 1963, National Theatre Archive, Box 40, closed file. With thanks to Barnabas Calder.
24. Table of Appointments for Interview, South Bank Theatre Board, 1963, as above.
25. Barnabas Calder, *Raw Concrete: The Beauty of Brutalism* (London: William Heinemann, 2016), p.49.
26. Robert Kirkman, interview with the author, April 2015.
27. DL&P memorandum, 1 October 1975, p.1. Note the sensitivity about Theatre Projects perhaps speaking out of turn!
28. Selection of architects, Evidence, 1963. South Bank Theatre Board, Box 13 Part 1. National Theatre Archive, closed file.
29. Barnabas Calder, *Committees and Concrete: The genesis and architecture of Denys Lasdun's National Theatre*, PhD Thesis, (University of Cambridge, 2007), p. 52-4.
30. Ibid, p.54.
31. Ibid, p.55.
32. Ibid, p.56.
33. Interview notoc, 24/25 October 1963, in South Bank Theatre Board, Box 13, part 1. National Theatre Archive, closed file.
34. Calder, 2007, p.58.
35. Ibid, p.61.
36. Ibid, p.58.
37. Calder, 2016, p.58.
38. Calder, 2007, p.60.
39. Richard Lynex to David McKenna and Lord Chandos, 29 October 1963, South Bank Theatre Board, Box 13, part 1. National Theatre Archive, closed file.
40. Laurence Olivier, *Confessions of an Actor* (London: Hodder and Stoughton, 1983), p.202.
41. Handwritten notes by Lasdun, 22 November 1963, Lasdun Archive, RIBA Collections, LaD/157/1.

2.2 - Design Begins: Meetings #16-21

42. Calder, 2007, p.60.
43. Denys Lasdun meeting with Kenneth Tynan, 28 January 1964, Lasdun Archive, RIBA Collections, LaD/166/1.
44. Denys Lasdun meeting with Michael Elliott, 11 February 1963, Lasdun Archive, RIBA Collections, LaD/164/4.
45. Denys Lasdun meeting with George Devine, 25 February 1963, Lasdun Archive, RIBA Collections, LaD/164/4.
46. Letter from George Devine to Sir Laurence Olivier, 28 February 1964, Laurence Olivier Archive, British Library Manuscripts, Add MS 80354.
47. Denys Lasdun meeting with George Devine, 23 March 1963, Lasdun Archive, RIBA Collections, LaD/164/2.
48. Denys Lasdun memorandum on meeting of the National Theatre Building Committee, 4 March 1964, Lasdun Archive, RIBA Collections. LaD/164/2.
49. Denys Lasdun notes on meeting with Peter Brook, 21 April 1964, Lasdun Archive, RIBA Collections, LaD/164/4.
50. Denys Lasdun notes on meeting with George Devine, 25 March 1964, Lasdun Archive, RIBA Collections, LaD/164/4.
51. Denys Lasdun notes on meeting with John Bury, 27 April 1964, Lasdun Archive, RIBA Collections, LaD/164/4.
52. Denys Lasdun notes on meeting with Peter Hall, 29 April 1964, Lasdun Archive, RIBA Collections, LaD/164/4.
53. Denys Lasdun notes on meeting with Peter Hall, 30 April 1964, Lasdun Archive, RIBA Collections, LaD/164/4.
54. Denys Lasdun memorandum on meeting with Peter Brook, 25 March 1964, Lasdun Archive, RIBA Collections, LaD/170/6.
55. Denys Lasdun memorandum, 4 May 1964, Lasdun Archive, RIBA Collections, LaD/166/3.
56. National Theatre Building Committee Minutes, 6 May 1964. National Theatre Archive, closed file.
57. Extract from the Minutes of the National Theatre Board Meeting, 11 May 1964, Lasdun Archive, RIBA Collections, LaD/166/6.
58. Denys Lasdun memorandum on meeting with Michel Saint-Denis and Kenneth Tynan, 12 May 1964, Lasdun Archive, RIBA Collections, LaD/164/4.
59. Lasdun memorandum on meeting with Norman Marshall, April 29 1964, Lasdun Archive, RIBA Collections, LaD/166/3.
60. South Bank Theatre Board minutes, 21 April 1965, National Theatre Archive, closed file.
61. Unconfirmed source.
62. Denys Lasdun memorandum, 22 February 1965, Lasdun Archive, RIBA Collections, LaD/164/4.
63. South Bank Theatre Board Minute 116, 21 February 1965. National Theatre Archive, closed file.
64. South Bank Theatre and Opera House Board Minute 125F, 4 May 1965, Lasdun Archive, RIBA Collections, LaD/159/3.
65. Notes on the architectural proposals, 26 May 1965, Lasdun Archive, RIBA Collections, LaD/190/1.
66. Letter from Lord Olivier to Denys Lasdun, 23 May 1965, Lasdun Archive, RIBA Collections, LaD/190/1.
67. Letter from the Treasury to the Greater London Council, 25 May 1965, South Bank Theatre and Opera House documents, National Archives, ED/221/34.
68. Denys Lasdun memorandum on meeting with Jennie Lee, 15 June 1965, Lasdun Archive, RIBA Collections, LaD/164/2.
69. South Bank Theatre Board Minutes, 20 October 1965, National Theatre Archive, closed file.
70. Coleman, 2006, p.371.
71. South Bank Theatre Board Minutes, 9 February 1966, National Theatre Archive, closed file.
72. Unconfirmed source.

2.3 - Blood Dripping from Concrete Walls: Meetings #24-29

73. South Bank Theatre and Opera House Board press handout. 9 March 1966. National Theatre Archive, closed file.
74. Josef Svoboda (1920-2002). Josef was an outstanding Czech scenographer, principal designer at the Czech National Theatre for over 30 years and famed internationally for his astonishing multimedia, lighting and technological innovations. Your author was honoured to light two productions for Josef at the The Old Vic: Ostrovsky's *The Storm*, directed by John Dexter and Chekhov's *Three Sisters*, directed by Sir Laurence.
75. Denys Lasdun memorandum of meeting with Sir Laurence Olivier, 26 April 1966, Lasdun Archive, RIBA Collections, LaD/171/2.
76. Kenneth Tynan letter to Sir Laurence Olivier, 4 May 1966, Laurence Olivier Archive, British Library, Add MS 80354.
77. Denys Lasdun memorandum of meeting, 5 May 1966, Lasdun Archive, RIBA Collections, LaD/171/2.
78. Denys Lasdun memorandum of meeting with Jocelyn Herbert, 18 May 1966, Lasdun Archive, RIBA Collections, LaD/171/2.
79. National Theatre Building Sub-Committee minutes, 3 June 1966, National Theatre Archive, closed file.
80. Denys Lasdun interviewed by Peter Hall, *Aquarius*, ITV, 29 February 1976.
81. National Theatre Building Sub-Committee minutes, 3 June 1966, National Theatre Archive, closed file.
82. Letter from Michel Saint-Denis to Sir Laurence Olivier, June 6 1966, Laurence Olivier Archive, British Library, Add MS 80354.
83. Unconfirmed source.
84. Denys Lasdun memorandum, 16 & 23 June 1966, Lasdun Archive, RIBA Collections, LaD/171/2.
85. Denys Lasdun memorandum of Building Sub-Committee meeting, 22 June 1966, Lasdun Archive, RIBA Collections, LaD/171/2.
86. Unconfirmed source.
87. Unconfirmed source.
88. Unconfirmed source.
89. Denys Lasdun memorandum on meeting with Peter Brook, 14 July 1966, Lasdun Archive, RIBA Collections, LaD/164/4.
90. Notes by Peter Brook for Sir Laurence Olivier, 1 August 1966, Peter Brook Archive, V&A Theatre and Performance Collections, GB 71 THM/452/3/119.
91. Letter from Sir Laurence Olivier to Peter Brook, 8 August 1966, Laurence Olivier Archive, British Library, Add MS 80367.
92. Denys Lasdun memorandum, 9 August 1966, Lasdun Archive, RIBA Collections, LaD/165/1.
93. South Bank Board Meeting minutes, 10 August 1966. National Theatre Archive, closed file.
94. Kenneth Rae's reports to Sir Laurence Olivier, 18 August 1966, Laurence Olivier Archive, British Library, Add MS 80354.
95. Letter from Peter Hall to Sir Laurence Olivier, 18 August 1966, Laurence Olivier Archive, British Library, Add MS 80354.
96. Coleman, 2005, p. 372.
97. Denys Lasdun memorandum, 16 September 1966, Lasdun Archive, RIBA Collections, LaD/171/2.]
98. Denys Lasdun memorandum on National Theatre Building Committee meeting, 19 August 1966, Lasdun Archive, RIBA Collections, LAD/171/2.
99. Denys Lasdun memorandum on Meeting on Scheme E, 21 September 1966, Lasdun Archive, RIBA Collections, LaD/171/2.
100. Denys Lasdun memorandum, 22 September 1966, Lasdun Archive, RIBA Collections, LaD/166/5.
101. Richard Pilbrow, *A Theatre Project* (New York: Plasa Media, 2011) p.133.
102. Barnabas Calder,

Committee and Concrete: The genesis and architecture of Denys Lasdun's National Theatre, University of Cambridge, unpublished thesis, 2007.
103. Denys Lasdun memorandum, 22 September 1966, Lasdun Archive, RIBA Collections, LaD/166/5.
104. The group name of three award-winning women English theatre designers, Margaret 'Percy' Harris (1904-2000), Sophie Harris (1900-1966) and Elizabeth Montgomery (1902-1993), who came to fame as John Gielgud's designers in the 1930s. They went on to distinguished careers at the Royal Shakespeare Theatre, the Old Vic, the West End and on Broadway.
105. Calder, p.113.
106. Letter from Jocelyn Herbert to Lord Olivier, 22 September 1966, Olivier Archives, British Library, Add MS BT80354.
107. Denys Lasdun memorandum on meeting with Bill Gaskill, 27 September 1966, Lasdun Archive, RIBA Collections, LAD/171/2.
108. Denys Lasdun memorandum on meeting, 29 September 1966, Lasdun Archive, RIBA Collections, LaD/171/2.
109. Denys Lasdun memorandum on meeting with Michael Elliott, 30 September 1966, Lasdun Archive, RIBA Collections, LaD/171/2.
110. Denys Lasdun memorandum on meeting with Peter Brook, 3 October 1966, Lasdun Archive, RIBA Collections, LaD/171/2.
111. Denys Lasdun memorandum on meeting with Peter Hall and Stephen Arlen, 4 October 1966, Lasdun Archive, RIBA Collections, LaD/171/2.
112. Denys Lasdun memorandum on National Theatre, 23 September 1966, Lasdun Archive, RIBA Collections, LaD/157/1.
113. Letter from Sir Laurence Olivier to Denys Lasdun, 26 September 1966.
114. Denys Lasdun memorandum on conversation with Lord Cottesloe, 27 September 1966, Lasdun Archive, RIBA Collections, LaD/157/2.
115. Denys Lasdun memorandum on conversation with Lord Cottesloe, 27 September 1966, Lasdun Archive, RIBA Collections, LaD/157/2.
116. Unconfirmed source.
117. Letter from Laurence Olivier to Peter Brook, 6 October 1966, Laurence Olivier Archives, British Library, Add MS 80354.
118. The play *US* was a 1966 experimental theatre play about the Vietnam war directed by Peter Brook for the RSC.
119. Letter from Kenneth Tynan to Sir Laurence Olivier, 11 October 1966, Laurence Olivier Archive, British Library, Add MS 80354.
120. Letter from Sir Laurence Olivier to the Building Committee, 14 October 1966, Laurence Olivier Archive, British Library, Add MS 80354.
121. Eric Jordan, Head of the Greater London Council's Theatre Department.
122. DL&P Memorandum on meeting between Lord Olivier and Peter Softley, 18 October 1966, Lasdun Archive, RIBA Collections, LaD/171/2.
123. South Bank Board Minute 155.
124. South Bank Board Minute 159.
125. Coleman, 2006, p.371-72.
126. A copy of the second questionnaire can be found in the Laurence Olivier Archive, British Library, Add MS 80354.
127. Memorandum from Yolande Bird to Laurence Olivier, 29 November 1966, Laurence Olivier Archive, British Library, Add MS 80354
128. Letter from Sir Laurence Olivier to Lord Chandos, 3 January 1967, Laurence Olivier Archive, British Library, Add MS 80354.
129. Letter from Richard Pilbrow to Sir Laurence Olivier, 1 November 1966, Laurence Olivier Archive, British Library, Add MS 80354.
130. Memorandum on teleconference with Kenneth Rae, May 1967, Lasdun archive, RIBA Collections, LaD/169/3.
131. Memorandum on teleconference with Lord Cottesloe, 25 October 1967, Lasdun archive, RIBA Collections, LaD/157/2.
132. Rosenthal, p.138.
133. Letter from Kenneth Rae to Sir Laurence Olivier, 14 November 1967, Laurence Olivier Archive, British Library, Add MS 80355.
134. Letter from Kenneth Rae to Sir Laurence Olivier, 21 November 1967, Laurence Olivier Archive, British Library, Add MS 80355.
135. Letter from Norman Marshall to Sir Laurence Olivier, 20 December 1967, Laurence Olivier Archive, British Library, Add MS 80355.
136. Denys Lasdun memorandum on teleconference with Lord Chandos, 6 February 1969, Lasdun Archive, RIBA Collections, LaD/165/2.
137. Extract from Hansard, 1 February 1968, included in the South Bank Theatre Board minutes 14 February 1968, Lasdun Archive, RIBA Collections, LaD/160/1.
138. Letter from Kenneth Rae to Sir Laurence Olivier, 11 March 1968, Laurence Olivier Archive, British Library, Add MS 80355.
139. Letter from Sir Laurence Olivier to the Building Committee, 11 March 1968, Laurence Olivier Archive, British Library, MS Add 80355.
140. Letter from William Gaskill to Sir Laurence Olivier, 5 April 1968, Laurence Olivier Archive, British Library, Add MS 80355.
141. Letter from Kenneth Rae to Sir Laurence Olivier, December 31 1968, Laurence Olivier Archive, British Library, MS Add 80355.
142. This meeting is incorrectly identified as the 28th in the records. It was actually the 30th - and final - meeting.
143. A large collection of theatrical memorabilia now with the theatrical collection of Bristol University.

2.4 - Full Scenic Capability
144. Richard Brett in conversation with the author, 1986.
145. Letter from Sir Laurence Olivier to Denys Lasdun, 6 December 1966, Laurence Olivier Archive, British Library, Add MS 80354.
146. Letter from Denys Lasdun to Sir Laurence Olivier, 21 December 1966, Laurence Olivier Archive, British Library, Add MS 80355.
147. Richard Pilbrow, extracts from *A Theatre Project* (New York: PLASA Media, 2011) p.133.

Part Three
3.1 - Peter Hall Takes Charge
1. Michael Billington, *The National Theatre at 50* in *The Guardian*, 18 October 2013.
2. South Bank Theatre Board Minutes, 9 August 1972. National Theatre Archive, closed file.
3. Letter from Anthony Easterbrook to Sir Laurence Olivier, 20 September 1972, Olivier Archives, British Library, Add MS 80355. Iain Mackintosh says he was always told 200 seats!
4. Lord Cottesloe's Topping Out Ceremony remarks, 2 May 1973, Lasdun Archive, RIBA Collections, LaD/161/1.
5. Statement from Peter Hall to the South Bank Theatre Board, 8 November 1973, National Theatre Archive, ED 245/28.
6. *Gomes* was by David Swift and Sidney Sheldon. It starred Rachel Kempson and Roy Dotrice and ran for a grand total of six performances!
7. Ginger Group Meeting, 19 November 1973, Laurence Olivier Archive, British Library, Add MS 80355.
8. Ginger Group Meeting, 3 April 1974, Laurence Olivier Archive, British Library, MS Add 80355.
9. Ginger Group Meeting, 11 June 1974, Laurence Olivier Archive, British Library, MS Add 80355.
10. Unconfirmed source.
11. Ginger Group Meeting, 16 July 1974, Laurence Olivier Archive, British Library, MS Add 80355.
12. Letter from Hugh Jenkins to Lord Cottesloe, 1 August 1974, South Bank Theatre Board. National Theatre Archive, closed file.
13. Unconfirmed source.
14. Ginger Group Meeting, 5 September 1974, Laurence Olivier Archive, British Library, Add MS 80355.
15. Letter from Linklaters and Paines to Peter Hall, 28 October 1974, Lasdun Archive, RIBA Collections, LaD/169/5.
16. Letter from Peter Hall to Linklater and Paines, 31 October 1974, Lasdun Archive, RIBA Collections, LaD/169/5.
17. Internal Memorandum from Simon Relph to Peter Hall and Peter Stevens, 6 November 1974, Lasdun Archive, RIBA Collections, LaD/169/5.
18. National Theatre Act 1949.
19. Ginger Group Meeting, 28 January 1975, Laurence Olivier Archive, British Library, Add MS 80355.
20. Denys Lasdun memorandum on 'McAlpine Lunch', 13 February 1975, Lasdun Archive, RIBA Collections, LaD/165/5.
21. Letter from Denys Lasdun to the author, 11 April 1975, Lasdun Archive, RIBA Collections, LaD/197/5.
22. Letter from Francis Reid to the author, 19 April 1975, Lasdun Archive, RIBA Collections, LaD/197/5.
23. Report by P.F. Jeffery, National Building's Agency, 4 September 1975, South Bank Theatre Board, closed file.
24. Peter Hall, ed. John Goodman, *Peter Hall's Diaries* (London: Hamish Hamilton, 1983) p.251.
25. Letter from Sir Laurence Olivier to Denys Lasdun, February 16 1972, Lasdun Archive, RIBA Collections, LaD/196/4.

3.2 - Her Majesty: "Is The Theatre Ready, Mr. Pilbrow?"
26. Peter Lewis, *The National, A Dream Made Concrete* (London: Methuen, 1990) p.118. And excluding his later 'virtual' performance

in the musical *Time*!
27 Email from Gawn Grainger to author, February 2018. Author's personal archive.
28 Tynan, *The Diaries of Kenneth Tynan*, edited by John Lahr. Bloomsbury, London & New York. 2001.
29 Ibid. p.126.
30 Ibid. p.190.
31 Ibid. p.224.
32 Ibid. p.267.
33 Ibid. p.343-344.
34 Ibid. p.384.
35 Unconfirmed source.
36 Maggie Riley to Sir Laurence Olivier, undated, British Library NT31/4 (7)
37 Victor Glasstone is an architect who has made theatre a life-long study. He is the author of *Victorian and Edwardian Theatres* (London: Thames and Hudson, 1973).
This extract is from the *Architect's Journal*, 12 January 1977 issue (Volume 165, number2).
38 Victor Glasstone, *Theatre Architecture in Britain*, RIBA Journal 50, 1968, p.505.
39 Ibid, p.405-406.
40 Bernard Levin, 13 July 1976, *The Times*.

Part Four
4.1 – Peter Hall
1 Letter from Peter Stevens to Mark Harrison, April 26 1977, Lasdun Archive, RIBA Collections, LaD/170/1.
2 South Bank Theatre Board Minutes, 4 May 1977, Lasdun Archive, RIBA Collections, LaD/162/2.
3 Letter from Mrs. A. Karet to the Managing Director of the National Theatre, 14 July 1977, Lasdun Archive, RIBA Collections, LaD/170/1.
4 Lasdun memorandum of teleconference with Peter Hall, 18 November 1977, Lasdun Archive, RIBA Collections, LaD/172/2.
5 Letter from Peter Hall to Denys Lasdun, 16 October 1978, Lasdun Archive, RIBA Collections, LaD/170/2.
6 Letter from Peter Hall to Denys Lasdun, February 18 1979, author's personal archives.
7 Respectively, Music Director and (at the time) Director of Productions at the Metropolitan Opera House, New York.
8 Union: National Association of Theatrical, Television and Kine Employees; became BECTU in 1985.
9 Letter from Harry Pugh to Michael Elliott, National Theatre Executive Director [distinct from the director Michael Elliott], 17 July 1980, Lasdun Archive, RIBA Collections, LaD/181/1.
10 Denys Lasdun notes on meeting with Jocelyn Herbert and Hayden Griffin, 22 February 1980, Lasdun Archive, RIBA Collections, LaD/181/4.
11 Letter from Denys Lasdun to Max Rayne, 1 June 1981, Lasdun Archive, RIBA Collections, LaD/180/4.
12 Letter from Denys Lasdun to Peter Hall, 23 October 1981, Lasdun Archive, RIBA Collections, LaD/170/2.
13 Letter from Denys Lasdun to Lord Rayne, 28 May 1982, Lasdun Archive, RIBA Collections, LaD/181/1.
14 Denys Ladun notes on teleconference, 20 October 1982, Lasdun Archive, RIBA Collections, LaD/181/1.
15 Letter from Denys Lasdun to Peter Hall, 22 October 1982, Lasdun Archive, RIBA Collections, LaD/181/1.
16 A British construction company.
17 Letter from Denys Lasdun to Peter Hall, 29 November 1982, Lasdun Archive, RIBA Collections, LaD/181/1.
18 Memorandum on meeting between Denys Lasdun and Jocelyn Herbert, 2 February 1983, Lasdun Archive, RIBA Collections, LaD/181/1.
19 Letter from Denys Lasdun to Max Rayne. 24 February 1983, Lasdun Archive, RIBA Collections, LAD/187/4.
20 Letter from Denys Lasdun to Peter Hall, 12 July 1983, Lasdun Archive, RIBA Collections, LaD/181/1.
21 Letter from Max Rayne to Lasdun, 12 August 1985. Lasdun Archive, RIBA Collections, LaD/187/4.
22 Letter from Denys Lasdun to Max Rayne, August 15 1985, Lasdun Archive, RIBA Collections, LaD/184/3.
23 Extracts from David Hare, *The Blue Touch Paper: A Memoir* (London: Faber & Faber, 2015).
24 Michael Blakemore. *Stage Blood: Five Tempestuous Years in the Early Life of the National Theatre* (London: Faber & Faber, 2013), p. 178-179.
25 I am grateful to Sir Alan for his permission to use this article about his NT adventures in the 1980s.
26 Alan Ayckbourn, *National Service* in the *Sunday Telegraph*, 21 February 1988.
27 Extracts from Simon Callow, *The National: The Theatre and its Work* (London: Nick Hern Books & National Theatre, 1997).

4.2 – Richard Eyre
28 Michael Billington, *The National Theatre at 50* in *The Guardian*, 18 October 2013.
29 Richard Eyre, *National Service: Diary of a Decade at the National Theatre* (London: Bloomsbury, 2003).
30 Teleconference Denys Lasdun and Richard Eyre, 23 May 1988, 19.30 hours. Lasdun Archive, RIBA Collections, LAD/187/4.
31 Letter from Richard Eyre to Denys Lasdun, 14 June 1988, Lasdun Archive, RIBA Collections, LaD/185/6.
32 Letter from Denys Lasdun to Lord Goodman, 4 July 1988, Lasdun Archive, RIBA Collections, LaD/185/8.
33 Memorandum from Paul Herbert to Lord Goodman, 17 August 1988, Lasdun Archive, RIBA Collections, LaD/185/8.
34 Letter from Richard Eyre to Max Rayne, 31 August 1988, Derek Mitchell Archive, National Theatre Archive, RNT/DM/21/31.
35 Letter from Gavin Stamp to Denys Lasdun, 24 October 1988, Lasdun Archive, RIBA Collections, LaD/183/1.
36 Letter from Serban Cantacuzino to Mr. S. Watts at Lambeth Bridge House, November 14 1988, Lasdun Archive, RIBA Collections, LaD/185/9.
37 Letter from Jocelyn Herbert to Denys Lasdun, 26 November 1988, Lasdun Archive, RIBA Collections, LaD/183/1.
38 Letter from Denys Lasdun to Jocelyn Herbert, 2 December 1988, Lasdun Archive, RIBA Collections, LaD/183/1.
39 Denys Lasdun memorandum, 6 February 1989, Lasdun Archive, RIBA Collections, LaD/185/4.
40 *Strategy for the Future*, April 1989, Lasdun Archive, RIBA Collections, LaD/183/ Loose Documents.
41 Letter from Mary Soames to Denys Lasdun, 5 December 1989, Lasdun Archive, RIBA Collections, LaD/184/2.
42 Letter from Stuart Lipton to Denys Lasdun, 30 March 1990, Lasdun Archive, RIBA Collections, LaD/183/2.
43 Letter from Denys Lasdun to Stuart Lipton, 20 April 1990, Lasdun Archive, RIBA Collections, LaD/183/2.
44 Letter from architects Stanton Williams to Denys Lasdun, 8 October 1990, Lasdun Archive, RIBA Collections, LaD/185/8.
45 Letter from Denys Lasdun to Mary Soames, 19 October 1993, Lasdun Archive, RIBA Collections, LaD/185/7.
46 Letter from Norman Lord St. John of Fawsley to Peter Brooke MP, 2 December 1993, Lasdun Archive, RIBA Collections, LaD/185/9.
47 Memorandum of meeting with the Royal Fine Art Commission, 17 February 1994, Lasdun Archive, RIBA Collections, LaD/185/9.
48 Letter from Lord St. John of Fawsley to Mary Soames, 2 March 1994, Lasdun Archive, RIBA Collections, LaD/185/9.
49 Minutes of the Royal National Theatre Building Development Committee, 10 May 1994, Derek Mitchell Archive, National Theatre Archive, RNT/DM/20/52.
50 Denys Lasdun notes on conversation with Richard Eyre, 20 June 1994, Lasdun Archive, RIBA Collections, LaD/185/6.
51 Introduction by Richard Eyre to *Proposed Plans for the Future Development of the Building*, prepared by Alan Stanton and Paul Williams of Stanton Williams, 23 June 1994, National Theatre Archive, RNT/PR/2/3/121.
52 Press release from the Department of National Heritage, 23 June 1994, National Theatre Archive, RNT/PR/2/3/121.
53 Letter to Denys Lasdun from Mary Soames, 31 January 1995, Lasdun Archive, RIBA Collections, LaD/185/7.
54 Letter from Richard Eyre to many, 2 February 1995, in Daniel Rosenthal, *Dramatic Exchanges: The Lives and Letters of the National Theatre* (London: Profile Books Limited, 2018), p.260.
55 Ibid, p.261
56 Letter from Denys Lasdun to George Perkin, former editor of *Concrete Quarterly*, 26 July 1995, Lasdun Archive, RIBA Collections, LaD/196/2.
57 Letter from Denys Lasdun to Christopher Hogg, 23 November 1995, Lasdun Archive, RIBA Collections LaD/186/9.
58 Letter from Christopher Hogg to Denys Lasdun, / February 1996, Lasdun Archive, RIBA Collections, LaD/186/8.
59 Letter from Denys Lasdun to Christopher Hogg, 14 May 1996, Lasdun Archive, RIBA Collections, LaD/183/3.
60 Letter from Denys Lasdun to Christopher Hogg, 18 October 1998, Lasdun Archive, RIBA Collections, LaD/189/1.
61 Letter from Denys Lasdun to Christopher Hogg, December 9 1996, Lasdun Archive, RIBA Collections, LaD/183/4.
62 Letter from Richard Eyre to Clinton Greyn of the Twentieth Century Society, 29 January 1997, Lasdun Archive, RIBA Collections, LaD/185/6.
63 Letter from Denys Lasdun to Richard Eyre, 28 May 1997, Lasdun Archive, RIBA Collections, LaD/185/6.
64 Bill Dudley, interview with the author.
65 Richard Eyre letter, 1994.

66 Unconfirmed source. National Theatre Mission Statement 2007-2008.
67 *Conservation Management Plan for the National Theatre*, Haworth Tompkins, Barnabas Calder, William Fawcett, 2008, p.61.

4.3 – Trevor Nunn
68 Michael Billington, *The National Theatre at 50* in *The Guardian*, 18 October 2013.
69 Trevor Nunn interviewed by Andrew Dickson, *The Guardian*, 18 October 2011.
70 Richard Cowell, Arup Acoustics, memo on acoustics, 27 October 1995, Christopher Hogg files (privately held).
71 Letter from David Hare to Christopher Hogg, 6 October 1995, Christopher Hogg files (privately held).
72 Trevor Nunn in *The Independent*, 1 November 2013.
73 Rosenthal, p.613.
74 Ibid, p.611.
75 Trevor Nunn, interview with Daniel Rosenthal.
76 Fax from David Hancock to Christopher Hogg, 3 August 2001, Christopher Hogg files (privately held).
77 National Theatre Board Minutes, 29 January 1999, National Theatre Archive, closed files.
78 National Theatre Board Minutes, 29 March 1999, National Theatre Archive, closed files.
79 Letter from Trevor Nunn to Christopher Hogg, 31 March 1999, Christopher Hogg files (privately held).
80 Trevor Nunn, *Daily Telegraph*, 31 March 1999.
81 John Caird, interview with Daniel Rosenthal.
82 Note by Christopher Hogg on meeting with Declan Donnellan, 6 September 2001, Christopher Hogg files (privately held).
83 Rosenthal, p.618.
84 Ibid, p.635.
85 Ibid, p. 647-648.
86 Ibid, p. 657.
87 National Theatre Board Minutes, 27 November 2000, National Theatre Archive, closed files.
88 Rosenthal, p.654.
89 Ibid, p. 659.
90 Transformation Season Press Release, March 2002, Royal National Theatre documents, National Theatre Archive, RNT/PR/2/4/182.
91 Rosenthal, p.685.
92 Transformation Season Press Release, March 2002, Royal National Theatre documents, National Theatre Archive, RNT/PR/2/4/182.
93 Unconfirmed source.
94 James Lasdun in *The Guardian*, 29 November 2003.

4.4 – Nicholas Hytner
95 Michael Billington, *The National Theatre at 50* in *The Guardian*, 18 October 2013.
96 Nicholas Hytner, *Balancing Acts: Behind the Scenes at the National Theatre* (London: Vintage, 2017), p.20.
97 Alistair Smith, *Nicholas Hytner: The Final Lap* in *The Stage*, 20 October 2013.
98 Hytner, *Balancing Acts*, p.38.
99 Ibid, p.249.
100 Ibid, p.207.
101 *Intelligent Life* magazine, May/June 2015, via www.jameskane.org/revamp-of-the-national-theatre.
102 Nicholas Hytner interviewed by Rachel Cooke in *The Observer*, 23 April 2017.
103 Hytner, *Balancing Acts*, p.34.
104 Ibid, p.34.
105 Ibid, p.34.
106 Ibid, p.34.

4.5 – Rufus Norris
107 Michael Billington, *The National Theatre at 50* in *The Guardian*, 18 October 2013.

Part Five
5.1 – Our Theatres Examined in a Changing World
1 Mark Rylance, Foreword from *London Theatres* by Michael Coveney (London: Frances Lincoln, 2017).

5.2 – The Shape of Theatre
2 Paul Arditti, letter to NT artistic director and associates regarding use of microphones and problems of background noise in theatre, October 2018.

5.4 – Designing Theatres
3 Stephen Joseph, *A Brains Trust*, in *Actor and Audience*, ed. Stephen Joseph (Manchester: Manchester University Press, 1964), p.103.
4 Charles Marowitz, Introduction to *Accommodating the Lively Arts: An Architect's View*, ed. Martin Bloom (Smith and Kraus, New Hampshire, 1997), p.ix.
5 Tom Morris in, *The Art of the Artistic Director: Conversations with Leading Practitioners* by Christopher Haydn (London: Methuen Drama, 2019).
6 Interviewed, along with a number of other designers, for the article *National Treasures* in *Light&Sound International* magazine, November 2017.
7 Ibid.
8 Lisa Marie Bowler, *Theatre Architecture as Embodied Space: A Phenomenology of Theatre Buildings in Performance*, dissertation, München, 2015.
9 Ibid. p.20.
10 Dominic Dromgoole. Artistic Director of Shakespeare's Globe Theatre, London, in conversation on 14 February 2013, p.2.
11 Bowler, p.3.
12 Ibid, p.34.
13 Ibid, p.39.
14 Ibid, p.44.
15 Ibid, p.45.
16 Rikard Küller, *Psycho-Physiological Conditions in Theatre Construction*, in *Theatre Space: 8. World Congress*, Munich, 18–25 September 1977, ed. James F. Arnott (Munich: Prestel, 1977), p175.
17 Ibid, p.92.
18 Ibid, p.164.
19 Ibid, p.194.

5.5 – Theatres for People
6 Peter Brook, interview January 1989.
7 Unconfirmed source.
8 *National Treasures*, covering four decades of technology at the National, in *Light&Sound International* magazine, November 2017. lsionline.com/magazine/digital.
3 Interviewed for *National Treasures* in *Light&Sound International* magazine, November 2017.
4 Interviewed for *Inventing The Future: The Story of the National Theatre's Lightboard*, a presentation at the 2016 PLASA Show in London, available via theatrecrafts.com.
5 Theatrecrafts.com is an invaluable resource for information about all of this lighting equipment, historic and current.
6 Interviewed, along with a number of other designers, for the article *National Treasures* in *Light&Sound International* magazine, November 2017.
7 Ibid.
8 Ibid.
9 Ibid.
10 Ibid.

6.4 – Theatre Makers and Architecture
11 Quoted in Simon Callow, *The National: The Theatre and its Work* (London: Nick Hern Books & National Theatre, 1997), p.6.
12 Mark Rylance, Foreword from *London Theatres* by Michael Coveney (London: Frances Lincoln, 2017).
13 *Red*, a play by John Logan about the artist Mark Rothko, premiered at the Donmar Warehouse in 2009, transferring to Broadway the next year. This production was revived at the Wyndham's Theatre in 2018.
14 Your author admits with great pride that he co-produced, with Hal Prince, this production at the Palace Theatre starring Judi as the definitive Sally Bowles.
15 One of the largest – and perhaps ugliest – multi-purpose theatres in the US.
16 Symposium at the National Theatre, 30 October 2016, proceedings published as *The National Theatre A Place for Plays* (Cambridge: Entertainment Technology Press, 2016).
17 Peter Brook, *The Empty Space* (New York: Simon & Schuster, 1996; originally published 1968).
18 Scene/Change: www.scene-change.com.
19 Leonard Tucker (1928-2023), Lennie to all, was chief electrician at the Old Vic from 1954, continued in that role when the National arrived, and moved with the company to the South Bank in 1976. He lit many productions for the NT including Olivier's *Othello*. "He basked in my spotlight, I basked in his," he recalled of Olivier. He remained at the National until 1985, then enjoyed a successful freelance lighting career.
20 Freelancers Make Theatre Work campaigned on behalf of freelance theatre workers during Covid and continues to do so beyond. freelancersmaketheatrework.com.

Part Six
6.2 – Technical Evolution
1 *NT+10*, in *Cue* issue 50, Nov/Dec 1987 (Oxford: Twynam Publishing Ltd), available via theatrecrafts.com.
2 Interviewed for the article

The Characters In The Story
The remarkable power of the internet allows you to hear some of the characters in this book share their views on the National Theatre in their own voices:

Richard Pilbrow:
https://bit.ly/3tRG3Uh
https://bit.ly/3tPYvww
https://bit.ly/3U6CuE8

Laurence Olivier:
https://bit.ly/3HsXOMQ

Denys Lasdun:
https://bit.ly/3ObUBVk
https://bit.ly/3Hyf2rP

Peter Hall:
https://bit.ly/3vlMARD

The Story:
The story of the creation of the National Theatre has also been told in a BBC radio play, with Richard featured as a character!
https://bbc.in/49ewjCd

Index

This Index is also available online at www.asenseoftheatre.com.
References in *italic* are to illustrations. 'n.' denotes Endnote numbers.
Theatres and other locations are generally arranged by their city, so theatres in London are subheadings under 'London.'
Shakespeare's plays are listed under Shakespeare, William. The initialism 'LO' denotes Sir Laurence Olivier as distinct from the Olivier Theatre.

A

The Absence of War 300, *300*
Absolute Hell 468
Academy Awards (Oscars) 362, 416, 458, 467
ACAS (Advisory, Conciliation and Arbitration Service) 244
Act for the Punishment of Vagabonds (1572) 26
Action Man Trilogy 64
actor/audience relationships 323–24, 405, 428–29, 468, 480, 481–82
Adam, Robert 34, 36
Adams, Polly 286
Adrian, Max 105
Aeschylus 431
Afore Night Comes 355
Ager, Mark 445
Ahrends, Burton and Koralek 97, 101
Aida 346
Air Traffic Control System (UK) 206
Aka (vital force) 480
Albert Speer 352
Albery, Sir Bronson 13, 14
Albery, Donald 13
Aldwych Company 109
Algarotti, Count Francesco, *An Essay on the Opera* 35
Alice Ltd (audio company) 448
Alice's Adventures Under Ground 346
All My Sons 318
Allam, Roger 376, 377, 463
Allen, Carol 425
Allio, Rene 56, 105
Almey, Cy 425
Altec loudspeakers 448
Amadeus viii, 261, 268, *268*, 361, *361*, 367, 385, *437*, 474
American Beauty (film) 318
An American in Paris 346
Amos, Tori, *The Light Princess* 364
Anderson, Bob 77, *77*, 443–44
Anderson, Paul 358, 371, *436*
Angels in America 301, *301*, 306, 347, 349, *362*, 363, *439*
Annals, Michael 56, 142
Annan, Noel 296
Annand, Simon 340
Antwerp 109
Anything Goes 436
Appia, Adolphe 43–44, 44
Aquarius (TV show) 241, 246
Arcadia 308
Archer, William 4–5, 13
  Scheme & Estimates for a National Theatre (with Harley Granville-Barker) 4, 4
Archie (clerk of works) 245

Archigram 97
The Architect and the Emperor of Assyria 276, 435
Architects Co-Partnership 97, 101
Architects' Journal 255, 424
Architects Registration Act (1938) 294
Architectural Design (journal) 101
Arden, John 147
Arditti, Paul 271, 339, 340, 341, 358, 359, 360, 361, 391, 452–53, *452*
arena stage 46, 307
Argand lamp 36
Arlen, Stephen 12, 76, *76*, 78–141, 175, 182–84, 185, 216
Armstrong's Last Goodnight 147, 170
Arnaud, Yvonne 286
Arnold, Matthew 4
art theatre movement 44–45, 48
Arthur, Chris 51
arts centres 421
Arts Council 9, 11, 14, 14–15, 47, 76, 81, 96, 166, 234, 243, 262–63, 315, 411, 477
  Drama Panel 81, 85, 96
Arup Acoustics 314, 453
Arup Associates 97
Ascot Royal Meeting, Berkshire 236
Ashcroft, Dame Peggy 238, 243, 247, 250, 273, 379
Ashmore, Catherine 323, 342
Ashwell, Lena 7
Association of British Theatre Technicians (ABTT) 72, 82, 101, 157
Association of Lighting Designers 310
Athens 221, 410
  Acropolis 240
  Niarchos Cultural Center 422, *422*
Attlee, Clement 10
Atwell, Hayley 332
audience density 40
Aukin, David 293
Austin, Jeremy 338
Austin, Neil 342, 353, *353*, 371, *436*, *437*, *438*, 440, *411*
Australia 145, 325
Austria 3
Avery, Brian 425
Avon, River 21
Ayckbourn, Alan 46, 263, 274, 285–87, *285*, 407
Aymonino, Carlo 401

B

Baal 74, 75
Babel (film) 352
Baby Doll 350
The Bacchai 436
Back to the Future: The Musical 311
Back to Methuselah 52
backstage community 470
Backup Tech 310
Badger, Richard 5
BAFTA Awards 458
Bagenal, Hope 21
Bain, Alan 487
Baker Barrios Architects *416*, 424
Balanchine, George 101
Balfour, Charles 359, *439*
Balmoral Castle, Aberdeenshire 237, 241
Bano, Tim 363
Barabino, Carlo 398, 399, 402
Barber, John 15
Barbican Theatre 264
  Anthony Ward on 323
  Bob Crowley on 347
    costs 143
  David Hersey on 276
  Judi Dench on 470
  LO on 167
  Michael Billington on 381
  model 167
  Peter Brook on 161–62
  Peter Hall on 151, 244, 263–64, 265
  Richard York on 245
  Royal Shakespeare Company and 171
  Simon Russell Beale on 464, 465
  Stephen Daldry on 305
  Trevor Nunn and 262
Barda, Clive 300, 302
Bardon, Henry 23
Barker, Felix 15, 267
Barmouth, North Wales, Dragon Theatre 47
Barnard, Rob 208, 268, 330, 448, 487
Barnes, Clive 57
Barnes, Jason 277, *277*
Barnett, Mike 212
Barrault, Jean-Louis 294
Barrie, J. M., *Peter Pan* 281
Barry, Edward Middleton 43
Bart, Lionel 75, 407
Bartholomew Fair 291
Barton Myers Associates *416*, 424
Bath, Theatre Royal 40
Bartlett, Neil *441*

Bauhaus 459
Bausor, Jon *437*
Baylis, Lilian 6–7, *7*, 9, 63
Bayreuth, Festspielhaus 19, 41, 41, 43, 281, 400, 430
BBC (British Broadcasting Corporation) 5, 17, 197–98, 202, 237
  Arena 65
BBC Films 355
Beale, Simon Russell 317, 332, 363, 463–66, *463*
The Beatles 51
Beattie, Rosie 247–48, *247*
Beaumont, Francis 30, 79
Beaumont, Hugh 132
The Beaux' Stratagem 367
Beckenham Children's Theatre Centre 197
Beckett, Samuel 231, 244, 304, 477
Bedroom Farce 285, *287*
Beech, Julian 267
Beeston, Christopher 30
The Beggar's Opera 34, 294, *491*
Behind the Beautiful Forevers 437, 458
Bel Geddes, Norman 166
Belfast 331
Bell, Robert 488
Benedict, David 321
Benn, Brian, cartoon on NT opening *257*
Benn, Tony (Anthony Wedgwood Benn) 14
Bennett, Alan 352, 468, 486
Bennett, Hubert 88, 96, 98
Bennetts Associates 24
Benthall, Michael 13–14, 70, 74, *74*, 78–141, 149–54, 155–62, 163, 182, 188, 192–93
Bergamo 399, 401
Berlin
  Deutsche Oper 207
  Freie Volksbühne 148, 170, 172, 200
  Grosses Schauspielhaus 44
  Philharmonie (Philharmonic Hall) 119–20, *120*, 417
  Theater am Schiffbauerdamm 110, *110*
Berliner Ensemble 106, 110, 123, 139, 170
Bernstein, Leonard 321
Bernstein, Sidney Bernstein, Baron 8–9, 14–15
Bertenshaw, David 206
Betaplan *422*
Betrayal 310
Betterton, Thomas 33
Bevin, Ernest 11

The Big Picnic 282
Bilkey, Dominic 448–49
Billingham, Forum Theatre 47
Billington, Michael 379–81, *379*, 486
  on LO and Peter Hall 65, 231
  on NT 263
  on Richard Eyre 289, 300
  on Rufus Norris 355, 357, 358
  theatre reviews 262, 301, 317, 322, 330, 339, 361, 362, 371
  on year 1963 51
  State of the Nation 486
Billy Elliot: the Musical 303, 306, 310
Billy Elliot (film) 303, 318
Bird, Yolande 71, 76, 173, 175, 187, 486
Birmingham, Repertory Theatre 21, 44, 47, 49, 107, 191, 197, 254, 278, 409, 412, *412*, 413, 509n.74
Birtwistle, Harrison 269
Black Comedy 54, 147, 161
Blair, Tony 313
Blakely, Colin 54, 57, 105
Blakemore, Michael 54, 63, 243, 250, 272, 283, 488
  Stage Blood 283, 306, 487
Les Blancs 360, *360*, 380, 464
Blane, Sue 269, *436*
Blessed, Brian 352
Blithe Spirit 244
Blitz! 53, 74, 206, 407, 408
The Blue Touch Paper 272
Blue/Orange 310, 317
Bochum 96
Boddington, Diana xvi, *61*, 62, 198, 247
Boeing 747 aircraft 443
Bogdanov, Michael 64, 64
Bolt, Beranel and Newman 408
A Bond Honoured 163
Bourne, Matthew 310, 315, 322, 324, 370
Bovis Construction 266
Bowen, Will 319
Bowler, Lisa, *Theatre Architecture as Embodied Space: A Phenomenology of Performance* 430–31
boxes 429
Boyd, Michael 23–24
Boyle, Danny 332
Bracegirdle, Anne 262
Brahms, Johannes 327
Branagh, Sir Kenneth 331, 353, 464, 467
Brand 409
Brantley, Ben 317, 341

Brazil 81
Brecht, Bertolt 45, 74, 75, 110, 171, 278, 293, 360, 477
Bremerhaven, Stadttheater 21
Brenner, Marc 361
Brett, Richard *xvii*, *77*, *202*, *232*, *251*
  author's last meeting with 333
  and Bastille project 403
  and Derngate Centre 424
  and design of NT 202–5, 236, 237–38, 239, 250, 251
  and general facilities panels 208
  and Genoa project 399–400
  on meeting LO 195
  report on progress (1982) 212
  report on progress (2013) 212–13
  and Theatre Projects 197–99, 398
Bretton Hall College of Education, Yorkshire 367
Brexit 473, 476
Brideshead Revisited (TV production) 49, 284
Bridge of Spies (film) 458
Bridges-Adams, William 9, 20, 21
Bridget Jones: The Edge of Reason (film) 352
Bridgwater Shepheard & Epstein 97, 101
Brighton xi
  Theatre Royal 413
Brinkhoff/Mögenburg 359
Bristol
  Old Vic 11, 64, 278, 280, 352, 414
  Theatre School 346
  Theatre Royal 35, *35*, 37
British Drama League 8
British Library 216, 486
  Olivier Archives 195–97
The Broken Heart 17, 70
Brook, Peter 73, *73*, *126*, *180*
  and Barbican Theatre 265
  conflict with Denys Lasdun 125
  David Hare on 276
  Denys Lasdun on 217, 218
  experimental work 233
  LO and 71, 180–81
  and NT Building Committee 70, 78, 84–162, 182–92
  and *Oedipus* 54
  Peter Hall on 262
  Richard Eyre on 290
  on Scheme B 189
  on seat prices 329
  on theatre design x, 296, 297, 381, 431, 471
  warning 182–83
  William Dudley on 281
Brooke, Peter (MP) 294, 295
Brooks, Rebekah 332
Brotherston, Lez *322*
Brown, Paul 369, *436*, 440, 497
Brown, Tony 206
Brutalist architecture 274, 477

Bryan, Robert 270
Bryant, Michael 248, 254, 268, 275
Bryden, Bill xxiii, 261, 262, 267, 272, 274, 281, 282, 289, 380
Bucharest 249
  Bulandra Theatre 294
Buckingham, George Villiers, Duke of 70
Buckle, J.G. 42
Budapest 120
Buggy, Niall 301
The Builder magazine 40
Building Research Laboratory 183, 184
Bulgakov, Mikhail 279
Bull, Diane 286
Bulwer-Lytton, Edward 317, 323
Bundy, Bill 264, 398
Burbage, Cuthbert 27
Burbage, James 27, 28
Burbage, Richard 27, *27*, 49, 54
Burge, Stewart 274
Burger, Lisa 333, *333*, 378, 487
Burnet, Tait & Lorne 97, 101
Burnt by the Sun 370, *438*
Burrell, John 10, 11
Burrows, Abe 269
Bury, John *126*, 269
  and *Amadeus* 268
  and Barbican Theatre 263, 265
  and Cottesloe 282
  and Lasdun 127, 265, 266
  LO on 134
  and NT design 233, 234, 241
  on Olivier Theatre flying system 212
  postcard *213*
  at Stratford East 20, 127
  and *Tamburlaine* 243, 244
Bury St Edmunds, Theatre Royal 39
Butler, Samuel 36
Byam Shaw, Glen 10–12, 15, 73, 262
Byng, John (later Viscount Torrington) 38

C
Cabanel, Rudolph 39, 40
Cabaret 355, 408, 467, 469
Cadac audio console 448
Cadle, Giles 338, *436*
Caesar and Cleopatra 74
Caird, John 315, 317, *440*
Calais, Jungle Refugee Camp, Good Chance Theatre 305
Calder, Barnabas 174, 215
  Raw Concrete: The Beauty of Brutalism 487
Calderón de la Barca, Pedro 28
Calgary, Alberta
  Arts Commons 421
  Martha Cohen Theatre 421, *421*
  Max Bell Theatre 421, *421*

Callow, Simon 56, 65, 267, 268, 269, 287
  The National - The Theatre and its Work 487
Cambridge
  Arts Theatre 45
  Festival Theatre (formerly Theatre Royal, Barnwell, Cambridge) 45, 134, 142
Cambridge, University of 318, 368, 463
  St Catharine's College 15
Campbell, Ken 380
Candide 321
Cantacuzino, Serban 291, 295
The Captain of Köpenick 323
The Caretaker 134
Carousel 302, *302*, 346, 460
Carry On films 332, 341
Carte Blanche 76
Carter, Lucy 358
Carter, Peter 97
Carter, Philip 342, 435, 487
Carveth, Jennifer 61
Casson, Hugh 97, 101
Casson, Sir Lewis 9, 13, 17, 70
Casson and Conder 97
The Cat in the Hat 344
Cat on a Hot Tin Roof 278
Cats 276, 313–14, *314*
Cattaneo Emilio & Figlio 398, 399, 401
The Caucasian Chalk Circle 298, 299
CCT Lighting, Silhouette spotlight 207
Ceausescu, Nicolae 249
César Pelli Associates *423*
Chalk, Warren 97
Chamberlin, Peter 244, 263
The Chances 17, 70, 86
Chandos, Oliver Lyttelton, Lord
  and appointment of TPC 187
  as chair of South Bank Board 76, *76*, 84, 85, 130, 142, 143–44, 153
  as Conservative minister 10
  and Frank Dunlop 64
  and GLC meeting 189, 191
  and Joint Council of NT and Old Vic 15, 16
  and LO 54, 84, 85, 89
  Lord Goodman and 166
  Lyttelton Theatre named for xxi, 5
  and NT board 54
  and plans for NT 16
  and *Soldiers* 54
Channel 4 News 296
Chapman, George 30
Charcoalblue 24, 446
Charles II, King 31, 32
Charles III, King (earlier Prince of Wales) xvi, 239, 291, 352, 473
Charleson, Ian *xii*
Charlie and the Chocolate Factory (musical) 308

Charlotte, North Carolina, Belk Theatre *423*, *423*
Charon, Jacques 54, *63*, 198
Charteris, Martin 237
Chatto, Ros 412–13
Chekhov, Anton 126, 130, 134, 275, 278–79
The Cherry Orchard 278–79, 353, *437*
Chiang, Dawn 488
Chicago
  Goodman Theatre 44, 509n.74
  Goodman Theatre Company 44
  Lyric Opera 344, 350
  Shakespeare Theater 23, 418, 420, *420*
  Steppenwolf Theatre Company 305, 416, *416*
Chichester Festival Theatre *17*, 80, *81*, *93*, *112*, *113*, 496
  and Building Committee 70–71, 78–82, 86, 106–9, 111, 119, 128, 133, 149, 151–52, 161
  concrete balcony 173
  Denys Lasdun and 389
  Denys Lasdun on 115, 161, 165–66
  first season 69
  fourth year 147
  Howard Davies on 280
  Judi Dench and 469
  lighting xvi
  LO and xv–xvi, 49, 100, 122, 151, 309, 390, 469, *496*
  Michael Elliott on 149
  Michael Grandage on 461
  opening xv, 17
  Powell & Moya and 97
  productions at 17, 55, 56, 147, 151
  see also Uncle Vanya
  Richard Cowell on 454
  second season 100
  section *112*
  Stephen Daldry on 305
  thrust stage *80*, 256
  William Gaskill on 133
Children of the Sun 350, *438*
China 28, 413, 413
Chips with Everything 134, 163
Chitty, Alison 271, *37*, *476*
Chocolat (film) 467
A Chorus of Disapproval 285
Chris Arthur: Scenes from National Life 51
Christie, Agatha, *The Mousetrap* 250
Christie, Bunny 341, 349, 350–51, *350*, 358, 370, *437*, 460, *476*
Churchill, Winston 5, 10, 54, 63, 293
Cibber, Colley 35
  An Apology for the Life of Mr. Colley Cibber 33
Cincinnati, Ohio 423
cinema 45, 48
Cirque du Soleil 341
Clachan, Lizzie *437*, 497
Clapp, Susannah 339, 341, 342

Clark, Jon 342, 361, 363, 367, *367*, *437*, *439*
Clark, Sir Kenneth 64, 132
Clark, Nobby 267, 268, *269*, 270, 271
Clarke, Sharon D. 359
Clayton, Laurie 248–50, *249*, 267
Cleo, Camping, Emanuelle And Dick 316
Clore Learning Centre *336*
Closer 311
Clough, Arthur xi, 292
coalminers' strike 211
The Coast of Utopia trilogy: *Voyage*, *Shipwreck*, *Salvage* 281, 319, 322, *322*, 435, *436*, 449
Codron, Michael 101
Cold War 51
Coll, Isle of 409
collaboration 425
Collaborators 352, 465
Collcutt, T. E. 42
Colley, Steve 444
Collison, David 53, 55, 77, *77*, 95, 104, 207–8, *232*, 409, 448
Cologne, Oper der Stadt 48
Comédie Française 4, 120, 132, 174
Compagnie des Quinze 73
Company 348, 350, 353, 408
computers 203–5
concert halls 417
Concorde 195, 443
Concrete Quarterly 297
concrete, use of
  and acoustics x, 391, 448–49, 451–53
  Albert Finney on x, 290, 291
  auditoria 24
  and carpet 219, 220, 227, 297
  at Chichester 129, 173
  Declan Donnellan on 414
  Denys Lasdun and xi, 127, 160, 210, 216–17, 220–23, 225, 265, 274, 292, 297, 335, 390, 400, 409, 463
  John Gunter on xi
  King Charles on xvi–xvii
  and lighting 447
  limitations and criticism of xvii, 230, 290, 430, 458
  LO on ix
  at Lyttelton Theatre xi, xxi, 310, 335, 395, 481
  Mark Thompson on 303
  at Olivier Theatre xix, xxvii, 175, 212, 276, 282, 311, 346, 370, 374, 447
  painting of 265–66
  Paule Constable on 370
  Peter Hall on 233, 375
  qualities of 390
  reducing 261
  Victor Glasstone on 256
Congreve, William 17, 410
Conrad (engineer) 250
Cons, Emma 6
Consent 310

Conservative Party (UK) 10, 13, 229
Constable, Paule *322*, 338, 339, 340, 341, 359, 360, 362, 363, 370–71, *370*, *436*, *437*, *438*, *439*, *440*
  Bunny Christie on 351
  discussion with Steve Tompkins 471
  environmental views 447
  and Freelancers Make Theatre Work 476
  on imagination 481
  Michael Grandage on 460
  on Olivier Theatre xix
  Susanna Clapp on 339
Contant, Clément, *Parallèle des Principaux Théâtres Modernes de l'Europe* 36
Cooke, Dominic 359, 363, *439*
Cookson, Sally *439*
Copeau, Jacques 73
Copenhagen 315–16, 317
Coram Boy 332, 370
Coram Boy (radio play) 332
Corbett, Tony 174
Corden, James 332, 341
Cork, Adam 360
Cork, Ireland 346
Corke, Sarah 487
Cornelissen, Douglas 212, 246
Cottesloe, John Fremantle, 4th Baron 76, *76*
  and architects 9, 99, 145, 166
  as chairman of Arts Council xxiii, 15–16
  and Denys Lasdun 176, 216
  at House of Lords lunch 145
  Hugh Jenkins and 237
  Kenneth Rae on 89
  as leader of NT/Old Vic Joint Council xv, xxiii, 15
  LO on 145, 172, 191, 195
  and plans for NT 16, 166, 189–91, 235, 236
  speech at South Bank Board meeting 243
  at topping-out ceremony 233
Cottesloe (later Dorfman) Theatre *xxiv*, *337*, *377*, *387*
  acoustics 317, 454
  as afterthought ix
  Alan Ayckbourn and 285
  Alex Jennings on 352
  Alison Chitty on 376
  Ben Power on 368–69
  Bill Bryden season 282
  Bob Crowley on 347
  and Bridge Theatre 419
  budget 264
  Bunny Christie on 350
  closed for remodelling 332
  as courtyard theatre 418
  David Hare on 275–76
  The Deck 446, *492*
  Declan Donnellan and Nick Ormerod on 376
  design xxiii, 231, 384, 397, 413, 482
  entrance 446
  estimates 239
  flexibility of 373
  foyer 299
  Husbands & Sons at 348
  Iain Mackintosh and 397
  Jason Barnes on 277
  Judi Dench on 373
  lighting 446–48
  lobby *336*
  Marianne Elliott on 349
  Mark Thompson on 309
  Michael Billington on 380
  model *219*, *235*
  and *The Mysteries* 281
  Neil Austin on 353
  opening 246, 248–49
  Paule Constable on 371
  Peter Hall on xxiii
  Peter Mumford on 325
  plans *xxiii*, *494*
  productions 440–41
  promenade productions 27
  Rae Smith on 366
  renaming of 333, 371, 378
  Richard Eyre on 376
  Rick Fisher on 310
  Ronnie Mulryne and Margaret Shewring on 376
  Rufus Norris and 353
  seating system 343, 446
  Simon Russell Beale on 465
  as studio theatre xxvii, 11, 23, 191
  success of xi
  Tim Hatley on 311
  Trevor Nunn and 315
  Trevor Nunn on 376
  Vicki Mortimer on 344
  Vincent Canby on 301
  William Dudloy on xxiii
Council for the Encouragement of Music and Arts (CEMA) 9
Country Life magazine 8
The Country Wife 262
Countrymania 458
courtyard theatre 234, 413, 418–19, *418–19*, 424, 454
Coveney, Michael 297, 340, 486
  London Theatres 457
Coventry 81
  Belgrade Theatre 47, 84
  City Architect's Department 47
Covid-19 pandemic 378, 445, 447, 449, 473–74, 476–77
Coward, Noël, 49
Cowell, Richard 314, 393, 454–55
Cox, Flora 487, 488
Cox, Jane *441*
Cox, Ronald *60*, 198
Coyne, John 425
Cracknell, Carrie 361, *439*
Craig, Edward Gordon 43, *43*, 225, 307
  Master of the Art and Science of the Theatre 407
Cranston, Bryan 362
Crayford Reading Circle, Kent 7–8
Crewe, Bertie 9, 42
Crickmay, Anthony 57
Cripps, Sir Stafford 11, 13
Critics' Circle Theatre Awards 350, 355
Crompton, Dennis 97
Cromwell, Oliver 31
Crosby, Theo 97, 510n.91
Crosland, Anthony 145
Crossfield, Scott 425
Crowley, Bob 275, 279, 300, 302, 339, 346–47, *346*, *436*, *441*, 476, 497
Crown (electrical firm) 236
The Crown (TV series) 303, 352
The Crucible 142
Cubitt, James 97, 101
Cue magazine 443
CultureWhisper 358
Cumberland, Richard, *Memoirs* 38
Cummins, Kevin 339
The Curious Incident of the Dog in the Night-Time 74, 329, 332, 334, 341, *341*, 343, 348, 349, *349*, 350
Curtis, William J.R., *Denys Lasdun - Architecture, City, Landscape* 487
Cutler, Horace 263
cycloconverters 203–5
Cyprus, National Theatre 427, *427–28*
Cyrano de Bergerac 10, *436*

D

da Costa, Liz 271
Daily Express 317
Daily Mail 413, 486
Daily Telegraph 15, 22, 291, 300, 316, 323, 324, 338, 340, 359, 360, 361
Dakin, Mark 331
Daldry, Stephen 302, 303–5, *303*
  and *An Inspector Calls* 289, 301, 306, 310, 460
  Jon Clark and 367
  Lynn Gardner on 301
  and *Machinal* 294, 310
  Michael Billington on 289
  Richard Eyre on 294
  Rufus Norris on 356
  and Steve Tompkins 334
  in succession debate 315, 318
  Trevor Nunn on 315
Dallas, Texas
  Kalita Humphreys Theater 256
  State Fair Music Hall 467
  Theatre 47 46
  Winspear Opera 422, *422*
  Wyly Theatre 418, *418*, 422
Dance of Death 254
Dando, Walter Pfeffer 42
Dandy Dick 163
d'Annunzio, Gabriele 4
Danton's Death 442, 460, *460*
Dara 438
The Dark Lady of the Sonnets 6
Dasso, Marco 402
D'Avenant (Davenant), William 31
Davey, Chris *438*, *441*
Davidson, Randall Thomas, 1st Baron Davidson of Lambeth, Archbishop of Canterbury 5
Davies, Elidir 48, 97, 101
Davies, Howard 271, 278–80, *278*, 281, 290, 318, 323, 342, 346, 351, 353, *436*, *437*, *438*, *440*, 460
Davies, Thomas 34
Davis, Belfield & Everest 77, 233
Davis, Ernie *61*
Dawson, Beatrice 55
Dayton, Ohio, Mead Theatre 423, *423*
de Jongh, Nicholas 302, 377
de Nobili, Lila 57, 148, 198
de Valois, Ninette 45
De Witt, Johannes 27
Dean, Basil 7, 9, 44, 47, 409
Dear England 367, 474
Death of England 474
Death of a Salesman 108, 310
DEC (Digital Equipment Corp) 207
The Deep Blue Sea 361, *361*, 368, *439*
Dekker, Thomas 30
Delphi 107, 108
Democracy 331
Dempster, Rory 270
Dench, Dame Judi xxvii, 271, 275, 463, 467–70, *467*, *469*, *470*
Denmark 3
Derby 47
Devine, George xvi, 11–12, 19, 70, 73, *73*, 75, 78–141, *115*, 149, 150, 164, 217, 262, 461, 486
Devlin, Es 363, *439*
de Rouw, Theo *66*
Dexter, John 73, *73*, *251*
  death 268
  and LO 53
  and NT Building committee xvi, 94–141, 149–76, 182, 185, 188, 192–93
  Peter Hall on 268
  Peter Shaffer on 56
  productions 54, 56, 142, 147, 183
  Richard Brett on 198
D'Huys, An 362
Dickens, Charles 3
Dickinson, Ian 341, 358, 362
DiGiCo audio console 448
Digital, Culture, Media and Sport, Department of, Culture Recovery Fund 474
Dillon, Patrick *333*, 334, 378
  on Denys Lasdun 335
  Concrete Reality: Denys Lasdun and the National Theatre 335, 487
  The Green Book 335
Dines, Rick 206
Disney (Walt Disney Company) 346, 353
Dispatches 261, 264
Diss, Eileen *438*
Dittmann, Michaël 403
DL&P (Denys Lasdun & Partners) *132*, *138*
  archives 125, 486
and Bastille project 403
discussion with Peter Hall 262
final report 176
Harry Pugh and 242
Kenneth Tynan on 154
meeting with Royal Fine Arts Commission 294
model of NT 191
notes 110, 127, 162, 173, 292, 295
and Scheme B 143
study sketches *132–33*, *138*
and Theatre Projects 397
DLK Architects 420
Dodd, Ken 405, *405*
Dodgshun, Edward 20
Dominic, Zoë 57, 268, 270
Donnell, Paddy 237–38
Donnellan, Declan 301, 317, 376, 414
Dorfman, Lloyd xxiii, 331, 446
Dorfman Theatre *see* Cottesloe (later Dorfman) Theatre
Dotrice, Roy 512n.6
Douet, Mark 363
Douglas, Archibald Campbell 382, 384
Down Cemetery Road 468
Dowson, Philip 97
Dowton, William 38
DP Architects 421
Draghici, Marina *437*
drama, theatres for 416
Drama Desk Awards 315–16, 346, 364, 452
Dresden 48, 54, 398
Driscoll, Jon 371
Dromgoole, Dominic 510n.91
drum revolve xvii, xxi, *194*, 202–5, 209–10, 212, *232*, 233, 235, 248, 250, 261, 271, 278, 281, 308–9, 311, 318, 323, 331, 333, 339, 351, 353, 356, 359, 375, 444–5, 449, 490, 495, 497
Drury, Matt 445, 447, 487
Dryden, John 32
Dublin, Abbey Theatre 342
Duckworth and Company 4
Dudley, William 281–82, *281*
  on Cottesloe Theatre xviii
  on Denys Lasdun 298–99
  Howard Davies on 278
  Jason Barnes on 277
  and Lyttelton Theatre 316, 377
  Peter Hall on 262
  Peter Hepple on 271
  productions 249, 317–19, 322, 435, *436*, 449
  and *The Shaughraun* and drum revolve 211, 261, 271, 278, 281, 290, 449, 497
  Variety on 322
Duff, Anne-Marie 339
Duffy, Carol Ann 307, 358
Dukes, Ashley 8–9
Duke's Company 31, 32
Dulwich College 197
Dumont, Gabriel Pierre Martin 387

Parallele de Plans des plus Belles Salles de Spectacles d'Italie et de France 36
Dunlop, Frank 15, 46, 51, 54, 64–65, 101, 188–91, 209, 407–8, *407*, 418
The Dutch Courtesan 133, 134

E

Ealing comedies 332
East Anglia, University of 100
Easterbrook, Anthony 76, 192–93, 209–10, 233, 245
The Economist 335
Eden End 273
Edgar, David 352
Edinburgh
  Assembly Hall 46, 420
  Festival 64, 303
  Royal Lyceum 364, *414*
Edis, Steven 321, 323
Edmond 331, 464
Education and Science, Department of 166
Edward II 234, 411, *437*
Edward II, King 25
Edward VIII, King 352
Edwards, Freya 301
Egeraat, Erick van 23
Egypt 220
Ehrenkrantz Ekstut Khan *416*
Ejiofor, Chiwetel 358
Elgar, Edward 5
Eliot, T.S. 216
Elizabeth I, Queen 6, 26, 27
Elizabeth II, Queen *244, 252*
  enquires about NT opening date 239, 241
  opening of Barbican Theatre 264
  opening of NT xix, 234, 237–38, 246, 253, 255, 397
  and site of NT 14
Elizabeth, Queen, the Queen Mother 14, 16, 239, 247
Elizabethan Stage Society 42
Elizabethan theatre 115, 133
Ellerbe Becket Architects *415*
Elliott, Marianne 74, 332, 339, 340, 341, 348–49, 353, 358, 362, 366, *436, 438, 439, 441*
Elliott, Michael (director) 74, *74*, *409*
  author on 383, 409
  and Manchester Royal Exchange 244, 348, 409, 417
  manifesto 410–11
  in meeting with NT design 173, 202
  and *Miss Julie* 147
  and NT Building Committee 70, 71, 78–141, 149–53, 155, 163, 182–93, 348
  and Old Vic company 409
  on Scheme E 175
Elliott, Michael (NT executive director) 265
Ellis, Ruth 22
Elmina's Kitchen 331, 350
Elsinore Castle (Kronborg),

Denmark 17, 45
Elsom, John, *The History of the National Theatre* 487
Emden, Walter 42
EMI Group 233
Emil and the Detectives 350
Emperor and Galilean 332, 368, 369, *436, 497*
Encore magazine 15
An Enemy of the People 314
England People Very Nice 331, 353
English Heritage 294
English National Opera 42
English Stage Company 19–20, 73
ENSA (Entertainments National Service Association) 9
The Entertainer 49
Epidaurus, ancient theatre x, xix, 223, 227, 240, *240*, 275, 291, 496
Equity (formerly British Actors' Equity Association) 16
Equus 54, 254, 264, 474
Esher, Oliver Brett, 3rd Viscount 5, 11–12, 15, 54
L'Espresso 402
ETC (Electronic Theatre Controls), Eos consoles (lighting control system) 447
Euripides 181
Evans, Dame Edith 105
Evans, Eldred 97
Evening News 15
Evening Standard 302, 340
  Theatre Awards 315, 355
Evening at the Talkhouse 441
Evershed Power Optics 205, 212, 445
Evershed-Martin, Leslie 17
Everyman 307, *307*, 358, *358*, 465
Evita 276
Exeter, Theatre Royal 42
Exit the King 134, 323
experimental theatre 17, 45, 79, 96, 112–13, 121, 131–33, 140, 189–91, 275, 327
Eyre, Sir Richard ix, xix, 269, 274, 281, *289*, 300, 343, 356, 368, *438, 440*
  and Alan Bennett 331
  Alan Bennett on 368
  conflict with Denys Lasdun ix, xi–xii, 289–99, 375, 466, 480
  on Cottesloe 376
  and David Hare Trilogy 300
  as director of NT 249, 289–99, 318, 444, 448, 497
  and *Guys and Dolls* 448
  and *An Inspector Calls* 303
  on Lyttelton 292
  Nick Starr and 343
  Richard Cowell on 454–55
  and temporary conversion of Olivier Theatre 274, 356, 375, 497
  Trevor Nunn on 314–15
  and *Vincent in Brixton* 319
  and William Dudley 281
  National Service: Diary of a Decade at the National Theatre 289, 487

F

Fair, Alistair, *Modern Playhouses* 47
Fall, Nadia *437, 438*
The False Servant 440
fan-shaped theatre 13, 19, 32, 41, 48, *48*, 69–70, 112, 114, 118, 119, 304, 423
Farber, Yaël 360, *437*
Farncombe, James *437, 441*, 448
Farrell, Terry 293
Fela! 437
Fellner & Helmer (Ferdinand Fellner and Hermann Helmer) 387
Fenwick, Oliver *439*
Feraby, Clare 425
Fernald, John 15
Festen 355
Festival of Britain 13, 510n.20
  Dome of Discovery, Skylon, Royal Festival Hall *68*
Fiddler on the Roof 317, 408
Fiennes, Ralph 463
59 Productions 340, 341, 359
59 Theatre Company 74, 409
Financial Times 300, 317, 358, 361, 486
Finbow, Acatia 487, 488
Findlater, Richard 15, *15*, 486
  The Unholy Trade 486
Findlay, Polly *437*
Fine Arts Commission 265
Finlay, Frank 53, 105
Finney, Albert x, 105, 147, 238, 242, 267, 290, 352, 376, 377, 379
fire and safety 40
Firth, Tazeena 238
Fisher, Jules 76
Fisher, Rick 301, 302, 310, *310*
Fisher of Lambeth, Geoffrey Fisher, Baron, Archbishop of Canterbury 14
Fiske, Sir William (W.B.) 142, 184
Fix Up 440
A Flea in Her Ear 54, 62, 254
Flecknoe, Richard, *A Short Discourse on the English Stage* 26
Fleming, Kate 254
Fletcher, John 17, 30, 79
The Flick 441
flies 8, 112–13, 114, 119–24
Flight 311
Flint & Neill 77, 175, 236
Flower, Archibald 20
Flower, Edward Fordham 15, 16
Follies 344, 363, *363*, 370, 458, 481
Forbes-Robertson, Johnson 5
Ford, John 287
Forster, E.M. 314
Foster + Partners *422*
Foster, Norman 274, 402, 425
Foster, Tim 425
Foucault, Michel 481–82
Four Baboons Adoring the Sun 72
'fourth wall' 462
Foy, Kenneth 440
Fram 436
France 7, 64
  national theatre 3

Frankenstein 329, 332
Frankfurt 96
Frankcom, Sarah 441
Fredericks, Kon 244
Freelancers Make Theatre Work 476
Freeland, Brian 56
Fresnel spotlights 207
Friel, Brian 371
Friese-Greene, William 281
From Morning to Midnight 438
The Front Page 51, 54, 254
Frost/Nixon 353
Frozen 353
Fry, Gareth 342
Fuente Ovejuna 491
A Funny Thing Happened on the Way to the Forum 408
Furse, Roger 70, 74, *74*, 78–141
Further than the Furthest Thing 148

G

Gailey, Dennis 97
Gaines, Barbara 23
Galaxy (lighting control system) 207
Gambon, Sir Michael 60, 105, 268, 275, 285–86, 287, 463, 468
Gardelle, Ignazio 402
Gardner, Herb 412
Gardner, Lynn 301
Garnier, Charles 41, 403
Garrick, David 33, 34, *34*, 35, 36, 38, 49, 54
Gascoigne, Bamber 56
Gaskill, William 56, 74, *74*
  and LO 83, 191
  and NT Building Committee 84–112, 149–54, 155, 163–76, 182, 185–87, 192
  on plans for NT 62
  and *The Recruiting Officer* 54, 56
  Richard Brett 198
  at Royal Court 53
Gavin, Jamila 332
Gay, John 34
GBBN Architects *423*
Gehry, Frank 402, 417, 425, 481
Gelsenkirchen, Germany 202
  Musiktheater *93*, 96, 101, 111, 112, *112*, 113, 114, 389
general facilities panels (GFPs) 208, *208*
Genoa
  Opera House (1828) 398, 399
  opera house project *396*, 397–403, *397, 399–403*, 415, 422
Gensler and Associates *416*
geometry 117, 118, 154, 157, 161, 175, 219, 220, 227, 240, 390, 420, 455
George, Colin 47, 420
George VI, King 8, 12, 14
Germany
  Nazism 203
  theatre in 20, 21, 25, 44, 45, 48, 76, 89, *93*, 96, 102, 107, 110, 175, 183, 188, 200, 203, 207, 249, 256, 305, 389, 399, 400, 430
Gesamtkunstwerk 41

Ghetto 346, 352
Gibberd, Frederick 97
Gibbs, Vic 206
Gibson, Donald 47
Gielgud, Sir John 49, 54, 238, 256, 276, 464, 469, 512n.104
Gilbert, W.S. and Sir Arthur Sullivan 7
Gill, Peter 274
Gillibrand, Nicky 358, 362
Gillon, Tom 60
Gilmour, Soutra 360, *437*, *438*
Gilson, Peggy 197
'Ginger Group' 233–36, 238, 239, 241
Girouard, Mark 376
Gladwell, Philip *437*
Glasgow 281, 282
  Citizens Theatre 351, 364, 382, *383*, 458
  Theatre Royal 383
  Tron Theatre 364
The Glass Menagerie 286
Glasstone, Victor 255–56
Gluckstein, Sir Louis 189
Glyndebourne, Festival Opera 281, 323, 344, 345, 422, *422*, 462
Godley, Adam 363
Godwin, Edward William 43
Goldby, Derek 57
The Golden Touch (musical) 101
Goldfinger, Ernö 97, 101
Goldoni, Carlo 341
Goldsmith, Oliver 410
Gollancz, Israel 5
Gomes (play) 234
Goodman, Arnold Goodman, Baron 16, 65, 166, 189–90, 234, 243, 246, 263, 290, 291
Goodman, Henry 317
Goodman Derrick & Co 291
Goodwin, John 241
Goodwin, Simon *437*
Gold, Sam *437*
Goldbym Derek 57
Goold, Rupert 368
Gordon, Coeks xvi, 154, 192–93, 198
Gore-Langton, Robert 317
Goring, Marius 12
Gorky, Maxim 279
Goulding, Andrzej 311
Graham, Elspeth 510n.91
Grainger, Gawn 242, 254
Granada cinema chain 9
Granada Television 348
Grandage, Michael 353, 459–62, *459*
Granville-Barker, Harley xv, 3–8, 4, 12–13, 19, 20, 43, 218
  The Exemplary Theatre 8
  The Madras House 261
  Prefaces to Shakespeare 7
  and William Archer, *Scheme & Estimates for a National Theatre* (later *A National Theatre: Scheme and Estimates*, the *Blue Book*) 4–5, 8
Gray, Terence 45
Great Britain (play) 311, 332

Greater London Council (GLC) 142, 144, 145, 147, 149, 184, 190–91, 235, 250–51, 263, 409
Greece 217, 220
  theatre 106–7, 114, 115, 121, 223, 227, 240, 282, 324, 410, 496
Greek National Opera 422
Green, Ric 268, 269
Green, Ti *441*
Greene, Robert 29
Greenfield, Jon 510n.91, 510n.92
Grenfell 474
Grey, Terence 72
Greyn, Clinton 298
Griffin, Hayden 264, 265, 270, 273, 274, 275
Griffiths, Richard 339
Griffiths, Trevor 63
Grimmer, Mark 449
Groothuis, Paul 271, 300, 301, 302, 323, 324, 338, 342, 363
Gropius, Walter 45
Grosser, Helmut 400
The Guardian 301, 317, 330, 339, 342, 358, 361, 363, 379, 413, 486
The Guide (play) 234
Gunter, John x–xi, 269, 270, 291, 298, *436*
Guthrie, Sir Tyrone
  in charge of Old Vic and Sadler's Wells Opera and Ballet 9, 10–12, 63, 64
  Frank Dunlop on 64
  Kenneth Rae on 190
  Kenneth Tynan on 110
  and plans for NT 13–14, 16–17
  Richard Brett on 198
  and scenery 173
  and Sheffield Crucible 70, 420
  and Tanya Moiseiwitsch 75, 83
  and thrust stage 24, 37, 45–48, 75, 384, 391, 420, 461
Guys and Dolls x–xi, *xii*, 212, 261, 269, *269*, 275, 310, 369, 448, 466, 474, 481
Gwynn, Nell 32

H

The Habit of Art 331, 368
Hadid, Zaha 382
Haill, Lynn 487
Half Life 491
Half a Sixpence 73
Hall, Brian 425
Hall, Jacqueline 263
Hall, John 206
Hall, Lady (Nicki) 487
Hall, Sir Peter 15, *72*, *126*, *230*, *231*, *261*, 269, *436*
  as absentee director 246
  and Aldwych Theatre 15
  and *Amadeus* 268
  and *Antony and Cleopatra* 271
  Ayckbourn on 285, 287
  and Barbican Theatre 244, 246, 305
  character and personality 72, 452, 466
  conflict with LO 16, 254
  and Cottesloe 412
  on Cottesloe as studio theatre xxvii
  David Hare on 272, 273–74
  diaries 231–44, 261–66, 306
  as director of NT 231, 245, 254, 375, 470
  and Dorfman Theatre 366
  Felix Barker on 15, 267
  and 'Ginger Group' 233
  and *Happy Days* 250
  Howard Davies on 278
  on John Dexter 268
  Laurie Clayton on 249
  LO and 15, 16, 254
  and McAlpines 238–39
  Michael Billington on 65, 379, 380
  Michael Blakemore on 243
  in New York 264
  and noise at rehearsal 247
  and NT Building Committee 70, 78–143, 149–53, 155, 163–70, 182–85, 188–91, 192, 217
  on Olivier stage xix
  and Olivier stage 22–23, 375, 444
  and Olivier Theatre opening 253–54
  and *The Oresteia* 269
  and planning for stages 204, 233
  Private Eye on 16
  on rehearsal rooms xxvii
  at rehearsals 248
  replaced as NT director by Richard Eyre 249
  Richard Brett on 250
  and *Ring* cycle 281
  at Rose Theatre 293
  and Shakespeare Memorial Theatre 15, 19, 72
  succeeds LO as director of NT 54, 65, 231, 245, 254
  and *Tamburlaine the Great* 244, 253, 261, 267
  and technical equipment 443
  and Trevor Nunn 313
  Trevor Nunn on 314
Hall, Sir Peter, and John Goodwin, *Peter Hall's Diaries: The Story of a Dramatic Battle* 487
Hall Stage Equipment 203, 236
Halliday, Rob 206–7
Hallifax, Michael 62
Halls, Luke 363, *439*
Ham, Roderick 409
Hamburg, Opera 207
Hamilton, Victoria 460
hanamichi (in Japanese theatre) 469
Handel, George Frideric 33, 332
Handley, Paul 445, 448, 487
Handspring Puppet Company 340
Hannen, Nicholas 9
Hansard (record of parliamentary debates) 190
Happy Days 243, 250, 273, 379, *438*
The Hard Problem 441
Hardy, Hugh 425
Hardy, Thomas 5
Hare, David 270, 272–75, *272*, 300, 314, 477
  on LO and Peter Hall 272–74, 276
  on Michael Gambon 275
  on Olivier Theatre 274–75
  on Peter Brook 276
Harlan, Manuel 341, 358
Harris, Margaret 174, 512n.104
Harris, Sophie 512n.104
Harrison, Mark 246, 261
Harrison, Tony 267, *436*
Harry Potter and the Cursed Child 353
Hart, Sir William 76, 142, 189
Hatley, Tim 310, 311, *311*, 317, 319, 338, *438*, 440, 476
Hauptmann, Gerhart 4
Havergal, Giles 364, 368, 382–85, *382*
Hawkins, Vincent 468
Hawksmoor, Nicholas 219, 220, 227, 480
Haworth Tompkins 334, 335, *416*, 419, *419*, 446, 491, *492*
Hayles, Andy 24
Haynes, Gabby 270
Haynes, John 269, 271, 300, 301, 324
Hayward, Sir Isaac 16, 76, 142
HB Hardy Collaborative Architecture *418*
Headlong company 368
Hedda Gabler 292, *439*
Heeley, Desmond 55, 57
Heilpern, John 244
Heisenberg 350
Hellerau, Festspielhaus 44, *44*
Helm, Nicholas 510n.92
Helpmann Award 325
Hemming, Lindy 270
Henderson, Harry *61*, 62, 253
Henderson, Mark 271, 300, 338, 339, 341, 353 *436*, *438*, 440, *441*
Henry IV (Pirandello) 353, 381
Henry V (film) 49, 74
Henry VIII, King 30, 326
Henslowe, Philip 28, 29, 407
Hepburn, Katharine 74
Hepple, Peter 271
Herbert, Jocelyn 74, 75, *75*, 105, 134, 150, 155–62, *162*, 163–76, 181, 182–84, 185–87, 188–91, 192, 197, 265, 266, 268, 269, 275, 291, 346, 497
Herbert, Paul 291
Herford, Robin 287
Herrin, Jeremy 441
Herron, Ron 97
Hersey, David 241, 248, *251*, 267, 269, 276, *276*, 323, 435, *436*, 448
Hersey, Dimitri *251*
Hertzog & de Meuron 425
heterotopia, theatre as 482
Heywood, Thomas 30
Hiawatha 353
Hicks, Greg 468
Higgott, Gordon 510n.91
Hildy, Franklin J. 430
Hilferty, Susan *437*
Hill-Gibbons, Joe *437*
Hiller, Wendy 247
His Dark Materials 329, 331, 332, 338, *338*, 370, *436*, 444
His Girl Friday 331
Historic England 295
The History Boys 329, 331, 339, *339*, 346, 347, *347*
Hitchcock, Alfred 49
HKS (architects) *416*, 424
Hoare, Guy 361, *439*
Hobson, Harold 55, 57, 262
Hobson's Choice 54, 107, 108, 170
Hochhuth, Rolf 54
Hodge, John, *Collaborators* 352
Hodge, Patricia *469*
Hogan, James 487
Hogarth, William 34
Hogg, Christopher 297, 298, 314, 318
Holford, Sir William 96
Holinshed, Raphael 25
Holland, Henry 37, 38
Holloway, Baliol 22
Holloway, G.H. 42
Holm, Ian *61*
The Homecoming 163
Hoover, Richard 315
Hopkins, Anthony 62, 105, 270, 271, 274–75, 275, 296, 470
Hopkins, Michael 402, *422*, 425
Hornsby, Paul 445
horseshoe theatre 8, 20, 21, 41, 44, 45, 48, 118, 284, 308, 345, 379, 398, 414, 416
Horsham, Christ's Hospital School Theatre 23, 101, 234, 407–8, 418, *418*
Hoskins, Bob *xii*
Houghton, Stanley 7
House and Garden 317
Houston, Canada, Astrodome 285
Houston, Texas
  Alley Theatre 46
  Grand Opera 350
  Playhouse Theatre 46
How the Other Half Loves 287
Howard, Alan 464
Howell, Bill 64, 65, 101, 234, 407, *418*
Howell Killick Partridge and Amis 97, *418*
Hughes, Mick 301, *438*, *441*
Hull, University of, Gulbenkian Theatre 101
The Humorous Lieutenant 32
Humphries, Fred 407
Humphries, Henry R. 77, 183, 184, 451, 453
Hunt, Hugh 11–12, 13
Huntington, Helen 7
Husbands & Sons 348, 349, 350, 358, *358*, 368
Husserl, Edmund 430
Hytner, Sir Nicholas xix, 249–50, 274, 275, 279, 300, 302, 318, *329*, 338, 339, 341, 342, 346, 352, 353, 497
  Alex Jennings on 352
  Ben Power on 369
  and Bridge Theatre 333, 343, 419, *436*, *438*, 441
  and *Carousel* 460
  Charles Spencer on 338
  and Cottesloe Theatre 465
  David Hare on 274, 275
  as director of NT 315, 319, 329–33, 375, 444, 497
  and ENO 346
  Howard Davies on 279
  Laurie Clayton on 249–50
  Madelaine North on 338
  Michael Billington on 330, 339
  Michael Grandage on 460
  Neil Austin and 353
  and NT 50th anniversary 463
  and NT Future scheme 326, 378
  and Olivier acoustics 455
  and Olivier drum revolve 444
  and Olivier lighting 453
  and Olivier stage xix
  Paule Constable on 370
  Rae Smith on 366
  Rob Barnard on 444
  Simon Russell Beale on 463–64, 466
  and Steve Tompkins 334
  and succession debate 316
  Susannah Clapp on 342
  and sustainability 447
  on West End theatres 461–62
  Balancing Acts 487

I

Ian Ritchie Architects 24
Ibsen, Henrik 4, 126, 130
The Iceman Cometh 279
Icke, Robert 276, *439*
Il Campiello 246, 255
Illuminatus! 380
Illustrated London News 291
I'm Not Rappaport 412
The Independent 302, 316, 318, 321, 338, 358, 361, 463
Independent on Sunday 316
India 331, 413, 458
The Inheritance 367
Ink 350
Innsbruck 202
An Inspector Calls 289, 301, *301*, 303, 306, 310, *310*, 370, 460
The Invention of Love 325
Inverness, Eden Court Theatre 234, 411, *411*
iPhone 206

Ipswich Town (football club) 340
Iraq, war in 329, 331
Iris (film) 467
Irish Times 357
Irving, Sir Henry 3, 4, 5, 43, *43*, 49, 54, 256
Italy, communist party 401
Izenour, George 48, 114

J

Jackson, Angus 440
Jackson, Sir Barry 21, 44, 47, 254, 409
Jacobi, Alan 198, *251*
Jacobi, Derek 53, 105
James Bond films 467
James I, King 27
James III 437
James, Morris & Kutyla 416
James, Sid 316
Jane Eyre 439
Japan 28, 115, 344, 413
  Japanese company 468
Jenkins, Hugh 16, 190, 237
Jenkins, Natasha 441
Jenkins, Paul 398–401, 403, 425
Jennings, Alex 352, *352*
Jerry Springer - The Opera 310, 329, *330*, 331
John Gabriel Borkman 238, 242, 247, 379
Johns, Margo 46
Johnson, Philip 97, 101, 216
Johnson, Russell 398, 399, 400, 401, 408, *408*
Johnson, Samuel 34
Johnson, Terry 316
Joint Stock Theatre Group 74
Jonathan, Mark 447
Jones, Basil 340
Jones, Bill T. 437
Jones, Inigo 28, 30, 31
Jones, Nic 270
Jones, Robert *439*
Jonson, Ben 28, 30
Jordan, Eric 182, 186, 409, 425
Jordan, Matthew 510n.91
Joseph and the Amazing Technicolor Dreamcoat 308
Joseph, Stephen 46, 407, *407*
Jourdain, Francis 44
Journey's End 49, 264
Jouvet, Louis 44
Jozefowski, Paul 487
Jubilee Walkway, 491
Jumpers 54
The Jungle 367
Juno and the Paycock 148

K

Kafka, George 335
Kalman, Jean *436*, *438*
Kander, John, and Fred Ebb 355
Kansas City, Kauffman Center *423*
Kantrowitz, Jason 440
Kaufmann, Oskar 21
Kean, Charles 39
Kean, Edmund 6, 39, *39*, 49, 54
Keenan, Roger 212, 445

Kemble, Charles 3
Kemble, John Philip 39
Kempson, Rachel 512n.6
Kennedy, John F. 103
Kenny, Sean 75, *75*, *314*, 407, *407*, *436*, 440
  and architecture 95
  B.A. Young on 55
  and Chichester 55, 100
  design for *Hamlet* at NT 55, *95*
  designs for *Oliver!* and *Blitz!* 407
  at Dunes Hotel, Las Vegas 95
  and NT Building Committee 70, 78–82, 84–89, 92, 94
  and OL 95, 279
  and Old Vic 53, 55, 105
  in Paris 123
  Peter Hall and 22–23
  Peter Shaffer on 55
  Richard Brett on 198
Kent, Jonathan 280, *369*, *436*, 440
Khan-Din, Ayub 329
Kickstarter 488
Killigrew, Thomas 31, 32
King Bastard (film) 355
King Kong (musical) 325
King's Company 32
King's Men 28, 31
Kinnear, Rory 332, 342, 369
Kirkman, Robert 77, 215
Kneehigh Theatre (company) 373
Knight, Esmond 348
Knight, Rosalind 348
Kohler, Adrian 340
Koltai, Ralph 254, 325
Komisarjevsky, Theodore 21
Koolhaas, Rem 425
KPF Architecture 427
Krapp, Herbert J. 387
Kubrick, Stanley 49
Kushner, Tony 301
Kuszell, Stefan 399, 400
Kuwabara Payne McKenna Blumberg Architects 420
Kwei-Armah, Kwame 329, 331
Kyncl, Ivan 301, 302, 324, 338, 339

L

Labour Party (UK) 10, 16, 19, 229
The Lady in the Van 352
Lamb, Thomas W. 387
LAMDA (London Academy of Music and Dramatic Art) 80, 121, 122, 131, 136, 257
Lamford, Chloe 361, *437*, *441*
Landscape with Weapon 441
Langley, John 487
Lark Rise to Candleford 261, 262
Larkin, Philip 51
Las Vegas
  Dunes Hotel 95
  Sphere 45
Lasdun, Sir Denys *ii*, *66*, *77*, *100*, *104*, *193*, *215*
  appointment as architect for NT xv, xxiii, 103, 389–90
  and appointment of Pilbrow

as consultant to NT 195–97
as architect 22
author and xvi
Ben Power on 368
and 'Blue Book' 5
character and personality xi, 100, 103, 326–27, 405, 480, 487
conflict with Richard Eyre xi–xii, 289–99
and construction of NT 210, 238, 241, 255–56, 274, 282, 473
correspondence with LO 176, 195–97, 251
and courtyard theatre concept 234–35
David Hare on 274, 477
death 313, 317–18, 326
Deborah Warner on 319
design of NT ix
  auditorium designs 215
  ceiling 183, 390
  design process 215–25
  front of house design x, 305
  general design principles 218–19, 471
  lighting 223–25
  Olivier acoustics 184, 455
on Olivier Theatre 292
and public areas NT x, xxv, 380, 463
on 'fourth theatre' xxv, 100, 215, 221–23, *223*, 482, 487
and Frank Dunlop 65
and Genoa project *396*, 397–403, 415
and George Devine 73, 164
and 'Ginger Group' 233, 235, 238
Harold Hobson on 262
as host to Peter Hall 263
and IBM building 264–65, 446, *492*
James Lasdun on 326–27
Jocelyn Herbert and 346
Kenneth Rae on 209
Kenneth Tynan on 186
knighthood 397
and LO 83, 154
LO on 103
notes on meeting with Jocelyn Herbert 162
notes on NTBC meeting 172–73
on NT Building Committee 70
and NT Building Committee 106–54, 155–63, 185–87, 192–93
and Olivier Theatre opening 253–54
Patrick Dillon on 335
Paule Constable on 371
and Peter Brook 73, 276
and Peter Hall 263–66, 375
Peter Hall on 233, 244
Peter Moro on 103
and press 237
on proscenium theatre 185
responses to questions from South Bank Board 210–11
restaurant named after 449
'The Room' *126*

and Royal College of Physicians 100, 216, 266, 274, 326, 477
on Saint-Denis 389–90
Scheme A 13, 114, *114*, 118, *118*, 119, *121*, *123*, *124*, 125, 132, 143, 156, 157, 159
Scheme B 105, 126–45, *126*, *127*, *129*, 130, *133*, *134*, *135*, *136*, *138*, *139*, *141*, 147–54, *151*, *153*, 155, 157–62, *158*, *165*, 166–68, *167*, 217
  questionnaire on 168–72
Scheme C *156*, *157*, 158, 160, *160*, 168–72, *172*, 178–79
Schemes D and E 172–75, *172*, *174*, *179*, 182–84, 189, 480
and selection of architect for NT 97, 102–3, 105
and The Shed 378
site model of NT-Opera House scheme *144*
sketch for Genoa *396*
sketch of site *221*
and South Bank Board 245, 263
speech to Royal Society of Arts 220–23
Steve Tompkins on 471
and 'theatre of confrontation' 303, 309, 311, 356, 379, 390, 394, 480
on use of concrete 297
and Young Vic 65
Strategy for the Future 292, *292*
Lasdun, James 100, 313
The Master Builder 326–27
Lasdun, Lady (Susan) 217–18, 220, 263, 321
The Last of the Haussmans 344
Latham, Charles Latham, 1st Baron 9
Laurence Olivier Awards 319, 346, 350, 352, 353, 364, 452, 458, 463
Lauve, Jules 488
Lavery, Bryony, *Treasure Island* 385
Law & Dunbar-Naismith 411
Lawrence of Arabia 104
Lawrence, D. H. 348, 368
le Carré, John, *The Spy Who Came in from the Cold* 51
Le Corbusier (Charles-Édouard Jeanneret) 220, 227, 299, 335, 480
Le Havre 7
Leatherhead, Surrey
  Repertory Theatre 197
  Thorndike Theatre *47*
LED lighting fixtures 447
LED technology 449
Lee, Erin 487
Lee, Jennie (later Baroness Lee) 16, 145, 166, 189–91, 327
Leeds
  Grand Theatre 383
  West Yorkshire Playhouse (later Leeds Playhouse) 305

The Lehman Trilogy 314, 363, *363*, 368, *439*, *466*, 481
Leicester
  Council 384
  Curve theatre 277, 385, 446
Leigh, Vivien 74
Leighton, Pat *60*
Leitermann, Gene, *Theater Planning* 481, 481–82
Lester, Adrian 329, 331, 332, 342
Lester, Mylan 444–45
Levin, Bernard 55, 256
Levine, James 264
Levitt Bernstein Associates 411, *417*, 425
Lewis, Peter 57
The National, A Dream Made Concrete 487
Les Liaisons Dangereuses 278, 346
Liebermann, Rolf 403
The Life and Adventures of Nicholas Nickleby (play, after novel by Charles Dickens) 300, *300*, 313, 347
The Life of Galileo 261, 268, *268*, 275, 278, *279*, 459
Life of Pi (after book by Yann Martel) 311
Light Palette (lighting control system) 207
Light Shining in Buckinghamshire 439
Lightboard (lighting control system) 205–7, *206*, 241, 250, *251*, 276, 446–47
  sketch *208*
Lighthouse Acting Studio 469
lighting 446–49
Lillie, Beatrice 122
limited facility panels (LFPs) 208
Lincoln, Theatre Royal 42
Lindsay, Katrina 340, 359, 363, 371, *437*, *438*, *441*
Linklater and Paines 238
Liolà 324, *438*
Lipton, Sir Stuart 292, 293, 294–95, 297–98
A Little Night Music 408, 467, 468, 470, 472
Littler, Prince 15, 76
Littlewood, Joan 20, 127
Littmann, Max 21, 44
Liverpool 47
  Empire Theatre 82
  Everyman Theatre 334
  John Moores University 510n.92
  New Shakespeare Theatre 27, 510n.90
  Playhouse 303
Llewellyn-Davies, Richard 97, 101
Lloyd, Jamie 367
Lloyd, Selwyn (later Baron Selwyn-Lloyd) 16, 145
Lloyd Webber, Andrew 314, 449
Lockwood, Edwin 206
Lockwood, Sir Joseph 233, 234, 236, 243, 246, 263

London
  Adelphi Theatre 39
  Aldwych Theatre 15, 43, 109, 168, 262, 284, 285, 286–87, 347
  Almeida Theatre 278, 279, 330, 343, 344, 350, 373, 380, 381, 461, 462
  Apollo Theatre 334, 343, *413*
  Aquinas Street 53, *53*, 63, 83, *94*, 198, 238, 241, 246
  Arts Theatre 15, 272
  Bankside 26
  Barbican: see B: Barbican
  Battersea Arts Centre 332, 334
  Bel Savage Inn 26
  Bell inn 26
  Belvedere Road 137
  Blackfriars Theatre 28, 29
  Blitz 9
  Bloomsbury 8
  Bridge Theatre 333, 334, 343, 350, 419, *419*
  British Museum 4, 6, 9
  Bull inn 26
  Cambridge Theatre 54
  The Cenotaph 9
  Central Saint Martins College of Art and Design 311
  Central School of Art 325, 350
  Central School of Speech and Drama xi, 49, 407, 410
  Charing Cross Bridge 8, 10
  Charing Cross Road 42
  Cockpit Theatre, Drury Lane (later Phoenix) 30, *30*
  Cockpit-in-Court, Whitehall 30, 510n.92
  Comedy Theatre 40
  County Hall 8, 9, 14, 96, 144, 145, 251
  Courtyard Theatre 28
  Covent Garden Market 389
  Criterion Theatre 40
  Cromwell Gardens 9
  Cromwell Tower, Barbican 246
  Cross Keys inn 26
  The Curtain 27, 509–10n.86
  Dome of Discovery *68*
  Donmar Warehouse 308, 313, 330, 347, 350, 353, 373, 380, 381, 459, 461, 462
  The Dorchester xvi, 83, 237, 243
  Duchess Theatre 315
  Duke of York's Theatre 42, 171
  Duke's Theatre, Dorset Garden 32
  ENO (English National Opera) 281, 344, 346, 350
  Fortune Playhouse 64
  Fortune Theatre 28, 29, 30, 407
  Gaiety Theatre 40
  Garrick Theatre 42, 353
  Gate Theatre 303, 319
  George Street 233
  Gibbon's Tennis Court 31
  Gielgud Theatre (formerly
  Globe Theatre) 43, 234, 343
  Globe Theatre (1599, 1613) 27, 28, 29, 30, *30*, 410
  Globe Theatre (Shakespeare's Globe, 1997) x, 24, 29, *29*, 30, 240, 305, 323–24, 344, 382, 384–85, 430, 458, *458*, 509–10n.86, 510n.92
  Wanamaker Playhouse 30, 510n.91, 510n.92
  Goodwin's Court 203
  Great Fire (1666) 31
  Great Plague (1665) 31
  Guildhall School 463
  Haymarket Theatre (Theatre Royal, Haymarket) 381, 385, *385*, 469
  Hayward Gallery 254
    exhibition on NT 254
  Her Majesty's Theatre 8, 42, 75, 385, *385*, 408
  House of Commons 13, 14, 366
  House of Lords 13, 16, 243
  Houses of Parliament 365
  Hungerford Bridge 96, 145
  IBM building *264*, *265*, 446, 491, *492*
  Kensington Gardens 281
  Keppel Street 6
  King's Head Theatre 350
  King's Reach 218, 220
  King's Theatre, Haymarket 37
  Kingsway Theatre 5
  Lambeth Council Planning Department 296
  Lasdun restaurant 449
  Leicester Square 8
  Lincoln's Inn Fields 31, 33, 34, 94
  Lisle's Tennis Court 31
  Little Theatre 5
  London Contemporary School of Dance 327
  Lyceum Theatre 5, 8, 39, 42, 43, 267
  Lyric, Hammersmith 367, 409
  Lyric, Shaftesbury Avenue 305
  Mahatma Gandhi Hill, Euston 407
  Menier Chocolate Factory 305, 373
  Mermaid Theatre 48, *48*, 70–71, 97, 101, 107, 118, 122, 130
  Middlesex Hospital 317
  Morley College 6
  National Gallery 3, 9, 291
  Neal's Yard, Covent Garden 198, 407
  New London Theatre (later Gillian Lynne Theatre) 75, *314*, 334
  Noël Coward Theatre, earlier New Theatre, Albery Theatre) 8, 10, 43, 54, 65, 389, 394–95, *394–95*
  Novello Theatre (earlier Strand Theatre) 43, 392–93, *392–93*
  Old Bailey 332
  Old Vic see O: Old Vic
  Old Vic Centre 73
  Olympics (2012) 303
  Orange Tree Theatre 383, 384
  Palace Theatre 323, 469
  Palladium 276
  Paul's Cross 28
  Phoenix Theatre, Charing Cross Road 9, 30, *30*, 75, 510n.91
  The Place 325
  population 25
  Portland Place 5
  Prince's Meadow 189, 216
  Promenade Concerts 27
  Queen's Theatre, Haymarket (later King's Theatre) 33, 37, 40, 125
  Queen's Theatre (now Sondheim Theatre) 43
  Rose Theatre 24, 27, 28, 29, *29*, 292–93, 509n.86
  Roundhouse 276
  Royal Academy 9
  Royal Albert Hall 350
  Royal Ballet 7, 45
  Royal College of Physicians 100, 216, 266, 274, 477
  Royal Court Theatre 11, 12, 14, 42, 43, 49, 53, 73, 74, 75, 89, 105, 117, 281, 282, 303, 305, 308, 324, 334, *334*, 346, 347, 348, 349, 356, 367, 373, 414, 416, 452
    acoustics 453, 454
  Royal Court Upstairs 319
  Royal English Opera House (later Palace Theatre) 42
  Royal Festival Hall 13, *68*, 82, 101, 294
  Royal Opera House 7, 32, 40, 43, 171, 207, 281, 344, 346, 381, 398
  Royalty Theatre 40, 86
  Sadler's Wells Opera and Ballet 8, 16, 42, 69, 76, 79, 85, 88, 92, 145, 398
  Salisbury Court, *31*
  St. James Theatre 5
  St. Paul's Cathedral xi, 32, 219, 293, 326
  St. Paul's Cathedral School 463
  St. Paul's Theatre 28
  Savoy Theatre 5, 42
  Scala Theatre 40
  Shaftesbury Avenue 42
  Shaftesbury Theatre 42
  Shell Building 144
  Shoreditch 26
  Skylon *68*
  Slade School of Arts 344
  Somerset House xi, 219, 326
  South Bank 9, 12, 15, 16, 28, 65, *68*, 69, 81, 241, 296, *354*, 422, 474, 480
  Southwark 294
  Stoll Theatre 121
  Stratford East 20, 127, 303
  Strawberry Hill 121
  Swan Theatre *26*, 27
  Tate Modern 446, 493
  Tate Museum 34
  The Theatre, Finsbury Fields 27
  Theatre Royal, Covent Garden 32, 33, 34, 37, 38, *38*, 39, 40
  Theatre Royal, Drury Lane x, 4, 8, 9, 31–39, *31*, *32*, *36*, *37*, 43, 166, 256, 282, 284, 305, 324, 334, *334*, 352, 390
  Theatre Royal Richmond 36
  Theatre Royal Stratford East 20
  Tivoli Theatre 42
  Tricycle Theatre (later Kiln Theatre) 305, 373, 381, *418*, 462
  Vaudeville Theatre 40
  Victoria and Albert Museum 9, 486
  Victoria Palace Theatre 455
  Wanamaker Playhouse, *457*
  Waterloo Bridge xi, 10, 12, 189, *191*, 218, 293, 296, 299, 326, *493*
  Waterloo Road 132, 198
  Waterloo station 250
  Westminster Abbey 9, 34, 219, 293
  Whitehall 9
  Wyndham's Theatre 8, 43, 347, 462
  Young Vic Theatre 11, 12, 14, 46, 51, 54, 64–65, *64*, 101, 234, 284, 344, 345, 350, 355, 355–56, 367, 371, 380, 381, 397, 407, 418, 509n.92
  Youth Theatre (Young Vic) 65
London Contemporary Dance Theatre 325
London County Council (LCC) 9, 13, 16, 69, *76*, 82, 84, 96, 115, 134, 137, 142
London Road 329, 331, 340, *340*, 355, 441
London Theatre Studio 10, 12
London Weekend Television, *Aquarius* 255–56
Long Day's Journey into Night 54, 62, 63, 254
Long, Robert *63*
Longhurst, Michael 361, *437*
Look Back in Anger 19–20, 130, 134
Lope de Vega, Félix 28, 413
Los Angeles 368
  Ahmanson Theatre *415*
  Dolby (formerly Kodak) Theatre 416, *416*
  Hollywood Bowl 182
  Opera 350
  Walt Disney Concert Hall 417, *417*
Los Angeles Times 362
Lotherbourg, Philippe-Jacques de 36
Love 441
Love for Love 33, 51, 54, 57, *57*, 62, 148, 200
Lucking, Peter 425
Lumière, Auguste and Louis 281

Luther 82
Lutkin, Tim 360, *437*
Lutyens, Sir Edwin 9–10, *9*, 22, 216
Lynex, Richard 76, 103, 145, 166
Lynn, Ralph 286
Lyttelton, Alfred xxi, 5, 10
Lyttelton, Edith xxi, 5, 10
Lyttelton Theatre *xxii*, *377*
  acoustics 241–42, 274, 276, *377*, 390–91, 451, 453, 455, 458, 465
  air inlets 239
  air-conditioning 244, 248
  Alan Ayckbourn on 285
  Albert Finney on 377
  Alex Jennings on 352
  Anthony Ward on 323, 324
  auditorium 11, *20*, 238, 275, 299, *395*, 481, 482
  balcony 275
  Ben Power on 368, 369
  Bob Crowley on 346–47
  buffet counter 265
  Bunny Christie on 351
  capacity 395
  circle 385, 481
  circle lobby *336*
  David Hare on 272, 304
  Declan Donnellan on 414
  Denys Lasdun on 100, 164
  design xxi, 200, 211, 220–21, 373
  Diana Quick on 284
  dress rehearsals at 242, 243, 247
  and drum road 211
  Dudley on 282
  elevators 212
  first performance (*Blithe Spirit*) 244
  fly tower 220, 449
  flying system 445–46
  foyer 256, 297, 299
  front of house 298
  Giles Havergal on 385
  grid 445–46
  Hamlet at 241, 242, 247
  Hayden Griffin and 273
  Howard Davies and 278
  Howard Davies on 278–79
  An Inspector Calls at 306
  Jerry Springer – The Opera at 330, *331*
  John Gielgud on 256
  Jon Clark on 367
  Judi Dench on 468
  Lasdun and 390–91, 480
  laser scans *394–95*
  lighting 205, 248, 256
  as listed building 366
  lobby 332, *336*
  The Loft 313, 315, 319, *319*
  Machinal at 306, 370
  manual flying system 242
  Marianne Elliott on 348, 349
  Mark Thompson on 309
  and Max Bell Theatre, Calgary 421

Index 521

Michael Billington on 362, 379
Michael Blakemore on 282
Michael Grandage on 460
Michael Radcliffe on 377
model *184*, *219*, *257*
as movie studio 449
named after Lyttelton family 5
Neil Austin on 353
Nicholas de Jongh on 377
Rick Fisher on 310
and NT Future renovation 333
opening 250, 253, 272
Paul Arditti on 453
Paule Constable on 370
plans *200*, *494*
plans for improvement 291
problems with 292
productions at *438–39*
prompt corner 247
proscenium 200, 231, 256, 279, 306, 316, 394, 453
Rae Smith on 364–65
reflection to stalls *455*
Richard Brett at 250
Richard Cowell on 455
Richard Eyre on 292
Roger Allam on 377
Rufus Norris on 356
seating 48, 274
Simon Russell Beale on 465–66
sketch *199*
sound console *208*, 448
stage 278–79, 304, 305, 306, *394*, *395*
stage equipment 195
stalls 308
Stephen Daldry on 460
Steve Tompkins on 334, 471
Tim Hatley on 311
'Transformation' 315, 318–19, *320*, 370, 375
Trevor Nunn and 375
Trevor Nunn on 316
under construction 237, 245
Vicki Mortimer on 344
view of river from 296
view of stage 261
William Dudley on 377
Lytton, Victor Bulwer-Lytton, 2nd Earl of 5, 11

M

M&E 399
Ma Rainey's Black Bottom 359, *359*, *439*
Macauley, Alastair 317
McAlpine, Sir Edward 237, 243
McAlpine, Sir Robert, and Sons 64, 77, 190, 210, 212, 235–43, 245, 246, 250
McBean, Angus 55, 56
McCafferty, Owen 331
McCarthy, Lillah (Mrs. Harley Granville-Barker) 5
McCrory, Helen 368
McCurdy, Peter 510n.92
McDiarmid, Ian 280
MacDonald, Robert David 382

McElfatrick, William H. 387, 429
McEwan, Geraldine *63*, 105
McGoohan, Patrick 409
Machinal 294, 302, *302*, 303, 306, 310, 370, 377
McKellen, Sir Ian 105, 234, 249, 274, *293*, 314, 316, 411
McKenna, David 76
McKenzie, Julia *xii*
McKintosh, Peter *437*
Mackintosh, Charles Rennie 220, 480
Mackintosh, Iain 77, *77*, 488, 510n.89, 510n.91
Architecture, Actor and Audience 487
on *The Beggar's Opera* 34
on Cottesloe auditorium xi
on Cottesloe design xxiii, 77, 231, 277, 282, 397
and Denys Lasdun 235
early career 411–12
and Eden Court Theatre, Inverness 234, 411
Paul Arditti on 454
Peter Hall on 234
and Royal Shakespeare Theatre 23
Rufus Norris on 356
Stephen Daldry and 303, 305, 397
Steve Tompkins on 334 and Theatre Projects Consultants 412, 425, 486–87
McLeish, Iona 497
Macmillan, Harold (later Earl of Stockton) 15
MacNeil, Ian 294, 301, 302, 306–7, *306*, 310, 358, 362, 370, *439*
McPherson, Conor *440*
Macready, William 39
Madama Butterfly 477
Made in Dagenham 350
Madison, Wisconsin, Overture Center 423, *423*
The Madness of George III 308, 331, 346
Madrid, Teatro Real 477
The Magic Flute 346
Major Barbara 332
Malleson, Miles 57
Malone, Aideen *439*
Mamma Mia! 308
Manchester 47
International Festival 359
Library Theatre 303
Opera House 82
Piccolo Theatre 64
Royal Exchange Theatre 74, 244, 280, 284, 308, 309, 347, 349, 364, 383, 397, 411, *411*, *417*, *417*
University Theatre 409
Manchester Theatre Project section *410*
Mander and Mitchenson

Collection 193
Mannheim 202
A Map of the World 274
Marat/Sade 161
Margaret, Princess 247–48
Margate, Theatre Royal 40
Market Boy 355
Marlowe, Christopher 30, 383
Marowitz, Charles 414
Marriott, R.B. 56
Marshall, Norman i, 13, 45, 70, 72, *72*, 76, 78–142, 148, 149–62, 163, 172, 182–84, 185–87, 188–91, 192–93, 195
Martin, Leslie 97, 510n. 19
Mary Poppins (musical) 346
Masey, Cecil 9, 10, 13
Massinger, Philip 30
Massini, Stefano 363, 368
The Master Builder 62, 133, 163
Master of the Revels 31
Matcham, Frank
and acoustics 453
appreciation of 389, 416
auditoria 10, 394
boxes and balconies 275, 377, 397
design principles 356
expertise as designer 387, 429
horseshoe shape 308, 377
and Jethro T. Robinson 6, 40
and Lyceum, Edinburgh 364
and modern theatres 382
Paul Arditti on 452
and proscenium theatre 118, 279, 307, 424
Rae Smith on 364, 365
Steve Tompkins and 334 and Theatre Royal, Nottingham 42, 405, 416
use of cantilever 42
Matcham and Co. 42
Mathews, E.D. Jefferiss 89
Mathias, Sean 316
Matthew, Sir Robert 96, 98
Maurice Pinder 441
May, Val 74
Maybanks, Helen 362
Medea 181, 368
Melia, Michael 241
Mendes, Sam 315, 318, 323, 363, 367, *439*, 459
Metamorphosis 289
Methodism 4, 39, 47
Meyer, Carl 5
Michael Grandage Company 459
Michael Wilford & Partners *421*
Michell, Roger 441
microphones, use of 208, 316–17, 352, 392, 448, 451, 452, 464, 467
Middle 310
Middleton McMillan *423*
Middleton, Thomas 30
Mielziner, Jo 83, 95
Mies van der Rohe, Ludwig 454
Milan, La Scala 398, 399
Miles, Ben 363
Miles, Bernard 70–71

Miles, Sarah 70
Miller, Jonathan 54, 63, 239, 272
Miller, Kenny 364
The Millionairess 74
Minjoodt, Malcolm 66, 77, 115–17, 128, 137–41, 155, 160, 163, 173, 215
Minneapolis, Guthrie Theater 24, 46, 75, 79, 107, 111, *112*, *113*, 115, 420
Minors, Anne 425
Mirren, Dame Helen 316, 332, 464
mirror neuron 480
The Misanthrope 254
Les Misérables 276, 314, 370, 520
Mishcon, Victor Mishcon, Baron 263
Miss Julie 54, 147
Miss Saigon 276
Missing Theatre Project 472
Mitchell, Bill *440*
Mitchell, Katie 329, 332, 344, 367, *438*, *440*, 449
modernism 387
Moderwell, Hiram Kelly, *The Theatre of Today* 44
Moiseiwitsch, Tanya 46, 47, 70, 75, *75*, 78–82, 83, 94–131, 188–91, 198, 420, 459
Mole Richardson *194*, 203, 212, 236, 444
Molière (Jean-Baptiste Poquelin) 28, 108
Money 317, 321
Montgomery, Chris 267
Montgomery, Elizabeth 512n.104
Moore, Henry 99
Moore, Martin 205, 206, 248
Moore, Rowan 227
Moore, Stephen 287
Morley, Christopher 23
Morley, Lewis 56
Morley, Sheridan 255
Moro, Peter 97, 101, 103, 409
Morpurgo, Michael 332
Morris Architects *423*
Morris, Tom 332, 340, 348, 414
Morrison, Conall 317
Morrison, Herbert 88
Mortimer, John 62
Mortimer, Vicki 342, 344–45, *344*, 360, 363, 370, *438*, *440*
Morton, Neil 425
Moscow 148
Art Theatre 43
Kremlevsky Teatr 54, *54*, 57, 148
Moshe Safdie Architects *423*
Moss, Larry 440
The Mother 350
Mother Clap's Molly House 318, *318*
Mother Courage 436, 470
*The Motherf**ker with the Hat 439*
The Motive and the Cue 367
Motley (designer) 134, 174, 509n.52
Motta, Fabrizio Carini, *Trattato Sopra la Struttura de' Teatri e Scene* 32

Mourning Becomes Electra 331
Moving Being 325
Mozart, Wolfgang Amadeus 265
Mrs Brown (film) 467
Mrs Henderson Presents (film) 467
Msamati, Lucian *viii*
Mulryne, Ronnie 376
multi-form halls 424, *424*
multipurpose halls 423, *423*
Mumford, Peter 323, 325, *325*, 476–77, *436*, *440*
Munich 48, 202, 400
Kammerspiele 140
Künstlertheater 21, 44, 47
National Theatre 398
Prinzregententheater 41, 44
Murfin, Daniel 445
Murmuring Judges 275, 300
Murphy, Arthur 34
Murphy, Joe 305
Musicians' Union 207
Mutabilitie 315
My Fair Lady 323, 324, *324*, 352
Myers, Barton *see also* Barton Myers Associates, 402, 424, 425
Myers, Scott 300
The Mysteries 27, 249, 261, 267, *267*, 277, *277*, 281, 317, 419

N

Nadeem, Shahid, *Dara* 331
Napier, Elise 322
Napier, John xix, 23, 313, 315, 316, 322, 375, 444, 497
Napoleonic wars 39
Napoli Milionaria 323
National Building Agency, report on sabotage at the NT 240
The National Health 54, 254, 283
National Health Service (UK) 10, 474
National Heritage, Department of 295
National Insurance 10
National Lottery 295
National Theatre Act (1949) 239
National Theatre Company 1, 19, 53, 105, 158, 171, 245, 311, 335, 375, 382, 475
National Theatre and Museum of London Act (1973) 239
National Theatre (NT) 22, *94*. *222*
acoustics 261–62, 451–56
actor contracts 236
Anthony Ward on 324
architectural lighting 223–25, *224*
archives 13, 208
auditoria 218, 225
backstage *xxvi*, 219
backstage tours xxvii
Baylis Terrace 290
behind the scenes xxviii
Board xv, 17, 19, 54, 69, 76, 84, 291, 318
bookshop 299
box office 299

522   A Sense of Theatre

Building #1 9
Building #2 9–10
Building #3 10, 12
Building Committee/Panel (NTBC) xv, xvi, 69–75, 76, 143, 356, 409, 457
 1st meeting 78–82
 2nd meeting 84–89, 91
 7th meeting 92
 10th meeting 97
 11th and 12th meetings 98
 13th and 14th meetings 101
 16th meeting 106–9
 17th meeting 111–13
 18th meeting 119–24
 19th meeting 128–29
 20th meeting 131–36
 21st meeting 137–41
 24th–30th meetings 149–92
 demise of 209
 informal meeting 192–93
 minutes 71, 71, 486
 Nick Starr on 343
 questionnaire and responses on Scheme B 168–72
 recommendations 90
 seating plan 103
 second questionnaire 186–87
Building Development Committee 295, 318
cafe extension 337
Ceefax sign 266
Company formed 104, 158
Conservation Management Plan 378
contracts department 285–86
costs 144–45
David Hare on 477
design 48
design of building 215–25
DL&P model 191
dressing rooms xxvii, 463–64, 465
drum road xxvi, 211
exterior 219, 375, 388, 449, 482
50th anniversary 333, 463
final site 68
foundation stone 12, 14, 15, 16, 253
foyers 335
funding 474
Grade II* listing of building 295, 296, 297
Henry V at 338
His Dark Materials at 338, 369, 370
idea of experimental theatre 96, 112–13, 121, 131–33, 189–91, 275
interior xxv
internal politics 245
Joint Council (with Old Vic) 15
John Dexter on 264
Judi Dench on xxvii, 470
lighting team 445
listing 375
load in xxvi
main entrance with sign 337
maintenance 444

Max Rayne Production Centre xxvi, 336, 378, 446, 492
Mezzanine restaurant 294
Michael Billington on 263
Michael Blakemore on 283
model of Opera House scheme 136
models 191, 215–16, 219, 245
night view 260
north east corner buttresses 214
NT Ensemble 316
NT Future renovation (2013–2016) xxvii, 211, 225, 326, 332–36, 333, 336–37, 343, 378, 444, 446, 487, 491, 492
NT Live 329, 332, 345, 357, 381, 449
opening 253–57, 397, 486
orders and deliveries of equipment 246
O'Rorke concept 12
plans 10, 490-6
porte-cochère 298, 299, 320
Preliminary Report 198–99, 199
projected opening dates 238–39
proposal (1924) 7
public spaces ('Fourth Theatre') xxv, xxvi, xxvi, 100, 220, 221–23, 223, 482, 487
rehearsal rooms 79, 129, 133, 137, 139–41, 154, 211, 213, 284, 464, 468
reports of sabotage at site 240
Rowan Moore on 227
section 10
selection of architect 102–3, 103
The Shed 332, 333, 350, 368, 373, 378, 378
shortage of materials 246
sign posting 246
sound systems 448–49
staff on terraces 357
stage door xxvi
stages 219
strike by stage staff 244
Studio workshop 332
Technical Sub-Committee 98, 145, 150, 154, 187, 192, 195
technology and technical facilities 443–49
Terrace Café 299
Theatre Square 296, 299, 332
thrust stage theatre 12
topping-out ceremony 233
under construction 236
The Understudy pub 337
use of concrete see concrete, use of
view from Waterloo Bridge 219, 493
walkway 446
wardrobe department 246
website 487
workshop 337, 446, 491
National Theatre (NT) see also Cottesloe (later Dorfman) Theatre; Lyttelton Theatre;

Olivier Theatre
National Theatre of Scotland 355
National Theatre Wales 355
NATTKE (National Association of Theatrical Television and Kine Employees) 244, 245, 264
Negri, Richard 64, 73, 74, 147, 409–10, 409
Neil, J.A. 233, 235
Nelson, Jeannette 455, 487
Network 362, 362, 439, 481
Neville, John 262
neuroaesthetics 480
New York 325, 344, 368, 408
 Alvin Theatre 54, 57, 198
 Broadway 19, 278, 279–80, 305, 311, 315, 329, 350, 423, 462, 473
 Central Park 412
 Ethel Barrymore Theatre 343
 Lincoln Center 17, 101, 107, 109, 111, 113, 119
  Avery Fisher Hall 408
 Metropolitan Opera 73, 264, 281, 364, 366, 381
  Opera Live 381
 Music Box Theater 341
 New Amsterdam Theatre 406, 416
 Polonsky Shakespeare Center 418, 418
 Royale Theatre 315
 Shubert Theatre 122
 Vivian Beaumont Theater 72, 83, 83, 95, 112, 389, 455
New York Drama Critics' Circle Award 316
New York Times 301, 302, 317, 341, 360
News of the World 332
Nighy, Bill 275
No Man's Land 438
Noble, Adrian 23
Noel-Baker, Philip 14
Nolan, Sidney 234
The Norman Conquests 285
Norris, Rufus 355, 437, 441
 as associate director of NT 355, 447
 as director of NT 355–57
  end of tenure 474
  and Lyttelton Theatre 368
  on Lyttelton Theatre 356, 378
  and Mark Rylance 458
  Michael Billington on 340, 355, 357, 358, 379
  on Olivier Theatre 378
  on post-pandemic era 477
  Simon Russell Beale on 464, 465
  and Small Island 371
  succeeds Nicholas Hytner 250, 315
  The Telegraph on 359
  on theatres (Lyttelton, Olivier, Royal Court, Old Vic and Coliseum) 356, 378
  Time Out on 360
  Trevor Nunn on 315, 331
  Variety on 358

The National Theatre: A Place for Plays 357
North, Madelaine 338
Northampton, Derngate Theatre 407, 424, 424
Not About Nightingales 315
Notes on a Scandal (film) 467
Nottingham
 Playhouse 64, 85, 97, 101, 139, 262, 427
 Theatre Royal 42, 86, 397, 404, 405, 405, 413, 416
Novello, Ivor 8
Novosolieski, Michael 37
Nunn, Trevor 313, 436
 Alex Jennings on 352
 announced as successor to Richard Eyre 298
 Anthony Ward on 324
 Billington on 313
 on Cottesloe 376
 David Hare on 272
 as director of NT 313–19, 375, 444, 497
 Howard Davies on 278, 321
 The Independent on 321
 Laurie Clayton on 249
 and Lyttelton 319
 and musicals 313–14
 Nick Starr on 343
 and Oklahoma! 323, 326
 and Olivier Theatre xix
 and Peter Hall 240, 262–63, 272
 and Peter Pan 315
 Richard Cowell on 455
 and Royal Shakespeare Company 23
 succeeded by Nicholas Hytner 319
 The Telegraph on 321
 and use of microphones 455, 464
 Variety on 321, 322
Nye 474

O
O'Brien, Timothy 238
The Observer 17, 270, 341, 486
O'Casey, Sean 344
The Ocean at the End of the Lane 370
Oedipus Rex 10, 54
Oh! Calcutta! 76
Oh, What a Lovely War! 20, 51
oil crisis, Mid-East 211, 229
Okhlopkov, Nikolay 46
Oklahoma! 321, 321, 323, 324, 369, 468, 481
Old Vic Company 74, 409, 467
Old Vic (earlier Royal Coburg) Theatre 94, 512n.104
 air space 305
 auditorium 2, 52, 79, 109, 128, 132
 discussed by NT Building Committee 107–8, 113, 119, 128, 132, 134, 151–52, 155
 dress rehearsals at 198
 fly floor 53, 91

forestage 168, 200
history of 6–7, 39, 40
Howard Davies on 279
industrial relations 245
Joint Council (with SMNT) 10, 13, 14, 16
Judi Dench on 467, 468–69
lighting department 51, 198, 473
and LO's Hamlet at Elsinore 17, 45
Michael Blakemore and 63
National Theatre Company at xvi, 389
NT productions at 54, 55–57, 105, 148, 183–84, 248
Peter Hall on 78
and Pilbrow 'PROJECT' 173, 174
plan for new centre (1944) 10–11
productions for NT 236, 237, 238, 241, 242, 272–73
prompt corner 91
proscenium 71
renovation 101
School 14, 64, 73
Sean Kenny and 75
section 112
stage 91, 410
stage crew 248
stage door 468
stage equipment 198, 210
Tyrone Guthrie and 10–12, 63
under LO, Ralph Richardson and John Burrell 10–12, 49, 262
under Michael Elliott 409
Oliver! 75, 407
Olivier, Sir Laurence ii, 11, 49, 51, 54, 58, 63, 72, 180, 193, 226, 230, 251, 252, 257
 archives 486
 and audience 405, 469, 480
 and author xv–xvi, 195–97
 on Broadway 74
 on Burbage 27
 and Chandos 54
 and Chichester Festival Theatre xv–xvi, 17, 49, 100, 122, 151, 309, 309, 390, 469, 496
 childhood memories 49
 conflict with Peter Hall 16, 254
 contemporaries on 62–63
 correspondence with Denys Lasdun 176, 195–97, 251
 on curves 303
 David Hare on 272, 273
 death 198, 293
 and Denys Lasdun 103, 321, 409, 480
 as director of NT (1963–73) 17, 51–62, 65, 69–72, 240, 355, 413
 and Eden End 273
 on Edmund Kean 39
 and Garrick 34
 on George Devine xvi
 and Hamlet xvi, 45, 55, 74, 105
 on Henry Irving 43

Index 523

and *Henry V* 74, 83
on human element of theatres 457
illness 253, 254
inspection of NT site 241
joins Joint Council of NT and Old Vic 15
Kenneth Tynan and 181
and *King Lear* 173
last stage performance 54
letter to Denys Lasdun *197*
in *Long Day's Journey into Night* 54
in Los Angeles 255
made a life peer 54
memorial service 293
on NT ix
 and NT Building Committee/Panel xv, 19, 24, 70–72, 76, 78–89, 92, 94, 96, 97, 98, 101–9, 111, 119–24, 128–29, 131–45, 457
and NT design 48, 282
and Old Vic 10–12, 49
on Old Vic 59
and Old Vic 279, 394
Olivier Theatre named after xix
and Olivier Theatre opening 253–54
and *Othello* 54, 63, 105, 129, 135, 142, 148, 254, 329
Paule Constable on 471
performance style 451
personal problems 145
and Peter Brook 71, 180–81
relations with South Bank Board 246
and Richard Brett 195
and *Richard III* 74
and Scheme E 181
and Sheffield Crucible 47
and Sixties planning experiment for NT 389
and South Bank Board 274
speech on Olivier Theatre stage 254–55
speech at topping-out ceremony 233
succeeded by Peter Hall as director of NT 231
at *Tamburlaine* preview 244
and *Three Sisters* 198
and *Titus Andronicus* 121
and *Uncle Vanya* 70, 79, 80, 100, 105, 107, 112, 134, 136, 139, 254
On Acting 27
see also National Theatre, Building Committee/Panel (NTBC)
Olivier Theatre x, xi, *xx*, ci, 48, 147, 191, 195–204, 355, *374*
 acoustics x, 243, 244, 256, 261, 263, 264, 265, 284, 290, 292, 314, 316, 392–93, 451, 467
 Paul Arditti on 452–53
 Richard Cowell on 454–55
 air space 305, 449
 air-conditioning 243

Albert Finney on 376
Amadeus at 268
Anthony Ward on 323
Antony and Cleopatra at 271
auditorium x, 275, 282, 298, 356, 371, *374*, 384, 409, 452, 481, 482
axonometric view 393, *393*
Alan Ayckbourn and 285, 286, 287
Ben Power on 368, 369
Bob Crowley on 346
Bunny Christie on 351
ceiling 183, 451, *451*
ceiling reflectors 453, 455
circle 305, 306, 314, 316, 346, 349, 368, 370, 452–53
compared to Novello Theatre 392–93
compared to Royal Court 453
Coram Boy at 332
cycloconverters and computers 203–5
David Hare on 274, 314
David Hersey on 276
Declan Donnellan and Nick Ormerod on 376
Declan Donnellan on 414
delays to completion 242–44
Denis Quilley on 376
design xix, xxi, 211, 216, 220, 282, 291, 373, 495-7
Diana Quick on 284
distance to stage 393, *393*
dressing rooms 468
drum revolve xvii, xxi, 194, *202*, *213*, *232*, *495*
 Bunny Christie on 351
 commissioned 250
 concept and planning 202–5, 209–10
 discussed by NT Building Committee 13
 first use (*The Shaughraun*) 211, 248, 271, 278, 281, 449
 Judi Dench on 468
 McAlpines and 235
 model *xvii*, *202*
 Neil Austin on 353
 Nicholas Hytner and 331, 333
 repairs to 444–45
 Richard Brett on installation 212
 Richard Brett's design for 204–5
 Richard Eyre on 290
 Rufus Norris on 356
 and Trevor Nunn's redesign 316, 375, 497
 wear and tear on 444–45
 William Dudley on 281–82
during fit-up 434
exterior 219, *221*
fly tower 213, 220, 221, 397, 452
flying system xxi, 201–2, 203, *204*, 212, 250, 445
foyer 256
Giles Havergal on 382

grid 201, 204, *204*, *213*, 219, *251*, 445
ground plan 409
Guys and Dolls at x–xi, *xii*, 275, 369
Hedda Gabler at 292
Helen Mirren on 316
Henry V at 331
An Inspector Calls at 306
Jon Clark on 367
Judi Dench on 467–68, 469–70
Lasdun on 292
laser scans 392–93, *392–93*
The Life of Galileo at 268, 459, *497*
lighting 205–6, 256, 308, 447
lighting bridge 183, 375
lighting walkway 447
as listed building 366
Marianne Elliott on 348–49
Mark Girouard on 376
Mark Rylance on 458
masking screens 204, *204*
Masterplan 314
Max Stafford-Clark on 318
Michael Billington on 379–80, 381
'Michael Bryant spot' 248
Michael Gambon on 376
Michael Grandage on 459–60, 461
models *181*, *219*, 291
Neil Austin on 353
Nicholas Hytner on 330, 332
and NT Future renovation 333
Oklahoma! at 325, 369
open stage xvii, 201–3, 390
open stage *see also* open stage (main entry)
opening 253–54, 267
painting of concrete 265–66
Paule Constable on 370
Peter Hall on xix
Peter Mumford on 325
plans *xix*, *196*, *201*, *391*, *495-7*
productions at *436–37*
proposal to darken 266
proscenium 452
Rae Smith on 365, 366
redesign 316
Rick Fisher on 310
'ripple rows' / 'ripple seats' 128, 185, 200, 316, 375, 497
The Rivals at 270
Roger Allam on 376
roof panels above auditorium 450, *451*, 453
Rufus Norris on 356
seating 48, 452, 481
section 10, *201*
Simon Russell Beale on 464, 465–66
sketch *202*
Small Island at 371
sound desk 448
stage 175–76, 231, 253–54, 268, 278, 282, 309, 316, 371, 375, 385, 390, 391, 480
stage from lighting bridge and

'stalactite' (lighting) *213*
stage staff 244
stalls 278, 308
Stephen Daldry on 304
Steve Tompkins on 334, 471
'Sweet Spot' 254
temporary arena 274
as theatre-in-the-round 121, 298, 299, *299*, 375, 378, 407
Tim Hatley on 311
Treasure Island at 385
Trevor Nunn on 316
under construction 210, *210*, 236, 239, 243
Vicki Mortimer on 344–45
view of stage 261
view to stage from grid 213, *442*
William Dudley on 81–82
One Man, Two Guvnors 308, 329, 332, 341, *341*, 353, 385
O'Neill, Eugene 477
open stage
 at Chichester 17, 71, 454
 construction 175
 Denys Lasdun and 390
 discussed by NT Building Committee 80–81, 86, 96–112, 139–93
 George Devine on 118
 LO on 168, 180
 Lord Goodman and 166
 Michael Elliott on 114
 movement towards 44, 47, 48, 106
 at New London Theatre 334
 Norman Marshall on 142, 168
 Peter Hall on 127, 130
 plans for xvii, 145, 169, 170–71, 199, 202, 210, 390
 Tyrone Guthrie on 16–17
opera houses 422, *422*
Opera North 325
Or You Could Kiss Me 441
Oram, Christopher 321, 323, 353, 459, 460
The Oresteia 261, 269, *269*, 369
Orlando, Florida
 Dr. Phillips Center
 Disney Theatre 416, *416*, 424
 Steinmetz Hall 424, *424*
Ormerod, Nick 301, 376
O'Rorke, Brian 12, 13, 14, 22, 69, 85, 97, 114, 216
Orrell, John 510n.89, 510n.91
Ortel, Sven 338, *449*
Osborne, John 272, 477
Oscars *see* Academy Awards
Oslo, Opera House (Den Norske Opera) 422, *422*
O'Toole, Peter xvi, 53, 54, 101, 104
Ott, Carlos 403
Our Country's Good 353, *437*
The Overwhelming 440
Oxford, Playhouse 234, 411
The Oxford Magazine 35
Oxford, University of, Worcester College 30

P
Pacific Domes Company 305
pandemics 473
Pani 207
Parade 353
Paris 76, 123
 Chaillot 82
 Odéon 294
 Opera 41, *41*
 Opéra Bastille 403
 Opéra Garnier 403
 Théâtre des Bouffes du Nord 73, 381
 Théâtre des Champs Élysées 21
 Théâtre du Vieux-Colombier 44
 Théâtre National de Chaillot 82, *82*
 Théâtre National Populaire (TNP) 249
Parker, Donna 487
Parry, Chris 315
Parry, Natasha 71
Parsifal 325
The Party 54
The Passion 262
Pate, Tom 62, 251
Paton, Maureen 271
Patti, Pierre 387
 Essai sur l'architecture théâtrale 35
Paul 440
Pawson, Terry 425
Payne, Tony 206
Peck, Bob 287
Peer Gynt 10, *11*, 17, 310, 317, 352, 410
Pelli, César 402, 425
Penang, Malaysia 463
People 331
People, Places and Things 350, *441*
Pepys, Samuel 32
performance space, feasibility 425
Perkin, George 297
Perret, Auguste and Gustave 21
Persson, Johan 341, 342, 359, 363
Peter Grimes 477
Peter, John 317
Peter Pan 315, *318*
Petherbridge, Edward 105
Phèdre 332
phenomenology 430
Philadelphia 310
Philip, Prince, Duke of Edinburgh 239
Philips/Signify 449
Phillips, Andy *251*, 268
Philomena (film) 467
Phipps, C.J. 40, 42, 387, 405, 416, *416*
Piaf 278
Piano, Renzo 402, 425
Pickup, Ronald 53, 105
Pilbrow & Partners 487
Pilbrow, Daisy 488
Pilbrow, Fred 425, 427, 487, 488

Pilbrow, Richard *xiii*, *75*, *77*, *183*, *202*, *232*, *489*
  appointment as theatre consultant 187, 195
  B. A. Young on 55
  career 75
  conversation with Laurie Clayton 248–50
  death 488
  and delays to completion of Olivier Theatre 242
  and Denys Lasdun 147
  and 'Ginger Group' 233, 235–36, 239
  invited to join NT Building Committee 150, 153
  letter to LO 209
  lighting design for NT 57, 205–7
  and NT Building Committee 154–56, 163–76, 182–84, 185–93
  'PROJECT' 173, *173*, 176
  response to questionnaire on Scheme B 170
  Richard Eyre on xii
  and shortage of electricians 238
  and studio theatre 234
  Stage Lighting (book) 72
  A Theatre Project (book) 488
Pilcher, John 77, *77*
Pillars of the Community 438
Pinero, Sir Arthur 5
Pink, Colin 339
Pinter, Harold 239, 379, 383, *438*
Piper, John 96
Piper, Tom 24
Piranesi, Giovanni Battista 335
Piscator, Erwin 45
Pitt, William 35
place, sense of 431
Platonov 73
Play (Beckett) 134
Play Without Words 320, 370
players, itinerant 25
playhouse design 19–49
Plays and Players 486
Plenty 274
Plessey 207
Plowright, Joan (later Baroness Olivier, Dame Joan Plowright) 17, 65, 70, 100, 105, 145, 254, 255
Plummer, 189
Plunder 242, 379
Poel, William 20, 42
Poet, Bruno 340, 438, *439*, *441*
The Point 149–50
Polaris submarines 206
Ponis, Alberto 399, 400–401, 402
Port of London Authority 76
Portable Theatre Company 272
Portoghesi, Paolo 401
Portzamparc, Christian de 402, 425
Potter Lawson & Fladd Architects *423*
Poughkeepsie, New York, Frances Lehman Loeb Art Center (The Loeb) 109

Powell and Moya 97
Powell, Nick 363
Power, Ben 368–69, *368*
Powell, Nick 363
power flying 445
  see also Olivier Theatre, flying system
PDP11 minicomputer (DEC) 447
Prana (vital force) 480
Pravda 261, 270, *270*, 274, 275
Prescot, Merseyside, Shakespeare North Playhouse 30, 510n.92
Present Laughter 438
President of an Empty Room 440
Price, Cedric 97
Prince, Harold *408*, 514n.14
The Prince and the Showgirl (film) 74
Private Eye 16
Private Lives, 49
Profumo, John 51
promenade format 419
proscenium theatre *163–64*
  acceptance of 40
  advantages of 134, 136, 139, 186, 305
  approval of 185
  defining 132
  Denys Lasdun on 113, 164, 390
  discussed by NT Building Committee 101, 108, 109, 113, 115, 130, 133, 136, 142, 155, 163–64, 170–71
  at Drury Lane 34, 38
  Howard Davies on 279
  Ian MacNeil on 357
  LO on 79, 83, 89
  at Lyttelton Theatre 379
  movement against 44, 47, 48
  new model 185–86
  at Old Vic 62, 78, 409–10
  Paul Arditti on 454
  Peter Hall on 86, 172
  Peter Softley's summary 164
  seating in 190
  Stephen Daldry on 265
  at Stratford 21–22
  Terence Gray and 45
  Tim Hatley on 311
  Trevor Nunn and 319
  Tyrone Guthrie and 13, 16
Prospect Theatre Company 234, 411
Provincial Theatre Council 12
Prowse, Philip 364, 382, 383
PTF control panel 207
Pugh, Harry 77, *77*, 192–93, 215, 233, 242, 245
Pullman, Philip 331
Punch 270
Punchdrunk (theatre company) 329, 373
Puritans, Puritan Revolution 25, 26, 28, 31, 40, 477
Pyant, Paul 300, 302, 317, *436*
Pye, Tom *436*, *438*

Q
Qi (vita force) 480
Quay Brothers *441*
Quayle, Sir Anthony 19, 22
The Queen (film) 352
Quick, Diana 284, *284*
Quilley, Denis 376

R
Race Seating 236, 237, 446
Racing Demon 300
RADA (Royal Academy of Dramatic Art) 355, 384
Radcliffe, Michael 377
radio 48
Radmore, Peter 198, 290, *290*, 294, 447
Rae, Kenneth
  Cecil Masey and 13
  and LO 209
  Lord Esher and 15
  and NT Building Committee 78–141, 148, 149–53, 155, 163–76, 182–84, 187–91, 195
  and NT royal opening 237
  and Scheme E 175
  as secretary of South Bank Theatre Board 71, 76
  summary of responses to questionnaire 172
Rafta, Rafta... 311, *438*
Raines Finlayson Barrett and Partners *421*
Ralph's Rocket 463
Rambert 325
Ramsdell, Roger *61*
Rank Organisation 316
Rank Strand *see* Strand Lighting
rational theatre 48
Rattigan, Terence 361
Rawn, William 402, 425
Rayne, Sir Max (later Lord Rayne) 54, 65, 233–36, *233*, 237, 239, 243, 246, 262, 263, 265, 266, 291
Rea, Stephen 271, 290
Read, John B. 55
Reardon, Michael 23
Rebecca (film) 49
The Recruiting Officer 54, 56, *56*, 74, 105, 108, 134, 163
Red 353, 462
The Red Barn 276, 350, *439*
Redgrave, Lynn 57
Redgrave, Sir Michael 17, 53, 55, 70, 105
Redgrave, Vanessa 72, 409
Rees, Llewellyn 11, 64
Reformation 326
Reid, Francis 239
Reinhardt, Max 20, 44, 110
The Relapse 352, *436*
Relph, Simon 239, 244, 273
Remember This 317
Renaissance, Italian 31
Renton Howard Wood Levin 404, 416, *416*, *420*, 424, 425

Renzo Piano Building Workshop *422*
repertory theatre 47
Restoration 31–33
Restoration comedy 148
  playhouses 262
Rex/OMA *418*
Rhymes, Rupert *60*, 192–93
Rice, Emma 344, *440*
Rice, Peter 361
Rich, Christopher 33
Rich, Frank 302
Rich, John 34
Richard III (film) 74
Richardson, Sir Ralph 11, *11*, 12, 49, 238, 247, 262, 264
  Ralph's Rocket 463
Rickman, Alan 316
Rickson, Ian *441*
Ridley, Brian 198, 293, *293*, 294
Rigg, Dame Diana 238
Riley, Maggie 255
Ring cycle 281, 325
ripple seating 185, 200, 316, 375
The Rivals 261, 270, *270*
The Roaring Girl 30
Robertson, Joe 305
Robertson, Patrick 64
Robinson, Jethro T. 6, 40, 42
Robson & Partners 97, 101
Rocket (locomotive) 39
Rockwell Associates 416
Rodenburg, Patsy 316
Rodgers, Richard, and Oscar Hammerstein 323
Rollins, Howard 412
Rome 28
Ron and Arthur (GLC surveyors) 250–51
Ronder, Tanya 355
"The Room" 114, *126*, 182
Rosencrantz and Guildenstern are Dead 51, 54, *54*, 57, 198
Rosenthal, Daniel 321
  The National Theatre Story 3, 487
Rosenthal, Jean 408
Rosner, Tal 358
Ross, Finn 341
Rossi, Aldo 400–402
Rothko, Mark 462, 514n.13
Rowan, Sir Leslie 76
Rowbottom, George xvi, 76, 128, 131, 149, 154, 155–62, 163–76, 182–84, 185–87, 188–91, 198
Royal Ballet 346
Royal Fine Arts Commission 291, 294
The Royal Hunt of the Sun 51, 54, 56, *56*, 142
Royal Institute of British Architects (RIBA) 20, 78–93, 136, 486
Royal Opera 350
Royal Shakespeare Company
  Alex Jennings and 352
  and Barbican Theatre 143, 171, 263–64, 381
  Bob Crowley and 346

and Christ's Hospital School Theatre 23, 407–8, 418
comparisons with NT 160–61, 171, 206
Jocelyn Herbert and 75
Judi Dench and 467
lighting 206, 276
Mark Thompson and 308
and *Nicholas Nickleby* 300
and NT Building Committee 70, 89, 160–61
Peter Brook and 73, 161
Peter Hall and 19, 72
  at Stratford 356
Tom Hatley and 311
Trevor Nunn and 313
William Dudley and 281
Rubasingham, Indhu *439*, 488
Rugg, Sir Percy 76
Ruhnau, Walter 97, 101, 216
Rules for Living 441
Runia, John 425, 487
Russell, Wally 207, 408
Russia 148
Rutherford and Son 344
Rylance, Sir Mark 382, 415, 457, *457*, 458, 482, 510n.90, 510n.91

S
Sabel, David 332
Sachs, Edwin 43
  Modern Opera Houses and Theatres 4, 387
Sacred Geometry 400
Sadler's Wells Committee 99
Sadler's Wells Trust 76
Safdie, Moshe 402, 425
St. Andrews, University of 350
Saint Joan 100, 105, 329, 332, 339, 348–49, 364, 365–66, 370
St. John of Fawsley, Norman St John-Stevas, Baron 294, 295
Saint-Denis, Michel 11–12, 64, 70, 73, *73*, 78–141, 163, 171, 174, 182, 185, 188, 217, 262, 389–90
Salome 437
San Francisco 294
  American Conservatory Theater (ACT) 384
  Geary Theater (now Toni Rembe Theater) *416*
Sansom, Laurie *437*
Saunders, George, *A Treatise on Theatres* 37
Saunders, James 35
Scapino 64
Scarborough
  public library 285
  Stephen Joseph Theatre 46, *46*, 285, 286, 287, 407
Scarfe, Gerald 286
Scarpa, Carlo 399, 400
Scene/Change (collective) 476
Scenes from an Execution 325
Scenes from a Big Picture 331
scenographic space 482

Schiller, Friedrich 383
Schlesinger, John 264
The School for Scandal 36, 54
Scobie, Harry 487
Scofield, Paul 238, 268, 287, 347, 412–13
Scott, Elisabeth 19, 20–23, *21*, 380, 391, 481
Scutt, Tom 361, *439*
The Seafarer 364, *440*
The Seagull 134
seat sales 431
Second Stride 325
Sellars, Peter 380
Semper, Gottfried 101
The Servant of Two Masters 332, 341
Shaffer, Peter 54, 55, 56, 57, 147, 254, 264, 267, 268, 269, 270, 271, 274
Shakespeare Council 15
Shakespeare Globe Trust 510n.90
Shakespeare, William 3, 4, 5, 14, 17, 27, 28, 79, 122, 342, 382, 383
 birthday 234
 death 30
 and Elizabethan theatre 27, 382
 First Folio 7, 74
 Giles Havergal on 383
 Henry Irving and 4
 as inspiration to theatre-lovers 3, 4
 LO on 79, 123
 and NT foundation stone 14
 Peter Hall on 240, 293
 plan for statue of 5
 retirement 30
 Robert Greene on 29
 Rufus Norris on 477
 Simon Russell Beale on 465
 Trevor Nunn and 313–14
 Tyrone Guthrie on 17
Antony and Cleopatra 74, 261, 271, *271*, 316, 468
As You Like It 72, 74, 409, *437*, 459–60
Coriolanus 15
Hamlet xvi, 17, 27, 39, 43, 45, 51, 53, 54, 55, *55*, 64, 74, 95, 101, 104, 241, 242, 247, 248, 249, 317, 332, 352, 369, 379, 464, 467
Henry IV Part 1 353
Henry IV Part 2 309, 353, *436*
Henry V 49, 74, 83, 311, 329, 331, 338, *338*
Henry VI 468
Henry VIII 38
Julius Caesar 254, 419
King Lear 27, 115, 120, 123, 163, 173, 249, 323, 476, 477
Macbeth 39, 163, 467
The Merchant of Venice 62, 317, 321, 325
A Midsummer Night's Dream 42, 347, 419, 465
Much Ado About Nothing 142, 254, 332, 465, 466, *466*
Othello 27, 39, 51, 54, 54, 63, 105, 109, 129, 135, 136, 142, 148, 254, 329, 332, 342, *342*, 345, 367
The Plantagenets (adaptation) 346
Richard II 74, 234, 411
Richard III 6, 10, 11, *11*, 27, 34, 39, 62, 64, 74, 106, 108, 153, 249, *294*
Romeo and Juliet 317, 449, 467, 470
The Tempest 28, *64*, 254, 464
Timon of Athens 275, 311
Titus Andronicus 121
Troilus and Cressida 316, 317, 321
Twelfth Night 437
The Winter's Tale 353, 467
Shakespeare Institute 64
Shakespeare in Love (film) 467
Shakespeare Memorial National Theatre (SMNT)
 Committee 5–6, 8, 9, 10
 Joint Council (with Old Vic) 10, 13, 14, 16
Sharoun, Hans 417
The Shaughraun 211, 248, 249, 261, 271, *271*, 275, 278, 281, 282, *282*, 290, 449, 481, *497*
Shaw, Fiona 294
Shaw, George Bernard 3, 4, 5, 9, *9*, 10, 14, 20, 43, 130, 274, 315
She Stoops to Conquer 36
Sheffield
 Crucible Theatre 24, 46, *46*, 47, 70–71, 75, 191, 303, 305, 311, 381, 391, *391*, 420, *420*, 454, 460, 461, 462
 Theatres 459
Sheldon, Sidney 512n.6
Shell plc 96
Sheppard, Richard 97, 101
Sher, Antony 381
Sheridan, Richard Brinsley 17
Shewring, Margaret 376
The Ship 282
Shortall, Tim *440*
Show Boat 408
Shulman, Milton 268, 269
Shunt (theatre company) 329
Shutt, Christopher 302, *322*, 340
Shuttleworth, Christine 488
SIAP acoustic enhancement system 448, 452
Sibella, Angelo 402
Sickert, Walter 305, 462
 The Old Bedford 42, 456
Siddons, Sarah 38, 39
The Siege of Rhodes 31
The Silver Tassie 342, *342*, 344, 345, 353, 370
Simpson, Christian 192–93
Singapore, Esplanade Arts Centre 421, *421*
Siobhan Davies Company 325

Slater, Simon 361
Sleichim, Eric 362
A Small Family Business 286, 287
Small Island 371
Smirke, Sir Robert 32
Smith, Greg 364
Smith, Dame Maggie 105, 147, 290, 463
Smith, Rae 339, 340, 359, 364–66, *364*, 370, 371, *436*, *438*, *440*, *441*
Smith, Richard Hubert 358, 360, 361
Smith, William 27
Snøhetta 402, *422*, 425
Snyder, Bruce 270
Soames, Mary Soames, Baroness 248, 293–96
Softley, Peter *66*, 77, *77*, 106–9, 111–290
 memorandum 176
Soldiers 54
Somerville, William Lyon 8
Somme, battle of 390
Sondheim, Stephen 307
Sonrel, Pierre 11
sound and communications 207–8, 448–49
Sound Research Laboratories 77, 454
South Bank National Theatre and Opera House Board 17, 69, 70
South Bank Theatre Board
 and appointment of Denys Lasdun 103
 and choice of architects 84, 87, 98
 and cost of NT project 142, 207, 235, 243, 444
 Kenneth Rae and 76, 81
 LO on 78, 85, 139
 NT Building Committee and 83–89, 91, 98, 106, 176
 and Olivier Theatre acoustics 261
 Peter Hall on 241–42
 and proscenium theatre 274
 and Scheme B 149
 and target dates and delays 235–36, 240–44, 263
South Pacific 322, *322*
South-East Asia 421
Southern, Richard 13
space stage 201, 216
Spacey, Kevin 279
Spain 413
Spartacus (film) 49
Speer, Albert 10
Spence (architect) 97
Spencer, Charles 322
Spencer, Terence 64, 97
Spot Me lighting system 447
Spotlight 21
Sprague, W.G.R. 43, 392, 394
Square Rounds, 497
Stafford-Clark, Max 74, 318, 440

The Stage 40, 338
Stage Technologies 445
Stalin, Joseph 148, 273
Stamp, Gavin 291
Standing at the Sky's Edge 474
Stanislavski, Konstantin 43
Stanley 325, *440*
Stansted Airport 274
Stanton, Robert 257
Stanton Williams (architects) 288, 293–94, 296, 299, 326, 491, *491*
Staples, David 425
Starlight Express 145
Starr, Nick 249, 274, 280, 332, 333, 334, 343, *343*, 351, 378, 419, 444, 466
Stasio, Marilyn 341
State of the Nation 314
Stein, Gertrude x
Stein, Peter 249
Stephens, Robert 53, 54, 56, 105
Stephenson, Robert 39
Sterling, Jo 269
Stevens, Peter 261
Still, Melly 332, 370, *438*
Stirling and Gowan 97, 101
Stockwood, John 28
Stoppard, Tom 198, 254, 319, 322, 449
The Storm 148, 183, 198
Straker, Dick 322, 338, 339, 449
Strand Lighting (later Rank Strand) 205–6, 206, 207, 236, 248
 Galaxy (lighting control system) 447
 Lightboard (lighting system) 205–7, *206*, 241, 250, *251*, 276, 446–47
 sketch *208*
 Light Palette (lighting control system) 207
Stranger Things (stage production) 303, 367
Stranger Things (TV show) 303
Stratford Herald 22
Stratford, Ontario 17, 46
 Festival Theatre 13, 17, 24, 75, 79, 80, 83, *83*, 108, *110*, 124, 216, 309, 420
Stratford-upon-Avon 477
 Courtyard Theatre 367, 380
 The Other Place 24, 313
 Royal Shakespeare Theatre 23–24, *23*, 84, 109, 282, 316, 356, 367, 384, 391, 512n.104
 Shakespeare Jubilee (1769) 34
 Shakespeare Memorial Theatre 14, 16, 19, 20–23, *21*, *22*, 352, 454, 481
 balcony *21*
 Shakespeare Theatre (1879) 20, *20*
 Swan Theatre *22*, 23–24, 101, 305, 313, 345, 408, 418, 469

Street of Crocodiles 364
Street, Peter 27
A Streetcar Named Desire 319, 367
Stride, John 53
Strindberg, August 126
Stroman, Susan 323
Stroomer, Mark 425
studio theatre (as concept)
 Bunny Christie on 351
 discussed by NT Building Committee 90, 139, 141, 173, 190–91, 192, 199
 Peter Hall and 231, 233–35, 239, 412
 see also Cottesloe (later Dorfman) Theatre
Stuff Happens 275, 331
Suffolk, Jonathan 487
Sullivan, Dan 412–13
Sullivan, Peter, *The National Theatre Plan - and how it evolved* (*Sunday Times*) 142–43, *142*
Summerfolk 249, 316–17, 321, *321*, 325
Sunday Express 340
Sunday Telegraph 299
Sunday Times 142–43, *142*, 145, 147, 238, 317
Supple, Tim 317
Sussex University, Gardner Arts Centre 75
Svoboda, Josef 148, 150, 183–84, 198, 367, 371
Sweden 3, 344
Sweet Bird of Youth 323
Swift, David 512n.6
Swift, Jonathan 296
Swindon, Wiltshire 47
Sydney, Australia, Opera House 145, 238, 425, 509n.84
Sylvester, Suzan 286
Syringa Tree 440

T

TABS magazine (Strand), 499
TAIT (technical supplier) 444–45
Talbot, Sir Robert 35
Tales from the Vienna Woods 331
Tamburlaine the Great 28, 243, 244, 249, 253, 261, 267, *267*, 276, 284, 352, 379, 383
Tanner, Flip 24
Tannoy loudspeakers 448
Tarzan (musical) 346
Taylor, Ben 339
Taylor, Fred *61*
Taylor, Kevin 445
Taylor, Paul 302, 316
Tchaikovsky, Pyotr Ilyich, *Swan Lake* 310
technology, theatre 425
Tele-Stage Associates 212, 236, 445
Tennant, H.M. 132
Terry, Ellen 5, 42, 43, *43*, 49

Tessenow, Heinrich 44
Thames, River 9, 321, 446, 482
Thatcher, Margaret 289, 315
theatre, sense of 461
Theatre of Cruelty 121
theatre design, key concepts 428–31, *430–31*
Theatre Projects Consultants (TPC), later Theatre Projects (TP)
 and actor/audience relationship 413
 aims and principles 415
 archives 486
 and auditoria 451
 and Bastille project 403
 Brian Benn and *257*
 collaborations 425
 conflict with DL&P 397
 and Cottesloe Cockpit xxiii, 235
 and Cottesloe Theatre design 231, 234, *235*, 239, 412
 courtyard theatres 380
 David Hersey and 276
 and Denys Lasdun 215
 electrical work 208
 first client and early projects 47
 and Genoa opera house project 398–403
 lighting design team xvi, 276
 lighting rental store 407
 and Lyttelton Theatre 250–51
 NT Building Committee on 187
 and NT timetable 236
 Richard Brett and 197–98, 250
 in Singapore and Canada 421
 and sound systems 448
 and stage equipment 210
 Steve Tompkins and 334, 356
 and studio theatre design 191
 training course 257
 in US 23, 95, 418
Theatre Regulations Act (1843) 40
theatre, shape of 387–96
 and appointment of Lasdun 389–90
 comparative studies 387
 'modern era' 387
 pattern of change 390
 silence and acoustics 391
 in Sixties 387–89
Theatreplan 212
Theatrical Representations Act (1788) 36
Thérèse Raquin 353
theta-drum revolve *see* drum revolve
This House 364, 366
Thompson, Mark 300, 308–9, *308*, 341, *436*
Thompson, Neville xvi, 154, 198
Thompson, Nick 47, 425
Thorn Lighting Group, Q-File lighting control system 206
Thorndike, Daniel 241
Thorndike, Dame Sybil 9, 17, 70
Three Sisters 108, 163, 198, 254, 331, 344, *345*, *438*

3 Winters 278, 311
three-day week 211, 229, 231, 235
The Threepenny Opera 344, 360, *360*, 464–65
thrust stage 11, *12*, 17, 19, 23–24, 45, 46, 47, 75, 83, 111, 150, 201, 234, 307, 384, 390, 391, 419, 469, 509–10n.86
Time Out 360, 361, 413
The Times 5, 296
Tim Foster Architects *418*
Tina: The Tina Turner Musical 308
Tinker, Jack 271
'Tis Pity She's a Whore 287
Toguri, David 269
Tolhurst, Linda 468, 487
Tomalin, Nicholas 487
Tompkins, Steve 303, 332, *333*, 334, *334*, 343, 356, 378, 419, 425, 471, 481
Toms, Carl 64
Tons of Money 285, 286, 287
Tony Awards 310, 311, 315, 316, 346, 350, 353, 364, 452, 458
Too Clever by Half 352
Tooley, Sir John 398
Toomey, Tanya 322
Total Theatre 45, *45*, 56
Tourneur, Cyril 30
Town, Johanna *440*
Trades Union Congress 16
Trafalgar, Battle of 39
Transfer of Functions Order (1965) 239
Translations 371
Travelex ticket scheme 329, 331, 356, 375
Travers, Ben 255
Travesties 347
La Traviata 346
Treadwell, Sophie 302
Treasure Island (play) 385
Treasury (UK) 12, 13, 76, 85, 112, 144, 145, 149, 166, 210, 239, 263
Tree, Sir Herbert Beerbohm 5, 42
Trelawny of the "Wells" 147, 151
Trench, Michael Le Poer 323
Tristan and Yseult 440
The Trojans 347
Tucker, Leonard xvi, 55, *60*, 62, 198, 447, 474
Turner, J.M.W. 281
Turner, Lyndsey *439*
Turner, Peter 77
Twentieth Century Society 298
Tynan, Kathleen 294
Tynan, Kenneth 15, 76, *76*
 on Aquinas Street offices 53
 on Brecht's Berliner Ensemble 110
 conflict with LO 17
 critical observations on NT 254
 and Denys Lasdun 110
 on front cover of *Encore* 15
 as literary advisor to NT 76
 on LO's *Othello* 63
 and NT Building Committee 131–41, 149–54, 155, 185–93

at NT topping-out ceremony 233
and Peter Brook 125
responses to questionnaire 172
on Scheme B 130
on Scheme E 175

U
Ulrich (Treasury representative) 263
Ultz 359, *439*
Uncle Vanya 17, 51, 55, 70, 79, 80, 83, 100, 105, 107, 112, 121, 134, 136, 139, 254
Unicorn Publishing Group 488
United Company 32
United States of America 39, 46, 114
 'Broadway' theatre 416
Unruh, Walther 76
Unsworth, William Frederick 20
Uruguay 403
US (play) 512n.118
Ustinov, Peter 64
Utzon, Jørn 425

V
The Vagina Monologues 350
Vale, Michael *439*
van Hove, Ivo 362
Vanbrugh, Sir John 33
Vance, Nina 46
Vanity Fair 317
Vanstone, Hugh *438*
Varah, Kate 487
Variety 321, 322, 341, 358, 360
Vedrenne, J.E. 4, 5, 43
Venables, Clare 303
Venice, La Fenice theatre 470
Verdi, Giuseppe 400, 401
Verity, Thomas 40
Vernon, John 237
Versweyveld, Jan 362, *439*
Victoria, Queen 39
video design 449
video projectors 453
Vienna
 Burgtheater 202, 207
 Redoutensaal 44
 Staatsoper 344, 477
A View from the Bridge 285, 286, 287
viewing distance 429
The Villains' Opera 317
Villeurbanne, France, Théâtre National Populaire 108
Vincent in Brixton 310, 311, 319, 325, *440*
Virgile & Stone 294
The Visit 364
Volpone 454
The Voysey Inheritance 491

W
Waagner-Biro 202, 203
Wagner, Richard 19, 41, 43, 47, 48, 101, 400, 430
Waiting for Godot 15
Walker, Mike 302
Walls, Tom 286
Walsh, Enda, *Once* 346
Walton, Tony 408, 413

Wanamaker, Sam 30
 death 510n.91
Wanamaker, Zoë 332, 466
War Horse 314, *340*, *366*, *436*
 as commercial hit 435, 444, 475
 Michael Elliott and 74
 at New London Theatre 334
 Nicholas Hytner and 329, 382
 at Olivier Theatre 310, 332, 340, 348, 369, 481
 Paule Constable and 370
 Rae Smith on 364, 365
 Simon Russell Beale on 465
 video element 449
Ward, Anthony 323–24, *323*, *438*
Wardle, Alex *440*
Wardle, Irving 10–11, 486
 The Theatres of George Devine 486
Warner, Deborah 315, 319, *436*, *438*
Warner, Helen 340
Warner, Leo 449
Warsaw, National Theatre 265, *266*
Warwick 47
Washington, USA
 Kennedy Center 380
 Penthouse Theatre 46
 University of, School of Drama 46
Watch It Come Down 379
Waterloo, Battle of 39
Watts, Roger 419
Watts, S. 291
Waves 449
Way, John 468
Way Upstream 285, 446
The Way of the World 34
Weapons of Happiness 272
Webb, John 30, 31
Webster, John 30
Weeks, John 101
Weill, Kurt 360
Welsh National Opera (WNO) 325
Welton Becket Associates *415*
Wentworth, Stephen 271
Wever, Klaus 203
The White Guard 280, 350, 351, *351*, 353
Whitmore, John 464
Whitworth, Geoffrey i, 7–8, 9, 9, 10, 14
 The History of the Stage 7
Wierzel, Robert *437*
Wilde, Oscar 17
Wilford, Michael 402, 425
Wilkins, William 45
Wilkinson, Norman 21
Willatt, Hugh 16
Williams, Keith 425
Williams, Kenneth 316
Williams, Marc 441, *445*
Williams, Roy 329
Williams, Tennessee 315
Williams, Sir William Emrys 16
Wilson, August 359

Wilson, Effingham, *A House for Shakespeare: A Proposition for the Consideration of the Nation* 3
Wilson, Harold (later Baron Wilson of Rievaulx) 190, 327
Wimbledon School of Art (later Wimbledon College of Arts) 51, 323, 410
The Wind in the Willows 248, 300, *300*, 308, 331, 444
Windsor Castle, Berkshire 34, 327
The Wings of the Dove (film) 352
Winteringham, Graham 47, 409
The Winter's Tale (ballet) 346
The Witches, 497
Wise Children (theatre company) 344
The Woman (play) 264
The Woman in White (musical) 449
Women Beware Women 86
Women of Troy 332, 367, *497*
wonder.land 359, *359*, 364
Wood, Peter 51, 54, 57, 62, 148, 270
 on LO 255
Wood, Philip *66*, 77, 215–16
Wood, Renton Howard 47, 405
Wood, Stephen 487
World War I 7, 182
World War II 9, 47, 48, 49, 54, 73, 76, 287, 387, 398, 405, 430, 477
Worthington, Sir Hubert 10
Wren, Sir Christopher 32
Wright, Frank Lloyd 75, 256, 407, 425
Wright, John 206
The Wrong Side of the Park 72
Wuthering Heights (film) 49
Wyatt, Benjamin Dean, *Observations on the Design of the Theatre Royal Drury Lane* 38

Y
Yale Center for British Art 34
Yarden, Tal 362
YMCA 7
York, Michael 105
York, Richard 233, 245–46, *245*, 250–51
Yorke, Rosenberg Mardell 97, 101
Young, B.A. 55
Young, Ian 212

Z
Zactrack (lighting system) 447
Zaghi, Athos 425
Zeffirelli, Franco 63, 142, 198, 470
Zeldin, Alexander 441
Zevi, Bruno 401, 403
Zieba, Derrick 269, 448
Zorba 408

527

Rob Halliday

Rob began lighting at school inspired by Richard Pilbrow's book *Stage Lighting*, and grew up watching shows standing at the back of the Olivier and Lyttelton at the National Theatre, fascinated by this building that was so different from London's more traditional theatres. He is therefore thrilled to have worked with Richard on *A Sense of Theatre*.

Rob trained at the National Youth Theatre, and from there has gone on to a career in entertainment lighting and production that over the last thirty-five years has spanned the world, working as a lighting designer on his own shows and as a lighting programmer and associate lighting designer to other designers.

His favourite shows working with others include *Les Misérables* and the National Theatre's *Oklahoma!* and *My Fair Lady* for David Hersey, *Billy Elliot* for Rick Fisher and *Red* for Neil Austin.

His own designs include the acclaimed dance show *Tree of Codes*, created with Wayne McGregor, Olafur Eliasson and Jamie xx which debuted at the Manchester International Festival in 2015 and has been seen around the world since.

Rob also writes extensively about lighting and production for a range of publications including *Light+Sound International*, *Lighting & Sound America*, *Live Design* and *The Stage*, and in the books *Entertainment In Production* and *Theatre Lighting Design: Conversations on the Art, Craft and Life*. He has spoken about lighting at trade shows, conferences and drama schools worldwide, and served as lighting consultant to new theatres including Leicester's Curve and Chester's Storyhouse.

www.robhalliday.com

Fred Pilbrow

Fred is an architect with over twenty-five years' experience designing award-winning projects in the UK and abroad.

Fred worked as a designer in the professional theatre before training to be an architect – including designing a show, *The Strangeness of Others*, in the Cottesloe at the National Theatre. This background gives him a unique insight into the quality of performance space design, which as an architect informed the design of the new National Theatre of Cyprus undertaken by Fred whilst a partner at KPF.

After time at KPF, working on projects such as the Heron Tower in the City of London, and as a partner at PLP Architecture, working on projects including the Francis Crick Institute in St Pancras, Fred founded the London-based Pilbrow & Partners in 2013 with Tal Ben Amar, Keb Garavito-Bruhn, Sam Yousif, and Clare Ralph.

Since its establishment, the practice has grown to a team of over sixty architects and urban planners with a reputation for delivering innovative solutions to a range of demanding and diverse project briefs.

Fred has particular experience working on complex mixed-use projects in sensitive historic environments. Significant projects like the Greenwich Peninsula Riverside Masterplan, the redevelopment of 8 Albert Embankment and the completed renovation of a Grade II-listed private residence in Bayswater clearly reflect his interests in these fields. Other key projects include the new University College London Hospital (UCLH), the design of The Market Building at Canary Wharf's new Wood Wharf district and the £17-million restoration of the former EMD Cinema in Waltham Forest for Soho Theatres.

www.pilbrowandpartners.com

Richard Pilbrow

Richard Pilbrow (1933-2023) was one of the world's leading theatre design consultants, a theatre, film, and television producer, an author, and a stage lighting designer. Under his leadership Theatre Projects, the company he founded in 1957, became the pre-eminent theatre consulting organisation in the world, with over 1800 projects in 80 countries to its credit. Richard was chosen by Sir Laurence Olivier to be theatre consultant to the National Theatre of Great Britain. He was also consultant to the RSC's Barbican Theatre, to the Royal Opera House Covent Garden and to many other arts buildings in North America, Europe, Hong Kong, China, and the Middle East.

Richard was a pioneer of modern stage lighting in Britain, lighting many shows for the National Theatre and in the West End. He was the first British lighting designer to light a musical on Broadway, *Zorba*. Subsequent shows in New York included *The Rothschilds*, the transfer of the National Theatre's *Rosencrantz and Guildenstern Are Dead*, *Four Baboons Adoring The Sun* (Tony Award nomination), the Cy Coleman musical *The Life* (Tony Award nomination), *A Tale of Two Cities* (Drama Desk Award nomination) and *Our Town* with Paul Newman, also for high-definition video for PBS. His lighting for the Hal Prince revival of *Show Boat* was seen on Broadway (Drama Desk Award, Outer Circle Critics Award), in Toronto (Dora Award) and on tour throughout the US (NAACP Award). Richard lit Sir Peter Hall's *The Magic Flute* for Los Angeles, Seattle, & Washington Operas and the 1999 Shakespeare Season at the Ahmanson Theatre in Los Angeles. In 2007-11, Richard was lighting designer (with Dawn Chiang) for American Ballet Theatre's *Sleeping Beauty* at the Metropolitan Opera and on tour. In 2017, he was lighting designer for the revival of *My Fair Lady* directed by Julie Andrews, with the original scenic and costume designs of Oliver Smith and Cecil Beaton, at the Sydney Opera House.

As a theatrical producer, his partnership with Hal Prince included the West End productions of *A Funny Thing Happened on the Way to the Forum, She Loves Me, Cabaret, Company* and *A Little Night Music*. He was responsible as producer for many other British productions, and producer of the feature film of Arthur Ransome's *Swallows and Amazons*, the TV series *All You Need is Love – The Story of Popular Music* and, with the BBC, *Swallows and Amazons Forever*.

Published in 1970, his book, *Stage Lighting*, featuring a foreword by Lord Olivier, became a standard international text, also published in China. A second book, *Stage Lighting Design: The Art, The Craft, The Life,* with a foreword by Hal Prince, was published in 1997. In 2003, Richard co-authored (with Patricia MacKay) *The Walt Disney Concert Hall – The Backstage Story. A Theatre Project*, published in 2011, was described by Michael Coveney as "An absolute joy to read... A history of theatre from an entirely new and fresh perspective." The book won the 2013 USITT Golden Pen Award. In 2016, Richard edited *The National Theatre, A Place for Plays*, the publication of a Symposium presented by the ABTT at the National Theatre.

In 2005, Richard was honoured as Lighting Designer of the Year by *Lighting Dimensions* magazine. In the premier edition of *LiveDesign* magazine in December 2005, he was named as one of the ten visionaries among designers and artists, who were the most influential people in the world of visual design for live events. In 2010, *LiveDesign* voted Richard "one of the fifty most powerful people in the entertainment technology industry."

In 1982, Richard received an award from the United States Institute for Theatre Technology (USITT) for "His many years' contribution to the art of lighting, as designer, entrepreneur, and consultant in both England and America," and a Distinguished Achievement Award from USITT in 1999. In 2018, he was awarded the Joel E Rubin Founder's Award from USITT. In 2000, he also received from the Association of British Theatre Technicians (ABTT) its annual Technician of the Year Award. He served as director-at-large on the USITT board from 2000-2006, and was elected a fellow in 2001 for "his truly astounding contribution to the theatre and the work of the institute." Richard was recipient of the 2008 Wally Russell Lifetime Achievement Award.

www.richardpilbrow.com   www.atheatreproject.com

"This is more than a proper job. We create art. We do what we say we're going to do. And we deliver on time! It's a much more complicated industry than any other I can think of. We're not just making six different versions of a chocolate bar. Every single product that we produce is handcrafted and unique."

Jonathan Suffolk, ex-technical director, National Theatre

"What we eventually got, when the architects, pressure groups, quacks, and empirics had finished, was a theatre, of all the theatres in England, in which it is hardest to make an audience laugh or cry."

William Bridges-Adams (1889-1965), director, about the Shakespeare Memorial Theatre, 1932

"I realised the single most important lesson I have ever learnt as an actor. I must play with the audience, not at them, for them or to them… with them, with their imagination, as fellow players. I was amongst them, part of a circle, a storytelling circle."

Mark Rylance, actor, first artistic director of the modern Globe Theatre

"That is the holy temple out there and people have paid you the greatest compliment in the world by coming to see you."

Ken Dodd (1927-2018), British comedian

"It is through collaboration that this knockabout art of theatre survives and kicks. It was true at The Globe, The Curtain, The Crown, and in the 'illustrious theatre' of Molière and it can work here, today."

Joan Littlewood (1914-2002), director, founder of Theatre Workshop

"That is why the Theatre, old as she is, remains the never-to-be-superseded great mother of all drama and entertainment, the everlasting fount of dramatic experience and inspiration."

J.B. Priestley (1894-1984), 1947

"If you were asked to imagine what a theatre looks like, chances are you would never imagine the National. The building suggests the first element of theatre: surprise."

Patrick Marber, dramatist

"There is a mysterious sense, called a 'sense of theatre', which is vital. With it, the curtain can be made to act as much as any actor, and lights can be made to talk as eloquently as any poetry… From the man who works the tabs to the girl who designs the crown for King Lear, each of these people is an artist just as much as the producer or designer."

George Devine (1910-1965), director